Marina Spiazzi
Marina Tavella Margaret Layton

Compact Performer Culture & Literature

- LEARN LANGUAGE WITH AND THROUGH CULTURE
- TRAIN AND REVISE FOR THE FIRST CERTIFICATE AND THE STATE EXAM
- STUDY THE MAJOR MILESTONES OF LITERATURE

Per sapere quali risorse digitali integrano il tuo libro, e come fare ad averle, connettiti a Internet e vai su:

http://my.zanichelli.it/risorsedigitali

Segui le istruzioni e tieni il tuo libro a portata di mano: avrai bisogno del codice ISBN*, che trovi nell'ultima pagina della copertina, in basso a sinistra.

- L'accesso alle risorse digitali protette è personale: non potrai condividerlo o cederlo.
- L'accesso a eventuali risorse digitali online protette è limitato nel tempo: alla pagina http://my.zanichelli.it/risorsedigitali trovi informazioni sulla durata della licenza.

* Se questo libro fa parte di una confezione, l'ISBN si trova nella quarta di copertina dell'ultimo libro nella confezione.

LINGUE ZANICHELLI

Compact Performer, Culture & Literature deriva da *Spiazzi, Tavella, Layton, Performer, Culture & Literature vol 1-2-3*, Zanichelli 2012

Realizzazione editoriale:
- Redazione e ricerca iconografica: Lindy Russell, Chiara comunicazione, Parma
- Progetto grafico e impaginazione: Dario Zannier, Studio Indaco, Milano

Contributi:
- Indice analitico: Ginevra Massari

Realizzazione delle risorse digitali:
- Redazione: Lindy Russell e Federica Gusmeroli
- Progettazione esecutiva e sviluppo software: duDAT srl, Bologna

Copertina:
- Progetto grafico: Miguel Sal & C., Bologna
- Realizzazione: Roberto Marchetti e Francesca Ponti

Prima edizione: marzo 2015

Ristampa:

5 4 3 2015 2016 2017 2018 2019

Zanichelli garantisce che le risorse digitali di questo volume sotto il suo controllo saranno accessibili, a partire dall'acquisto dell'esemplare nuovo, per tutta la durata della normale utilizzazione didattica dell'opera. Passato questo periodo, alcune o tutte le risorse potrebbero non essere più accessibili o disponibili: per maggiori informazioni, leggi my.zanichelli.it/fuoricatalogo

File per sintesi vocale
L'editore mette a disposizione degli studenti non vedenti, ipovedenti, disabili motori o con disturbi specifici di apprendimento i file pdf in cui sono memorizzate le pagine di questo libro. Il formato del file permette l'ingrandimento dei caratteri del testo e la lettura mediante software screen reader. Le informazioni su come ottenere i file sono sul sito http://www.zanichelli.it/scuola/bisogni-educativi-speciali

Suggerimenti e segnalazione degli errori
Realizzare un libro è un'operazione complessa, che richiede numerosi controlli: sul testo, sulle immagini e sulle relazioni che si stabiliscono tra essi. L'esperienza suggerisce che è praticamente impossibile pubblicare un libro privo di errori. Saremo quindi grati ai lettori che vorranno segnalarceli. Per segnalazioni o suggerimenti relativi a questo libro scrivere al seguente indirizzo:

divisioneaz@zanichelli.it

Le correzioni di eventuali errori presenti nel testo sono pubblicate nel sito www.zanichelli.it/aggiornamenti

Zanichelli editore S.p.A. opera con sistema qualità certificato CertiCarGraf n. 477 secondo la norma UNI EN ISO 9001:2008

Questo libro è stampato su carta che rispetta le foreste.
www.zanichelli.it/la-casa-editrice/carta-e-ambiente/

Fotocomposizione: Fratelli Sala

Stampa: L.E.G.O. S.p.A.
Via Galileo Galilei 11, 38015 Lavis
per conto di Zanichelli editore S.p.A.
Via Irnerio 34, 40126 Bologna

Specification 1

The Making of the Nation

Specification 2

The English Renaissance

Specification 3

Shaping the English Character

Com'è fatto il libro

Culture

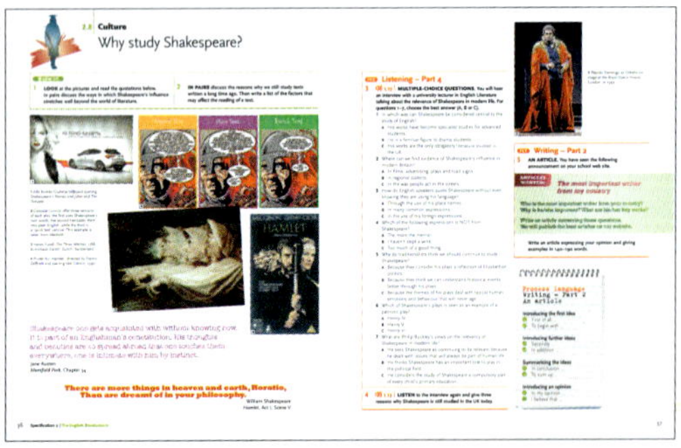

Approfondimento o analisi critica di aspetti relativi alla cultura dei diversi periodi storico-sociali.

Two Films About...

La relazione tra linguaggio letterario e cinematografico nell'analisi di due film per ogni *Specification*.

History

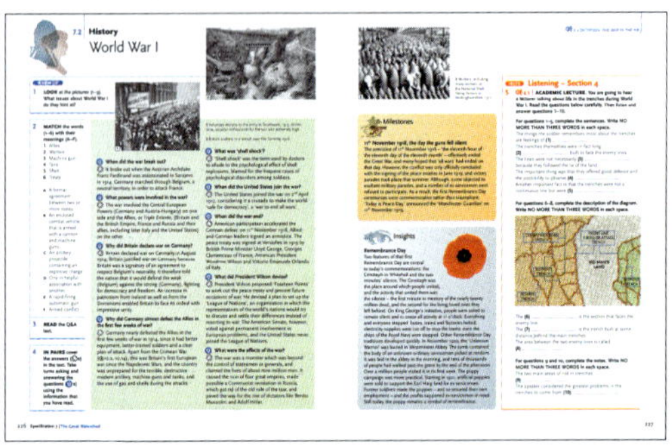

Introduzione al contesto storico e sociale con esercizi legati alle certificazioni internazionali. La rubrica ***Insights*** approfondisce un argomento di civiltà e ***Milestones*** un anno significativo dal punto di vista storico-sociale.

Cultural Issues

Approfondimenti di temi non solo letterari con mappe visive introduttive e analisi di testi da opere contemporanee.

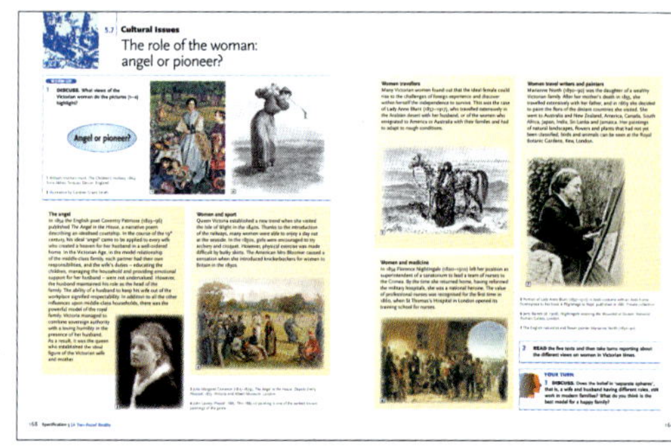

Literature

Autori presentati tematicamente e testi dalle opere più significative. Nelle Specifications 7–9 esercizi legati all'*Esame di Stato*.

Literary Genre Reference

Per i generi letterari *Literary Language*, una sorta di *information store*, e la sezione finale del volume *Literary Language Reference*. Con in più 6 pagine di *Literary Genre Reference*.

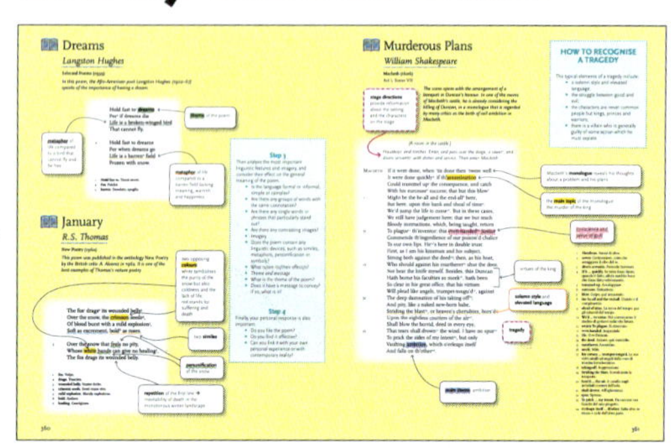

The Arts

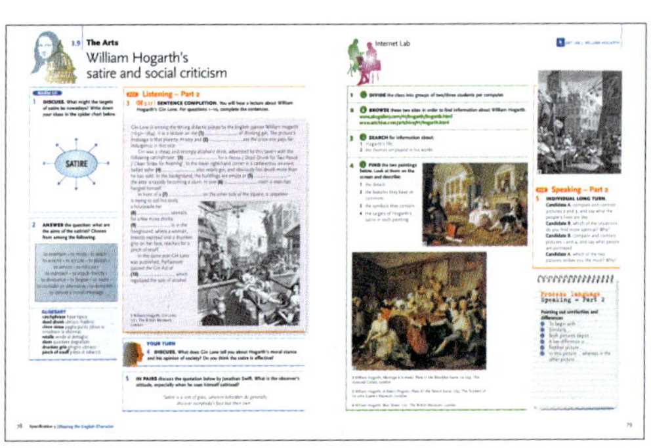

Analisi di opere d'arte per temi o autori anche con esercizi legati alle certificazioni internazionali. ***Internet Lab*** propone itinerari guidati in Internet.

Esame di Stato

Nelle Specifications 7–9 esercizi sulla *Terza Prova* e sulla *Prova Orale*, accompagnati da *Exam Description* e *Tips*. A fine volume 4 pagine di *Exam Reference*.

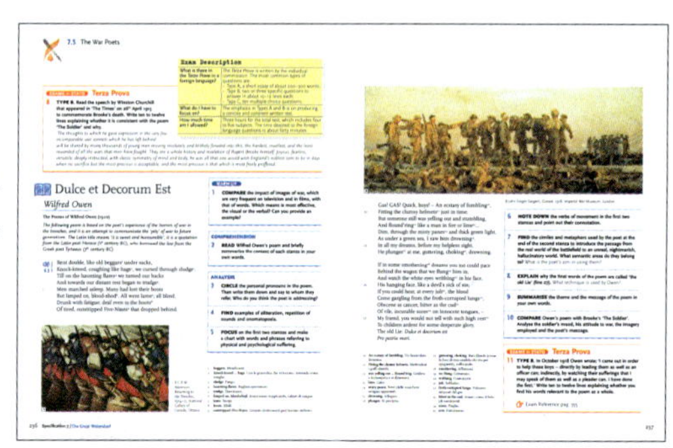

The Making of the Nation

Specification 1 | Homepage

Top News

927 Anglo-Saxon King Athelstan makes England

1215 John Lackland signs the Magna Carta

Top Issue

Giving identity a voice

Most Popular News

1154
The Plantagenets get the English throne

1348
The Black Death hits the country

Spotlight

1387–1400 Chaucer portrays English society

Cinema

See Robin Hood on screen

The Arts

Gothic cathedrals are built

Mapping History

Visit the places of the Norman invasion

EXPLORE THE CULTURE

Literature | History | Society | The Arts | Two Films About... | Cultural Issues

1.1 History

Meet the Celts

WARM-UP

1 **LOOK** at the pictures (1–4) and match them with the captions (A–D).

- A An iron weapon. ....
- B Queen Boadicea. ....
- C A hill fort. ....
- D A hut. ....

2 **IN PAIRS** discuss what the pictures tell you about the Celts.

3 **READ** the Q&A text below.

GLOSSARY

settled si stabilirono
ironworking lavorazione del ferro
ditch fossato
surrounding che recintavano
timber legno, legname
thatched di paglia
plough aratro
worship culto
wells sorgenti, pozzi
springs fonti

1

2

During the Iron Age (ca 600 BC–50 AD), a Celtic culture established itself throughout the British Isles.

Q Who were the Celts?

A The 'Celts' were tribes of warriors who shared a similar language, religion and culture. The Romans, who fought against them, reported about their culture but presented them as barbarians.

Q When did they come to Britain?

A It is not correct to say that they invaded Britain. They gradually settled in the country between about 500 and 100 BC.

Q What did they bring to the British Isles?

A They brought ironworking to the British Isles, which had amazing effects. It affected trade and helped develop local independence because iron was quite cheap and easily available.

Q Did the Celts build hill forts?

A We don't know if the hill forts were built by the Celts as they moved into hostile territory or by the native Britons to defend themselves. Hill forts consisted of a small ditch and bank surrounding a hilltop.

Q What was the basic unit of Celtic life?

A It was the clan, which was like today's extended family.

Q Were clans bound together?

A Yes, clans joined together with other clans to form tribes, each with its own social structure and customs.

Q Where did the Celts live?

A They lived in huts made of timber with thatched roofs.

Q Were they farmers?

A The Celts practised agriculture when they were not fighting in wars. They introduced the iron plough, which made the cultivation of the soil easier. In the countryside in Britain it is still possible to see the long and narrow pattern of the Celtic field.

Q What was the role of women?

A They were almost equal to men. They could choose the man they wanted to marry and retained their own property. They could also lead other warriors in war, like Boadicea – a warrior queen of the early Britons who fought against the Romans.

3

4

Insights

The origins of Halloween

October 31st is Halloween. This festivity has Celtic origins: in the 5th century BC, the Celts believed that summer ended on October 31st. The holiday was called *Samhain* and celebrated the start of winter and of the new year. The Celts believed that ghosts and witches returned on that night and that evil spirits entered the body of a person or animal. This is why they used to wear frightening costumes and make big fires to send the spirits away. Later, Christian practices replaced pagan ones; the Roman Catholic Church decided to call November 1st 'All Hollows Day' or 'All Saints Day' and the evening of October 31st became 'All Hollows Eve' – that is, Halloween.

Nowadays at Halloween children and teenagers wear skeleton, witch, ghost and monster costumes for parties and 'trick or treating'. They visit their neighbours' houses and, when the door opens, they say 'Trick or treat?' and people usually give them sweets or money. This custom originated in the 9th century in Ireland, where on November 2nd – All Souls Day – Christians used to walk from village to village begging for 'soul cakes', made of bread with currants. The more 'soul cakes' the beggars received, the more prayers they promised to say for dead relatives. The custom of buying a big pumpkin and making a lantern comes from Irish folklore. Irish people put lit, hollowed-out turnips in front of their windows and in their garden to frighten evil spirits away.

4 IN PAIRS cover the answers (A s) in the text. Take turns asking and answering the questions (Q s) using the information that you have read.

Q Did the Celts write literature?

A They depended on the oral transmission of culture, especially through bards. Much of what we know of their traditions comes to us today through the old stories and poems that were passed down for generations before being written down.

Q What did they worship?

A They worshipped the natural elements, like the sun, the moon and water. They held their religious rites in the woods and near the sacred water of wells and springs.

1 Maiden Castle, an Iron Age site in Dorchester, Dorset, England.

2 Spearhead found in the River Thames, England. Iron Age, 200–50 BC. The spearhead has been decorated with four strips of bronze in the La Tène style. The decoration may mean that the spear was not made for use in battle or hunting.

3 Bronze statue near Westminster Pier, London, as commissioned by Prince Albert and executed by Thomas Thornycroft, completed in 1905.

4 Reconstructed Celtic village, Castell Henllys, Wales.

FCE Writing – Part 1

5 AN ESSAY. Your teacher has asked you to write an essay for homework. Write your essay in 140–190 words using all the notes and giving reasons for your point of view.

Halloween has become a popular and commercially significant festivity in lots of countries.
How is Halloween celebrated in your country?

Notes

Write about:

1 how this festivity is celebrated in your country
2 its symbols
3 .... (your own opinion)

Process language
Writing – Part 1
An essay

Introducing a point
- In my opinion ...
- I think ...
- It is clear that ...

Developing an argument
- Moreover ...
- In addition ...
- It is also true that ...

Concluding
- Finally ...
- To conclude ...
- In conclusion ...

From the Romans to the Anglo-Saxons

WARM-UP

1 **DISCUSS.** Do you know when the Romans invaded Britain and if they conquered the whole of the British Isles? Where did the Anglo-Saxons come from?

2 **READ** the text and say where the term 'Anglo-Saxon' came from.

3 **READ** the text and the Milestones and take notes on the following points:
1. Roman towns and roads;
2. Londinium;
3. the origin of the name England;
4. Anglo-Saxon society;
5. Anglo-Saxon values;
6. the monk Augustine;
7. Alfred the Great;
8. Athelstan and the year 927.

1 Roman mosaic floor in the Corinium Museum, Cirencester, Gloucestershire, England.

2 A section of Hadrian's Wall in England.

3 Whitby Abbey, in Yorkshire, England. The first monastery here was founded in 657 AD by the Anglo-Saxon king of Northumbria.

The Roman invasion

In 55 BC Julius Caesar (ca 100–44 BC) invaded Britain, but it was under Emperor Claudius (10 BC–54 AD) that the real conquest of the country took place, in the years 43–47 AD. The Romans involved the conquered tribes in the administration of the province, and they encouraged the growth of towns near their army bases. They persuaded the ruling class of Celtic aristocrats to live in the towns, which became centres of commercial activity. The towns were usually surrounded by stone walls and had a regular network of streets. The centre contained a *forum*, or civic centre, with access to the *basilica*, or town hall, which is where courts of justice or merchants assemblies were held. There were also public baths, which were used as spas and meeting places in every town.

The Roman influence on Britain

The Romans built over 9,600 kilometres of roads in Britain. They were extremely well built and served to join the towns and facilitate the movement of troops and commercial goods. They also built an extraordinary defence fortification and barrier from the east coast to the west coast, between England and Scotland, known as Hadrian's Wall. The Roman invasion also marked the beginning of the importance of London. The Romans built the first 'London Bridge'. This crossing place proved a convenient central point for the new network of roads, and the Roman settlement on the north side of the bridge, called 'Londinium', quickly became important as a trading centre.

The Anglo-Saxons arrive

When the Roman army withdrew from Britain in 410 AD, the Romanised Celts were left alone to fight against groups from Germany and Scandinavia who invaded the island in the 5th century and destroyed the Roman British towns. These people were the Angles, the Saxons and the Jutes, and they gave the larger part of Britain its current name: England, that is, 'the land of the Angles'. The Anglo-Saxon invaders were mainly farmers or fishermen who were also organised into family groups called 'clans'. For these clans, the most important social bond was loyalty to their king and tribe. They exalted physical courage and personal freedom. They also created fine artwork and ornaments, and enjoyed feasts and drinking.

The Christianisation of Britain

At the end of the 6th century, Pope Gregory I the Great (590–604) sent a monk, Augustine, to bring Christianity to England. Augustine first went to Canterbury and became the first Archbishop of Canterbury. Soon monasteries were built and turned into important centres of communal life and culture.

The Kingdom of England

At this time, the land now known as England was divided and ruled in small areas under different tribes. This was the situation until 865, when Danish armies, commonly known as Vikings, began to invade. They quickly conquered northern, eastern, southern and part of the central areas of England, until Alfred the Great of Wessex (871–899) intervened and halted the Danish advance. In ca 879 a

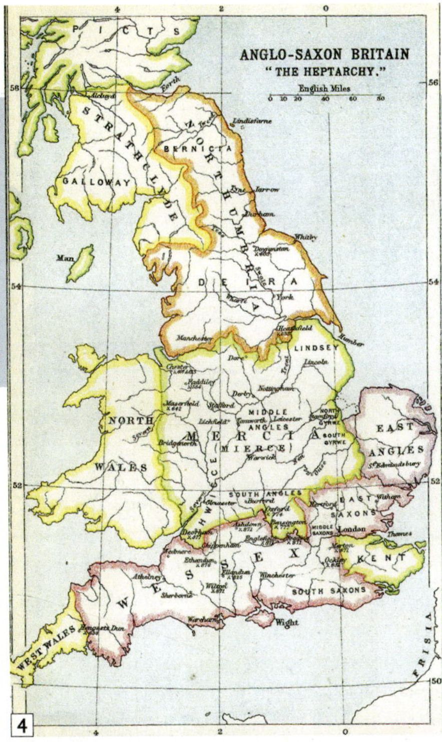

4

'kingdom of Anglo-Saxons', joining Wessex (the West Saxons, in southern England) and Mercia (the Angles, in central England), was born under Alfred's lordship. Alfred's vision was for a kingdom built over generations, with developments in state-building, local organisation, the construction of towns, the distribution of coins, the making of English law and the promotion of learning and literacy. Alfred's son Edward (899–924) extended their power into the Midlands and East Anglia, and Edward's son Athelstan completed the task of creating England by conquering Northumbria in 927.

4 The Heptarchy, a name applied to the seven Anglo-Saxon kingdoms.

Milestones

927, Athelstan made England
Few English kings have as direct a claim as Athelstan to be described as the father of the English state. 927 AD was a turning point, the year when he created a kingdom of all of England by establishing the idea of royal authority, law and coinage. Diplomacy was a fascinating aspect of his rule. Disorder was the great terror of the age. He tried to achieve peace across western Europe through a series of diplomatic alliances, including the marriage of four of his sisters to European rulers. This is why in the 12th century Athelstan was remembered as a kind of English Charlemagne – an image echoed in several medieval romances and even on the Elizabethan stage.

FCE Reading and Use of English – Part 5

4 MULTIPLE-CHOICE QUESTIONS. Read the text about British history again. For questions 1–6, choose the answer (A, B, C or D) which you think fits best according to the text.

1 The Roman invaders in Britain persuaded the conquered tribe leaders to
- **A** build new army bases within the towns.
- **B** avoid trading with Rome.
- **C** move into the towns.
- **D** give up their previous lands and occupations.

2 What evidence of Roman influence remained in Britain?
- **A** Hadrian's Bridge, a small network of roads and a new town in Londinium.
- **B** disorganised communication systems.
- **C** fortified farms and towns without a proper centre.
- **D** an extensive network of roads, a formidable customs barrier and fortified towns.

3 What happened after the Roman army withdrew from Britain?
- **A** The Romanised Celts destroyed the British Roman towns.
- **B** The island was invaded by the Angles, the Saxons and the Jutes.
- **C** The Romanised Celts returned to Ireland and Wales.
- **D** The Romanised Celts successfully defended the British Roman towns from invasion.

4 Anglo-Saxon culture was characterised by many aspects but NOT
- **A** physical courage.
- **B** artistic beauty.
- **C** feasting and drinking.
- **D** lack of personal freedom.

5 What was Alfred the Great's important achievement in the 9th century?
- **A** He halted the advance of the Vikings' conquests in England.
- **B** He conquered Northumbria.
- **C** He brought Christianity to England.
- **D** He extended his power into the Midlands and East Anglia.

6 In 927 ... completed the task of creating England by conquering Northumbria.
- **A** Alfred
- **B** Alfred's son, Edward,
- **C** Edward's son, Athelstan,
- **D** a Viking king

1.3 | **History**

The Norman Conquest and feudalism

INTERACTIVE MAP 1: *THE NORMAN INVASION*

WARM-UP

1 MATCH the words with their Italian equivalent.

1 baron	**A** vescovo
2 bishop	**B** cavaliere
3 abbot	**C** contadino
4 knight	**D** feudatario
5 peasant	**E** abate

2 READ the text and match each heading (A–D) with a paragraph (1–4).

1 A new social order
2 Defeat and conquest
3 Wealth and taxation
4 Interdependence

1 ....

On October 14th 1066, William, Duke of Normandy, defeated the Anglo-Saxon king, Harold II, at Hastings. On Christmas Day of that year, William was crowned as William I (1066–87) in Westminster Abbey. He had conquered the South East, but it took five more years to subjugate the rest of England.

2 ....

First, William created a new aristocracy, which replaced the Anglo-Saxon aristocracy. The king kept the best lands, the towns and the forests. He distributed the rest of the lands to his Norman followers and to a few trusted Saxons. The feudal system was established: the barons obtained their land by becoming the king's tenants, and they paid their 'rent' in military services to the king. They built castles to demonstrate and maintain their power.

3 ....

The barons were able to sub-let their lands to the knights in return for their services. Thus the barons and knights provided the military service, and the agricultural work was done by the peasants, who belonged to the land of all the tenants. This system guaranteed security and food, and so peace and prosperity.

1 A close-up showing William I the Conqueror from the Bayeux Tapestry, ca 11th–12th centuries, Normandy (France), at the Musée de la Tapisserie de Bayeux.

2 A page of the *Domesday Book* (1086–87) for the county of Warwickshire, in the West Midlands region of England. The *Domesday Book* is now held by the National Archives.

1

4 ....

Twenty years after the Conquest, William sent his men throughout England to make a complete survey of the economic life of the country. The survey, which was written down in the *Domesday Book*, had two objectives: first, to provide the necessary information for collecting the 'geld' or property tax, and second, to give the king detailed knowledge of the extent and distribution of the wealth of his tenants.

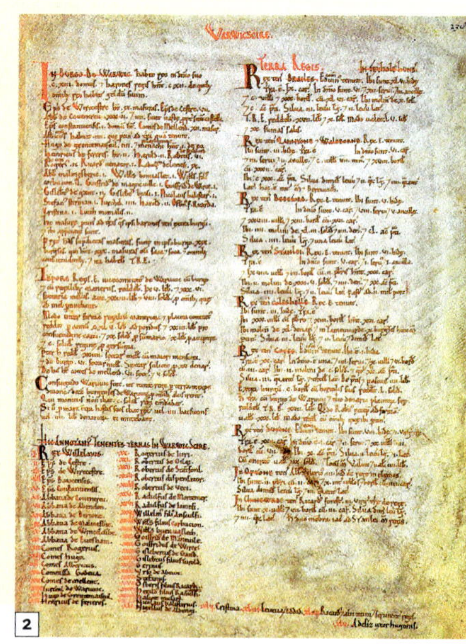

2

3 ANSWER the following questions.

1 Who did William defeat?
2 Where and when was William I crowned?
3 What did the king own?
4 What did the barons obtain from the king? What did they have to pay the king?
5 What system guaranteed security and prosperity?
6 What was the *Domesday Book*? Why was the survey carried out?

FCE Speaking – Part 1

4 INTERVIEW. Answer the following questions.

1 Do you like studying history? Why is it important?
2 Does the place where you live have historical relevance?
3 Can you name places that are important in your national history?
4 Have you ever been to England? Have you visited any of the places you have studied? Which ones would you like to visit? Why?

Henry II: the first Plantagenet king

1 AS YOU READ, write a heading for each paragraph (1–5).

GLOSSARY
shrine tempio
barefoot scalzo

2 ANSWER the questions about the text.

1 What was Henry II's reign like?
2 After scutage was introduced, did all knights fight in battles?
3 How was justice administered?
4 What was 'common law' and how did it differ from the law in other European countries?
5 What was Henry II's relationship with the Church?
6 Did making Thomas Becket head of the Church in England have the result that the king intended?
7 How did people react to Becket's murder?

1 ……………

In the years after the Norman Conquest, there were no set laws to decide who should replace a dead monarch. Thus this was a time when the throne was fiercely contested, with several different people asserting their claims to be the ruler of England. The members of the aristocracy became tired of the lack of an effective monarch. They refused to battle each other and obliged the various contenders to come to an arrangement in 1153.

2 ……………

Henry II was the first king of the Plantagenet dynasty. The Plantagenets were kings of France and England. Henry II's reign (1154–89) was successful in bringing order and stability. His first task was to reduce the power of the barons. He did this with the help of professional soldiers. Knights could now pay the king a sum of money, or 'scutage', instead of giving military service, and with this money the king was able to hire mercenaries, or professional soldiers.

3 ……………

Henry II sent travelling judges round the land to the largest towns in each county. The law they administered became known as 'common law', because it was used everywhere. In other parts of Europe, legal practice was based on the Civil Law of the Roman Empire or the Canon Law of the Church. English lawyers created an entirely different system of law based on custom, comparisons, previous cases and previous decisions. This mixture of experience and custom is the basis of law in England even today.

4 ……………

The king also wanted to reduce the power of the Church. Henry II thought that the easiest way of controlling the Church would be to make Thomas Becket (1118–70), his chancellor and friend, head of the Church in England. However, once he became Archbishop of Canterbury, Becket became an opponent of the king, who had considerable authority because he chose the bishops. The conflict lasted for a long time, until Becket was murdered in Canterbury Cathedral by four knights on 29th December 1170.

5 ……………

Becket's murder shocked all of Europe. He was soon regarded as a martyr and was canonised as St Thomas in 1173. Pilgrims from all over England and Europe visited his shrine in Canterbury Cathedral, and Henry II himself walked barefoot to his tomb. St Thomas's shrine was also the destination of the pilgrims portrayed by Geoffrey Chaucer in *The Canterbury Tales* (ca 1387).

1 *Henry II* from *The Four Kings of England*, from *Abbreviatio chronicorum Angliae*, British Library, London.

2 *The Murder of Thomas Becket* from *Historia Anglorum*, British Library, London.

The Gothic cathedral

WARM-UP

1 **DISCUSS.** What do you generally associate the adjective 'Gothic' with?

2 **READ** the text below and answer the questions.
1. When was there a large cathedral-campaign in England?
2. When was a church called a 'cathedral'?
3. What materials were used to build Gothic cathedrals?

The building of Gothic cathedrals in England

The end of the 12th century witnessed a large cathedral-campaign in England. There were different reasons for this. First, the construction of new roads and bridges improved the transportation of materials. Urban growth created a diversity of labourers and craftsmen. Ecclesiastical incomes increased as a result of more efficiency of management and administration. At that time, a church was called a 'cathedral' when it contained a *cathedra*, or 'throne', for a bishop and the most important materials employed to build it were timber, stone (the most common was limestone), marble and glass.

3 **READ** the first sentence in the following brochure for Canterbury Cathedral. What word would you use to fill in the blank?

FCE **Listening – Part 2**

4 1.2 | **SENTENCE COMPLETION.** You will hear part of a radio talk about Canterbury Cathedral in Kent. For questions 1–10, complete the sentences in the brochure.

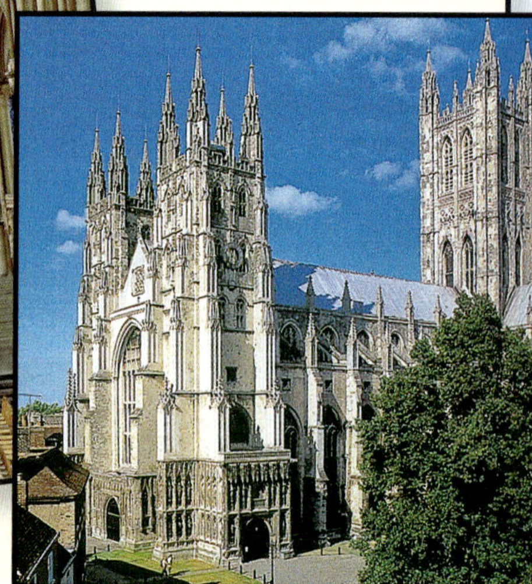

Canterbury has been the most important spiritual centre in England for **(1)** ………………………… .

St Augustine was sent to Kent as **(2)** ………………………… in 597 AD and given a church at Canterbury.

Until the 10th century, the Cathedral community was a **(3)** ………………………… of Benedictine monks.

The wealth and power of the Cathedral increased in the 12th century thanks to the **(4)** ………………………… .

It is now regarded as one of the finest examples of **(5)** ………………………… art.

The Cathedral was seriously damaged by the severe earthquake of 1382, losing its bells and campanile. The nave was rebuilt in the Perpendicular style of English Gothic, but the Norman and Early English east end was left in place.

Today nearly **(6)** ………………………… are held each year.

'Save Canterbury Cathedral' was the banner launching an appeal to **(7)** ………………………… in 2006.

This appeal wanted to protect the future of the Cathedral as a **(8)** ………………………… centre.

A combination of centuries of **(9)** ………………………… and constant use had produced serious damage problems at Canterbury Cathedral that needed urgent action.

The structural review wants to guarantee **(10)** ………………………… of the pilgrims and tourists visiting the Cathedral every year.

1.6 **History**

King John and the Magna Carta

1 **SCAN** the following texts and see if you can explain why John is popularly known as 'Bad King John'.

GLOSSARY
drain prosciugare
defy sfidare
seal sigillare
indictment accusa scritta
seizure confisca
wage dichiarare (guerra)

FCE Reading and Use of English – Part 1

2 **MULTIPLE-CHOICE CLOZE.** For questions 1–8, read the text and decide which answer (A, B, C or D) best fits each gap. There is an example at the beginning (0).

Richard I **(0)** SUCCEEDED his father, Henry II, in 1189. He spent less **(1)** .... a year of his reign in England, because he **(2)** .... for the Holy Land to take part in the Third Crusade. During his absence, his brother John tried to usurp his place. When Richard **(3)** .... without an heir in 1199, the English and Norman barons chose John as king.

In the popular perception, John is 'Bad King John' – an image that has been reinforced by his negative presentation on the screen in Robin Hood films or TV series like *Ivanhoe*, where he always **(4)** .... as a cowardly, cruel and reprehensible monarch.

The rebellion that started in England in 1215 had John as its cause. His defence of the French territories was ineffective, and the constant collection of taxes **(5)** .... the incomes of the barons and increased their discontent. It seemed that no one was safe from his arbitrary rule. The barons **(6)** .... to pay scutage and conspired to resist the king. By May 1215 war had broken out. The rebels, under the name 'the Army of God', **(7)** .... the king and occupied London. John agreed **(8)** .... them and sealed the Magna Carta.

0	**A** succeeded	**B** succeeds	**C** has succeeded	**D** had succeeded
1	**A** more	**B** then	**C** about	**D** than
2	**A** has left	**B** left	**C** leaved	**D** had left
3	**A** dyed	**B** has died	**C** died	**D** had died
4	**A** appeared	**B** has appeared	**C** appear	**D** appears
5	**A** drains	**B** had drained	**C** did not drain	**D** has drained
6	**A** refuse	**B** refusing	**C** refused	**D** has refused
7	**A** defy	**B** have defied	**C** defyed	**D** defied
8	**A** to meet	**B** meet	**C** met	**D** meeting

1 Battle between Crusaders and Muslims. Bibliothèque Nationale, Alinari Archives, Paris.

Milestones

1215, the Magna Carta
The clauses of the Magna Carta were indictments against John's rule. Among them, the Magna Carta called for a guarantee of protection to all free men from illegal imprisonment and seizure of property. It also asked for swift justice and scutage limitations. The charter established a committee of twenty-five barons with a mandate to wage war on the king if he failed to respect the agreement.

3 **READ** the texts again and get ready to report orally on the following points:
1 Richard I;
2 the reasons for John's unpopularity;
3 the barons' reaction to John's rule;
4 the clauses of the Magna Carta.

TEXT BANK 3: *ROBIN HOOD*

FCE Reading and Use of English – Part 2

4 OPEN CLOZE. For questions 1–8, read the text below and write the word which best fits each gap. Use only one word in each gap. There is an example at the beginning (0).

MEDIEVAL OUTLAWS

THE MEDIEVAL OUTLAW IS A FAMILIAR FIGURE IN (0) ....THE.... MODERN IMAGINATION. THIS IS DUE (1) .... THE POPULARITY OF THE LEGEND OF ROBIN HOOD. WE TEND TO IMAGINE ROBIN AND OUTLAWS (2) .... FUGITIVES BECAUSE THEY DEFIED THE KING'S OFFICIALS AND OPERATED OUTSIDE THE LAW IN THE GREAT FORESTS OF THE KINGDOM. WHAT WE FORGET IS THAT (3) .... WAS AN ESTABLISHED PROCESS BEHIND THE CREATION OF OUTLAWS. MEN (4) .... NOT CHOOSE TO BECOME OUTLAWS: THEY WERE MADE OUTLAWS. THIS WAS A TOOL FREQUENTLY EMPLOYED (5) .... HENRY II, RICHARD I AND JOHN TO ENFORCE THE EXILE OF INDIVIDUALS FOUND GUILTY OR SUSPECTED OF ROBBERY, THEFT OR MURDER. SUCH INDIVIDUALS WERE OBLIGED TO LEAVE THE KINGDOM IN EITHER EIGHT DAYS (6) .... FORTY DAYS. IF THEY RETURNED, THEY WERE TO BE ARRESTED AS OUTLAWS. THIS MEANT IMMEDIATE EXECUTION. MEN WERE OUTLAWED FOR TREASON, (7) .... MADE IT A POWERFUL TOOL FOR THE PUNISHMENT AND REMOVAL OF THE KING'S ENEMIES. CLAUSE 39 OF THE MAGNA CARTA ADDRESSED THE OPERATION OF OUTLAWRY: (8) .... FREE MAN WAS TO BE IMPRISONED, DISPOSSESSED OF HIS PROPERTY AND EXILED, OUTLAWED OR RUINED 'EXCEPT BY THE LAWFUL JUDGEMENT OF HIS PEERS OR BY THE LAW OF THE LAND'.

5 DESCRIBE the process of outlawry using the following words:

defy • tool • exile • guilty • execution • treason • imprisoned • dispossessed • peers

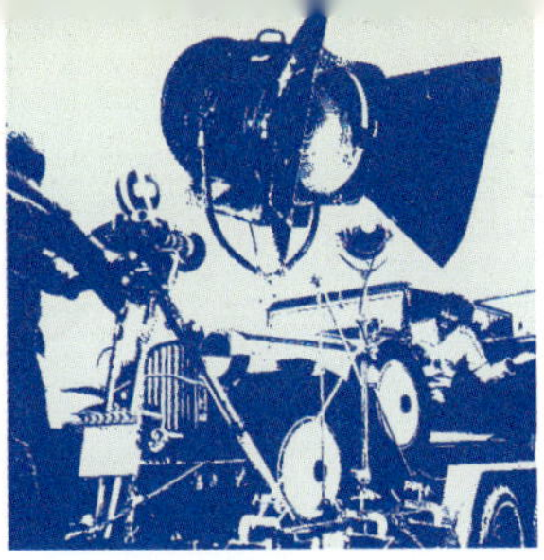

1.7 Two Films About...

Robin Hood

WARM-UP

1 **DISCUSS the questions.**

1. What do you know about Robin Hood?
2. Why was he famous?
3. How was he traditionally dressed?
4. Who was his enemy?
5. Do you know the names of some of his friends?

Robin Hood, Prince of Thieves

Directed by Kevin Reynolds; USA 1991.
With Kevin Kostner (Robin of Locksley); Mary Elizabeth Mastrantonio (Maid Marian); Sean Connery (King Richard); Morgan Freeman (the Moor).

The young nobleman Robin of Locksley escapes from a hellish prison in the Holy Land and makes his way home to England with a Moor, Azeem. Once home, Robin discovers that his father has been murdered and the wicked sheriff of Nottingham is frightening the country. While travelling through Sherwood Forest, Robin is ambushed by a gang of thieves, but he soon learns that they are honest men and women who have been driven from their homes by the sheriff's cruelty. Robin wins their trust and becomes their leader. He falls in love with Maid Marian, a relative of King Richard. Eventually, the sheriff dies and Robin and Marian get married with the blessing of the king.

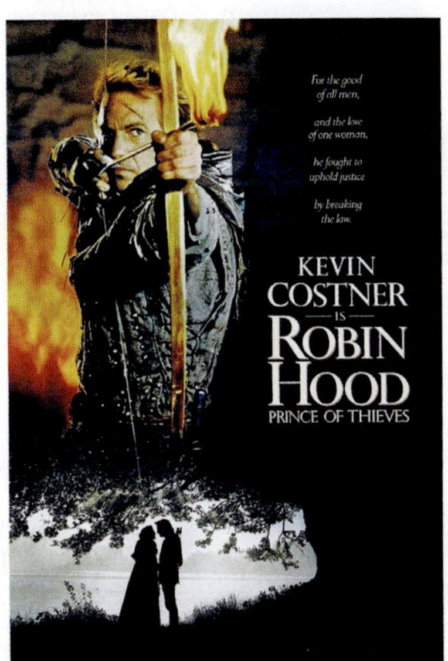

What about accuracy?
The film presents an accurate portrayal of medieval Europe: there are horses and carriages for transport; the Church is highly respected; there are both good and bad knights; and public torture is used for the people's amusement. But there are also some inaccuracies. Although the film is set during King Richard's absence from England, Prince John does not appear and it is the sheriff of Nottingham who tries to fill the vacuum of power.

Robin Hood

Directed by Ridley Scott; USA 2010.
With Russell Crowe (Robin Hood); Cate Blanchett (Lady Marion); Max von Sydow (Robin's father).

This version of 'Robin Hood' differs from previous ones: it tells of Robin Hood's transformation from Robin Longstride, the son of a stonemason and an archer in King Richard's army, into a leader of English soldiers against an invading French army and, finally, into a rebel against King John.

The climax of the film is the French army's invasion of England's Dover Beach, where they are opposed by an English army. The English are victorious, but in the final scenes King John declares Robin an outlaw. In response to this, Robin moves to Sherwood Forest with his friends to form what will become the Merry Men of Sherwood Forest.

What about accuracy?
Warfare is presented as exceptionally brutal, fought with swords, arrows, boiling oil and fire. Life in England, except for the rich, was hard at that time, with most people living in huts. Even those with land and titles, like Lady Marion, had to face grain shortages, do hard labour and live in cold, barren castles. The film makes Robin responsible for the Magna Carta, which was historically impossible.

1.8 **Literature**

The medieval ballad

Literary language
The ballad

Here are the most important features of the ballad:

- short stanzas of two or four lines;
- repetition of words or lines;
- mixture of dialogue and narration;
- narrative as a series of rapid flashes;
- both real and supernatural characters;
- themes of the supernatural, love, war, domestic tragedy, outlawry.

WARM-UP

1 **REFER to the introduction on ballads and make predictions about:**

1 the content of the ballad;
2 the characters involved;
3 the stylistic devices.

1 A young woman dancing to the sound of the troubadour's music, ca 1300. University Library, Heidelberg, Germany.

Ballads were produced anonymously and sung with or without accompaniment or dance. They were transmitted orally and written down between the 13th and 14th centuries. They were later collected and published by Bishop Thomas Percy in his famous *Reliques of Ancient English Poetry* in 1765.

Lord Randal

Anonymous

First published in the 19th century

The poem you are going to read is a traditional ballad. It is a folk narrative poem which was very popular in the late Middle Ages. It was originally adapted for singing and dancing.

1.3

O where ha'[1] you been, Lord Randal my son?
And where ha' you been, my handsome young man?
I ha' been at the greenwood[2]; mother, mak[3] my bed soon,
For I'm wearied wi'[4] hunting and fain wad[5] lie down.

An' wha[6] met ye[7] there, Lord Randal my son?
An' wha met you there; my handsome young man?
O I met wi' my true-love; mother, mak my bed soon,
For I'm wearied wi' huntin'[8] and fain wad lie down.

And what did she give you, Lord Randal my son?
And what did she give you, my handsome young man?
Eels fried[9] in a pan; mother, mak my bed soon,
For I'm wearied wi' huntin' and fain wad lie down.

And wha gat your leavins[10], Lord Randal my son?
And wha gat your leavins, my handsome young man?
My hawks and my hounds; mother, mak my bed soon,
For I'm wearied wi' huntin' and fain wad lie down.

And what becam[11] of them, Lord Randal my son?
And what becam of them, my handsome young man?
They stretched their legs out an' died; mother, mak my bed soon,
For I'm wearied wi' huntin' and fain wad lie down.

O I fear you are poisoned, Lord Randal my son,
I fear you are poisoned, my handsome young man.
O yes, I am poisoned; mother, mak my bed soon,
For I'm sick at the heart and I fain wad lie down.

What d'ye[12] leave to your mother, Lord Randal my son?
What d'ye leave to your mother, my handsome young man?
Four and twenty milk kye[13]; mother, mak my bed soon,
For I'm sick at the heart and fain wad lie down.

1 **ha'**. *Have.*
2 **greenwood.** Bosco.
3 **mak.** *Make.*
4 **wi'**. *With.*
5 **fain wad.** Gradirei (*wad = would*).
6 **An' wha.** *And who.*
7 **ye.** *You.*
8 **huntin'**. *Hunting.*
9 **Eels fried.** Anguille fritte.
10 **wha gat your leavings.** *Who got your leavings.* Chi ebbe gli avanzi del pasto.
11 **becam.** *Became.*
12 **d'ye.** *Do you.*
13 **kye.** *Cows.*

REDBURN

What d'ye leave to your sister, Lord Randal my son?
What d'ye leave to your sister, my handsome young man?
My gold and my silver; mother, make my bed soon,
For I'm sick at the heart and I fain wad lie down.

What d'ye leave to your brother, Lord Randal my son?
What d'ye leave to your brother, my handsome young man?
My houses and my lands; mother, mak my bed soon,
For I'm sick at the heart and I fain wad lie down.

What d'ye leave to your true-love, Lord Randal my son?
What d'ye leave to your true-love, my handsome young man?
I leave her hell and fire; mother, mak my bed soon,
For I'm sick at the heart and I fain wad lie down.

COMPREHENSION

2 READ the ballad carefully and answer the following questions.

1. Who is speaking?
2. Can you infer when and where the story is set?
3. Where has Lord Randal been? Why?
4. Who did he meet?
5. What was he given?
6. What did he take with him?
7. What happened to him?

ANALYSIS

3 FOCUS on the sound pattern of the poem to understand its musical quality.

1. Write down the rhyme scheme using the letters of the alphabet. Is it regular? If it is, why?
2. Point out all the repeated words. Are there many? You will notice they are repeated without any variation from stanza to stanza. **This sort of repetition involves the use of a sort of fixed formula called 'refrain'.**
3. Find examples of alliteration, underlining the words that start with the same consonant sound.
4. Discuss the effect of rhyme, repetition and alliteration. Tick as appropriate and justify your choice.
   - ◻ They help the listener to memorise.
   - ◻ They create a musical effect.
   - ◻ They link words and lines.
   - ◻ They emphasise important details.

4 FOCUS on the layout of the poem, that is, its organisation on the page.

1. How many stanzas are there?
2. How many lines are there in each stanza?
3. What is the function of the apostrophes?

5 CONSIDER the language of the poem.

1. Decide whether the nouns are concrete or abstract. To what purpose? Tick and give reasons:
   - ◻ To convey the psychology of the characters.
   - ◻ To describe events.
   - ◻ To express feelings.
2. Each stanza (from 1 to 6) contains an alternation of sense and sound. Lines 1 and 3 provide information about the storyline; lines 2 and 4 contribute to the sound quality of the poem through repetition. The third line of stanzas 1–6 contains key words. Write them down below. The first has been provided.
   - stanza 1 *greenwood*
   - stanza 2 ....
   - stanza 3 ....
   - stanza 4 ....
   - stanza 5 ....
   - stanza 6 ....

   In this way we get to know the story; here is its beginning. Complete it using your own words.
   Lord Randal has been hunting in the wood and he has met...
3. Say where the turning point, or climax, is. Which stanza is it in?
4. The climax of the story affects the tone of the dialogue between Lord Randal and his mother in the last four stanzas. In fact they contain another device typical of the ballad: the oral testament. Explain how it works.

6 FIND evidence in the text for the following:

- hunting, as a resource;
- the absence of the horse, which helps you understand that *Lord Randal* is a very old ballad, witnessing an age when hunting was carried out on foot;
- the wood, as a main feature of landscape but, at the same time, as a mysterious and magic place;
- hawks and hounds, as the assistants of the hunter.

YOUR TURN

7 DISCUSS in pairs. The ballad is still used in modern pop and folk music. Can you think of examples of modern ballads sung by famous singers? How do they differ from medieval ballads?

1.9 **History**

The birth of Parliament

WARM-UP

1 **DISCUSS.** What do you know about today's English Parliament?

On John's death, his nine-year-old son, Henry III (1207–72), became king, and England was governed by a group of barons until he came of age. It was in his reign that parliament began to create a structure of permanent control over the king's policies. The term 'parliament' comes from the French word meaning 'discussion', and in fact his council included barons, knights and, for the first time, two representatives from each town.

Henry's son, Edward I (1239–1307), continued the experiment when he became king in 1272. The meeting of his council, known as the 'Model Parliament' of 1295, included representatives of the barons, the clergy, two knights from each county and two citizens from each town. The system of the future two Houses of Parliament – the House of Lords and the House of Commons – was already in place.

1 The English Parliament meets before Edward, ca 1300.

2 A photo of a Parliamentary session of the House of Commons today.

3 The British Houses of Parliament in the Palace of Westminster on the north bank of the River Thames.

Internet Lab

TYPE in the website www.parliament.uk and carry out a research project on the following:

1 Parliament's role;
2 its composition;
3 checking the work of government;
4 rules and customs;
5 Parliament and the Crown;
6 the birth of the two-chamber system;
7 the increase of the Commons' power;
8 the clash between Parliament and the Crown;
9 the supremacy of Parliament over the Crown;
10 the growth of the size of Parliament and devolution.

1.10 **Society**

The three orders of medieval society

WARM-UP

1 **READ the title of the section (1.10). Then look at the pictures below and write the names of the three orders of medieval society under them.**

peasants
nobles
clergy

1 ....

2 ....

3 ....

FCE Listening – Part 1

2 1.4 | **EXTRACTS WITH MULTIPLE-CHOICE QUESTIONS. You will hear people talking about medieval society. For questions 1–8, choose the best answer (A, B or C).**

1 You hear a lecturer talking about medieval society. What was it like?
- A It was fixed and hierarchical.
- B It was characterised by mobility.
- C It was powerful and free.

1–2 Occupations of the months from a manuscript of ca 1280.

2 You hear a professor explaining the nobility in feudal society. What did a lord need to maintain his power?
- A Hereditary titles.
- B The king.
- C Castles and vassals.

3 You hear a student answering the teacher's question about medieval society. Who were vassals?
- A They were the king's friends.
- B They were men who had taken an oath to the king.
- C They were the king's guards.

4 You hear part of a history lesson at school. What linked the clergy to the noble estate?
- A They both prayed.
- B The eldest male heirs who inherited the estates and titles.
- C The younger sons of noble families who entered religious life.

5 You hear a radio talk about the controversial aspects of a clergyman's life. What were its contradictions?
- A Many clergymen had properties and children.
- B All clergymen were poor and chaste.
- C Most clergymen were poor but not chaste.

6 You hear an extract from a history programme about medieval society. What percentage of the population were peasants?
- A 5%.
- B 10%.
- C 95%.

7 You hear part of a history lesson at school. What did serfdom also imply?
- A Being born on the manor.
- B Paying taxes and being subject to the lord's permission to get married.
- C Having basic individual rights.

8 You hear two people discussing the breakdown of the three orders, or estates, of medieval society. When did some social mobility start?
- A After the Black Death had killed up to half of the population.
- B After Chaucer wrote *The Canterbury Tales*.
- C In the 13th century.

3 **EXPLAIN what each order, or estate, did in medieval society.**

1.11 **Literature**

Geoffrey Chaucer's portrait of English society

WARM-UP

1 **DISCUSS. Geoffrey Chaucer is regarded as the 'father of English literature'. Can you think of the possible reasons why? Can you guess what he chose to write about?**

1 Pier Paolo Pasolini as Chaucer in the film 'The Canterbury Tales', directed by Pasolini himself in 1972.

2 A mural by Ezra Winter illustrating the characters in *The Canterbury Tales*. Library of Congress, Washington DC, US. This mural shows (left to right): The Miller; the Host of Tabard Inn; the Knight, followed by his son, the Squire; a Yeoman; the Doctor of Physic; Chaucer, riding with his back to the observer, as he talks to the Lawyer; the Clerk of Oxenford; the Manciple; the Sailor; the Prioress; the Nun; and three priests.

Geoffrey Chaucer's life

Born about 1343, Geoffrey Chaucer (ca 1343–1400) was the son of a wine merchant and the relative wealth of his family enabled him to receive an excellent education. He found employment in the house of John of Gaunt, son of King Edward III of England and the wealthiest man in the land. In response to the death of John of Gaunt's first wife, he wrote one of his most important works, *The Book of the Duchess*. It was his skill and inventiveness as a writer, combined with a clever mind and practical skills, that raised his social status. He worked as a controller of the customs for the Port of London and took part in important diplomatic missions. He died in 1400 and was the first poet to be buried in Westminster Abbey, in what was to become Poets' Corner.

The Canterbury Tales (ca 1387–1400)

In his unfinished narrative poem *The Canterbury Tales* Chaucer used the structure of the three orders of society. This work belongs to a genre of writing known as 'estates satire', in which stock characters or stereotypes were represented, such as a dishonest miller, a lascivious friar and a virtuous knight. Chaucer, however, also included a significant number of figures representing the rising merchant class of his day.

The premise of *The Canterbury Tales*

The story is about thirty people, including Chaucer as narrator, who meet at the Tabard Inn in London. They are all there to join a pilgrimage to Canterbury Cathedral and the shrine of Thomas Becket . The innkeeper decides to make things interesting by suggesting that every pilgrim should tell two stories on the way to Canterbury and two on the way back; the pilgrim who tells the best story will win a free dinner. The various tales are both religious and humorous, moral and satirical. Before the storytelling begins, however, Chaucer gives us portraits of each of the travellers in a 'General Prologue'.

The three estates

Chaucer begins his character description with a knight who, with his son, is the only representative of the noble estate on this particular pilgrimage. His description is almost entirely focused on the numerous military campaigns he has fought. He represents the warlike aspect of the noble classes – the original source of their power and status. By contrast, the knight's son represents a noble character with courtly and chivalric attributes.

Ridiculing the religious

In the 'General Prologue', Chaucer then moves from the nobility to the clergy. The character of the prioress, a kind of nun, is described next, but instead of a description highlighting her faith and devotion, Chaucer's narrator describes the prioress's singing, her ability to speak French, her elegant table manners and her love of small animals. At Chaucer's time it was dangerous to criticise the king, but

writers made fun of monks, nuns, friars and pardoners. The medieval Church claimed to be all-powerful. It was strong culturally, but by modern standards it was weak as an organisation. Ordinary people often ignored Church laws and some attacked Church property. When a dissident movement (the Lollards, led by John Wycliffe) emerged in the 1380s, the authorities became watchful for heresy, but only a few opinions were classified as heretical.

Overcoming the three estates

One of the most fascinating aspects of Chaucer's version of the estates satire is that he includes several pilgrims – the Doctor, the Shipman, the Cook, to name just three – who do not fit neatly into the three estates model. The figure that best displays this is the Wife of Bath, whose status as a widow and a merchant contradicts traditional medieval ideas of both gender and class – demonstrating how the social structure was changing. Five times married, she is perhaps the most entertaining of the pilgrims. She, like so many others among this group, seems to regard the pilgrimage as a kind of social activity, as she has been to all the major pilgrimage sites of the medieval world: Jerusalem, Rome, Boulogne, Santiago de Compostella and Cologne. She has visited some of these sites more than once. This suggests a remarkable freedom of movement and access to wealth that was unusual in the Middle Ages, but still common enough to confound and complicate the ideal of the three orders.

The pilgrimage

Chaucer used the idea of pilgrimage as an organising principle for his collection of tales. Pilgrimages to religious sites were an important feature of medieval religious life for members of all social classes. Although Chaucer's pilgrims seem more interested in socialising than spirituality, thousands of medieval people felt obliged to make journeys to places as far away as Jerusalem and as close as the next village in search of forgiveness, to give thanks or simply to demonstrate their faith.

Chaucer's language

During the Middle Ages, three languages were spoken in England: French, Anglo-Saxon and Latin. It was from the blend of these three that Middle English (1100–1450) originated. For about two centuries after the Norman Conquest, the ruling classes and the aristocracy used Norman French, while the conquered continued to speak in their native Anglo-Saxon language; Latin was mainly used by the Church and as the language of learning.

By the time Chaucer wrote *The Canterbury Tales*, English had replaced French as the language of instruction in local schools. English was also becoming the language of government, and there was a growing demand for literary works in English. However, Chaucer knew the problem of writing poetry in English: it demanded a new form of the language – a literary language – shaped largely by French and Latin models but built upon the old popular tradition and on a deep knowledge of actual speech, which formed the basis of Chaucer's dramatic style.

Literary language
The narrative poem

Narrative poems tell stories in verse. The greatest example of a narrative poem is Geoffrey Chaucer's *The Canterbury Tales*.

Here are the features of the narrative poem:

- variety of narrative elements (such as: the setting in time and place; the description of characters; the use of a narrator, often in the first person);
- links with the moral views of the time;
- insight into individual characters as regards their lifestyles, their psychology and their experiences.

2 READ the text about Geoffrey Chaucer's life and works and answer the questions.

1 What class did Chaucer belong to?
2 What made him successful during his life?
3 Where was he buried?
4 What genre does *The Canterbury Tales* belong to? What did Chaucer add?
5 What is the story about?
6 Did Chaucer follow the three orders of society in his presentation?
7 What was the purpose of a pilgrimage in medieval times?
8 What languages were spoken in England in the Middle Ages?
9 How was language changing when Chaucer began to write?
10 What formed the basis of his style?

1.11 Geoffrey Chaucer's portrait of English society

1 An illustration of Geoffrey Chaucer.

WARM-UP

1 **DISCUSS.** What do you associate the season of spring with? How do you feel in this period of the year? What do you feel like doing?

When in April

Geoffrey Chaucer

The Canterbury Tales (ca 1387–1400)

General Prologue, lines 1–42

This is the opening of The Canterbury Tales. *These are perhaps Chaucer's best-known lines. They introduce the framework to the poem and also establish the sense of 'variety within unity', 'disorder within order' which characterises Chaucer's masterpiece.*

1.5

When in April the sweet showers[1] fall
And pierce the drought[2] of March to the root, and all
The veins are bathed in liquor of such power
As brings about the engendering[3] of the flower,
When also Zephyrus[4] with his sweet breath
Exhales an air in every grove and heath[5]
Upon the tender shoots[6], and the young sun
His half-course in the sign of the Ram[7] has run,
And the small fowl[8] are making melody
That sleep away the night with open eye
(So nature pricks them[9] and their heart engages)
Then people long to[10] go on pilgrimages
And palmers[11] long to seek the stranger strands[12]
Of far-off saints, hallowed[13] in sundry[14] lands,
And specially, from every shire[15]'s end
Of England, down to Canterbury they wend[16]
To seek the holy blissful martyr[17], quick
To give his help to them when they were sick.
It happened in that season that one day
In Southwark, at The Tabard, as I lay
Ready to go on pilgrimage and start
For Canterbury, most devout at heart,
At night there came into that hostelry[18]
Some nine and twenty in a company
Of sundry folk happening then to fall
In fellowship[19], and they were pilgrims all
That towards Canterbury meant to ride.
The rooms and stables[20] of the inn were wide;
They made us easy, all was of the best.
And, briefly, when the sun had gone to rest,
I'd spoken to them all upon the trip
And was soon one with them in fellowship,
Pledged[21] to rise early and to take the way
To Canterbury, as you heard me say.
But none the less[22], while I have time and space,
Before my story takes a further pace[23],
It seems a reasonable thing to say
What their condition was, the full array[24]
Of each of them, as it appeared to me,
According to profession and degree[25],
And what apparel[26] they were riding in;
And at a Knight I therefore will begin.

1 **showers.** Piogge.
2 **pierce the drought.** Penetrano la siccità.
3 **brings about the engendering.** Genera.
4 **Zephyrus.** Zeffiro.
5 **grove and heath.** Bosco e brughiera.
6 **shoots.** Germogli.
7 **the Ram.** L'Ariete.
8 **fowl.** Uccelli.
9 **pricks them.** Li punge.
10 **long to.** Sentono il desiderio.
11 **palmers.** Palmieri, pellegrini.
12 **to seek the stranger strands.** Cercare i lidi forestieri.
13 **hallowed.** Venerati.
14 **sundry.** Diverse.
15 **shire.** Contea.
16 **wend.** (*Arc.*) Si dirigono.
17 **blissful martyr.** Beato martire, San Tommaso di Canterbury.
18 **hostelry.** Locanda.
19 **fellowship.** Compagnia.
20 **stables.** Stalle.
21 **pledged.** Con la promessa, l'impegno.
22 **none the less.** Tuttavia.
23 **takes a further pace.** Proceda.
24 **array.** Schiera.
25 **degree.** Ceto.
26 **apparel.** Abbigliamento.

COMPREHENSION

2 **READ the first 18 lines and answer the following questions.**

1. What does April bring about?
2. What is the west wind called? What action does it perform?
3. What are the little birds doing?
4. What effect does spring have on people?
5. Where do English people decide to go? Why?

3 **READ up to line 34 and make notes about:**

- the place setting;
- the speaker's disposition;
- the setting in time;
- the number of people involved;
- their relationship.

4 **READ the text to the end and explain what method of description the poet is going to employ.**

5 **SAY in your own words what the story is about.**

ANALYSIS

6 **SAY if the lines rhyme. What rhyme scheme can you identify?**

7 **FOCUS on the opening lines. They convey a sense of growth and energy. Find the words referring to these fields:**

- Growth ....
- Energy ....

Now explain the connection between spring and the pilgrimage.

8 **FIND examples of personification, that is, giving a personal nature or human characteristics to something that is not human, or the representation of an abstract quality in human form. Explain how they are achieved.**

9 **FOCUS on the figure of the narrator.**

1. Underline the first explicit reference to his presence.
2. Find where the voice of Chaucer the poet is heard in the opening lines.
3. Say where the narrator becomes a pilgrim himself.

YOUR TURN

10 **PICK OUT the main features of the narrative poem in the text.**

WARM-UP

1 **CONSIDER the title of the passage. What information do the words 'wife' and 'Bath' provide?**

2 Laura Betti as the Wife of Bath in the film 'The Canterbury Tales', directed by Pier Paolo Pasolini in 1972.

The Wife of Bath

Geoffrey Chaucer

The Canterbury Tales (ca 1387–1400)
General Prologue, lines 455–486

In this passage you will read about a pilgrim. Her name is Dame Alice. 'Wife' is her status in society; she is actually a widow. 'Bath' is the town she comes from. She really enjoys going on pilgrimages. She represents worldly, earthy qualities as well as a female point of view.

1.6

A worthy woman from beside Bath city
Was with us[1], somewhat deaf[2], which was a pity[3].
In making cloth she showed so great a bent[4]
She bettered those of Ypres and of Ghent[5].
In all the parish not a dame dared stir
Towards the altar steps in front of her[6],
And if indeed they did, so wrath[7] was she
As to be quite put out of charity.
Her kerchiefs[8] were of finely woven ground;
I dared have sworn they weighed a good ten pound,
The ones she wore on Sunday, on her head.
Her hose[9] were of the finest scarlet red
And gartered[10] tight; her shoes were soft and new.
Bold was her face, handsome, and red in hue.
A worthy woman all her life, what's more

1 **with us.** Con noi (l'autore è uno dei pellegrini).
2 **somewhat deaf.** Un po' sorda.
3 **which was a pity.** Il che (il fatto che fosse sorda) era un peccato.
4 **so great a bent.** Molta predisposizione.
5 **of Ypres and of Ghent.** Città delle Fiandre celebri per la manifattura e il commercio della lana.
6 **dared stir ... in front of her.** Osava precederla.
7 **wrath.** Furiosa.
8 **kerchiefs.** Sciarpe.
9 **hose.** Calze.
10 **gartered.** Fermate con la giarrettiera.

1.11 Geoffrey Chaucer's portrait of English society

She'd had five husbands, all at the church door,
Apart from other company in youth;
No need just now to speak of that, forsooth[11].
And she had thrice been to Jerusalem,
Seen many strange rivers and passed over them;
She'd been to Rome and also to Boulogne,
St James of Compostella and Cologne,
And she was skilled in wandering by the way.
She had gap-teeth[12], set widely, truth to say.
Easily on an ambling[13] horse she sat
Well wimpled up[14], and on her head a hat
As broad as is a buckler or a shield[15];
She had a flowing mantle that concealed[16]
Large hips, her heels spurred[17] sharply under that.
In company she liked to laugh and chat
And knew the remedies for love's mischances,
An art in which she knew the oldest dances.

1 Laura Betti as the Wife of Bath in the film 'The Canterbury Tales', directed by Pier Paolo Pasolini in 1972.

11 **forsooth.** (*Arc.*) In verità.
12 **gap-teeth.** Spazi tra i denti (segno di temperamento sensuale e amore per i viaggi secondo la fisiognomica).
13 **ambling.** Che andava al passo.
14 **Well wimpled up.** Ben avvolta da un soggolo.
15 **a buckler or a shield.** Un brocchiere (piccolo scudo circolare) o uno scudo.
16 **concealed.** Nascondeva.
17 **spurred.** Incitavano (il cavallo) con gli speroni.

COMPREHENSION

2 **AS YOU READ** the passage, find the lines where Chaucer describes the Wife of Bath's economic skills and those linked to her social skills. What were her skills and abilities?

3 **FIND** the details regarding her clothes. What do they suggest about her social status?

4 **UNDERLINE** all the physical descriptions of the Wife. Are they positive or negative?

5 **TWO NUMBERS** are mentioned. What are they and what do they refer to?

ANALYSIS

6 **WRITE** down the rhyme scheme. You have just learnt to recognise a rhyming couplet, the rhyme pattern used by Chaucer.

7 **WHAT COLOUR** is mentioned and associated with this character? What do we normally associate with this colour?

8 **FIND** where Chaucer uses exaggeration in his description of the Wife. Here are some key words to help you find the exaggerations: first, kerchiefs, numbers, hat. What effect do these four exaggerated descriptions have on our idea of what the Wife of Bath was like?

9 **IRONY** is the use of words to convey a meaning that is the opposite of its literal meaning. Find some examples of irony in the text. Do you get the impression the Wife of Bath went on pilgrimages because she was very pious?

YOUR TURN

10 **DISCUSS.** Do you think the description of this character is a stereotype or the picture of an individual? Does this pilgrim fit into one of the three orders of medieval society?

1.12 **Cultural Issues**

Giving identity a voice

1 Poet Patience Agbabi reads one of her poems about climate change in London, 2007. Photo by Suzanne Plunkett.

WARM-UP

1 **IMAGINE you have to write your own version of 'The Wife of Bath'. What type of woman and occupation might you choose?**

The stories in *The Canterbury Tales* are very much about entertainment, and the teller of the best tale is promised a free meal at the end of the pilgrimage. In this way, it resembles a modern-day poetry slam, where poets perform and compete for a prize. British performance poet Patience Agbabi (1965–) is a self-confessed lover of Chaucer's work. In her poem 'The Wife of Bafa', she has refashioned 'The Wife of Bath' into a sassy, contemporary Nigerian businesswoman.

FCE Speaking – Part 2

2 **INDIVIDUAL LONG TURN. Here are two sets of two photos showing women at work. In pairs decide which of you is A and which is B.**

- **Candidate A:** Look at the photos for A. Compare the photos and say which place you would choose to work in and why. Speak for about one minute.
- **Candidate B:** Look at the photos for B. Compare the pictures and say what qualities you think are needed to do the job shown. Speak for about one minute.

At the end of each description, answer an extra question.

- **Extra question for A:** Do you think women have more or fewer work opportunities than men?
- **Extra question for B:** Do you think people work better alone or as part of a team?

A

B

The Wife of Bafa

Patience Agbabi

2010

1.7

My name is Mrs Alice Ebi Bafa.
I come from Nigeria.
I'm very fine, isn't it.
My next birthday I'll be ... twenty-nine.
I'm business woman.
Would you like to buy some cloth?
I've all the latest styles from Lagos,
Italian shoe and handbag to match,
lace, linen[1] and Dutch wax.
I only buy the best
and I travel first class.

Some say I have blood on my hands
'cause I like to paint my nails red
but others call me femme fatale.
My father had four wives
so I've had five husbands.
I cast a spell[2] with my gap-toothed smile
and my bottom[3] power.
Three were good and two were bad.

The first three were old and rich
and I was young and fit.
They died of exhaustion.
The fourth one was ladies' man.
I could not count his women on one hand
but he'd rage[4] if I looked at another man.
I was very wild when I was young.
They called me Miss Highlife,

1 **lace, linen.** Pizzo, lino.
2 **I cast a spell.** Ho lanciato un incantesimo.
3 **bottom.** Fondoschiena.
4 **he'd rage.** Si arrabbiava.

I was not considered a good wife
but I always respected my husband.
He died when I returned from this London.

The fifth one I married for love.
He was studying law at University of Ibadon.
He was not yet twenty-one,
wicked[5] in bed and so handsome
but he liked pornographic magazine.
His favourite was Playboy.
One day I threw it on fire
to teach him a lesson.
He turned into wife batterer[6].
He was to regret his action.
I beat him till he begged for his ancestors.
Now we get on like house on fire.

Some say I'm a witchcraft[7]
'cause I did not bear them children.
They do not understand your Western medicine.

You like my headtie[8].
It's the latest fashion.
They sell like hot cake[9] on Victoria Island.
Fifty pounds.
I give you discount 'cause I like your smile.
The quality is very good.
If I take off more I will not make profit
and I travel to Lagos next week.
Make it my lucky day.
Please, I beg you.

COMPREHENSION

1 **READ** the poem and complete the table below.

Name	
Nationality	
Age	
Job	
Physical appearance	
Clothes	

5 **wicked.** Perverso.
6 **wife batterer.** Uomo violento che picchia la moglie.
7 **witchcraft.** Stregoneria.
8 **headtie.** Foulard.
9 **like hot cake.** Molto.

1 Woman carrying a water jug on her head in Niger. Photo by Karen Kasmauski.

2 **ANSWER these questions about the poem.**
1. How many husbands did she have? What were they like?
2. What did the first three have in common?
3. What about the fourth? Did she love him?
4. What happened to her last husband?
5. Has she got any children?
6. What is she doing in the last stanza?

ANALYSIS

3 **EXPLAIN. How is 'The Wife of Bafa' narrated? How does it reveal the Wife's character?**

4 **DECIDE. Do the lines rhyme?**

5 **PICK OUT examples from the poem in which Agbabi wanted to replicate Nigerian English. What effect is achieved?**

6 **ANALYSE. Has the poet changed Chaucer's original?**

7 **TICK as appropriate. What was the poet's aim?**
- ☐ To make a caricature of West African women.
- ☐ To celebrate a timeless, complex character that exists in all cultures.

YOUR TURN

8 **CREATE 'a modern pilgrim' in Chaucerian style and get ready to perform in front of the class. Follow the prompts below.**
- Present your pilgrim with concrete details (clothes, physical features to reflect social status and personality).
- Use irony.
- Choose a modern occupation.
- Show respect for the pilgrim.

1.13 **History**

The Black Death: a great human tragedy

WARM-UP

1 **READ** the title of this section (1.13). Do you know what the Black Death was? Why was it called 'Black'?

FCE Reading and Use of English – Part 6

2 **GAPPED TEXT.** You are going to read a text about the Black Death. Six sentences have been removed from the text. Choose from the sentences A–G the one which best fits each gap (1–6). There is one extra sentence which you do not need to use.

- **A** The idea was simple enough: remove yourself from those areas which were affected.
- **B** On the other hand, most people who caught the plague were dead within a few days.
- **C** Normally it takes ten to fourteen days before the plague has killed off most of a contaminated rat colony.
- **D** This plague, known as the 'Black Death' because the body went dark-coloured after death, was caused by fleas living on black rats which infested ships trading with Europe.
- **E** But for almost everyone, the plague was a sign of God's anger.
- **F** The actual plague bacillus was discovered only in the middle of the 19th century.
- **G** The plague could take out an entire side of one street, the entire street or just one house on the street.

3 **ANSWER** the following questions about the text.

1. What were the causes of the bubonic plague?
2. How did men and women react to the disease?
3. Who was responsible for the plague, according to common people?
4. What were the main consequences of the Black Death?

The Black Death was one of the greatest human tragedies ever experienced in Europe. **1** ____ The apparent virulence of the outbreak in 1347–50 was linked to a lack of immunity among the population, but also to the fact that the bubonic form was accompanied by outbreaks of pneumonic plague, which was spread by direct contact between humans and gave no chance of survival.

Rich or poor, young or old, fit or ill, man or woman, the plague, like a tornado, made no distinction when it came. **2** ____ It sometimes happened that a victim would catch the plague but recover. **3** ____

Flight from infected areas was the most common response, especially among those who could afford to flee. **4** ____ This usually meant fleeing from the city to the countryside, as did the wealthy storytellers in Boccaccio's *The Decameron* (1348–53). Here is Boccaccio's description of the plague symptoms:

'[I]n men and women alike there appeared, at the beginning of the malady, certain swellings, either on the groin or under the armpits, whereof some waxed to the bigness of a common apple, others to the size of an egg, some more and some less, and these the vulgar named plague-boils.'

General ignorance about the causes of the plague did nothing to dispel fear and terror. The creatures responsible for the spread of the plague – rats and fleas – were not suspected for one very simple reason: they were common and familiar in the 14th century. **5** ____ The earthquake of 1348 was blamed for corrupting the air with foul odours, thus precipitating the plague. There were other theories too. **6** ____

The Black Death was responsible for the death of a third of England's population. The economic and social effects were enormous. Labour was scarce, so wages rose, prices dropped and the condition of those peasants who survived improved since they were able to demand payment for work done on their lord's land.

1–2 Images depicting England at the time of the Black Death.

1 Overview

Test what you know

1 DECIDE if the following statements are true or false. Correct the false ones.

1 Henry II increased the power of the barons. T F
2 The knights paid Henry II a sum of money instead of giving him military service. T F
3 Common Law was based on a written code. T F
4 Thomas Becket was a supporter of the king. T F
5 King John left for the Holy Land to take part in the Third Crusade. T F
6 With the Magna Carta, the king agreed that no tax could be imposed without the consent of the committee of twenty-five barons. T F
7 The first parliament was formed during the reign of Henry II. T F

2 PROVIDE an explanation for each of the following.

1 Scutage: ....
2 Common Law: ....
3 Magna Carta: ....
4 Model Parliament: ....

Can you do it?

3 EXPLAIN the link between Halloween and the Celts.

4 DESCRIBE Anglo-Saxon society.

5 SAY why Canterbury Cathedral is so important and what the most important features of its architectural style are.

6 TRACE the process behind the creation of outlaws.

7 REVISE your knowledge about Geoffrey Chaucer's *The Canterbury Tales* and complete the notes below.

1 The premise..
2 The three estates ....
3 The organising principle for his tales ....
4 The language ....

8 READ the text 'The Knight' from the 'General Prologue' of *The Canterbury Tales* and do the activities below.

1 Read the first four lines and write down what values the Knight is associated with.
2 What details does Chaucer give about the Knight's appearance? Why?
3 Circle all the adjectives used to describe the Knight. Are they consistent with the values he is associated with at the beginning of the passage?
4 What do you think is Chaucer's attitude towards the Knight and the values he represents?

There was a Knight, a most distinguished man,
Who from the day on which he first began
To ride abroad[1] had followed chivalry,
Truth, honour, generousness and courtesy.
He had done nobly in his sovereign's war
And ridden into battle, no man more,
As well in Christian as in heathen[2] places,
And ever honoured for his noble graces. [...]

He was of sovereign value in all eyes.
And though so much distinguished, he was wise
And in his bearing[3] modest as a maid.
He never yet a boorish[4] thing had said
In all his life to any, come what might;
He was a true, a perfect gentle-knight.
Speaking of his equipment, he possessed
Fine horses, but he was not gaily dressed.
He wore a fustian[5] tunic stained[6] and dark
With smudges[7] where his armour had left mark;
Just home from service, he had joined our ranks
To do his pilgrimage and render thanks.

1 **abroad.** *Qui*: fuori dal suo paese, in giro.
2 **heathen.** Pagani.
3 **bearing.** Portamento.
4 **boorish.** Volgare.
5 **fustian.** Di fustagno.
6 **stained.** Macchiata.
7 **smudges.** Sbavature, macchie.

Oral test

9 IMAGINE your teacher asks you the following questions in an oral test. For each question, prepare a one-minute turn.

1 What was the position of women in Celtic society?
2 What did the Romans introduce into Britain?
3 Why can we say that Athelstan made England?
4 What changes did Norman rule bring to society?
5 What was the *Domesday Book*?
6 Why is Henry II remembered as a great reformer?
7 Why can we consider 1215 a milestone in English history?
8 What are the most important features of medieval ballads?
9 Why is *The Canterbury Tales* an estates satire?
10 What were the economic and social effects of the Black Death?

The English Renaissance

Specification 2 | Homepage

Top News

1534
Henry VIII breaks with Rome

Top Issue

Woman, lady, mistress

Most Popular News

1558 Elizabeth I ascends the English throne

1588 England defeats the Invincible Armada

1564 William Shakespeare, England's genius, is born

Spotlight

Why study Shakespeare?

Cinema

See *Romeo and Juliet* on screen

The Arts

Elizabeth's portraits: the symbolism of power

Mapping History

Visit the places of the Gunpowder Plot

EXPLORE THE CULTURE

Culture | Literature | History | The Arts | Science | Two Films About... | Cultural Issues

2.1 History
Meet the Tudors

WARM-UP

1 **LOOK at the pictures (1–4) and match them with a caption (A–D). Then discuss what you think were the main problems the Tudor dynasty had to face.**

A The queen's progress. ....
B England defeats Spain. ....
C England begins to expand abroad. ....
D The king orders his son to maintain the Anglican faith. ....

1

2

3

4

FCE Reading and Use of English – Part 7

2 **MULTIPLE MATCHING. Read the text about the Tudor dynasty. For questions 1–10, choose from the people (A–D). The people may be chosen more than once.**

Which king/queen

used marriage as a political weapon?	1	2
persecuted Protestants?		3
created the basis of English naval power?		4
did not have any children?	5	6
deeply affected the fate of monasteries?		7
created a myth of the monarch?		8
created the Anglican Church?		9
encouraged the arts?		10

A. Henry VII

Henry VII (1457–1509), who came to the English throne when the Wars of the Roses ended, was the first king of the Tudor dynasty. He tried to consolidate his position through: a treaty with France, giving him recognition; a trade treaty with the Netherlands; and the dynastic marriage in 1501 between his son Arthur and the Spanish princess, Catherine of Aragon. During his reign he turned England into a modern state which he administered like a businessman. He also laid the foundations of English naval power by increasing spending on shipbuilding so that England could have its own merchant fleet and extend its military power.

B. Henry VIII

Henry VIII (1491–1547) was Henry VII's second son. From an early age he was a known figure at court, and in his youth he was a natural sportsman, which made him popular both with the English elite and with the English public. He was called the 'Golden Prince' both for his natural good looks and for his chivalry and education. In 1521 he was granted the title of 'Defender of the Faith' by the pope in recognition of his Latin treatise defending the sacraments. This title has been maintained by English monarchs ever since and is on English coins still today.

After the death of his brother Arthur, Henry married his widow, Catherine of Aragon, by special dispensation. In twenty years of marriage Catherine only produced a daughter, Mary, and Henry desperately wanted a male heir to keep the country united and strong. He began to consider marriage to his pregnant mistress Anne Boleyn, and asked the pope for a divorce in order to marry her. When it was clear that the pope would not declare his first marriage invalid, Henry broke with Rome and declared himself 'Supreme Head on Earth of the Church of England' by means of the Act of Supremacy (1534). This meant that he had the right to appoint bishops, decide on articles of faith and impose his will on the monasteries. The king soon dissolved the monasteries, taking their wealth, and social charities – such as schools and hospitals for the poor – mostly disappeared. Another consequence of Henry's policy was that Ireland remained a Catholic country and this marked the beginning of the Irish question. Henry married

GLOSSARY

treaty trattato, patto
fleet flotta
treatise dissertazione
tried processata
treason tradimento

Anne Boleyn in 1533, and she gave him a second daughter, Elizabeth. She fell out of favour, however, and was tried and executed for treason in 1536, leaving the king free to remarry. Henry went on to have four more wives in quick succession and one son, Edward, from his third wife, Jane Seymour.

C. Mary I

Mary I (1516–58) was born in 1516, the only surviving child of Henry VIII and Catherine of Aragon. Rejection by her father and the cruel treatment of her mother were to have a fundamental influence on her life. Her resentment took on a religious connotation when Henry also rejected the pope. She refused to abandon her own traditional faith, and when she became queen in 1553, she believed herself to be the agent of a Counter-Reformation. This attempt to restore England to papal obedience, her marriage to the Catholic Philip of Spain and the burning of Protestants, earned her the nickname 'Bloody Mary' and alienated public opinion. Mary's end was tragic: deserted by her husband, without an heir, her foreign and domestic policies were a failure, and her country was still divided over religion when she died.

D. Elizabeth I

In 1558 Elizabeth (1533–1603), Henry VIII and Anne Boleyn's daughter, became queen of a divided nation – the majority of which was anti-Catholic and anti-Spanish. She was twenty-five and had a strong personality, a lively intelligence and a passionate character. She had received an excellent education and could speak French, Latin and Italian with ease, but above all she was a political genius of the first order.

As queen she faced the problems of marriage and succession, religious division, domestic discontent and foreign threats. Her Church of England restored the country firmly to Protestantism, yet she granted Catholics freedom of worship. She was unmarried and used this as a political weapon, encouraging the hopes of European princes with whom it was important to keep on good terms. She often repeated that 'the Queen was married to her people'; eventually the people accepted this idea and began to make a cult of their 'Virgin Queen'. She wore magnificent clothes adorned with rich jewels to impress her subjects; she went on royal progresses to be seen and to get to know her people. She had numerous portraits painted and copies widely distributed. The spirit emanating from the queen inspired literature, music, drama and poetry.

She recognised Spain as her main trade rival and enemy. At first, open war was avoided and exploration and overseas trade expanded, making England a commercial and sea power. English sea captains, like Francis Drake (ca 1540–96), were secretly encouraged by the queen in their piracy against Spanish ships, and she took a share of the profits. They captured ships carrying precious metals, tobacco and slaves from America and Africa. In 1588 the Spanish decided to invade England and sent a great armada of 130 galleons to the English Channel, but the English defeated the Spanish Armada. Supremacy at sea enabled Elizabeth to lay the basis of England's empire, chartering seven companies to colonise in the name of trade.

Milestones

1534, the Act of Supremacy

The name 'Act of Supremacy' is used for two separate acts of the English Parliament, one passed in 1534 and the other in 1559. Both acts had the same purpose: to firmly establish the English monarch as the official head of the Church of England, supplanting the power of the Catholic pope in Rome.

In 1534 Henry VIII completed his break with the pope by getting Parliament to acknowledge him as 'Supreme Head on Earth of the Church of England'. By tying the church and monarchy so closely together, support for Catholicism became not simply a statement of personal religious conviction, but a repudiation of the authority of the monarch, and as such, an act of treason punishable by death.

Milestones

1588, the defeat of the Spanish Armada

In August 1588 the fleet of the Spanish Armada lay in the English Channel, close to the cliffs of Calais. The Spanish hoped that a success for their 'Invincible Armada' would mean that Queen Elizabeth, viewed as a Protestant heretic, would be deposed and the English people subjugated to Spanish rule and converted to Catholicism. There were many more Spanish ships than English vessels, but the English ships were smaller, faster and heavily armed. On the night of 7th August, the English filled eight ships with flammable material and set fire to them. They sent in the burning ships to create panic among the Spaniards and scatter the Armada's formation. The Spanish panicked and fled to the open sea, becoming easy targets for the English artillery.

Another important reason why the English were able to defeat the Armada was that the wind blew the Spanish ships northwards. Strong winds and terrible rain forced many ships onto rocks near Ireland. The outcome of 1588 was a European turning point because England's successful resistance showed that Spain was not 'invincible'.

2.2 The Arts

Portraits of Queen Elizabeth I

WARM-UP

1 **DISCUSS.** Why were so many portraits of Queen Elizabeth I painted?

FCE Reading and Use of English – Part 1

2 **MULTIPLE-CHOICE CLOZE.** For questions 1–8, read the extract from a biography of Queen Elizabeth I and decide which answer (A, B, C or D) best fits each gap.

The Symbolism of Power

When Elizabeth I came to the **(1)** .... in 1558 after the death of her sister Mary, she needed the support of all her people. Monarchs used to make a tour of the country and show themselves to the people; this was called a 'progress'. However, Elizabeth had many Catholic enemies, and when it was not considered **(2)** .... for her to travel around the country, she chose, instead, to use **(3)** .... to show herself to her people and impress their imagination. Pictures of Elizabeth were copied and distributed throughout the land, and the nobility would have a portrait in their great houses as a symbol of **(4)** .... to her.

The way the queen was painted changed over the course of her reign. In the early years, the queen was portrayed very simply, with little symbolism or even majesty to convey that she was the monarch. In some paintings she looks perhaps like any other wealthy Elizabethan woman. The combination of the Renaissance style and the queen's almost mythical **(5)** .... resulted in later portraits that are full of symbolism and are part of what has been called the 'Cult of Elizabeth, the Virgin Queen'.

The portraits give us some idea of the queen's physical appearance. While the pale-faced woman with reddish-gold hair is common to all of them, it seems that every painter has **(6)** .... a slightly different image of her. We can be **(7)** .... completely certain that her hair was a golden red, her eyes dark brown, her nose ridged or hooked in the middle, her lips rather thin and her cheekbones pronounced. Her hair was also probably naturally curly or at least wavy. She may well have had freckles on her pale skin, but like all Elizabethan ladies she would have taken care to avoid **(8)** .... the sun on her face, and the make-up she wore for most of her life would have protected her delicate skin from a suntan. White skin was fashionable in Tudor times as it was what distinguished the rich from the poor. If a person had white skin, it showed that he or she did not have to work outdoors for a living.

1	A monarchy	B crown	C throne	D royalty
2	A safe	B certain	C sure	D confident
3	A statues	B photos	C descriptions	D portraits
4	A loyalty	B sympathy	C kindness	D friendship
5	A success	B popularity	C love	D devotion
6	A held	B kept	C taken	D captured
7	A almost	B not	C but	D rather
8	A taking	B getting	C reaching	D shining

3 **LOOK** at the two portraits of the queen. What features do they have in common? Consider:

- lines;
- colours;
- line of sight;
- the queen's appearance;
- the queen's clothes.

1

2

1 Unknown artist, *Coronation Portrait*, ca 1600. The National Portrait Gallery, London.

2 George Gower, *Armada Portrait*, ca 1588. The Marquess of Salisbury, Hatfield House, Hatfield, England.

INTERACTIVE MAP 2: *THE GUNPOWDER PLOT*

King by divine right

1 **LOOK** at the title of the section (2.3) and then skim the text on the right quickly. In pairs discuss whether the English might have been happy with the new monarch or not.

2 **READ** the text carefully and get ready to report orally on the following points:
1. the role of Parliament;
2. the religious issue;
3. James I's financial policy;
4. the king's interest;
5. the Pilgrim Fathers;
6. the plot to blow up the Houses of Parliament.

GLOSSARY
rule governare
summon convocare
levy imporre, riscuotere
bar vietare l'accesso a
fine multare
apply for richiedere
patent esclusiva, brevetto
plot complottare
blow up far saltare in aria

With the death of Elizabeth I in 1603, the Tudor line died out and James VI (1566–1625) of Scotland became the first Stuart king in England, with the title of James I. He was a Protestant, and instead of basing his rule on 'the love of his people', he based it on the theory of the 'divine right of kings'. He believed that, as a monarch, he was the representative of God on earth. He summoned Parliament only to ask for money, but its members refused to levy any taxes unless the money was needed for war. He was interested in witchcraft and the supernatural, and in his treatise *Daemonologie* (1597) he declared his belief in black magic.

As in the early days of Elizabeth I, religion was the most urgent problem of the new reign. Catholics were barred from public life and were fined if they refused to attend the Church of England; extreme Protestants, called Puritans, disapproved of both the rites and the bishops of the Church of England. These Puritans had a high sense of duty and morality and they did not want to live in a country which they believed was going to fall into moral decline. So a hundred of them, the Pilgrim Fathers, applied for a government patent to colonise New England. In 1620 they left England for America on the Mayflower and founded New Plymouth.

King James authorised a new translation of the Bible in 1604. Nearly fifty scholars, influenced by Humanists and using the original Hebrew and Greek, worked on the translation for seven years. Unlike earlier texts, which were for scholars, this version would be heard and read by laymen. The Protestant religion actively encouraged personal knowledge of the Bible, and this version, the King James Bible, would be used by the Church of England for more than three hundred years, greatly influencing the spread of literacy and writing.

In 1605, some radical Catholics, led by Guy Fawkes, plotted to blow up the king in the Houses of Parliament. The failure of the 'Gunpowder Plot' is still commemorated in England on 5th November.

1 Portrait of James I of England, painted by Paulus van Somer. Museo del Prado, Madrid, Spain.

Insights

The origin of Thanksgiving Day
The first Thanksgiving was celebrated by the Pilgrim Fathers (early settlers of America) in 1621 to thank God for their first good harvest. They celebrated it with the local Wampanoag Indians, who had helped them survive and taught them how to plant their crops. That first feast lasted three days and included a wide variety of animals as well as fruits and vegetables from the autumn harvest. Americans did not all celebrate Thanksgiving at the same time until 1863, when President Abraham Lincoln declared the last Thursday in November a day of thanksgiving.

Today Americans celebrate Thanksgiving on the fourth Thursday of November. There is no school and most businesses close. Families and friends join together to eat roast turkey with cranberry sauce, potatoes, pumpkin pie and apple pie.

Insights

Guys Fawkes and Bonfire Night
Bonfire Night celebrations begin two or three days before 5th November. Children make puppet-like figures of Guy Fawkes, which are called 'Guys'. Some children even continue an old tradition of walking in the streets, carrying the 'Guy' they have just made and asking passersby for 'a penny for the Guy'. The kids then use the money to buy fireworks for the evening festivities.

On the night itself, the Guy is placed on the top of a bonfire, which is then set on fire, and firework displays fill the sky.

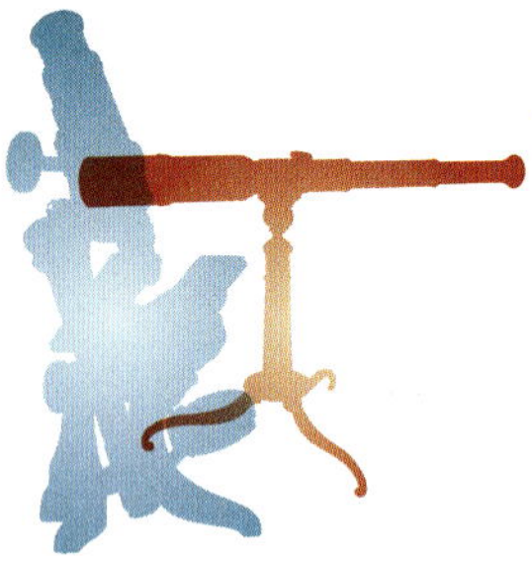

2.4 Science

An expanding world

WARM-UP

1 **READ** the title of the section (2.4). Do you know what the contemporary view of the universe was in Elizabethan times? What was it called?

The restlessness of the 16th century was increased by new geographical and scientific discoveries which weakened the old models of the world and the universe. By around 150 AD, the Alexandrian astronomer Ptolemy (2nd century AD) had written the *Geography*, which defined the discipline of geography and laid down the principles of global mapping. It had allowed scholars to map the world for the first time. Renaissance geographers produced new editions of the *Geography* and employed Ptolemy's principles to try to map the expanding world.

In Ptolemy's view of the universe, the sun and the planets revolved around a stationary earth. Below the moon was the world of mutability; above it, that of permanence. This old order of ideas was weakened by new cultural influences, such as the theories of Nicolaus Copernicus (1473–1543).

Copernicus was born in Poland but studied in Italy. It was in Bologna that a mathematics professor inspired him to question the medieval astronomical dogma. He created a new model of the solar system in which the sun was at the centre, with the earth and the other planets moving around it. The invention of the telescope by Galileo Galilei (1564–1642) proved that the earth turns around the sun; moreover, the Italian astronomer established the scientific method, that is, the study of the physical world by sensory observation, experiment and by mathematical measurement.

Astrology, however, continued to be taught at universities. Traditional medicine linked bodily rhythms and diseases to the motions of the seven planets and the influence of the twelve signs of the zodiac. The human microcosm could be understood by reference to the macrocosm of all creation. An entire hierarchical system linked the different orders of life – from minerals to angels.

Here is the chain as it was commonly understood in the 16th century.

- First there was the inanimate class: the elements, liquids and metals.
- Next there was the vegetative class.
- Then there was the animal class, with man at the top, as he had not only existence, life and feeling, but also understanding.
- Finally there were the angels, linked to man because of understanding, but freed from attachment to the lower faculties.

The position of man in the chain was extremely interesting. Given his double nature of matter and spirit, he had the unique function of linking all creation together, especially in the conflict between passion and reason.

1 Portrait of Galileo Galilei by Justus Sustermans, painted in 1636. National Maritime Museum, London.

2 **ANSWER** these questions about the text.

1 What was the cultural importance of Ptolemy's *Geography*?
2 How was the concept of mutability connected with Ptolemy's view of the universe?
3 How did Copernicus question Ptolemy's view of the universe?
4 What was Galileo's contribution to the development of astronomy?
5 How was the microcosm studied at universities?
6 How was the chain of being organised?
7 What position did man occupy in the chain?

FCE Listening – Part 3

3 1.8 | **MULTIPLE MATCHING. You will hear five people talking about Galileo. For questions 1–5, choose which of the opinions (A–H) each speaker expresses. Use each opinion only once. There are three extra letters which you do not need to use.**

A Although Galileo's discovery did not prove the Copernican theory, it certainly undermined 'natural philosophy'.
B Galileo suggested the presence of plants, animals and, maybe, rational inhabitants on the moon.
C Many nationalities, including the French, claimed the moon as their territory.
D Galileo can be compared to a new and greater Columbus.
E Galileo confirmed the previous views of the universe.
F Galileo's explorations of the heavens with his telescope overturned the old astronomers' views.
G The telescope helped to bring the moon down to earth.
H Galileo's discovery changed our understanding even more than the first landing on the moon.

Speaker 1	1
Speaker 2	2
Speaker 3	3
Speaker 4	4
Speaker 5	5

2.5 **Literature**

1.9 DICTATION: *ERASMUS OF ROTTERDAM*

The English Renaissance

WARM-UP

1 **IN PAIRS** list some of the main features of the Italian Renaissance, which flourished a century before the English one; mention some writers and painters you have studied.

2 **AS YOU READ** the text, write notes about the following:

1. the historical period covered by the English Renaissance;
2. its main feature;
3. how the English literature of the period differed from Italian literature;
4. what Humanism was called in England;
5. what it encouraged;
6. its contribution to the development of the English language;
7. Erasmus of Rotterdam's influence on the development of New Learning.

The English Renaissance

The English Renaissance covers the historical period from 1509, the year Henry VIII ascended the throne, to 1660, the year which marked the beginning of the Restoration. The English Renaissance developed later than its European equivalents and was an original, typically English movement. Its main feature was its strong Protestant basis, influenced by the Reformation under the reign of Henry VIII, who broke with Rome and declared that the king was the head of the English Church. The English literature of the period lacked the pagan serenity of the Italian Renaissance and was less linked to the visual arts.

New Learning

England fought to free itself from the Italian influence, which was identified with Rome and the papacy. The new literature was also influenced by the training in classical imitation of a number of Humanist scholars and translators, reaching back to the time of Erasmus of Rotterdam (ca 1469–1536). At the beginning of the century, he had stressed the importance of studying classical literature for the Christian student. The 'New Learning', as Humanism was also called, was established in grammar schools all over the country and in the two universities, Oxford and Cambridge. It encouraged confidence in the power of human reason to interpret man and nature, in the value of literature as an instrument of reason and in the dignity of modern English as a literary medium.

1 John Faed, *Shakespeare and his Friends at the Mermaid Tavern*, ca 1850. The Mermaid Tavern was located east of St Paul's Cathedral. It was the site of the so-called 'Friday Street Club'. The club, meeting monthly, was allegedly founded by Sir Walter Raleigh in 1603, and included some leading literary figures, such as Ben Jonson, John Donne and, perhaps, William Shakespeare.

2 A view of Trinity College in Cambridge. In 1209, students escaping from Oxford fled to Cambridge and formed a university there. The oldest college, Peterhouse, which still exists, was founded in 1284.

3 **COMPLETE** the table below with words from the text.

Noun	Verb
ascent	
development	
	feature
declaration	
lack	
encouragement	

4 **REPORT** on the English Renaissance, using the words in the table above.

The sonnet

ART LAB 2: *NICHOLAS HILLIARD*
TEXT BANK 7–8: *SHAKESPEARE'S SONNETS*
TEXT BANK 9: *JOHN DONNE*

WARM-UP

1 BEFORE READING the text below, look at the pictures (1–4) and answer these questions in pairs.
1 Who do the pictures represent?
2 What themes do they introduce?

2 DISCUSS the questions.
1 Do you know what a sonnet is?
2 Which Italian sonneteers do you know?
3 What feelings does a sonnet describe?

1

2

3

4

The Renaissance is considered the 'golden age' of poetry because of the flourishing of love songs and sonnets. The sonnet was introduced into England by Sir Thomas Wyatt (1503–42) and Henry Howard, Earl of Surrey (1517–47), from Italy, where it had been experimented with and refined by Dante (1265–1321) and Petrarch (1304–74), whose *Canzoniere* (1342–74) had become the model for all European Renaissance poets. This Petrarchan tradition found fertile ground in England because of the veneration of Queen Elizabeth I, who was referred to as 'the Faerie Queene'.

As a metrical form, the sonnet is composed of fourteen lines. The 'Italian', or 'Petrarchan', sonnet is divided into one octave plus a sestet. The most frequent rhyme schemes are: ABBA ABBA CDE CDE or ABBA ABBA CDC DCD. The octave generally presents an issue or a situation, while the sestet contains the solution of the problem or personal reflections. This kind of sonnet often shows a turning point at the end of the eighth line, and the ninth is sometimes introduced by words like: *and, if, so, but, yet.*

After a period of evolution, the English sonnet came to be identified with the Shakespearean model. It consists of three quatrains and a final couplet; the rhyme scheme is ABAB CDCD EFEF GG. Through this structure, the poet can use the quatrains to present a theme or three different arguments and draw a conclusion in the final couplet. The traditional subjects of the sonnet are love, faith, beauty, art and the destructive action of time.

In the 17th century, in England, important writers like John Milton (1608–74) and John Donne (1572–1631) wrote sonnets concerning religion and subjective experiences but preferred the Petrarchan sonnet to the Shakespearean one.

3 READ the text and explain how the English sonnet differs from the Italian one.

Literary language
The sonnet

Here are the most important features of the sonnet:

Italian sonnet	English or Shakespearean sonnet
14 lines of iambic pentameter	14 lines of iambic pentameter
Division into 2 sections: the octave presents a problem or situation; the sestet solves or clarifies the situation	Division into 4 sections: 3 quatrains that present a problem or situation and a couplet that solves or summarises the problem
Rhyme scheme: ABBAABBA for the octave CDECDE or CDCDCD for the sestet	Rhyme scheme: Quatrain I: ABAB Quatrain II: CDCD Quatrain II: EFEF Couplet: GG
Turning point: at the end of the eighth line and the ninth (sometimes introduced by words like: *and, if, so, but, then, when*)	Turning point: at the end of the eighth line and the ninth (sometimes introduced by words like: *and, if, so, but, then, when*)
Themes: love and faith, beauty	Themes: love and faith, beauty and art

1 Portrait of Petrarch by Altichiero da Zevio, ca 1370. Reggia Carrarese, Padua, Italy.

2 An anonymous portrait of Elizabeth Vernon, Countess of Southampton, ca 1600.

3 Nicholas Hilliard, *Young Man Among Roses*, ca 1588. Victoria and Albert Museum, London.

4 *Illuminations of Dante's Divine Comedy* by Giovanni di Paolo, 1440–50.

2.7 **Cultural Issues**

Woman, lady, mistress

WARM-UP

1 **LOOK UP** the three words in the title of this section (2.7) in the dictionary and write down their definitions.

FCE Reading and Use of English – Part 3

2 **WORD FORMATION.** For questions 1–8, read the text below. Use the word given in capitals at the end of some of the lines to form a word that fits the gap in the same line. There is an example at the beginning (0).

The **(0)** IDEALISATION of the woman has been one of the main topics	**IDEALISE**
of **(1)** .... literature since the works in ancient Greek	**WEST**
and Latin. In the Middle Ages the **(2)** .... of love varied	**TREAT**
according to the genre of the literary work: from Provençal poetry to the	
French metrical romances, in which the woman was a lady whom the author	
(3) .... like the Virgin Mary. Love for this ideal woman was	**WORSHIP**
linked with the ideals of **(4)** .... , sacrifice, renunciation and	**LOYAL**
reward.	
Mystery and adultery were popular ingredients due to the social	
(5) .... of marriage in feudal society. At that time, the lady	**REAL**
often lived with her lord in an **(6)** .... castle and married	**ISOLATE**
for **(7)** .... or political reasons. Thus marriage was rarely a	**ECONOMY**
synonym for passion. The lady **(8)** .... tempted the few men	**INEVITABLE**
she came into contact with, usually knights or men visiting the castle but	
belonging to a lower class.	

Spiritual elevation was the new theme connected with love in the poetry of the Italian (*dolce*) *stil novo*, or 'the new style'. Love was no longer mere courtship; the woman was no longer a metaphor, but became an angel, an intermediary creature between the earth and heaven. Her presence led man closer to God. This poetic trend started with works by Guido Guinizzelli (ca 1230–76), and found its highest expression in the poetry of Guido Cavalcanti (ca 1259–1300) and Dante Alighieri (1265–1321).

During the Renaissance, the poet confronted the clash between ideal love, leading to perfection, and real love, which was irrational, passionate and led to folly and perdition. The figure of Petrarch (1304–74) stood between the dying medieval period and the Renaissance.

William Shakespeare (1564–1616) tried to separate the different aspects of love that had been fused in Petrarch, in order to reassign them to two opposed types of love-relationship. To achieve this goal he needed to rewrite the Petrarchan archetype. He inverted the conventional presentation of the woman. As a result, the woman is given dark hair and eyes and an unattractive face.

3 **READ** the rest of the text and explain the following:

1. the new theme connected with love and the new figure of the woman in the Italian *stil novo*;
2. the clash the Renaissance poet had to face;
3. the difference between Petrarch and Shakespeare as regards love.

1 Frank Cadogan Cowper, *La Belle Dame Sans Merci*, 1926. Private collection.

2 Frank Dicksee, *La Belle Dame Sans Merci*, 1902. City of Bristol Art Gallery, Bristol, England.

3 John William Waterhouse, *La Belle Dame Sans Merci*, 1893. Hessisches Landesmuseum Darmstadt, Germany.

TEXT BANK 7–8: *SHAKESPEARE'S SONNETS*

WARM-UP

1 **DISCUSS** in pairs. What is beauty, in your opinion? Why do we love a person?

My Mistress' Eyes

William Shakespeare

Sonnet CXXX (1609)

In this sonnet, which belongs to the sequence addressed to 'the dark lady', Shakespeare talks about his lover in an unusual way.

1.10

My mistress' eyes are nothing like the sun;
Coral is far more red than her lips' red;
If snow be white, why then her breasts are dun[1];
If hairs be wires[2], black wires grow on her head;

I have seen roses damasked[3], red and white,
But no such roses see I in her cheeks;
And in some perfumes is there more delight
Than in the breath[4] that from my mistress reeks[5];

I love to hear her speak, yet well I know
That music hath a far more pleasing sound;
I grant[6] I never saw a goddess[7] go.
(My mistress when she walks treads on[8] the ground).

And yet by heaven[9] I think my love as rare
As any she belied with false compare[10].

1 **her breasts are dun.** Il suo seno è grigiastro.
2 **wires.** Setole.
3 **damasked.** Screziate.
4 **breath.** Alito.
5 **reeks.** Emana.
6 **grant.** Ammetto.
7 **goddess.** Dea.
8 **treads on.** Calpesta.
9 **by heaven.** In nome del cielo.
10 **As any ... compare.** Come qualsiasi donna falsamente decantata.

COMPREHENSION

2 **READ** the sonnet and complete the chart with details from the poem.

Her eyes	nothing like the sun
Her lips	not so red
Her breasts	
Her hair	
Her cheeks	
Her breath	

Now try to describe the lady in your own words.

ANALYSIS

3 **POINT OUT** the features of the Shakespearean sonnet in the poem:
- Layout ....
- Rhyme scheme ....
- Turning point ....

4 **FOCUS** on the first twelve lines. Shakespeare carries out the description of the lady using a series of comparisons.
Circle the terms of comparison and say:
1 what common feature they share or do not share;
2 what their effect is on the reader's expectations.

5 **SAY** what feeling the poet expresses in the final couplet.

6 **DECIDE.** How does this sonnet compare to the Petrarchan tradition?

YOUR TURN

7 **DISCUSS.** Shakespeare's assumption in the poem is that love and beauty are not necessarily related. Do you agree or disagree?

8 **WRITE.** Shakespeare dramatically describes his love by saying what she is not. Think of the modern clichés in love songs, films, etc. and write a paragraph of what, in your opinion, your love is not.

1 Pablo Picasso, *Portrait of Dora Maar*, ca 1937. Dora Maar was a French photographer, poet and painter, best known for being a lover and muse of Picasso.

WARM-UP

1 **LOOK** at the picture of Anne Hathaway's cottage in Stratford-upon-Avon. Do you know who she was married to?

Anne Hathaway

Carol Ann Duffy

The World's Wife (1999)

Carol Ann Duffy (1955–) is the UK's twentieth Poet Laureate. In her poem entitled 'Anne Hathaway', Duffy adopts the persona of Shakespeare's widow. It is a very passionate love sonnet, but it does not take the traditional form of a conventional sonnet. Duffy's approach is more romantic than Shakespeare's unconventional approach to his feelings for his lover in sonnet CXXX.

1.11

The bed we loved in was a spinning[1] world
of forests, castles, torchlight, clifftops, seas
where we would dive for pearls. My lover's words
were shooting stars[2] which fell to earth as kisses

on these lips; my body now a softer rhyme
to his, now echo, assonance; his touch
a verb dancing in the centre of a noun.
Some nights, I dreamed he'd written me, the bed

a page beneath his writer's hands. Romance
and drama played by touch, by scent[3], by taste.
In the other bed, the best, our guests dozed on[4],
dribbling[5] their prose. My living laughing love –

I hold him in the casket[6] of my widow's head
as he held me upon that next best bed.

1 **spinning.** Che gira vorticosamente.
2 **shooting stars.** Stelle cadenti.
3 **scent.** Olfatto.
4 **dozed on.** Sonnecchiavano.
5 **dribbling.** Dribblando.
6 **casket.** Scrigno.

COMPREHENSION

2 **READ** the sonnet and answer these questions.
1 What is the focus of the first quatrain?
2 What are the two lovers compared to in line 3?
3 How does she describe her body in line 5?
4 What did she use to dream some nights?
5 How was love experienced by the two lovers?
6 Who slept in the best bed?
7 What memory does she keep?

ANALYSIS

3 **DECIDE.** How well does the poet adapt the sonnet form here?

4 **FIND** the metaphor in the first two lines.

5 **READ** lines 3–4. What are Shakespeare's words compared to?

6 **FOCUS** on the second quatrain and underline the words related to the fact that Anne's husband was a writer.

7 **READ** lines 6–7. What is personified?

8 **FOCUS** on the third quatrain.
1 Highlight the contrast to the magic world of love introduced in the octave.
2 Find a beautiful example of alliteration.

9 **EXPLAIN.** What comparison is established in the couplet?

YOUR TURN

10 **DISCUSS.** Is this poem more about Anne or her husband, or is it about them both as a couple?

11 **DISCUSS.** What does this poem say about the nature of imagination?

2.8 **Culture**

Why study Shakespeare?

WARM-UP

1 **LOOK** at the pictures and read the quotations below. In pairs discuss the ways in which Shakespeare's influence stretches well beyond the world of literature.

2 **IN PAIRS** discuss the reasons why we still study texts written a long time ago. Then write a list of the factors that may affect the reading of a text.

1 Alfa Romeo Giulietta billboard quoting Shakespeare's *Romeo and Juliet* and *The Tempest*.

2 Classical Comics offer three versions of each play: the first uses Shakespeare's own words, the second translates them into plain English, while the third is a 'quick text' version. This example is taken from *Macbeth*.

3 Henry Fuseli, *The Three Witches*, 1788. Kunsthaus Zürich, Zurich, Switzerland.

4 Poster for 'Hamlet', directed by Franco Zeffirelli and starring Mel Gibson, 1990.

Shakespeare one gets acquainted with without knowing how. It is part of an Englishman's constitution. His thoughts and beauties are so spread abroad that one touches them everywhere, one is intimate with him by instinct.

Jane Austen
Mansfield Park, Chapter 34

There are more things in heaven and earth, Horatio,
Than are dreamt of in your philosophy.

William Shakespeare
Hamlet, Act I, Scene V

FCE Listening – Part 4

3 1.12 | **MULTIPLE-CHOICE QUESTIONS. You will hear an interview with a university lecturer in English Literature talking about the relevance of Shakespeare in modern life. For questions 1–7, choose the best answer (A, B or C).**

1 In which way can Shakespeare be considered central to the study of English?
- **A** His works have become specialist studies for advanced students.
- **B** He is a familiar figure to drama students.
- **C** His works are the only obligatory literature studied in the UK.

2 Where can we find evidence of Shakespeare's influence in modern Britain?
- **A** In films, advertising, plays and road signs.
- **B** In regional dialects.
- **C** In the way people act in the streets.

3 How do English speakers quote Shakespeare without even knowing they are using his language?
- **A** Through the use of his place names.
- **B** In many common expressions.
- **C** In the use of his foreign expressions.

4 Which of the following expressions is NOT from Shakespeare?
- **A** The more the merrier.
- **B** I haven't slept a wink.
- **C** Too much of a good thing.

5 Why do traditionalists think we should continue to study Shakespeare?
- **A** Because they consider his plays a reflection of Elizabethan politics.
- **B** Because they think we can understand historical events better through his plays.
- **C** Because the themes of his plays deal with typical human emotions and behaviour that will never age.

6 Which of Shakespeare's plays is seen as an example of a patriotic play?
- **A** Henry IV.
- **B** Henry V.
- **C** Henry VI.

7 What are Philip Buckley's views on the relevancy of Shakespeare in modern life?
- **A** He sees Shakespeare as continuing to be relevant because he dealt with issues that will always be part of human life.
- **B** He thinks Shakespeare has an important role to play in the political field.
- **C** He considers the study of Shakespeare a compulsory part of every child's primary education.

4 1.12 | **LISTEN to the interview again and give three reasons why Shakespeare is still studied in the UK today.**

5 Plácido Domingo as Othello on stage at the Royal Opera House, London, in 1992.

FCE Writing – Part 2

5 **AN ARTICLE. You have seen the following announcement on your school web site.**

ARTICLES WANTED:

The most important writer from my country

Who is the most important writer from your country? Why is he/she important? What are his/her key works?

Write an article answering these questions. We will publish the best articles on our website.

Write an article expressing your opinion and giving examples in 140–190 words.

Process language
Writing – Part 2
An article

Introducing the first idea
- First of all ...
- To begin with ...

Introducing further ideas
- Secondly ...
- In addition ...

Summarising the ideas
- In conclusion ...
- To sum up ...

Introducing an opinion
- In my opinion ...
- I believe that ...

William Shakespeare: England's genius

1 **READ** Shakespeare's biography and collect data in the table below.

Family	
Education	
Experiences	
First works	
Later works	

2 **IN PAIRS** choose one of the bubbles and prepare to report to the class about its content.

William Shakespeare's life

William Shakespeare was born in Stratford-upon-Avon in April 1564, possibly on 23rd April, which is also said to be the date of his death. His father was a yeoman (a successful tradesman), until he met with financial difficulties. William was the eldest son and attended the local grammar school, which gave him a thorough grounding in the use of language and classical authors. He married Anne Hathaway when he was only eighteen and she was twenty-six and pregnant with their daughter.

In 1584 he left Stratford and went to London. It was at that time that he first experienced the playhouse. He was received into one of the acting companies at a very minor level at first, but his admirable wit soon distinguished him – if not as a great actor, as an excellent writer. In 1593 the London theatres were closed because of the plague, and Shakespeare needed the support of a private patron. He found it in a young nobleman, the Earl of Southampton, to whom he dedicated his poems. When the theatres reopened, Shakespeare became a shareholder and the main playwright of the most successful company of actors in London: the Lord Chamberlain's Men. In 1599 his company built the Globe Theatre, where most of his plays were performed.

Between 1590 and 1596 he mainly wrote historical dramas. Overlapping with the history plays, between 1593 and 1600, he put ten comedies onto the stage, ranging from farce to romance. The great tragedies were written between 1595 and 1605.

The latter part of his life was spent in retirement in Stratford. He died in 1616 when he was 52 years old and was buried in the local church. Seven years after his death, some of his friends and fellow actors published an edition of thirty-six of his plays in one volume – the famous *First Folio*.

The actor and the playwright

Shakespeare was a playwright, a poet, an actor and a shareholder in his theatre company – a company that might perform for anyone who could afford a penny to stand and watch a play at the Globe one week, and for the fashionable courts of Queen Elizabeth or King James I the next. He understood how to take a familiar story and create tragic, hilarious, suspenseful, philosophical and challenging dramas with which people all over the world continue to identify.

The language genius

Shakespeare was writing at a time before theatre technologies and complex stage design created visual worlds for theatre audiences – he created those worlds through language. He coined new words and phrases that we still use today, and his rich, theatrical and poetic language can be both strikingly resonant and a challenge to access. When young people watch or read Shakespeare today, they are pulled into a world that is both alien and familiar to them. In one scene, his treatment of love, jealousy, racism, mourning or power can seem remarkably relevant; in the next moment, the audience or reader might have to engage with concepts of religion, family or fashion that are completely different to their own. Shakespeare constantly challenges and confounds us: we might be asked to laugh in a painful scene, or engage with profound philosophical questions in a comic one.

The poet

Shakespeare's sonnets were published in 1609, although they were probably written in the 1590s. The collection included 154 sonnets in decasyllables. Shakespeare did not use the Italian form, an octave and a sestet; instead, he employed three quatrains and a final couplet. However, the development of the argument in many of his sonnets follows the 'two-poem' structure of the Petrarchan form since there is a turning point in the ninth line.

The 154 sonnets included in the 1609 publication were not necessarily chronological, as there is good reason to believe from their style, method and content. They can be divided into two sections. The first 126 sonnets are addressed to a 'fair youth' – probably Shakespeare's young patron, the Earl of Southampton. The poet encourages the young man to marry and preserve his virtues and beauty through his children. The rest of the poems, except the last two, are addressed to a 'dark lady' or 'black woman' who, though physically unattractive, is irresistibly desirable.

TEXT BANK 10–13: *A MIDSUMMER NIGHT'S DREAM*
TEXT BANK 14: *JULIUS CAESAR*

The comedian

Shakespeare's comedies follow a certain set of conventions including: disguise, frustrated love, mistaken identity, marital and romantic misunderstandings. They end in multiple marriages, and they all seem to have in common the preoccupation with the journey of young women – and sometimes men – from the state of virginity to that of marriage. Whereas tragedy works towards death, comedy traces the passage of young people out of their parents' control and into marriage.

The historian

Shakespeare's history plays were closely based on serious records like the Tudors' chronicles. Even so, they did not only deal with kings, queens and lords; they generally gave some sort of portrait of the nation as a whole – with peasants, workers and soldiers having roles to play. It was during this period that the idea of England as a 'nation' was gaining strength. The history plays themselves were part of a process by which people came to see themselves as belonging to 'England', rather than to families, households, village communities or local lords. They tell the story of the civil wars between the Houses of York and Lancaster.

Shakespeare's history plays are usually divided into two 'tetralogies' (a tetralogy is a group of four plays). The first tetralogy includes *Henry VI* Parts One, Two and Three (1590–92) and *Richard III* (1592–93); the second tetralogy, written at the height of Shakespeare's powers, consists of *Richard II* (1595–96), *Henry IV* Parts One and Two (1597–98) and *Henry V* (1598–99).

The tragic playwright

The historical moment of transition between the medieval and modern worlds helped create the nature of tragedies in Shakespeare's work. There is no evidence that Shakespeare had any direct acquaintance with the conventions of classical tragedy, identified by the Greek philosopher Aristotle in his *Poetics*. Shakespeare set out to tell a story in a recognised dramatic genre that would be attractive to London theatregoers, only a minority of whom would have been familiar with classical tragedy. In telling these stories within the genre of tragedy, he made statements about many aspects of human life, but mainly about the nature of political power and the problems of the powerful in a world that was changing.

1 Photo of Shakespeare's Birthplace.

Insights

Stratford-upon-Avon: Shakespeare's birthplace

Stratford-upon-Avon is a beautiful town situated on the river Avon, with characteristic black and white timber-framed buildings. The town centre offers a good selection of shops, restaurants and tearooms.

A great way to explore the town and the neighbouring villages of Shottery and Wilmcote, home to Anne Hathaway's Cottage and Shakespeare's mother Mary Arden's, is with City Sightseeing's 'Hop On Hop Off' buses. You can also see Stratford by relaxing on a cruise along the river. Anyone interested in Tudor history won't want to miss The Falstaff Experience, a living museum where history is brought to life with theatrical settings and atmosphere. No visit to Stratford-upon-Avon would be complete without seeing a production by the Royal Shakespeare Company at its own theatre.

The best of Stratford's architectural heritage is located along a centuries-old walking route leading from Shakespeare's Birthplace in Henley Street to Holy Trinity Church in the Old Town. Holy Trinity Church has the added fame of being the place where Shakespeare was both baptised and buried. A monument erected here in his memory makes it one of the most famous churches in the country.

The most important building in Henley Street is Shakespeare's Birthplace, a timber-framed building dating from the 16th century, owned and lived in by Shakespeare's father until his death in 1601, and where Shakespeare himself was born. On the other side of the street there are some timber-framed buildings. The first is Hall's Croft, believed to be the home of John Hall and his wife Susanna, Shakespeare's daughter. Its earliest surviving features date back to the early 17th century.

2.10 **Literature**

The structure of theatres

WARM-UP

1 **LOOK** at the pictures (1–2) below and in pairs discuss their most important differences.

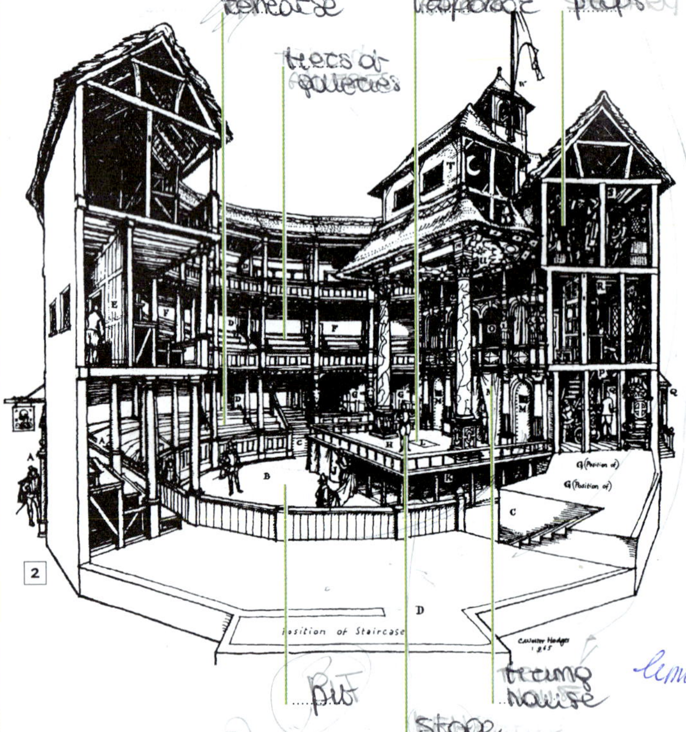

During the 16th century, the first permanent playhouses were built in London.

Q Which were the first playhouses built in London?

A The Theatre was the first playhouse to be built, in 1576, followed by the Curtain in 1577, the Swan in 1595 and the Globe in 1599.

Q What was the architecture of these theatres like?

A These playhouses were round or octagonal in shape, twelve metres high and with a diameter of twenty-five metres. They could hold up to 3,000 people.

Q How wide was the stage?

A The rectangular stage was twelve metres wide. Such a restricted space did not allow more than twelve actors to appear on the stage at a time.

1 The Royal Theatre in Brighton, England. The theatre opened on 27th June 1807 with a performance of Shakespeare's *Hamlet*.

2 A conjectural reconstruction of the Globe Theatre built in London in 1599.

3 An illustration of the Globe Theatre in London from 1616.

2 **LOOK** at the sketch of the Globe Theatre above and label its parts using the words from the glossary.

GLOSSARY
- **pit** platea
- **tiers of galleries** file di gallerie
- **trap door** botola
- **tiring house** camerino
- **scenery** scenario
- **props** materiale scenico
- **rehearse** provare

Q What was the stage like?

A The stage had no curtain; it was supported by two pillars and was roofed over to protect the actors and their costumes. It projected into an uncovered central area, called 'the pit', surrounded by three roofed tiers of galleries. The gallery above the stage could be used either by the audience or by the musicians, or as an additional part of the stage for scenes such as 'the balcony scene' in *Romeo and Juliet*.

Q What other elements were there? How were they used?

A There was a trap door, used for devilish apparitions, disappearances and also for burials. A balcony crowned by a gable on the upper floor housed the stage machinery. It was from there that gods and goddesses and other special effects descended onto the stage. During a performance a flag with the emblem of the theatre flew above the roof.

Q Where did the actors change their clothes?

A The actors' tiring house, that is to say, the place where the actors changed their attire, was at the rear of the stage. There were two doors for entrances and exits.

Q What sort of scenery was employed?

A There was no scenery, and plays were acted in daylight. Performances required a limited number of props: tables, chairs, swords, canvasses of the sun and moon, and also a tree of golden apples and a series of dragons. For night scenes a simple candle or torch symbolically transported the audience into the night world. Thus the theatre relied on the audience's imagination, and the text was enough to bring the play to life.

Q When did a scene end?

A The action was continuous. A scene ended when all the actors had gone off the stage and a new set of characters came on. There was thus a quick continuity of performance, with no break in the illusion.

Q Did the Elizabethan actor prepare his performance over a long period?

A The Elizabethan actor was a busy man, constantly rehearsing new plays. He had little time for long and elaborate preparations, but he belonged to a team and the trained actor was ready to improvise in an emergency.

Q Who acted female roles?

A In Shakespeare's time there were no female actresses; the parts of young women were acted by boys.

4

5

3 READ the Q&A text.

4 IN PAIRS cover the answers (**A**s) in the text. Take turns asking and answering the questions (**Q**s) using the information that you have read.

5 WRITE some key ideas to describe the Elizabethan playhouse.

4 Gwyneth Paltrow using a trap door in a scene from John Madden's film 'Shakespeare in Love', 1998.

5 Joseph Fiennes and Ben Affleck in a scene from John Madden's film 'Shakespeare in Love', 1998. The still illustrates the proximity of the Elizabethan stage actors to the audience.

Internet Lab

FCE Reading and Use of English – Part 2

6 OPEN CLOZE. For questions 1–8, read the text about Elizabethan audiences and think of the word which best fits each gap. Use only one word in each gap. There is an example at the beginning (0).

The Audiences

(0) QUEEN Elizabeth I loved watching **(1)** ...., but these were generally performed in indoor playhouses for her pleasure. She would not have attended the plays performed at the playhouses such **(2)** .... the Globe.

The upper-class nobles would have paid for the better seats in the 'Lord's rooms', paying 5p for the privilege. The 'groundlings' were the standing members of the audience. For one penny, **(3)** .... was the price of a loaf of bread, they could stand in the open yard. They used **(4)** .... put the money in a box at the theatre entrance, hence the term 'box office'. The gentry would pay to sit in the galleries, often using cushions for comfort. Rich nobles could watch the play from a chair set on the side of the stage itself. The crowd of spectators ate and drank during the performance and freely expressed their emotions. They loved metaphor and extremes and **(5)** .... deeply moved by long speeches and soliloquies. Horror, macabre scenes and revenge tragedies were very popular, as **(6)** .... as history plays where heroic deeds, battles and weapons evoked strong feelings.

People used to applaud any notable event during the play, but it was only **(7)** .... the end that they could be really noisy. There was often a 'jig', a comic song and dance story, and the company would announce the next play in the repertoire. The audience would show their approval or disapproval of the choice by calling **(8)** ...., whistling and even throwing things.

7 WRITE some key words and phrases to describe the Elizabethan audiences.

Milestones

1599, the Globe

The Globe was also known as the Shakespeare Globe Theatre since it was the playhouse where Shakespeare performed many of his greatest plays. Built from oak, this famous playhouse had a large circular structure, three stories high. A small straw thatched roof only partially covered the circular structure, giving it an appearance very much like a modern day football stadium where the centre is uncovered. To advertise the arrival of the new playhouse, the Lord Chamberlain's Men used a flying flag with Hercules carrying a Globe on his shoulders to announce the imminent performance of Shakespeare's play *Julius Caesar.* Above the main entrance were inscribed the words *Totus mundus agit histrionem* ('the whole world is a playhouse'), a phrase echoed in *As You Like It* ('All the world's a stage').

1 LOOK at the picture. The New Globe Theatre in London is a faithful reconstruction of the open-air playhouse designed in 1599.

2 BROWSE the site **www.shakespearesglobe.com** and carry out the following activities.

1. Find information about:
   - A the location of the New Globe;
   - B how it can be reached;
   - C how you can book a performance.
2. Visit the exhibition. What insights does it give you into Shakespeare's theatre? Make notes and write down a short summary.
3. Find information about:
   - A London playhouses in the 16th and 17th centuries;
   - B the history of the Old Globe.

   Draw a timeline pointing out the most important events.
4. Collect information about the *frons scenae* as regards:
   - A the decoration of the stage wall;
   - B the heavens (what it was and how it was decorated);
   - C what there was behind the stage;
   - D what covered the surface of the stage and why.

1 A scene depicting a theatre audience in John Madden's film 'Shakespeare in Love', 1998.

2 The New Globe Theatre.

2.11 **Literature**

The world of drama

WARM-UP

1 **DISCUSS** in pairs.

1 What makes dramatic works unique?
2 How many people are involved in the communication of dramatic works?

The Elizabethan theatre reached its peak of vitality and splendour with Shakespeare's works. You will now be introduced to the genre of drama, its conventions and particular features through a series of four short dramatic extracts.

Literary language
A dramatic technique: the dialogue

The dialogue is the main support of drama since:

- it creates the action;
- it provides details about the characters and their relationships;
- it shows what a character thinks about another;
- it gives information about the past and can foreshadow subsequent events.

What shall I swear by?

William Shakespeare

Romeo and Juliet (1594–96)
Act II, Scene I

2.1

ROMEO Lady, by yonder blessed[1] moon I swear[2]
That tips with silver all these fruit-tree tops[3] –
JULIET O, swear not by the moon, the inconstant moon,
That monthly changes in her circled orb,
Lest that[4] thy love prove likewise[5] variable.
ROMEO What shall I swear by?
JULIET Do not swear at all;
Or, if thou wilt[6], swear by thy gracious self,
Which is the god of my idolatry,
And I'll believe thee.

1 **yonder blessed.** Quella sacra.
2 **I swear.** Giuro.
3 **That ... tops.** Che copre d'argento le cime del frutteto.
4 **Lest that.** Per paura che.
5 **likewise.** Altrettanto.
6 **wilt.** *Will.*

2 **READ the dialogue between Romeo and Juliet. Choose from the following adjectives to express the impression you get of the two characters.**

aggressive • frightened • romantic • gentle • modern • passionate • conventional • lively

1 Richard Beymer and Natalie Wood in the film version of the musical 'West Side Story', 1961. 'West Side Story' is a modernised version of *Romeo and Juliet* in which the lovers come from two rival street gangs in New York City.

TEXT BANK 15–16: *HAMLET*

Literary language
A dramatic technique: the monologue / the soliloquy

The monologue is a speech uttered by a speaker who is heard by other characters present on the stage; however, the speaker ignores them. The soliloquy is a speech uttered by a character who is alone on the stage. These devices enable the playwright to let the audience know the character's:

- thoughts about a specific problem;
- plans for the future;
- feelings and reactions;
- explanation of what happens between scenes.

To be or not to be

William Shakespeare

Hamlet (1601)
Act III, Scene I

2.2

HAMLET To be, or not to be: that is the question:
Whether 'tis nobler in the mind to suffer
The slings and arrows of outrageous fortune[1],
Or to take arms against a sea of troubles,
And by opposing end them? To die, to sleep
No more; and by a sleep to say we end
The heartache, and the thousand natural shocks
That flesh is heir to, 'tis a consummation
Devoutly to be wish'd[2].

1 **The slings ... fortune.** I colpi e dardi della sorte nefasta.
2 **a consummation ... wish'd.** Un completamento da desiderare con tutto il cuore.

3 **READ Hamlet's famous soliloquy and tick the correct answer.**
Hamlet's speech provides insight into his
- □ thoughts about a specific problem.
- □ plans for the future.
- □ feelings and reactions.

4 **DISCUSS. What is Hamlet concerned with?**

1 Andy Warhol, *Skull*, 1976. Private Collection.

Literary language
A dramatic technique: the aside

The aside is a short comment made by a character for the audience alone, usually occurring in or between speeches. Its purpose can be:

- to reveal the nature of the speaker;
- to draw the attention of the audience to the importance of what has been said or to explain developments;
- to create humour by introducing the unexpected.

5 READ **this short extract and explain the function of Shylock's aside.**

The bond

William Shakespeare

The Merchant of Venice (1597)
Act I, Scene III

2.3

BASSANIO This is Signor Antonio.
SHYLOCK [*Aside*] How like a fawning publican[1] he looks!
I hate him for he is a Christian;
But more for that in low simplicity
He lends out money gratis, and brings down
The rate of usance[2] here with us in Venice.
If I can catch him once upon the hip[3],
I will feed fat the ancient grudge I bear him[4].
He hates our sacred nation and he rails[5]
Even there where merchants most do congregate
On me, my bargains, and my well-won thrift[6],
Which he calls interest. Cursèd be my tribe
If I forgive him!

1 **fawning publican.** Servile pubblicano (i pubblicani erano anche esattori delle tasse durante il dominio romano).
2 **rate of usance.** Tasso di interesse.
3 **upon the hip.** Di fianco, cioè in una posizione di svantaggio.
4 **I will ... bear him.** Ingrasserò l'antico rancore che gli porto.
5 **rails.** Inveisce.
6 **do congregate ... thrift.** Si radunano contro di me, i miei affari, il mio ben guadagnato profitto.

Literary language
A dramatic technique: stage directions

Stage directions are open interventions, usually written in italics, intermingled in the script of the play. They provide information about the places, characters and visual and sound effects.

6 READ **the extract from *Macbeth* and state what information the stage directions provide.**

My hands are of your colour

William Shakespeare

Macbeth (1606)
Act II, Scene II

2.4

Re-enter Lady Macbeth.

LADY MACBETH My hands are of your colour; but I shame
To wear a heart so white. [*Knock*] I hear a knocking
At the south entry: – retire we to our chamber.
A little water clears us of this deed:
How easy is it then! Your constancy
Hath left you unattended[1]. – [*Knock*] Hark! more knocking.
Get on your night-gown, lest[2] occasion call us,
And show us be watchers. – Be not lost
So poorly in your thoughts.
MACBETH To know my deed, 'twere best not know myself. [*Knock*]
Wake Duncan with thy knocking: I would thou couldst[3]!

Exeunt.

1 **Your constancy ... unattended.** La tua risolutezza ti ha abbandonato.
2 **lest.** Dovesse.
3 **I ... couldst!** Vorrei che tu lo potessi!

Literary language

Comedy

- ....
- ....
- ....
- ....
- ....

Literary language

Tragedy

- ....
- ....
- ....
- ....
- ....

1 Poster of the film 'Maqbool', an Indian adaptation of *Macbeth*, directed by Vishal Bhardwaj in 2004.

7 COMPLETE the Literary language boxes about comedy and tragedy above, using the points given in scrambled order below.

1 The plots are mainly based on love and rely on witty dialogue.
2 It begins with misfortune, but does not end with the death of the main character.
3 It employs the concept of *catharsis* – a Greek word meaning 'purification' – a process in which strong emotions are experienced by the audience through identification with the characters so that, in the end, these passions lose their power.
4 It generally deals with ordinary characters set in everyday situations in an amusing way.
5 It uses a solemn style and elevated language.
6 The heroes / heroines – who are never common people, but kings, princes and warriors – are not free, but dominated by fate.
7 The playwright generally mocks the vices and follies of the society he belongs to.
8 Specific sets of comic characters are developed; they do not evolve in the course of the play, and their names sometimes reveal their nature.
9 The hero sometimes presents a flaw – ambition, weakness, jealousy – which leads him to suffering, madness or suicide. In this case the character is called a 'tragic hero' because, after coming close to success and showing courage, he experiences destruction.
10 There is generally a villain who is guilty of some action which he must expiate through death.

8 STUDY the features of comedy and those of tragedy. In pairs ask and answer questions about each using the prompts:

1 style and language;
2 the hero / the heroine;
3 the tragic hero;
4 the villain;
5 the playwright's aim;
6 the story / plot.

9 WRITE a short essay about the origins of drama and the meaning of the words comedy and tragedy.

TEXT BANK 19: *ROMEO AND JULIET*

Romeo and Juliet: the tragedy of not knowing

Romeo and Juliet (1594–96)

The plot

The setting is Verona, where two families, the Montagues and the Capulets, are locked in a violent feud.

First Act. The first act covers a whole day and it opens in a street in Verona. This act is composed of a series of dialogues about the courtly concept of love, which was linked to melancholy, holy devotion and the idealisation of the object of desire. It ends with the scene of the masque and the meeting of the main characters, Romeo, the son of Lord Montague, and Juliet, Lord Capulet's daughter.

Second Act. The second act concentrates on the development of the relationship between Romeo and Juliet. The dialogue between the two lovers deals with the theme of love in a way that departs from courtly conventions, especially in Juliet's language. This act ends with the secret wedding of the two lovers in the chapel by the friendly priest, Friar Laurence.

Third Act. The pace of events increases. It is the longest act and can be divided into two parts: that of public events, full of action and movement, and the part devoted to private events. Mercutio, Romeo's friend, is killed by Tybalt, Juliet's cousin, during a street fight. In revenge Romeo kills Tybalt and is banished from Verona to Mantua. The act ends with Romeo and Juliet's wedding night at the Capulets' house.

Fourth Act. It is the preparatory act to the final tragedy. To avoid her marriage to Count Paris organised by her father, Juliet takes a drug given to her by Friar Laurence. This potion makes her seem dead. The friar sends a messenger to Mantua, but before he arrives, Romeo is told that Juliet is dead and decides to come back to Verona.

Fifth Act. The fifth act consists of three scenes. The first breaks the unity of place, moving from Verona to Mantua. In the last scene Romeo poisons himself after seeing Juliet apparently dead in the tomb, while Juliet, waking from her trance, sees Romeo dead and stabs herself with his dagger. Unlike most Shakespearean heroes, Romeo and Juliet will never know the truth about their death.

Themes

The main themes of the play are:

- The lack of knowledge which necessarily derives from bad communication: *Romeo and Juliet* is a tragedy of not knowing and unawareness; it cannot be summed up as the tragedy of 'old hate' and 'young love', since the tragic final destruction results from a pattern which includes the elements of chance and the more pervading one of unawareness.
- The reflection upon language made by Juliet, who shows a tendency to realism in her use of language: though she is set within the courtly love convention and she stands for innocence, she returns Romeo's love. She belongs to no characterisation, classification or idealisation: she is a real woman. Her language is not only influenced by her being atypical, but also by the plot. She is in love with Romeo, and the first obstacle to their love is 'his name', a name which does not correspond to the 'real Romeo'. Therefore she reflects upon the symbolic order of language and its links to 'reality'.

1 Lord Frederic Leighton, *Dead Bodies of Romeo and Juliet*, 1852–55. Agnes Scott College, Decatur, Georgia, US.

1 **ANSWER** the following questions about the plot of ***Romeo and Juliet.***

1. What are Romeo's and Juliet's surnames?
2. Where does the play take place?
3. How does the play open?
4. How does the first act end?
5. What does the dialogue between the two lovers deal with?
6. Who marries Romeo and Juliet?
7. Who is Mercutio? Who kills him in the third act?
8. Where is Romeo exiled after killing Tybalt?
9. Who gives Juliet a drug to make her seem dead?
10. What does Romeo do after seeing Juliet apparently dead in the tomb?
11. How does Juliet kill herself?

2 **READ** about the themes of ***Romeo and Juliet*** and state:

1. what the most important themes are;
2. what kind of woman Juliet is.

WARM-UP

1 **WRITE** a definition of 'prologue' in your own words. Then write a list of the things you expect to be told by a playwright in the prologue to a play.

Two households

William Shakespeare

Romeo and Juliet (1594–96)
Prologue

Romeo and Juliet *begins with a prologue spoken by the Chorus, which was usually performed by a single actor. The social context to the emotional experience of the two lovers is introduced together with the ideas of destiny and death.*

THE PROLOGUE

Enter Chorus

2.5

CHORUS Two households[1] both alike[2] in dignity
In fair Verona (where we lay our scene)
From ancient grudge[3] break to new mutiny[4],
Where civil blood makes civil hands unclean[5]
From forth the fatal loins[6] of these two foes[7]
A pair of star-cross'd lovers[8] take their life,
Whose misadventur'd piteous[9] overthrows[10]
Doth with their death bury their parents' strife[11].
The fearful passage of their death-mark'd love[12]
And the continuance of their parents' rage[13],
Which, but their children's end, nought[14] could remove,
Is now the two hours' traffic[15] of our stage;
The which, if you with patient ears attend,
What here shall miss, our toil[16] shall strive[17] to mend[18].
[*Exit*]

1 **households.** Casate.
2 **alike.** Pari.
3 **grudge.** Rancore.
4 **mutiny.** Disordine.
5 **makes ... unclean.** Rende sporche mani fraterne.
6 **fatal loins.** Lombi fatali.
7 **foes.** Nemici.
8 **star-cross'd lovers.** Amanti avversati dalle stelle.
9 **misadventur'd piteous.** Miserande pietose.
10 **overthrows.** Avventure.
11 **strife.** Contesa, lotta.
12 **death-mark'd love.** Amore contrassegnato dalla morte.
13 **rage.** Odio.
14 **nought.** Nulla.
15 **traffic.** Armeggio; *qui:* recitazione.
16 **toil.** Fatica.
17 **shall strive.** Si sforzerà.
18 **to mend.** Di riparare.

COMPREHENSION

2 **READ** the prologue and say:
1 where the story takes place;
2 what troubles the town;
3 who the two lovers are;
4 what will happen to them;
5 how their love will affect their families;
6 how long the play is going to last.

ANALYSIS

3 **MARK** the rhyme scheme. What poetic form is the prologue?

4 **THE CHORUS** establishes a relationship between 'we' and 'you'. Who are 'we' and 'you'?

5 **UNDERLINE** the words which emphasise the idea of symmetry in the story.

6 **TICK** the most appropriate solution(s) and justify your choice quoting from the text. What is the function of the prologue in this play?
- ☐ To introduce the characters.
- ☐ To engage the audience's active cooperation in the drama.
- ☐ To introduce the story.
- ☐ To comment on the events objectively.
- ☐ To set the scene.
- ☐ To point out that the story does not belong to reality.

YOUR TURN

7 **LIST** these elements in order of priority, from the most important to the least important. Explain your order. What order of priority would an Elizabethan audience have given?
- the details of the plot
- the individual characters
- the poetry of the language
- the action (fights, love scenes)

8 **WRITE** the plot of *Romeo and Juliet* as stated in the prologue, using your own words.

The ball

William Shakespeare

Romeo and Juliet (1595–96)
Act I, Scene V

Love is one of the most important aspects of Romeo and Juliet. When Romeo first sees Juliet at the Capulets' great ball, it is love at first sight.

1 Leonardo DiCaprio and Claire Danes in 'Romeo + Juliet', directed by Baz Luhrmann in 1996.

2.6

ROMEO O she doth[1] teach the torches to burn bright!
It seems she hangs upon the cheek of night
As a rich jewel in an Ethiop's ear –
Beauty too rich for use, for earth too dear!
So shows a snowy dove trooping[2] with crows[3],
As yonder[4] lady o'er her fellows shows.
The measure done, I'll watch her place of stand,
And, touching hers, make blessèd my rude hand.
Did my heart love till now? Forswear[5] it, sight!
For I ne'er saw true beauty till this night. [...]

ROMEO [*To Juliet, touching her hand*]
If I profane with my unworthiest hand
This holy shrine[6], the gentle sin is this:
My lips, two blushing[7] pilgrims, ready stand
To smooth[8] that rough touch[9] with a tender kiss.
JULIET Good pilgrim, you do wrong your hand too much,
Which mannerly[10] devotion shows in this:
For saints have hands that pilgrim's hands do touch,
And palm to palm[11] is holy palmers' kiss[12].
ROMEO Have not saints lips, and holy palmers too?
JULIET Ay, pilgrim, lips that they must use in prayer.
ROMEO O then, dear saint, let lips do what hands do,
They pray: grant thou[13], lest[14] faith turn to despair.
JULIET Saints do not move, though grant for prayers' sake.
ROMEO Then move not, while my prayer's effect I take.
[*He kisses her*]
Thus from my lips by thine my sin is purged[15].

1 **doth.** *Arc.: does.*
2 **trooping.** Che si unisce.
3 **crows.** Corvi.
4 **yonder.** Quella.
5 **Forswear.** Rinnega.
6 **shrine.** Reliquiario.
7 **blushing.** Arrossiti (di vergogna).
8 **To smooth.** Lisciare.
9 **rough touch.** Tocco rude.
10 **mannerly.** Cortese, educata; *qui*: giusta.
11 **palm to palm.** Palmo contro palmo.
12 **palmers' kiss.** Il bacio dei palmieri (pellegrini diretti in terra santa).
13 **grant thou.** Concedilo.
14 **lest.** Per paura che.
15 **is purged.** Viene tolto.

WARM-UP

1 DISCUSS. What has the term 'Romeo' become universal for?

COMPREHENSION

2 ANSWER the following questions.
1 When is the scene set?
2 Who is Romeo speaking about in his monologue (lines 1–10)?
3 What happens when Romeo and Juliet meet?
4 Can you recognise a fixed poetic form in lines 11–24? What words mark the beginning of the various sections?
5 What in the dialogue between Romeo and Juliet shows that they are both very young?

ANALYSIS

3 DESCRIBE. What mood does Shakespeare create with the language of this scene?

4 DISCUSS. Romeo embodies the Renaissance code of courtly love. Decide whether this is apparent from his monologue. Justify your answer with reference to the text.

5 POINT OUT the metaphors used in lines 11–13 and discuss their connotation.

6 FIND words appealing to the sense of 'touch'; discuss the meaning they suggest.

7 IN PAIRS discuss what kind of girl Juliet is.

YOUR TURN

8 WRITE a short dialogue between a boy and a girl in which he declares his love. Decide whether she returns his feelings or not.

2.12 *Romeo and Juliet*: the tragedy of not knowing

WARM-UP

1 **DISCUSS** in pairs. How could a 'balcony scene' have been performed at the Globe Theatre?

The balcony scene

William Shakespeare

Romeo and Juliet (1594–96)
Act II, Scene 1

This is the famous 'balcony scene' where the two lovers declare their love to each other. While Romeo praises Juliet's beauty with neo-platonic images in the style of the courtly tradition, Juliet's declaration is quite different.

2.7

JULIET 'Tis but thy name that is my enemy.
Thou art thy self, though not a Montague.
O be some other name! What's Montague?
It is nor hand, nor foot, nor arm, nor face,
Nor any other part belonging to a man.
What's in a name? That which we call a rose
By any other name would smell as sweet.
So Romeo would, were he not Romeo called,
Retain that dear perfection which he owes,
Without that title[1]. Romeo, doff[2] thy name;
And for thy name, which is no part of thee,
Take all myself.
ROMEO I take thee at thy word:
Call me but love, and I'll be new baptised;
Henceforth I never will be Romeo.
JULIET What man art thou that, thus bescreened[3] in night,
So stumblest on my counsel[4]?
ROMEO By a name
I know not how to tell thee who I am.
My name, dear saint, is hateful to myself
Because it is an enemy to thee.
Had I it written, I would tear the word.
[...]
JULIET Thou knowest the mask of night is on my face;
Else would a maiden[5] blush bepaint my cheek,
For that which thou hast heard me speak tonight.
Fain would I dwell on form[6]; fain, fain deny
What I have spoke: but farewell compliment[7]!
Dost thou love me? I know thou wilt say 'Ay',
And I will take thy word. Yet, if thou swearst,
Thou mayst prove false. At lovers' perjuries[8]
They say Jove laughs. O gentle Romeo,

COMPREHENSION

2 **SAY** which lines show that Juliet did not realise that Romeo was there at first.

3 **EXPLAIN** whether Romeo tells her his name.

4 **READ** lines 23–44. Find the lines or phrases that Juliet speaks which mean the following:

- *I'm glad it is dark and you cannot see me blush.*
- *I cannot deny what I have said.*
- *Perhaps I should have been more discrete.*
- *Do not think because I'm giving in to you, that my feelings are only superficial.*

ANALYSIS

5 **STATE** the theme of Juliet's monologue. Remember that a monologue is a speech uttered by a single character with others on stage who do not speak.

6 **FOCUS** on line 13, where there is the transition from monologue to dialogue. What impact do you think it has on the audience?

7 **CONCENTRATE** on the two young lovers. Which adjectives would you use to describe Romeo, and which for Juliet?

tender • impulsive • personal
romantic • direct •
artless • artful • passionate • practical

8 **LOOK BACK** at the excerpt from Act I, 'The ball', and again at this part of Act 2.

1 How have Romeo's and Juliet's characters and their relationship developed?
2 Which sense is significant here, and which provides tension by not being possible?

1 **Without that title.** Senza quel nome.
2 **doff.** Butta via.
3 **bescreened.** Nascosto alla vista.
4 **So stumblest on my counsel?** Inciampi nel mio pensiero segreto?
5 **maiden.** Verginale, puro.
6 **Fain would I dwell on form.** Vorrei tanto salvare le apparenze.
7 **farewell compliment.** Addio formalità.
8 **perjuries.** Spergiuri.

If thou dost love, pronounce it faithfully.
Or, if thou think'st I am too quickly won,
I'll frown and be perverse and say thee nay[9],
So thou wilt woo[10]; but else, not for the world.
In truth, fair Montague, I am too fond,
And therefore thou mayst think my haviour light[11];
But trust me, gentleman, I'll prove more true
Than those that have more cunning to be strange[12].
I should have been more strange, I must confess
But that thou overheardst, ere I was ware[13],
My true-love passion. Therefore pardon me,
And not impute this yielding[14] to light love,
Which the dark night hath so discoveréd.

9 **I'll frown and be perverse and say thee nay.** Aggrotterò le ciglia e sarò spietata e ti dirò di no.
10 **wilt woo.** Corteggerai.
11 **my haviour light.** Che la mia condotta sia leggera.
12 **that … strange.** Che sono più esperte di me nel fingere ritrosia.
13 **ere I was ware.** Prima che io ne fossi consapevole.
14 **yielding.** Cedere.

1 John Stride and Judi Dench in Franco Zeffirelli's first stage production of *Romeo and Juliet*. Photo by Houston Rogers, 1960.

9 RE-READ lines 1–22.

1 Fill in the table below with words and phrases linked to reality and appearance.

Reality	
Appearance	

2 How does Juliet's reflection upon the language shake the medieval code?

10 FOCUS on lines 23–44. Juliet reflects upon the conventional code of behaviour.

1 Fill in the table below.

Conventional behaviour	
Juliet's behaviour	

2 Do you think Romeo shares Juliet's view (see lines 18–22), and if so, is he conscious of it?

YOUR TURN

11 DISCUSS. The story of Romeo and Juliet has been retold in other contexts, such as the musical 'West Side Story' (1961) and Baz Luhrmann's film 'Romeo + Juliet' (1996), set in modern American gang land. Can you think of another modern context in which the story would still resonate?

2.13 Two Films About... *Romeo and Juliet*

WARM-UP

1 **DISCUSS in pairs. Do you think Shakespeare's works should be adapted in order to be appreciated by a young audience? Or should teens be encouraged to appreciate his plays in their original form?**

Romeo and Juliet

Directed by Franco Zeffirelli;
UK/Italy 1968.
With Leonard Whiting (Romeo); Olivia Hussey (Juliet); Laurence Olivier (Prologue Narrator).

This version of Romeo and Juliet's famous love story was very successful because it contained more action, more humour and more sensuality than had ever been used before. It was filmed in Tuscany, in Pienza, Gubbio, Artena and in a palace once owned by the Borgias. It was the first time the two teenagers had been played by two unknown young actors whose age was very close to that of the lovers. Laurence Olivier lent his voice to the narrator, but the director was the real star since he managed to film the most stirring crowd scenes, public fights full of action and some unforgettable romantic moments, including Romeo and Juliet naked on their wedding night. The film won Oscars for costume design and cinematography.

What about accuracy?

While based on the original play, numerous small details were changed in the film's story. For example, near the end of the play, following Romeo's and Juliet's respective suicides, Friar Laurence is arrested and brought back to the tomb, where he reveals the truth about Romeo and Juliet's clandestine wedding and his plans to unite them. In the film version, the Friar is not seen or heard after fleeing in terror from the tomb, and thus the revelation of the secret marriage is never shown.

Romeo + Juliet

Directed by Baz Luhrmann;
USA 1996.
With Leonardo DiCaprio (Romeo); Claire Danes (Juliet).

Luhrmann's is an unconventional adaptation of the classical love story of Romeo and Juliet. Even though the actors speak with an American accent and the script cuts out some scenes from Shakespeare's play, the iambic pentameter is not lost and the dialogue employs street language just as the playwright intended in his own time. Key sentences are also visualised on boards and the names of the two families, the Capulets and the Montagues, are written in lights on buildings. The setting is not 16th-century Verona, but contemporary Verona Beach, California, patrolled by police helicopters which try to keep the brawls between rival gangs under control.

What about accuracy?

Swords become handguns in the film. Another major departure from the source occurs in the final scene, in which Juliet wakes before Romeo dies: if Romeo had just turned around before drinking the poison; if only Juliet had cried out in time! The sense of doomed tragedy that this change adds makes the ending more heartbreaking and even more cynical. Another crucial final difference is that Luhrmann never shows the families reuniting. In the play, Capulet and Montague agree to end their feud; in Zeffirelli's film, the families converge visually. In the 1996 version, the parents have been relegated to the background all the way through, brought in only to reinforce their short-sighted authoritarianism.

2.14 **Literature**

Macbeth: the tragedy of ambition

Macbeth (1606)

The plot

First Act. The play opens with the news that the attempted invasion by the Norwegians, helped by the traitor the thane of Cawdor, has failed thanks to Macbeth's courage. While returning from the battle, Macbeth and his friend Banquo meet three witches who greet Macbeth as 'Thane of Cawdor' and say that he will become king of Scotland. They also promise Banquo that a line of kings will come from him. Later, they meet the king's messenger, who tells Macbeth that the king has decided to reward him with the title of 'Thane of Cawdor'. The witches' prophecy begins to work on Macbeth's ambition. He invites the king to his castle and writes a letter to his wife to inform her. She carries out a plan to kill Duncan and sweeps away Macbeth's doubts with her determination.

Second Act. Duncan is murdered and the blame is put on the king's servants who were sleeping outside the room. The king's sons leave Macbeth's castle, fearing for their lives. Macbeth is now on the throne, but Macduff and Banquo suspect him.

Third Act. Macbeth does not feel safe because the prophecy is for the throne to fall to the heirs of Banquo. He decides to kill Banquo and his son, Fleance, but Fleance escapes and Banquo's ghost begins to haunt Macbeth.

Fourth Act. The three witches warn Macbeth to beware of Macduff; this will lead to the murder of Macduff's wife and children. The witches also predict that Macbeth will be safe as long as Birnam Wood does not move towards him and that 'none of woman borne shall harm' him.

Fifth Act. This act opens with the sight of Lady Macbeth's madness: she walks in her sleep trying to wash away Duncan's blood from her hands. Meanwhile Malcolm, Duncan's son, is marching into Scotland with an army. His soldiers cut branches from the trees of Birnam Wood to advance on Dunsinane Castle hidden behind the leaves. Macbeth is alone because all the lords have allied with Malcolm, who represents order and stability. Macduff, to whom the phrase 'none of woman borne' refers, since he was 'torn' from his mother by a surgeon before he was due to be born, kills Macbeth. The play ends with Macduff carrying Macbeth's head and proclaiming Malcolm king of Scotland.

Themes

Macbeth is the shortest of Shakespeare's tragedies; it is simple in its plot but complex in its psychological analysis of what takes place in the mind of the criminal. There is no villain standing against the hero – actually, it is the hero who starts the play as a brave, heroic character and ends up as a murderous tyrant as a result of his 'ambition' and thirst for power.

The main themes of the tragedy are:

- Regicide, which is an act against nature, bringing about chaos, catastrophe and terrible weather conditions. The terms 'blood', 'bloody', 'to bleed' are the most frequently used words in the play, repeated more than a hundred times.

- The reversal of values – 'Fair is foul, and foul is fair' – introduced by the three witches. It represents the darkest, most dangerous aspect of 'equivocation'. Closely related to the theme of equivocation is the one of 'false appearance'. Shakespeare explores the difference between what is true and what only seems to be true. Besides its connection with the three witches, this theme also finds expression through the chain of metaphors connected with 'clothing', especially clothes that do not fit, and in the repetition of the verb 'to seem'.
- Time: the fundamental question is whether the future is pre-ordained or not inevitable, not fixed, the result of individual activity. This theme is associated with a chain of images concerned with 'growth': babies, seeds, plants, trees.

1 Sam Worthington as Macbeth with the three witches in the 2006 Australian film adaptation of *Macbeth* directed by Geoffrey Wright.

1 ANSWER the following questions about the plot of *Macbeth*.

1 Who does Macbeth meet while returning from battle?
2 What title is Macbeth given at the beginning of the play?
3 Who is his first victim?
4 Whose ghost haunts Macbeth?
5 Who does Macbeth murder at last?
6 What is the name of the wood that will have to move before Macbeth is defeated?
7 Who is Duncan's son?
8 What covers Lady Macbeth's hands in her imagination?
9 Who was 'none of woman borne'?
10 Who becomes king of Scotland at the end?

2 READ about the themes of *Macbeth* and state:

1 what *Macbeth* mainly analyses;
2 if there is a villain;
3 what the most frequent words are in the play;
4 what characters and images are connected with the theme of equivocation;
5 how Shakespeare deals with the theme of time in the play.

The three witches

William Shakespeare

Macbeth (1606)

Act I, Scene I

The opening scene of the play introduces the three witches. They are vital poetic symbols in the play, essential manifestations of the moral atmosphere of Macbeth's world.

[*An open place*]

Thunder[1] *and lightning. Enter three Witches.*

2.8

1st Witch — When shall we three meet again?
In thunder, lightning, or in rain?
2nd Witch — When the hurlyburly[2]'s done,
When the battle's lost and won.
3rd Witch — That will be ere the set of sun[3].
1st Witch — Where the place?
2nd Witch — Upon the heath[4].
3rd Witch — There to meet with Macbeth.
1st Witch — I come, Graymalkin[5]!
All — Paddock[6] calls.
3rd Witch — Anon[7]!
All — Fair is foul, and foul is fair:
Hover[8] through the fog and filthy[9] air. [*Exeunt*]

1 **Thunder.** Tuoni.
2 **hurlyburly.** Tumulto, confusione.
3 **ere the set of sun.** Prima del tramonto.
4 **heath.** Brughiera.
5 **Graymalkin.** È il nome di un gatto grigio.
6 **Paddock.** È il nome di un rospo.
7 **Anon!** Subito!
8 **Hover.** Planiamo.
9 **filthy.** Impura.

1 The three witches from the film 'Macbeth', directed by Orson Welles in 1948.

WARM-UP

1 **LOOK** at the title of the extract and complete the spider chart with what you associate witches with.

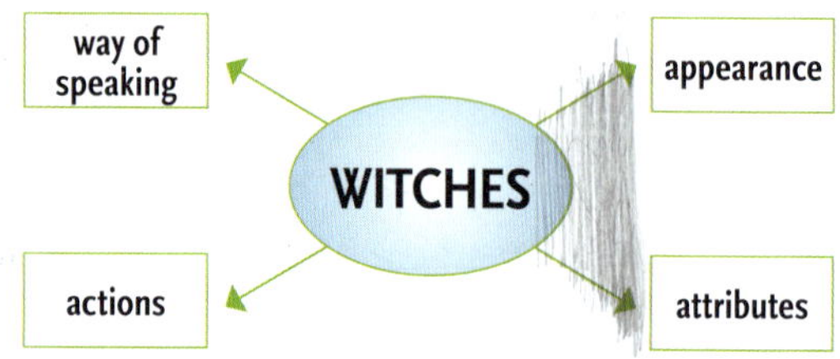

COMPREHENSION

2 **READ** the extract and answer the following questions.

1 What are the atmospheric conditions like?
2 Who appears on the stage?
3 What is the first word in the play connected with? What does the first witch ask?
4 What does the second witch reply?
5 When will that happen?
6 Where will they meet?
7 What animals are linked to the witches?
8 How do the witches move?

ANALYSIS

3 **DECIDE.** What does the stage direction 'An open place' imply?

4 **DESCRIBE.** What is bad weather generally associated with?

5 **HYPOTHESISE.** Where do you think the three witches entered from?

6 **DECIDE.** Can they be regarded as hallucinations?

7 **UNDERLINE** the words associated with the themes of confusion and the reversal of values.

YOUR TURN

8 **IMAGINE** you are a theatre director. How would you stage Shakespeare's witches? Would they be old or young, male or female, attractive or ugly?

WARM-UP

1 COMPLETE the chart. Macbeth is a man with positive qualities, but he is ruined by ambition and the thirst for power. What do you associate ambition with?

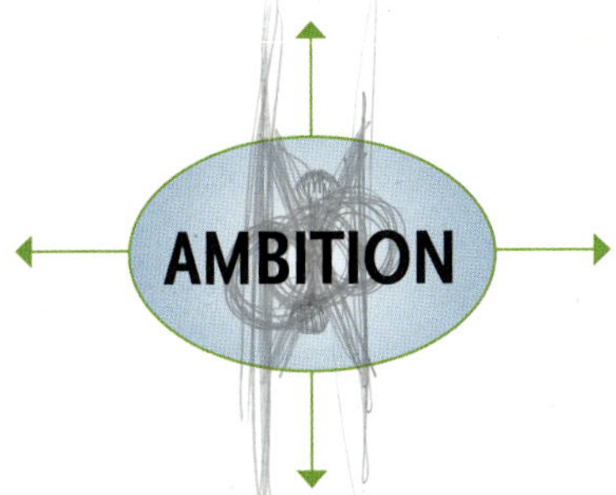

2 DISCUSS in pairs. Is ambition always negative or are there any circumstances when it is a good thing?

3 READ the introduction to the extract. Before reading the dialogue, discuss with the rest of the class how you think Duncan has been killed.

Duncan's murder

William Shakespeare

Macbeth (1606)
Act II, Scene II

An atmosphere of horror and guilt is built up in this scene, which deals with the murder of King Duncan by Macbeth. The realisation that what has been done cannot be undone arouses different thoughts and reactions in Macbeth and his wife.

2.9

MACBETH I have done the deed. – Didst thou not hear a noise?
LADY MACBETH I heard the owl scream, and the crickets cry[1].
Did not you speak?
MACBETH When?
LADY MACBETH Now.
MACBETH As I descended?
LADY MACBETH Ay.
MACBETH Hark!
Who lies i'th'second chamber?
LADY MACBETH Donalbain.
MACBETH This is a sorry[2] sight.
LADY MACBETH A foolish thought to say a sorry sight.
MACBETH There's one did laugh in's sleep, and one cried, 'Murther!'
That they did wake each other: I stood and heard them;
But they did say their prayers, and address'd them
Again to sleep.
LADY MACBETH There are two lodg'd together.
MACBETH One cried, 'God bless us!' and, 'Amen,' the other,
As they had seen me with these hangman[3]'s hands.
List'ning their fear, I could not say, 'Amen,'
When they did say, 'God bless us.'
LADY MACBETH Consider it not so deeply.
MACBETH But wherefore[4] could not I pronounce 'Amen'?
I had most need of blessing, and 'Amen'
Stuck in my throat[5].
LADY MACBETH These deeds must not be thought
After these ways: so, it will make us mad.
MACBETH Methought[6], I heard a voice cry, 'Sleep no more!
Macbeth does murther Sleep,' – the innocent Sleep;
Sleep, that knits up the ravell'd sleave of care[7],
The death of each day's life, sore labour's bath[8],
Balm[9] of hurt minds, great Nature's second course,
Chief nourisher in life's feast; –
LADY MACBETH What do you mean?
MACBETH Still it cried, 'Sleep no more!' to all the house:
'Glamis hath murther'd Sleep, and therefore Cawdor
Shall sleep no more, Macbeth shall sleep no more!'
LADY MACBETH Who was it that thus cried? Why, worthy[10] Thane,

1 **the crickets cry.** I grilli cantare.
2 **sorry.** Penosa.
3 **hangman.** Boia, carnefice.
4 **wherefore.** Perché.
5 **Stuck in my throat.** Mi si è bloccato in gola.
6 **Methought.** Mi è sembrato.
7 **knits ... care.** Avvolge la matassa aggrovigliata delle preoccupazioni.
8 **sore labour's bath.** Bagno ristoratore dell'affanno.
9 **Balm.** Balsamo.
10 **worthy.** Valoroso.

1 Henry Fuseli, *Lady Macbeth seizing the daggers*, 1812. Tate Gallery, London.

2 Scene from the film 'The Tragedy of Macbeth', directed by Roman Polanski in 1971.

You do unbend[11] your noble strength, to think
So brainsickly[12] of things. Go, get some water,
And wash this filthy witness from your hand. –
Why did you bring these daggers from the place?
They must lie there: go, carry them, and smear[13]
The sleepy grooms with blood.

MACBETH — I'll go no more:
I am afraid to think what I have done;
Look on't again I dare not.

LADY MACBETH — Infirm of purpose[14]!
Give me the daggers. The sleeping, and the dead,
Are but as pictures; 'tis the eye of childhood
That fears a painted devil. If he do bleed,
I'll gild[15] the faces of the grooms withal[16],
For it must seem their guilt.
[*Exit – Knocking within*]

11 **You do unbend.** Indebolisci, allenti.
12 **brainsickly.** In modo dissennato.
13 **smear.** Imbratta.
14 **Infirm of purpose.** Privo di fermezza.
15 **I'll gild.** Dorerò.
16 **withal.** Inoltre, pure.

COMPREHENSION

4 **READ** the dialogue and write down what Macbeth and Lady Macbeth hear.

5 **MAKE** a list of what Lady Macbeth advises her husband to do.

ANALYSIS

6 **FOCUS** on Macbeth's character. Write down the terms he uses to define the crime and himself. Why doesn't he mention the crime explicitly?

7 **WRITE** a few sentences about the relationship between Macbeth and Lady Macbeth and their different states of mind using the material you have gathered so far.

8 **IMAGERY** is a very important element in the play since it introduces the various themes. Analyse the most remarkable images in this passage:

- **Sleep**
  Macbeth refers to sleep by means of a series of metaphors. Underline them. What common idea do they share? How do they foreshadow Macbeth's punishment?
- **Madness**
  Madness, instead, will be Lady Macbeth's punishment later in the play. Point out the lines that foreshadow her destiny.
- **Blood and water**
  What does each image symbolise?

YOUR TURN

9 **DISCUSS.** Duncan's murder takes place off stage.

1 Can you think of any reason why?
2 Was this device effective for the Elizabethan audience?
3 Would it still be effective for a modern audience?
4 If you were a director, how would you stage this scene?

WARM-UP

1 DISCUSS. What would you expect Macbeth's last words to be?

COMPREHENSION

2 READ the text and discuss these questions.

1. Why are the women crying?
2. What is Macbeth's reaction? How would he have reacted in the past?
3. What has he almost forgotten? Why?

ANALYSIS

3 UNDERLINE the expressions referring to time. How does Macbeth convey the idea that time is an invincible, ineluctable power?

4 DECIDE. When referring to man in relation to time, Macbeth uses the term 'fools'. What do you think he has realised about man's power to change his destiny?

5 ANALYSE the metaphors Macbeth uses to describe life and the ideas they introduce. What conclusion about the meaning of life does Macbeth come to?

YOUR TURN

6 DISCUSS. If you were a film director, how would you stage the last act of this tragedy? What stage directions would you use? What suggestions would you give your actors?

Macbeth's last monologue

William Shakespeare

Macbeth (1606)
Act V, Scene V

The news of his wife's death is received by Macbeth with a famous monologue, almost at the end of the play. The country has risen in revolt against Macbeth and his castle is under siege.

[*Dunsinane. Within the castle*]

A cry within, of women.

2.10

MACBETH [...] What is that noise?
SEYTON It is the cry of women, my good Lord. [*Exit*]
MACBETH I have almost forgot the taste of fears.
The time has been, my senses would have cool'd
To hear a night-shriek; and my fell of hair[1]
Would at a dismal treatise[2] rouse, and stir[3],
As life were in't. I have supp'd full[4] with horrors:
Direness[5], familiar to my slaughterous[6] thoughts,
Cannot once start me[7].

Re-enter Seyton.

Wherefore[8] was that cry?
SEYTON The Queen, my Lord, is dead.
MACBETH She should have died hereafter[9]:
There would have been a time for such a word.–
To-morrow, and to-morrow, and to-morrow,
Creeps in this petty pace[10] from day to day,
To the last syllable of recorded time[11];
And all our yesterdays have lighted fools[12]
The way to dusty death. Out, out, brief candle!
Life's but[13] a walking shadow, a poor player,
That struts and frets[14] his hour upon the stage,
And then is heard no more: it is a tale
Told by an idiot, full of sound and fury,
Signifying nothing.

1 **fell of hair.** Capelli.
2 **dismal treatise.** Storia raccapricciante.
3 **rouse, and stir.** Drizzarsi e agitarsi.
4 **have supp'd full.** Mi sono saziato.
5 **Direness.** Spavento.
6 **slaughterous.** Omicidi.
7 **Cannot ... me.** Non può più farmi trasalire.
8 **Wherefore.** Perché.
9 **hereafter.** Prima o poi.
10 **Creeps ... pace.** Striscia a piccoli passi.
11 **recorded time.** *Lett.*: il tempo documentato; *qui*: la durata della vita.
12 **have lighted fools.** Hanno illuminato agli sciocchi.
13 **Life's but.** La vita non è altro che.
14 **struts and frets.** Si pavoneggia e si agita.

2.15 **Literature**

The Tempest: the comedy of forgiveness

The Tempest (1611)

The plot

First Act. The play begins with a tempest near an enchanted island. Shipwrecked, Alonso King of Naples, his son Ferdinand, Antonio Duke of Milan and their court are magically washed up on this island. This is all the plan of Prospero, a magician who lives on the island with his daughter Miranda. He explains to her that he was the rightful Duke of Milan who, being devoted more to the study of philosophy and magic than to affairs of state, was deposed twelve years earlier and set adrift with her on a boat on the orders of his brother Antonio. They finally reached an island which had been the refuge of the witch Sycorax and was inhabited by her son Caliban, a strange creature of brute intelligence, and Ariel, a gentle spirit of the air whom Sycorax had imprisoned. Prospero released Ariel and made him his agent.

Second Act. King Alonso is desperate because he thinks his son has drowned. Ferdinand, instead, is wandering all over the island, moved by Ariel's singing; he meets Miranda and falls in love with her.

Third Act. To test Ferdinand, Prospero makes him perform menial tasks. Caliban meets Trinculo, the king's jester, and Stephano, the royal butler, and they plan to kill Prospero. Ariel hears them and reports the plan to Prospero.

Fourth Act. It is a sort of interlude to entertain Miranda and Ferdinand while Prospero completes his plans of reward and punishment.

Fifth Act. The play ends in an atmosphere of general reconciliation: Miranda and Ferdinand marry, Prospero forgives his brother and returns to Milan to take possession of his lost dukedom. Caliban is left alone on the island and Ariel is released, free to wander as he wishes.

Themes

The Tempest belongs to the last period of Shakespeare's work and it is characterised by a 'serenity' which casts sweetness and light over human relations. Shakespeare seems much more concerned with human destiny as a whole rather than with individual peculiarities, more eager to show that good may come of evil. There is, in fact, no tragic ending: not only are the criminals prevented from causing death, but they are forgiven. Forgiveness seems to be one of the main themes: all ends in peace and reconciliation, with music intensifying the atmosphere of enchantment. Miranda is not a suffering heroine; she embodies womanly perfection through her ethereal beauty and unspoilt innocence.

There is another element in the play that was certainly of great interest for the contemporary audience: the wild, exotic setting, the relationship between natives and invaders, the problem of forced labour and the traffic in liquor. However, the most interesting theme of the play is certainly the 'element of magic' and its representation as 'theatrical illusion'. There are two types of magic in the play: maleficent and beneficent. The former, that of the witch Sycorax, tends to work evil on its victims and is usually the result of a pact with the devil. The latter, that of Prospero, derives from study and is used only for good purposes. The attributes of magic used by Prospero are his books, which are his chief power and represent his supernatural knowledge; his robe, which he puts on when he is working as a magician and takes off when he is an ordinary man; and his wand, which represents his instrument of power.

1 Helen Mirren as Prospera creating the storm in the 2010 film adaptation of *The Tempest* directed by Julie Taymor.

1 **ANSWER the following questions about the plot of *The Tempest*.**

1. What is the name of the magician who used to be Duke of Milan?
2. Who is Miranda?
3. Have Prospero and his daughter been on the island for six, twelve or eighteen years?
4. Who is Propsero's brother: Sebastian, Alonso or Antonio?
5. Who is Sycorax?
6. Who is Caliban?
7. Which character helps Prospero in his work as a magician?
8. What does Prospero force Ferdinand to do?
9. Who are the two characters that Caliban meets after the storm?
10. Who marries Miranda?

2 **READ about the themes of *The Tempest* and state:**

1. in what sense the play is characterised by 'serenity';
2. what the role of music is;
3. how many types of magic there are;
4. what the symbols of Prospero's power are.

WARM-UP

1 BEFORE READING the extract, work in pairs to fill in some ideas in the table about various aspects of the performance of the tempest in the first scene.

Sound effects	
Stage set	
Lighting	
Costumes	
Acting (gestures, tone of voice)	

The tempest

William Shakespeare

The Tempest (1611)
Act I, Scene I

A terrible storm hits the ship of Alonso, King of Naples, and his court. They have just come from Tunis, in Africa, where Alonso's daughter, Claribel, has been married to the prince.

The characters

Alonso: King of Naples who has conspired to usurp Prospero's dukedom of Milan.
Gonzalo: an old counsellor who has shown compassion for Prospero and his daughter Miranda.
Antonio: Prospero's brother, the usurping Duke of Milan.
Sebastian: Alonso's brother.
Ship-master: master or captain of the ship.
Boatswain: the ship's officer in charge of the crew and the rigging of the sails.
Mariners: the ship's crew who take orders from the Boatswain.

[*On a ship at sea*]: *a tempestuous noise of thunder and lightning heard.*
Enter a Ship-Master and a Boatswain[1].

2.11

Master — Boatswain!
Boatswain — Here, master: what cheer?[2]
Master — Good, speak to th' mariners: fall to 't, yarely[3],
Or we run ourselves aground: bestir[4], bestir. [*Exit*]

Enter Mariners.

Boatswain — Heigh, my hearts! cheerly, cheerly, my hearts! yare, yare!
Take in the topsail. Tend to th' master's whistle.
Blow, till thou burst thy wind, if room enough[5]!

Enter Alonso, Sebastian, Antonio, Ferdinand, Gonzalo, and others.

Alonso — Good boatswain, have care. Where's the master? Play the men.
Boatswain — I pray now, keep below.
Antonio — Where is the master, boatswain?
Boatswain — Do you not hear him? You mar[6] our labour: keep your cabins:
You do assist the storm.
Gonzalo — Nay, good, be patient.
Boatswain — When the sea is. Hence! What cares these roarers[7]
For the name of king? To cabin: silence! trouble us not.
Gonzalo — Good, yet remember whom thou hast aboard.
Boatswain — None that I more love than myself. You are a counsellor;
If you can command these elements to silence,
And work the peace of the present, we will not
Hand a rope more[8]; use your authority: if you cannot,
Give thanks you have lived so long, and make yourself ready
In your cabin for the mischance[9] of the hour, if it so hap[10].
Cheerly, good hearts! Out of our way, I say. [*Exit*]
Gonzalo — I have great comfort from this fellow: methinks[11]

1 **Boatswain.** Nostromo.
2 **what cheer?** Che c'è?
3 **fall to 't, yarely.** Presto, datti da fare.
4 **bestir.** Muoversi.
5 **if room enough.** Purché lasci spazio di manovra.
6 **You mar.** Intralciate.
7 **What ... roarers.** Che importa a queste onde urlanti.
8 **we will not hand a rope more.** Non toccheremo più una fune.
9 **mischance.** Disastro.
10 **hap.** Destino.
11 **methinks.** Mi sembra.

2.15 *The Tempest*: the comedy of forgiveness

He hath no drowning mark[12] upon him;
His complexion is perfect gallows[13].
Stand fast, good Fate, to his hanging: make the rope
of his destiny our cable[14], for our own doth little advantage.
If he be not born to be hanged, our case is miserable.

Exeunt.

Re-enter Boatswain.

BOATSWAIN Down with the topmast! yare! lower, lower!
Bring her to try with main-course. [*A cry within*]
A plague upon this howling[15]!
They are louder than the weather or our office.

Re-enter Sebastian, Antonio, and Gonzalo.

Yet again! what do you here? Shall we give o'er
And drown? Have you a mind to sink?
SEBASTIAN A pox o' your throat, you bawling[16], blasphemous,
Incharitable dog!
BOATSWAIN Work you then.
ANTONIO Hang, cur[17]! hang, you whoreson, insolent noise maker!
We are less afraid to be drowned than thou art.
GONZALO I'll warrant him for drowning[18]; though the ship were no stronger
Than a nutshell and as leaky as an unstanched wench[19].
BOATSWAIN Lay her a-hold, a-hold! set her two courses off to sea again;
Lay her off[20].

Enter Mariners wet.

MARINERS All lost! to prayers, to prayers! all lost!
BOATSWAIN What, must our mouths be cold?
GONZALO The King and Prince at prayers! Let's assist them,
For our case is as theirs.
SEBASTIAN I'm out of patience.
ANTONIO We are merely cheated[21] of our lives by drunkards[22]:
This wide-chapp'd rascal[23] – would thou mightst lie drowning
The washing of ten tides[24]!
GONZALO He'll be hang'd yet,
Though every drop of water swear against it,
And gape at widest to glut him[25].
[*A confused noise within*] 'Mercy on us!' –
'We split[26], we split!' – 'Farewell, my wife and children!' –
'Farewell, brother!' – 'We split, we split, we split!'
ANTONIO Let's all sink with the King.
SEBASTIAN Let's take leave of him.

Exeunt Antonio and Sebastian.

GONZALO Now would I give a thousand furlongs[27] of sea for an
Acre of barren ground, long heath, broom, furze[28],
Anything. The wills above be done! but I would fain[29]
Die a dry death.

Exeunt.

12 **drowning mark.** Segno di annegamento.
13 **His ... gallows.** Ha l'aria di chi deve finire sulla forca.
14 **cable.** Gomena di salvezza.
15 **plague ... howling.** Al diavolo queste urla.
16 **A pox ... bawling.** Ti venga un cancro in gola, urlante.
17 **Hang, cur.** Che ti impicchino, bastardo.
18 **I'll ... drowning.** Garantisco che non annegherà.
19 **as ... wench.** Facesse acqua come una prostituta sfondata.
20 **Lay ... off.** Serrate, serrate! abbassate le vele; andiamo al largo; serrate.
21 **cheated.** Truffati.
22 **drunkards.** Ubriaconi.
23 **wide-chapp'd rascal.** Farabutto sboccato.
24 **would ... tides.** Potessi annegare lentamente sciacquato da dieci maree.
25 **And gape ... him.** E si allargasse all'infinito per inghiottirlo.
26 **We split.** Andiamo in pezzi.
27 **furlongs.** Iugeri, unità di misura di lunghezza equivalente a circa 201 metri.
28 **long heath, broom, furze.** Coperto di eriche, ginestre, sterpi.
29 **I would fain.** Avrei preferito.

COMPREHENSION

2 **AS YOU READ the extract, answer the following questions.**

1 What do the stage directions suggest?
2 Where does the first scene take place, according to the first word?
3 What does the Boatswain order his men to do?
4 Who does Alonso want to see?
5 What does the Boatswain complain about?
6 What does Gonzalo think of the Boatswain? What about the other characters?
7 What do the mariners cry at the end?
8 What would Gonzalo have preferred?

ANALYSIS

3 **FOCUS on the language.**

1 What helps create the fury of the waves and wind?
2 What words convey a sense of fear and crisis?
3 What expresses the challenge to traditional authority?
4 How do the men on the deck react? Do they try to save their lives, are they well disciplined or do they panic?

YOUR TURN

4 **DIVIDE into groups of three or four and carry out the following activities.**

1 Choose one of the opening scenes from this Specification – *Romeo and Juliet* ('Two households'), *Macbeth* ('The three witches') or *The Tempest* – and discuss why it is your favourite.
2 Read it again and summarise its content in your own words. Then get ready to act it out.
3 Use the diagram below to draw comparisons among the opening scenes that you have read. What do they have in common? How do they differ?

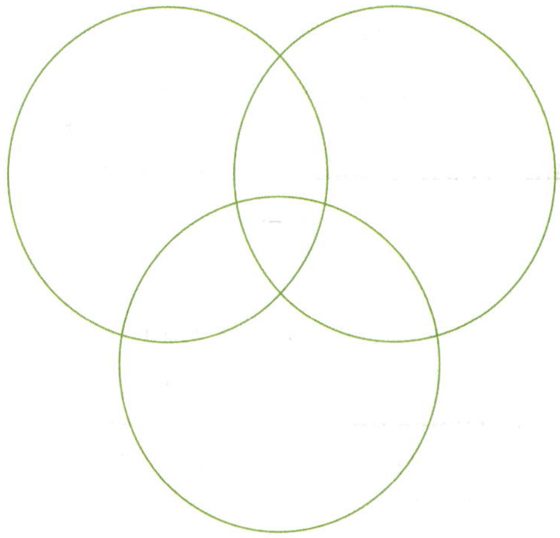

1 George Romney, engraving for *The Tempest*, Act I, Scene I, 1797.

2.15 *The Tempest*: the comedy of forgiveness

WARM-UP

1 **DESCRIBE** this picture. What is the most important contrast between Caliban and the two female characters?

2 **DISCUSS.** What does the word 'Caliban' make you think of?

1 Film still from 'The Tempest', directed by Julia Taymor in 2010.

Prospero and Caliban

William Shakespeare

The Tempest (1611)
Act I, Scene II

The passage below provides insight into the character of Caliban, Prospero's slave on the island.

2.12

PROSPERO Thou poisonous slave, got by the devil himself
Upon thy wicked dam[1], come forth[2]!

Enter Caliban.

CALIBAN As wicked dew[3] as e'er my mother brush'd
With raven's feather from unwholesome fen[4]
Drop on you both! a south-west blow on ye[5]
And blister you all o'er[6]!

PROSPERO For this, be sure, to-night thou shalt have cramps,
Side-stitches that shall pen thy breath up[7]; urchins[8]
Shall, for that vast of night that they may work,
All exercise on thee; thou shalt be pinch'd[9]
As thick as honeycomb[10], each pinch more stinging
Than bees that made 'em.

CALIBAN I must eat my dinner.
This island's mine, by Sycorax my mother,
Which thou tak'st from me. When thou cam'st first,
Thou strok'st[11] me, and made much of me[12]; wouldst give me
Water with berries in 't; and teach me how
To name the bigger light, and how the less[13],
That burn by day and night: and then I lov'd thee,
And show'd thee all the qualities o' th' isle,
The fresh springs, brine-pits[14], barren place and fertile:
Curs'd be I that did so! All the charms
Of Sycorax, toads, beetles, bats, light on you!
For I am all the subjects that you have,
Which first was mine own King: and here you sty me[15]
In this hard rock, whiles you do keep from me
The rest o' th' island.

1 **dam.** Madre (detto di animale).
2 **come forth.** Vieni fuori.
3 **wicked dew.** Perfida rugiada.
4 **brush'd ... fen.** Raccoglieva con penna di corvo da una malsana palude.
5 **on ye.** Su di voi.
6 **blister you all o'er.** Vi ricopra di vesciche.
7 **Side-stitches ... up.** Fitte ai fianchi che ti mozzeranno il respiro.
8 **urchins.** Folletti.
9 **pinch'd.** Pizzicato, punto.
10 **honeycomb.** Alveare.
11 **strok'st.** Accarezzavi.
12 **made ... me.** Mi tenevi in gran conto.
13 **the less.** La (luce) più piccola.
14 **fresh springs, brine-pits.** Sorgenti d'acqua dolce, pozze d'acqua salata.
15 **you sty me.** *Lett.*: mi hai messo in gabbia; *qui*: mi hai confinato.

PROSPERO Thou most lying slave,
Whom stripes[16] may move, not kindness! I have us'd thee,
Filth[17] as thou art, with human care; and lodg'd thee
In mine own cell, till thou didst seek to violate
The honour of my child.

CALIBAN O ho, O ho! would 't had been done!
Thou didst prevent me; I had peopled else[18]
This isle with Calibans.

PROSPERO Abhorred slave,
Which any print of goodness wilt not take,
Being capable of all ill! I pitied thee,
Took pains to make thee speak, taught thee each hour
One thing or other: when thou didst not, savage,
Know thine own meaning, but wouldst gabble[19] like
A thing most brutish, I endow'd thy purposes[20]
With words that made them known. But thy vile race,
Though thou didst learn, had that in 't which good natures
Could not abide[21] to be with; therefore wast thou
Deservedly confin'd into this rock,
Who hadst deserv'd more than a prison.

CALIBAN You taught me language; and my profit on 't
Is, I know how to curse. The red plague rid you[22]
For learning me your language!

PROSPERO Hag-seed, hence[23]!
Fetch us in fuel[24]; and be quick, thou 'rt best,
To answer other business. Shrug'st[25] thou, malice[26]?
If thou neglect'st[27], or dost unwillingly
What I command, I'll rack thee[28] with old cramps,
Fill all thy bones with aches, make thee roar[29],
That beasts shall tremble at thy din[30].

CALIBAN No, pray thee.
[*Aside*] I must obey: his Art is of such pow'r,
It would control my dam's god, Setebos,
And make a vassal of him.

PROSPERO So, slave; hence!

Exit Caliban.

16 **stripes.** Frustate.
17 **Filth.** Immondizia, sudiciume.
18 **I ... else.** Avrei popolato altrimenti.
19 **gabble.** Parlare in modo inarticolato, farfugliare.
20 **I ... purposes.** Fornii i tuoi propositi.
21 **Could not abide.** Non possono tollerare.
22 **The red plague rid you.** La peste rossa ti distrugga.
23 **Hag-seed, hence.** Seme di strega, via di qui.
24 **fuel.** Legna da ardere.
25 **Shrug'st.** Scuoti le spalle.
26 **malice.** Malizia, malignità.
27 **neglect'st.** Disdegni, tralasci.
28 **I'll rack thee.** Ti tormenterò.
29 **roar.** Urlare, ruggire.
30 **din.** Rumore, frastuono.

COMPREHENSION

3 READ the extract and explain:

1 what Caliban's origin is;
2 what physical punishment Prospero threatens him with;
3 the way Caliban behaved to Prospero when he arrived on the island;
4 what Prospero tried to teach him;
5 what Caliban did to spoil their relationship;
6 why Caliban has to obey Prospero.

ANALYSIS

4 THE DIALOGUE contains Caliban's opening speech and it gives us insight into his character.

1 Point out the expressions used to describe Caliban and who uses them.
2 State what Caliban's condition is and, considering the adjectives used by Prospero, what this is associated with.

5 THE SCENE presents Caliban mainly as a beast. However, there are at least three elements that make him more human. What are they?

line 19 ....
lines 20–21 ....
lines 58–59 ....

6 TICK as appropriate. What impression do you get of the character of Caliban?

- ☐ He is material, brutal and coarse.
- ☐ He combines animal and human traits.
- ☐ He is innocent and natural, but completely amoral and ungrateful.

7 DECIDE. What feelings do you think the character of Caliban aroused in the Elizabethan audience? Choose from among the following and explain why.

- ☐ Disgust.
- ☐ Curiosity.
- ☐ Sympathy.
- ☐ Repulsion.

WARM-UP

1 DISCUSS in pairs. Why do you think Prospero gives up his magic powers?

Prospero renounces his magic powers

William Shakespeare

The Tempest (1611)
Act V, Scene I

Prospero is preparing to leave the island and give up his magic powers in order to return to his dukedom.

2.13

PROSPERO
Ye elves of hills, brooks, standing lakes, and groves[1];
And ye that on the sands with printless foot
Do chase the ebbing Neptune[2], and do fly him
When he comes back; you demi-puppets[3] that
By moonshine do the green sour ringlets[4] make,
Whereof[5] the ewe[6] not bites; and you whose pastime
Is to make midnight mushrooms[7], that rejoice
To hear the solemn curfew[8], by whose aid –
Weak masters though ye be – I have bedimm'd[9]
The noontide sun, call'd forth[10] the mutinous[11] winds,
And 'twixt[12] the green sea and the azur'd vault
Set roaring war: to the dread rattling[13] thunder
Have I given fire, and rifted Jove's stout oak[14]
With his own bolt[15]; the strong-bas'd promontory
Have I made shake, and by the spurs pluck'd up[16]
The pine and cedar: graves at my command
Have wak'd their sleepers, op'd, and let 'em forth
By my so potent Art. But this rough[17] magic
I here abjure; and, when I have requir'd
Some heavenly music, – which even now I do, –
To work mine end upon their senses, that
This airy charm is for, I'll break my staff[18],
Bury it certain fadoms[19] in the earth,
And deeper than did ever plummet sound[20]
I'll drown my book.
[*Solemn music*]

1 **Ye ... groves.** Voi, o elfi delle colline, dei ruscelli, dei laghi immobili, e dei boschi.
2 **with ... Neptune.** Con passo senza orma inseguite la marea di Nettuno.
3 **demi-puppets.** Mezzi burattini.
4 **green sour ringlets.** Piccoli cerchi di erba amara.
5 **Whereof.** Da cui.
6 **the ewe.** La pecora.
7 **to make midnight mushrooms.** Far crescere i funghi a mezzanotte.
8 **curfew.** Coprifuoco.
9 **I have bedimm'd.** Ho velato.
10 **call'd forth.** *Lett.*: suscitato; *qui*: fatto soffiare.
11 **mutinous.** Ribelli.
12 **'twixt.** Tra.
13 **rattling.** Rumoreggiante, strepitante.
14 **rifted Jove's stout oak.** Ho spaccato la forte quercia di Giove.
15 **bolt.** Fulmine.
16 **by the spurs pluck'd up.** Dalle radici (*lett.*: speroni) ho divelto.
17 **rough.** Primitiva, rozza.
18 **staff.** *Lett.*: bastone; *qui*: bacchetta magica.
19 **certain fadoms.** In profondità.
20 **did ever plummet sound.** Sia mai sceso uno scandaglio.

COMPREHENSION

2 DECIDE. Who does Prospero address?

3 CHOOSE the correct option to complete the sentence. Prospero's gaze

- **A** turns inwards.
- **B** turns towards his immediate surroundings.
- **C** contemplates the invisible.

4 DISCUSS. What does Prospero decide to do in the end?

ANALYSIS

5 COMPLETE the table with the images of nature and the supernatural.

Nature	Supernatural

6 FIND words referring to the senses. What is their effect on the audience?

7 DECIDE. Why does Prospero give up his magic powers and call magic 'rough'?

8 DISCUSS. What is the role of music in this scene?

FCE Speaking – Part 3

9 **COLLABORATIVE TASK.** **Imagine that a Shakespeare festival is taking place in your town. Here are some of the plays that are being performed. Talk to each other about which play you would definitely see with your class and which you would not recommend to a group of teenagers. You have two minutes to discuss the plays and one minute to make a decision.**

A MIDSUMMER NIGHT'S DREAM
A tale of magic and romance, of fairies and lovers, of misunderstanding and laughter.

THE TEMPEST
A tale of revenge and hatred, of philosophy, magic and love.

Which play would you definitely see with your class and which would you not recommend to a group of teenagers?

MACBETH
Ambition is the driving force of this action-packed play where kings are murdered and ghosts are uninvited guests.

HAMLET
A king is dead and his son is called to avenge his murder, but his enemy is his mother's new husband. Which force is greater, love or hate?

ROMEO AND JULIET
The most famous romantic tragedy ever written. What cruel destiny lies ahead for those who dare to love an enemy?

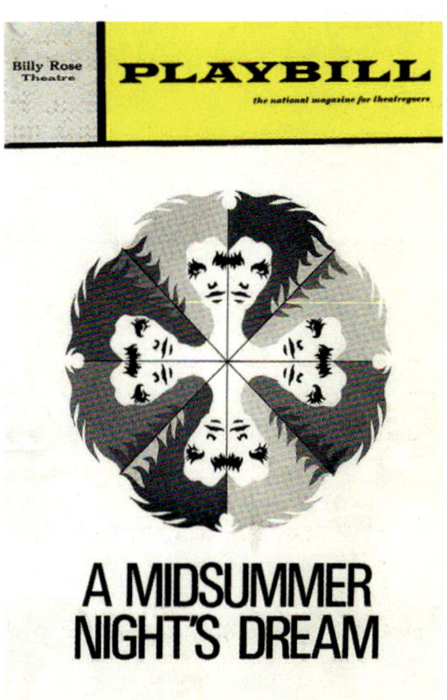

Process language
Speaking – Part 3

Involving the other candidate
- How about ... ?
- Why don't we ... ?
- I'd suggest (+ *-ing* form) ...

Agreeing
- I completely agree and ...
- I partly agree, but ...

Disagreeing
- I'm afraid I disagree because ...
- But don't you think ... ?

Making a decision
- To sum up, we have chosen ...

2 Overview

Test what you know

1 CORRECT the mistake in the following statements.

1. The purpose of the Act of Supremacy was to recognise the power of the pope in Rome.
2. During the reign of Henry VIII, support for Catholicism became simply a statement of personal religious conviction.
3. Mary I refused to abandon her traditional Protestant faith.
4. The English set fire to the ships of the Spanish Armada.
5. The ships of the Spanish Armada were more numerous and better armed than the English ships.
6. James I's reign was marked by the cooperation with Parliament.
7. The Gunpowder Plot was organised by Puritan volunteers.
8. Copernicus created a new model of the solar system in which the earth was at the centre.

Can you do it?

2 LIST the ways in which Henry VII tried to consolidate his position.

3 EXPLAIN the meaning of Henry VIII's title 'Defender of the Faith'.

4 COMPLETE the following table.

	Mary I	Elizabeth I
Daughter of		
Religion professed		
Home policy		
Foreign policy		
Popularity		

5 TRACE the symbolism of power in the portraits of Elizabeth I that you have studied.

6 EXPLAIN the importance of the Act of Supremacy.

7 COMPARE Ptolemy's and Copernicus's views of the universe.

8 DRAW a comparison between the Italian and the English sonnet.

9 READ 'Sonnet LX' by William Shakespeare and answer the questions.

1. What are the minutes of man's life compared to in the first quatrain?
2. What ages of man are opposed in the second quatrain?
3. What is the action of time? What is the function of poetry?
4. What is the theme of the poem?

Like as the waves make towards the pebbled shore[1],
So do our minutes hasten[2] to their end,
Each changing place with that which goes before
In sequent toil[3] all forwards do contend[4].

Nativity, once in the main of light[5],
Crawls[6] to maturity, wherewith, being crowned[7],
Crooked[8] eclipses 'gainst his glory fight
And Time that gave, doth now his gift confound.

Time doth transfix the flourish[9] set on youth,
And delves the parallels in beauty's brow[10],
Feeds on the rarities of natures truth,
And nothing stands but for his scythe to mow[11];

And yet, to times, in hope, my verse shall stand,
Praising thy worth, despite his cruel hand.

1 **pebbled shore.** Riva di ciottoli.
2 **hasten.** Si affrettano, corrono.
3 **toil.** Lavoro, affanno.
4 **forwards do contend.** Lottano in avanti.
5 **in the main of light.** Venuta alla luce.
6 **Crawls.** Avanza con fatica.
7 **wherewith, being crowned.** Dopo averla incoronata.
8 **Crooked.** Insidiose.
9 **doth transfix the flourish.** Travolge il fiore.
10 **delves the parallels in beauty's brow.** Scava rughe profonde sulla fronte della bellezza.
11 **stands but for his scythe to mow.** È risparmiato al mietere della sua falce.

10 DESCRIBE the structure of an Elizabethan playhouse.

Oral test

11 IMAGINE your teacher asks you the following questions in an oral test. For each question, prepare a one-minute turn.

1. What were the reasons for and the consequences of the English Reformation?
2. How can Henry VIII be defined?
3. How did Elizabeth I create the cult of the 'Virgin Queen'?
4. How did she handle the internal religious struggle?
5. How did Shakespeare describe his mistress in Sonnet CXXX? What is the basic assumption of the poem?
6. What are the differences between the Elizabethan theatre and the modern one?
7. What are the differences between comedy and tragedy?
8. What are the themes developed in the play *Romeo and Juliet*?
9. What role is played by ambition, fate and superstition in *Macbeth*?
10. Which element in *The Tempest* was of great interest to a Renaissance audience?

Shaping the English Character

Specification 3 | Homepage

Top News

1642 The Civil War breaks out

1707 Scotland is joined to England

Top Issue

Tourists, travellers and movers

Most Popular News

1649 Charles I is executed

1688 William and Mary are crowned joint monarchs

1679–80 The Tory and Whig Parties are founded

Spotlight

1719 Daniel Defoe publishes *Robinson Crusoe*

The Arts

William Hogarth: satire and social criticism

Cinema

See the Civil War on screen

Mapping Society

Visit England's landscape gardens

EXPLORE THE CULTURE

Literature | History | Society | The Arts | Science | Two Films About... | Cultural Issues

3.1 **History**

The Civil War

1 Anthony van Dyck, *Equestrian Portrait of Charles I*, 1637–38. National Portrait Gallery, London.

2 Robert Walker, *Portrait of Cromwell*, 1634. National Portrait Gallery, London.

WARM-UP

1 **LOOK** at the pictures (1–4) and match them with the captions (A–D).

A Oliver Cromwell, Lord Protector of England, Scotland and Ireland.

B Puritan leaders.

C The execution of King Charles I, 30th January 1649.

D King Charles I on horseback.

2 **DISCUSS** the differences in pose and dress in the various images. What do you think these differences might suggest about the changing attitudes and values of the times?

3 **READ** the Q&A text below.

3 Gillis van Tilborch, *Group Portrait of Academicians in a Picture Gallery, with a Self-Portrait of the Artist on the Right*, 17th century.

4 Gonzales Cocker, *Decapitation of Charles I at Whitehall*, 17th century. Musée de Picardie, Amiens, France.

During the 17th century, Britain went through a republican experiment that was to be reversed in 1660.

Q Who became king when James I died?

A Charles I (1600–49) succeeded his father, James I, in 1625.

Q What did Charles I have to face when he became king?

A He could not avoid direct confrontation with the Puritan party, which had given rise to a social and political movement holding a considerable majority in Parliament, and whose members mainly belonged to the middle classes.

Q Who were the Puritans?

A Puritan was the name given to the more extreme Protestants within the Church of England who thought the English Reformation had not done enough to reform the doctrines and structure of the Church. They wanted to purify their national Church by eliminating every trace of Catholic influence. The Puritans eventually went on to attempt purification of the self and society as well.

Q Why did the Civil War break out?

A Puritans wanted a true balance of power between the king and Parliament, but Charles I firmly believed he was king by divine right. His reign was therefore troubled by a continuous clash with Parliament. In 1642 the king was asked to give up his command of the armed forces; he refused and the Civil War broke out.

Q What factions were involved in the war?

A The forces were divided into Royalists, who sided with the king, and supporters of Parliament, called Parliamentarians, led by Oliver Cromwell (1599–1658). The former let their hair grow long and were also known as 'Cavaliers'. They included the lords, the gentry and officials of the Church of England. The latter were called 'Roundheads' because they considered long hair sinful and cut theirs short. London, the ports, the navy, the new gentry and small landowners, artisans and Puritans sided with Parliament.

Q How did the war end?

A The king was taken prisoner in 1647. Cromwell took control of London and expelled or arrested more than 100 Members of the House of Lords. The remaining members voted for the execution of the king on 30th January 1649. After Charles I's execution, the monarchy was abolished and the country was ruled as a republic, known as 'the Commonwealth'.

4 **IN PAIRS** cover the answers (As) in the text and take turns asking and answering the questions (Qs) using the information that you have read.

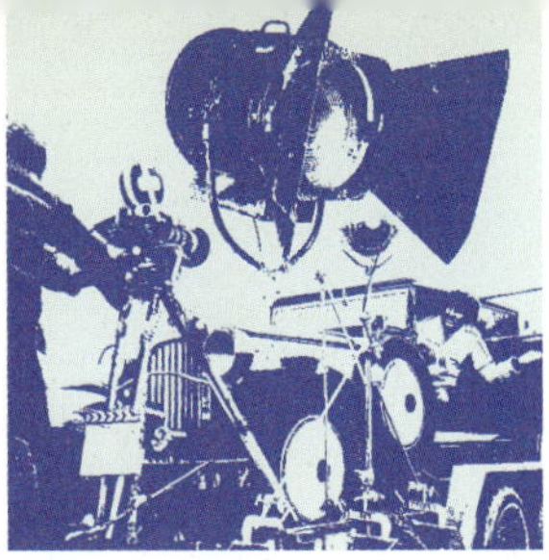

3.2 Two Films About...
The Civil War

WARM-UP

1 **DISCUSS** the following sentence in pairs: 'History is written in blood.' State whether these words could be applied to the Civil War.

Cromwell

Directed by Ken Hughes;
USA 1970.
With Richard Harris (Cromwell); Alec Guinness (King Charles I); Timothy Dalton (Prince Rupert).

This film is based on the life of Oliver Cromwell who, disgusted with the policies of King Charles I, plans to take his family to the New World. But on the eve of their departure, he is persuaded by his friends to stay and resume a role in politics. He leads the Parliamentary forces during the English Civil War and, as Lord Protector, rules Great Britain and Ireland in the 1650s.

What about accuracy?
The film does not fully explain the causes of the Civil War or the differences between the Parliamentarians and the Royalists. It portrays the Royalist forces as the well-equipped and stronger element, when in reality the Parliamentary forces were not only much more numerous, but usually much better equipped. The film also portrays Cromwell as too important from the start. Rather than being one of the key leaders from the beginning, he actually started as a military commander and became important over time. Finally, Cromwell, despite some of his autocratic tendencies, is too often shown to be a reluctant, noble hero, while nothing is mentioned of his willingness to shed the blood of Royalists and Catholics.

To Kill a King

Directed by Mike Barker;
UK 2003.
With Tim Roth (Oliver Cromwell); Dougray Scott (Sir Thomas Fairfax); Rupert Everett (King Charles I).

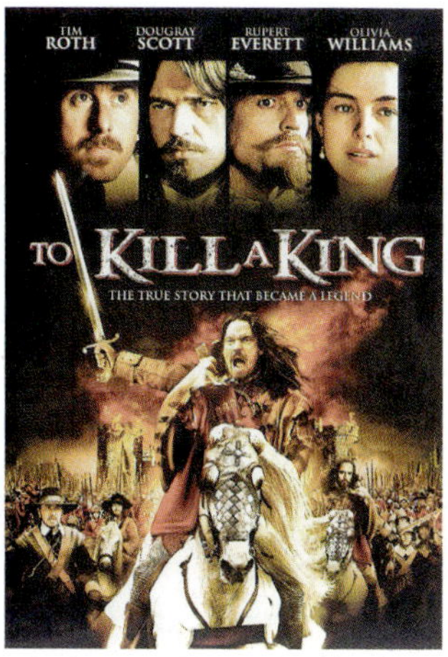

The film presents the relationship between General Fairfax and Oliver Cromwell as they try to face the consequences of deposing King Charles I. Thomas Fairfax is presented as the military genius and architect of the victories of the Parliamentarians.

What about accuracy?
By starting the film in 1645, when the war was almost over, the film fails to show why there was a war and why King Charles I had to be executed. The king's tyranny, his intrigues and plots are not even dealt with, and Charles I is portrayed more as a victim than the tyrant he really was. On the contrary, Oliver Cromwell is depicted as a bloodthirsty tyrant, lusting for power at all costs and having corpses hung publicly for display. Actually, it was never the practice of the Puritans to show such contempt for human life. It was, however, the practice of both Charles I and his son, Charles II, to have the corpses of 'traitors' hung and left in public.

3.3 Society
The Puritans

WARM-UP

1 MATCH the statements (A–G) with the pictures (1–2).

Cavaliers

1

A They liked bright colours.
B They wore plain clothes with a conservative cut.
C They wore their hair short.
D They dressed in elegant silks and velvets.
E They had long hair.
F They neither wore ornaments nor used perfume.
G They liked lace and scented their hair.

Roundheads

2

2 2.14 | **LISTEN** to an extract on the origins and beliefs of Puritanism. Tick the words employed by the speaker.

- ☐ Theology
- ☐ Intolerance
- ☐ Salvation
- ☐ Worship
- ☐ Mercy
- ☐ Saved
- ☐ Authority
- ☐ Bible
- ☐ Faith
- ☐ Sober
- ☐ Grace
- ☐ Scripture

1 Sir Anthony van Dyck, *Lord John Stuart and his brother, Lord Bernard Stuart*, ca 1638. The National Gallery, London.

2 John Pettie, *Puritan, Roundhead*. Sheffield Galleries and Museums Trust, Sheffield, England.

3 US agents enforcing the law against bootleg liquor in the 1930s.

FCE **Listening – Part 2**

3 2.14 | **SENTENCE COMPLETION.** Listen to the extract on the origins and beliefs of Puritanism again. For questions 1–10, complete the sentences.

The Puritan Mind

The English Puritans criticised the **(1)** .... made during the reign of Elizabeth I.
Many of them had studied at Cambridge University.
(2) .... was the field in which they tried to change the most.
James I rejected their proposal of **(3)** ....
During the Civil War, they supported the **(4)** ....
Their theological roots stretch back to **(5)** ....
The 'Pilgrims' established the Plymouth Colony in 1620.
The Puritans believed that **(6)** .... depended on God.
They regarded the Bible as a **(7)** .... to life.
They encouraged personal acts of **(8)** ....
The Puritans' reputation has been damaged by a unified view of society implying **(9)** ....
Puritanism provided the foundation for the **(10)** .... in modern times.

Insights

The Puritan heritage in America
The ideology of Puritanism is not a simple one. There were many different ways of being a Puritan and they changed often during the 100 years of their existence in England. These differences were exported to New England with the early settlers, where discussions and argument over the use of authority took place. Witness Roger Williams, for example, was expelled from the Massachusetts Bay Colony because he thought the government still had too much control. He went on to found Providence, Rhode Island, a haven for religious freedom.

There is a certain irony in the fact that while in England the basic tenets of Puritanism eventually lost out to the Church of England, in America their impact has remained strong. The concepts of freedom, religion, expression and congregationalism, as well as salvation and the related Calvinist movement, took hold in the New World. Whereas the Church of England has never taken a strong foothold in America, the Puritan heritage is part of their everyday life. Many of the American thoughts and beliefs today are an indirect result of the Puritan beliefs of the 'Pilgrims'.

3

John Milton: Satan's speech

WARM-UP

1 **LOOK at the pictures (1–3) and discuss. John Milton is regarded as 'England's epic genius'. Can you guess what he chose to write about?**

John Milton's life

John Milton (1608–74) was the author of the greatest epic poem in English, *Paradise Lost* (1667), but he was also a reforming prose writer, a member of the revolutionary government and the victim of censorship. As a poet and as a politically engaged writer, he struggled in defense of liberty. He despised all forms of tyranny, from political to religious, to domestic. When the monarchy was abolished in 1649, he served the republican government, justifying the execution of the king to the rest of Europe in his writings. After the return of the monarchy in 1660, his republican writings were condemned to be burnt and the author was sent to prison. He was later pardoned and released from prison. This experience of political and personal loss was recreated in his great poem, *Paradise Lost*, written after the Restoration of the monarchy.

3

1

2

Paradise Lost

A religious epic poem

Milton chose the epic genre for his masterpiece because of the greatness of his subject, and he followed the typical epic conventions. In fact, *Paradise Lost* opens with a precise statement of the theme of the epic – 'Of Man's First Disobedience' – as do all traditional epics. This epic takes place in the universe: in Heaven, Hell and Eden. There, God, Satan, Christ, Man and many fallen angels are met, and they echo the several warriors and heroes created by Homer. The typical character of the epic hero was altered by Milton to suit the changing spirit of the age: no longer a warrior like Achilles, seeking glory on the battlefield, but a more philosophical hero who must learn to control himself before he is judged fit to found an empire. The style is elevated and complex, with Latin syntax and difficult vocabulary.

The universe of *Paradise Lost*

Although Milton was familiar with Copernican cosmology, which established the sun, and not the earth, as the centre of the universe, he based his universe on the more traditional Ptolemaic system. In Milton's Heaven, God sits on his throne surrounded by the nine orders of angels; the tenth one, who revolted under Satan, has been hurled down into a dreadful realm, Hell, which is below Chaos and which is in antithesis with God's world. Out of Chaos, God created the earth, fixed in the centre of the universe, and around it the spheres.

Satan as an epic hero

At the beginning of the poem, Satan has many of the characteristics of the epic hero: leadership, the courage which refuses to accept defeat and a willingness to undertake the desperate enterprise to escape from Hell and attack God's creation – Man. Satan embodies the figure of the rebel against authority.

The story

Paradise Lost tells the biblical story of Adam and Eve, with God and Satan (Lucifer), who is thrown out of Heaven and later tries to corrupt humankind. Satan, the most beautiful of the angels, is hurled into Hell with his stunned followers as a consequence of his defeat in the war in Heaven.

2 **READ the text about John Milton and *Paradise Lost* and answer these questions.**

1 What did Milton despise?
2 What happened to him after the Restoration of the monarchy?
3 Why did he choose the epic form for his masterpiece?
4 Where does his epic take place?
5 What features does Satan share with the epic hero?

1–2 Gustave Doré, illustrations for *Paradise Lost*, ca 1866.

3 Unknown artist, *Portrait of John Milton*, ca 1629. National Portrait Gallery, London.

WARM-UP

1 **MAKE** predictions about the tone employed by Satan in his speech.

COMPREHENSION

2 **ANSWER** the following questions.

1 Who is speaking? Is he alone?
2 What does he hail?
3 How does Satan react to the fall from Heaven?
4 Does he feel equal to God? Why is the power of reason so important?

ANALYSIS

3 **HELL** is described in contrast with Heaven.

1 List any reference to the features of Heaven and Hell.
2 State which semantic area all the antitheses belong to. Then try to recognise the message they convey.

4 **FOCUS** on the hero Satan.

1 Underline any words or phrases in which Satan refers to God. How does Satan see God?
2 What are Satan's feelings about his new situation?
3 Can you consider Satan an epic hero? Why?

5 **CONCENTRATE** on the style.

1 This poem is written in **blank verse, that is, unrhymed verse, usually in lines of 5 iambic feet**. However, Milton varies: the number of syllables in a line; the number of stresses; the succession of unstressed-stressed syllables. Find examples of these variations.
2 Milton was a great Latin scholar. This can be inferred from his use of long sentences, deviation from the normal English order of words and Latinised words. Find examples of each. Then state the effect achieved by the use of this Latinate syntax.

Satan's speech

John Milton

Paradise Lost (1667)
Book I, lines 242–270

The passage you are going to read deals with Satan's arrival in his new kingdom, Hell.

2.15

'Is this the Region, this the Soil, the Clime,'
Said then the lost Arch Angel[1], 'this the seat[2]
That we must change for Heav'n, this mournful gloom[3]
For that celestial light? Be it so, since he
Who now is Sovran can dispose and bid
What shall be right: farthest from him is best
Whom reason hath equall'd, force hath made supreme
Above his equals. Farewell happy Fields
Where Joy for ever dwells: Hail[4] horrors, hail
Infernal world, and thou[5] profoundest Hell
Receive thy[6] new Possessor: One who brings
A mind[7] not to be chang'd by Place or Time.
The mind is its own place[8], and in itself
Can make a Heav'n of Hell, a Hell of Heav'n.
What matter where, if I be still the same,
And what I should be, all but less than he[9]
Whom Thunder hath made[10] greater? Here at least
We shall be free; th'Almighty hath not built
Here for his envy, will not drive us hence[11]:
Here we may reign secure, and in my choice
To reign is worth ambition though in Hell:
Better to reign in Hell, than serve in Heav'n.
But wherefore[12] let we then our faithful friends,
Th'associates[13] and co-partners of our loss
Lie thus astonisht[14] on th'oblivious Pool[15],
And call them not to share with us their part
In this unhappy Mansion[16], or once more
With rallied Arms[17] to try what may be yet
Regain'd in Heav'n, or what more lost in Hell?'

1 **Arch Angel.** Arcangelo; *qui*: Satana.
2 **seat.** Dimora.
3 **mournful gloom.** Triste oscurità.
4 **Hail.** Salve.
5 **thou.** *You*: tu.
6 **thy.** *Your*: tuo.
7 **One who brings A mind.** Uno che reca uno spirito.
8 **The mind is its own place.** La mente è la sua dimora.
9 **all but ... he.** Tutto tranne che lui (Dio).
10 **hath made.** Ha reso.
11 **hence.** Di qui.
12 **wherefore.** Perché.
13 **Th'associates.** I compagni.
14 **astonisht.** Attoniti.
15 **oblivious Pool.** Stagno dell'oblio.
16 **Mansion.** Sede, dimora.
17 **rallied Arms.** Armi raccolte.

YOUR TURN

6 **THINK** of other descriptions of hell that you have studied in literature or art or seen in films, and draw a comparison with Milton's Hell.

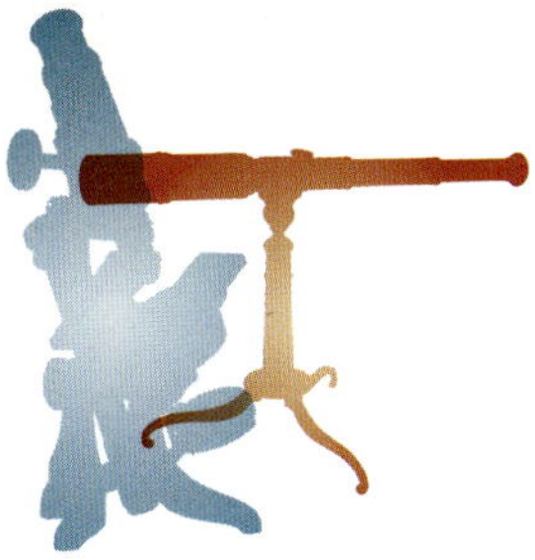

The scientific revolution

2.16 DICTATION: *THE ROYAL SOCIETY*

WARM-UP

1 READ the definition of the term 'method' below. In what fields is a method applied?

'Method means a procedure, technique or a set of rules employed in an activity or to approach the problems of truth and knowledge.'

FCE Reading and Use of English – Part 2

2 OPEN CLOZE. For questions 1–8, read the text below and think of the word which best fits each gap. Use only one word in each gap. There is an example at the beginning (0).

NEW SCIENTIFIC METHODS

The first half of the 17th century in Europe represented a critical stage in the replacement of one world view with another.

The concept of method probably came **(0)** ...FROM... the Greek philosopher Socrates (ca 469–399 BC). The Socratic method was applied in philosophical conversations with pupils to clarify thinking both on ethics **(1)** .... on politics.

Three different approaches to the study of phenomena in nature can **(2)** .... identified. The first is the deductive method, employed in logic, mathematics and geometry, in which the conclusion necessarily follows from the premises. The second is the experimental method, applied to physics, chemistry and biology, **(3)** .... is founded on the formulation of hypotheses and their verification through experience. The third is the method of classification, typical of biology, which is based on placing any organism into a group, class or family according to its biochemical, anatomical or physiological characteristics.

The process that we now call the scientific method – **(4)** .... is, the study of the physical world by sensory observation and experiment, by mathematical measurement and inductive reasoning – had **(5)** .... established by the activities of men **(6)** .... the Italian astronomer Galileo Galilei (1564–1642) and the German mathematician Johannes Kepler (1571–1630). This first age of science culminated in England with the work of Isaac Newton (1642–1727), with his demonstration of the laws of gravity and motion by which the planets move in their orderly courses.

The experimental method goes further **(7)** .... that by making a hypothesis, that is, the description of what has been observed. Predictions are tested by experiments or further observation, and finally there is the clarification of the theory concerning the phenomenon. Therefore the experimental method moves **(8)** .... the particular to the universal.

3 READ the text again and say:

1. how many kinds of approaches to the study of phenomena there are and how they differ;
2. what the scientific method is;
3. why the experimental method goes further than the scientific method.

The Royal Society

The centre of the development of the new scientific philosophy was London, where in 1662 the Royal Society was founded with King Charles II's patronage. The motto of the Society, *nullius in verba* ('nothing by words'), was a direct challenge to the dependence of the old philosophy on written authorities.

The useful and the simple replaced the ornate, the rich and the complex, which had characterised the previous age. It was from 1660 onwards that some of the typical traits of the English character began to emerge: a materialistic and practical mind, tolerance, reasonableness and common sense. These traits were to become the key words of the 18th century.

1 Somerset House, home to the Royal Society during the 18th and 19th centuries.

4 ANSWER the questions.

1. What did the members of the Royal Society challenge?
2. What typical features of the English character began to emerge?

Insights

The Royal Society today

The Royal Society is a fellowship of the world's preeminent scientists. It is the oldest scientific academy in continuous existence. It aims to expand the frontiers of knowledge by the development and use of science, mathematics, engineering and medicine for the benefit of humanity and the good of the planet.

Today there are approximately 1,500 Fellows and Foreign Members, including more than 70 Nobel Laureates. The Society has three roles: it is the UK's academy of science, promoting the natural and applied sciences; it is a learned society; and it is a funding agency.

As the UK's independent national academy, the Society represents the British scientific community within Britain and in relation to individuals and groups of scientists throughout the world.

3.6 **History**

The Restoration of the monarchy

1 **READ** the text. Then put the pictures 1–4 in chronological order.

2 **REPORT** on the Restoration of the monarchy using the pictures.

Milestones

1688, the Glorious Revolution
After the bloodless revolution of 1688, William and Mary's subsequent coronation as joint monarchs represented the first truly modern revolution. This revolution was a clash between two contrasting modernisation programmes: one developed by the Catholic James II and heavily modelled on Louis XIV's France; the other promoted by members of the Whig party and strongly influenced by the Dutch Republic. While James and his Catholic advisers opposed religious pluralism, William and the Whigs were committed to toleration. While James tried to increase Britain's international power through empire and the exploitation of landed wealth, the Whigs wanted to create a trading nation, using commerce as the route to national greatness. Both sides wanted a powerful, interventionist state, but while James saw this as being directed largely by the king and his court, the Whigs favoured a contractual, participatory model of government.

In 1660 Parliament invited Charles II (1630–85) to return to his kingdom from his exile in France and the republic was over. The Restoration of the monarchy was greeted with relief by most Englishmen, who had felt oppressed in their everyday life by the strict rules of the Puritans.

Charles II's court was the most immoral in English history, so when the two catastrophes of the plague and the Great Fire hit the country, the Puritans interpreted them as God's punishment for the king's immorality. London was struck in 1665 by an outbreak of bubonic plague, during which more than 100,000 people died. A year later, a fire destroyed most of the city in four days.

Charles II's brother, James II (1633–1701), succeeded him in 1685. He had converted to Catholicism in 1660, and his attempts to give civic equality to Roman Catholic and Protestant dissenters led to conflict with Parliament. In 1688, James's second wife, Mary of Modena, gave birth to a son. Fearing that a Catholic succession was now assured, a group of Protestant nobles appealed to William of Orange (1650–1702), the husband of James's older, and Protestant, daughter Mary (1662–94). In November, William landed with an army in Devon, while James II fled abroad. Cooperation between the crown and Parliament became effective with the so-called Glorious Revolution. Its name celebrates the bloodlessness of the event, which saw William of Orange and his wife Mary established as joint monarchs in 1689. The reign of William III and Mary II was a time of economic progress for England; London was becoming the financial capital of the world and the Bill of Rights of 1689, which prevented the king from raising taxes or keeping an army without the agreement of Parliament, represented the victory of a parliamentary, or constitutional, monarchy.

1

2

3

4

1 The arrival of William of Orange on 5th November 1688 in Brixham, Devon. The Royal Collection.

2 Dutch School, *The Great Fire of London*, ca 1666. Museum of London, London.

3 Dirck Stoop, *Charles II's cavalcade through the City of London, 22nd April, 1661*, 1662. Museum of London, London.

4 Sir Paul Lely, *King James II* (detail), 1660s. National Portrait Gallery, London.

3.7 **History**

The birth of political parties

2

1

3

4

WARM-UP

1 **LOOK at the pictures (1–4) and match them with the captions (A–D).**

A A political satire of the Seven Years' War. In the centre King George III is trying to put out the fire of the war, while William Pitt is fuelling the flames.

B Figures in a tavern or coffee house.

C William Pitt addressing the House of Commons.

D 10 Downing Street, the official residence of the prime minister.

2 **DISCUSS. What do you think these pictures tell us about the changes in government and lifestyle taking place at this time?**

3 **READ the Q&A text.**

GLOSSARY

customs duties diritti doganali
raw materials materie prime
smuggling contrabbando
bribery corruzione

1 William Hogarth, ca 1750. Yale Center for British Art, New Haven, Connecticut, US.

2 Karl Anton Hickel, 1793–95. National Portrait Gallery, London.

3 William Hogarth, 1762.

4 Illustration, early 18th century.

At the beginning of the 18th century, the Hanover dynasty succeeded that of the Stuarts.

Q Who came to the throne when William III died in 1702?

A Queen Anne (1665–1714) succeeded her brother-in-law, William III, and her sister Mary. During her reign, Scotland became officially united with England with the Act of Union of 1707. Many Scots emigrated to England and the expanding colonies.

Q Who was the first prime minister?

A The Whigs and the Tories were the first political parties in Britain, and the first prime minister was the Whig Sir Robert Walpole (1676–1745), who was in power for over twenty years (1721–42).

Q How did Walpole improve the finances of the nation?

A He managed to keep England out of foreign conflicts so that trade could flourish and taxes could be kept down. Trade was stimulated by the removal of customs duties on exports and on imports of raw materials, but in 1723 tea, coffee and chocolate became subject to taxation. This kept smuggling under control and at the same time increased government income.

Q What was Walpole accused of?

A From 1726 Walpole and his government were accused of corruption and bribery during elections. He had, however, survived a change of monarch when George I of Hanover (1660–1727) died and was succeeded by his son, George II (1683–1760). The new king relied more and more on Walpole and gave him a house in Westminster, 10 Downing Street, which is still the official residence of the prime minister today.

Q What happened when William Pitt became prime minister?

A In 1735 the Whig William Pitt entered Parliament as an opponent of Walpole, and became prime minister in 1766. He started a mercantilist policy to make England a strong and economically competitive country. This led to the establishment of a new set of values based on power, wealth and prestige. The new middle-class man of Pitt's age would be reflected in Daniel Defoe's *Robinson Crusoe*. In this period, England expanded its possessions in India, North America and the Caribbean.

4 **IN PAIRS cover the answers (A s) in the text above. Take turns asking and answering the questions (Q s) using the information that you have read.**

Milestones

1707, the Act of Union

In a poorly attended Scottish Parliament, the Scottish Members of Parliament (MPs) voted to join the Union, and on 16th January 1707 the Act of Union was signed. The Scottish Parliament was dissolved, and England and Scotland became one country. Scotland kept its independence with respect to its legal and religious systems, but currency, taxation, sovereignty, trade, parliament and flag became one. The red cross of St George combined with the blue and white cross of St Andrew, resulting in the 'old' union flag.

However, there were and there are significant differences between the two countries in culture, education, religion and even language. The Scots speak English, but with their own accent and with different words, like *kirk* for church, *wee* for small, *bonnie* for attractive, *burn* for stream and many others.

FCE Reading and Use of English – Part 2

5 OPEN CLOZE. For questions 1–8, read the text below about the two main political parties during the 18th century and think of the word which best fits each gap. Use only one word in each gap. There is an example at the beginning (0).

The Tories and the Whigs

The Tories were formed in 1679–80. **(0)** ...THEY... came **(1)** .... the Royalists, and their name derived from the 17th-century Irish outlaws **(2)** .... killed English settlers. They believed **(3)** .... the divine right of the monarch and opposed religious toleration. The Church of England and the landowners supported them. They became the Conservative Party in 1832.

The Whigs' name derived from 'cattle drivers'. They **(4)** .... descendants of the Parliamentarians. They were supported **(5)** .... the wealthy and commercial classes; they fought **(6)** .... industrial and commercial development, a vigorous foreign policy and religious toleration. They eventually became the Liberal Party in the 1860s. The meetings of Whig ministers gave origin to the Cabinet.

(7) .... parties were founded on rich politicians, more than on popular votes; there were elections to the House of Commons, but a small number of men controlled **(8)** .... of the voters.

6 COMPLETE the table below about the Tories and the Whigs.

	Tories	Whigs
Descendants of		
Supporters of		
Believers in		

Insights

Modern political parties

Nowadays the two main parties are the Conservative Party, whose beginning dates back to the 19th century, and the Labour Party, which was formed in 1900. A third important party is the Liberal Democrat Party, formed in 1988 when the Liberal Party, which also began in the 19th century, joined with the Social Democratic Party, founded in 1981, after a split in the Labour Party. Traditionally the Conservative Party represents private enterprise, the ruling classes and nationalistic values, while the Labour Party, which grew out of the Trade Union Movement, represents the working classes, social values and state-run institutions. Other parties include two national parties: Plaid Cymru, the Party of Wales (founded in 1925), and the Scottish National Party (founded in 1934). Northern Ireland has a number of parties: the Ulster Unionists (formed in the early 20th century), the Democratic Unionists (founded in 1971), the Social Democratic and Labour Party (founded in 1970) and Sinn Féin, considered the political face of the IRA.

The prime minister and the Cabinet

Unlike the US president, British voters do not choose their prime minister (PM). He or she is elected within their political party. After a general election, the leader of the political party with the most MPs in the House of Commons is asked by the Queen to become prime minister and to form a government that will manage the country. Today there are two parties in power. In the 2010 general election, no party won an overall majority of seats. David Cameron, the leader of the Conservative Party, formed a new government in coalition with Nick Clegg, the leader of the Liberal Democrats. The prime minister leads the government and appoints ministers, who head individual government departments. The most important ministers are called secretaries of state and form the Cabinet.

1 The first British prime minister, the Whig Sir Robert Walpole. Portrait by John Wooton and Jonathan Richardson, pre-1764.

3.8 **Society**

A golden age

INTERACTIVE MAP 3: *THE ENGLISH LANDSCAPE GARDEN*

WARM-UP

1 **DISCUSS.** What are the key ideas you generally associate with a 'golden age'?

2 **COMPLETE** the table below with the correct word.

Noun	Adjective
	stable
traditionalism / tradition	
	elegant
	witty
materialism	
world	
pragmatism	
	responsive
hierarchy	
heredity	
	privileged
	individualistic
pessimism	
	optimistic

FCE **Reading and Use of English – Part 3**

3 **WORD FORMATION.** For questions 1–8, read the text below. Use the word given in capitals at the end of some of the lines to form a word that fits in the gap in the same line. There is an example at the beginning (0).

Reason and common sense

Generally regarded as a golden age, the 18th century in England was called 'Augustan' after the period of Roman history which had achieved political **(0)** STABILITY and power as well as a flourishing of the arts. **STABLE**

In fact, it was an age of wise **(1)** .... , of elegance and wit, but also a distinctive moment in the making of modern England. It was a **(2)** .... society – worldly, pragmatic, **(3)** .... to economic pressure. **TRADITION** **MATERIAL** **RESPONSE**

Yet, its political institutions were **(4)** .... , hereditary and privileged. Elections were largely controlled by the local landowners since voting was not secret; politicians were not concerned about winning over the electorate, but with **(5)** .... it either with money or with the promise of jobs. **HIERARCHY** **BRIBE**

Society in the 18th century championed **(6)** .... , seizing opportunities in the sectors of economy which provided scope for initiative, enterprise and enrichment. **INDIVIDUAL**

It was in many ways an **(7)** .... free and open age. Enlightened thinkers, from the philosopher John Locke (1632–1704) to journalists such as Joseph Addison (1672–1719), rejected the strict and pessimistic values of Puritanism, like original sin and the depravity of man. Liberal thought influenced the new view of the world and affirmed free will, salvation for all, the goodness of mankind and its capacity for progress. **ORDINARY**

(8) .... encouraged faith in progress and human perfectibility, and made people eager to try new ways, trusting their own powers: reason, which made them different from animals, and common sense. **OPTIMISTIC**

1 Johann Zoffany, *Charles Towneley in his Sculpture Gallery*, 1782. Towneley Hall Art Gallery and Museum, Burnley, Lancashire, England.

2 A scene from the film 'Tom Jones' (1963), an adaptation of Henry Fielding's *The History of Tom Jones, a Foundling* (1749).

4 **AFTER READING** the text 'Reason and common sense', explain:

1 why the 18th century was called 'Augustan';
2 what the main features of the age were;
3 what society was like at that time;
4 who controlled the elections and how;
5 what values characterised the age.

3.9 **The Arts**

William Hogarth's satire and social criticism

WARM-UP

1 **DISCUSS.** What might the targets of satire be nowadays? Write down your ideas in the spider chart below.

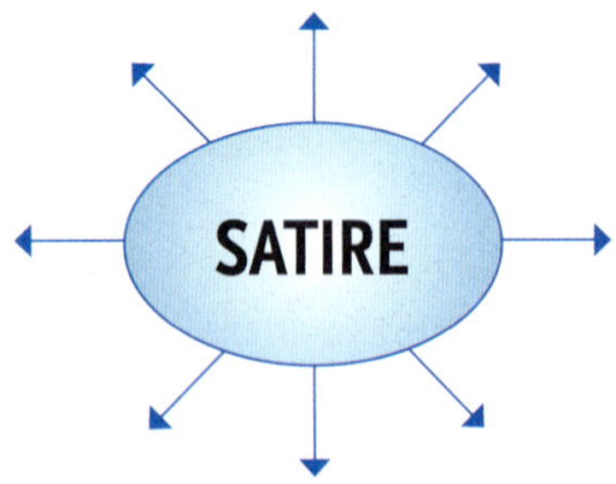

2 **ANSWER** the question: what are the aims of the satirist? Choose from among the following.

to entertain • to mock • to teach • to amend • to accuse • to punish • to amuse • to ridicule • to reproach • to attack directly • to denounce • to forgive • to invite • to consider an alternative • to demolish • to convey a moral message

GLOSSARY

catchphrase frase tipica
dead drunk ubriaco fradicio
clean straw paglia pulita (dove si smaltisce la sbornia)
retails vende al dettaglio
slum quartiere degradato
drunken grin ghigno ubriaco
pinch of snuff presa di tabacco

FCE Listening – Part 2

3 2.17 | **SENTENCE COMPLETION.** You will hear a lecture about William Hogarth's *Gin Lane*. For questions 1–10, complete the sentences.

Gin Lane is among the strong didactic pieces by the English painter William Hogarth (1697–1764). It is a lecture on the **(1)** .... of drinking gin. The picture's message is that poverty, misery and **(2)** .... are the price one pays for indulgence in this vice.

Gin was a cheap and strongly alcoholic drink, advertised by this tavern with the following catchphrase: '**(3)** .... for a Penny / Dead Drunk for Two Pence / Clean Straw for Nothing'. In the lower right-hand corner is a cadaverous itinerant ballad seller **(4)** .... also retails gin, and obviously has drunk more than he has sold. In the background, the buildings are empty or **(5)** .... – the area is rapidly becoming a slum. In one **(6)** .... room a man has hanged himself.

In front of a **(7)** .... on the other side of the square, a carpenter is trying to sell his tools, a housewife her **(8)** .... utensils for a few more drinks. **(9)** .... is in the foreground, where a woman, breasts exposed and a drunken grin on her face, reaches for a pinch of snuff.

In the same year *Gin Lane* was published, Parliament passed the Gin Act of **(10)** .... , which regulated the sale of alcohol.

1 William Hogarth, *Gin Lane*, 1751. The British Museum, London.

YOUR TURN

4 **DISCUSS.** What does *Gin Lane* tell you about Hogarth's moral stance and his opinion of society? Do you think the satire is effective?

5 **IN PAIRS** discuss the quotation below by Jonathan Swift. What is the observer's attitude, especially when he sees himself satirised?

'Satire is a sort of glass, wherein beholders do generally discover everybody's face but their own.'

Internet Lab

1 **DIVIDE** the class into groups of two/three students per computer.

2 **BROWSE** these two sites in order to find information about William Hogarth.
www.abcgallery.com/H/hogarth/hogarth.html
www.artchive.com/archive/H/hogarth.html

3 **SEARCH** for information about:
1 Hogarth's life;
2 the themes employed in his works.

4 **FIND** the two paintings below. Look at them on the screen and describe:
1 the details;
2 the features they have in common;
3 the symbols they contain;
4 the targets of Hogarth's satire in each painting.

2

3

4

2 William Hogarth, *Marriage à la mode, Plate II: the Breakfast Scene*, ca 1743. The National Gallery, London.

3 William Hogarth, *A Rake's Progress, Plate III: the Tavern Scene*, 1735. The Trustees of Sir John Soane's Museum, London.

4 William Hogarth, *Beer Street*, 1751. The British Museum, London.

FCE Speaking – Part 2

5 **INDIVIDUAL LONG TURN.**
Candidate A, compare and contrast pictures 2 and 3, and say what the people's lives are like.
Candidate B, which of the situations do you find more satirical? Why?
Candidate B, compare and contrast pictures 1 and 4, and say what people are portrayed.
Candidate A, which of the two pictures strikes you the most? Why?

Process language
Speaking – Part 2

Pointing out similarities and differences
- To begin with ...
- Similarly, ...
- Both pictures depict ...
- A key difference is ...
- Neither picture ...
- In this picture ... whereas in the other picture ...

3.10 **Literature**

The means for cultural debate

WARM-UP

1 **DISCUSS** in pairs. Where can you find the latest business and foreign news, keep up to date with politics and find out what others think of a new book or film?

1 Coffeehouse in London, late 17th century. The Mansell Collection, London.

2 James Gillray's caricature of William Pitt as *The Giant-Factotum amusing himself*, issued in January 1797.

The spread of cultural debate in the 18th century brought about the need for new means of expression and for the circulation of ideas. This phenomenon was strictly linked to the Enlightenment and the affirmation of rationalistic ideas which, though begun in England, found development in France at first and later in the rest of Europe.

During the 17th century, there had been an increase in the publication of journals and pamphlets; however, it was in the 18th century that journalism took on its specific features. **1** ______ The first English periodical, 'A Current of General News', was published in London, in 1622, by the printers Archer and Bourne. The first daily newspaper, 'Leipziger Zeitung', however, appeared in Germany in 1660.

2 ______ Unlike the previous political journals, it deliberately avoided controversial tones aimed at the moralisation of public opinion, especially because it addressed a middle-class public.

Among the pioneers of journalism was Daniel Defoe with his periodical 'The Review', a weekly, and later a thrice-weekly, publication (1704–13). **3** ______ It also dealt with religion, trade, manners and morals. Its influence can be clearly seen in the gentle didacticism of Richard Steele's 'The Tatler' (1709) and Joseph Addison's 'The Spectator' (1711).

The spread of journalism began to worry politicians, who were afraid that the masses could somehow get access to power. **4** ______ This led to an increase in price which caused many newspapers to lose some of their readers. Advertisements became a means of survival for dailies, such as 'The Daily Courant' or 'The Daily Advertiser'.

Throughout the century, English journalists fought to defend liberal principles and the right to cover Parliamentary debates. From 1772 newspapers were allowed to send their reporters to attend Parliamentary sessions and write about them. Then, 'The Morning Post' introduced the use of bigger type to distinguish the titles of the most important articles, and in 1785 'The Daily Universal Register', which became 'The Times' in 1788, was founded.

Another significant trait of England's social life was the coffeehouse. **5** ______ They were associated with news and gossip and provided entertainment, so their function was very similar to that of the theatre in the Elizabethan age. With the beginning of a postal system at the end of the 17th century, they took on a new role as circulation centres. **6** ______ In the Augustan age, fashionable and artistic people began to attend the houses, which became gathering points where people exchanged opinions. It was mainly through the coffeehouses that public opinion and journalism began to evolve. The coffeehouses were almost exclusively attended by men, though women were slowly showing signs of emancipation.

FCE Reading and Use of English – Part 6

2 **GAPPED TEXT.** You are going to read an article about journalism and debate in 18th-century England. Six sentences have been removed from the article. Choose from the sentences A–G the one which fits each gap (1–6). There is one extra sentence that you do not need to use.

A It was the main government organ, as its political line mirrored that of the Whigs.

B They served as a box number for advertisers in the newspapers and as meeting places for the most important companies.

C Under the Commonwealth a number of coffeehouses had been opened in London.

D England was the first country where journalism developed as a free profession, encouraging the struggle for political and individual freedom.

E The circulation of newspapers was very limited until the political parties developed.

F They therefore tried to impose new limitations, such as the obligation to use special paper with a stamp on it.

G The modern periodical took shape in the first half of the 18th century in England.

TEXT BANK 20: *HENRY FIELDING*

The rise of the novel

WARM-UP

1 DISCUSS what features you look for when you buy a novel.

The literature of the 18th century reflected the economic and intellectual progress of the period and an increasing popular interest in reading. Lending, or circulating, libraries acquired great importance and since subscriptions were moderately priced, they led to an increase in the reading public. More printed items were produced, literacy increased (60% of the adult male and 40% of the adult female population could read) and more and more readers belonged to the middle and lower classes. People preferred prose to verse and drama. They liked reading about the practical needs of different trades, stories of pirates and thieves, books dealing with journeys to distant countries, accounts of crime, political pamphlets and newspapers. Writing became a profession ruled by economic criteria, and the value of an author depended on the number of pages he or she wrote. The belief in the power of reason and the individual's trust in his own abilities found expression in the novel.

By definition, a novel is 'a long prose narrative about largely fictional, if usually realistic, characters and plausible events'.

The 18th-century novelist was the spokesman of the middle class. The realism of the novel was not linked to the kind of life presented, but to the way it was shown. The writer's primary aim was to write in a simple way in order to be understood even by less well-educated readers. The novel, which was primarily concerned with everything that could alter social status, was particularly appealing to the practical-minded tradesman, who was self-made and self-reliant. The sense of reward and punishment, which was the 'message' of the novel itself, was related to the Puritan ethics of the middle classes.

1 A portable bookstall, ca 1700. The British Library, London.

2 Unknown artist, *Jonathan Wild unkennelling the butler*, 18th century.

2 READ the text about the rise of the novel in the 18th century and the Literary language box, and do the following activities.

1. List the reasons that led to the increase in the reading public.
2. Explain what kind of people read and what they enjoyed reading.
3. Complete the chart below.

The 18th-century novel

- Story
- Setting
- Characters
- Narrator

3 SUM UP the 18th-century writer's aim and the message he wanted to convey.

Literary language
The 18th-century novel

18th-century novels shared the following features:

- Events were usually narrated in chronological sequence.
- Narration was in the 1st person (the narrator and the protagonist are the same person) or the 3rd person (the narrator is omniscient).
- The setting was given great attention, with specific references to names of countries, streets and towns.
- References were made to particular times of the year or of the day.
- All the characters were given contemporary names and surnames to reinforce the impression of realism, and they struggled either for survival or for social success.
- The hero of the novel was always the 'bourgeois man', with his problems. He was generally the mouthpiece of his author and the reader was expected to sympathise with him.
- The language was simple and factual.

TEXT BANK 21–22: *ROBINSON CRUSOE*

Daniel Defoe and the realistic novel

Writers, whose profession was now becoming profitable, began to write to please a public of middle- and upper-class people who wanted to read about their own problems and individual experiences. The novel, therefore, became more and more a picture of real life and came to be defined as 'realistic', not only because of 'what' it presented, but above all because of 'how' it presented it. Authors began to use 'clock time' and 'physical setting'; descriptions contained primary qualities, such as colour, size, solidity, extension and number. A new type of 'hero' developed – practical, self-made and self-reliant, guided by common sense. Greater importance was given to bourgeois values, such as money and the improvement of one's social status. Daniel Defoe (1660–1731) was the first novelist to create this new type of fiction.

Daniel Defoe's life

Daniel Defoe was born in 1660 into a family of Dissenters, a Protestant sect which refused the authority of the Church of England. He started to write in Whig papers. As a journalist his greatest achievement was 'The Review', the periodical which he published two or three times a week from 1704 to 1713. He became a famous and well-paid intellectual by writing political essays and pamphlets up till the reign of Queen Anne. The queen did not like his critical attitude and had him arrested, tried and imprisoned. He even made three appearances in the pillory, which were meant to degrade him publicly, but were turned into a triumph when some of his friends threw flowers at him instead of rocks or rotten eggs. In order to regain his freedom he denied his Whig ideas and became a secret agent for the new government. When he was about sixty, he started to write novels which were very successful. In 1719 he published his first novel, *Robinson Crusoe*, which was followed by *Captain Singleton* in 1720. In 1722 he published *Moll Flanders* and *Colonel Jack*. Defoe's last novel was *The Fortunate Mistress*, better known as *Roxana* (1724). Thanks to the money he earned with these works, he could afford a comfortable standard of life, but his old creditors haunted him and pushed him into numerous adventures till his death in 1731.

people wanted/read something concrete

1

1 READ Defoe's biography and provide evidence to justify these statements about his reputation:

1. he was a prolific writer;
2. he was one of the greatest journalists of the age;
3. he sold his pen to the political party which governed the country;
4. he was an outsider;
5. he always held his head high.

1 Michael Van der Gucht, *Daniel Defoe*, 1706. National Portrait Gallery, London.

2 Frontispiece to *Robinson Crusoe* (1719).

Robinson Crusoe (1719)

Defoe's most famous novel is *Robinson Crusoe*. It was based on the real experiences of Alexander Selkirk, a seaman who in 1704 was put ashore on the desert island of Juan Fernández, in the Pacific Ocean, from which he was rescued in 1709. Defoe also drew inspiration from some of the travel books that were so successful in his time.

The new middle-class hero

Robinson Crusoe belongs to the middle class, 'the middle state', which his father praises as 'the best state in the world, the most suited to human happiness, not exposed to the miseries and hardships, the labour and sufferings of the mechanick part of mankind, and not embarass'd with the pride, luxury, ambition and envy of the upper part of mankind'. What Robinson has in common with the classical heroes of travel literature is his restlessness, the search for his own identity in alternative to the model provided by his father.

The story

Robinson Crusoe consists of three separate sections. The first section tells how, in spite of his father's warning, Robinson leaves his family when he is nineteen and goes to sea to make his fortune. After several adventures, he lands in Brazil, where he starts a successful plantation. One day, during an expedition to Africa to buy some slaves for his plantation, he is shipwrecked on a remote island where he spends twenty-eight years, two months and nineteen days. The second section is actually in the form of a diary-like account of Robinson's experiences on the island. It tells how he is able to partly recreate the world he has left behind him, how he eventually saves a young savage from cannibals and makes him his servant with the name of Man Friday, and how he is finally rescued by an English ship. In the third section Robinson returns to England, where he learns that his plantation in Brazil has made him rich.

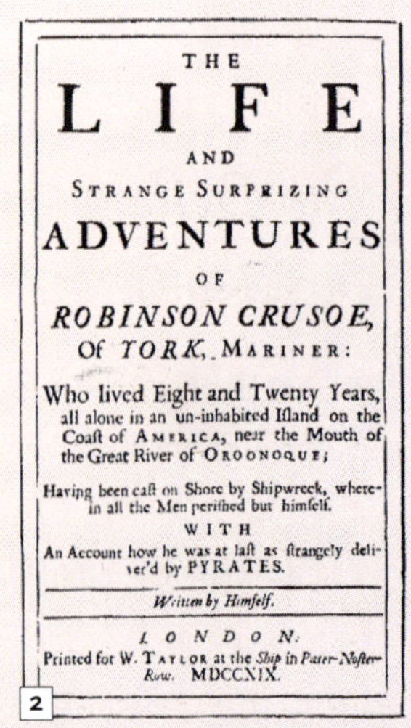

THE LIFE AND STRANGE SURPRIZING ADVENTURES OF ROBINSON CRUSOE, Of YORK, MARINER:

Who lived Eight and Twenty Years, all alone in an un-inhabited Island on the Coast of AMERICA, near the Mouth of the Great River of OROONOQUE;

Having been cast on Shore by Shipwreck, wherein all the Men perished but himself.

WITH An Account how he was at last as strangely deliver'd by PYRATES.

Written by Himself.

LONDON: Printed for W. TAYLOR at the *Ship* in *Pater-Noster-Row*. MDCCXIX.

2

A spiritual autobiography

The novel is full of religious references to God, sin, Providence and salvation. It can be read as a spiritual autobiography in which the hero reads the Bible to find comfort and guidance, experiences the constant conflict between good and evil, and keeps a diary to record events in order to see God's will in them. What Defoe explores is the conflict between economic motivation and spiritual salvation.

The island

The setting of most of the story – the island – is the ideal place for Robinson to prove his qualities, to demonstrate that he deserved to be saved by God's Providence. On the island Robinson organises a primitive empire, thus becoming the prototype of the English coloniser: his stay on the island is not seen as a return to a natural state, but as a chance to exploit and dominate nature.

The individual and society

The hero's life on the island puts forward the issue of the relationship between the individual and society, between the 'private' and the 'public' spheres. The society Robinson creates on the island is not an alternative to the English one; on the contrary, it can be read as an exaltation of 18th-century England and its ideals of mobility, material productiveness and individualism. Defoe shows that, though God is the prime cause of everything, the individual can shape his destiny through action. Robinson has a pragmatic and individualistic outlook. He applies a rational method to every situation: he always starts by observing the situation, then he makes a list of all possible solutions, he considers the pros and cons and he chooses the best alternative.

3 A scene from Robert Zemeckis's film 'Cast Away' (2000), based on the story of *Robinson Crusoe*, starring Tom Hanks.

2 **IN PAIRS take turns asking and answering the following questions about *Robinson Crusoe*.**

1. What social class does Robinson belong to?
2. What does he have in common with other heroes of travel literature?
3. In what sense can the novel be read as a spiritual autobiography?
4. What is the function of the island in the novel?
5. What kind of society does Robinson create on the island?
6. What is Robinson's attitude to reality?

The journal

Daniel Defoe

Robinson Crusoe (1719)
Chapter V, Builds a House

The following extract is from the second section of the novel. Robinson finds himself shipwrecked on a desert island and begins to keep a journal.

WARM-UP

1 **DISCUSS the questions with the rest of the class.**

1. What would you do if you were shipwrecked on a desert island and found yourself in Robinson's situation?
2. What would you miss most?
3. What do you think you would appreciate?

2.18

September 30, 1659. I, poor miserable Robinson Crusoe, being shipwrecked, during a dreadful storm, in the offing[1], came on shore on this dismal[2] unfortunate island, which I called the Island of Despair, all the rest of the ship's company being drowned, and myself almost dead.

All the rest of the day I spent in afflicting myself at the dismal circumstances I was brought to, viz[3]. I had neither food, house, clothes, weapon, nor place to fly to, and in despair of any relief[4], saw nothing but death before me, either that I should be devoured by wild beasts, murthered by savages, or starved to death for want[5] of food. At the approach of night, I slept in a tree for fear of wild creatures, but slept soundly, tho'[6] it rained all night.

1 **in the offing.** Al largo (ma in vista della terra).
2 **dismal.** Orribile, squallida.
3 **viz.** Cioè.
4 **relief.** Soccorso, ristoro.
5 **want.** Mancanza.
6 **soundly, tho'.** Profondamente, sebbene.

1 Illustration to *Robinson Crusoe*, 1951.

October 1. In the morning I saw to my great surprise, the ship had floated with the high tide[7], and was driven on shore again much nearer the island, which as it was some comfort on one hand, for[8] seeing her sit upright, and not broken to pieces, I hoped, if the wind abated[9], I might get on board, and get some food and necessaries out of her for my relief; so on the other hand, it renewed my grief[10] at the loss of my comrades, who I imagined if we had all stayed on board might have saved the ship, or at least that they would not have been all drowned as they were; and that had the men been saved, we might perhaps have built us a boat out of the ruins of the ship to have carried us to some other part of the world. I spent great part of this day in perplexing myself on these things; but at length seeing the ship almost dry, I went upon the sand as near as I could, and then swam on board; this day also it continued raining, tho' with no wind at all.

From the 1st of October to the 24th. All these days entirely spent in many several voyages to get all I could out of the ship, which I brought on shore, every tide of flood, upon rafts[11]. Much rain also in the days, tho' with some intervals of fair weather: but, it seems, this was the rainy season.

Oct. 20. I overset[12] my raft and all the goods I had got upon it, but being in shoal[13] water, and the things being chiefly heavy, I recovered many of them when the tide was out.

Oct. 25. It rained all night and all day, with some gusts[14] of wind, during which time the ship broke in pieces, the wind blowing a little harder than before, and was no more to be seen, except the wreck[15] of her, and that only at low water. I spent this day in covering and securing the goods which I had saved, that the rain might not spoil them.

Oct. 26. I walked about the shore almost all day to find out a place to fix my habitation, greatly concerned to secure my self from any attack in the night, either from wild beasts or men. Towards night I fixed upon a proper[16] place under a rock, and marked out a semicircle for my encampment, which I resolved to strengthen[17] with a work, wall, or fortification made of double piles[18], lined within with cables[19], and without with turf[20].

From the 26th to the 30th. I worked very hard in carrying all my goods to my new habitation, tho' some part of the time it rained exceedingly hard.

The 31st. in the morning, I went out into the island with my gun to see for[21] some food, and discover the country, when I killed a she-goat, and her kid followed me home, which I afterwards killed also because it would not feed.

November 1. I set up my tent under a rock, and lay there for the first night, making it as large as I could with stakes driven in to swing my hammock upon[22].

Nov. 2. I set up all my chests and boards[23], and the pieces of timber[24] which made my rafts, and with them formed a fence[25] round me, a little within the place I had marked out for my fortification.

7 **tide.** Marea.
8 **for.** Poiché.
9 **abated.** Diminuiva.
10 **grief.** Dolore.
11 **rafts.** Zattere.
12 **I overset.** Capovolsi.
13 **shoal.** Bassa.
14 **gusts.** Raffiche.
15 **wreck.** Relitto.
16 **proper.** Adatto.
17 **I resolved to strengthen.** Decisi di rafforzare.
18 **double piles.** Una doppia palificazione.
19 **lined within with cables.** Rivestito all'interno con dei funi.
20 **without with turf.** All'esterno con delle zolle erbose.
21 **to see for.** A cercare.
22 **with stakes ... upon.** Piantando dei pali a cui appendere la mia amaca.
23 **chests and boards.** Casse e assi.
24 **timber.** Legno.
25 **fence.** Staccionata.

COMPREHENSION

2 READ the extract and reorder the events by numbering them from 1 to 11.

- .... Robinson managed to reach the shore after the shipwreck.
- .... He continued to carry goods from the ship to the shore.
- .... He swam to the ship to get some provisions.
- .... He found shelter in a tree in order to spend the night.
- .... He found the right place to build his house.
- .... He tried to store the goods so as not to have them spoilt by the rain.
- .... The raft overturned and he had to recover many of the goods when the tide was low.
- .... He carried all the goods to his 'house'.
- .... He built a fence around his tent.
- .... He looked for food.
- .... He slept in his new fortification.

ANALYSIS

3 FIND references to the setting in time and place.

4 DECIDE. Who tells the story? What do you call the kind of narrative technique where the narrator and the protagonist are the same person? What are its advantages?

5 TICK the correct answer. How are the events described?

- ☐ Through flashbacks.
- ☐ In chronological order.
- ☐ Through flashforwards.

6 FOCUS on the character of Robinson. He manages to overcome the obstacles he is faced with thanks to his physical and rational efforts.

1. There is a moment when he seems upset. Find where this happens and explain the reasons for his sadness. How does he end his reflection?
2. Provide examples of his change of mood by quoting from the text.
3. What sentences emphasise Robinson's efforts to survive?
4. Does Robinson have time for intellectual speculation?
5. What kind of man is Robinson? Write a short paragraph.

7 DESCRIBE. The main lexical items in this extract are the sea, the ship and the fortification. What are they connected with?

The sea → ....

The ship → ....

The fortification → ....

YOUR TURN

8 LOOK at the picture on the previous page. What do you think were the main problems Robinson Crusoe had to face on the island? Why do you think he began to keep a diary?

WARM-UP

1 LOOK at the picture on the following page and describe both Robinson's and the native's attitude.

Man Friday

Daniel Defoe

Robinson Crusoe (1719)

Chapter 14, A Dream Realized

This extract deals with the description of the native that Robinson has rescued from a group of cannibals who came to the island to perform their rites.

2.19

He was a comely[1] handsome fellow, perfectly well made; with straight strong limbs[2], not too large; tall and well-shaped, and, as I reckon[3], about twenty-six years of age. He had a very good countenance[4], not a fierce and surly[5] aspect; but seemed to have something very manly in his face, and yet he had all the sweetness and softness of an European in his countenance too, especially when he smiled. His hair was long and black, not curled like wool; his forehead very high and large, and a great vivacity and sparkling[6] sharpness[7] in his eyes. The colour of his skin was not quite black, but very tawny[8]; and yet not of an ugly yellow nauseous tawny, as the Brasilians, and Virginians, and other natives of America are; but of a bright kind of a dun[9] olive colour, that had in it something very agreeable, tho'[10] not very easy to describe. His face was round and plump; his nose small, not flat like the negroes, a very good

1 **comely.** Attraente.
2 **limbs.** Membra, arti.
3 **I reckon.** Credo.
4 **countenance.** Espressione.
5 **surly.** Scontroso.
6 **sparkling.** Vivace.
7 **sharpness.** Acutezza.
8 **tawny.** Bruno.
9 **dun.** Bigio, opaco.
10 **tho'.** *Though*, sebbene.

3.12 Daniel Defoe and the realistic novel

mouth, thin lips, and his fine teeth well set, and white as ivory. After he had slumbered[11], rather than slept, about half an hour, he waked again, and comes out of the cave to me; for I had been milking my goats, which I had in the enclosure just by; when he espy'd[12] me, he came running to me, laying himself down again upon the ground, with all the possible signs of an humble thankful disposition, making a many antick gestures to show it. At last he lays his head flat upon the ground, close to my foot, and sets my other foot upon his head, as he had done before; and after this, made all the signs to me of subjection, servitude, and submission imaginable, to let me know how he would serve me as long as he lived. I understood him in many things, and let him know I was very well pleased with him; in a little time I began to speak to him, and teach him to speak to me; and first, I made him know his name should be Friday, which was the day I saved his life; I called him so for the memory of the time; I likewise[13] taught him to say Master, and then let him know, that was to be my name; I likewise taught him to say yes and no, and to know the meaning of them; I gave him some milk in an earthen pot, and let him see me drink it before him, and sop[14] my bread in it; and I gave him a cake of bread to do the like, which he quickly comply'd with[15], and made signs that it was very good for him.

I kept there with him all that night; but as soon as it was day, I beckoned to him[16] to come with me, and let him know I would give him some cloaths, at which he seemed very glad, for he was stark naked[17]. As we went by the place where he had bury'd the two men, he pointed exactly to the place, and shewed me the marks that he had made to find them again, making signs to me that we should dig them up again, and eat them; at this I appeared very angry, expressed my abhorrence of it, made as if I would vomit at the thoughts of it, and beckoned with my hand to him to come away, which he did immediately, with great submission.

1 Illustration to *Robinson Crusoe*, 1951.

11 **slumbered.** Sonnecchiato.
12 **espy'd.** Vide.
13 **likewise.** Allo stesso modo.
14 **sop.** Intingere.
15 **comply'd with.** Obbedì.
16 **I beckoned to him.** Gli feci un cenno.
17 **stark naked.** Completamente nudo.

COMPREHENSION

2 WRITE a caption summarising each section of the extract.

Section 1 (lines 1–12): ....
Section 2 (lines 12–21): ....
Section 3 (lines 21–37): ....

3 ANSWER the questions.

1 What was Robinson doing while the young savage was sleeping?
2 What did the young man do when he saw Robinson?
3 How did Robinson react? What name did he call him? Why?
4 What English words did Robinson teach him?
5 What did he give him?
6 Did he let the man live according to his people's traditions and customs? Why or why not?

ANALYSIS

4 ANALYSE the extract by doing the following activities.

1 Write down the details of Friday's description.
Build ....
Face ....
Hair ....
Forehead ....
Eyes ....
Skin ....
Nose ....
Teeth ....
2 Decide if the details stressed by Robinson are mainly positive or negative.
3 Discuss what leads Robinson to define Friday as 'handsome'.
4 List the other native peoples mentioned as terms of comparison in the description of Friday.
5 Focus on Friday's behaviour. How would you define it? What will his relationship with Robinson be like?
6 Say what the theme of the passage is.
7 Explain why Robinson could be regarded as the prototype of the English coloniser.

YOUR TURN

5 EXPLAIN how Robinson's approach to his new condition reflects the ideology of the 18th century.

Jonathan Swift and the satirical novel

Jonathan Swift's life

Although his family was English, Jonathan Swift (1667–1745) was born and educated in Dublin. He left Ireland for England at the time of the Revolution in 1688. He started to work for Sir William Temple, a scholar and Whig statesman who encouraged him to write his first satirical works. Among his best satires were *The Battle of the Books* and *A Tale of a Tub*, both published in 1704. In 1694 Swift returned to Ireland and became an ordained Anglican priest. From 1708 to 1714 he was mainly in London, where he made friends with other leading writers. He produced a great deal of writings for the Tory administration, which found his talent for argument useful. In April 1713 he was made Dean of St Patrick's Cathedral in Dublin, where he remained for the next thirty years. In 1726 he published his masterpiece, *Travels into Several Remote Nations of the World*, known as *Gulliver's Travels*. In 1729 *A Modest Proposal* appeared, in which, with irony and bitterness, Swift suggested that the poverty of the Irish people should be relieved by the sale of their children as food for the rich. Swift's later years were marked by the decay of his mental faculties, due to labyrinthine vertigo, and by deafness. He died in 1745.

A controversial writer

Swift is without doubt one of the most controversial among great English writers. He has been labelled alternatively as a misanthrope, a monster or a lover of mankind. What clearly emerges from his works is that he was seriously concerned with politics and society, and that his attitude was conservative. It is also clear that he did not share the optimism of his age or the pride in England of his contemporaries. According to Swift, reason is an instrument that must be used properly; too intensive a use of reason is an error of judgement and therefore unreasonable. Thus he insisted on the need to take a common-sense view of life. Swift found in irony and satire the means that suited his temperament and his interests. He usually achieved the effect of parody, combining ironic intent with the simplicity of his style and his diction.

1 **DECIDE whether the following statements about Swift's life and works are true or false. Correct the false ones.**

1. Swift's family was of Irish origin but was forced to leave Ireland at the time of the Revolution of 1688. T F
2. He found a job at the house of Sir William Temple, a retired Whig statesman. T F
3. He went back to Ireland, determined to take his orders. T F
4. Swift became the Dean of St Paul's Cathedral. T F
5. He supported the English rule in Ireland. T F
6. He made serious proposals to improve the situation of the poor in Ireland. T F

2 **EXPLAIN in your own words:**

1. how Swift has been labelled;
2. what his attitude to his contemporary society was;
3. how he viewed reason;
4. what his favourite means of expression was.

Gulliver's Travels (1721–25)

Gulliver's Travels was printed in London in 1726, though most of it was certainly written in the years 1721–25. It consists of four books, each dealing with the various adventures of the ship's surgeon, Lemuel Gulliver, and illustrated by maps of the places he visited.

The story

In Book 1 Gulliver sails from Bristol, and after six months, is shipwrecked somewhere in the South Pacific. He is cast upon the shore of 'Lilliput', whose inhabitants, the 'Lilliputians', are only six inches tall. After many amusing experiences, he manages to return to England.

In Book 2 Gulliver sails for India, but finds himself in 'Brobdingnag', a country Swift located in Alaska. Here the natives are giants twelve times as tall as Gulliver. His size causes him many misadventures and he finally becomes the King's pet, kept in a cage. One day Gulliver's cage is lifted up by a huge bird and dropped in the middle of the ocean. He is rescued by a ship and returns to England.

In Book 3 Gulliver's ship is attacked by pirates who set him adrift on a small boat. He finds himself on the flying island of 'Laputa', whose inhabitants are absent-minded astronomers, philosophers and scientists who carry out absurd experiments. The island drops Gulliver on Japan and he manages to go back to England.

In Book 4 Gulliver's last voyage leads him to the island inhabited by the 'Houyhnhnms', rational horses that rule over the 'Yahoos', a vile species of animal resembling human beings. When the horses banish him, he builds a canoe and leaves for England. Once back in civilisation, he joins his wife and children but cannot stand their human smell. He therefore goes to live in the stable, among the animals that remind him of the nobility of the Houyhnhnms.

1 Charles Jervas, *Jonathan Swift*, ca 1718. National Portrait Gallery, London.

3.13 Jonathan Swift and the satirical novel

TEXT BANK 23: *GULLIVER'S TRAVELS*

1 James Gillray, *The King of Brobdingnag and Gulliver* from *Swift's Gulliver: Voyage to Brobdingnag*, after Lt Col Braddyll. Published by Hannah Humphrey, 26th June 1803.

2 The Classic Comics version of *Gulliver's Travels*, 1943.

The sources

Swift looked to the extensive literature of travel, both real and imaginary. The scientific projects described in Book 3, on the other hand, display an acquaintance with the work of the Royal Society. Finally, there are recognisable elements of political allegory through allusions to people and events in the England of Anne I and George I.

Throughout the 17th century the imaginary voyage had been used by French writers as a vehicle for their theories. The traveller usually discovered some happy society where men lived a simple, uncorrupted life, following their natural instincts and the innate light of reason. From these utopias, the European man was seen as the victim of civilisation. In addition, there are more general themes of moral satire: man's concern with unimportant matters and greed (Book 1), his pride (Book 2), the representation of pure reason (Book 4), the absurdities and evils of the various professions (Book 3).

The character of Gulliver

Gulliver is middle-aged, well-educated, sensible and a careful observer. He takes care of his family and runs his business prudently. He has experience of the world and he fully supports the culture which has produced him. During the four voyages he is the reader's contact, and by the end he is completely different from the person he was at the beginning. Gulliver differs from the typical traveller because the people he meets during his voyages are in no sense children of nature. They all live in highly organised societies and are governed by institutions. If in the end he is disgusted by everything at home, it is because Europe is losing its civilisation and falling into a state of corruption, expressed in the novel by the constant opposition between rationality and animality.

Swift's originality lies in his creating a series of experiences, of which the latest is in contrast with those which preceded it. Gulliver always finds himself displaced – first in relation to little men and then to big ones, and finally and suddenly forced into comparison not with men but with animals. Gulliver tells his experiences in the first person, in a prose style which is matter-of-fact and free of literary colouring, and records observed details with the precision of a scientific instrument. Gulliver is not Swift himself; he is an invented character, an object as much as an instrument of satire.

Swift's masterpiece can be read on different levels. It has been widely read as a tale for children because of Gulliver's amusing and absurd adventures, especially in the first two Books. It can also be read as a political allegory of Swift's time, as a parody of voyage literature or as a masterpiece of misanthropy and a reflection on the aberrations of human reason.

3 IN PAIRS take turns to ask and answer the following questions about *Gulliver's Travels*.

1. What lands does Gulliver visit?
2. What people does he meet?
3. Why does Gulliver differ from traditional travellers?
4. What constant opposition is expressed in the novel?
5. What sort of character is Gulliver?
6. What is his function in the text?
7. How can the novel be interpreted?

WARM-UP

1 **IN PAIRS discuss the following questions.**

1. What is satire? What makes it an effective form of criticism?
2. Is there anything that should be free from attack by satire?
3. In *Gulliver's Travels*, Jonathan Swift examines the essence of human nature. Do you think humans are basically rational and good beings, or impulsive and cruel beasts?

3 Ted Danson as Lemuel Gulliver in 'Gulliver's Travels', directed by Charles Sturridge in 1996.

Gulliver and the Lilliputians

Jonathan Swift

Gulliver's Travels (1721–25)
Book 1, Chapter 2

In this passage, Gulliver's ship is caught by a storm and wrecks in a strange region called Lilliput. After the shipwreck Gulliver falls asleep. When he wakes up, he finds that he has been tied up by the Lilliputians, tiny men who are now inspecting his clothes.

2.20

I took up the two officers in my hands, put them first into my coat-pockets, and then into every other pocket about me, except my two fobs[1], and another secret pocket which I had no mind should be searched[2], wherein I had some little necessaries of no consequence[3] to any but myself. In one of my fobs there was a silver watch, and in the other a small quantity of gold in a purse. These gentlemen, having pen, ink and paper about them, made an exact inventory[4] of everything they saw; and when they had done, desired I would set them down[5], that they might deliver it to the Emperor. This inventory I afterwards translated into English, and is word for word as follows.

IMPRIMIS, In the right coat-pocket of the Great Man-Mountain (for so I interpret the words *Quinbus Flestrin*) after the strictest search, we found only one great piece of coarse cloth[6], large enough to be a foot-cloth for your Majesty's chief room of state. In the left pocket, we saw a huge silver chest[7], with a cover of the same metal, which we the searchers were not able to lift[8]. We desired it should be opened, and one of us stepping into[9] it, found himself up to the mid leg in a sort of dust, some part whereof flying up to our faces set us both a sneezing[10] for several times together. In his right waistcoat-pocket[11], we found a prodigious bundle[12] of white thin substances, folded[13] one over another, about the bigness of three men, tied with a strong cable, and marked with black figures; which we humbly conceive[14] to be writings, every letter almost half as large as the palm of our hands. In the left, there was a sort of engine, from the back of which were extended twenty long poles[15], resembling the palisados[16] before your Majesty's Court; wherewith we conjecture the Man-Mountain combs his head, for we did not always trouble him with questions, because we found it a great difficulty to make him understand us. [...]

1 **fobs.** Taschini per l'orologio.
2 **searched.** Ispezionata.
3 **consequence.** Importanza.
4 **inventory.** Inventario.
5 **I would set them down.** Che li mettessi giù.
6 **coarse cloth.** Stoffa grezza, non pregiata.
7 **chest.** Scrigno, forziere.
8 **lift.** Sollevare.
9 **stepping into.** Essendovi entrato.
10 **sneezing.** Starnutire.
11 **waistcoat-pocket.** Taschino del panciotto, gilè.
12 **bundle.** Fascio, fagotto.
13 **folded.** Piegate.
14 **we humbly conceive.** Umilmente riteniamo.
15 **poles.** Pali.
16 **palisados.** Palizzate, steccati.

There were two pockets which we could not enter: these he called his fobs; they were two large slits[17] cut into the top of his middle cover, but squeezed close by the pressure of his belly[18]. Out of the right fob hung a great silver chain, with a wonderful kind of engine at the bottom. We directed him to draw out whatever was at the end of that chain; which appeared to be a globe, half silver, and half of some transparent metal: for on the transparent side we saw certain strange figures circularly drawn, and thought we could touch them, till we found our fingers stopped with that lucid substance. He put this engine to our ears, which made an incessant noise like that of a watermill. And we conjecture it is either some unknown animal, or the god that he worships: but we are more inclined to the latter[19] opinion, because he assured us (if we understood him right, for he expressed himself very imperfectly), that he seldom did anything without consulting it. He called it his oracle, and said it pointed out the time for every action of his life.

17 **slits.** Fessure.
18 **belly.** Ventre.
19 **the latter.** La seconda.

COMPREHENSION

2 READ the passage and make notes about:

1 where the Lilliputians are while making the inventory;
2 the name the Lilliputians give Gulliver;
3 what they find in his right coat-pocket;
4 what they find in his left coat-pocket;
5 what they find in his right waistcoat-pocket;
6 what they find in his left waistcoat-pocket;
7 what hung out of the right fob;
8 why they think he carries the god he worships.

ANALYSIS

3 DECIDE. Who is the narrator? Does he interpret what he sees for the reader or does he just describe what he sees?

4 FOCUS on the description of the inventory. How would you define it?
☐ Vague.
☐ Realistic.
☐ Rambling.
☐ Detailed.
☐ Precise.

5 FILL IN the following table. To the impression of realism conveyed by the description of the objects, Swift adds a twist of absurdity through the distorted perspective of the Lilliputians.

Lilliputians' description	What they actually find

6 UNDERLINE the words referring to the Lilliputians' behaviour. What is the main feature that strikes Gulliver?

7 SAY what name is given to Gulliver. What does he stand for, in contrast to the Lilliputians?

8 TICK as appropriate. What do you think the author's aim is?
☒ To amuse the reader.
☐ To moralise.
☐ To satirise some aspects of his society.

YOUR TURN

9 DISCUSS the following questions.

1 What do you believe Jonathan Swift was trying to say regarding the society of his day?
2 What would Swift think of life in this century?
3 What aspects of modern institutions do you think he would approve or disapprove of?

10 WRITE. Political cartoons have been a common and effective form of satire for centuries. Collect some political cartoons from newspapers and magazines. Write an analysis of the issue being satirised and the cartoonist's attitude on the issue.

1 James Gillray (1757–1815), political satire. The Royal Collection.

3.14 **Cultural Issues**

Tourists, travellers and movers

WARM-UP

1 COMPLETE the diagrams below with what you associate with the verbs 'travel' and 'move'.

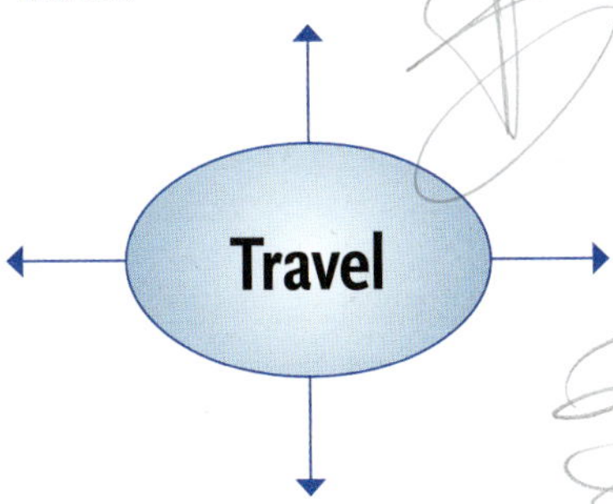

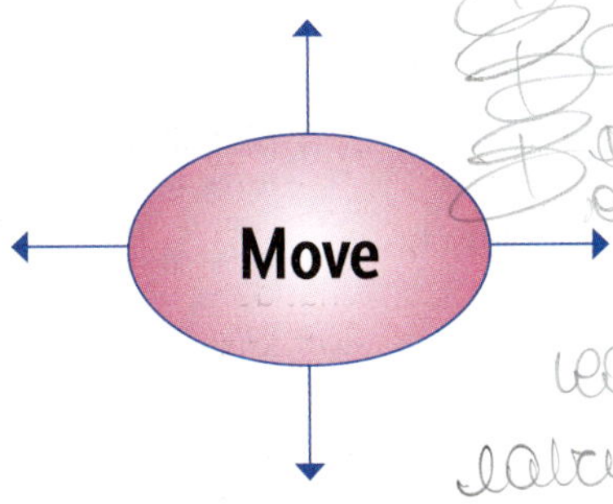

When *Robinson Crusoe* and *Gulliver's Travels* were written, European explorers were travelling across the Atlantic Ocean and around the African continent, looking for new lands to colonise and new sea routes for trade. The geography of the world was expanding. New maps of the world were being made. Many 18th-century novels took place in the unknown regions of the Pacific Ocean, where Europeans had little geographical understanding.

Travelling became a common experience in 18th-century society because of the expansion of trade and the rise of a new, more enterprising middle class. The heroes of novels were presented as restless travellers driven by their desire to improve their social standing and to conquer new worlds.

There are many aspects of a journey: your destination, the means of transport and who you travel with. Travelling is certainly an adventure leading to better self-knowledge, and to the discovery of one's limits and strengths, which allows new personal awareness.

2 LOOK at the pictures and list some reasons why people travel nowadays.

3 DISCUSS. What do you think is the best way of travelling? How would you plan a journey?

4 FILL IN the table. What are the benefits of travelling, in your opinion?

Physical	Psychological

5 EXPLAIN. Is there a difference between a traveller, a tourist and a mover?

About movers

Salman Rushdie

Shame (1983)

Shame is a novel about Pakistan and the people who ruled Pakistan. In one of the interludes Salman Rushdie's (1947–) narrator makes in the midst of the story, he compares emigration to anti-gravitation.

2.21

I, too, know something of this immigrant business. I am an emigrant from one country (India) and a newcomer in two (England, where I live, and Pakistan, to which my family moved against my will). And I have a theory that the resentments we *mohajirs* engender[1] have something to do with our conquest of the force of gravity. We have performed the act of which all men anciently dream, the thing for which they envy the birds; that is to say, we have flown.

I am comparing gravity with belonging. Both phenomena observably exist: my feet stay on the ground, and I have never been angrier than on the day my father told me he had sold my childhood home in Bombay. But neither is understood. We know the force of gravity, but not its origins; and to explain why we become attached to our birthplaces we pretend that we are trees and speak of roots. Look under your feet. You will not find gnarled growths spouting through the soles[2]. Roots, I sometimes think, are a conservative myth, designed to keep us in our places.

The anti-myths of gravity and of belonging bear the same name: flight. *Migration, n., moving, for instance in flight*[3]*, from one place to another.* To fly and to flee[4]: both are ways of seeking freedom ... an odd thing about gravity, incidentally, is that while it remains uncomprehended everybody seems to find it easy to comprehend the notion of its theoretical counter-force: anti-gravity. But anti-belonging is not accepted by modern science ... suppose ICI or Ciba-Geigy or Pfizer or Roche[5] or even, I guess, NASA came up with an anti-gravity pill. The world's airlines would go broke overnight[6], of course. Pill-poppers would come unstuck[7] from the ground and float upwards until they sank into the clouds. It would be necessary to devise special water-proof flying garments[8]. And when the effects of the pill wore off[9] one would simply sink gently down to earth again, but in a different place, because of prevailing windspeeds[10] and planetary rotation. Personalized international travel could be made possible by manufacturing pills of different strengths for different lengths of journey. Some kind of directional booster-engine[11] would have to be constructed, perhaps in back-pack form. Mass production could bring this within the reach of every household. You see the connection between gravity and 'roots': the pill would make migrants of us all. We would float upwards, use our boosters to get ourselves to the right latitude, and let the rotating planet do the rest.

When individuals come unstuck from their native land, they are called migrants. When nations do the same (Bangladesh), the act is called secession. What is the best thing about migrant peoples and seceded nations? I think it is their hopefulness . . . And what's the worst thing? It is the emptiness of one's luggage. I'm speaking of invisible suitcases, not the physical, perhaps cardboard, variety containing a few meaning-drained mementoes[12]: we have come unstuck from more than land. We have floated upwards from history from memory, from Time.

1 Indian-British novelist and essayist Salman Rushdie.

1 **we *mohajirs* engender.** Noi emigrati suscitiamo.
2 **gnarled ... soles.** Escrescenze nodose che spuntano dalle suole.
3 ***flight*.** 'Volo' e anche 'fuga'.
4 **to flee.** Fuggire.
5 **ICI or Ciba-Geigy or Pfizer or Roche.** Nomi di case farmaceutiche.
6 **would go broke overnight.** Fallirebbero da un giorno all'altro.
7 **Pill-poppers would come unstuck.** Gli ingoiatori di pillole si staccherebbero.
8 **garments.** Abiti.
9 **wore off.** Si esaurissero.
10 **prevailing windspeeds.** Venti prevalenti.
11 **directional booster-engine.** Motore di spinta direzionale.
12 **meaning-drained mementoes.** Ricordi svuotati di significato.

COMPREHENSION

1 **READ the extract and find out:**

1. who the speaker is;
2. what theory he has;
3. what he compares gravity to;
4. what he thinks of roots;
5. the two ways of looking for freedom;
6. the supposition he makes;
7. its consequences;
8. what it would be necessary to devise;
9. the connection between gravity and roots;
10. the best and worst things about migrant people.

ANALYSIS

2 **DESCRIBE.** What double condition does the speaker experience?

3 **FIND** the metaphor upon which the whole text is built.

4 **EXPLAIN** the connection between gravity and belonging.

5 **DISCUSS.** What words and concepts does the speaker play with in the third paragraph?

6 **EXPLAIN** in your own words the fantastic situation which reminds one of Swift's world that the narrator describes in the fourth paragraph. What is the effect of this type of description?

7 **DISCUSS.** Do you get the impression the narrator is in favour of or against migration?

FCE Speaking – Part 3

8 **COLLABORATIVE TASK.** Talk to each other about some rules to follow to become a responsible tourist or traveller. You have two minutes to discuss the positive and negative aspects of the following ideas and one minute to make a decision.

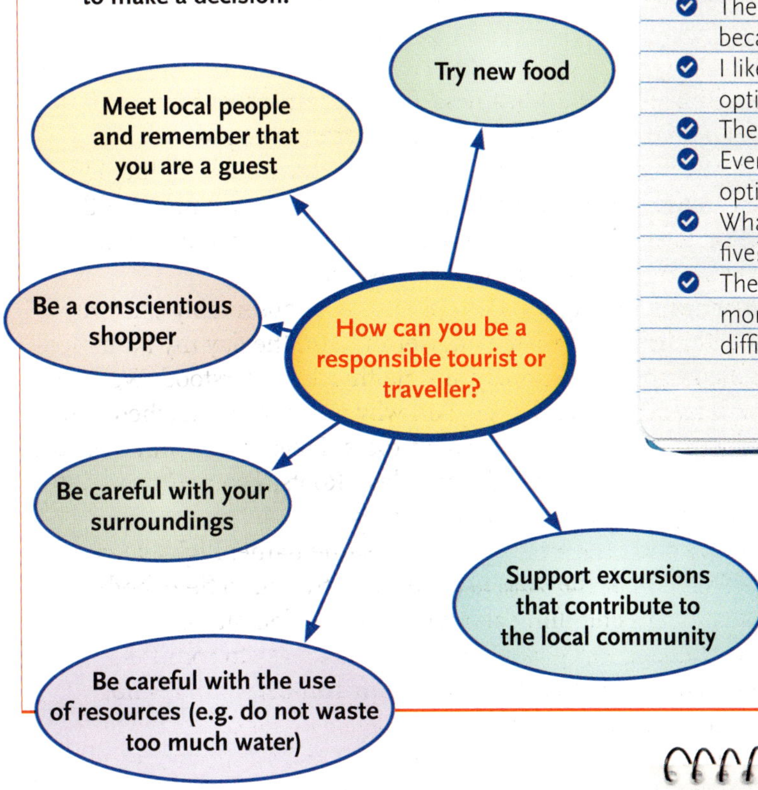

Process language
Speaking – Part 3

Describing and comparing the options

- The first option is interesting because it ...
- I like the idea of the second option because ...
- The third option can be done ...
- Everyone would enjoy the fourth option because ...
- What do you think about option five?
- The idea of option ... is certainly more effective/challenging/difficult than that of option ...

FCE Writing – Part 2

9 **A STORY.** You have decided to enter a competition organised by the local council in which you have to write a story about a journey in extreme circumstances. Your story must begin with the following sentence. Write your story in 140–190 words.

No one could possibly have imagined what would happen before the journey ended.

Process language
Writing – Part 2
A story

Beginning

- It all began ...
- A few months ago ...
- One day ...

Sequence of events

- First ...
- Then ...
- Next ...
- After that ...

Consequences

- In the end ...
- For all these reasons ...
- And that's why ...

3 Overview

Test what you know

1 DECIDE whether the following sentences are true or false. Correct the false ones.

1. Charles I's reign was marked by the cooperation with Parliament. T F
2. The Puritans wanted a true balance of power between the king and Parliament. T F
3. Charles I escaped to France. T F
4. He fought against the aristocracy and the High Clergy. T F
5. Oliver Cromwell expelled the Puritan members of the Parliament. T F
6. Cromwell was sentenced to death by the Parliament in 1649. T F
7. The monarchy was replaced by a republic, known as the Commonwealth. T F
8. During the Glorious Revolution, William of Orange entered London without shedding blood. T F

2 CORRECT these statements about Walpole and Pitt.

1. Robert Walpole was a Tory landowner.
2. During his government taxes were raised.
3. Walpole was not accused of corruption by the opposition.
4. His government ended when George II came to the throne.
5. He went to live at Buckingham Palace.
6. William Pitt was a Tory.
7. England did not expand during Pitt's government.

3 COMPLETE these statements about the age.

1. It was a .... society.
2. Its political institutions were ....
3. Elections were largely controlled by ....
4. Politicians often practised .... either with money or with the promise of jobs.
5. Eighteenth-century society championed ....

Can you do it?

4 HIGHLIGHT the main features of the two factions involved in the Civil War, the Cavaliers and the Roundheads.

5 LIST the key ideas of Puritanism.

6 EXPLAIN in what sense Milton was a 'reforming writer'.

7 SAY why the year 1707 is a milestone in British history.

8 TRACE the origin of the name 'Augustan'.

9 READ this extract from *Robinson Crusoe* by Daniel Defoe. Then focus on what you know about this novel and do the activities below.

1. Who is the narrator? Where is he? What is he doing? How does he feel?
2. Explain the features of the narrator's character. Justify your answer by quoting from the text.
3. Write down which themes of the novel can be found in this short text.

I cast[1] my eyes to the stranded vessel[2], when the breach and froth[3] of the sea being so big, I could hardly[4] see it, it lay so far off, and considered, Lord! How was it possible I could get on shore?

After I had solaced[5] my mind with the comfortable part of my condition, I began to look round me to see what kind of place I was in, and what was next to be done, and I soon found my comforts abate[6], and that in a word I had a dreadful deliverance[7]: for I was wet, had no clothes to shift me[8], nor any thing either to eat or drink to comfort me, neither did I see any prospect before me, but[9] that of perishing with hunger[10], or being devoured by wild beasts; [...]

1 **cast.** Posai.
2 **stranded vessel.** Nave arenata.
3 **the breach and froth.** Il frangersi delle onde e la schiuma.
4 **hardly.** A malapena.
5 **solaced.** Consolato.
6 **abate.** Cessare.
7 **dreadful deliverance.** Terribile condizione.
8 **to shift me.** Per cambiarmi.
9 **but.** Eccetto.
10 **hunger.** Fame.

Oral test

10 IMAGINE your teacher asks you the following questions in an oral test. For each question, prepare a one-minute turn.

1. Who were the Puritans and what did they want?
2. Which of the basic tenets of Puritanism had a great impact in America?
3. What does the character of Satan embody in *Paradise Lost*? Provide examples from the text 'Satan's Speech'.
4. What is the experimental method and who established it?
5. What are the two main parties in the United Kingdom nowadays?
6. What were the targets of William Hogarth's satire?
7. What was the function of coffeehouses?
8. What are the most important features of the 18th-century novel?
9. What novels did Defoe write and what narrative technique did he employ?
10. How does *Robinson Crusoe* present the relationship between the individual and society?
11. How does Gulliver change throughout the novel *Gulliver's Travels*?

Revolutions and the Romantic Spirit

Specification 4 | Homepage

Top News

1776 America declares independence

Top Issue

Who invented marriage?

Most Popular News

1794 William Blake publishes *Songs of Experience*

1798 Wordsworth and Coleridge publish *Lyrical Ballads*

Spotlight

1813 Jane Austen's *Pride and Prejudice* is published

Cinema

See *Pride and Prejudice* on screen

The Arts

Visions of the sublime

Mapping History

Visit the places where technology was invented

EXPLORE THE CULTURE

Culture | Literature | History | Society | The Arts | Philosophy | Two Films About... | Cultural Issues

4.1 | **History**

An age of revolutions

WARM-UP

1 **MATCH** each picture (1–3) with the corresponding revolution.

A The Agrarian Revolution. ....?

B The Industrial Revolution. ....?

C The French Revolution. ....?

2 Mechanical horse-drawn reaper invented by Rev. Patrick Bell around 1828 in Scotland.

1 Eugène Delacroix, *Liberty leading the people*, 1830. Musée du Louvre, Paris, France.

3 Cotton factory in Preston, Lancashire, in 1830. Private Collection.

2 **READ** the Q&A text.

The last decades of the 18th century were marked by great revolutions: the Agrarian and Industrial Revolutions reshaped the social and political background of Britain; the British colonies on the other side of the Atlantic became a new and free nation, and the French Revolution, followed by the Napoleonic conquests, spread ideas of freedom and equality all over Europe. All this was naturally to affect all the cultural and literary aspects of life.

Q What changes were there in Britain at the end of the 18th century?

A Britain changed from a mainly farming country into an industrial one.

Q What caused this change?

A Towards 1750 there was a great increase in population, which meant a greater demand for pots, beer and, above all, clothes. The times really required quicker, more efficient production.

Q What did the 'Industrial Revolution' imply?

A It implied new technologies and inventions, the development of the factory system, new sources of power and of transport.

Q What were the most important inventions?

A The most important inventions regarded machinery for cloth-making, such as James Hargreaves's 'spinning jenny' and Richard Arkwright's 'water frame'. These machines allowed one man or woman to produce what had once required many workers.

4 Sir Richard Arkwright's Masson Mills, Derbyshire, England, photographed by Gillian Darley.

5 James Nasmyth, *A Steam Hammer at Work*, ca 1871. Science Museum, London.

Q What fuelled these machines?

A At first most of the power used to drive machinery came from water, but the need for more energy brought the development of steam power. In 1775 James Watt (1736–1819) patented an engine that was more powerful and wasted less fuel than its predecessors.

6

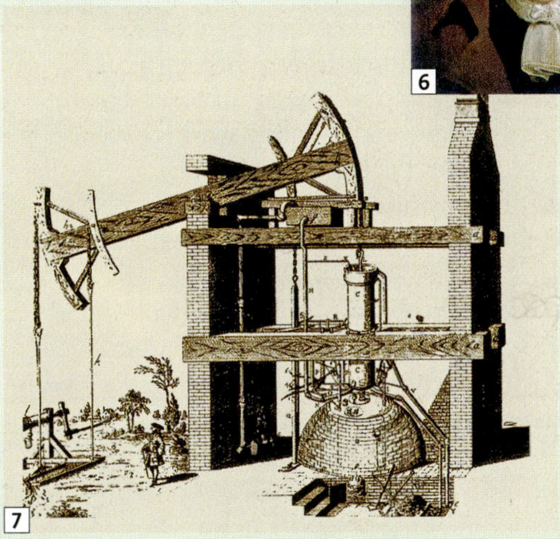

7

Q What was the effect of Watt's invention?

A As a result of the introduction of the steam engine, new factories were built on the coal and iron fields of Lancashire, Yorkshire, central Scotland and South Wales. These new factories allowed Britain to manufacture cloth more cheaply than elsewhere, but also put many people out of work.

Q How did changes in transport affect the Revolution?

A Goods became cheaper as transport was made more efficient. New waterways were built and road conditions were improved. Fast road travel and cheap transport by canal made the economic success of the Industrial Revolution possible.

Q What changes occurred in agriculture?

A There were also great changes in agriculture. The Agrarian Revolution was connected to the Industrial Revolution because they both used technological inventions.

Q What forms did the Agrarian Revolution take?

A It took two principal forms: the widespread enclosure of 'open fields' and common land to make larger, more efficient farms; improvements in the selective breeding of cattle to produce more meat, and in farming techniques such as crop rotation and mechanisation.

3 IN PAIRS cover the answers (**A**s) in the text and take turns asking and answering the questions (**Q**s) using the information that you have read.

4 MATCH the halves to make words and phrases about the Industrial and Agrarian Revolutions.

1 technol	A ments
2 invent	B engine
3 sources of	C ogies
4 steam	D sure
5 manu	E power
6 water	F facture
7 enclo	G ways
8 improve	H ions

5 MAKE sentences about the Industrial and Agrarian Revolutions using the words and phrases from exercise 4.

6 Henry Howard, *Portrait of James Watt*, 1797. National Portrait Gallery, London.

7 Newcomen's steam engine, 18th century.

8 English School, *Countryside around Dixton*, ca 1715. Cheltenham Art Gallery & Museum, Cheltenham, England.

8

INTERACTIVE MAP 4: *HEROES OF INVENTION*

Industrial society

WARM-UP

1 **DISCUSS** in pairs. The poet William Blake used the phrase 'dark satanic mills' to refer to the effects of the early Industrial Revolution on people's lives. What are the possible ways in which industrialisation affected the life of urban people?

2 **READ** the text; then look for these words and write down the noun, adjective or phrase they are associated with. Use the phrases you have made to report orally about industrial society.

1. population
2. coal fields
3. towns
4. women and children
5. working hours
6. living conditions
7. public services
8. air and water
9. houses
10. life expectancy

GLOSSARY
filth sporcizia
life expectancy aspettativa di vita
toil lavoro duro, fatica

During the 18th century, there was a shifting of population from the agricultural and commercial areas of the south to the north and the midlands, where new factories were built near the coal fields which provided them with fuel. Small towns, the so-called 'mushroom towns', were constructed to house the workers.

Women and children were increasingly employed because they could be paid less and were easier to control. For the labourers the city environment meant long working hours and terrible living conditions. Industrial cities lacked elementary public services; the air and water were polluted by smoke and filth; the houses, built in endless rows, were overcrowded. The workers' lives were revolutionised because of the mechanisation and the rational division of labour.

The life expectancy of the poor inhabitants of industrial cities was well below twenty years, due to incessant toil, disease and heavy drinking to bear the fatigue and alienation. At the beginning of the 19th century, however, the level of unemployment rose in consequence of the new technologies and the Napoleonic wars. Spreading discontent meant that the first three decades of the century were a period of political stagnation and repression.

1 Philippe-Jacques de Loutherbourg, *Coalbrookdale by night*, 1801. Science Museum, London.

2 *Boy Chimney Sweep*, illustration by H. W. Petherick (1839-1919) for a children's book published in London ca 1875.

FCE Reading and Use of English – Part 2

3 **OPEN CLOZE.** For questions 1–8, read the text about the exploitation of children during the 18th century and think of the word which best fits each gap. Use only one word in each gap. There is an example at the beginning (0).

HOW CHILD LABOUR CHANGED THE WORLD

Child labour was a crucial ingredient **(0)** WHICH allowed Britain's Industrial Revolution **(1)** .... succeed. By the early 19th century, England had **(2)** .... than a million child workers accounting for 15 per cent of the total labour force.

Early factory owners – located in the countryside so that they **(3)** .... exploit power from rivers – found that local labour **(4)** .... scarce and that those agricultural workers **(5)** .... were available were unsuitable for industrial production. They therefore decided to create a new work force composed of children, tailor-made for their factories.

Factory owners were looking for cheap, malleable and fast-learning work forces – and found them ready-made **(6)** .... the children of the urban workhouses. They weren't paid – simply fed and given dormitory accommodation. The exploitation of children massively increased as newly emerging factories began their operations in the late 18th century.

The use of working-class children to provide much of the labour force for the Industrial Revolution was, **(7)** ...., merely an expansion and extension of an already long-established practice of working-class children employed **(8)** .... farmers or artisans.

(Abridged from 'The Independent', *Revealed: Industrial Revolution was powered by child slaves* by David Keys, 2nd August 2010)

4 **ANSWER** these questions about the text above.

1. What was the percentage of child workers during the Industrial Revolution?
2. Why were they chosen as a work force?
3. Was this a new practice?

ART LAB 4: *WILLIAM BLAKE*
TEXT BANK 24–27: *WILLIAM BLAKE*

William Blake and the victims of industrialisation

William Blake's life

William Blake was born in London in 1757 and died there in 1827. His origins were humble and he remained poor all his life. Trained as an engraver, he practised this craft until he died. He was deeply aware of the great political and social issues of his age. A political freethinker, he supported the French Revolution and remained a radical throughout his life. He witnessed the evil effects of industrial development on man's soul, and it was probably this which convinced him that the artist should have a new role: he should become the guardian of the spirit and imagination. The most important literary influence in his life was the Bible because it presented a complete vision of the world and its history.

He had many acquaintances but very few intimate friends. One was his wife, Catherine Boucher, the illiterate daughter of a market gardener, who shared his interest in the spiritual and assisted him in the production of his works. The other was his younger brother Robert, who died at the age of twenty. Blake began to have visions of his dead brother and claimed that he showed him the unique printing method he employed for his original work.

Blake the artist

When he was ten years old, his father sent him to a drawing school where, working from statues, he became acquainted with the works of Raphael and Michelangelo. The influence of Michelangelo is clear in Blake's works, especially in the exaggerated muscular forms in his best-known illustrations. After completing his apprenticeship, he studied at the Royal Academy of Art. Painters were expected to conform to standards of realistic representation, to respect perspective and proportions and to produce works which fell into categories or genres. Blake broke with these conventions and created a new kind of art which emphasised the power of the imagination. He created his own method for making prints that combined picture and poetic text called 'illuminated printing'. For him painting was not simply the illustration of poetry – it was its counterpart.

1 AFTER READING 'Blake the artist', describe the pictures on this page and the next page and use them to provide evidence of the most important features of Blake's work.

Blake the poet

His experiences as a craftsman, visionary and radical contributed to the development of his poetry, which is regarded as early Romantic because he rejected the neoclassical literary style and themes. He stressed the importance of imagination over reason and believed that ideal forms should be created not from observations of nature but from inner visions.

The collections of short lyrical verses *Songs of Innocence* (1789) and *Songs of Experience* (1794) are the most accessible of Blake's works. The first is in the pastoral mode; the narrator is a shepherd who receives inspiration from a child in a cloud to pipe his songs celebrating the divine in all creation. The imagery of the poems is full of lambs, flowers and children playing on the village green; it deals with childhood as the symbol of innocence, a state of the soul connected with happiness, freedom and imagination. The language is simple and musical.

While *Songs of Innocence* was produced before the outbreak of the French Revolution, when Blake's enthusiasm for liberal ideas was high, *Songs of Experience* appeared when the period of the Terror (1793–94) was at its height in France. Blake did not reject the songs of the innocent shepherd, but he created its contrary in the form of the bard who questions the themes of the previous collection. A more pessimistic view of life emerges in these 'Songs', which are intended to be read together with *Songs of Innocence*, so that the paired poems comment on each other, sometimes managing to convey an ironical view of the situation presented. 'Experience', identified with adulthood, coexists with and completes 'Innocence', thus providing another point of view on reality.

Blake the prophet

Blake was also very active in publishing prophetic books, in which he created a complex personal mythology and invented his own symbolic characters to reflect his social interests and denounce authority. The most famous was *The Marriage of Heaven and Hell* (1790), a prose work, a mixture of aphorisms, anecdotes and proverbs, in which Hell and Satan represent liberty and energy, while Heaven is the place of lawgiving. Desire and energy gain supremacy over restraint and reason. All the proverbs directly attack the repression of human energies by conventions and emphasise the need to experience joy and freedom of thought and expression.

1 John Linnell, *William Blake wearing a hat*, ca 1825.

2 William Blake, frontispiece for *Vision of the Daughters of Albion*, ca 1795. Tate Britain, London.

4.3 William Blake and the victims of industrialisation

2 AFTER READING 'Blake the poet' and 'Blake the prophet' on page 99, complete the following statements.

1 Blake thought that the poet drew inspiration from .... to create ideal forms.
2 The tone of *Songs of Innocence* is ....
3 Its narrator is a .... inspired by a ....
4 Its language is ....
5 *Songs of Experience* was written when ....
6 Its narrator is a ....
7 Its view of life is ....
8 *The Marriage of Heaven and Hell* is a ....
9 Blake's proverbs attack ....

1

2

'Complementary opposites'

Blake's Christianity was not liturgical or moralistic. He believed in the reality of a spiritual world but regarded Christianity, and the Church especially, as responsible for the fragmentation of consciousness and the dualism characterising man's life. To this dualistic view he substituted a vision made up not of 'contraries', but of 'complementary opposites': good and evil, male and female, reason and imagination, cruelty and kindness. He stated: 'Without Contraries there is no Progression. Attraction and Repulsion, Reason and Energy, Love and Hate are necessary to Human Existence.' The possibility of progress, of achieving the knowledge of what we are, lies in the tension between opposite states of mind, not in their resolution by one gaining supremacy over the other.

Imagination and the poet

Blake considered imagination, and not sense perceptions, as the means through which man could know the world. Imagination, or 'the Divine Vision', means 'to see more, beyond material reality, into the life of things'. God, the child and the poet share this power of vision, which is also the power of creating things. The poet therefore becomes a sort of prophet who can see more deeply into reality and who also tries to warn man of the evils of society.

Blake's interest in social problems

Blake was very much concerned with the political and social problems of his time: he supported the abolition of slavery and shared other intellectuals' enthusiasm for the egalitarian principles which came to the fore during the French Revolution. He believed in revolution as purifying violence, necessary for the redemption of man. Later, disillusioned, he focused his attention on the evil consequences of the Industrial Revolution – the injustices caused by a materialistic attitude and the commercial exploitation of human beings. In his poems he sympathised with the victims of industrial society, such as children and prostitutes, as well as with the victims of oppression by institutions, such as orphans and soldiers.

Style

Blake's poems present a very simple structure and a highly individual use of symbols. He employed a central group of symbols to form a context for all the minor symbols in the Songs; these are: the child, the father and Christ, representing the states of innocence, experience and a higher innocence. His verse is linear and rhythmical; it shows a close relationship between sound and meaning and is characterised by the frequent use of repetition.

3 REVISE your knowledge about Blake's thought and works by writing notes under the following headings.

1 What he meant by 'complementary opposites';
2 His concept of imagination and the poet;
3 His concern about society;
4 The main features of his style.

3

1 William Blake, *Songs of Innocence: The Lamb*, 1789. The British Museum, London.

2 William Blake, frontispiece for *The Marriage of Heaven and Hell*, ca 1790–93.

3 William Blake, *The Circle of the Lustful: Paolo and Francesca*, ca 1824–27.

WARM-UP

1 LOOK at the pictures and point out the features of the industrial town. Which ones do you find in the poem?

4 Gustave Doré and Blanchard Jerrold, *Over London by Rail*, *from London: A Pilgrimage*, published in 1872.

COMPREHENSION

2 READ the poem and say in your own words:

1 who 'I' is;
2 what the setting in time and place is;
3 through what senses the speaker perceives the scene;
4 what the living conditions of the people he sees are.

ANALYSIS

3 WORK OUT the rhyme scheme of the poem and say if it is regular or not.

4 PROVIDE examples of Blake's considerable use of repetition in the poem. He repeats sounds, words and concepts. Say what effect they create, choosing from the following suggestions:

- ☐ They underline the condition of suffering and disease surrounding the poet.
- ☐ They create a sense of obsession and anxiety.
- ☐ They increase the musicality.

5 DISCUSS. What symbolic meaning does the word 'chartered' acquire if applied to the streets and the river Thames?

6 LINE 8 contains a very powerful metaphor.

1 Analyse its terms.
2 With whom or what does Blake identify the 'manacles' in the poem?
3 What does this metaphor reveal about Blake's attitude to the society of his time?

7 DECIDE. In the third and fourth stanzas Blake points out some victims of the industrialised town. Who are they?

London

William Blake

Songs of Experience (1794)

One of his greatest, this poem conveys Blake's view of the city – of the disease and suffering brought about by industrialisation.

3.2

I wander thro'[1] each charter'd[2] street
Near where the charter'd Thames does flow,
And mark[3] in every face I meet
Marks of weakness, marks of woe[4].

In every cry of every Man,
In every Infant's cry of fear,
In every voice, in every ban[5],
The mind-forg'd manacles[6] I hear.

How the Chimney-sweeper's cry
Every black'ning Church appalls[7],
And the hapless Soldier's sigh[8]
Runs in blood down Palace walls.

But most thro' midnight streets I hear
How the youthful Harlot's curse[9]
Blasts[10] the new born Infant's tear,
And blights with plagues[11] the Marriage hearse[12].

1 **thro'.** Lungo.
2 **charter'd.** Monopolizzata.
3 **mark.** Vedo, colgo.
4 **woe.** Dolore.
5 **ban.** Divieto.
6 **mind-forg'd manacles.** Manette forgiate dalla mente.
7 **appalls.** Sgomenta, fa inorridire.
8 **hapless Soldier's sigh.** Il sospiro del soldato infelice.
9 **youthful Harlot's curse.** La maledizione della giovane prostituta.
10 **Blasts.** Maledice.
11 **blights with plagues.** Infetta di pestilenze (possibile accenno alla cecità causata dalla sifilide).
12 **hearse.** Carro funebre.

8 DEFINE the tone of the poem. Choose from the following:

sad • indignant • sorrowful • sympathetic • emotional • angry • accusing • prophetic • nostalgic • bitter

YOUR TURN

9 DISCUSS. What were your reactions to the poem? Think about the metaphor you analysed. What kind of constraints have you experienced in life so far? What 'manacles' have you felt imprisoned by?

4.4 **History**

The American War of Independence

WARM-UP

1 **MATCH** pictures 1–3 with the corresponding heading (A–C).

A Loyalists and Patriots. ....
B The Boston Tea Party. ....
C The creation of the American flag. ....

2 **DISCUSS.** What do you think these pictures tell us about the changing political ideas of this time?

3 **READ** the Q&A text below.

1

1 The Sons of Liberty, dressed as Indians, throw cases of tea into Boston Harbor.

2 John Singleton Copley, *The Death of Major Peirson*, 1783. Tate Gallery, London.

3 John Ward Dunsmore, *Betsy Ross showing the first American flag to George Washington*, 1920.

In 1760 the American colonies were rich and populated by educated religious and political refugees and economic migrants.

Q What was the situation in Britain when George III came to the throne?

A When George III (1738–1820) came to the throne in 1760, Britain was in control of the seas and was enjoying a period of domestic stability and economic expansion.

Q What caused the conflict between the American colonies and Britain?

A The British government wanted the American colonies to help pay for their defence and imposed new taxes. These taxes were the catalyst for the rebellion. One such tax was on the importation of tea. At the Boston Tea Party in 1773, rebels, dressed as Native Americans, threw the hated tea from Britain into the Boston Harbor. The rebels maintained that the taxes were unjust, as the colonies had no political power; they said, 'No taxation without representation.'

Q Did any people in England support the American cause?

A In England, Edmund Burke recognised the justice of the American cause and Thomas Paine's *Common Sense* (1776) stimulated the desire for a republic.

Q What was the difference between the 'Patriots' and 'Loyalists'?

A The Americans were divided into 'Patriots' and 'Loyalists' when the War of Independence, or Revolutionary War, began in 1775. While the Patriots had no army, they knew the land. The British Loyalists had an army, but it was too small to both attack and defend what it had won, and was two months' distance from supplies and orders. A deciding factor was the support of the French for the Patriots; the French fleet prevented the British navy from aiding the Loyalists.

2

Q What happened on 4th July 1776?

A On 4th July 1776 in Philadelphia, the Continental Congress signed the 'Declaration of Independence', written by Thomas Jefferson (1743–1826), a lawyer from Virginia. It was more than a statement that the colonies were a new nation, since it claimed that all men had a natural right to 'life, liberty, and the pursuit of happiness'. It also stated that governments can only claim the right to rule if they have the approval of those they govern – 'the consent of the governed'.

Milestones

1776, the American Declaration of Independence
The signing of the American Declaration of Independence on 4th July 1776 was a key moment in the history not only of North America but also of Britain and the English-speaking world. The rejection of British authority was symbolic as well as constitutional. On 9th July 1776, after the colonial assembly of New York gave its assent to the Declaration of Independence, the inhabitants of New York City pulled down an equestrian statue of King George III erected in 1770, and the royal arms were taken down all over the town and usually treated with contempt. The king's name was removed from government and legal documents and royal portraits were reversed or destroyed.

Q What did the Treaty of Versailles recognise?

A With the Treaty of Versailles in 1783, Britain recognised the independence of its former colonies. The new republic of the United States of America adopted a federal constitution in 1787, and George Washington (1732–99) became the first president in 1789.

4 IN PAIRS cover the answers (As) in the text and take turns asking and answering the questions (Qs) using the information that you have read.

Insights

America's birthday
Across America people celebrate the July 4th holiday with parades and spectacular fireworks shows. Cities like New York City, Boston and Chicago organise large-scale fireworks displays which are often broadcast on television. Families and groups of friends gather and organise elaborate barbecues and picnics with hamburgers, hot dogs, potato salads and chocolate cakes to celebrate Independence Day.

Internet Lab

1 SURF the web site www.whitehouse.gov to learn how America's federal, state and local governments work to enact the will of the people, and how the president and his administration collaborate with the legislative and judicial branches to govern the United States.

2 CARRY OUT a research project on the following:
1 the legislative branch;
2 the executive branch;
3 the judicial branch;
4 elections and voting;
5 state and local government.

4 John Trumbull, *Declaration of Independence*, 1819. The United States Capitol, Washington DC, US.

5 A Fourth of July parade.

The Sublime: a new sensibility

WARM-UP

1 **IN PAIRS** write down in the chart what you associate with the term 'sublime'.

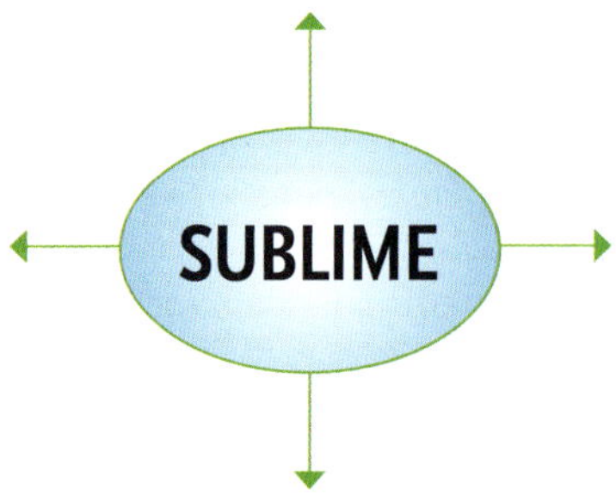

1 John Constable, *Hadleigh Castle*, 1829. Tate Gallery, London.

2 Henry Fuseli, *The Artist Moved by the Grandeur of Antique Fragments*, 1778–79. Kunsthaus Zürich, Zurich, Switzerland.

FCE Reading and Use of English – Part 7

2 **MULTIPLE MATCHING. You are going to read an article in which four people describe the sublime. For questions 1–10, choose from the people (A–D). The people may be chosen more than once.**

Which person

deals with the importance of the perceiver?	1	2
links the sublime with an idea of terror?	3	4
refers to classical views of the sublime?	5	6
emphasises the importance of nature in generating the sublime?		7
introduces the distinction between the beautiful and the sublime?	8	9
deals with the primary and secondary feelings produced by the sublime?		10

1

A. A journalist

Scholars have debated the term 'sublime' in the field of aesthetics for centuries. But what is the sublime? Is it a thing, a feeling, an event or a state of mind? The term, of Latin origin, refers to a linguistic, literary or artistic form which expresses noble or elevated feelings and behaviour. The concept of sublime was analysed by an unknown rhetorician of the 1st century AD, who identified the sublime with the beautiful and found its origin not in the perfection of the style but in the passion of inspiration echoing in the soul.

In his journal 'The Spectator', Joseph Addison made the distinction between the beautiful and the sublime, which became a main theme of 18th-century aesthetics. The most interesting development of this idea can be found in Edmund Burke's *A Philosophical Enquiry into the Origin of Our Ideas of the Sublime and Beautiful* (1757), where he regarded the beautiful and the sublime as opposed.

2

B. A gallery owner

The writings of Burke contained two themes which are particularly important to conceptions of the sublime. The first was that the sublime should be discussed in terms of its effects upon the perceiver. For the first time the person who enjoys sublimity became more important than the qualities of the pleasing object. Classical, Renaissance and 18th-century aestheticians defined the beautiful in terms of the qualities of the beautiful object. Thus, the proportions of the *Venus de Milo* and the proper mixture of unity and variety which it incorporates, were, for these critics, the sources of its beauty.

ART LAB 5: *HENRY FUSELI*
ART LAB 6: *J.M.W. TURNER*
ART LAB 7: *JOHN CONSTABLE*

C. A teacher

In his *Philosophical Enquiry* Burke generates a conception of the sublime in connection with our encounter with nature as well as art. The sublime now becomes what causes astonishment, 'that state of the soul in which all its motions are suspended, with some degree of horror'. In lesser degrees, the sublime produces admiration, reverence and respect. In greater degrees, the sublime is that which produces terror. So Burke's question then becomes: what terrifies us? Subjectively, it is the fear of pain. Objectively, we are terrified by the vastness of the ocean; by obscurity, which hides the full extent of a danger from us; by what is powerful; and by what is infinite. In relation to art, Burke lists as sources of sublimity: magnitude, for example of a building; unfinishedness, as in preparatory sketches; difficulty, as when we imagine the immense force necessary to build Stonehenge; magnificence, especially when to some extent in a state of confusion; and colour – the sublime excludes white, green, yellow, blue, pale red, violet and requires 'sad and fuscous colours like black, or brown, or deep purple'.

3 Henry Fuseli, *Thor battering the Midgard Serpent*, 1790. The Royal Academy, London.

4 J.M.W. Turner, *The Slave Ship or Slavers Throwing overboard the Dead and Dying – Typhoon coming on*, ca 1840. Museum of Fine Arts, Boston, US.

D. A lecturer

The sublime does neither arise from the pleasure produced by beautiful forms nor from the detached contemplation of the object, but has its roots in the feelings of fear and horror created by what is infinite and terrible. For example, void, obscurity, loneliness and silence are sublime; the tall oaks are sublime, while flowerbeds are beautiful, the night is sublime, whereas the day is beautiful. This 'horrible beauty', identified by Burke, affected the literature of the end of the 18th century. The taste for obscurity, terror and introspection became the distinguishing feature of the Gothic novel.

Burke's theory was further developed by the German philosopher Immanuel Kant (1724–1804) in his *Critique of Judgement* (1790). In this work, he stated that the sublime does not derive, like the beautiful, from the free interplay between sensibility and intellect, but from the free conflict between sensibility and reason. Hence the mixture of horror and pleasure created either by what is great and immeasurable in time and space, or by those natural sceneries and phenomena which underline the frailty of man. However, Kant's originality lies in his identification of the origin of the sublime with the subject who perceives it, rather than with the object contemplated.

3 READ the text again and do the following activities.

1 Write down the cause and effects of the sublime as explained by Burke.

Cause	Effects
	Major:
	Minor:

2 Burke says that the sublime results in the passion of 'astonishment'. What is the observer then not able to do?

3 Give examples of what stimulates a sublime reaction.

4 Explain the sources that most arouse the sublime in art.

5 Complete the following statement: *Burke's conclusion is that the great and the sublime are more effective than the beautiful in art because* ....

4.6 **Literature**

The Gothic novel

WARM-UP

1 **DISCUSS. What do you generally associate with the adjective 'Gothic'?**

1 *A drawing depicting the Gothic staircase at Strawberry Hill*, near London. Strawberry Hill is the fancifully Gothic castle purchased by the writer Horace Walpole in 1748.

The concept of the sublime influenced the so-called Gothic novels which gained popularity at the end of the 18th century. The interest in such novels was extraordinary and common to all social classes also thanks to circulating libraries. The Gothic influence, however, did not cease after this period. Today's ghost and horror novels and films, which are so keenly read and watched all over the world, come from the 18th-century Gothic novel.

The adjective 'Gothic' was first applied to architecture long before it connoted literature. The writer Horace Walpole (1717–97) was the first to establish a link between the two; his obsession with his beloved miniature castle at Strawberry Hill was the inspiration for his novel *The Castle of Otranto* (1764), and the book's subtitle, 'A Gothic Story', marks the first time that the term was used in a literary context.

Gothic novels aimed to arouse fear in the reader – a threat of the realisation of all the potentialities of one's mind beyond reason. The nature of this fear seemed to reflect this specific historical moment, characterised by increasing disillusionment with Enlightenment rationality and by the bloody Revolutions in America and France.

The first novel of this kind, *The Castle of Otranto*, was followed by *The Mysteries of Udolpho* (1794) by Ann Radcliffe (1764–1823), *The Monk* (1796) by Matthew Lewis (1775–1818) and *Frankenstein* (1818) by Mary Shelley (1797–1851).

2 Jonathan Barry, *Udolpho Castle*, 1993. Private Collection.

Literary language
The Gothic novel

The most common features of Gothic novels are:

- the great importance given to terror and horror as two different ingredients: the former characterised by obscurity and uncertainty, and the latter by evil and atrocity;
- the night as the most important setting, because darkness is a powerful element that helps to create an atmosphere of gloom, oppression and mystery;
- ancient settings, like isolated castles, mysterious abbeys and convents;
- complex plots, often complicated by embedded narratives;
- the use of supernatural beings, like vampires, monsters, ghosts and witches;
- heroines who are dominated by exaggerated passions and by fear of imprisonment, rape and personal violation;
- sensitive, honourable heroes who save heroines from villains that are terrifying male characters, victims of their negative impulses.

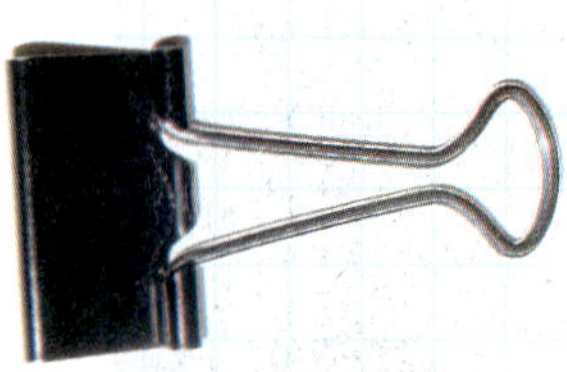

2 **READ the text about the Gothic novel and do the following activities.**

1 Say when Gothic novels became popular.
2 Highlight the connotation of the word 'Gothic'.
3 Complete the chart below:

The ingredients of the Gothic novel

Plot	Setting in place / setting in time	Characters	Hero / heroine

Mary Shelley and a new interest in science

Mary Shelley's life

Mary Shelley was born in 1797, the daughter of the pioneer feminist Mary Wollstonecraft (1759–97) and the radical thinker William Godwin (1756–1836). Both her parents had been heavily influenced by the ideas of the French Revolution, and were part of a small radical group which included other important men of letters of the time such as William Blake. Ten days after Mary's birth, her mother died, and two years later her father married Jane Clairmont. If Mary's emotional life was troubled, intellectual stimulus was not wanting; in fact, Godwin's house was visited by some of the most famous writers of the day, like the Romantic poets Samuel Coleridge and Percy Bysshe Shelley. In July 1814, Mary and Shelley fled to France, and later the poet decided to rent a country house on the banks of Lake Geneva near Villa Diodati. It was there that the writing of *Frankenstein, or the Modern Prometheus* took place. The initial inspiration of this novel burst into Mary's consciousness as a waking dream or nightmare, as a result of the intellectual stimulation of Shelley and the Romantic poet Byron, together with her own deep anxieties and uncertainties. In 1816 Mary Shelley began to write *Frankenstein*, which was published anonymously in 1818. In 1822 the Shelleys moved to Lerici, where Percy set sail in a storm and was found drowned ten days later. Mary returned to England in 1823, where she died in 1851.

1 READ Mary Shelley's biography and provide evidence to justify these statements.

1 She was heavily influenced by her parents.
2 She eloped with Percy Shelley.
3 The origin of her novel *Frankenstein* was a nightmare.

1 Richard Rothwell, *Portrait of Mary Shelley* (detail), 1840. The National Portrait Gallery, London.

2 Poster for the 1931 film 'Frankenstein', directed by James Whale.

3 Boris Karloff as Frankenstein's monster in James Whale's 1931 film.

Frankenstein (1818)

The influence of science

Mary Shelley dedicated *Frankenstein* to Godwin and used many of the ideas held by her parents, including social justice and education. She clearly sympathises with the monster, but she is afraid of the consequences of his actions. In this, there is tension between the fear of revolution and interest in revolutionary ideas – two attitudes which were characteristic of English intellectuals in the years between 1789 and 1832.

Even the influence of Percy Bysshe Shelley was important. He and Mary were interested in science, and particularly chemistry, so that by the time she wrote *Frankenstein*, she was aware of the latest scientific theories and experiments of the day in the fields of chemistry, evolutionism and electricity. These sources provided contrasting scientific attitudes important to Mary Shelley's conception of science in *Frankenstein*, whose protagonist is the first embodiment of the theme of science and its responsibility to mankind. In fact, Frankenstein tries to create a human being through the use of electricity and chemistry without respecting the rules of nature as far as creation and life are concerned.

The story

Doctor Victor Frankenstein, a Swiss scientist, manages to create a human being by joining parts selected from corpses. Despite careful preparation, the result of the experiment is ugly and revolting; the monster becomes a murderer, and in the end he destroys his creator. The story is not told chronologically and is introduced to us by a series of letters written by Walton, a young explorer on a voyage of expedition to the North Pole, to his sister, Margaret Saville.

4.7 Mary Shelley and a new interest in science

Literary influences

The monster can be considered Rousseau's natural man, that is, a man in a primitive state, not influenced by civilisation; he, however, rapidly discovers the limitations both of the state of nature and of civilisation.

The ghost stories read at Villa Diodati provided an immediate stimulus, even if *Frankenstein* differs from the Gothic tradition, since it is not set in a dark castle and does not deal with supernatural events.

The myth of Prometheus is also important. Prometheus in Greek mythology was a giant who stole fire from the gods in order to give it to man. In so doing, he challenged the divine authority and freed men from the gods' power. He is a clear example of an overreacher, just like Dr Frankenstein.

Narrative structure

This novel is told by different narrators:

1 At first, Walton informs his sister, whose initials are the same as those of Mary Shelley (MS), that is, Margaret Saville.

2 Then, Frankenstein informs Walton, who informs his sister.

3 Finally, the monster informs Frankenstein, who informs Walton, who informs his sister.

Thus the whole novel has Walton's sister as the receiver, but presents three different points of view. The form of the novel is epistolary – perhaps the writer wanted to disguise her own voice as a woman by hiding behind three male narrators.

Themes

The main themes of the novel are:

- the quest for forbidden knowledge, which is present throughout;
- the overreacher, in the characters of Walton and Dr Frankenstein;
- the double – the three most important characters of the novel are all linked to the theme of the double (Walton is a double of Frankenstein, since he manifests the same ambition – the desire to overcome human limits in his travelling towards the unknown – and the same wish for loneliness and pride in being different. Frankenstein and his creature are complementary. They both suffer from a sense of alienation and isolation; both begin with a desire to be good, but become obsessed with hate and revenge.);
- the penetration of nature's secrets, which is related to the theme of the overreacher;
- the usurpation of the female role, since the creation of human beings becomes possible without the participation of women;
- social prejudices, through the figure of the monster as an outcast.

1 Robert De Niro in 'Mary Shelley's Frankenstein', directed by Kenneth Branagh in 1994.

2 Robert De Niro during a make-up session for the film 'Mary Shelley's Frankenstein'.

2 IN PAIRS take turns asking and answering the following questions about *Frankenstein*.

1 How did science influence the writer?
2 What literary and philosophical influences can be recognised in this novel?
3 Who are the main characters?
4 What narrative technique is employed?
5 What themes are developed?

WARM-UP

1 **FILL IN** the spider chart below with the physical features and other associations linked to the word 'monster'.

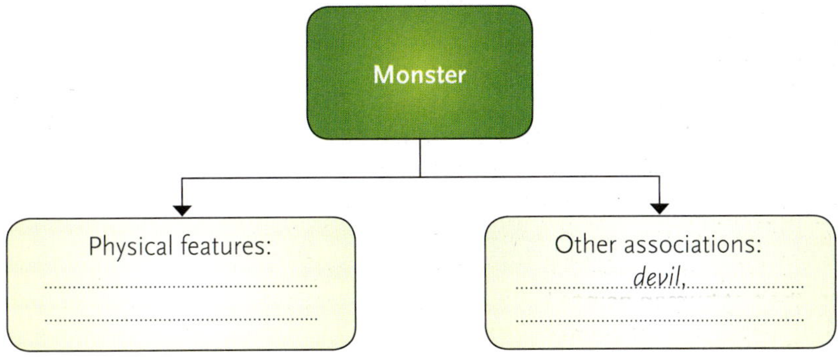

3 Black and white poster for James Whale's 1931 film 'Frankenstein'.

The creation of the monster

Mary Shelley

Frankenstein, or the Modern Prometheus (1818)

Chapter 5

Dr Frankenstein is in the German town of Ingolstadt. He is doing some research on human physiology in the local university laboratory. The following extract describes the creation of the new 'human being'.

3.3

It was on a dreary[1] night of November that I beheld the accomplishment[2] of my toils. With an anxiety that almost amounted to agony, I collected the instruments of life around me, that I might infuse a spark[3] of being into the lifeless thing that lay at my feet. It was already one in the morning; the rain pattered dismally[4] against the panes, and my candle was nearly burnt out, when, by the glimmer of the half-extinguished light, I saw the dull[5] yellow eye of the creature open; it breathed hard, and a convulsive motion agitated its limbs.

How can I describe my emotions at this catastrophe, or how delineate the wretch[6] whom with such infinite pains and care I had endeavoured to form? His limbs were in proportion, and I had selected his features as beautiful. Beautiful! Great God! His yellow skin scarcely covered the work of muscles and arteries beneath; his hair was of a lustrous[7] black, and flowing; his teeth of a pearly whiteness; but these luxuriances[8] only formed a more horrid contrast with his watery eyes, that seemed almost of the same colour as the dun-white sockets[9] in which they were set, his shrivelled complexion[10] and straight black lips.

The different accidents of life are not so changeable as the feelings of human nature. I had worked hard for nearly two years, for the sole purpose of infusing life into an inanimate body. For this I had deprived myself of rest and health. I had desired it with an ardour that far exceeded moderation; but now that I had finished, the beauty of the dream vanished, and breathless horror and disgust filled my heart. Unable to endure the aspect of the being I had created, I rushed out of the room and continued a

1 **dreary.** Deprimente.
2 **accomplishment.** Coronamento.
3 **spark.** Scintilla.
4 **dismally.** Lugubramente.
5 **dull.** Smorto, inespressivo.
6 **wretch.** Infelice, miserabile.
7 **lustrous.** Lucente.
8 **luxuriances.** *Lett.*: ornamenti; *qui*: particolari.
9 **dun-white sockets.** Orbite grigiastre.
10 **shrivelled complexion.** Pelle grinzosa.

long time traversing my bedchamber, unable to compose my mind to sleep. At length lassitude[11] succeeded to the tumult I had before endured, and I threw myself on the bed in my clothes, endeavouring to seek a few moments of forgetfulness. But it was in vain; I slept, indeed, but I was disturbed by the wildest dreams. I thought I saw Elizabeth, in the bloom of health, walking in the streets of Ingolstadt. Delighted and surprised, I embraced her, but as I imprinted the first kiss on her lips, they became livid with the hue of death; her features appeared to change, and I thought that I held the corpse of my dead mother in my arms; a shroud[12] enveloped her form, and I saw the grave-worms[13] crawling in the folds of the flannel. I started from my sleep with horror; a cold dew[14] covered my forehead, my teeth chattered, and every limb became convulsed; when, by the dim and yellow light of the moon, as it forced its way through the window shutters, I beheld the wretch – the miserable monster whom I had created. He held up the curtain of the bed; and his eyes, if eyes they may be called, were fixed on me. His jaws opened, and he muttered some inarticulate sounds, while a grin wrinkled his cheeks. He might have spoken, but I did not hear; one hand was stretched out, seemingly to detain[15] me, but I escaped and rushed downstairs.

11 **lassitude.** Stanchezza.
12 **shroud.** Sudario.
13 **grave-worms.** I vermi della tomba.
14 **dew.** Sudore.
15 **to detain.** Per trattenere.

1 Robert De Niro and Kenneth Branagh in 'Mary Shelley's Frankenstein', 1994.

COMPREHENSION

2 READ the first two paragraphs and fill in the table below.

When	Who	Actions

3 ANSWER the following questions.

1. What feelings replace the 'beauty' of Frankenstein's dream in the third paragraph?
2. What nightmare disturbs Frankenstein during his sleep?
3. Who wakes him up?
4. Why does Frankenstein run away?

ANALYSIS

4 SAY who the narrator is. Whose point of view do you share?

5 LIST the details of the description which refer to the creature.

Eyes		Skin	
Hair		Teeth	
Eye Sockets		Lips	
Breath		Movements	

What do these expressions connote? What feelings does this detailed description of the monster reinforce?

6 FOCUS on Frankenstein. Frankenstein's mood changes before and after the creation. Complete the table below.

	Words related to Frankenstein's feelings	Frankenstein's mood
Before the creation		
After the creation		

7 DISCUSS. What is the monster a symbol of?

YOUR TURN

8 DISCUSS with the rest of the class. What do you think of organ transplants? Is a human body made up of transplanted organs possible, in your opinion?

4.8 Culture

Is it Romantic?

WARM-UP

1 **DISCUSS** in pairs. What is Romanticism? Say what ideas the word conveys and write them in the chart below.

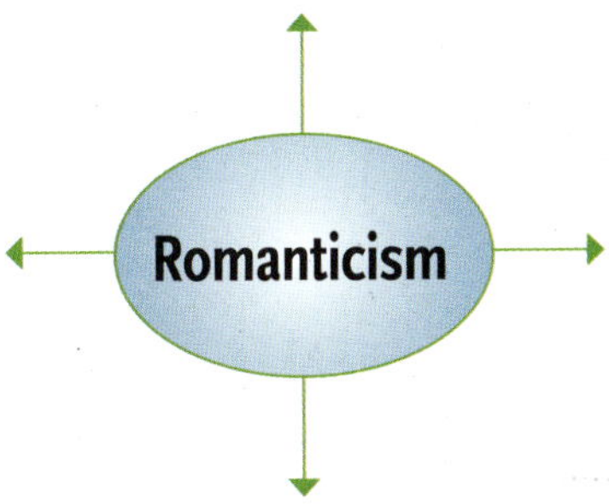

The word 'Romantic' was adopted in the last decades of the 18th century and, although it was widely debated, few would have agreed on a general meaning. When speaking of a 'Romantic age', we identify a period in which certain ideas and attitudes arose in reaction to the 18th-century Enlightenment and became dominant in most intellectual areas. That is, they became the main means of expression. Expression was perhaps everything to the Romantics – expression in art, music, poetry, drama, literature and philosophy. In most cases, these ideas were created by a sense of dissatisfaction with the dominant ideals of the Enlightenment and the society that had produced them.

FCE Speaking – Part 2

2 **INDIVIDUAL LONG TURN.** Here are two photographs showing different ways of being romantic. Compare them and say how the people are feeling. You have one minute to do this.

How do you think these people are feeling?

Process language
Speaking - Part 2

Describing pictures
- In the first picture there is ...
- What strikes me in the first / second picture is that ...
- The ... appears to be ...

Making comparisons
- One similarity is that ...
- A way in which they differ is that ...

1 The DVD cover of the film 'Casablanca', directed by Michael Curtiz in 1942.

2 Joseph Severn, *Shelley in the Baths of Caracalla*, 1845. Keats-Shelley Memorial House, Rome.

4.9 **Literature**

Emotion vs reason

WARM-UP

1 **READ** the following quotations from English Romantic writers and discuss what key ideas about Romanticism they express.

'"How despicably have I acted!" she cried. – "I, who have prided myself on my discernment! ... Till this moment, I never knew myself."'

Jane Austen, *Pride and Prejudice*, Chapter XXXV

'My mind feels as if it ached to behold and know something great, something one and indivisible – and it is only in the faith of this that rocks or waterfalls, mountains or caverns, give me the sense of sublimity or majesty!'

Samuel Taylor Coleridge to John Thelwall, 14th October 1797

'Bathe in the waters of life'

William Blake, *Milton*, 1804–09

English Romanticism

English Romanticism covers the period between the French Revolution and the coronation of Queen Victoria in 1837. It was never a unified movement, although there were certain features that distinguish it from the age of Enlightenment.

Where the Enlightenment had emphasised objectivity and reason, Romanticism valued the subjective and irrational parts of human nature: emotion, imagination, introspection and a relationship with nature.

Apart from the poet William Blake, in English literature there were two great generations of poets: William Wordsworth and Samuel Taylor Coleridge in the first; Lord Byron, John Keats and Percy Bysshe Shelley in the second. These writers never formed a movement, but they shared a feeling that they were giving voice to a period of political, social and intellectual change.

'Man is born free and everywhere he is in chains'

Jean-Jacques Rousseau, *The Social Contract*, 1762

'O for a life of sensations rather than of thoughts'

John Keats to Benjamin Bailey, 22nd November 1817

'We live among such philosophers and poets as surpass beyond comparison any who have appeared since the last national struggle for civil and religious liberty.'

P.B. Shelley, *A Defence of Poetry*, 1821

2 **DISCUSS.** What does this picture suggest to you? What relationship is established between man and nature?

1 Caspar David Friedrich, *Wanderer above the Sea of Fog*, 1818. Hamburger Kunsthalle, Hamburg, Germany.

3 **COMPLETE** the table below with the correct word.

Noun	Adjective
	sensible
dominance	
	romantic
	introspective
	nostalgic
	emotional
growth	
philosophy	
	willing
	sensitive

FCE Reading and Use of English – Part 3

4 **WORD FORMATION.** **For questions 1–8, read the text 'A new sensibility'. Use the word given in capitals at the end of some of the lines to form a word that fits in the gap in the same line.**

5 **READ** the text 'A new sensibility' again and carry out the following activities.

1 Explain the new sensibility that arose around 1770.

2 Complete the table. In column A list the new interests which defined the new sensibility at the end of the 18th century. In column B write down what they were in opposition with.

A	B

3 Say what key role was played by imagination.

4 Focus on the revaluation of childhood and point out what the child was associated with in the diagram below.

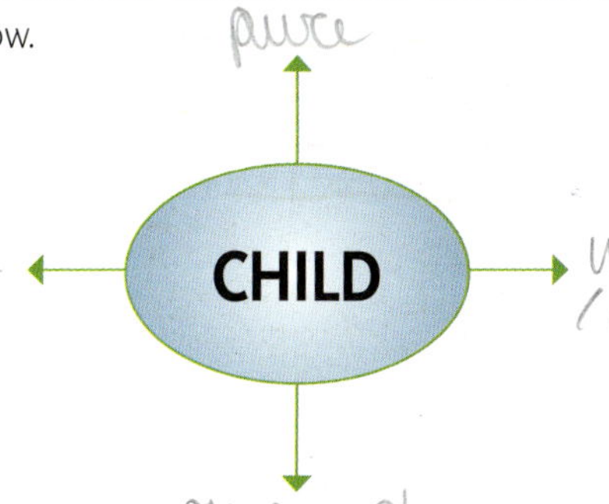

A new sensibility

In the last thirty years of the 18th century
a new **(1)** .... became **SENSIBLE**
(2) .... which came **DOMINANCE**
to be known in literature as
'Romanticism', claiming the supremacy
of feelings and emotions.
It included elements of
(3) .... nostalgia, **INTROSPECTIVE**
(4) .... and individualism, **EMOTIONAL**
and it led to a new way of considering the
role of man in the universe.

The new appeal to the heart and to the relationship between reason and emotions expressed itself in various ways.
There was a **(5)** .... interest **GROW**
in humble and everyday life, and great attention was paid to the countryside as a place where there could still be a relationship with nature, as opposed to
the **(6)** .... town. **INDUSTRIAL**

A new taste for the desolate – the love of ruins – was part of a revival of a past perceived as contrasting with present reality. There was also a revolution in the concept of nature. It was no longer
an abstract and **(7)** .... **PHILOSOPHY**
concept, something which man could control thanks to his faculty of reason; slowly, it began to be perceived as a manifestation of a divine power on earth. Imagination assumed a key role as a means of giving expression to emotional experience not strictly accountable to reason.

The willingness to explore less conscious aspects of feeling was accompanied by a serious concern about the experience of childhood. To a Romantic, a child was purer than an adult because he was unspoilt by civilisation.
His uncorrupted **(8)** .... **SENSITIVE**
meant he was even closer to God and the sources of creation, therefore childhood was a state to be admired and cultivated.

1

2

6 **READ the text 'The emphasis on the individual' below and make notes about:**
- what forms of individualism the Romantics exalted;
- what view of society they had;
- what current of thought encouraged this view;
- the meaning of the 'cult of the exotic'.

7 **FIND these words in the text below and write down either the noun(s) or the adjective(s) they are associated with. Then use them to discuss the Romantic emphasis on the individual and the cult of the exotic.**

universe • symbols for • emphasis on • cult of • view that • idea that • far away • unfamiliar in • appeal of

The emphasis on the individual

The Romantics thought that the universe was expanding, that it was organic and alive. They looked for their soul in the experience of life, which was positively exhilarating and liberating. Great emphasis was laid on the significance of the individual. The Romantics were fond of introspection. They saw the individual essentially in a solitary state; they exalted the atypical, the outcast, the rebel. This attitude led, on the one hand, to the cult of the hero – the 'rebel' in Coleridge and the 'Byronic hero' – and, on the other hand, to the view that the habits, values, rules and standards imposed by a society grounded in reason had to be abandoned.

The current of thought represented by Jean-Jacques Rousseau (1712–78) encouraged the idea that the conventions of civilisation represented intolerable restrictions on the individual personality and produced every kind of corruption and evil. It followed that 'natural' behaviour, that is to say, unrestrained and impulsive, was good.

Rousseau's theories also influenced the 'cult of the exotic', the veneration of what is far away both in space and in time. Not only did they welcome picturesque and frightening features and appearances, but also the remote and the unfamiliar in custom and social outlook. The remotest parts of Europe and the Near East had the appeal of being strange and unpredictable; danger and disaster, adventure and the inexplicable became symbols for other modes of human experience, as is shown in *The Rime of the Ancient Mariner* by Coleridge.

1 John Martin, *The Bard*, 1817. Yale Center for British Art, New Haven, Connecticut, US.

2 John Sell Cotman, *Croyland Abbey*, 1804. British Museum, London.

William Wordsworth and nature

WARM-UP

1 **DISCUSS** in pairs. What is nature for you? Write down some notes.

How the Romantics understood nature

The Romantics admired the power of living nature and looked especially for its moral and emotional relationship to mankind. The warmth of the heart was found and encouraged by communion with nature. The heart was a source of knowledge – the location of ideas 'felt' as sensations rather than thoughts. Men could learn more through intuition and feelings, by learning to trust their instincts. And the interest in the humble and uncultured is an example of how the Romantics reinterpreted the irrational aspect of reality – the imagination.

A Guide to the Romantic Understanding of Nature

The Romantics considered nature as

- opposed to institutionalised practices of thought;
- a substitute for traditional religion;
- a vehicle for self-consciousness: nature allows people to discover what they truly are;
- a source of sensations;
- a provocation to a state of imagination and vision;
- an expressive language: natural images provide the poet with a way of thinking about human feelings and the self.

William Wordsworth's life

William Wordsworth (1770–1850) was born in Cumberland (now called Cumbria) in the English Lake District in 1770. He was educated at St John's College, Cambridge, and in 1790 he went on a walking tour of France and the Alps. His experience in Revolutionary France filled him with enthusiasm for democratic ideals which he hoped could lead to a new and just social order. He returned to France and fell in love with Annette Vallon, who bore him a daughter, Caroline.

The brutal developments of the Revolution and the war between England and France brought him to the edge of a nervous breakdown. The despair and disillusionment of these years were healed by contact with nature, which he rediscovered in Dorset, where he went to live with his sister Dorothy in 1795. She remained his most faithful friend: she constantly supported his poetry, she copied down his poems and recorded their life in her *Journals*, which sometimes provide interesting insight into the experiences which generated Wordsworth's poems.

In the same year he moved to Somerset to be near Samuel Taylor Coleridge. Their friendship proved crucial to the development of English Romantic poetry: they produced a collection of poems called *Lyrical Ballads*, which appeared anonymously in 1798. The second edition of 1800 contained Wordsworth's famous 'Preface', which was to become the 'Manifesto of English Romanticism'.

In 1799 William and Dorothy settled in the Lake District, and in 1802 William married a childhood friend, Mary Hutchinson, who bore him five children. In 1805 he finished his masterpiece *The Prelude*, a long autobiographical poem in 14 books, subtitled 'Growth of a Poet's Mind', which was published only after his death.

His reputation as a poet grew steadily and, in 1843, he was made Poet Laureate. The last years of his life were marked by the growing conservatism of his political views and the decline of his creative powers. However, he continued to write poems until his death, in 1850, at the age of eighty.

1 A portrait of William Wordsworth.

2 Margaret Gillies, *Portrait of William and Mary Wordsworth*, 1839. Dove Cottage Trust, Grasmere, Cumbria, England.

2 **READ** Wordsworth's biography and write the questions to the following answers.

1. In Cumberland, in 1770.
2. At St John's College.
3. On a walking tour of France and the Alps.
4. Because he thought it could lead to justice.
5. Annette Vallon.
6. Yes, she bore him a daughter, Caroline.
7. He suffered from a nervous breakdown.
8. Contact with nature.
9. His sister Dorothy.
10. To the production of a collection of poems called *Lyrical Ballads*.
11. Yes, and he had five children.
12. *The Prelude*.
13. He became conservative.
14. He was eighty.

4.10 William Wordsworth and nature

Wordsworth and the relationship with nature

Wordsworth was interested in the relationship between the natural world and human consciousness. His poetry therefore offers a detailed account of the complex interaction between man and nature, of the influences, insights, emotions and sensations which arise from this contact rather than precise and objective observation of natural phenomena. When a natural object is described, the main focus of interest is actually the poet's response to that object. Indeed, one of the most consistent concepts in Wordsworth's work is the idea that man and nature are inseparable; man exists not outside the natural world, but as an active participant in it, so that 'nature' to Wordsworth means something that includes both inanimate and human nature – each being part of the same whole. Nature comforts man in sorrow; it is a source of pleasure and joy. It teaches man to love and to act in a moral way; it is the seat of the spirit of the universe.

The importance of the senses

Nature also means the world of sense perceptions. Wordsworth exploited above all the sensibility of the eye and ear, through which he could perceive both the 'beauteous forms' of nature and the sounds of the winds or waters, or the silence of secluded places. Sensations lead to simple thoughts, which later combine into complex and organised ideas.

Insights

The Lake District

The Lake District is a mountainous region situated in the North West of England. Since Victorian times it has been famous for its beautiful scenery and its associations with Romantic poetry and the writings of William Wordsworth and the Lake Poets. The most popular area is the Lake District National Park, which became a national park in 1951. It lies completely within the modern county of Cumbria; it contains all the land in England higher than 3,000 feet above sea level as well as the deepest and longest lakes.

Recollection in tranquillity

All genuine poetry 'takes its origin from emotion recollected in tranquillity' so that what we read in the poem results from the active, vital relationship between present and past experience. Through the re-creative power of memory, an emotion is reproduced and purified in poetic form so that a second emotion, 'kindred' to the first one, is generated.

The whole process could be described as in the sequence below:

object → poet → sensory experience → emotion → memory = recollection in tranquillity → 'kindred' emotion → poem → reader → emotion

The poet's task

The poet, though a common man, has a greater sensibility and the ability to penetrate the heart of things. The power of imagination enables him to communicate his knowledge, so that he becomes a teacher who shows men how to understand their feelings and improve their moral being. His task consists in drawing attention to the ordinary things of life, to the humblest people, where the deepest emotions and truths are to be found.

Milestones

1798, *Lyrical Ballads*: the Manifesto of English Romanticism

While planning *Lyrical Ballads*, Wordsworth agreed that he would write on the beauty of nature and ordinary things, with the aim of making them interesting for the reader; Coleridge, instead, would deal with visionary topics, the supernatural and mystery.

Wordsworth did not want to write following the standards of 18th-century poetry. His strongest objection to it was its artificial, elevated language, which he called 'poetic diction'. In his 'Preface' he stated that poetry should deal with everyday situations or incidents and with ordinary people, especially humble, rural people; even the language should be simple, the objects mentioned homely and called by their ordinary names. The reason for Wordsworth's choice lies in the fact that he believed that in low and rustic life man is more direct, nearer to his own purer passions. Therefore the poet is a man among men, writing about what interests mankind.

3 **REVISE your knowledge about Wordsworth's work using the following headings.**

1 What he stated in the 'Preface' to *Lyrical Ballads*;
2 What view he had of nature and man;
3 How poetry originates;
4 What the poet's task is.

Daffodils

William Wordsworth

Poems in Two Volumes (1807)

This poem records the experience of a walk the poet went for with his sister Dorothy near their home in the Lake District. It is one of Wordsworth's most famous poems, in which he vividly conveys his love for nature. Written in 1804, it was published in 1807.

3.4

I wandered lonely as a cloud
That floats[1] on high o'er vales and hills,
When all at once I saw a crowd,
A host, of golden daffodils[2];
Beside the lake, beneath[3] the trees,
Fluttering and dancing in the breeze[4].

Continuous as the stars that shine
And twinkle[5] on the milky way[6],
They stretched in never-ending line
Along the margin of a bay:
Ten thousand saw I at a glance,
Tossing[7] their heads in sprightly[8] dance.

The waves beside them danced; but they
Outdid the sparkling waves[9] in glee[10];
A poet could not but be gay,
In such a jocund company;
I gazed[11] – and gazed – but little thought
What wealth the show to me had brought:

For oft, when on my couch[12] I lie
In vacant[13] or in pensive mood,
They flash upon that inward[14] eye
Which is the bliss[15] of solitude;
And then my heart with pleasure fills,
And dances with the daffodils.

1 **floats.** Galleggia.
2 **host, of golden daffodils.** Moltitudine di giunchiglie dorate.
3 **beneath.** Al di sotto di.
4 **Fluttering and dancing in the breeze.** Ondeggianti e danzanti nella brezza.
5 **twinkle.** Scintillano.
6 **the milky way.** La via lattea.
7 **Tossing.** Che scuotevano.
8 **sprightly.** Allegra, briosa.
9 **Outdid the sparkling waves.** Superavano le onde spumeggianti.
10 **glee.** Gaiezza.
11 **gazed.** Guardavo, fissavo.
12 **couch.** Divano.
13 **vacant.** Ozioso, distratto.
14 **inward.** Interiore.
15 **bliss.** Beatitudine.

1 Walter Crane, *La Primavera*, 1883. Private collection.

WARM-UP

1 THINK of a scene, either in the country or in a town, that particularly struck you. Describe the scene as carefully as you can, saying what senses were involved in the experience. What makes it memorable for you? How do you feel when you remember it?

COMPREHENSION

2 READ the poem and answer the questions.

First stanza

- What was the poet doing? What was his mood?
- What broke this mood suddenly?
- Where were the flowers?

Second stanza

- What did the poet associate them with?
- How many did he see? Is that possible?

Third stanza

- What was the environment like?
- How did the poet feel? Why does the author say 'A poet' in line 15?

Fourth stanza

- What kind of state does the poet describe?
- Is this solitude similar to the loneliness of the first stanza?
- What is the result of this experience?

ANALYSIS

3 ANSWER the questions about the poem.

1 How are the daffodils introduced in the first stanza? What is this literary device called?
2 What effect is achieved by showing the daffodils as part of the universal order in the second stanza?
3 What view of nature is conveyed by Wordsworth in the second and third stanzas?
4 How are perception and thought related in the third stanza?
5 Lines 19–24 provide an exception to the use of the past tense which characterises the whole poem. State what tense appears in these lines and what its function is.

YOUR TURN

4 EXPLAIN how Wordsworth's idea of poetic composition applies to this poem.

4.11 **Literature**

Samuel Taylor Coleridge and sublime nature

Coleridge's life

Samuel Taylor Coleridge was born in Devonshire in 1772. At the age of ten, he was sent to Christ's Hospital School in London, and then he went to Cambridge, where he never graduated. He was heavily influenced by French Revolutionary ideals, which made him an enthusiastic republican.

After the disillusionment with the French Revolution, he planned to establish a utopian community in Pennsylvania under the name of 'Pantisocracy', where every economic activity would be done communally and private ownership would not exist, in order to provide labour and peace and create the best possible environment for everyone. In the end this project failed.

In 1797 he met the poet William Wordsworth and an important collaboration started. Together they published the collection *Lyrical Ballads*, which includes his masterpiece, *The Rime of the Ancient Mariner*, written in 1798. In 1799 he joined Wordsworth and his sister in the Lake District, and later he began a career lecturing on literary concerns and journalism. The lectures he gave on Shakespeare between 1808 and 1818 laid the foundations of Shakespearean criticism.

Finally, he settled in London, where he produced *Biographia Literaria* (1817), a classic text of literary criticism and autobiography. Here he explained the dual task which he and Wordsworth had set themselves in *Lyrical Ballads*. In contrast to Wordsworth's preoccupation with subjects from ordinary life, his own task was to write about extraordinary events in a credible way. He died in 1834.

Imagination and fancy

Like Blake and Wordsworth, Coleridge stressed the role of the imagination, and his critical essays did much to assert the idea of this faculty as the sovereign creative power. He distinguished between 'primary' and 'secondary' imagination. He described primary imagination as a fusion of perception and the human individual power to produce images. It was also the power to give chaos a certain order, to give the material of perception a certain shape. Secondary imagination was something more, it was the poetic faculty which not only gave shape and order to a given world, but built new worlds.

Imagination was more important than fancy, which, though on a higher level than mere perception, was based on the power of association of material already provided and subject to the rational law of judgement. A practical example is offered by what Coleridge does in *The Rime of the Ancient Mariner*; he uses several details that had impressed him during his readings, and he shapes them into something else. Thus fancy enabled the poet to blend various 'ingredients' into beautiful images.

Coleridge's view of nature

Unlike Wordsworth, Coleridge did not view nature as a moral guide or a source of consolation and happiness. His contemplation of nature was always accompanied by the awareness of the presence of the ideal in the real. His strong Christian faith, however, did not allow him to identify nature with the divine – the form of pantheism which Wordsworth adopted. Rather, he saw nature and the material world as the projection of the 'real' world of ideas on the flux of time. Thus Coleridge believed that natural images carried abstract meanings and he used them in his most visionary poems.

1 A portrait of Samuel Taylor Coleridge.

2 Wordsworth and Coleridge in *The Travellers Breakfast* by Edward Villiers Rippingille, 1824.

1 PROVIDE evidence to justify these statements about Coleridge's life and works.

1 He was disillusioned with the French Revolution.
2 His friendship with William Wordsworth was crucial.
3 He became a literary critic.
4 He explained his task as a poet in *Biographia Literaria*.

2 ANSWER these questions.

1 What role did the imagination play, according to the poet?
2 What was the difference between 'primary' and 'secondary' imagination?
3 What was fancy?
4 How did Coleridge view nature?

The Rime of the Ancient Mariner (1798)

The story

The ballad *The Rime of the Ancient Mariner* is made up of seven parts and is set in a boundless sea with days of pitiless sun and nights lit by the moon. It is introduced by an 'Argument' containing a short summary of the whole poem and consists of two narratives: one is made up of the captions to the right of the stanzas, which constitute the framework and introduce the protagonist and his listener; the other is the poem itself.

3 **MATCH each sentence (A–F) to the correct illustration (1–6) by the French engraver Gustave Doré (1832–83) to summarise the main events of *The Rime of the Ancient Mariner*.**

A At the end, the Ancient Mariner leaves the wedding guest after teaching him to love all living beings through his tale. ....

B Eventually, a phantom ship came closer to the doomed crew and was identified as a skeleton ship. On board, Death and Life-in-Death cast dice; the former won the Mariner's fellow sailors and the latter won the Mariner's life. ....

C After the storm, an albatross appeared and led them out of the Antarctic; despite this he was killed by the Mariner. (The shooting of a bird may seem a matter of little moment, but Coleridge makes it significant in two ways. First of all, he does not say why the Mariner kills the albatross and what matters is precisely the uncertainty of the Mariner's motives, which suggests the essential irrationality of the crime. Secondly, this action is against nature and breaks a sacred law of life.) ....

D All the Mariner's fellow sailors died. ....

E The Mariner stops a wedding guest to tell him his dreadful tale. He narrates how he and his fellow mariners reached the equator and the polar regions after a violent storm. ....

F The Mariner, now alone, blessed some water snakes and began to re-establish a relationship with nature. The bodies of the crew rose again and steered the ship back home. ....

1

2

3

4

5

6

4.11 Samuel Taylor Coleridge and sublime nature

The natural world

The atmosphere of the whole poem is mysterious because of the combination of the supernatural and the real – dream-like elements and visual realism. At times nature seems to be a character itself, based on the way it interacts with the Ancient Mariner. When the Mariner kills the albatross, he offends the spirit of the 'rime'. In fact, like all natural things, the Albatross is linked to the spiritual world, and thus the Ancient Mariner's punishment through nature itself begins. The wind dies, the sun becomes hotter and hotter, it does not rain. The ocean becomes revolting, rotten, peopled with 'slimy' creatures. It is only at the end of the poem that the Ancient Mariner preaches respect for the natural world, because one must respect all natural creatures in order to respect God.

4 **IN PAIRS** **take turns asking and answering the following questions about *The Rime of the Ancient Mariner*.**

1 What atmosphere characterises the whole poem?
2 How is the Ancient Mariner punished after killing the Albatross?
3 Why can't the Mariner be considered a real character?
4 What features does *The Rime* share with traditional medieval ballads?
5 What makes it a Romantic ballad?

The characters

The Mariner and his fellow sailors are hardly characters in any dramatic sense. They are more types than human beings and their agonies are simply universally human. The Mariner does not speak as a moral agent; he is passive in guilt and remorse. When he acts, he does so blindly, under compulsion. From his paralysis of conscience the Mariner succeeds in gaining his authority, though he pays for it by remaining in the condition of an outcast. Coleridge makes him spectator as well as actor in the drama, so that he can tell even of his worst terrors with the calm of lucid retrospection.

The Rime and traditional ballads

This poem contains many of the features traditionally associated with ballads, that is: the combination of dialogue and narration; the four-line stanza; archaic language, rich in alliteration, repetition and onomatopoeia; the theme of travel and wandering; and supernatural elements. However, the presence of a moral at the end makes *The Rime of the Ancient Mariner* a Romantic ballad.

1 Frontispiece to *The Rime of the Ancient Mariner*, 1876.

WARM-UP

1 **IMAGINE you are on a holiday voyage to an unknown place. How would you feel if a violent storm broke out during your journey? Describe both your reactions and those of all the other people on board.**

The killing of the Albatross

Samuel Taylor Coleridge

The Rime of the Ancient Mariner (1798)
Part I, Lines 1–82

The extract you are going to read is full of suspense from the very first line: an old, lonely Mariner appears from nowhere and forces one in a crowd, on his way to a wedding party, to listen to his story. The Mariner's tale is about a sea voyage, which soon turns out to be a voyage with no return because of the uncontrollable powers of nature.

ARGUMENT

How a Ship having passed the Line[1] was driven by storms to the cold Country towards the South Pole; and how from thence[2] she made her course[3] to the tropical Latitude of the Great Pacific Ocean; and of the strange things that befell[4]; and in what manner the ancyent Marinere came back to his own Country.

An ancient Mariner meeteth three Gallants bidden to a wedding-feast, and detaineth[5] one.

3.5

It is an ancient Mariner,
And he stoppeth[6] one of three.
'By thy[7] long grey beard and glittering eye,
Now wherefore[8] stopp'st thou[9] me?

1 **Line.** Linea dell'Equatore.
2 **thence.** *Arc.: there.*
3 **course.** Rotta.
4 **befell.** Accaddero.
5 **detaineth.** (*Arc.*) Trattiene ('-th' è la desinenza di terza persona singolare).
6 **stoppeth.** *Stops.*
7 **thy.** *Arc.: your.*
8 **wherefore.** Perché.
9 **thou.** *Arc.: you.*

The Bridegroom[10]'s doors are opened wide,
And I am next of kin[11],
The guests are met, the feast is set:
May'st hear the merry din[12].

He holds him with his skinny hand,
'There was a ship' quoth he[13].
'Hold off![14] unhand me, grey-beard loon[15]!
Eftsoons his hand dropt he[16].

The Wedding-Guest is spellbound by the eye of the old seafaring man, and constrained to hear his tale.

He holds him with his glittering eye –
The Wedding-Guest stood still,
And listens like a three years' child:
The Mariner hath his will.

The Wedding-Guest sat on a stone:
He cannot choose but hear;
And thus spake[17] on that ancient man,
The bright-eyed Mariner.
'The ship was cheered[18], the harbour cleared[19],
Merrily did we drop
Below the kirk[20], below the hill,
Below the lighthouse top.

The Mariner tells how the ship sailed southward with a good wind and fair weather, till it reached the line.

The sun came up upon the left,
Out of the sea came he!
And he shone bright, and on the right
Went down into the sea.

Higher and higher every day,
Till over the mast[21] at noon –'
The Wedding-Guest here beat his breast,
For he heard the loud bassoon[22].

The Wedding-Guest heareth the bridal music; but the Mariner continueth his tale.

The bride hath paced[23] into the hall,
Red as a rose is she;
Nodding their heads before her goes
The merry minstrelsy[24].

The Wedding-Guest he beat his breast,
Yet he cannot choose but hear;

2 Angus McBride, illustrations based on the poem *The Rime of the Ancient Mariner* by Samuel Taylor Coleridge, 20th century.

10 **Bridegroom.** Sposo.
11 **I am next of kin.** Io sono un parente stretto.
12 **din.** Chiasso.
13 **quoth he.** Lui disse ('quoth' è forma arcaica di 'said').
14 **Hold off!** Stammi lontano!
15 **grey-beard loon.** Vecchio matto.
16 **Eftsoons ... he.** Subito lasciò cadere la sua mano.
17 **spake.** (*Arc.*) Parlò.
18 **cheered.** Salutata.
19 **the harbour cleared.** Il porto (fu) lasciato.
20 **the kirk.** La chiesa. ('kirk' è forma arcaica di 'church').
21 **Till ... mast.** Finché a picco sull'albero maestro.
22 **the loud bassoon.** Il forte suono del fagotto.
23 **paced.** Entrata.
24 **minstrelsy.** Menestrelli.

4.11 Samuel Taylor Coleridge and sublime nature

And thus spake on that ancient man,
The bright-eyed Mariner.

The ship driven by a storm toward the south pole.

'And now the storm-blast[25] came, and he
Was tyrannous and strong:
He struck with his o'ertaking[26] wings,
And chased us south along.

With sloping masts and dipping prow[27],
As who pursued[28] with yell and blow
Still treads the shadow of his foe[29],
And forward bends his head,
The ship drove fast, loud roared the blast,
And southward aye we fled.

And now there came both mist and snow,
And it grew wondrous cold[30]:
And ice, mast-high, came floating by,
As green as emerald.

The land of ice, and of fearful sounds where no living thing was to be seen.

And through the drifts the snowy clifts[31]
Did send a dismal sheen[32].
Nor shapes of men nor beasts we ken[33] –
The ice was all between.

The ice was here, the ice was there,
The ice was all around:
It cracked and growled, and roared and howled,
Like noises in a swound[34]!

Till a great sea-bird, called the Albatross came through the snow-fog, and was received with great joy and hospitality.

At length did cross an Albatross,
Thorough[35] the fog it came;
As if it had been a Christian soul,
We hailed it in God's name.

It ate the food it ne'er had eat,
And round and round it flew.
The ice did split with a thunder-fit;
The helmsman[36] steered us through!

And lo! the Albatross proveth a bird of good omen, and followeth the ship as it returned northward through fog and floating ice.

1 English School, *Albatross*, 20th century.

2 Some critics claim that Watchet harbour, in Somerset, is the port from which the Ancient Mariner by S.T. Coleridge set sail. In 2003 a sculpture of the Ancient Mariner with the albatross hung around his neck was unveiled at Watchet harbour as a tribute to the poet.

25 **storm-blast.** Tempesta.
26 **o'ertaking.** Travolgenti.
27 **sloping ... prow.** Alberi inclinati e la prua immersa nell'acqua.
28 **pursued.** Inseguito.
29 **foe.** Nemico.
30 **it ... cold.** Divenne terribilmente freddo.
31 **snowy clifts.** Rocce innevate.
32 **Did ... sheen.** Inviavano un bagliore assai lugubre.
33 **Nor shapes ... ken.** Non vedevamo forme di uomini o bestie.
34 **swound.** Svenimento.
35 **Thorough.** Attraverso.
36 **helmsman.** Timoniere.

And a good south wind sprung up behind;
The Albatross did follow,
And every day, for food or play,
Came to the mariners' hollo!

In mist or cloud, on mast or shroud,
It perched[37] for vespers nine;
Whiles all the night, through fog-smoke white,
Glimmered the white moon-shine.'

The ancient Mariner inhospitably killeth the pious bird of good omen.

'God save thee, ancient Mariner!
From the fiends, that plague thee thus! –
Why look'st thou so?' – With my cross-bow
I shot[38] the albatross.

37 **perched.** Stette appollaiato.
38 **With ... shot.** Con la balestra uccisi.

2

COMPREHENSION

2 AS YOU READ the extract, note down:
1 the setting in time and place;
2 the characters involved.

3 FOCUS on the Ancient Mariner's description; then complete the sentences below.
1 The Ancient Mariner is ....
2 His beard is .... ; his eyes are .... and .... ; his hands are ....
3 He turns out to be a .... character since he hypnotises the ....

4 COMPLETE the table about the Mariner's voyage.

	Direction of the ship	Place reached
After leaving the harbour		
During the storm		
After the appearance of the Albatross		

5 WRITE down, in your own words, what happens at the end.

ANALYSIS

6 EXPLAIN. ***The Rime*** **is a ballad. Which of the characteristics of the old ballad form does it contain?**

7 THE NARRATION of the voyage is interrupted twice by the other character – the wedding guest.
1 Underline the two occasions – one of which is external to the narration, while the other is a sort of comment.
2 Describe the listener's attitude on these occasions.

8 FOCUS on the natural elements the ship meets at the beginning of the voyage.
1 How is the storm represented (lines 41–50)? What poetic device does the poet use?
2 What other elements come next (lines 51–62)?
3 How are they connoted and how can they be interpreted?
4 What side of nature does the albatross represent?

YOUR TURN

9 COMPARE Coleridge's vision of nature to Wordsworth's. Discuss with the rest of the class.

4.12 **History**

The Napoleonic Wars

3.6 DICTATION: *THE PETERLOO MASSACRE*

WARM-UP

1 **LOOK** at picture 1. Who are these characters? What do you think they are doing?

2 **READ** the Q&A text.

GLOSSARY
offset against compensate da
outbursts scoppi
on the verge sull'orlo
smashed rotto, frantumato
starvation fame
power loom telaio meccanico

Milestones

1819, the Peterloo Massacre

On 16th August over 60,000 peaceful pro-democracy and anti-poverty protesters converged on what is now St Peter's Square, Manchester. From towns and villages these groups marched peacefully, each group headed by its own banner with their demands. The authorities, filled with alarm at what they believed would be the result of this immense demonstration, sent in the cavalry, who charged into the densely packed mass with swords drawn. Defenceless, the crowd tried to disperse; as the field cleared, all that remained were the dead and injured. Eleven people were killed and four hundred were wounded. The incident quickly became known as the 'Peterloo Massacre', an allusion to the Battle of Waterloo four years earlier.

3 **IN PAIRS** cover the answers (A s) in the text and take turns asking and answering the questions (Q s) using the information that you have read.

The French Revolution was followed by Napoleon's ascent.

Q Where did Britain decide to fight against Napoleon's France?

A In 1793 France declared war and Britain, who feared an invasion and relied on a stronger navy, decided to fight France at sea. The great hero of the British navy was Admiral Horatio Nelson (1758–1805), who defeated the French-Spanish fleet off Cape Trafalgar on the Atlantic coast of southern Spain in 1805.

Q Where was Napoleon defeated?

A The total defeat of Napoleon happened in 1815 at the Battle of Waterloo, in Belgium, where the British troops, commanded by Arthur Wellesley, the first Duke of Wellington (1769–1852), were able to overcome Napoleon, weakened by his disastrous invasion of Russia.

Q What were the consequences of the Napoleonic Wars?

A Despite the victory over France, Britain had gained relatively little from a long and exhausting war. The acquisition of the Cape of Good Hope, Trinidad, Singapore, Ceylon and Malta was of considerable strategic interest but had to be offset against the enormous financial costs of the war.

Q What were the social conditions in Britain after the wars?

A Britain's internal situation was far from happy. The country was on the verge of starvation, bankruptcy and revolution.

Q What was welcomed by the Romantics in 1807?

A In 1807 the abolition of slave-trading with British ships was welcomed by the Romantics, many of whom had been expressing Abolitionist ideas in their works for several years. Blake, in particular, had opposed the slave trade, describing in *London* the revulsion he experienced when hearing the sound of the 'mind-forg'd manacles'. Shelley's *Prometheus Unbound* contains symbols linked to the anti-slavery movement, and Byron's Oriental slavery in works such as *Don Juan* is often interpreted as a protest against slavery in the colonies.

1

Q What were the Luddite riots?

A Inhuman working conditions in factories and severe unemployment, arising both from the sudden fall in demand for British goods and from the increasing use of machinery, led to outbursts of machine-breaking, culminating in the Luddite riots (named after Ned Ludd who, in 1779, had smashed a power loom for making stockings) of 1811–12. The Luddites caused so much alarm, however, that large numbers of troops hunted them down and the government made machine-breaking punishable by death.

Q What happened in 1819?

A In 1819, during a peaceful public meeting in Manchester, soldiers fired into a crowd and eleven people were killed in the so-called 'Peterloo Massacre'.

Q What changes occurred in the political situation around the 1830s?

A The period which covered the end of the Napoleonic Wars (1811–20) was called 'the Regency', since the Prince Regent, later to become George IV, acted as monarch during the illness of his father George III (1760–1820). In 1830 William IV succeeded his brother and his short reign saw a new political awareness, leading to a new age of reforms. This was the background when Queen Victoria ascended the throne in 1837.

1 An example of political satire against the division of the world between England and France.

George Gordon Byron and the stormy ocean

1 **READ** the text in the green box on the right and fill in the table.

VIEW OF NATURE	
Wordsworth	
Coleridge	
Byron	
Shelley	
Keats	

2 **LOOK** at the pictures of Byron on pages 125–127. What do they tell you about his life? Where is he? What do you think about his appearance and style of dress?

Nature in the second generation of Romantic poets

The Romantic poets of the first generation gave great importance to nature. Wordsworth considered nature as a source of joy, inspiration and knowledge, a mother and a moral guide. Nature was apprehended by Coleridge from a pantheistic dimension as a universal force which sheds light on man's spirituality. For him nature was the representation of God's will and love, so man had to respect it, otherwise he could offend God. The poets of the second generation were also attracted to the beauty of nature. For Byron's hero it was the companion of his loneliness or the counterpart of his stormy feelings when it was violently upset. Shelley had a passionate devotion to nature, which was a source of enjoyment and inspiration. He thought that nature was pervaded by a guiding power leading man to love. Keats thought of natural phenomena as therapeutic to human health: the creative and philosophical mind benefits immensely from the beauty of the natural landscape more than from institutionalised learning. Nature serves as a kind of muse to the poet's artistic quest towards more complex levels of awareness and creativity.

George Gordon Byron's life

Handsome and unconventional, George Gordon, 6th Baron Byron, (1788–1824) descended from two aristocratic families and, to many of his contemporaries, his poetry and life embodied the Romantic spirit. He began to write at Trinity College, Cambridge, and in 1807 he published *Hours of Idleness*, a small volume of lyric poems, which was attacked in the pages of the 'Edinburgh Review'. Byron replied with *English Bards and Scotch Reviewers*, where he showed his taste for satire.

In 1809 he set out on a tour of Spain, Portugal, Malta, Albania, Greece and the Middle East, where he gathered the experiences which gave rise to the first two cantos of *Childe Harold's Pilgrimage*, which he published after his return to England in 1812. The cantos were so successful that Byron became a literary and social celebrity. His reputation increased even further when he published a series of verse narratives, *The Giaour*, *The Corsair* and *Lara*, which were popular with the public for their exotic settings and descriptions of foreign customs. In 1815 Byron married Annabella Milbanke, but the marriage collapsed a year later because of Byron's incestuous relationship with his half-sister Augusta Leigh. Surrounded by scandal and debts, he left England in 1816 never to return. He lived in Geneva, where he became a close friend of the poet Percy Bysshe Shelley and wrote the third canto of *Childe Harold*. Then he moved to Venice, where he produced the fourth and last canto of *Childe Harold* (1818), the tragedy *Manfred* (1817), and began his masterpiece, the mock-epic *Don Juan*.

In 1819 he moved to Milan, where he became involved in the patriotic plots against Austrian rule; then he decided to commit himself to the Greek struggle for independence from Turkey. He organised an expedition and devoted himself to training the troops in the town of Missolonghi, where he died in 1824, struck by a severe fever. His heart is buried in Greece, where he is still regarded as a national hero, while his body is interred in the family tomb in England.

1

2

1 Thomas Phillips, *George Gordon Byron*, 1835. National Portrait Gallery, London.

2 Joseph-Denis Odevaere, *Byron on his Death Bed*, ca 1826. Groeninge Museum, Bruges, Belgium.

4.13 George Gordon Byron and the stormy ocean

1 Giacomo Trécourt, *Poet Lord George Byron on the Greek coastline*, ca 1850. Musei Civici di Pavia, Pavia, Italy.

The Romantic rebel

Although Byron never considered himself a Romantic poet, he was the only English poet of his age to achieve a European reputation and exert a significant influence on other writers, such as the Russians Aleksandr Sergeyevich Pushkin (1799–1837) and Fyodor Dostoyevsky (1821–81), the German Johann Wolfgang von Goethe (1749–1832) and the Frenchman Honoré de Balzac (1799–1850). His verse and drama also inspired the works of Franz Liszt, Hector Berlioz and Giuseppe Verdi. With his life and his works he popularised the 'Byronic hero', a moody, restless and mysterious Romantic rebel who hides some horrible sin or secret in his past. He is characterised by proud individualism and rejects the conventional moral rules of society. He is an outsider, isolated and attractive at the same time. He is of noble birth but wild in his manners; his looks are hard but handsome. He has a great sensibility to nature and beauty, but has grown bored with the excesses and excitements of the world. Women cannot resist him, but he refuses their love; men either admire or envy him. This blend of hidden suffering, rebelliousness and eroticism, which can be seen in the first two cantos of *Childe Harold* and in his later poems and tragedies, was irresistible in Byron's age.

Byron's individualism

The figure of the Byronic hero originated in a complex and contradictory personality. Byron firmly believed in individual liberty and hated any sort of constraint; he wished to be himself without compromises. As well as this, he wanted all men to be free and so went to fight against tyrants. He denounced the evils of society by using the witty style of 18th-century poetry to convey a satirical aim. However, his mood and the choice of his themes were Romantic. In the foreground there is always an isolated man whose feelings are reflected in the wildest and most exotic natural landscapes. So nature is not a source of consolation and joy; it does not embody any theory, nor does it have any message to convey.

3 IN PAIRS ask and answer these questions.

1 What were the main features of the Byronic hero?
2 How did Byron's personality influence the Byronic hero?
3 What was nature, according to Byron?
4 Was his poetry Romantic or classical?

FCE Listening – Part 2

4 3.7 | **SENTENCE COMPLETION. You will hear a lecture about Byron's *Childe Harold's Pilgrimage*. For questions 1–10, complete the sentences.**

Childe Harold's Pilgrimage (1812–18)

The poem is made up of **(1)** ....
The term 'Childe' means a **(2)** .... awaiting knighthood.
In Cantos I and II there are descriptions of the familiar, the **(3)** ....
Harold meditates on **(4)** .... and the vanity of life.
The background to the third canto is **(5)** ....
The fourth canto contains descriptions of **(6)** .... especially of **(7)** ....
The poet's **(8)** .... are reflected by nature.
The popularity of the four cantos derived from their articulation of the 'world-weariness' after the **(9)** ....
The quest for moral and intellectual certainty passes through **(10)** ....

2 Sir William Allan, *Lord Byron reposing in the house of a fisherman having swum the Hellespont*, 1831.

3 John Sanders, *George Gordon Sixth Lord Byron*, 1846. The Royal Collection, London.

WARM-UP

1 **TICK as appropriate. What is an apostrophe?**

- ☐ A type of punctuation mark.
- ☐ A technique which involves speaking to an imaginary or absent person, or to inanimate objects.
- ☐ A reproach or warning.

Apostrophe to the ocean

George Gordon Byron

Childe Harold's Pilgrimage (1812–18)

Canto IV

Written in the middle of the Romantic period, Byron's 'apostrophe' conveys the view of the sea as powerful and sublime. The poet addresses his wild emotions to the ocean as if it were the woman he loved and desired.

CLXXVIII

3.8

There is a pleasure in the pathless[1] woods,
There is a rapture on the lonely shore,
There is society where none intrudes,
By the deep Sea, and music in its roar:
I love not Man the less, but Nature more,
From these our interviews[2], in which I steal
From all I may be, or have been before,
To mingle[3] with the Universe, and feel
What I can ne'er express, yet cannot all conceal[4].

CLXXIX

Roll on, thou deep and dark blue Ocean – roll!
Ten thousand fleets sweep over thee in vain;
Man marks the earth with ruin – his control
Stops with the shore; – upon the watery plain
The wrecks are all thy deed[5], nor doth remain
A shadow of man's ravage[6], save his own,
When for a moment, like a drop of rain,
He sinks into thy depths with bubbling groan[7],
Without a grave, unknelled, uncoffined[8], and unknown.

1 **pathless.** Impenetrabili, inesplorati.
2 **interviews.** Incontri, scambi.
3 **To mingle.** Per mescolarmi.
4 **yet ... conceal.** Tuttavia ... nascondere.
5 **The wrecks are all thy deed.** Le carcasse (dei naufragi) sono tutte le tue imprese.
6 **ravage.** Devastazione.
7 **bubbling groan.** Lamento gorgogliante.
8 **unknelled, uncoffined.** Non annunciato dai rintocchi funebri, non posto nella bara.

4.13 George Gordon Byron and the stormy ocean

CLXXX

His steps are not upon thy paths, – thy fields
Are not a spoil[9] for him, – thou dost arise
And shake him from thee; the vile strength he wields[10]
For earth's destruction thou dost all despise[11],
Spurning him from thy bosom[12] to the skies,
And send'st him, shivering[13] in thy playful spray
And howling, to his gods, where haply lies
His petty hope[14] in some near port or bay,
And dashest him[15] again to earth: – there let him lay.

CLXXXIV

And I have loved thee, Ocean! and my joy
Of youthful sports was on thy breast to be
Borne[16] like thy bubbles, onward: from a boy
I wantoned with thy breakers[17] – they to me
Were a delight; and if the freshening sea
Made them a terror – 'twas a pleasing fear,
For I was as it were a child of thee,
And trusted to thy billows[18] far and near,
And laid my hand upon thy mane[19] – as I do here.

9 **a spoil.** Spoglie.
10 **the vile strength he wields.** Esercita la vile forza.
11 **thou dost all despise.** Tu disprezzi tutto.
12 **Spurning him from thy bosom.** Respingendolo dal tuo petto.
13 **shivering.** Tremante.
14 **haply lies / His petty hope.** Giace accidentalmente / La sua piccola speranza.
15 **dashest him.** Lo scagli.
16 **Of youthful ... / Borne.** Di svaghi giovanili doveva essere trasportata dal tuo seno.
17 **I wantoned with thy breakers.** Scherzavo con le tue onde.
18 **trusted to thy billows.** Mi affidavo ai tuoi marosi.
19 **thy mane.** La tua criniera.

COMPREHENSION

2 **AS YOU READ** the extract, answer the questions about each stanza.

Stanza CLXXVIII
- What kind of scene is presented in the first three lines?
- What is the speaker's attitude towards society and nature?

Stanza CLXXIX
- How does the speaker contrast man's power with that of the sea?
- How does he describe our power's oblivion?

Stanza CLXXX
- How does the ocean behave towards mankind?

Stanza CLXXXIV
- What are the speaker's feelings towards the ocean?

ANALYSIS

3 **WRITE** down the rhyme scheme of stanza CLXXVIII.

4 **UNDERLINE** examples of the following in the poem:
- **assonance** (stanza CLXXIX)
- **alliteration** (stanza CLXXX)
- **parallelism, that is, the similarity of structure in a pair or series of related words, phrases or clauses** (stanza CLXXVIII)
- **paradox** (stanza CLXXVIII)
- **apostrophe**
- **personification, that is, a type of metaphor which attributes to abstract things or to inanimate objects the characteristics of a living being.** Provide examples of personification of the ocean.
- **simile**. Man sinks like a ... (stanza CLXXIX)
- **solecism, that is, a mistake in grammar.** What solecism is found in the last line of stanza CLXXX?
- **oxymoron** (stanza CLXXXIV)
- **metaphor** (stanza CLXXXIV)

5 **WRITE** a few sentences to state the theme and the mood of the extract.

YOUR TURN

6 **QUOTE** the lines from the poem that impressed you most. Justify your answer.

7 **DISCUSS.** Do you admire the possibilities of the ocean? If not, what other natural element do you find worthy of admiration?

8 **DESCRIBE** how Byron's spirit exemplified the Romantic spirit.

4.14 **Literature**

TEXT BANK 33: *JOHN KEATS*

John Keats and unchanging nature

John Keats's life

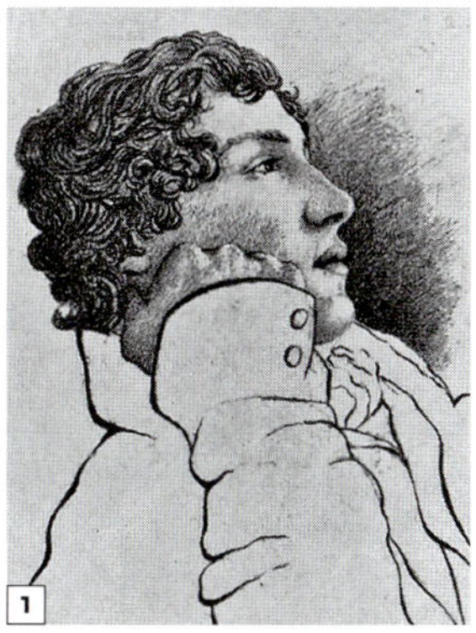

John Keats (1795–1821) is perhaps the greatest member of that group of the second generation of Romantic poets who blossomed early and died young. He is Romantic in his relish of sensation, his feeling for the Middle Ages, his love for the Greek civilisation and his concept of the writer, but the synthesis he made of all these elements was very much his own.

Keats was born in London in 1795 to a humble but well-off family. The first of five children, he attended a private school in Enfield and, following the early deaths of his father (killed in a riding accident) and mother (of tuberculosis – a family illness), he decided to study to become a surgeon in 1810. Six years later, in spite of precarious finances, he gave up medicine for poetry. Helped in his quest by the poet and radical editor of 'The Examiner', Leigh Hunt, Keats soon became a friend of the leading writers and artists of the period, including Percy Bysshe Shelley. In 1818 *Endymion*, a long, mythological poem, appeared. This was a difficult time for Keats; his ever-frail health deteriorated rapidly following a walking tour in the Highlands in 1818.

In 1820, Keats coughed up blood and the symptoms of tuberculosis became evident. In September of the same year, he travelled to Italy in an effort to recover his health but died in Rome in February 1821. He was buried in the Protestant Cemetery in Rome.

The substance of his poetry

His lyrical poems are not fragments of a continual spiritual autobiography, like the lyrics of Shelley and Byron. Certainly there is some deeply felt personal experience behind the odes of 1818, but the significant fact is that this experience is 'behind' the odes, not their substance. Moreover, the poetical personal pronoun 'I' does not stand for a human being linked to the events of his time, but for a universal one. Another feature of Keats's striking departure from the central creed of Romanticism is indicated by his remark that 'scenery is fine, but human nature is finer'. The common Romantic tendency to identify scenes and landscapes with subjective moods and emotions is rarely present in his poetry; it has nothing of the Wordsworthian pantheistic conviction and no sense of mystery.

Milestones

1818, Keats's Great Year

September 1818 marked the beginning of what has come to be called the Great Year. Keats wrote, consecutively, *The Eve of St Agnes*, characterised by those features which are conventionally called 'Romantic'; *The Eve of St Mark*; *Ode to Psyche*; *La Belle Dame Sans Merci*, where the poet recorded a dream in which he met a beautiful woman in a magic place which turned out to be filled with pallid, enslaved lovers; *Ode to a Nightingale*; *Ode on a Grecian Urn*, where he admires a moment of beauty held forever in a work of art; *Ode on Melancholy*, *Ode on Indolence*, *Lamia*, *The Fall of Hyperion* and *To Autumn*. This outpouring of major poetry is unmatched in English literature.

The role of imagination

It was Keats's belief in the supreme value of imagination which made him a Romantic poet. His imagination takes two main forms: firstly, the world of his poetry is predominantly artificial, one that he imagines; secondly, his poetry comes from imagination in the sense that a great deal of his work, even of the odes, is a vision of what he would like human life to be like, stimulated by his own experiences of pain and misery.

Beauty and art

What strikes his imagination most is beauty, and it is his disinterested love for it that differentiates him from the other Romantic writers and makes him the forerunner of Victorian writers. His first apprehension of beauty proceeds from the senses, from concrete physical sensations. All the senses, not only the nobler ones, sight and hearing, as in Wordsworth's poetry, are involved in this process. This 'physical beauty' is caught in all the forms nature acquires, in the colours it displays, in the sweetness of its perfumes, in the curves of a flower, in a woman. Beauty can also produce a much deeper experience of joy, which introduces a sort of 'spiritual beauty', that is one of love, friendship and poetry. These two kinds of beauty are closely linked, since the former – linked to life, enjoyment, decay and death – is the expression of the latter, which is related to eternity. Moreover, Keats identifies beauty and truth as the only true types of knowledge.

Negative capability

The poet, in Keats's view, has what he called 'negative capability': negativity refers to the capability the poet has to deny his certainties and personality in order to identify himself with the object which is the source of his inspiration and the place where truth resides. When the poet can rely on this negative capability, he is able to seek sensation, which is the basis of knowledge since it leads to beauty and truth, and allows him to render it through poetry. This was a new view of the poet's task.

1 **MAKE NOTES under the following headings to organise your knowledge about the work of John Keats.**

1. The family problems which affected his poetic output;
2. His great year;
3. The substance of his poetry;
4. The role of imagination;
5. The central theme of his works;
6. The figure of the poet and his task.

1 A portrait of John Keats, 1817.

WARM-UP

1 DISCUSS the questions.
1 What does the title of this poem suggest to you?
2 Have you ever turned to a natural element to express your true feelings?

COMPREHENSION

2 READ the poem and say:
1 who the poet addresses;
2 what he wishes;
3 whether he wishes to live by himself;
4 what the poet could see if he were a bright star;
5 whether the poet really wants to look at a pastoral scene;
6 what the poet describes in lines 11–12;
7 how the poet concludes his poem.

ANALYSIS

3 WORK OUT the rhyme scheme. What kind of sonnet is *Bright Star*?

4 FOCUS on lines 1–8 and do the activities below.
1 Underline all the words and phrases referring to the 'star'. How is it connoted?
2 What device is used in line 3?
3 What is the star compared to in line 4?
4 What is the effect of 'waters' (lines 5–6) on earth?
5 Explain the metaphor in line 7.

5 DECIDE. Where is the turning point of this sonnet? What does the repetition of 'still' underline?

6 THE LAST LINE contains a paradox. Can you explain it?

7 DESCRIBE. What is the theme of the sonnet?

Bright Star

John Keats

1819

In the summer of 1819 Keats fell in love with Fanny Brawne. The poet wrote her several letters and this sonnet, in which he expressed his wish to be with his lover for eternity.

3.9

Bright Star, would I were stedfast[1] as thou art –
Not in lone splendour hung aloft the night[2]
And watching, with eternal lids[3] apart,
Like nature's patient, sleepless Eremite[4],
The moving waters at their priestlike task[5]
Of pure ablution[6] round earth's human shores,
Or gazing on the new soft-fallen mask[7]
Of snow upon the mountains and the moors[8] –
No – yet still stedfast, still unchangeable,
Pillow'd upon my fair love's ripening breast[9],
To feel for ever its soft fall and swell[10],
Awake for ever in a sweet unrest[11],
Still, still to hear her tender-taken breath,
And so live ever – or else swoon to death[12].

1 **stedfast.** Costante.
2 **Not ... night.** Non in solitario splendore sospeso alto nella notte.
3 **lids.** Palpebre.
4 **sleepless Eremite.** Insonne Eremita.
5 **priestlike task.** Dovere sacerdotale (il poeta si riferisce all'alzarsi ed abbassarsi delle acque per le maree).
6 **ablution.** Abluzione.
7 **soft-fallen mask.** Maschera dolcemente caduta.
8 **moors.** Brughiere.
9 **Pillow'd ... breast.** Vorrei riposare sul guanciale del puro seno del mio amore.
10 **swell.** Sollevarsi.
11 **unrest.** Inquietitudine.
12 **else ... to death.** O altrimenti svenire nella morte.

1 Still from the film 'Bright Star' directed by Jane Campion in 2009.

8 DEFINE the role nature plays in this poem.

YOUR TURN

9 DISCUSS. Have you ever experienced a moment of ecstasy either due to love, a religious experience or a sports victory? Can you describe your feelings?

4.15 **Literature**

Percy Bysshe Shelley and the free spirit of nature

Percy Bysshe Shelley's life

Percy Bysshe Shelley, born in Sussex in 1792, was the eldest son of a wealthy, conservative Member of Parliament, and heir to a considerable fortune. In 1810 he was expelled from Oxford University because of his radical pamphlet *The Necessity of Atheism* (1811), challenging the existence of God.

At the age of nineteen, he married sixteen-year-old Harriet Westbrooke. They had two children and moved from place to place, including Ireland, where Shelley made revolutionary propaganda against Catholicism and English rule. In that period, the idealistic drive of the French Revolution had already been exhausted and was followed by a nationalistic wave both in France and in other European countries. Shelley, therefore, lived in an atmosphere of conservatism which was hostile not only to any radical ideas but even to political moderation. He rebelled against existing religions, laws and customs; he became a republican, a vegetarian and an advocate of free love. He later eloped with Mary Wollstonecraft Godwin, the daughter of the radical philosopher William Godwin. They went to Switzerland, where they met Byron. In 1818 the Shelleys left England and went to live in Italy, in voluntary exile, during which much of his best work was composed: *Ode to the West Wind*, written in 1819; *To a Skylark*, written in 1820; *The Cenci* (1819), a verse tragedy; *Prometheus Unbound* (1820), a lyrical drama dealing with the theme of intellectual rebellion, the desire for spiritual liberty and the belief that evil would be overcome by the power of love; *A Defence of Poetry* (1821); and an unfinished essay concerning the importance of poetry.

In 1822 Shelley's intense life was cut short by an accident: while sailing near Livorno, he drowned during a storm. Shelley's grave is in the Protestant Cemetery in Rome.

1

Freedom and love

Almost all works by Shelley show his restless spirit, his refusal of social conventions, political oppression, any form of tyranny, and his faith in a better future. Less disciplined and methodical than Wordsworth or Coleridge, he remains nevertheless a poet of great conviction and powerful musicality, and the author of some of the finest lyric poetry in English literature. Shelley believed strongly in the principles of freedom and love, which he regarded as remedies for the faults and evils of society. Through love, he believed man could overcome any political, moral or social convention.

The role of imagination

Shelley's belief in nature and the function of poetry is mainly expressed in his essay *A Defence of Poetry*; it consists of an exalted defence of poetry as the expression of imagination and understood as revolutionary creativity, seriously meant to change the reality of an increasingly material world.

Nature

The nature Shelley describes is not the real world of Wordsworth's poems, but a beautiful veil that hides the eternal truth of the divine spirit. His approach to nature is also instrumental, since it provides him with images, such as the wind and the clouds and symbols for the creation of his cosmic schemes. Finally, nature represents his favourite refuge from the disappointment and injustice of the ordinary world, the interlocutor of his melancholy dreams and of his hopes for a better future.

The poet's task

The poet, for Shelley, is at the same time a prophet and a titan challenging the cosmos; his task is to help mankind to reach an ideal world where freedom, love and beauty are delivered from their enemies, such as tyranny, destruction and alienation.

2

1 William Powell Frith, *The Lover's Seat: Shelley and Mary Godwin in Old St Pancras Churchyard*, 1877.

2 Louis Édouard Fournier, *The Cremation of Shelley*, 1889. Walker Art Gallery, Liverpool, England.

1 WHILE READING the previous text about Shelley's life and works, make notes under the following headings.

- His political ideas;
- The central themes of his works;
- The role of imagination;
- His view of nature;
- The task of the poet.

WARM-UP

1 **LOOK** at the painting below and answer the questions.

1 What does it represent?
2 What impression do you get of the wind?
3 Why do you think the wind fascinated the Romantic poets?

Ode to the West Wind

Percy Bysshe Shelley

1819

An 'ode' is a lyric composition with an elevated tone, full of archaisms, invocations and personifications. This ode, published with Prometheus Unbound, *identifies Shelley with his heroic Titan. By stealing fire from heaven, Prometheus enabled humanity to found civilisation. In punishment, Zeus chained Prometheus to a mountain and gave him unending torment – an eagle fed from his constantly restored liver. Like Prometheus, Shelley hopes that his fire, a liberal philosophy, will enlighten humanity and liberate it from intellectual and moral imprisonment. He writes about his hopes for the future.*

3.10

O wild West Wind, thou[1] breath of Autumn's being[2],
Thou, from whose unseen presence the leaves dead
Are driven, like ghosts from an enchanter fleeing[3],

Yellow, and black, and pale, and hectic red[4],
Pestilence-stricken multitudes: O thou,
Who chariotest to their dark wintry bed[5]

The wingèd seeds[6], where they lie cold and low,
Each like a corpse within its grave, until
Thine azure sister of the Spring[7] shall blow

Her clarion[8] o'er[9] the dreaming earth and fill
(Driving sweet buds[10] like flocks[11] to feed in air)
With living hues and odours plain and hill[12]:

Wild Spirit, which art[13] moving everywhere;
Destroyer and PRESERVER; hear, oh, hear!

1 **thou.** *Arc.: you.*
2 **being.** Essenza.
3 **fleeing.** Che fuggono.
4 **hectic red.** Del rossore della febbre.
5 **O thou ... bed.** Oh tu che guidi ai loro letti oscuri invernali.
6 **wingèd seeds.** Semi alati.
7 **Thine ... Spring.** La tua sorella azzurra della primavera (cioè il vento Zefiro).
8 **clarion.** Tromba.
9 **o'er.** Forma poetica per *over.*
10 **Driving sweet buds.** Spingendo le dolci gemme.
11 **flocks.** Greggi.
12 **With living ... hill.** Di profumi e di colori vividi pianura e collina.
13 **art.** *Arc.: are.*

1 J.M.W. Turner, *Waves Breaking against the Wind*, 1835. Tate Gallery, London.

Thou on whose stream, mid the steep sky's commotion[14],
Loose[15] clouds like earth's decaying leaves are shed,
Shook from the tangled boughs[16] of Heaven and Ocean,

Angels of rain and lightning[17]: there are spread[18]
On the blue surface of thine aëry surge[19],
Like the bright hair uplifted from the head

Of some fierce Maenad[20], even from the dim verge
Of the horizon to the zenith's height[21],
The locks[22] of the approaching storm. Thou dirge

Of the dying year[23] to which this closing night
Will be the dome[24] of a vast sepulchre,
Vaulted with all thy congregated might[25]

Of vapours[26], from whose solid atmosphere
Black rain, and fire, and hail will burst: oh, hear!

Thou who didst[27] waken from his summer dreams
The blue Mediterranean, where he lay,
Lulled by the coil of his crystàlline streams[28],

Beside a pumice isle in Baiae's bay[29],
And saw in sleep old palaces and towers
Quivering within the wave's intenser day[30],

All overgrown[31] with azure moss[32] and flowers
So sweet, the sense faints picturing them! Thou
For whose path the Atlantic's level powers

Cleave themselves into chasms[33], while far below
The sea-blooms[34] and the oozy[35] woods which wear
The sapless foliage[36] of the ocean, know

Thy voice, and suddenly grow gray with fear,
And tremble and despoil[37] themselves: oh, hear!

14 **mid the steep sky's commotion.** In mezzo al tumulto degli alti cieli.
15 **Loose.** Disperse.
16 **Shook ... boughs.** Scosse dai rami intricati.
17 **Angels ... lightning.** Angeli della pioggia e del fulmine (le nubi).
18 **there ... spread.** Si spargono là.
19 **On ... surge.** Sull'azzurra superficie delle tue onde d'aria.
20 **Of ... Maenad.** Di una fiera Menade; le Menadi erano anche chiamati Baccanti, sacerdotesse del dio greco Dionisio (il latino Bacco).
21 **dim ... height.** Dal limite fioco dell'orizzonte fino alle altezze estreme dello zenit.
22 **locks.** Avvisaglie.
23 **dirge ... year.** Canto funebre dell'anno che muore.
24 **dome.** Cupola.
25 **with all thy congregated might.** Con tutta la tua concentrata potenza.
26 **vapours.** *Lett.*: vapori; *qui*: nuvole.
27 **didst.** *Arc.*: *did.*
28 **Lulled ... streams.** Cullato dal moto dei flutti cristallini.
29 **pumice ... bay.** Isola di pomice del golfo di Baia (località del golfo di Pozzuoli, in Campania).
30 **Quivering ... day.** Tremolanti nella luce più intensa (riflessa dalla superficie) del mare.
31 **overgrown.** Ricoperti.
32 **moss.** Muschio.
33 **For whose path ... chasms.** Per il cui sentiero la possente superficie dell'Atlantico si squarcia in abissi.
34 **sea-blooms.** Fiori del mare.
35 **oozy.** Limacciosi.
36 **sapless foliage.** Il fogliame senza linfa.
37 **despoil.** Spogliano.

COMPREHENSION

2 **READ lines 1–42 and complete the sentences.**

1. The opening three stanzas invoke the ... as a ... over ... , in the ... and under ... and beg it ... the poet in lines 14, 28, 42.
2. In the first stanza the wind as ... and ... (line 14) drives ... ... to ... (line 4) and ... ... to the ... ... (lines 8–12).
3. The second and third stanzas extend the image of ... ... In fact the sky's clouds are like '...' (line 16) and '... of ... and ...' (line 18).
4. In the third stanza the wind penetrates the '...' (line 37) and causes the ... and the ... (line 39) to ... ... (line 42), that is, to shed sea-leaves.
5. In this way the forests implicit in the ... stanza become the '... of Heaven and Ocean' in the ... , and '...' in the third.

4.15 Percy Bysshe Shelley and the free spirit of nature

If I were a dead leaf thou mightest[38] bear;
If I were a swift cloud to fly with thee[39];
A wave to pant[40] beneath thy power, and share

The impulse of thy strength, only less free
Than thou, O uncontrollable! If even
I were as in my boyhood, and could be

The comrade of thy[41] wanderings over Heaven,
As then, when to outstrip thy skiey speed
Scarce seemed a vision[42]; I would ne'er have striven

As thus with thee in prayer[43] in my sore need[44].
Oh, lift me as a wave, a leaf, a cloud!
I fall upon the thorns[45] of life! I bleed!

A heavy weight of hours has chained and bowed
One too like thee: tameless[46], and swift, and proud.

Make me thy lyre, even as the forest is:
What if[47] my leaves are falling like its own!
The tumult of thy mighty harmonies

Will take from both[48] a deep, autumnal tone,
Sweet though in sadness. Be thou, Spirit fierce,
My spirit! Be thou me, impetuous one!

Drive my dead thoughts over the universe
Like withered leaves[49] to quicken a new birth[50]!
And, by the incantation of this verse,

Scatter[51], as from an unextinguished hearth[52]
Ashes and sparks, my words among mankind!
Be through my lips to unawakened earth

The trumpet of a prophecy! O, Wind,
If Winter comes, can Spring be far behind?

38 **mightest.** *Arc.: might.*
39 **thee.** *Arc.: you.*
40 **to pant.** Ansimare.
41 **thy.** *Arc.: your.*
42 **when ... a vision.** Quando superare la tua eterea velocità non sembrava un'illusione.
43 **I would ... prayer.** Non mi rivolgerei a te in preghiera.
44 **sore need.** Estremo bisogno.
45 **thorns.** Spine.
46 **tameless.** Indomito.
47 **What if.** Che importa se.
48 **both.** Entrambi (il poeta e la foresta).
49 **withered leaves.** Foglie appassite.
50 **to quicken a new birth.** Per affrettare una nuova nascita.
51 **Scatter.** Spargi.
52 **unextinguished hearth.** Focolare non spento.

3 THE LAST TWO STANZAS shift from the forest's nature to Shelley's.
1 What are the things the poet says he is not but would like to be?
2 How would you describe the poet's state of mind in the fourth stanza?
3 What requests does he make to the wind in the last stanza?

ANALYSIS

4 THE LANGUAGE employed in this ode is highly figurative.
1 What images can you find in the first two sections? Summarise what the wind brings about.
2 Which semantic area do the images of the third section belong to? What disturbs them?
3 Stanza 4 introduces a new element. What is it? What does the poet have in common with the natural elements described in the previous stanzas?
4 In the last stanza every natural element and the poet have been turned into symbols through a series of similes and metaphors. Identify them. Who would the poet like to identify himself with? What could he do then?

5 THE WIND is vividly personified throughout the poem. Justify this statement quoting from the text.

6 DECIDE. What is the wind a symbol of? What is the message of the whole poem?

7 DISCUSS. The poem leads to a statement of personal, even spiritual, crisis, yet it concludes with great optimism.
1 How is this achieved?
2 Can we now interpret the poem's famous ending beyond its general popular meaning?
3 What figure of the poet emerges?

YOUR TURN

8 DISCUSS. The wind is described as 'destroyer' and 'preserver' by the poet. Does the world we live in today require something similar to this creative/destructive force?

TEXT·BANK 34–35: *SENSE AND SENSIBILITY*

Jane Austen and the theme of love

1 A portrait of Jane Austen, ca 1805.

Jane Austen: an uneventful life

Jane Austen (1775–1817) is acknowledged to be one of the great English novelists. She was born in 1775 in Steventon, Hampshire, a small village in the southwest of England where her father was rector of the local church. The sixth of seven children, she spent her short, uneventful life within the circle of her very close, affectionate family. Her lifelong, inseparable companion was her sister Cassandra, who, like Jane, never married.

She was educated at home by her father, and showed an interest in literature and writing at a very early age. Her earliest writings date from 1787. She went on to produce a large output of prose, and, between 1795 and 1796, she completed *Elinor and Marianne*, which would become the basis of *Sense and Sensibility*, published in 1811, and *First Impressions*, which, later revised, became *Pride and Prejudice*, published in 1813. In 1798 she wrote *Northanger Abbey*, which was published posthumously.

When her father died, Jane, her sister and her mother settled in Chawton, a small country village a few miles from her birthplace. There, Jane produced her most mature works: *Mansfield Park*, begun in 1811 and published in 1814; *Emma*, begun in 1814 and published in 1816; and *Persuasion*, begun in 1815 and published in 1818, after her death. She died in Winchester in 1817, probably of Addison's disease, and was buried in Winchester Cathedral.

All her novels were originally published anonymously; her identity was revealed by her brother Henry, who supervised the publication of *Northanger Abbey* and *Persuasion*, adding a 'Biographical Notice of the Author'. Jane's fame, however, was already well established: among her contemporaries, Sir Walter Scott was one of the first to realise her greatness in his review of *Emma*, where he pointed out her 'exquisite touch which renders ordinary commonplace things and characters interesting'.

The debt to the 18th-century novel

Jane Austen owes much to the 18th-century novelists, from whom she learnt how to give insight into the psychology of characters and the subtleties of ordinary events, like balls, walks, tea parties and visits to friends and neighbours. From Henry Fielding in particular, she derived the omniscient narrator and the technique of bringing the character into existence through dialogue. Her style was also characterised by the use of verbal and situational irony, rather than by open interpretation or comment on the action. Unlike the Augustan writers, however, she restricted her view to the world of the country gentry which she knew best: 'three or four country families,' she said, 'is the very thing to work on.'

The national marriage market

The traditional values of these families – such as property, decorum, money and marriage – provided the basis of the plots and settings of her novels. Austen's novels take place in England, there is no Scotland, Wales or Ireland, and not even the industrial north of England. She writes about the oldest England, based on the possession of land, parks and country houses; in her stories, people from different counties get married as a result of growing social mobility. The marriage market takes place in London, Bath and some seaside resorts where people used to gather and carry out their business. It is in these places that all the troubles of Austen's world occur: gossip, flirtations, seductions, adulteries. This happens because the marriage market has also produced a range of villains: unscrupulous relatives, seducers and social climbers.

Austen's treatment of love

Austen had no place for great passion; her real concern was with people and the analysis of character and conduct. She remained fully committed to the common sense and moral principles of the previous generation but checked them through her own direct observation and spontaneous feeling. Therefore her work is very amusing and, at the same time, deals with the serious matters of love, marriage and parenthood. The happy ending is a romantic element to her novels: they all end in the marriage of the hero and heroine. What makes them interesting is the concentration on the steps through which the protagonists successfully reach this stage in their lives.

Romantic love gives Jane Austen a focus from which individual values can achieve high definition, usually in conflict with the social code that encourages marriages for money and social standing. Her treatment of love and sexual attraction is in line with her general view that strong impulses and intensely emotional states should be regulated, controlled and brought to order by private reflection – not in favour of some abstract standard of reason but to fulfil a social obligation. The heroine's reflection after a crisis or climax is a common feature of the novels because understanding and coming to terms with her private feelings allows her personal judgement to establish itself and secures her own moral autonomy.

1 **READ Jane Austen's biography and provide evidence that her life was uneventful.**

2 **IN PAIRS ask and answer the following questions about Austen's works.**

1. What did Austen learn from the 18th-century novelists?
2. What were the features of her style?
3. What geographical and social setting did she choose for her novels?
4. What themes did she deal with?

4.16 Jane Austen and the theme of love

Pride and Prejudice (1813)

The themes in the novel

- The relationship between the individual and society: how could conflict between the individual's desires and the individual's responsibility to society be resolved?
- The use that the individual makes of freedom and its consequences.
- The contrast between imagination and reason.
- Love, courtship and marriage.

The story

The plot of *Pride and Prejudice* is that of a romantic comedy: it concerns the fortunes of young lovers – their trials, misunderstandings, reversals, triumphs – and ends in happy marriages.

It is set in Longbourn, a small country village in Hertfordshire, where Mr and Mrs Bennet live with their five daughters: Jane, Elizabeth, Mary, Lydia and Kitty. A rich bachelor, Charles Bingley, and his two sisters arrive to rent a large estate in the neighbourhood, called Netherfield Park. After a series of balls and parties that bring the members of this little society together, Mr Bingley falls in love with Jane, and his best friend, the wealthy landowner Fitzwilliam Darcy, begins to feel attracted to Elizabeth. She, however, has deliberately cultivated a dislike towards him for his initial rejection of her as a dancing partner and for his snobbish behaviour. When Mr Darcy declares his love, he cannot help showing contempt for her inferior social position; thus Elizabeth rejects him, accuses him of separating her sister and Bingley, and of ill-treating George Wickham, a young officer who was the son of Darcy's former steward. Darcy writes her a letter where he reveals that Wickham is an unscrupulous adventurer. Meanwhile, Wickham elopes with Lydia. Darcy traces them and organises their marriage thus showing Elizabeth her 'prejudice' was unjustified. She accepts Darcy's renewed proposal in spite of the opposition of Lady Catherine De Bourgh, Darcy's arrogant aunt. Bingley returns and becomes engaged to Jane, so the novel ends with the happy marriages of the two couples.

Elizabeth and Darcy

The heroine, Elizabeth Bennet, and the hero, Mr Darcy, have great qualities but also great weaknesses. They appear to have been conceived and developed in critical antithesis to the conventional heroes and heroines of the sentimental novels of the period. Darcy knows the principles of correct conduct, but is selfish and unsociable. Elizabeth has a lively mind, one of the qualities that attracts Darcy to her; she is capable of complex impressions and ideas. She has a strong spirit of independence: she refuses to take on the roles which her family or socially superior people try to impose on her. Both Elizabeth and Darcy set out with an imperfect understanding of themselves and each other. She accuses him of pride and he accuses her of prejudice. These accusations are partly just, but they also work in reverse: she is proud, and her pride blinds her to his virtues; he is prejudiced by his upbringing and is disgusted by the vulgar behaviour of Elizabeth's mother and younger sisters.

1

Not simply a love story

The novel is not simply a love story because through Austen's irony it develops economic, sociological and philosophical themes. There are elements of social realism, dealing with marriage as a means of social mobility of the bourgeoisie and the aristocracy during the era of the Napoleonic wars and at the beginning of the Industrial Revolution. The author seems interested in the balance between the social and economic need of securing a marriage and the desire to follow idealism and feeling. Through the character of Elizabeth, her romantic independence and individualism, Austen tells the struggle to find one's place within the conservative social institution of marriage. The marriage between Darcy and Elizabeth reveals the characteristics that make a marriage successful. Feeling cannot be brought on by appearances and must gradually develop between the two people as they get to know each other. The message of the novel seems to be the search for a balance through the gradual change of the main traits of the characters' personalities that will lead to a reconciliation of the themes that they represent.

1 The novels of Jane Austen have been adapted in a great number of films and television series. *Pride and Prejudice* has been the most reproduced of her works, with six films; the 2005 adaptation, seen here, was directed by Joe Wright, starring Keira Knightley, Donald Sutherland and Dame Judi Dench.

3 **ANSWER these questions about *Pride and Prejudice*.**

1. What are the central themes of the novel?
2. Are Elizabeth and Darcy the typical heroine and hero of a sentimental novel? Why or why not?
3. Why is the novel not simply a love story?
4. What makes a marriage successful, according to Austen?

Mr and Mrs Bennet

Jane Austen

Pride and Prejudice (1813)
Chapter 1

These are the first pages of the novel – perhaps Jane Austen's most quoted lines – where the Bennet family is introduced.

3.11

It is a truth universally acknowledged[1], that a single man in possession of a good fortune, must be in want[2] of a wife. However little known the feelings or views of such a man may be on his first entering a neighbourhood[3], this truth is so well fixed in the minds of the surrounding families, that he is considered as the rightful property of some one or other of their daughters.

'My dear Mr Bennet,' said his lady to him one day, 'have you heard that Netherfield Park is let[4] at last?'

Mr Bennet replied that he had not.

'But it is,' returned she; 'for Mrs Long has just been here, and she told me all about it.'

Mr Bennet made no answer.

'Do not you want to know who has taken it?' cried his wife impatiently.

'*You* want to tell me, and I have no objection to hearing it.'

This was invitation enough.

'Why, my dear, you must know, Mrs Long says that Netherfield is taken by a young man of large fortune from the north of England; that he came down on Monday in a chaise and four[5] to see the place, and was so much delighted with it that he agreed with Mr Morris immediately; that he is to take possession before Michaelmas[6], and some of his servants are to be in the house by the end of next week.'

'What is his name?'

'Bingley.'

'Is he married or single?'

'Oh! Single, my dear, to be sure! A single man of large fortune; four or five thousand a year. What a fine thing for our girls!'

'How so? How can it affect them?'

'My dear Mr Bennet,' replied his wife, 'how can you be so tiresome[7]! You must know that I am thinking of his marrying one of them.'

'Is that his design in settling[8] here?'

'Design! Nonsense, how can you talk so! But it is very likely[9] that he *may* fall in love with one of them, and therefore you must visit him as soon as he comes.'

'I see no occasion for that. You and the girls may go, or you may send them by themselves, which perhaps will be still better, for as you are as handsome as any of them, Mr Bingley might like you the best of the party[10].'

'My dear, you flatter me[11]. I certainly *have* had my share of beauty, but I do not pretend to be any thing extraordinary now. When a woman has five grown-up daughters, she ought to give over[12] thinking of her own beauty.'

'In such cases, a woman has not often much beauty to think of.'

'But, my dear, you must indeed go and see Mr Bingley when he comes into the neighbourhood.'

'It is more than I engage for[13], I assure you.'

WARM-UP

1 DISCUSS. What do you associate the terms 'pride' and 'prejudice' with? How do you think they will be developed in the novel?

2 Illustration of Mrs Bennet from *Pride and Prejudice* by Hugh Thomson, 1894.

1 **acknowledged.** Riconosciuta.
2 **in want.** Alla ricerca.
3 **neighbourhood.** Comunità, società locale.
4 **let.** Affittato.
5 **in a chaise and four.** In una carrozza a quattro cavalli.
6 **before Michaelmas.** Prima del giorno di S. Michele (29 settembre).
7 **tiresome.** Irritante, noioso.
8 **his design in settling.** Il suo proposito nello stabilirsi.
9 **likely.** Probabile.
10 **party.** Gruppo.
11 **you flatter me.** Mi lusinghi.
12 **to give over.** Rinunciare, smettere.
13 **I engage for.** Possa ingegnarmi a fare.

4.16 Jane Austen and the theme of love

'But consider your daughters. Only think what an establishment it would be for one of them. Sir William and Lady Lucas are determined to go, merely on that account[14], for in general you know they visit no new comers. Indeed you must go, for it will be impossible for *us* to visit him, if you do not.'

'You are over scrupulous surely. I dare say Mr Bingley will be very glad to see you; and I will send a few lines by you to assure him of my hearty consent to his marrying which ever he chooses of the girls; though I must throw in[15] a good word for my little Lizzy.'

'I desire you will do no such thing. Lizzy is not a bit better than the others; and I am sure she is not half so handsome as Jane, nor half so good humoured as Lydia. But you are always giving *her* the preference.'

'They have none of them much to recommend them,' replied he; 'they are all silly and ignorant like other girls; but Lizzy has something more of quickness[16] than her sisters.'

'Mr Bennet, how can you abuse your own children in such a way? You take delight in vexing me[17]. You have no compassion on my poor nerves.'

'You mistake me, my dear. I have a high respect for your nerves. They are my old friends. I have heard you mention them[18] with consideration these twenty years at least.'

'Ah! You do not know what I suffer.'

'But I hope you will get over it, and live to see many young men of four thousand a year come into the neighbourhood.'

'It will be no use to us, if twenty such should come since you will not visit them.'

'Depend upon it[19], my dear, that when there are twenty, I will visit them all.'

Mr Bennet was so odd a mixture of quick parts[20], sarcastic humour, reserve, and caprice, that the experience of three and twenty years had been insufficient to make his wife understand his character. *Her* mind was less difficult to develop. She was a woman of mean understanding, little information, and uncertain temper. When she was discontented she fancied herself nervous. The business of her life was to get her daughters married; its solace[21] was visiting and news.

14 **merely on that account.** Solo per quel motivo.
15 **throw in.** Aggiungere.
16 **quickness.** Prontezza, vivacità.
17 **vexing me.** Contrariarmi, irritarmi.
18 **mention them.** Nominarli.
19 **Depend upon it.** Puoi contarci.
20 **quick parts.** Vivacità, impulsività.
21 **solace.** Consolazione, sollievo.

COMPREHENSION

2 READ the extract and answer the following questions.

1. What does Mrs Bennet want Mr Bennet to do?
2. How does he react?
3. What is Mrs Bennet's real worry?
4. How many daughters have they got?
5. Who is Mr Bennet's favourite? Why?

ANALYSIS

3 POINT OUT what the narrative mode is and the kind of narrator used.

4 CONSIDER the tone of the opening sentence.

1. How would you define it?
2. Analyse the terms of the sentence in lines 1–2 to see how Jane Austen's irony works:
   - 'truth'. What does this term imply?
   - 'universally acknowledged'. By whom?
   - 'a single man'. Why single?
   - 'in possession'. What does the term imply legally?
   - 'a good fortune'. How much is 'good'?
   - 'must be in want of a wife'. Does he lack, need or want a wife?
3. Briefly summarise what the author means.
4. Underline other examples of irony in the extract.

5 FOCUS on the characters of Mr and Mrs Bennet and suggest some adjectives to define both of them.

6 WRITE down the main themes introduced in the passage.

7 DISCUSS. Mr and Mrs Bennet provide the first 'example of marriage' in the novel.

1. What do you think their marriage was based on?
2. Do they provide an example of a well-matched couple?

YOUR TURN

8 DISCUSS. The opening chapter of the novel gives some insights into the characters' social class, their habits and their values. Find examples in the extract, and say if modern families have the same worries about their children.

WARM-UP

1 DISCUSS in pairs.

1 Do people still propose nowadays?
2 If so, how does it usually happen? Is it just a man's job?

Darcy proposes to Elizabeth

Jane Austen

Pride and Prejudice (1813)
Chapter XXXIV

The following passage represents a turning point in the novel. It deals with the heroine, Elizabeth Bennet, who has taken a prejudiced dislike to the hero, Mr Darcy, a wealthy aristocrat. Though he considers Elizabeth socially inferior, Darcy falls in love with her and finally decides to propose marriage to her.

3.12

After a silence of several minutes he came towards her in an agitated manner, and thus began:

'In vain have I struggled. It will not do. My feelings will not be repressed. You must allow me to tell you how ardently I admire and love you.'

Elizabeth's astonishment was beyond expression. She stared[1], coloured, doubted, and was silent. This he considered sufficient encouragement, and the avowal[2] of all that he felt and had long felt for her, immediately followed. He spoke well, but there were feelings besides those of the heart to be detailed[3], and he was not more eloquent on the subject of tenderness than of pride. His sense of her inferiority – of its being a degradation – of the family obstacles which judgment had always opposed to inclination, were dwelt on[4] with a warmth which seemed due to the consequence he was wounding[5], but was very unlikely to recommend his suit.

In spite of her deeply-rooted dislike, she could not be insensible to the compliment of such a man's affection, and though her intentions did not vary for an instant, she was at first sorry for the pain he was to receive; till, roused to resentment by his subsequent language, she lost all compassion in anger. She tried, however, to compose herself[6] to answer him with patience, when he should have done[7]. He concluded with representing to her the strength of that attachment which, in spite of all his endeavours[8], he had found impossible to conquer; and with expressing his hope that it would now be rewarded[9] by her acceptance of his hand. As he said this, she could easily see that he had no doubt of a favourable answer. He *spoke* of apprehension and anxiety, but his countenance[10] expressed real security. Such a circumstance could only exasperate farther, and when he ceased, the colour rose into her cheeks, and she said:

'In such cases as this, it is, I believe, the established[11] mode to express a sense of obligation for the sentiments avowed, however unequally they may be returned. It is natural that obligation should be felt, and if I could *feel* gratitude, I would now thank you. But I cannot – I have never desired your good opinion, and you have certainly bestowed[12] it most unwillingly...'

1 **She stared.** Sgranò gli occhi.
2 **avowal.** Dichiarazione.
3 **detailed.** Descritti, precisati.
4 **dwelt on.** Sottolineati.
5 **wounding.** Soffrendo.
6 **to compose herself.** Di calmarsi, di ricomporsi.
7 **done.** *Qui*: finito.
8 **endeavours.** Sforzi.
9 **rewarded.** Ricompensato.
10 **countenance.** Espressione del volto.
11 **established.** Convenzionale.
12 **bestowed.** Concessa, donata.

1 Keira Knightley and Matthew Macfadyen in the film version of *Pride and Prejudice* directed by Joe Wright in 2005.

COMPREHENSION

2 AS YOU READ the first part of the passage, note down:

- the characters involved;
- the situation;
- the expressions referring to the hero's manners;
- the expressions referring to the heroine's various feelings;
- the reasons behind the hero's struggle against his own feelings.

Mr Darcy, who was leaning[13] against the mantle-piece[14] with his eyes fixed on her face, seemed to catch her words with no less resentment than surprise. His complexion became pale with anger, and the disturbance of his mind was visible in every feature. He was struggling for the appearance of composure, and would not open his lips, till he believed himself to have attained it. The pause was to Elizabeth's feelings dreadful. At length, in a voice of forced calmness, he said,

'And this is all the reply which I am to have the honour of expecting! I might, perhaps, wish to be informed why, with so little *endeavour* at civility[15], I am thus rejected. But it is of small importance.'

'I might as well enquire,' replied she, 'why with so evident a design of offending and insulting me, you chose to tell me that you liked me against your will, against your reason, and even against your character? Was not this some excuse for incivility, if I *was* uncivil? But I have other provocations. You know I have. Had not my own feelings decided against you, had they been indifferent, or had they even been favourable, do you think that any consideration would tempt me to accept the man, who has been the means of ruining, perhaps for ever, the happiness of a most beloved sister?'

As she pronounced these words, Mr Darcy changed colour; but the emotion was short, and he listened without attempting to interrupt her while she continued.

'I have every reason in the world to think ill[16] of you. No motive can excuse the unjust and ungenerous part you acted *there*. You dare not, you cannot deny that you have been the principal, if not the only means of dividing them from each other, of exposing one to the censure of the world for caprice and instability, the other to its derision for disappointed hopes, and involving them both in misery of the acutest kind.'

She paused, and saw with no slight indignation that he was listening with an air which proved him wholly unmoved by any feeling of remorse. He even looked at her with a smile of affected incredulity.

'Can you deny that you have done it?' she repeated.

With assumed[17] tranquillity he then replied, 'I have no wish of denying that I did every thing in my power to separate my friend from your sister, or that I rejoice in my success. Towards *him* I have been kinder than towards myself.'

Elizabeth disdained the appearance of noticing this civil reflection, but its meaning did not escape, nor was it likely to conciliate her.

'But it is not merely this affair,' she continued, 'on which my dislike is founded. Long before it had taken place, my opinion of you was decided. Your character was unfolded[18] in the recital[19] which I received many months ago from Mr Wickham. On this subject, what can you have to say? In what imaginary act of friendship can you here defend yourself? or under what misrepresentation, can you here impose[20] upon others?'

'You take an eager interest in that gentleman's concerns,' said Darcy in a less tranquil tone, and with a heightened colour.

'Who that knows what his misfortunes have been, can help feeling an interest in him?'

'His misfortunes!' repeated Darcy contemptuously[21]; 'Yes, his misfortunes have been great indeed.'

'And of your infliction,' cried Elizabeth with energy. 'You have reduced him to his present state of poverty, comparative poverty. You have withheld the advantages, which you must know to have been designed for him. You have deprived the best years of his life, of that independence which was no less his due than his desert[22]. You have done all

1 English School, *Pride and Prejudice*'s Elizabeth and Mr Darcy, 20th century.

COMPREHENSION

3 READ the text to the end and answer the following questions.

1 Does Elizabeth accept Darcy's proposal?
2 What is his reaction?
3 Why does Elizabeth reject him?
4 What does Darcy accuse Elizabeth of?
5 What does Elizabeth accuse Darcy of?

13 **was leaning.** Era appoggiato.
14 **mantle-piece.** Mensola del caminetto.
15 **civility.** Educazione, cortesia.
16 **ill.** Male.
17 **assumed.** Simulata.
18 **unfolded.** Rivelato, svelato.
19 **recital.** Racconto.
20 **impose.** Approfittare di.
21 **contemptuously.** Sdegnosamente.
22 **desert.** Merito, ciò che gli spettava.

this! and yet you can treat the mention of his misfortunes with contempt and ridicule.'

'And this,' cried Darcy, as he walked with quick steps across the room, 'is your opinion of me! This is the estimation in which you hold me! I thank you for explaining it so fully. My faults, according to this calculation, are heavy indeed! But perhaps,' added he, stopping in his walk, and turning towards her, 'these offences might have been overlooked, had not your pride been hurt by my honest confession of the scruples that had long prevented my forming any serious design. These bitter accusations might have been suppressed, had I with greater policy[23] concealed my struggles, and flattered you into the belief of my being impelled by unqualified[24], unalloyed[25] inclination; by reason, by reflection, by every thing. But disguise of every sort is my abhorrence. Nor am I ashamed of the feelings I related. They were natural and just. Could you expect me to rejoice in the inferiority of your connections? To congratulate myself on the hope of relations, whose condition in life is so decidedly beneath my own?'

Elizabeth felt herself growing more angry every moment; yet she tried to the utmost to speak with composure when she said,

'You are mistaken, Mr Darcy, if you suppose that the mode of your declaration affected me in any other way, than as it spared me[26] the concern which I might have felt in refusing you, had you behaved in a more gentleman-like manner.'

She saw him start[27] at this, but he said nothing, and she continued,

'You could not have made me the offer of your hand in any possible way that would have tempted me to accept it.'

Again his astonishment was obvious; and he looked at her with an expression of mingled incredulity and mortification. She went on.

'From the very beginning, from the first moment I may almost say, of my acquaintance with you, your manners impressing me with the fullest belief of your arrogance, your conceit[28], and your selfish disdain of the feelings of others, were such as to form that ground-work[29] of disapprobation, on which succeeding events have built so immovable a dislike; and I had not known you a month before I felt that you were the last man in the world whom I could ever be prevailed on[30] to marry.'

23 **policy.** Accortezza, diplomazia.
24 **unqualified.** Incondizionata.
25 **unalloyed.** Pura.
26 **it spared me.** Mi ha risparmiato.
27 **start.** Trasalire.
28 **conceit.** Presunzione.
29 **ground-work.** Fondamento.
30 **prevailed on.** Persuasa.

2 Matthew Macfadyen and Keira Knightley as Mr Darcy and Elizabeth Bennet in the film 'Pride & Prejudice', directed by Joe Wright in 2005.

ANALYSIS

4 DECIDE. What kind of narrator is there? From whose point of view is the story mainly told?

5 TICK as appropriate. What is the effect of this choice?
- ☐ It subtly mitigates Darcy's offensive remarks.
- ☐ It gains control of the tone, guiding the reader to a correct interpretation.
- ☐ It prevents Darcy from making a fool of himself with his own words.
- ☐ It sustains the tension, mingling dialogue and narration.

6 CONSIDER the social condition of women at the beginning of the 19th century. What particular significance did the term 'proposal' acquire in that context?

7 WRITING. This passage provides a good insight into the hero's and heroine's characters. Write two short paragraphs about them.

8 CHAPTER XXXIV marks the worst moment in the relationship between Elizabeth and Darcy, and also clarifies the choice of the title of the novel. Explain it providing examples from the text.

YOUR TURN

9 DISCUSS. Elizabeth's rejection of Darcy acquires particular significance if one takes into account the social position of women at the beginning of the 19th century. Try to explain Jane Austen's aim.

10 DISCUSS. The novel actually ends with the marriage between Darcy and Elizabeth. Do you think it will be a happy marriage?

4.17 Two Films About... *Pride and Prejudice*

WARM-UP

1 DISCUSS in pairs.

1. What is your idea of a 'perfect' marriage?
2. Why do you think Austen's books continue to be made into successful films?

Pride and Prejudice

Directed by Simon Langton; UK 1995.
With Jennifer Ehle (Elizabeth Bennet); Colin Firth (Mr Darcy).

In this six-episode television adaptation of Jane Austen's novel, Elizabeth Bennett is a strong-willed but sensible young woman with four sisters, a loving father and a mother who is anxious to marry her daughters to wealthy young gentlemen. At a local ball, Elizabeth meets a wealthy young man, Mr Fitzwilliam Darcy, who is arrogant, cold and rude. As her eldest sister, Jane, falls in love with Mr Darcy's best friend, Mr Bingley, and her youngest sister, Lydia, flirts with anyone in a military uniform, Elizabeth learns that not all is quite as it seems and that Mr Darcy might not be so disagreeable after all.

What about accuracy?

This BBC dramatisation of *Pride and Prejudice* has turned many characters into caricatures. In fact, much of the comedy in the film is linked to the relationship between the most rounded characters and caricatures, as, for example, when Elizabeth is humiliated by her family's behaviour at the town ball. The character that has been expanded significantly is Colin Firth's Mr Darcy. His transformation is clear in the book, but the reader is left to imagine the details of how it took place. This television adaptation tries to fill in these gaps.

Pride & Prejudice

Directed by Joe Wright; UK 2005.
With Keira Knightley (Elizabeth Bennet); Matthew Macfadyen (Mr Darcy).

'Pride & Prejudice' depicts the romance between the smart, at times tempestuous and at times vulnerable, Elizabeth Bennet and the handsome Mr Darcy. At their first meeting, they form unfavorable impressions of each other but, as events continually bring them together, their opinions change and they fall in love with each other.

What about accuracy?

The book contains numerous subplots, which have been eliminated in the film version. For example, the relationship between Mr Bingley and Jane Bennet remains but in a condensed form, and only because it is necessary to the central love story. Most of the rest of *Pride and Prejudice* is left intact, and much of Austen's dialogue has been preserved.

4.18 **Cultural Issues**

Marriage

WARM-UP

1 **DISCUSS.** What is proper love? Is it intelligent love? What qualities and behaviour lead to a happy marriage?

2 **LOOK** at the pictures. What do they show? What do they have in common?

Who invented marriage?

The oldest historical record of laws concerning marriage dates back to the Mesopotamians and is to be found on the tablet called Codex Hammurabi.

Cultures around the world have their own theories on why this institution was created. Evolutionists argue that the need for survival was the main reason behind marriages coming into being. Other theories say that the institution was born to moderate the competition between men for access to women. Today, this institution still survives around the world and is controlled by local governments and cultures.

1

2

3

4

5

6

1 A traditional Jewish wedding ceremony.

2 A Russian Orthodox wedding ceremony in Ukraine.

3 A Pakistani bride's hands are adorned with henna during the *mehndi* ceremony a few days before her wedding.

4 A Japanese couple perform the ritual of drinking nine cups of sake during their wedding at a Shinto shrine.

5 Male guests wear traditional Highland outfits to a wedding in Scotland.

6 A Russian bridal couple releases a pair of white doves in St Petersburg.

3 **DISCUSS.**

1 Is marriage still popular in your country?
2 At what age do people get married?
3 What is the wedding ceremony like?

Brick Lane (2003)

Monica Ali (1967–)
Monica Ali was born in Dhaka, Bangladesh, in 1967 to a Bangladeshi father and an English mother. She was raised in Bolton, England, and graduated with a degree in Philosophy, Politics and Economics at the University of Oxford. She lives in South London with her husband Simon and their two children. *Brick Lane* (2003) is her first novel. It was adapted into a film in 2007.

The story
The focus of the novel is the Bangladeshi community in Tower Hamlets, London, where Brick Lane is. The protagonist is Nazneen, whose arranged marriage to Chanu, a man twenty years older, brings her at the age of eighteen from the rice fields of rural Bangladesh to England. Nazneen has always known that it is pointless to 'kick against fate', unlike her younger sister Hasina, who broke all the rules and ran away from her family for love. At first, Nazneen seldom leaves her flat, but when she does, she begins to observe London with the perplexed interest of an outsider.

Throughout the novel, the trials of Nazneen's life in Brick Lane are cut through by letters from home, from her sister Hasina, who was forced to leave her violent husband and try to survive on her own as a factory worker, a prostitute and a maid. At the same time, Ali describes how Nazneen's arranged marriage is threatened in a culture in which a woman is encouraged to grow beyond it.

The style
The story in *Brick Lane* is told mainly in the third person from Nazneen's point of view. Nazneen is not a 'complete' person when she arrives in London; Ali's prose grows with her, gaining in depth and complexity.

The book has a humane sense of comedy that still allows the protagonists room to live and breathe, since Ali never leaves the characters with only their absurd aspects to define them.

1 Poster for the film 'Brick Lane' directed by Sarah Gavron in 2007.

Any wife is better than no wife

Monica Ali

Brick Lane (2003)
Chapter 1

The following extract deals with one of the main themes of the novel: the role of fate in shaping the individual's destiny. At sixteen, Hasina, Nazneen's sister, eloped with a man for a marriage based on love. Unlike her, Nazneen did not protest to an arranged marriage to Chanu, a man who lived in London, where he had been working for two decades.

3.13

It worried her that Hasina kicked against fate. No good could come of it. Not a single person could say so. But then if you really looked into it, thought about it more deeply, how could you be sure that Hasina was not simply following her fate? If fate cannot be changed, no matter how you struggle against it, then perhaps Hasina was fated to run away with Malek. Maybe she struggled against *that*, and *that* was what she could not alter. Oh, you think it would be simple, having made the decision long, long ago, to be at the beck and call of fate[1], but how to know which way it is calling you? And

COMPREHENSION

1 **READ the extract and answer the following questions.**
1. What was Nazneen thinking about?
2. What was Chanu like?
3. What did he think of his wife? How did Nazneen know that?
4. What had Nazneen expected when she married her husband?

1 **to be ... of fate.** Essere agli ordini del destino.

there was each and every day to be got through. If Chanu came home this evening and found the place untidy and the spices not even ground[2], could she put her hands like so and say, 'Don't ask me why nothing is prepared, it was not I who decided it, it was fate.' A wife could reasonably be beaten for a lesser offence.

Chanu had not beaten her yet. He showed no signs of wanting to beat her. In fact, he was kind and gentle. Even so, it was foolish to assume he would never beat her. He thought she was a 'good worker' (she had overheard him on the telephone). He would be shocked if she lapsed[3].

'She is an unspoilt girl. From the village.'

She had got up one night to fetch[4] a glass of water. It was one week since they married. She had gone to bed and he was still up, talking on the telephone as she stood outside the door.

'No,' said Chanu. 'I would not say so. Not beautiful, but not so ugly either. The face is broad[5], big forehead. Eyes are a bit too close together.'

Nazneen put her hand up to her head. It was true.

The forehead was large. But she had never thought of her eyes being too close.

'Not tall. Not short. Around five foot two. Hips are a bit narrow[6] but wide enough, I think, to carry children. All things considered, I am satisfied. Perhaps when she gets older she'll grow a beard on her chin[7], but now she is only eighteen. And a blind uncle is better than no uncle. I waited too long to get a wife.'

Narrow hips! You could wish for such a fault[8], Nazneen said to herself, thinking of the rolls of fat that hung low from Chanu's stomach. It would be possible to tuck[9] all your hundred pens and pencils under those rolls and keep them safe and tight[10]. You could stuff[11] a book or two up there as well. If your spindle legs[12] could take the weight.

'What's more, she is a good worker. Cleaning and cooking and all that. The only complaint I could make is she can't put my files in order, because she has no English. I don't complain though. As I say, a girl from the village: totally unspoilt.'

Chanu went on talking but Nazneen crept away[13], back to bed. A blind uncle is better than no uncle. Her husband had a proverb for everything. Any wife is better than no wife. Something is better than nothing. What had she imagined? That he was in love with her? That he was grateful because she, young and graceful, had accepted him? That in sacrificing herself to him, she was owed[14] something? Yes. Yes. She realized in a stinging rush[15] she had imagined all these things. Such a foolish girl. Such high notions. What self-regard[16].

2 **ground.** Macinate.
3 **if she lapsed.** Se lei avesse mancato (di svolgere il suo lavoro).
4 **to fetch.** Per andare a prendere.
5 **broad.** Larga.
6 **Hips are a bit narrow.** I fianchi sono un po' stretti.
7 **she'll grow ... chin.** Le crescerà la barba sul mento.
8 **fault.** Difetto.
9 **to tuck.** Infilare.
10 **safe and tight.** Sane e salve.
11 **stuff.** Infilare.
12 **spindle legs.** Gambe lunghe e sottili.
13 **crept away.** Scivolò via furtivamente.
14 **she was owed.** Le spettasse.
15 **stinging rush.** Impeto doloroso.
16 **What self-regard.** Che considerazione di sé.

ANALYSIS

2 **DECIDE.** How is the text narrated?

3 **DESCRIBE.** How are the characters presented?

4 **FIND** examples of Ali's comic touch.

5 **EXPLAIN.** How is the theme of marriage developed?

YOUR TURN

6 **DISCUSS.** How do Elizabeth Bennet and Nazneen compare as regards marriage?

7 **DISCUSS.** Would you like to get married or would you prefer to live together with your partner unmarried?

8 **DISCUSS.** How would you feel about an arranged marriage? Can you see any advantages in it?

FCE Writing – Part 2

9 **A REVIEW.** This notice recently appeared in your school magazine.

We will give a prize to the best review of *Brick Lane* by Monica Ali, to appear in next month's school magazine. Compare Nazneen's view of marriage with the view of a classical character, like Elizabeth Bennet from Jane Austen's *Pride and Prejudice*. Also give your own views on traditional marriage, living together outside of marriage and arranged marriages.

Write your review in 140–190 words.

4 Overview

Test what you know

1 LIST the revolutions of the last decades of the 18th century.

2 SAY if the sentences are true or false. Correct the false ones.

1. The new sensibility argued for the supremacy of reason. T F
2. The new artists and men of letters were interested in the lofty subjects of Classicism and the town. T F
3. Britain declared war against Napoleon in order to extend its dominions. T F
4. Napoleon was defeated at Trafalgar. T F
5. During the Luddite riots eleven people were killed. T F
6. The first three decades of the 19th century were a period of reforms. T F

Can you do it?

3 TRACE the causes of the American Revolution.

4 EXPLAIN the importance of 1776 in American history.

5 STATE the cause and effects of the sublime as explained by Edmund Burke.

6 EXPLAIN the meaning of 'Gothic'. Then describe the main features of the Gothic novel and its aim.

7 DESCRIBE the narrative structure of the novel *Frankenstein*.

8 READ the lines (88–111) from 'Tintern Abbey' by William Wordsworth, which is one of the best expression of the poet's thoughts, and do the activities below.

1. What is the poet's response to the natural world? What does the word 'music' (line 91) suggest?
2. What religious belief emerges in these lines?
3. The poet is now an adult man. What is his relationship with nature?
4. What Romantic conception does the poet suggest in lines 106–107?
5. How does the section end?

... For I have learned
To look on nature, not as in the hour
Of thoughtless youth[1]; but hearing oftentimes
The still, sad music of humanity,
Nor harsh nor grating, though of ample power
To chasten and subdue[2]. And I have felt
A presence that disturbs me with the joy
Of elevated thoughts; a sense sublime
Of something far more deeply interfused[3],
Whose dwelling[4] is the light of setting[5] suns,
And the round ocean and the living air,
And the blue sky, and in the mind of man:
A motion and a spirit, that impels[6]
All thinking things, all objects of all thought,
And rolls through[7] all things. Therefore am I still
A lover of the meadows[8] and the woods,
And mountains; and of all that we behold
From this green earth; of all the mighty world
Of eye, and ear, both what they half create,
And what perceive; well pleased to recognise
In nature and the language of the sense,
The anchor of my purest thoughts, the nurse,
The guide, the guardian of my heart, and soul
Of all my moral being.

1 **in the ... youth.** Al tempo della giovinezza spensierata.
2 **Nor ... subdue.** Né aspra né stridente benché ampiamente capace di calmare e dominare (le passioni).
3 **interfused.** Infuso.
4 **dwelling.** Dimora.
5 **setting.** Al tramonto.
6 **that impels.** Che muove, spinge.
7 **And rolls through.** E percorre.
8 **meadows.** Prati.

9 HIGHLIGHT the way Byron deals with nature and compare it to Wordsworth's and Coleridge's styles.

10 STATE Shelley's most important themes, his thoughts about nature and his concept about the poet's task.

11 DESCRIBE the setting, themes and the contrast between the hero and the heroine in *Pride and Prejudice*.

Oral test

12 IMAGINE your teacher asks you the following questions in an oral test. For each question, prepare a one-minute turn.

1. Why did factory owners decide to create a new work force composed of children?
2. What symbols and metaphors does Blake use in his poem 'London' to convey his view of industrialisation?
3. Who and what influenced Mary Shelley in her novel *Frankenstein*?
4. What were the key ideas of English Romanticism?
5. How did Wordsworth interpret the relationship between man and nature?
6. Who is the poet, according to Wordsworth?
7. What are the differences and similarities between *The Rime of the Ancient Mariner* and traditional medieval ballads?
8. What features characterise the 'Byronic hero'?
9. What is the central theme of Keats's poetry?

A Two-Faced Reality

Specification 5 | Homepage

Top News

1837 Queen Victoria comes to the throne

Top Issue

Angels or pioneers?

Most Popular News

1871 Darwin publishes *The Descent of Man*

Spotlight

1837–39 Charles Dickens writes *Oliver Twist*

The Arts

The Pre-Raphaelite Brotherhood

Cinema

See the life of Oscar Wilde on screen

Mapping History

British imperial trading routes

EXPLORE THE CULTURE

Literature | History | Society | The Arts | Science | Two Films About... | Cultural Issues

5.1 **History**

The first half of Queen Victoria's reign

WARM-UP

1 **LOOK** at the pictures. What Victorian issues do they hint at?

2 **READ** the Q&A text.

Queen Victoria's reign was the longest in the history of England. She came to the throne in 1837 and died in 1901.

Q Why did the nation identify with the Queen?

A Her exemplary way of life and her strict code of behaviour made her beloved, especially by the middle classes, who shared her moral and religious views.

Q What were the first years of Victoria's reign like?

A It was a period of unprecedented material progress, imperial expansion and also one of political developments and social reforms, like the Ten Hours Act of 1847, which limited working hours to ten a day for all labourers.

Q What made these achievements possible?

A The merits of these achievements partly belonged to the queen, who, in marked contrast with other European monarchs, reigned constitutionally, avoiding the storm of revolution which spread all over Europe in 1848. She never overruled Parliament and became a mediator above party politics.

Q What were the main political parties during her reign?

A During her reign, the two main political parties were the Liberals (ex-Whigs) and the Conservatives, who alternated in government. The Liberals promoted a strong campaign for free trade that led to the repeal of the Corn Laws.

Q What were the Corn Laws?

A They were laws which maintained the price of corn artificially high to protect the landed interests.

Q Were there any working-class movements?

A Between 1838 and 1848 'Chartism' played an important role, drawing up the 'People's Charter' in 1838, which called for social reforms and the extension of the right to vote to all male adults.

1 The 'Penny Black', the world's first adhesive postage stamp.

2 The royal family at Osborne, 26th May 1857.

3 The Great Chartist Meeting on Kennington Common, April 10th, 1848, photograph by William Kilburn.

Q Was Chartism successful?

A Its demands were refused by the House of Commons, and the movement slowly died.

Q What about foreign policy?

A England was ready to fight wars to protect its trading routes. The First Opium War against China, in 1839–42, gained Britain access to five Chinese ports and the control of Hong Kong. Britain also supported Turkey during the Crimean War, between 1853 and 1856. There was also a dangerous crisis in India where native soldiers threatened British rule in 1857.

4 A satirical drawing by George Cruikshank illustrating the behaviour of the Whigs and the Tories during the creation of the Reform Act of 1832.

3 **IN PAIRS cover the answers (As) in the text above. Take turns asking and answering the questions (Qs) using the information that you have read.**

4 **MATCH the words in column A with those in column B to form key terms about the first half of Victoria's reign.**

A		B	
1	imperial	**A**	monarchy
2	political	**B**	movement
3	constitutional	**C**	expansion
4	party	**D**	development
5	working-class	**E**	reforms
6	technological	**F**	politics

Milestones

1851, the Great Exhibition

Social unrest did not prevent the increasing power of the middle classes or the expansion of industry and trade. Moreover, there were considerable scientific and technological developments. Britain's leading industrial and economic position in the world was symbolised by the 'Great Exhibition' of 1851, where goods from all the different countries of the Empire as well as from all over Britain were exhibited. It was housed in the Crystal Palace, built by Joseph Paxton in Hyde Park. It was the first building in iron and glass to be entirely prefabricated. The Great Exhibition was the first exhibition of this kind and attracted huge crowds. The profits were used for the establishment of the Science Museum, the Natural History Museum and the Victoria and Albert Museum.

5 Interior of the Crystal Palace, the cast-iron and glass building designed by Joseph Paxton was originally erected in Hyde Park, London, England, to house the Great Exhibition of 1851. Full-size, living elm trees were enclosed within the central exhibition hall near a 27-foot-tall (8 m) crystal fountain.

5.2 **Society**

Life in the Victorian town

By the middle of the 19th century, Britain had become a nation of town dwellers. This fact was mainly due to extraordinary industrial development. Finding a solution to problems linked to the overcrowded urban environment was at the heart of Victorian political and social reforms.

Housing for the majority of the poor in Victorian cities was famous for its overcrowding and squalor, disease and crime, particularly in the slum districts. The mortality rate was high and terrible working conditions in polluted atmospheres had a disastrous effect, especially on children's health. The Common Lodging Houses Act and Labouring Classes Lodging Houses Act (1851) were passed to prevent the worst squalor and to clean up the towns which had been devastated by cholera epidemics and tuberculosis. However, the changes were slow in coming and gradual in effect. As a result, for every grand public building the Victorians built, just around the corner there were lots of terraced houses and slum districts.

Medicine also underwent a radical change: professional organisations were founded to regulate and control medical education and research, and modern hospitals were built.

Other services were also introduced, such as: water, gas and lighting; paved roads; places of entertainment, like public houses, music halls, parks and stadiums; and shops. Even now, Victorian institutions, prisons, police stations, boarding schools and town halls can still be seen in British cities.

Law and order were among the major problems of the urban environment and modern police forces were needed to keep cities under control. In 1829–30 Prime Minister Robert Peel established the Metropolitan Police. It was from their founder's name that policemen were first known as 'Peelers' and then as 'Bobbies'.

1

2

1 William Logsdail, *St Paul's and Ludgate Hill*, 1887. Private collection.

2 Luke Fildes, *Applicants for Admission to a Casual Ward*, 1874. Royal Holloway Centre, Egham, Surrey, England.

1 **COMPLETE** the spider chart about city slums with words from the text above.

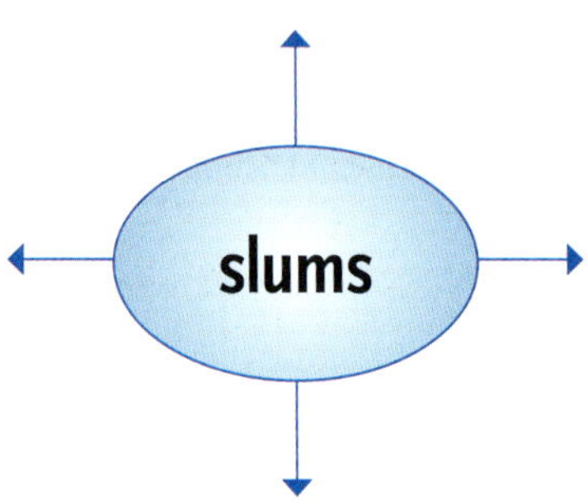

2 **IDENTIFY** the main features concerning urban life.

3 **SUMMARISE** the reforms enacted to improve the lives of many Victorians.

4 **LOOK** at the pictures (3–4). What do you think the main features of the Victorian high street, that is, the main street in the town, were?

3

4

FCE Reading and Use of English – Part 2

5 **OPEN CLOZE.** For questions 1–8, read the text about high streets in Victorian London and think of the word which best fits each gap. Use only one word in each gap. There is an example at the beginning (0).

The birth of the high street

The roots **(0)** ......OF...... the modern high street **(1)** .... be found in the era of rural self-sufficiency, when the vast majority of the population grew their **(2)** .... food and exchanged it for animals and services. At this time, baking, dressmaking, hairdressing and other tasks were part of the domestic economy.

This developed **(3)** .... a more urban pattern of itinerant salesmen and market stall holders selling goods **(4)** .... prices that were decided after the two parties had discussed about it. Next came fixed-location shops, selling goods at fixed prices.

Biweekly markets **(5)** .... sell perishable local foods: dairy produce, poultry and vegetables, as well as homemade pies and bread. The stalls on these markets were usually rented from a landlord, **(6)** .... could prohibit any competition within five miles.

After 1850, a rising population, improvements in transport, innovative manufacturing processes and a lack of tariffs all provided high-street shopkeepers **(7)** .... a wider range of goods to sell and more customers to buy them. While some butchers and fishmongers continued to sell through market stalls, other traders, **(8)** .... as grocers, invested in fixed buildings with goods displayed behind glass windows and shopkeepers to attend to customers' needs.

(Abridged from Philip Wilkinson, *Turn Back Time: The High Street – 100 Years of British Life Through the Shop Window*, 2010)

3 High Street, Kensington, a district of London, ca 1905.

4 Joseph Clark, *Buying a New Hat*, 1880. Bourne Gallery, Reigate, Surrey, England.

WARM-UP

1 **LOOK** at the pictures on pages 152–153. What characteristics of the urban habitat you have just read about are visible?

2 **READ** 'Coketown' and point out the features of the pictures on pages 152–153 in the passage.

Coketown

Charles Dickens

Hard Times (1854)
Book I, Chapter 5

Charles Dickens (1812–70) was the great Victorian novelist of cities. The following passage is from Dickens's novel Hard Times. *It is centred on the description of the industrial centre of Coketown, where the story is set and where Mr Gradgrind, the headmaster of the local school, and his friend Mr Bounderby are now walking.*

4.2

Coketown, to which Messrs Bounderby and Gradgrind now walked, was a triumph of fact; it had no greater taint of fancy[1] in it than Mrs Gradgrind herself. Let us strike the key-note[2], Coketown, before pursuing our tune.

It was a town of red brick, or of brick that would have been red if the smoke and ashes had allowed it; but, as matters stood it was a town of unnatural red and black like the painted face of a savage. It was a town of machinery and tall chimneys, out of which interminable serpents of smoke trailed themselves[3] for ever and ever, and never

1 **taint of fancy.** Tracce di fantasia.
2 **Let us strike the key-note.** Suoniamo la nota dominante.
3 **trailed themselves.** Si susseguivano.

5.2 Life in the Victorian town

got uncoiled[4]. It had a black canal in it, and a river that ran purple with ill-smelling dye[5], and vast piles of building full of windows where there was a rattling and a trembling all day long, and where the piston of the steam-engine worked monotonously up and down, like the head of an elephant in a state of melancholy madness. It contained several large streets all very like one another, and many small streets still more like one another, inhabited by people equally like one another, who all went in and out at the same hours, with the same sound upon the same pavements, to do the same work, and to whom every day was the same as yesterday and tomorrow, and every year the counterpart of the last and the next.

These attributes of Coketown were in the main inseparable from the work by which it was sustained; against them were to be set off, comforts of life which found their way all over the world, and elegancies of life which made, we will not ask how much of the fine lady, who could scarcely bear to hear the place mentioned. The rest of its features were voluntary, and they were these.

1 Back-to-back housing in Staithes, Yorkshire, England, late 19th century.

2 The industrial town of Sheffield, England, in the 19th century.

You saw nothing in Coketown but what was severely workful. If the members of a religious persuasion[6] built a chapel there – as the members of eighteen religious persuasions had done – they made it a pious warehouse[7] of red brick, with sometimes (but this only in highly ornamented examples) a bell in a bird-cage on the top of it. The solitary exception was the New Church; a stuccoed[8] edifice with a square steeple[9] over the door, terminating in four short pinnacles like florid wooden legs. All the public inscriptions in the town were painted alike, in severe characters of black and white. The jail[10] might have been the infirmary, the infirmary might have been the jail, the town-hall might have been either, or both, or anything else, for anything that appeared to the contrary in the graces of their construction. Fact, fact, fact, everywhere in the material aspect of the town; fact, fact, fact, everywhere in the immaterial. The M'Choakumchild school was all fact, and the school of design was all fact, and the relations between master and man were all fact, and everything was fact between the lying-in[11] hospital and the cemetery, and what you couldn't state in figures[12], or show to be purchaseable in the cheapest market and saleable in the dearest, was not, and never should be, world without end, Amen[13].

A town so sacred to fact, and so triumphant in its assertion, of course got on well? Why no, not quite well. No? Dear me!

No. Coketown did not come out of its own furnaces, in all respects like gold that had stood the fire. First, the perplexing mystery of the place was, Who belonged to the eighteen denominations[14]? Because, whoever did, the labouring people did not. It was very strange to walk through the streets on a Sunday morning, and note how few of *them* the barbarous jangling[15] of bells that was driving the sick and nervous mad, called away from their own quarter, from their own close rooms, from the corners of their own streets, where they lounged listlessly[16], gazing at all the church and chapel going, as at a thing with which they had no manner of concern. Nor was it merely the stranger who noticed this, because there was a native organization in Coketown itself, whose members were to be heard of in the House of Commons every session, indignantly petitioning for acts of parliament that should make these people religious by main force[17]. Then, came the Teetotal Society[18], who complained that these same people *would* get drunk, and showed in tabular statements[19] that they did get drunk, and proved at tea parties that no inducement, human or Divine (except a medal), would induce them to forego[20] their custom of getting drunk. Then, came the chemist and druggist, with other tabular statements, showing that when they didn't get drunk, they took opium. Then, came the experienced chaplain of the

4 **never got uncoiled.** Non finivano mai di srotolarsi.
5 **ill-smelling dye.** Tintura maleodorante.
6 **persuasion.** Setta, credo, convinzione.
7 **pious warehouse.** Pio magazzino.
8 **stuccoed.** Decorato a stucco.
9 **steeple.** Campanile.
10 **jail.** Prigione.
11 **lying-in.** Maternità.
12 **figures.** Cifre.
13 **world ... Amen.** Nei secoli dei secoli, Amen.
14 **denominations.** Sette religiose.
15 **barbarous jangling.** Barbaro stridio.
16 **lounged listlessly.** Si attardavano svogliatamente.
17 **by main force.** A viva forza.
18 **Teetotal Society.** Società degli astemi.
19 **showed ... statements.** Dimostrava in statistiche.
20 **to forego.** Ad astenersi da.

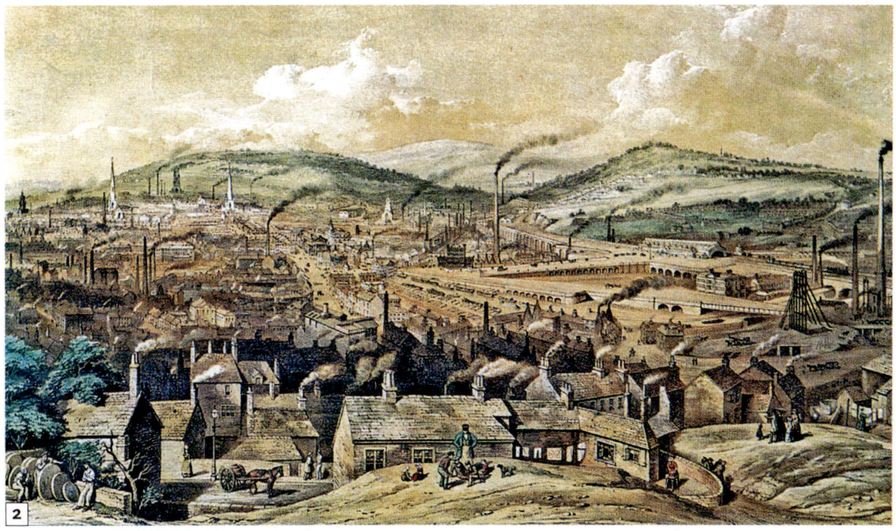
2

jail, with more tabular statements, outdoing all the previous tabular statements, and showing that the same people *would* resort to low haunts[21], hidden from the public eye, where they heard low singing[22] and saw low dancing[23], and mayhap[24] joined in it; and where A. B., aged twenty-four next birthday, and committed for eighteen months' solitary[25], had himself said (not that he had ever shown himself particularly worthy of belief) his ruin began, as he was perfectly sure and confident that otherwise he would have been a tip-top moral specimen[26]. Then, came Mr Gradgrind and Mr Bounderby, the two gentlemen at this present moment walking through Coketown, and both eminently practical, who could, on occasion, furnish more tabular statements derived from their own personal experience, and illustrated by cases they had known and seen, from which it clearly appeared – in short it was the only clear thing in the case – that these same people were a bad lot altogether, gentlemen; that do what you would for them they were never thankful for it, gentlemen; that they were restless[27], gentlemen; that they never knew what they wanted; that they lived upon the best, and bought fresh butter, and insisted on Mocha coffee, and rejected all but prime parts of meat, and yet were eternally dissatisfied and unmanageable[28].

21 **haunts.** Luoghi di ritrovo.
22 **low singing.** Canti indecenti.
23 **low dancing.** Balli indecenti.
24 **mayhap.** Forse.
25 **committed ... solitary.** Messo in cella di isolamento per diciotto mesi.
26 **tip-top moral specimen.** Eccellente esempio di moralità.
27 **restless.** Irrequieti.
28 **unmanageable.** Ribelli, intrattabili.

COMPREHENSION

3 READ up to line 18 and say what kind of town Coketown was and what it contained.

4 UNDERLINE the list of the public buildings in Coketown in the fourth paragraph and say if there are any differences among them.

5 ANSWER the following questions. **The last two paragraphs deal with the effect of such a town on its inhabitants.**

1 What did a native organisation of Coketown want to do?
2 What did the Teetotal Society show in tabular statements?
3 How did the chemist and druggist show that the inhabitants of Coketown took opium?
4 What was the aim of the jail chaplain?
5 What did Mr Gradgrind and Mr Bounderby want to prove?

ANALYSIS

6 DEFINE the type of narrator.

7 DECIDE. What is the keyword of this passage, in your opinion?

8 FIND the images used by Dickens to describe Coketown in the second paragraph and group them according to:

- similes: ....
- metaphors: ....

What do they have in common? Is the process of industrialisation approved of or criticised?

9 THE DESCRIPTION gradually takes on an interior quality, since it moves its focus from the street to the people (lines 13–18). The mechanical repetition of words and phrases and of the syntax combine to express the main psychological features of the inhabitants of Coketown.

1 Find and underline the repetitions in the text.
2 What aspects of the inhabitants of Coketown do these linguistic devices underline? Tick as appropriate and explain your choice(s).
   - ☐ Monotony.
   - ☐ Amusement.
   - ☐ Alienation.
   - ☐ Creativity.

YOUR TURN

10 DISCUSS what Victorian issues Dickens emphasises in this passage.

5.3 | **Society**

The Victorian compromise

WARM-UP

1 **DISCUSS.** What is the meaning of 'compromise'? Why do you think it is related to the Victorian Age?

2 **READ** the text and check if your predictions to exercise 1 were correct.

3 **COMPLETE** the table with the correct word.

Noun	Adjective
	stable
	dutiful
respectability	
comfort	
charity	
patriarchy	
	chaste
prudery	

FCE Reading and Use of English – Part 3

4 **WORD FORMATION.** For questions 1–8, read the text. Use the word given in capitals at the end of some of the lines to form a word that fits in the gap in the same line. There is an example at the beginning (0).

The Victorian Age was a complex and contradictory era: on the
one hand, it was an age of progress, **(0)** ......STABILITY...... **STABLE**
and great social reforms; on the other, it was also characterised
by poverty, injustice and social unrest.

The Victorians were great **(1)** .... : they faced a large **MORALISE**
number of problems on such a scale that they felt obliged to
support certain values which offered solutions or escapes.
Thus they promoted a code of values that reflected the world as
they wanted it to be, not as it really was, based on **(2)** .... **DUTY**
hard work, respectability and charity. These values were refined
by the upper and middle classes, who had political and economic
power, but they were of equal application to all strata of society.

In fact, one of the most important notions throughout the
19th century was the need to work hard. The idea of being
(3) .... distinguished the middle from the lower class. **RESPECT**
Respectability was a mixture of both morality and hypocrisy,
severity and conformity to social standards. It implied the
possession of good manners, the **(4)** .... of a comfortable **OWNER**
house with servants and a carriage, regular attendance at
church, and **(5)** .... activity. Philanthropy was a widespread **CHARITY**
phenomenon; it addressed itself to every kind of poverty, to 'stray
children, fallen women and **(6)** .... men' and absorbed the **DRINK**
energies of thousands of Victorians, large numbers of whom were
women.

Middle-class ideals dominated Victorian family life. The
family was a **(7)** .... unit where the husband represented **PATRIARCH**
authority and the key role of women concerned the education of
children and the managing of the house. Victorian society was
deeply concerned with female chastity, and single women with
a child suffered the worst of society's punishments: they were
emarginated as 'fallen women'. Sexuality was generally repressed
in its public and private forms, and being **(8)** .... in its **PRUDERY**
most extreme manifestations led to the denunciation of nudity
in art and the rejection of words with a sexual connotation from
everyday vocabulary.

1 George William Joy, *The Bayswater Omnibus*, 1895. Museum of London, London. The painting shows a group of passengers who represent respectable Victorian types: a mother and her children; a fashionable woman; a City gent reading a paper; a nurse; and a milliner. The advent of advertisements can be seen above their heads.

2 George Adolphus Storey, *The Orphans*, 1879. The Forbes Magazine collection, New York. The upper and middle classes often had a somewhat romantic perception of 'stray children' due to their prevalence in Victorian literature. However, orphans were also often treated with disdain and distrust – victims of classic 'Victorian contradictions'.

5 **ANSWER** the following questions about the text.

1 Why did the Victorians feel forced to promote a strict code of values?
2 Which social classes refined this code?
3 What did the Victorian code of values consist of? In your analysis consider the following concepts:
- respectability;
- work;
- family;
- sex.

4 What is the meaning of the word 'compromise' when applied to the Victorian way of life?

TEXT BANK 37: *EMILY BRONTË*
TEXT BANK 38: *THOMAS HARDY*

5.4 **Literature**

The Victorian novel

WARM-UP

1 **REFER** to the Victorian compromise and make predictions as regards the main features of the Victorian novel.

Literary language
The Victorian novel

The main features of the Victorian novel:

- The voice of the omniscient narrator provided a comment on the plot and erected a rigid barrier between 'right' and 'wrong', light and darkness.
- The setting chosen by most Victorian novelists was the city, which was the main symbol of industrial civilisation as well as the expression of anonymous lives and lost identities.
- The plot was long and often complicated by subplots.
- Victorian writers concentrated on the creation of characters and thus achieved deeper analysis of the characters' inner life.
- Retribution and punishment were to be found in the final chapter, where the whole texture of events, adventures and incidents had to be explained and justified.

During the Victorian Age, for the first time there was a communion of interests and opinions between writers and their readers. One reason for this was the enormous growth in the middle classes, who were avid consumers of literature. They borrowed books from circulating libraries and read various periodicals.

A great deal of Victorian literature was first published in instalments in the pages of periodicals, which allowed the writer to feel he was in constant contact with his public. The novel became the most popular form of literature and the main form of entertainment, since novels were read aloud within the family. The novelists felt they had a moral and social responsibility to fulfil: they aimed at reflecting the social changes that had been in progress for a long time, such as the Industrial Revolution, the struggle for democracy and the growth of towns. They depicted society as they saw it. They were aware of the evils of their society and denounced them; however, their criticism was not radical, it just aimed at making readers aware of social injustices.

It is important to underline that a great number of novels published during the middle period of Victorianism were written by women. This output is surprising if one thinks of the state of subjection of Victorian women. It is less surprising if one remembers that the majority of novel-buyers and readers were women, since they spent more time than men at home, where they could devote themselves to reading. However, it was not easy to publish, and some women used a male pseudonym in order to see their work in print; in fact, creative writing, like art and public activities, was considered 'masculine'.

From Jane Austen to George Eliot (the pen name of Mary Ann Evans, 1819–80), the woman's novel had moved in the direction of a realistic exploration of the daily lives and values of women within the family and the community.

The first part of the Victorian Age was linked to social and humanitarian novels, whose main representative was Charles Dickens (1812–70), and to psychological novels, with the works of Emily (1818–48) and Charlotte Brontë (1816–55).

Following Darwin's theories, the late-Victorian novel was nearer to the European development of 'Naturalism', an almost scientific look at human behaviour. Writers like Thomas Hardy (1840–1928), Robert Louis Stevenson (1850–94) and Oscar Wilde (1854–1900) reacted against the triumphant Victorian ideology and began to express a deep sense of dissatisfaction with the values of their age.

1 George Cruikshank, *Cold, misery, and want, destroy their youngest child*, 1847. Victoria and Albert Museum, London.

2 **ANSWER the following questions.**

1 Why was there a communion of interest between writers and readers during the Victorian Age?
2 How were lots of works published?
3 What did novelists want to reflect?
4 How did they depict society?
5 How many kinds of Victorian novels do you know?
6 What are the distinctive features of the Victorian novel?

5.5 **Literature**

Charles Dickens and children

Charles Dickens's life

Charles Dickens (1812–70) was born in Portsmouth, on the southern coast of England, in 1812. He had an unhappy childhood. His father was imprisoned for debt, and his wife and children, with the exception of Charles, who was put to work in a factory, joined him in the Marshalsea Prison. When the family finances improved and his father was released, the twelve-year-old Dickens was further wounded by his mother's insistence that he continue to work at the factory. At fifteen, he found employment as an office boy at a lawyer's and studied shorthand at night. By 1832, he had become a very successful reporter of Parliamentary debates in the House of Commons, and began to work as a reporter for a newspaper.

In 1833, his first story appeared, and in 1836, still a newspaper reporter, he adopted the pen name 'Boz', publishing *Sketches by 'Boz'*, a collection of articles describing London's people and scenes, written for the periodical 'Monthly Magazine'. It was immediately followed by *The Posthumous Papers of the Pickwick Club* (also known as *The Pickwick Papers*), which was published in episodes and revealed Dickens's humoristic and satirical qualities.

After the success of *The Pickwick Papers*, Dickens started a full-time career as a novelist, producing work of increasing complexity at an incredible rate, although he also continued his journalistic and editorial activities. *Oliver Twist* was begun in 1837 and continued in monthly parts until April 1839. *Nicholas Nickleby* was published in 1839. In 1842 he embarked on a visit to Canada and the United States in which he advocated international copyright and the abolition of slavery. His *American Notes* appeared in October of that year. *Martin Chuzzlewit*, part of which was set in America, appeared in 1844, and in December of the previous year *A Christmas Carol*, the first of Dickens's enormously successful Christmas books, was published.

The protagonists of his autobiographical novels, *Oliver Twist* (1837–39), *David Copperfield* (1849–50) and *Little Dorrit* (1855–57), became symbols of an exploited childhood confronted with the sad realities of slums and factories. Other works include *Bleak House* (1852–53), *Hard Times* (1854) and *Great Expectations* (1860–61), which deal with social issues such as the conditions of the poor and the working class in general.

He died in London in 1870 and is buried in Westminster Abbey.

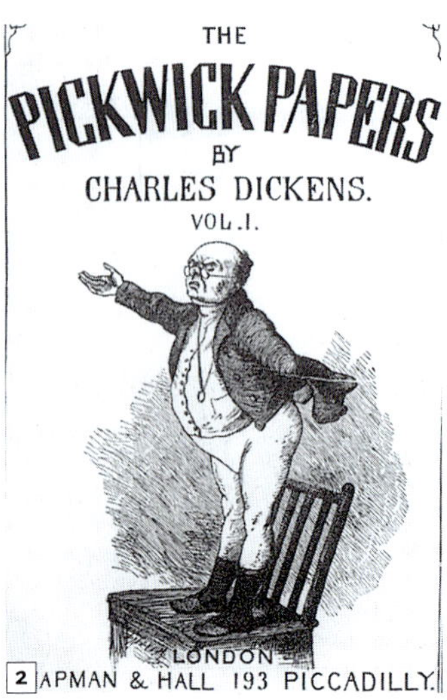

1 Robert William Buss, *Dickens's Dream*, 1875. The Charles Dickens Museum, London.

2 Frontispiece to the first volume of *The Pickwick Papers* by Charles Dickens.

1 COMPLETE **the table below with the information you have read to organise your knowledge about Charles Dickens's life.**

Place of birth	
Childhood	
Education	
Beginning of literary career	
Works	

3–4 Scenes from 'Oliver Twist', a film directed by Roman Polanski in 2005.

Oliver Twist (1837–39)

Childhood in the Victorian Age was generally a cruel experience. A lot of children from poor and working-class backgrounds who escaped an early death were obliged either to work in factories and mines, or as domestic servants and chimneysweeps. Others became criminals. Some government acts, like the Ten Hours Act (1847), tried to improve children's working conditions by limiting the hours worked by women and children to ten per day. Victorian literature played an important role in the sentimental portrayal of childhood. Dickens was obsessed with children, whom he presented as either innocent or corrupted by adults. At the beginning, they live through a negative situation but later rise to happy endings. The writer's nostalgia for the innocence of childhood is a critique of the oppressions associated with the world of adults.

London life

The most important setting of the novel is London, which is depicted at three different social levels. First, the parochial world of the workhouse is revealed. The inhabitants of this world, belonging to the lower-middle-class strata of society, are calculating and insensible to the feelings of the poor. Second, the criminal world is described, with pickpockets and murderers. Poverty drives them to crime and the weapon they use to achieve their end is violence. They live in dirty, squalid slums in a permanent state of fear and generally die a miserable death. Finally, the world of the Victorian middle class is presented. In this world, there live respectable people who show a regard for moral values and believe in the principle of human dignity.

The story

Oliver Twist first appeared in instalments in 1837 and was later published as a book. The novel reflects the economic insecurity and humiliation Dickens experienced as a child. The name 'Twist', though it is given to the protagonist by accident, represents the outrageous reversals of fortune that he will experience.

Oliver Twist is a poor boy of unknown parents; he is brought up in a workhouse in an inhuman way. He is later sold to an undertaker as an apprentice, but the cruelty and the unhappiness he experiences with his new master cause him to run away to London. There he falls into the hands of a gang of young pickpockets, led by the Artful Dodger and trained by the elderly Fagin, who try to make a thief out of him, but the boy is helped by an old gentleman. Oliver is eventually kidnapped by the gang and forced to commit burglary; during the job, he is shot and wounded. It is a middle-class family that adopts Oliver and shows kindness and affection towards him at last. Investigations are made about who the boy is and it is discovered he has noble origins. The gang of pickpockets and Oliver's half-brother, who paid the thieves in order to ruin Oliver and have their father's property all for himself, are arrested in the end.

The world of the workhouse

Dickens attacked the social evils of his times, such as poor houses, unjust courts and the underworld. With the rise in the level of poverty, workhouses run by parishes spread all over England to give relief to the poor. However, the conditions prevailing in the workhouses were appalling. Their residents were subject to hard regulations: labour was required, families were almost always separated and rations of food and clothing were small and poor. The idea upon which the workhouses were founded was that poverty was the consequence of laziness and that the terrible conditions in the workhouse would inspire the poor to improve their own conditions. Yet the economic dislocation of the Industrial Revolution made it impossible for many to do so, and the workhouses did not provide any means for social or economic advances. Furthermore, as Dickens points out, instead of alleviating the suffering of the poor, the officials who ran workhouses abused their rights as individuals and caused them further misery.

2 **ANSWER these questions about *Oliver Twist*.**

1 What was childhood like in the Victorian Age?
2 What does Dickens's nostalgia for an innocent childhood stand for?
3 What does *Oliver Twist* fictionalise?
4 Where is Oliver brought up?
5 Who eventually kidnaps Oliver?
6 Who adopts Oliver?
7 What is discovered at the end of the novel?
8 What is the setting of the novel? Which social classes are depicted?
9 What were Victorian workhouses like?
10 What did Dickens criticise about this social institution?

GLOSSARY
undertaker becchino
pickpockets borseggiatori
kidnapped rapito
burglary furto con scasso
half-brother fratellastro

5.5 Charles Dickens and children

WARM-UP

1 **LOOK** at the picture. What emotions and feelings can you see in the children's eyes?

1 George Cruikshank, *Oliver Twist asking for more food in the workhouse*, 1838. The British Library, London.

Oliver wants some more

Charles Dickens

Oliver Twist (1837–39)
Chapter 2

This extract reveals Dickens's awareness of the social problems of his time.

4.3

The room in which the boys were fed, was a large stone hall, with a copper[1] at one end: out of which the master, dressed in an apron for the purpose, and assisted by one or two women, ladled the gruel[2] at meal-times. Of this festive composition each boy had one porringer[3], and no more – except on occasions of great public rejoicing, when he had two ounces[4] and a quarter of bread besides. The bowls never wanted washing. The boys polished them with their spoons till they shone again; and when they had performed this operation (which never took very long, the spoons being nearly as large as the bowls), they would sit staring at the copper, with such eager eyes, as if they could have devoured the very bricks of which it was composed; employing themselves, meanwhile, in sucking their fingers most assiduously, with the view of catching up any stray splashes[5] of gruel that might have been cast thereon[6]. Boys have generally excellent appetites. Oliver Twist and his companions suffered the tortures of slow starvation[7] for three months: at last they got so voracious and wild with hunger, that one boy, who was tall for his age, and hadn't been used to that sort of thing (for his father had kept a small cookshop[8]), hinted darkly to his companions, that unless he had another basin of gruel *per diem*, he was afraid he might some night happen to eat the boy who slept next him, who happened to be a weakly youth of tender age. He had a wild, hungry eye; and they implicitly believed him. A council was held; lots were

1 **copper.** Paiolo di rame.
2 **ladled the gruel.** Scodellava la farinata (pappa di avena o orzo).
3 **porringer.** Scodella.
4 **ounces.** Once.
5 **splashes.** Schizzi.
6 **cast thereon.** Lasciati cadere sulle loro dita.
7 **starvation.** Inedia.
8 **cookshop.** Trattoria.

cast[9] who should walk up to the master after supper that evening, and ask for more; and it fell to Oliver Twist.

The evening arrived; the boys took their places. The master, in his cook's uniform, stationed himself at the copper; his pauper assistants ranged themselves behind him; the gruel was served out; and a long grace[10] was said over the short commons[11]. The gruel disappeared; the boys whispered to each other, and winked[12] at Oliver; while his next neighbours nudged[13] him. Child as he was, he was desperate with hunger, and reckless[14] with misery. He rose from the table; and advancing to the master, basin and spoon in hand, said, somewhat alarmed at his own temerity:

'Please, sir, I want some more.'

The master was a fat, healthy man; but he turned very pale. He gazed in stupefied astonishment on the small rebel for some seconds, and then clung[15] for support to the copper. The assistants were paralysed with wonder; the boys with fear.

'What!' said the master at length, in a faint voice.

'Please, sir,' replied Oliver, 'I want some more.'

The master aimed a blow at Oliver's head with the ladle; pinioned[16] him in his arms; and shrieked aloud for the beadle[17].

The board[18] were sitting in solemn conclave, when Mr Bumble rushed into the room in great excitement, and addressing the gentleman in the high chair, said,

'Mr Limbkins, I beg your pardon, sir! Oliver Twist has asked for more!'

There was a general start. Horror was depicted on every countenance[19].

'For *more*!' said Mr Limbkins. 'Compose yourself, Bumble, and answer me distinctly. Do I understand that he asked for more, after he had eaten the supper allotted[20] by the dietary?'

'He did, sir,' replied Bumble.

'That boy will be hung,' said the gentleman in the white waistcoat. 'I know that boy will be hung.'

Nobody controverted the prophetic gentleman's opinion. An animated discussion took place. Oliver was ordered into instant confinement[21]; and a bill was next morning pasted[22] on the outside of the gate, offering a reward of five pounds to anybody who would take Oliver Twist off the hands of the parish. In other words, five pounds and Oliver Twist were offered to any man or woman who wanted an apprentice to any trade, business, or calling[23].

2 Dinnertime in St Pancras Workhouse, London. Photograph from *The Queen's Empire* (Cassell, 1899).

9 **lots were cast.** Fu tirato a sorte.
10 **grace.** Preghiera di ringraziamento.
11 **over the short commons.** Per le scarse razioni di cibo.
12 **winked.** Strizzavano l'occhio.
13 **nudged.** Davano una leggera gomitata.
14 **reckless.** Imprudente.
15 **clung.** Si aggrappò.
16 **pinioned.** Immobilizzò.
17 **beadle.** Il sorvegliante.
18 **board.** Consiglio.
19 **countenance.** *Lett.*: espressione; *qui*: viso.
20 **allotted.** Concessa.
21 **confinement.** Isolamento.
22 **pasted.** Affisso.
23 **calling.** Mestiere.

COMPREHENSION

2 READ the passage and answer the questions.

1 Where does the scene take place?
2 What is the boys' greatest problem?
3 What is the main event of the passage?
4 What are the consequences of Oliver's request?

ANALYSIS

3 ANSWER the following questions.

1 Is the narrator a voice outside or inside the novel? Whose point of view is adopted?
2 How is the story developed?
3 Is the description detailed or vague? What is its function?
4 What is the function of the narration? And that of the dialogues?
5 Which feelings characterise the two worlds presented in the text?
6 What antithetical images and ideas can you find in the passage?

YOUR TURN

4 WRITE. Does this episode merely draw attention to the conditions of poor orphans or does it call for political action? If you think it calls for political action, what action do you think it is? Write a passage about it.

5.6 Literature

Charles Dickens and Charlotte Brontë and the theme of education

WARM-UP

1 **LOOK** at the picture. What aspects of Victorian education do you think it represents?

1

FCE Listening – Part 4

2 4.4 | **MULTIPLE-CHOICE QUESTIONS. You will hear an interview with an expert about Victorian education. For questions 1–7, choose the best answer (A, B or C).**

1 What is the target audience of the website Kate works for?
- A Experts in history.
- B High school students.
- C Anyone wanting to know more about Victorian times.

2 What does Kate say about children in early Victorian England?
- A They received a different education according to their social class.
- B They had a lot of learning possibilities.
- C They spent most of their time playing with toys.

3 Kate says that boys and girls from rich families
- A were only taught at home.
- B had the same kind of education.
- C were taught by a governess at first but then received different kinds if education.

4 How many hours did poor children work?
- A Sixteen per day.
- B Sixty per week.
- C Six per day.

5 What were 'ragged schools'?
- A Schools run by single women.
- B Schools run by charities.
- C Schools inside factories.

6 What method does Kate say Victorian teachers mainly used?
- A They dictated things to learn.
- B They wrote lists for pupils to copy.
- C They had pupils bring objects to put on their desks.

7 Kate explains that punishment was given through
- A only caning.
- B having children recite until they were word perfect.
- C caning or making pupils stand on a stool with a hat on.

Dickens and a critique of education

Charles Dickens was a pioneer in introducing the theme of education into his works. He strongly believed in universal education, though not necessarily under a state system. Dickens's own education, which he acknowledged to have been 'irregular', began in Chatham, where he was a pupil at a dame-school (a private establishment run by an unqualified woman). Dickens objected to church intervention in education and shared his concern for the poor and deprived with James Kay-Shuttleworth (1804–77), who laid the foundation for a national system of popular education. In 1843 Dickens began his frequent visits to 'ragged schools' and became one of their supporters, though he was also aware of their limitations – especially the lack of qualified teaching staff. Dickens also objected to certain educational methods.

One strategy singled out for criticism in *Hard Times* was the 'object lesson'. Originally conceived as a method of instruction arising from children's own experiences and suited to their particular stage of development, it was distorted in its introduction to English schools. Form acquired more importance than subject matter, leading to lessons whose vocabulary and content were not suited to children's experience. Dickens's critique is embodied in the exchange between the educator, Gradgrind, and the pupils, Bitzer and Sissy Jupe, over the proper definition of a horse. Bitzer, who has learned a definition by heart, classifies it as a 'Quadruped' and 'Gramnivorous', whereas Sissy, the horseman's daughter, called 'Girl number twenty', is reproached for possessing 'no facts, in reference to one of the commonest of animals'.

Dickens believed in the extension of education to all citizens but did not offer specific strategies for achieving this aim. He had a compromising attitude. He criticised abuses and deficiencies while praising what he believed were positive developments. In the year of his death, Parliament passed the Elementary Education Act (1870), which made education compulsory.

Hard Times (1854)

The story

This novel is set in an imaginary industrial town named Coketown. Thomas Gradgrind, an educator who believes in facts and statistics, has founded a school where his theories are taught, and he brings up his two children, Louisa and Tom, in the same way, repressing their imagination and feelings. He marries his daughter to Josiah Bounderby, a rich banker of the city, thirty years older than she is. The girl consents since she wishes to help her brother, who is given a job in Bounderby's bank, but the marriage proves to be unhappy. Tom, who is lazy and selfish, robs his employer. At first he succeeds in throwing the suspicion on an honest workman, but he is eventually discovered and obliged to leave the country.

WARM-UP

1 **DISCUSS.** How important do you think imagination and experience are in education? Provide examples.

The definition of a horse

Charles Dickens

Hard Times (1854)

Chapter 2, Murdering the Innocents

In the industrial city of Coketown – a place dominated by grim factories and oppressed by coils of black smoke – the dark-eyed, rigid man Thomas Gradgrind has established a school.

4.5

Thomas Gradgrind, sir. A man of realities. A man of fact and calculations. A man who proceeds upon the principle that two and two are four, and nothing over, and who is not to be talked into allowing for anything over[1]. Thomas Gradgrind, sir – peremptorily[2] Thomas – Thomas Gradgrind. With a rule and a pair of scales[3], and the multiplication table always in his pocket, sir, ready to weigh and measure any parcel of human nature, and tell you exactly what it comes to. It is a mere question of figures[4], a case of simple arithmetic. You might hope to get some other nonsensical belief into the head of George Gradgrind, or Augustus Gradgrind or John Gradgrind, or Joseph Gradgrind (all suppositious[5], no existent persons), but into the head of Thomas Gradgrind – no, sir!

In such terms Mr Gradgrind always mentally introduced himself, whether to his private circle of acquaintance[6], or to the public in general. In such terms, no doubt, substituting the words 'boys and girls', for 'sir', Thomas Gradgrind now presented Thomas Gradgrind to the little pitchers[7] before him, who were to be filled so full of facts.

Indeed, as he eagerly sparkled at them[8] from the cellarage[9] before mentioned, he seemed a kind of cannon loaded to the muzzle[10] with facts, and prepared to blow them clean out of the regions of childhood at one discharge[11]. He seemed a galvanizing apparatus[12], too, charged with a grim mechanical substitute[13] for the tender young imaginations that were to be stormed away[14].

'Girl number twenty,' said Mr Gradgrind, squarely pointing with his square forefinger, 'I don't know that girl. Who is that girl?'

1 **who is ... over.** Che non si lascia convincere ad ammettere niente di più.
2 **peremptorily.** Perentoriamente.
3 **a pair of scales.** Una bilancia.
4 **figures.** Cifre.
5 **suppositious.** Immaginarie.
6 **acquaintance.** Conoscenze.
7 **pitchers.** Recipienti.
8 **sparkled at them.** Li guardava.
9 **from the cellarage.** Dalle caverne (degli occhi).
10 **a kind ... muzzle.** Una specie di cannone caricato fino all'imboccatura.
11 **at one discharge.** Con una scarica.
12 **galvanizing apparatus.** Impianto elettrolitico.
13 **a grim mechanical substitute.** Un arcigno surrogato meccanico.
14 **stormed away.** Espugnate.

1 Theophile Emmanuel Duverger, *The naughty schoolchildren*, ca 1850.

2 Alberto Salinas, *Charles Dickens: His words brought the Victorian Age to life*, 1970.

'Sissy Jupe, sir,' explained number twenty, blushing[15], standing up, and curtseying[16].

'Sissy is not a name,' said Mr Gradgrind. 'Don't call yourself Sissy. Call yourself Cecilia.'

'It's father as calls me[17] Sissy. sir,' returned the young girl in a trembling voice, and with another curtsey.

'Then he has no business to do it,' said Mr. Gradgrind. 'Tell him he mustn't. Cecilia Jupe. Let me see. What is your father?'

'He belongs to the horse-riding, if you please, sir.'

Mr Gradgrind frowned[18], and waved off the objectionable calling with his hand[19].

'We don't want to know anything about that, here. You mustn't tell us about that, here. Your father breaks[20] horses, does he?'

'If you please, sir, when they can get any to break, they do break horses in the ring, sir.'

'You mustn't tell us about the ring, here. Very well, then. Describe your father as a horsebreaker. He doctors sick horses, I dare say?'

'Oh yes, sir.'

'Very well, then. He is a veterinary surgeon, a farrier and horsebreaker[21]. Give me your definition of a horse.'

(Sissy Jupe thrown into the greatest alarm[22] by this demand.)

'Girl number twenty unable to define a horse!' said Mr Gradgrind, for the general behoof[23] of all the little pitchers. 'Girl number twenty possessed of no facts, in reference to one of the commonest of animals! Some boy's definition of a horse. Bitzer, yours.'

The square finger, moving here and there, lighted suddenly on Bitzer, perhaps because he chanced to sit in the same ray of sunlight which, darting in[24] at one of the bare windows of the intensely whitewashed room, irradiated Sissy. For, the boys and girls sat on face of the inclined plane in two compact bodies, divided up the centre by a narrow interval[25]; and Sissy, being at the corner of a row on the other side, came in for the beginning of a sunbeam, of which Bitzer, being at the comer of a row on the other side, a few rows in advance, caught the end. But, whereas the girl was dark-eyed and dark-haired, that she seemed to receive a deeper and more lustrous colour from the sun when it shone upon her, the boy was so light-eyed and light-haired that the self-same rays appeared to draw out of him what little colour he ever possessed. His cold eyes

15 **blushing.** Arrossendo.
16 **curtseying.** Facendo un inchino.
17 **It's ... calls me.** E' mio padre che mi chiama.
18 **frowned.** Aggrottò le sopracciglia.
19 **waved ... his hand.** Liquidò la disdicevole professione con un gesto della mano.
20 **breaks.** Doma.
21 **veterinary ... horsebreaker.** Veterinario, maniscalco e domatore di cavalli.
22 **thrown ... alarm.** Enormemente allarmata.
23 **for the general behoof.** A beneficio.
24 **darting in.** Penetrando.
25 **a narrow interval.** Stretto spazio.

1 Alberto Salinas, *Charles Dickens: His words brought the Victorian Age to life*, 1970.

would hardly have been eyes, but for[26] the short ends of lashes[27] which, by bringing them into immediate contrast with something paler than themselves, expressed their form. His shortcropped[28] hair might have been a mere continuation of the sandy freckles[29] on his forehead and face. His skin was so unwholesomely[30] deficient in the natural tinge, that he looked as though, if he were cut, he would bleed white.

'Bitzer,' said Thomas Gradgrind. 'Your definition of a horse.'

'Quadruped. Graminivorous[31]. Forty teeth, namely twenty-four grinders[32], four eye-teeth, and twelve incisive. Sheds[33] coat in the spring; in marshy countries, sheds hoofs[34], too. Hoofs hard, but requiring to be shod[35] with iron. Age known by marks in mouth.' Thus (and much more) Bitzer.

'Now girl number twenty,' said Mr. Gradgrind. 'You know what a horse is.'

She curtseyed again, and would have blushed deeper, if she could have blushed deeper than she had blushed all this time. Bitzer, after rapidly blinking at[36] Thomas Gradgrind with both eyes at once, and so catching the light upon his quivering[37] ends of lashes that they looked like the antennae of busy insects, put his knuckles[38] to his freckled forehead, and sat down again.

26 **but for.** Se non fosse per.
27 **lashes.** Ciglia.
28 **shortcropped.** Corti.
29 **sandy freckles.** Lentiggini gialle.
30 **unwholesomely.** In modo malsano.
31 **Graminivorous.** Erbivoro.
32 **grinders.** Molari.
33 **Sheds.** Perde.
34 **hoofs.** Zoccoli.
35 **shod.** Ferrati.
36 **blinking at.** Aver guardato battendo le palpebre.
37 **quivering.** Tremanti.
38 **knuckles.** Nocche.

COMPREHENSION

2 AS YOU READ the passage, answer the following questions.

1 Where does the scene take place?
2 What is it like?
3 What is Thomas Gradgrind doing?
4 Who does he pick on?
5 What does Gradgrind object to about her?
6 What is the girl asked by Mr Gradgrind?
7 Who is Bitzer?
8 What is he remarkable for?
9 What does he provide?

2 An image for the BBC adaptation of *Hard Times*.

ANALYSIS

3 FOCUS on Mr Gradgrind.

1 Fill in the table below with words or phrases describing his physical appearance, interests and 'instruments of work'.

Physical appearance	Interests	Instruments of work

2 What overall impression do these details create?
3 What does he represent?
4 His name is composed of two words. Gradgrind = *grade* (a particular standard or level of quality of a product) + *grind* (to crush into powder). The onomatopoeic sound and the inferred meaning of this name suggest a lot about this educator's personality. Which definition would you choose to describe him?

4 CONSIDER the students and answer these questions.

1 How does Mr Gradgrind refer to them?
2 What does he call them?
3 How would you describe most of his students' personalities?
4 How does the girl differ from the other students? How is this difference underlined?

5 DECIDE. What is the theme of the extract?

YOUR TURN

6 DISCUSS in pairs your ideas about education. What do you think education should be like?

5.6 Charles Dickens and Charlotte Brontë and the theme of education

Charlotte Brontë's life

The daughter of an Anglican clergyman of Irish origin who exerted an important influence on her artistic inclinations, Charlotte Brontë (1816–55) spent most of her life in isolation in a remote part of Yorkshire, in Northern England. She did not receive a formal education; apart from some periods at school, she was mainly self-educated, reading widely from her father's library and drawing inspiration from the local public library or from periodicals.

Like many female writers of the period, she decided to use a pen-name to publish her novel *Jane Eyre* in 1847. It was immediately successful and was followed by other two novels, *Shirley* (1849) and *Villette* (1853). Charlotte married Reverend Arthur Nicholls in 1854 and died the following year, probably of an illness due to pregnancy.

1 COMPLETE the table below about Charlotte Brontë's life.

Father's role	
Education	
Beginning of literary career	
Works	
Death	

Jane Eyre (1847): an education novel

Charlotte Brontë's novel *Jane Eyre* is a perfect example of an education novel. The reader follows the main character's 'coming of age', as Jane passes from the innocence of childhood through the maturity of adulthood. During this journey, Jane undergoes the trial of education according to Victorian standards. She must constantly struggle for self-control as she moves through different places of residence, including Gateshead Hall, Lowood Institution, Thornfield, Moor House and Morton and Ferndean Manor, where she is, finally, fully educated.

The story

The story begins when Jane is living with the Reed family in their home at Gateshead Hall. Here, the theme of education develops immediately, as Jane is kept confined indoors on a cold winter day. The other children are 'gathered round their mother in the drawing-room', being taught, but Jane has been excluded from the group. Jane tries to educate herself by reading from Bewick's *History of British Birds*, but once again, she is held back from her attempt by the abuse of John Reed, who punishes her and throws the heavy book at her. In anger, Jane cries out, 'You are like a murderer – you are like a slave-driver.' Jane is blamed for the entire incident and is locked up in the 'red-room'. Jane is sent away by Mrs Reed to Lowood Institution, a boarding school for orphaned girls. Jane receives a school education, but is very much contained by the strict discipline and lifestyle as well as the harshness of the people there. However, she masters the Lowood curriculum with tenacity and hard work and later takes up employment as a governess at Thornfield Hall.

WARM-UP

1 DISCUSS. What qualities should a good teacher have?

Punishment

Charlotte Brontë

Jane Eyre (1847)
Chapter 7

Jane is sent away by Mrs Reed to Lowood Institution, a boarding school for orphaned girls. There she receives a scholastic education but is very much contained by the strict discipline and lifestyle as well as the harshness of certain prominent figures, such as Miss Scatcherd and Mr Brocklehurst, the institution's main benefactor.

4.6

'It is the new pupil, I perceive.' And before I could draw breath[1], 'I must not forget I have a word to say respecting her.' Then aloud: how loud it seemed to me! 'Let the child who broke her slate[2], come forward!'

Of my own accord I could not have stirred[3]; I was paralysed: but the two great girls who sat on each side of me, set me on my legs and pushed me towards the dread judge, and then Miss Temple[4] gently assisted me to his very feet, and I caught her whispered counsel[5].

'Don't be afraid, Jane, I saw it was an accident; you shall not be punished.'

The kind whisper went to my heart like a dagger[6].

1 **draw breath.** Respirare.
2 **slate.** Lavagnetta.
3 **stirred.** Muovermi.
4 **Miss Temple.** Insegnante con cui Jane instaura un legame di stima e affetto.
5 **whispered counsel.** Consiglio sussurrato.
6 **dagger.** Pugnale.

'Another minute, and she will despise me[7] for a hypocrite,' thought I; and an impulse of fury against Reed, Brocklehurst, and Co., bounded in my pulses at the conviction. I was no Helen Burns[8].

'Fetch that stool[9],' said Mr Brocklehurst, pointing to a very high one from which a monitor had just risen: it was brought.

'Place the child upon it.'

And I was placed there, by whom I don't know: I was in no condition to note particulars; I was only aware that they had hoisted me up[10] to the height of Mr. Brocklehurst's nose, that he was within a yard of me, and that a spread of shot orange and purple silk pelisses[11] and a cloud of silvery plumage extended and waved[12] below me.

Mr Brocklehurst hemmed[13].

'Ladies,' said he, turning to his family; 'Miss Temple, teachers, and children, you all see this girl?'

Of course they did; for I felt their eyes directed like burning-glasses against my scorched[14] skin.

'You see she is yet young; you observe she possesses the ordinary form of childhood; God has graciously given her the shape that He has given to all of us; no signal deformity points her out as a marked character. Who would think that the Evil One had already found a servant and agent in her? Yet such, I grieve[15] to say, is the case.'

A pause – in which I began to steady the palsy[16] of my nerves, and to feel that the Rubicon was passed; and that the trial, no longer to be shirked[17], must be firmly sustained.

'My dear children,' pursued[18] the black marble clergyman, with pathos, 'this is a sad, a melancholy occasion; for it becomes my duty to warn you, that this girl, who might be one of God's own lambs, is a little castaway[19]: not a member of the true flock[20], but evidently an interloper[21] and an alien. You must be on your guard against her; you must shun[22] her example; if necessary, avoid her company, exclude her from your sports, and shut her out from your converse. Teachers, you must watch her: keep your eyes on her movements, weigh well her words, scrutinise her actions, punish her body to save her soul; if, indeed, such salvation be possible, for (my tongue falters[23] while I tell it) this girl, this child, the native of a Christian land, worse than many a little heathen[24] who says its prayers to Brahma and kneels before Juggernaut[25] – this girl is – a liar[26]!'

Now came a pause of ten minutes, during which I, by this time in perfect possession of my wits[27], observed all the female Brocklehursts produce their pocket-handkerchiefs and apply them to their optics, while the elderly lady swayed herself to and fro[28], and the two younger ones whispered, 'How shocking!'

Mr Brocklehurst resumed[29].

'This I learned from her benefactress; from the pious and charitable lady who adopted her in her orphan state, reared her[30] as her own daughter, and whose kindness, whose generosity the unhappy girl repaid by an ingratitude so bad, so dreadful, that at last her excellent patroness was obliged to separate her from her own young ones, fearful lest[31] her vicious example should contaminate their purity: she has sent her here to be healed[32], even as the Jews of old sent their diseased to the troubled pool of Bethesda; and, teachers, superintendent, I beg of you not to allow the waters to stagnate round her.'

With this sublime conclusion, Mr Brocklehurst adjusted the top button of his surtout[33], muttered[34] something to his family, who rose, bowed[35] to Miss Temple, and then all the great people sailed in state from the room. Turning at the door, my judge said: –

1 George Richmond, *Charlotte Brontë (Mrs A.B. Nicholls)*, 1850. National Portrait Gallery, London.

7 **will despise me.** Mi disprezzerà.
8 **Helen Burns.** Una studentessa della scuola.
9 **Fetch that stool.** Andate a prendere quello sgabello.
10 **hoisted me up.** Issata.
11 **spread ... pelisses.** Una distesa di mantelle di seta cangiante arancione e porpora.
12 **silvery plumage ... waved.** Piume argentate ... ondeggiavano.
13 **hemmed.** Si schiarì la voce.
14 **scorched.** Scottata.
15 **I grieve.** Mi duole.
16 **to steady the palsy.** A fermare la paralisi.
17 **the trial ... to be shirked.** La prova non più da evitare.
18 **pursued.** Proseguì.
19 **castaway.** Reietta.
20 **flock.** Gregge.
21 **interloper.** Intrusa.
22 **shun.** Rifuggire.
23 **falters.** Tartaglia.
24 **heathen.** Ateo.
25 **Brahma ... Juggernaut.** Brahma (dio creatore dell'Induismo) ... Jagannath (divinità indù).
26 **liar.** Bugiarda.
27 **wits.** Facoltà mentali.
28 **swayed herself to and fro.** Si dondolava avanti e indietro.
29 **resumed.** Riprese a parlare.
30 **reared her.** La allevò.
31 **fearful lest.** Per paura che.
32 **healed.** Risanata.
33 **surtout.** Giacca.
34 **muttered.** Mormorò.
35 **bowed.** Si inchinò.

'Let her stand half an hour longer on that stool, and let no one speak to her during the remainder of the day.'

There was I, then, mounted aloft[36]; I, who had said I could not bear the shame of standing on my natural feet in the middle of the room, was now exposed to general view on a pedestal of infamy. What my sensations were, no language can describe; but just as they all rose, stifling my breath[37] and constricting my throat, a girl came up and passed me: in passing, she lifted her eyes. What a strange light inspired them! What an extraordinary sensation that ray sent through me! How the new feeling bore me up[38]! It was as if a martyr, a hero, had passed a slave or victim, and imparted strength in the transit. I mastered[39] the rising hysteria, lifted up my head, and took a firm stand on the stool. Helen Burns asked some slight question about her work of Miss Smith, was chidden for the triviality of the inquiry[40], returned to her place, and smiled at me as she again went by. What a smile! I remember it now, and I know that it was the effluence of fine intellect, of true courage; it lit up her marked lineaments, her thin face, her sunken[41] grey eye, like a reflection from the aspect of an angel. Yet at that moment Helen Burns wore on her arm 'the untidy badge[42]', scarcely an hour ago I had heard her condemned by Miss Scatcherd to a dinner of bread and water on the morrow, because she had blotted[43] an exercise in copying it out. Such is the imperfect nature of man! such spots[44] are there on the disc of the clearest planet; and eyes like Miss Scatcherd's can only see those minute defects, and are blind to the full brightness of the orb[45].

36 **aloft.** In alto.
37 **stifling my breath.** Trattenendo il respiro.
38 **bore me up.** Mi diede coraggio.
39 **mastered.** Controllai.
40 **was chidden ... inquiry.** Fu sgridata per la futilità della richiesta.
41 **sunken.** Infossato.
42 **'the untidy badge'.** Il distintivo del disordine.
43 **blotted.** Macchiato d'inchiostro.
44 **spots.** Macchie.
45 **orb.** Sfera.

1 Charlotte Gainsbourg in 'Jane Eyre', directed by Franco Zeffirelli in 1996.

COMPREHENSION

2 READ lines 1–42 and answer the questions.

1 What is Jane accused of?
2 How is she punished?
3 How does she react at first?
4 What are Mr Brocklehurst's warnings to the pupils and the teachers?
5 What does he think of Jane?

3 READ the passage to the end and find out:

1 the reaction of Mr Brocklehurst's family;
2 the reason why Jane was sent to Lowood;
3 Jane's sensations;
4 who came by her and how she felt;
5 the girl's punishment.

ANALYSIS

4 IDENTIFY the narrator and say whose point of view you share as a reader. What effect does the use of the first-person create?

5 LIST the phrases and the expressions referring to Mr Brocklehurst. What does he represent? What does he identify morality with?

6 FILL IN the table with words referring to Jane and those used to describe the other children.

Jane	Other children

7 UNDERLINE the phrases which mark the progression of Jane's feelings and say what she learns through the stool punishment. How is her character established in the passage?

8 DECIDE. What is the role of Miss Temple and Helen Burns in the passage?

YOUR TURN

9 DISCUSS. Would a pupil be punished for blotting an exercise or breaking something nowadays? How has the issue of punishment changed since Jane Eyre's times?

10 DISCUSS. What overall vision of Victorian education do you get from the texts you have read in this section?

1 **LOOK** at the picture below. What do you remember about Alice's stories from your childhood?

Alice's Adventures in Wonderland

The theme of education is widely developed in Lewis Carroll's *Alice's Adventures in Wonderland* (1865). The book both shows respect for and mocks learning. The things children learn at school are usually parodied in the book as impractical for real life. Alice listens to different lessons but has trouble understanding their real applications. Her knowledge seems to consist mainly of maxims and morals about obedience and safety, which are turned into nonsensical rules by Carroll. The duchess sums things up rather well when speaking to Alice, saying: 'Everything's got a moral, if only you can find it.' Carroll's rejection of typical Victorian education supports his idea that a child's imagination is really important.

John Tenniel, *Alice upsets the Jury Box*, illustration from *Alice's Adventures in Wonderland* by Lewis Carroll. Private collection.

2 **EXPLAIN how the theme of education is developed in *Alice's Adventures in Wonderland.***

3 **DIVIDE the class into groups of two to three students per computer.**

4 **BROWSE this site: www.alice-in-wonderland.net and carry out a research project about one of these topics:**

1. themes and motifs in Alice's stories;
2. characters' descriptions;
3. most famous quotations;
4. the real girl named Alice;
5. John Tenniel, the illustrator of *Alice*'s books;
6. Disney's *Alice in Wonderland*;
7. mad tea-party ideas.

5 **EACH GROUP will present their findings to the rest of the class.**

FCE Speaking – Part 2

6 **INDIVIDUAL LONG TURN. Here are two photographs. They show students studying. Compare these photos and say what you think the advantages and disadvantages are of studying in these ways.**

What do you think the advantages and disadvantages are of studying in these ways?

Process language
Speaking – Part 2

Describing the pictures

- This picture reminds me of ...
- Judging from the photo, (the students) ...
- From what we can see, (he / they) must ...
- Both photographs are quite similar because they show ...

5.7 **Cultural Issues**

The role of the woman: angel or pioneer?

WARM-UP

1 **DISCUSS.** What views of the Victorian woman do the pictures (1–2) highlight?

Angel or pioneer?

1 William Holman Hunt, *The Children's Holiday*, 1864. Torre Abbey, Torquay, Devon, England.

2 Illustration by Gardner Grant Smith.

The angel

In 1854 the English poet Coventry Patmore (1823–96) published *The Angel in the House*, a narrative poem describing an idealised courtship. In the course of the 19th century, his ideal 'angel' came to be applied to every wife who created a heaven for her husband in a well-ordered home. In the Victorian Age, in the model relationship of the middle-class family, each partner had their own responsibilities, and the wife's duties – educating the children, managing the household and providing emotional support for her husband – were not undervalued. However, the husband maintained his role as the head of the family. The ability of a husband to keep his wife out of the workplace signified respectability. In addition to all the other influences upon middle-class households, there was the powerful model of the royal family. Victoria managed to combine sovereign authority with a loving humility in the presence of her husband. As a result, it was the queen who established the ideal figure of the Victorian wife and mother.

Women and sport

Queen Victoria established a new trend when she visited the Isle of Wight in the 1840s. Thanks to the introduction of the railways, many women were able to enjoy a day out at the seaside. In the 1850s, girls were encouraged to try archery and croquet. However, physical exercise was made difficult by bulky skirts. The American Mrs Bloomer caused a sensation when she introduced knickerbockers for women to Britain in the 1850s.

3 Julia Margaret Cameron (1815–1879), *The Angel in the House. Depicts Emily Peacock*, 1873. Victoria and Albert Museum, London.

4 John Lavery, *Played!*, 1885. This 1885 oil painting is one of the earliest known paintings of the game.

Women travellers

Many Victorian women found out that the ideal female could rise to the challenges of foreign experience and discover within herself the independence to survive. This was the case of Lady Anne Blunt (1837–1917), who travelled extensively in the Arabian desert with her husband, or of the women who emigrated to America or Australia with their familes and had to adapt to rough conditions.

5

Women and medicine

In 1854 Florence Nightingale (1820–1910) left her position as superintendent of a sanatorium to lead a team of nurses to the Crimea. By the time she returned home, having reformed the military hospitals, she was a national heroine. The value of professional nurses was recognised for the first time in 1860, when St Thomas's Hospital in London opened its training school for nurses.

6

Women travel writers and painters

Marianne North (1830–90) was the daughter of a wealthy Victorian family. After her mother's death in 1855, she travelled extensively with her father, and in 1869 she decided to paint the flora of the distant countries she visited. She went to Australia and New Zealand, America, Canada, South Africa, Japan, India, Sri Lanka and Jamaica. Her paintings of natural landscapes, flowers and plants that had not yet been classified, birds and animals can be seen at the Royal Botanic Gardens, Kew, London.

7

5 Portrait of Lady Anne Blunt (1837–1917) in Arab costume with an Arab horse, frontispiece to her book *A Pilgrimage to Nejd*, published in 1881. Private collection.

6 Jerry Barrett (d. 1906), *Nightingale receiving the Wounded at Scutari*. National Portrait Gallery, London.

7 The English naturalist and flower painter Marianne North (1830–90).

2 **READ the five texts and then take turns reporting about the different views on women in Victorian times.**

YOUR TURN

3 **DISCUSS. Does the belief in 'separate spheres', that is, a wife and husband having different roles, still work in modern families? What do you think is the best model for a happy family?**

Florence Nightingale, founder of modern nursing, both military and civil, paved the way to a new conception of the potentiality and place in society of the trained and educated woman. This in turn led in the 1860s and 1870s to John Stuart Mill's movement for women's suffrage, which Miss Nightingale supported, and to the founding of women's colleges and the improvement of girls' schools, when at length some provision was made for the neglected higher education of one half of the queen's subjects. Later on, at the time of the two World Wars, women joined the nursing profession to take an active part in the war effort, as is narrated in contemporary British novelist Ian McEwan's (1948–) masterpiece *Atonement* (2001).

Atonement (2001)

The story

Atonement, the reader later discovers, is the novel Briony Tallis has been writing from 1940 to the present, 1999. It starts as a classic family saga set in a British country house in 1935. 13-year-old Briony witnesses an odd incident from her bedroom window. It regards her sister, Cecilia, who takes off her dress and steps into a fountain in the presence of Robbie Turner, the son of a family servant. Robbie has been educated at Cambridge under Mr Tallis's patronage, and wants to become a physician. He and Cecilia are in love, but Briony, unaware, suspects that Robbie Turner is forcing her sister into doing obscene things. When her young cousin Lola is raped in the garden, Briony accuses Robbie of the act, out of revenge and perhaps jealousy. Robbie is imprisoned and expelled from the family's estate. Cecilia, who believes in his innocence, breaks with her family.

The second part of the novel takes place in Normandy in May 1940. Robbie is serving as a soldier after his prison sentence. We follow him as he retreats with the rest of the British Expeditionary Force through northern France to Dunkirk. The only thing that keeps him alive is his hope to be united with Cecilia, who meanwhile has become a nurse. Briony, now eighteen, has realised that she made a mistake and is tormented by remorse.

In part three, Briony works as a trainee nurse at a London hospital, where the hard labour is a form of atonement for her. The novel ends in 1999 when the ageing Briony, now a successful novelist, becomes aware that she is developing progressive vascular dementia. Soon, her ability to remember and grasp reality will desert her. But she is at peace because she has finished writing her latest version of Robbie and Cecilia's story. Her atonement seems complete, until we learn that Robbie died in France and Cecilia in a bombing raid, and that the happy ending we read was simply Briony's atonement for what she did.

1

WARM-UP

1 **THINK** of the qualities that are important for becoming a nurse.

Becoming a nurse

Ian McEwan

Atonement (2001)

Part 3

In the following extract, the narrator describes Briony's experience as a nurse trainee under the assistance of Sister Drummond at a hospital in London, where her sister Cecilia also works as a nurse.

4.7

In those early months, Briony often thought that her only relationship was with Sister Drummond. She was always there, one moment at the end of the corridor, approaching with a terrible purpose, the next, at Briony's shoulder, murmuring in her ear that she had failed to pay attention during preliminary training to the correct procedures for blanket-bathing[1] male patients: only after the *second* change of washing water should the freshly soaped back flannel and back towel be passed to the patient so that he could 'finish off for himself'. Briony's state of mind largely depended on how she stood that hour in the ward sister's opinion. She felt a coolness in her stomach whenever Sister Drummond's gaze[2] fell on her. It was impossible to know whether you had done well. Briony dreaded her bad opinion. Praise[3] was unheard of. The best one could hope for was indifference.

1 **blanket-bathing.** Lavare (i pazienti) nel letto.
2 **gaze.** Sguardo.
3 **Praise.** Elogio.

1 Poster for the film 'Atonement', directed by Joe Wright in 2007.

2 Florence Nightingale surrounded by staff and students of the Nightingale Training School at St Thomas's.

3 Scene from the film 'Atonement', directed by Joe Wright in 2007. Briony stands in the foreground, wearing her nurse's uniform.

In the moments she had to herself, usually in the dark, minutes before falling asleep, Briony contemplated a ghostly[4] parallel life in which she was at Girton[5], reading Milton. She could have been at her sister's college, rather than her sister's hospital. Briony had thought she was joining the war effort[6]. In fact, she had narrowed her life to a relationship with a woman fifteen years older who assumed a power over her greater than that of a mother over an infant.

This narrowing, which was above all a stripping away[7] of identity, began weeks before she had even heard of Sister Drummond. On her first day of the two months' preliminary training, Briony's humiliation in front of the class had been instructive. This was how it was going to be. She had gone up to the sister to point out courteously that a mistake had been made with her name badge[8]. She was B. Tallis, not, as it said on the little rectangular brooch[9], N. Tallis.

The reply was calm. 'You are, and will remain, as you have been designated. Your Christian name is of no interest to me. Now kindly sit down, Nurse Tallis.'

The other girls would have laughed if they had dared[10], for[11] they all had the same initial, but they correctly sensed that permission had not been granted. This was the time of hygiene lectures, and of practising blanket-baths on life-size models – Mrs Mackintosh, Lady Chase, and baby George whose blandly impaired[12] physique allowed him to double as a baby girl. It was the time of adapting to unthinking obedience, of learning to carry bedpans in a stack[13], and remembering a fundamental rule: never walk up a ward[14] without bringing something back. Physical discomfort helped close down Briony's mental horizons. The high starched collars rubbed her neck raw[15]. Washing her hands a dozen times a day under stinging[16] cold water with a block of soda brought on her first chilblains[17]. The shoes she had to buy with her own money fiercely pinched her toes[18]. The uniform, like all uniforms, eroded identity, and the daily attention required – ironing pleats[19], pinning hats, straightening seams[20], shoe polishing, especially the heels[21] – began a process by which other concerns were slowly excluded. By the time the girls were ready to start their course as probationers[22], and to work in the wards (they were never to say 'on') under Sister Drummond, and to submit to the daily routine 'from bedpan to Bovril[23]', their previous lives were becoming indistinct. Their minds had emptied to some extent, their defences were down, so that they were easily persuaded of the absolute authority of the ward sister. There could be no resistance as she filled their vacated minds.

It was never said, but the model behind this process was military. Miss

4 **ghostly.** Spettrale, spirituale.
5 **Girton.** L'unico college di Oxford aperto alle donne.
6 **effort.** Sforzo.
7 **stripping away.** Privarsi, spogliarsi.
8 **badge.** Distintivo.
9 **brooch.** Spilla.
10 **dared.** Osato.
11 **for.** Poiché.
12 **blandly impaired.** Blandamente menomato.
13 **bedpans in a stack.** Padelle per ammalati impilate.
14 **ward.** Corsia.
15 **The high ... raw.** Gli alti colletti inamidati le ferivano il collo.
16 **stinging.** Pungente.
17 **chilblains.** Geloni.
18 **fiercely pinched her toes.** Le serravano ferocemente le dita dei piedi.
19 **ironing pleats.** Stirare le pieghe.
20 **straightening seams.** Raddrizzare cuciture.
21 **heels.** Tacchi.
22 **probationers.** Tirocinanti.
23 **Bovril.** Estratto di carne di bue usato per fare il brodo.

Nightingale, who was never to be referred to as Florence, had been in the Crimea long enough to see the value of discipline, strong lines of command and well-trained troops. So when she lay in the dark listening to Fiona[24] begin her nightlong snoring[25] – she slept on her back – Briony already sensed that the parallel life, which she could imagine so easily from her visits to Cambridge as a child to see Leon and Cecilia[26], would soon begin to diverge from her own. This was her student life now, these four years, this enveloping[27] regime, and she had no will, no freedom to leave. She was abandoning herself to a life of strictures, rules, obedience, housework, and a constant fear of disapproval. She was one of a batch[28] of probationers – there was a new intake every few months – and she had no identity beyond her badge. There were no tutorials[29] here, no one losing sleep over the precise course of her intellectual development. She emptied and sluiced[30] the bedpans, swept and polished floors, made cocoa and Bovril, fetched and carried[31] – and was delivered[32] from introspection. At some point in the future, she knew from listening to the second-year students, she would begin to take pleasure in her competence. She had had a taste of it lately, having been entrusted with taking a pulse and temperature under supervision and marking the readings on a chart. In the way of medical treatments, she had already dabbed gentian violet on ringworm[33], aquaflavine[34] emulsion on a cut, and painted lead lotion on a bruise[35]. But mostly, she was a maid, a skivvy[36] and, in her hours off, a crammer[37] of simple facts. She was happy to have little time to think of anything else. But when she stood on her landing in her dressing gown, last thing at night, and she looked across the river at the unlit city, she remembered the unease[38] that was out there in the streets as well as in the wards, and was like the darkness itself. Nothing in her routine, not even Sister Drummond, could protect her from it.

24 **Fiona.** La tirocinante che dormiva nel letto accanto a quello di Briony.
25 **snoring.** Russare.
26 **Leon and Cecilia.** Il fratello e la sorella maggiore di Briony, studenti a Cambridge.
27 **enveloping.** Avvolgente.
28 **batch.** Gruppo.
29 **tutorials.** Lezioni a piccoli gruppi.
30 **sluiced.** Risciacquava.
31 **fetched and carried.** Andava a prendere e portava.
32 **delivered.** Dispensata.
33 **dabbed ... ringworm.** Applicato tintura di genziana su tricofizia.
34 **aquaflavine.** Acriflavina (disinfettante).
35 **painted ... bruise.** Spalmato lozione al minio su una contusione.
36 **maid, a skivvy.** Serva, una sguattera.
37 **crammer.** Studente ripetitore.
38 **unease.** Disagio.

COMPREHENSION

2 **READ** the extract and write notes about:

1 Briony's most important relationship at the beginning of her training;
2 what Briony was afraid of;
3 the reason why Briony had decided to join a hospital rather than going to university;
4 what she complained about on the first day of her training;
5 the reply she received;
6 how the other girls reacted;
7 the fundamental rule she was taught;
8 the effect of physical discomfort;
9 the model which had inspired the training;
10 what feeling Briony perceived around her at night.

ANALYSIS

3 **FOCUS** on the character of Sister Drummond. What is her attitude towards the probationers?

4 **TRACE** Briony's reactions throughout the extract.

5 **SAY** what the first effect of the training is on Briony.

6 **FILL IN** the table with the physical and psychological aspects of the preliminary training.

Physical	Psychological

7 **BRIONY** thinks of a parallel life in order to bear the hard reality of the hospital. What does she think of and when does this happen?

FCE Writing – Part 2

8 **A REPORT.** You have been asked by your English teacher to write a report showing how Briony's experience during World War II in London reflects the influence of Victorian times. Remember to justify your findings with reference to the text and what you have studied in this Cultural Issue about women. Write your report in 140–190 words.

5.8 **History**

The British Empire

WARM-UP

1 **EXPLAIN** the difference between the title of 'queen' and that of 'empress'.

2 **LOOK** at the picture.
1 What might it suggest to someone living in Victorian Britain about the British Empire?
2 Queen Victoria is presenting the Bible to the man kneeling in front of her. What does this symbolise?

3 **READ** the Q&A text.

GLOSSARY
square miles miglia quadrate
scramble divisione
subdued sottomisero
burden fardello

1 Thomas Jones Barker, *The Secret of England's Greatness (Queen Victoria presenting a Bible in the Audience Chamber at Windsor)*, 1863. National Portrait Gallery, London.

During the reign of Queen Victoria, Great Britain ruled over a wide and powerful empire that brought the British in contact with various cultures.

Q What size did the British Empire reach during Victoria's reign?

A In the last decades of the 19th century, the British Empire occupied an area of 4 million square miles and more than 400 million people were ruled over by the British, although through the use of varying practices.

Q When may Britain's imperial activity be said to have begun?

A It may be said to have begun during the second half of the 16th century. This was the time when Queen Elizabeth I, and later James I, encouraged 'plantations' – the settling of English and Scottish people in Ireland on land forcibly taken from the native Irish. In 1600, Elizabeth I also chartered the British East India Company, a trading concern that was eventually to rule over much of today's India, Pakistan, Bangladesh and Sri Lanka.

Q What happened after the 1857 Indian Mutiny?

A India came under direct rule by Britain, and Queen Victoria was crowned Empress of India by the British prime minister, Benjamin Disraeli (1804–81), in 1877.

Q What other territories did the British occupy during the Victorian Age?

A The British also occupied Australia and New Zealand, seized parts of China – including Hong Kong in 1841 – and expanded their possessions in Africa and Southeast Asia – annexing Burma, for example, in 1886.

Q Did they also expand in Africa?

A Expansionist activity reached a crescendo with the 'scramble for Africa' in the 1880s and 1890s. This was a race among European powers to establish territorial rights to those parts of the continent as yet unclaimed. Britain took over Egypt to protect its routes to India through the Suez Canal in 1882 and then Sudan in 1884. From 1899 to 1902, Britain was at war in South Africa against the Dutch settlers, the Boers, over control of gold and diamond mines. The British eventually won, but with great difficulty.

Q What kind of empire did Britain create?

A Because the British came into contact with and subdued vastly different areas at different times, they were able to shape imperial and colonial policy gradually, adapting to different realities and producing an empire united in name but varied in fact.

Q Were there expressions of civic pride and national fervour among the British?

A Yes, they were frequent in the late 19th century. Patriotism was deeply influenced by ideas of racial superiority. The British had only to look at their empire – at the variety of races and peoples they governed – to find apparent confirmation of this view.

Q What did the British think of their role as colonisers?

A There was a belief that the 'races' of the world were divided by fundamental physical and intellectual differences – that some were destined to be led by others. It was thus an obligation, 'the white man's burden', imposed by God on the British to impose their superior way of life, their institutions, laws and politics on native peoples throughout the world.

1 Indian soldiers faithful to the British, commanded by Major William Hodson.

3 A picture of Aung San Suu Kyi, behind her the National League for Democracy flag.

4 **IN PAIRS** cover the answers (**A**s) in the text. Take turns asking and answering the questions (**Q**s), using the information that you have read.

Milestones

1877, Queen Victoria becomes Empress of India

The title Empress of India was given to Queen Victoria in 1877 when India was formally incorporated into the British Empire. Victoria's desire for such a title probably derived from jealousy of the imperial titles of some of her royal cousins in Germany and Russia. Prime Minister Benjamin Disraeli is usually credited with having given her the idea.

When Victoria died and her son Edward VII ascended the throne, his title became Emperor of India. The title continued until India became independent from the United Kingdom in 1947.

2 Alexander Bassano, *Queen Victoria*, 1882. National Portrait Gallery, London.

Insights

Burma: the price of independence

Burma was annexed as a province of British India in 1886 and Burmese customs were weakened. In 1941 the Japanese invaded Burma, promising independence if the British were defeated. At the end of World War II, the leader Aung San negotiated independence from Britain, which was granted in 1948.

From 1948 to 1962, Burma was a democratic republic, with U Nu as the first prime minister. In 1962 General Ne Win led a military *coup d'état*. He ruled for twenty-six years as a dictator, suspending the constitution and establishing military rule. Outside visitors were few and restricted to Rangoon, Mandalay and a handful of other tightly controlled towns close to the central plains.

In July 1988, demonstrations broke out across the country during the so-called 'Democracy Summer'. In 1988, Aung San Suu Kyi, daughter of the independence hero Aung San, founded the National League for Democracy (NLD). Her party quickly gathered country-wide support. Although committed to non-violence, Aung San Suu Kyi was placed under house arrest in July 1989 for 'endangering the state' and kept there for the next six years. Nevertheless, her party won the elections in 1990. In 1991 she was awarded the Nobel Peace Prize; in 2003, she was imprisoned once again and released in 2010.

The humanitarian situation in Burma is disastrous and civil war still ravages the border areas. The effect of military rule has been an impoverished and underdeveloped nation; Burma is rated as the second least developed nation on the United Nations Development Index. Peace, democracy and the most basic human rights do not exist.

5.9 **Society**

INTERACTIVE MAP 5: *BRITISH IMPERIAL TRADING ROUTES*

The mission of the coloniser

The concept of 'the white man's burden' was exalted in the works of colonial writers like Rudyard Kipling, and the expansion of the Empire was often regarded as a mission. Every time the British took control over a territory, they felt they brought civilisation to the barbarian, faith to the heathen, wealth to the poor and law and social order to primitive societies.

Rudyard Kipling's (1865–1936) poem 'The White Man's Burden', written in 1899 to give advice to the United States on the occasion of the annexation of the Philippines, contains the author's most famous phrase, 'the white man's burden', which made him the bard of the English Empire and came to symbolise the belief in the superiority of the Anglo-Saxon race.

The White Man's Burden[1]

Rudyard Kipling

The White Man's Burden (1899)

5.1

Take up the White Man's burden –
Send forth the best ye breed[2] –
Go bind[3] your sons to exile
To serve your captive's need;
To wait in heavy harness[4]
On fluttered folk[5] and wild –
Your new-caught, sullen[6] peoples,
Half devil and half child.

Take up the White Man's burden –
In patience to abide[7],
To veil the threat of terror
And check the show of pride;
By open speech and simple,
An hundred times made plain,
To seek another's profit,
And work another's gain[8].

Take up the White Man's burden –
The savage wars of peace –
Fill full the mouth of Famine
And bid[9] the sickness cease;
And when your goal is nearest
The end for others sought[10],
Watch Sloth and heathen Folly[11]
Bring all your hope to nought[12].

Take up the White Man's burden –
No tawdry[13] rule of kings,
But toil[14] of serf and sweeper –
The tale of common things,
The ports ye shall not enter,
The roads ye shall not tread[15],
Go make them with your living,
And mark them with your dead! [...]

1 India on the brain – *Mr Rudyard Kipling*, cartoon, ca 1892.

1 READ the poem and find out:

1. what Kipling actually means by 'burden';
2. how the colonised peoples are described;
3. what the advantages brought to them by imperialism are;
4. whether the mission of the coloniser implies reward.

2 FILL IN the table with the Victorian arguments for and against imperialism. Then share your ideas with the rest of the class.

Arguments for
Arguments against

1 **Burden.** Fardello.
2 **Send ... breed.** Mandate (in missione) i migliori che allevate.
3 **bind.** Legate, vincolate.
4 **harness.** Onere, lavoro.
5 **fluttered folk.** Gente agitata.
6 **sullen.** Astiosi o pigri.
7 **to abide.** Sopportare.
8 **gain.** Miglioramento.
9 **bid.** Ordina.
10 **sought.** Cercato.
11 **Sloth and heathen Folly.** La pigrizia e la follia dei pagani.
12 **nought.** Nulla.
13 **tawdry.** Pacchiano, da due soldi.
14 **toil.** Duro lavoro.
15 **tread.** Percorrere, calpestare.

5.10 **Science and Philosophy**

Charles Darwin and evolution

WARM-UP

1 **WRITE** a list of the ideas you associate with the name of Charles Darwin.

In the second half of the 19th century, Britain reached the peak of its power abroad; however, some ideological conflicts were beginning to undermine the self-confident attitude that had characterised the first part of Victoria's reign. Changes regarded several fields, especially scientific achievements, industrialisation, sexuality and religion, and a growing pessimism began to affect intellectuals and artists, who expressed in different ways their sense of doubt about the stability of Victorian society.

In 1859, Charles Darwin (1809–82) published his theory of evolution in *On the Origin of Species*. Although evolutionary ideas were not new to the Victorians (the work of Charles Lyell in 1830–33 and Robert Chambers in 1844 both held that organisms evolved from an original being created by God), Darwin's radical contribution was his theory of 'natural selection' and his stress on the godless element of chance involved in evolutionary variation.

While Darwin's theory discarded the version of creation given by the Bible, it also seemed to show that the strongest survived and the weakest deserved to be defeated. The philosopher Herbert Spencer (1820–1903) applied Darwin's ideas to social life, arguing that economic competition was the same as natural selection and that the poor and oppressed did not deserve compassion.

Milestones

1871, Darwin's The Descent of Man and Selection in Relation to Sex

In this seminal work Darwin developed the theory of evolution and natural selection, according to which:

- all living creatures in existence have taken their forms through a slow process of change and adaptation in a struggle for survival;
- favourable physical conditions determine the survival of a species, unfavourable ones its extinction;
- man evolved, like any other animal, from less highly organised forms, namely from a monkey.

Benjamin Waterhouse Hawkins, frontispiece to Thomas Henry Huxley's *Evidence as to Man's Place in Nature*, 1863.

1 Darwin with Charles Lyell. Lyell was the founder of modern geology and his studies greatly influenced Darwin's theories. The two scientists became close friends.

2 A satire of Darwin's theory of evolution, from 'The Illustrated Times', 1863.

3 Charles Darwin, photographed by Julia Margaret Cameron, 1868.

2 **LOOK at the cartoon below and, in pairs, discuss why Darwin was depicted like this.**

A Venerable Orang-outang, a caricature of Charles Darwin as an ape published in 'The Hornet', a satirical magazine, March 1871.

FCE Reading and Use of English – Part 6

3 **GAPPED TEXT. You are going to read an article about Darwin's theory of evolution. Six sentences have been removed from the article. Choose from the sentences A–G the one which fits each gap (1–6). There is one extra sentence which you do not need to use.**

- **A** Among the scientific community they ranged from contemptuous rejection to enthusiastic support.
- **B** Many suggested instead that the variations that natural selection picked out were themselves divinely guided or caused.
- **C** It is probably more fantasy than fact.
- **D** Scientists found that new avenues were thrown open to their particular fields of research.
- **E** Yet, close study of many thousands of organisms showed that there was a constant abundance of variety or slight differences between all individuals.
- **F** These had gradually changed as the environment changed around them.
- **G** Writers before Darwin had made connections between humans and apes and monkeys because of our obvious physical similarities.

Darwin vs **God?**

About two hundred years ago, Charles Darwin, the bearded Victorian sage on the ten pound note, was born. Many people believe he was the man who discovered that we come from monkeys. Yet, he did no such thing. **1** ______ Instead, Darwin set out to answer the questions: How are new species formed? Where do they come from? What is their origin? His theory was not about the origin of life itself. Although Darwin believed that this question too would turn out to have a perfectly natural explanation, he thought that it was, then, beyond the power of science to answer.

We often hear that when *On the Origin of Species* was published there was much protest and a historic clash of science and religion. But is that true? **2** ______ The Victorian public that first read or read about *On the Origin of Species* were, for the most part, not biblical literalists. For decades, the most enlightened writers in the fields of science and religion had accepted that much of the Old Testament, and Genesis in particular, had to be read in a metaphorical sense. So Victorian readers were confronted with one of the leading men of science of the day publishing a work that claimed that, contrary to long-held beliefs, new species were not somehow created in each new geological age to fit the new conditions. Instead, new species were the lineal descendants of earlier species. **3** ______ Thus all living and extinct species were related on a single genealogical family tree – the tree of life.

Darwin's theories inspired lots of reactions. **4** ______ Darwin's wide variety of arguments and evidence persuaded many that he had found the hidden bond that naturalists had been seeking which explained how all the different genera and species were related. Other writers felt that Darwin's views were an attack on the role of a Creator in nature. Instead of tracing a lineage to the son of God, Darwin's theory suggested that man had only beastly origins.

Others, like the Reverend Charles Kingsley, felt differently. He wrote enthusiastically to Darwin about his theory. To religious thinkers like Kingsley, Darwin had uncovered a new law by which God governed the natural world. For such thinkers, it was quite reasonable to reconcile Darwin's views with their religious beliefs. As the years passed and reviews and counter-reviews appeared, the fact of Darwinian evolution – the common descent of species – became increasingly recognised. Yet, the other key Darwinian idea – natural selection – was much less welcome. As scientific and non-scientific readers came increasingly to accept the Darwinian concept of common ancestry for species, the view that natural selection was the primary mechanism was often rejected. **5** ______ The bottom line seemed to be: was there a meaning or intention behind how life changed? According to Darwin, there were only natural reasons.

The fact that Darwin's views were largely accepted throughout the international community within ten to fifteen years is remarkable. **6** ______ Countless confirmations and refinements were published. New fossil forms were discovered which filled gaps between already known groups, just as Darwin had predicted.

(Abridged from 'BBC History', January 2009)

5.11 **Literature**

Robert Louis Stevenson: Victorian hypocrisy and the double in literature

WARM-UP

1 **DISCUSS** why most of the literature of the second half of the 19th century is based on the contrast between appearance and reality. You may also refer to section 5.3 to support your ideas.

The Scottish writer Robert Louis Stevenson (1850–94) captured the mood of change of the last decades of the 19th century and expressed the moral dichotomy between good and evil in his classic psychological novel *The Strange Case of Dr Jekyll and Mr Hyde* (1886), in which hypocrisy is embodied by the double. The double, or *doppelgänger*, is a second self or *alter ego*, which appears as a distinct and separate being perceived by the physical senses but existing in a dependent relation to the original. 'Dependent' does not mean 'subordinate'; in fact, the double often comes to dominate, control and usurp the functions of the subject. Stevenson created a symbiotic relationship between Dr Jekyll and Mr Hyde, the former locked in symbolic conflict with the sinister power he had released from within his own being.

Robert Louis Stevenson's life

Robert Louis Stevenson was born in Edinburgh in 1850. Because of his poor health, he spent most of his childhood in bed, terrified of the dark and tutored at home under the influence of his family's Calvinism.

In his adolescence he travelled a lot in search of a friendlier climate; he lived in the south of England, Germany, France and Italy. He took up engineering at university, following in his father's footsteps, but he was not enthusiastic about it. He was in conflict with his social environment, the respectable Victorian world; he grew his hair long, his manners were eccentric and he became one of the first examples of a 'bohemian' in Britain, openly rejecting his family's religious principles and their love for respectability.

After giving up engineering, he graduated in law in 1875 and decided to devote himself to writing. He married an American woman, and since his health was deteriorating, they moved to Australia and Tahiti, settling down at Vailima in Samoa. He died of a brain haemorrhage in 1894.

Stevenson became popular as a novelist in the 1880s, when he published *Treasure Island* (1883), *The Strange Case of Dr Jekyll and Mr Hyde* (1886), *Kidnapped* (1886) and *The Master of Ballantrae* (1889). His short stories, pervaded by a sense of suspense and supernatural, were collected as *New Arabian Nights* (1882).

1 A portrait of Robert Louis Stevenson, 1894. National Portrait Gallery, London.

The Strange Case of Dr Jekyll and Mr Hyde (1886)

The story

The plot of *Dr Jekyll and Mr Hyde* is quite simple: the protagonist is a man divided against himself into two distinct characters. The first is a respectable being, Jekyll, and the second an evil genius, Hyde. These two beings are in a perpetual struggle, and it is the same act of secret chemistry that releases Hyde and restores Jekyll. Once Hyde is released from hiding, he achieves domination over the Jekyll aspect, so that the individual has only two choices: the man may choose a life of crime and depravity, or Jekyll must eliminate Hyde in the only way left – by killing himself. Hence Jekyll's suicide is the final and only choice. Stevenson therefore implies that man's salvation is based on the annihilation of one part of his nature – if he lives in a civilised society.

2 Fredric March in the film 'Dr Jekyll and Mr Hyde', directed by Rouben Mamoulian in 1931.

2 **FILL IN** the table below to organise your knowledge about Stevenson's life.

Place of birth	
Childhood experiences	
Religious upbringing	
Education	
Journeys	
Attitude towards society	
Works	
Cause of death	

WARM-UP

1 **REFER to the description of 'The story' on the previous page and describe what you think Jekyll-Hyde's house and its door might look like. Then read the passage and check your predictions.**

The story of the door

Robert Louis Stevenson

The Strange Case of Dr Jekyll and Mr Hyde (1886)

Chapter I

In the following passage the third-person narrator, who tells most of the story, closely follows the movements of Mr Utterson and introduces the protagonist, the monster Hyde.

5.2

Mr Utterson the lawyer was a man of a rugged countenance[1], that was never lighted by a smile; cold, scanty[2] and embarrassed in discourse; backward in sentiment[3]; lean, long, dusty, dreary, and yet somehow lovable. At friendly meetings, and when the wine was to his taste, something eminently human beaconed[4] from his eye; something indeed which never found its way into his talk, but which spoke not only in these silent symbols of the after dinner face, but more often and loudly in the acts of his life. He was austere with himself: drank gin when he was alone, to mortify a taste for vintages[5]; and though he enjoyed the theatre, had not crossed the doors of one for twenty years. But he had an approved tolerance for others; sometimes wondering almost with envy, at the high pressure of spirits involved in their misdeeds[6]; and in any extremity inclined to help rather than to reprove. 'I incline to Cain's heresy,' he used to say quaintly[7]: 'I let my brother go to the devil in his own way.' In this character it was frequently his fortune to be the last reputable acquaintance and the last good influence in the lives of down-going men[8]. And to such as these, so long as they came about his chambers, he never marked a shade of change in his demeanour.

No doubt the feat[9] was easy to Mr Utterson; for he was undemonstrative at the best, and even his friendships seemed to be founded in a similar catholicity[10] of good-nature. It is the mark of a modest man to accept his friendly circle ready made from the hands of opportunity; and that was the lawyer's way. His friends were those of his own blood, or those whom he had known the longest; his affections, like ivy, were the growth of time, they implied no aptness[11] in the object. Hence, no doubt, the bond that united him to Mr Richard Enfield, his distant kinsman, the well-known man about town. It was a nut to crack for many[12], what these two could see in each other, or what subject they could find in common. It was reported by those who encountered them in their Sunday walks, that they said nothing, looked singularly dull[13], and would hail with obvious relief the appearance of a friend. For all that, the two men put the greatest store[14] by these excursions, counted them the chief jewel of each week, and not only set aside occasions of pleasure, but even resisted the calls of business, that they might enjoy them uninterrupted.

It chanced on one of these rambles that their way led them down a by street in a busy quarter of London. The street was small and what is called quiet, but it drove

3 A 1930 illustration for *The Strange Case of Dr Jekyll and Mr Hyde* by S.G. Hulme Beaman.

1 **rugged countenance.** Burbera espressione.
2 **scanty.** Reticente.
3 **backward in sentiment.** Introverso.
4 **beaconed.** Splendeva.
5 **vintages.** Vini eccellenti.
6 **misdeeds.** Misfatti.
7 **quaintly.** In modo bizzarro.
8 **down-going men.** Uomini sulla via della rovina.
9 **feat.** Impresa.
10 **catholicity.** Universalità, eclettismo.
11 **aptness.** Abilità, propensione.
12 **a nut to crack for many.** Problema difficile da risolvere per molti.
13 **dull.** Tristi.
14 **put the greatest store.** Davano la più grande importanza.

a thriving trade on the week-days. The inhabitants were all doing well, it seemed, and all emulously[15] hoping to do better still, and laying out the surplus of their gains in coquetry[16]; so that the shop fronts stood along that thoroughfare with an air of invitation, like rows of smiling saleswomen. Even on Sunday, when it veiled its more florid charms and lay comparatively empty of passage, the street shone out in contrast to its dingy neighbourhood, like a fire in a forest; and with its freshly painted shutters, well-polished brasses[17], and general cleanliness and gaiety of note, instantly caught and pleased the eye of the passenger.

Two doors from one corner, on the left hand going east, the line was broken by the entry of a court; and just at that point, a certain sinister block of building thrust forward its gable[18] on the street. It was two storeys high; showed no window, nothing but a door on the lower storey and a blind forehead of discoloured wall on the upper; and bore in every feature the marks of prolonged and sordid negligence. The door, which was equipped with neither bell nor knocker, was blistered and distained[19]. Tramps slouched[20] into the recess and struck matches on the panels; children kept shop upon the steps; the schoolboy had tried his knife on the mouldings[21]; and for close on a generation no one had appeared to drive away these random visitors or to repair their ravages[22].

Mr Enfield and the lawyer were on the other side of the by street; but when they came abreast[23] of the entry, the former lifted up his cane and pointed.

'Did you ever remark that door?' he asked; and when his companion had replied in the affirmative, 'It is connected in my mind,' added he, 'with a very odd story.'

'Indeed!' said Mr Utterson, with a slight change of voice, 'and what was that?'

'Well, it was this way,' returned Mr Enfield: 'I was coming home from some place at the end of the world, about three o'clock of a black winter morning, and my way lay through a part of town where there was literally nothing to be seen but lamps. Street after street, and all the folks asleep – street after street, all lighted up as if for a procession, and all as empty as a church – till at last I got into that state of mind when a man listens and listens and begins to long for the sight of a policeman. All at once, I saw two figures: one a little man who was stumping along[24] eastward at a good walk, and the other a girl of maybe eight or ten who was running as hard as she was able down a cross-street. Well, sir, the two ran into one another naturally enough at the corner; and then came the horrible part of the thing; for the man trampled calmly over[25] the child's body and left her screaming on the ground. It sounds nothing to hear, but it was hellish to see. It wasn't like a man; it was like some damned Juggernaut[26]. I gave a view halloa[27], took to my heels, collared my gentleman, and brought him back to where there was already quite a group about the screaming child. He was perfectly cool and made no resistance, but gave me one look, so ugly that it brought out the sweat on me like running. The people who had turned out were the girl's own family; and pretty soon the doctor, for whom she had been sent, put in his appearance. Well, the child was not much the worse, more frightened, according to the Sawbones[28]; and there you might have supposed would be an end to it. But there was one curious circumstance. I had taken a loathing[29] to my gentleman at first sight. So had the child's family, which was only natural. But the doctor's case was what struck me. He was the usual cut-and-dry apothecary[30], of no particular age and colour, with a strong Edinburgh accent, and

15 **emulously.** Ardentemente.
16 **laying ... in coquetry.** Investendo l'eccedenza dei propri guadagni in opere di abbellimento (*lett.*: civetteria).
17 **well-polished brasses.** Ottoni ben lucidati.
18 **gable.** Tetto a due spioventi.
19 **blistered and distained.** Screpolata e stinta.
20 **Tramps slouched.** Vagabondi stavano rannicchiati.
21 **mouldings.** Stipiti.
22 **ravages.** Rovine.
23 **abreast.** Fianco a fianco.
24 **stumping along.** Camminando.
25 **trampled ... over.** Calpestò.
26 **Juggernaut.** Idolo indù, che si trascinava per le vie su un grosso carro mentre i fanatici si gettavano sotto le ruote; si usa per indicare chi calpesta tutto quello che incontra sul cammino per raggiungere il proprio scopo.
27 **view halloa.** Forte urlo (incitamento usato nella caccia alla volpe).
28 **Sawbones.** Medico (termine dispregiativo; *lett.*: 'Segaossi').
29 **loathing.** Disgusto.
30 **apothecary.** Farmacista.

1 Spencer Tracy in the film 'Dr Jekyll and Mr Hyde', directed by Victor Fleming in 1941.

about as emotional as a bagpipe. Well, sir, he was like the rest of us: every time he looked at my prisoner, I saw that Sawbones turned sick and white with the desire to kill him, I knew what was in his mind, just as he knew what was in mine; and killing being out of the question, we did the next best. We told the man we could and would make such a scandal out of this, as should make his name stink[31] from one end of London to the other. If he had any friends or any credit, we undertook, that he should lose them. And all the time, as we were pitching it in red hot[32], we were keeping the women off him as best we could, for they were as wild as harpies. I never saw a circle of such hateful faces; and there was the man in the middle, with a kind of black sneering coolness – frightened too, I could see that – but carrying it off, sir, really like Satan.'

31 **stink.** *Lett.*: puzzare; *qui*: rendere odioso.

32 **pitching it in red hot.** Lo tenevamo sulle spine.

COMPREHENSION

2 READ the first three paragraphs and find out:

1 what Mr Utterson's job was;
2 what he was like;
3 who Mr Enfield was;
4 what Mr Utterson's relationship with Mr Enfield was like;
5 where they happened to wander one Sunday afternoon.

3 READ the description of the house in lines 41–50 and complete the notes below.

Height	The door ....
Number of windows	The panels ....
Number of doors	The steps ....
The façade	The mouldings ....

4 DESCRIBE the features of the 'by street' on weekdays and on Sundays. How do they differ?

5 DECIDE if the following sentences are true or false. Correct the false ones.

1 Mr Enfield had spent the night at his usual place. T F
2 The street he was walking along was dull. T F
3 He felt uneasy. T F
4 The little man was crippled. T F
5 The little man hurt the little girl. T F
6 The little man ran away with her. T F
7 The little man was not frightened at all. T F
8 The doctor was very sensitive. T F
9 Mr Enfield and the doctor decided to kill the little man to avenge the girl. T F

ANALYSIS

6 DECIDE. Who is the narrator? Whose points of view are adopted?

7 JUSTIFY this statement with reference to the text: Mr Utterson is the typical Victorian man.

8 THE NARRATOR tells us only three things about Mr Enfield:

1 He is Utterson's 'distant relative' (line 23).
2 He is 'the well-known man about town' (lines 23–24).
3 He gives great importance to his regular walks with Utterson even if 'they said nothing' (line 26) and 'they looked singularly dull' (line 26).

Consider these details and say what they suggest about the Utterson-Enfield relationship.

9 UNDERLINE all the expressions about 'the little man'.

1 What do they connote?
2 What kind of person do you think he is?
3 What feelings does this creature provoke in the others?
- □ Anguish.
- □ Decay.
- □ Fright.
- □ Curiosity.
- □ Repulsion.
- □ Imminent danger.
- □ Evil.

10 LINE 65 contains the expression 'two ... into one', which has a symbolic meaning. Can you explain it?

YOUR TURN

11 DISCUSS in pairs your personal opinions on the theme of the double. Do you know other stories based on the idea of a split personality?

5.12 | **The Arts**

New aesthetic theories

The Aesthetic Movement developed in the universities and intellectual circles in the last decades of the 19th century. It began in France with Théophile Gautier (1811–72) and reflected the sense of frustration and uncertainty of the artist, his reaction against the materialism and the restrictive moral code of the bourgeoisie and his need to re-define the role of art. As a result, French artists withdrew from the political and social scene and 'escaped' into aesthetic isolation, into what Gautier defined 'Art for Art's Sake'. The *bohémien* embodied his protest against the monotony and vulgarity of bourgeois life, leading an unconventional existence, pursuing sensation and excess, and cultivating art and beauty.

The origins of the English Aesthetic Movement can be traced back to the Pre-Raphaelite Dante Gabriel Rossetti (1828–82), who was a remarkable example of an artist dedicated wholly to his art.

1 READ the text on the left and make notes about:

1. where and when the Aesthetic Movement began;
2. what it reflected and reacted against;
3. what its motto was;
4. how the Aesthete lived.

FCE Reading and Use of English – Part 2

2 OPEN CLOZE. For questions 1–8, read the text below and think of the word which best fits each gap. Use only one word in each gap. There is an example at the beginning (0).

The Pre-Raphaelite Brotherhood

The term 'Pre-Raphaelite' came **(0)** ......INTO...... use when the young painters William Holman Hunt (1827–1910) and John Everett Millais (1829–96), criticising the style of Raphael and his followers, rejected academic taste and 'classical' doctrines and praised the purity and simplicity of the Italian art of the 13th and 14th centuries. The movement began at **(1)** .... end of the 1840s, **(2)** .... an attempt to introduce **(3)** .... visual art not only the qualities of medieval Italian painting but a concern with naturalistic accuracy of detail. The Pre-Raphaelite painters turned their eyes away **(4)** .... the ugly contemporary industrial and urban world and conceived the creation of beauty as a duty owed to society. Both a poet and a painter, Dante Gabriel Rossetti (1828–82) was the strongest personality and organiser of the group.

The second phase of Pre-Raphaelitism, **(5)** .... developed from the late 1850s under the direction of Rossetti, was Aesthetic Pre-Raphaelitism. It led to William Morris's Arts and Crafts Movement, which advocated the renewed use of handicraft and simple decoration in reaction **(6)** .... industrial machinery and contemporary aesthetic eclecticism. The firm designed and manufactured in a great variety of media, including stained glass, hand-painted tiles, tapestries and other woven textiles, embroideries, rugs and carpets, as **(7)** .... as hand-printed wallpapers and chintzes with which **(8)** .... of Victorian interiors were furnished.

A further development was the work of the Aesthetes and the Decadents. Rossetti and his follower Edward Burne-Jones (1833–98) emphasised medieval erotic themes, a combination of realism with elaborate symbolism and pictorial techniques which achieved a dreamy atmosphere.

1 Edward Burne-Jones, *The Golden Stairs*, 1876–80. Tate Gallery, London.

2 Dante Gabriel Rossetti, *Venus Verticordia*, 1863–68. Russell-Cotes Art Gallery and Museum, Bournemouth, England.

3 READ the text about the Pre-Raphaelite Brotherhood again and underline the key phrases. Then compare your work with a classmate.

GLOSSARY
handicraft artigianato
tiles piastrelle
tapestries arazzi
woven textiles tessuti artigianali
embroideries ricami
rugs tappetini
hand-printed stampate a mano
wallpapers carta da parati, tappezzerie
chintzes tessuti in cotone o seta, resi lucidi da una gommatura di fissaggio

Internet Lab

1 **DIVIDE the class into groups of two or three students per computer.**

2 **BROWSE this site:**
www.tate.org.uk

3 **CARRY OUT a research project, in your group, about one of these three paintings. The questions given below each painting may help you.**

3 Dante Gabriel Rossetti, *Ecce Ancilla Domini*, 1850. Tate Gallery, London.

1 Look at painting 3 and do the following activities.

- **A** Say where the scene takes place.
- **B** Describe the Virgin and her attitude.
- **C** Point out the details concerning the angel Gabriel.
- **D** The painting has a tall narrow shape. Highlight the elements which contribute to the vertical division of space. What elements move across this division?
- **E** The Pre-Raphaelites adopted the practice of painting over a pure white background. Comment on the use of colour in the picture.
- **F** The colours chosen are charged with symbolic meaning. What associations do they suggest?
- **G** Compare Rossetti's depiction of the Virgin with an example of traditional iconography and explain why the Victorian public found it shocking.

4 John Everett Millais, *Ophelia*, 1851–52. Tate Gallery, London.

2 Look at painting 4 and fill in the table below.

The source of the painting	
The painter's aim	
The model	
The technique	
The background	
Symbolism	

3 Look at painting 5 and answer the questions.

- **A** What is there on the carpet?
- **B** What does the girl's lack of a wedding ring emphasise?
- **C** Is there a window or a mirror in the background?
- **D** How is the room furnished?
- **E** What symbols explain the theme of the 'fallen woman'?
- **F** How are the image reflected in the mirror and the light in the right corner related?

4 **PRESENT your group's findings to the rest of the class.**

5 **DISCUSS with the rest of the class what aspects of Victorianism these paintings comment upon.**

5 William Holman Hunt, *The Awakening Conscience*, 1853. Tate Gallery, London.

5.13 **Literature**

Aestheticism

theme of art not connected with

AIM: ART for ART'S sake
get pleasure x art
no connection between art and morality

the artist must be free to express himself without following any rules and convention

Walter Pater and the Aesthetic Movement

Walter Pater (1839–94) is regarded as the theorist of the Aesthetic Movement in England. His *Studies in the History of the Renaissance* (1873) and his masterpiece *Marius the Epicurean* (1885) were immediately successful, especially with the young, because of their subversive and potentially 'demoralising' message. He rejected religious faith and said that art was the only means to stop time, the only certainty. He thought life should be lived in the spirit of art, namely 'as a work of art', filling each passing moment with intense experience, feeling all kinds of sensations. The task of the artist was to feel sensations, to be attentive to the 'attractive', the 'gracious'. So the artist was seen as the transcriber 'not of the world, not of mere fact, but of his sense of it'. The main implication of this new aesthetic position was that art had no reference to life, and therefore it had nothing to do with morality and did not need to be didactic.

Pater's works had a deep influence on the poets and writers of the 1890s, especially Oscar Wilde, who was, in his twenties, an exemplary Aesthete.

Literary language
Aestheticism

A number of features can be distinguished in the works of Aesthetic artists:

- evocative use of the language of the senses;
- excessive attention to the self;
- a hedonistic attitude;
- perversity in subject matter;
- disenchantment with contemporary society;
- absence of any didactic aim.

1 Aubrey Beardsley, front cover for 'The Yellow Book', January 1895. 'The Yellow Book' was a leading British journal of the 1890s which was associated with Aestheticism and Decadence. The magazine contained a wide range of literary and artistic genres, poetry, short stories, essays, book illustrations, portraits, and reproductions of paintings.

1 **READ the text about Walter Pater and the Aesthetic Movement and complete the following sentences.**

1 The message of his works was ....

2 The only way to stop time is ....

3 Life should be lived as ....

4 The writer's task is to ....

5 As a result, art does not have to ....

TEXT BANK 42: *THE PICTURE OF DORIAN GRAY*
TEXT BANK 43: *THE IMPORTANCE OF BEING EARNEST*

Oscar Wilde: the brilliant artist and Aesthete

Oscar Wilde's life

Oscar Wilde (1854–1900) was born in Dublin in 1854. After attending Trinity College in Dublin, he was sent to Oxford, where he gained a first class degree in classics and distinguished himself for his eccentricity. He became a disciple of Walter Pater, accepting the theory of 'Art for Art's Sake'. After graduating, he left Oxford and settled in London, where he soon became a fashionable dandy for his extraordinary wit and his extravagant way of dressing.

In 1881, Wilde edited, at his own expense, *Poems*, and was engaged for a tour in the United States, where he held some lectures about the Pre-Raphaelites and the Aesthetes. On his arrival in New York, he told reporters that Aestheticism was a search for the beautiful, a science through which men looked for the relationship existing between painting, sculpture and poetry, which were simply different forms of the same truth. The tour was a remarkable personal success for Wilde.

On his return to Europe in 1883, he married Constance Lloyd, who bore him two children, but he soon became tired of his marriage. At this point in his career he was most noted as a great speaker and wit: his presence became a social event and his remarks appeared in the most fashionable London magazines. As a tribute to his dandified Aestheticism, women wore lilies and many young men wore lilies in the buttonholes of their coats.

In the late 1880s, Wilde's literary talent was revealed by a series of short stories, *The Canterville Ghost*, *Lord Arthur Savile's Crime*, *The Happy Prince and Other Tales*, written for his children, and the novel *The Picture of Dorian Gray* (1891). After his first and only novel, he developed an interest in drama. In the 1890s, he produced a series of plays which were successful on the London stage, such as his masterpiece *The Importance of Being Earnest* (1895) and the tragedy in French *Salomé* (1893). However, both the novel and the tragedy damaged the writer's reputation: the former was considered immoral, and the latter was prevented from appearing on the London stage due to its presumed obscenity.

In 1891, Wilde met the handsome young nobleman Lord Alfred Douglas, with whom he had a homosexual affair. The boy's father forced a public trial and Wilde was convicted of homosexual practices and subsequently sentenced to two years of hard labour. While in prison, he wrote *De Profundis*, a long letter to explain his life and to condemn Lord Alfred Douglas for abandoning him; this work was published posthumously in 1905. After Wilde was released from prison, he lived in France under a pseudonym, as an outcast in poverty. He died of meningitis in Paris in 1900.

1

1 Oscar Wilde and Lord Alfred Douglas, 1893.

2 Oscar Wilde, photographed by Napoleon Sarony, 1882. Courtesy Merlin Holland, London.

2

1 **WHILE READING Wilde's biography, fill in the table below. Then use the information you have gathered to organise your knowledge about the author's life.**

Place of birth	
Education	
Influences	
Personal attitudes	
Prose works	
Drama	
Reputation	
Last years of life	
Death	

The Picture of Dorian Gray (1891) and the theme of beauty

The narrative technique

The story is told by an unobtrusive third-person narrator. The perspective adopted is internal, since Dorian's apparition is in the second chapter, and this allows a process of identification between the reader and the character. The settings are vividly described with words appealing to the senses. The characters reveal themselves through what they say or what other people say of them, a technique which is typical of drama.

Timeless beauty

The story is profoundly allegorical; it is a 19th-century version of the myth of Faust, the story of a man who sells his soul to the devil so that all his desires might be satisfied. In the novel, this soul is the picture, which records the signs of time, the corruption, the horror and the sins concealed under the mask of Dorian's timeless beauty. Wilde plays on the Renaissance idea of the correspondence existing between the physical and spiritual realms: beautiful people are moral people; ugly people are immoral people. His variation on this theme is his use of the magical portrait. The picture is not an autonomous self; it represents the dark side of Dorian's personality, his double, which he tries to forget by locking it in a room.

The moral of the novel is that every excess must be punished and reality cannot be escaped. When Dorian destroys the picture, he cannot avoid the punishment for all his sins, that is, death. The horrible, corrupted picture can be seen as a symbol of the immorality and bad conscience of the Victorian middle class, while Dorian and his pure, innocent appearance are symbols of bourgeois hypocrisy. Finally, the picture, restored to its original beauty, illustrates Wilde's theories of art: art survives people, art is eternal.

1 Hurd Hatfield as Dorian Gray in front of his corrupted portrait in the film 'The Picture of Dorian Gray', directed by Albert Lewin in 1945.

2 EXPLAIN:

1 where and when *The Picture of Dorian Gray* takes place;
2 who Dorian Gray is;
3 what narrative technique is employed in the novel;
4 what the picture symbolises;
5 what the moral of the novel is.

The story

The novel is set in London at the end of the 19th century. The protagonist is Dorian Gray, a young man. Dorian's beauty fascinates a painter, Basil Hallward, who decides to paint his portrait. The portrait satisfies the young man's desires, including that of eternal youth; the signs of age, experience and vice appear on the portrait. Dorian lives only for pleasure, making use of everybody and even letting people die because of his insensitivity. When the painter sees the corrupted image of the portrait, Dorian kills him. Later, Dorian wants to free himself of the portrait, witness to his spiritual corruption, and stabs it, but in doing so he mysteriously kills himself. In the very moment of his death, the picture returns to its original purity, and Dorian's face becomes 'withered, wrinkled, and loathsome'.

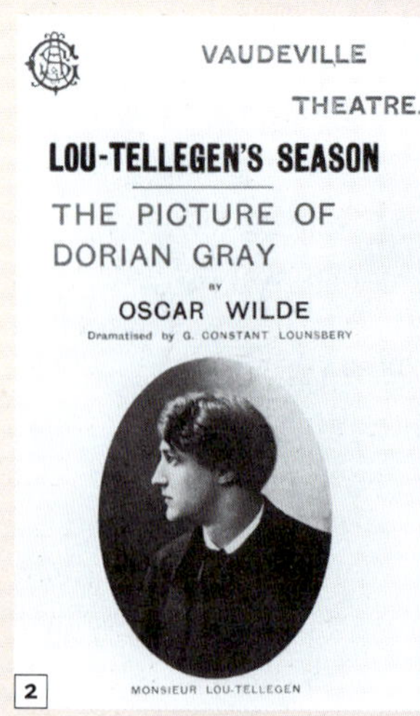

2 Theatre programme for a performance of *The Picture of Dorian Gray*, Vaudeville Theatre, 20th August 1913.

WARM-UP

1 **DISCUSS** with the rest of the class. Nowadays are we too dependent upon what things look like rather than what they really are?

Dorian's death

Oscar Wilde

The Picture of Dorian Gray (1891)
Chapter XX

The following passage is from the final chapter of the novel when the story reaches its climax in an unexpected and dramatic way with Dorian's dreadful metamorphosis.

3 John Singer Sargent, *Walford Graham Robertson*, 1894. Tate Gallery, London.

5.3

It was a lovely night, so warm that he threw his coat over his arm, and did not even put his silk scarf round his throat. As he strolled home, smoking his cigarette, two young men in evening dress passed him. He heard one of them whisper to the other, 'That is Dorian Gray.' He remembered how pleased he used to be when he was pointed out, or stared at, or talked about. He was tired of hearing his own name now. Half the charm of the little village where he had been so often lately was that no one knew who he was. He had often told the girl whom he had lured[1] to love him that he was poor, and she had believed him. He had told her once that he was wicked[2], and she had laughed at him, and answered that wicked people were always very old and very ugly. What a laugh she had! – just like a thrush[3] singing. And how pretty she had been in her cotton dress and her large hats! She knew nothing, but she had everything that he had lost.

When he reached home, he found his servant waiting up for him. He sent him to bed, and threw himself down on the sofa in the library, and began to think over some of the things that Lord Henry had said to him.

Was it really true that one could never change? He felt a wild longing[4] for the unstained purity of his boyhood – his rose-white boyhood, as Lord Henry had once called it. He knew that he had tarnished[5] himself, filled his mind with corruption, and given horror to his fancy; that he had been an evil influence to others, and had experienced a terrible joy in being so; and that, of the lives that had crossed his own, it had been the fairest and the most full of promise that he had brought to shame. But was it all irretrievable[6]? Was there no hope for him?

Ah! in what a monstrous moment of pride and passion he had prayed that the portrait should bear the burden[7] of his days, and he keep the unsullied splendour of eternal youth! All his failure had been due to that. Better for him that each sin of his life had brought its sure, swift penalty along with it. There was purification in punishment. Not 'Forgive us our sins,' but 'Smite[8] us for our iniquities,' should be the prayer of a man to a most just God.

The curiously carved mirror that Lord Henry had given to him, so many years ago now, was standing on the table, and the whitelimbed Cupids laughed round it as of old[9]. He took it up, as he had done on that night of horror, when he had first

1 **lured.** Indotto.
2 **wicked.** Malvagio.
3 **thrush.** Tordo.
4 **longing.** Desiderio intenso.
5 **had tarnished.** Aveva macchiato.
6 **irretrievable.** Irrecuperabile.
7 **bear the burden.** Sostenere il fardello.
8 **Smite.** Punisci.
9 **as of old.** Come un tempo.

noted … ear-dimmed eyes looked into its pol… oved him had written to him a mad l… world is changed because you are m… write history.' The phrases came back t… ver to himself. Then he loathed his ow… , crushed[10] it into silver splinters[11] benea… ed him, his beauty and the youth that he ha… his life might have been free from stain. His be… his youth but a mockery[12]. What was youth at bes… e of shallow moods[13] and sickly thoughts. Why had h… spoiled him.

It was better not to think of the past. Nothing could alter that. It was of himself, and of his own future, that he had to think. James Vane was hidden in a nameless grave in Selby Churchyard. Alan Campbell had shot himself one night in his laboratory, but had not revealed the secret that he had been forced to know. The excitement, such as it was, over Basil Hallward's disappearance would soon pass away. It was already waning[15]. He was perfectly safe there. Nor, indeed, was it the death of Basil Hallward that weighed most upon his mind. It was the living death of his own soul that troubled him. Basil had painted the portrait that had marred[16] his life. He could not forgive him that. It was the portrait that had done everything. Basil had said things to him that were unbearable, and that he had yet borne with patience. The murder had been simply the madness of a moment. As for Alan Campbell, his suicide had been his own act. He had chosen to do it. It was nothing to him.

A new life! That was what he wanted. That was what he was waiting for. Surely he had begun it already. He had spared one innocent thing, at any rate. He would never again tempt innocence. He would be good.

As he thought of Hetty Merton, he began to wonder if the portrait in the locked room had changed. Surely it was not still so horrible as it had been? Perhaps if his life became pure, he would be able to expel every sign of evil passion from the face. Perhaps the signs of evil had already gone away. He would go and look.

He took the lamp from the table and crept upstairs. As he unbarred[17] the door a smile of joy flitted[18] across his strangely young-looking face and lingered[19] for a moment about his lips. Yes, he would be good, and the hideous thing[20] that he had hidden away would no longer be a terror to him. He felt as if the load[21] had been lifted from him already.

He went in quietly, locking the door behind him, as was his custom, and dragged the purple hanging from the portrait. A cry of pain and indignation broke from him. He could see no change save that in the eyes there was a look of cunning[22], and in the mouth the curved wrinkle of the hypocrite. The thing was still loathsome[23] – more loathsome, if possible, than before – and the scarlet dew that spotted[24] the hand seemed brighter, and more like blood newly spilt. Then he trembled. Had it been merely vanity that had made him do his one good deed? Or the desire for a new sensation, as Lord Henry had hinted, with his mocking laugh? Or that passion to act a part that sometimes makes us do things finer than we are ourselves? Or, perhaps, all these? And why was the red stain larger than it had been? It seemed to have crept like a horrible disease over the wrinkled fingers. There was blood on the painted feet, as though the thing had dripped[25] – blood even on the hand that had not held the knife. Confess? Did it mean that he was to confess? To give himself up[26], and be put to death? He laughed. He felt that the idea was monstrous. Besides, even if he

10 **crushed.** *Lett.*: schiacciò; *qui*: ridusse.
11 **splinters.** Frammenti, schegge.
12 **mockery.** Beffa.
13 **shallow moods.** Umori frivoli.
14 **livery.** Livrea.
15 **waning.** Svanendo.
16 **had marred.** Aveva rovinato.
17 **unbarred.** Tolse il catenaccio.
18 **flitted.** Balenò.
19 **lingered.** Indugiò.
20 **hideous thing.** Cosa odiosa, ripugnante (il quadro).
21 **load.** Peso.
22 **cunning.** Astuzia.
23 **loathsome.** Orribile.
24 **spotted.** Macchiava.
25 **dripped.** Gocciolato.
26 **To give himself up.** Consegnarsi, costituirsi.

THEME of ART = he destroys the portrait.

did confess, who would believe him? There was no trace of the murdered man anywhere. Everything belonging to him had been destroyed. He himself had burned what had been below-stairs. The world would simply say that he was mad. They would shut him up if he persisted in his story... Yet it was his duty to confess, to suffer public shame, and to make public atonement[27]. There was a God who called upon men to tell their sins to earth as well as to heaven. Nothing that he could do would cleanse him till he had told his own sin. His sin? He shrugged his shoulders. The death of Basil Hallward seemed very little to him. He was thinking of Hetty Merton. For it was an unjust mirror, this mirror of his soul that he was looking at. Vanity? Curiosity? Hypocrisy? Had there been nothing more in his renunciation than that? There had been something more. At least he thought so. But who could tell?... No. There had been nothing more. Through vanity he had spared her. In hypocrisy he had worn the mask of goodness. For curiosity's sake he had tried the denial of self. He recognised that now.

1 Ben Barnes as Dorian Gray in front of his portrait in the film 'Dorian Gray', directed by Oliver Parker in 2009.

But this murder – was it to dog[28] him all his life? Was he always to be burdened by his past? Was he really to confess? Never. There was only one bit of evidence[29] left against him. The picture itself – that was evidence. He would destroy it. Why had he kept it so long? Once it had given him pleasure to watch it changing and growing old. Of late he had felt no such pleasure. It had kept him awake at night. When he had been away, he had been filled with terror lest[30] other eyes should look upon it. It had brought melancholy across his passions. Its mere memory had marred many moments of joy. It had been like conscience to him. Yes, it had been conscience. He would destroy it.

He looked round, and saw the knife that had stabbed Basil Hallward. He had cleaned it many times, till there was no stain left upon it. It was bright, and glistened[31]. As it had killed the painter, so it would kill the painter's work, and all that that meant. It would kill the past and when that was dead he would be free. It would kill this monstrous soul-life, and, without its hideous warnings, he would be at peace. He seized the thing, and stabbed the picture with it.

There was a cry heard, and a crash. The cry was so horrible in its agony that the frightened servants woke, and crept out of their rooms. Two gentlemen, who were passing in the Square below, stopped, and looked up at the great house. They walked on till they met a policeman, and brought him back. The man rang the bell several times, but there was no answer. Except for a light in one of the top windows, the house was all dark. After a time, he went away and stood in an adjoining portico and watched.

'Whose house is that, constable?' asked the elder of the two gentlemen.

'Mr Dorian Gray's, sir,' answered the policeman.

They looked at each other, as they walked away, and sneered[32]. One of them was Sir Henry Ashton's uncle.

Inside, in the servants' part of the house, the half-clad[33] domestics were talking in low whispers to each other. Old Mrs Leaf was crying and wringing her hands. Francis was as pale as death.

27 **atonement.** Espiazione.
28 **to dog.** Perseguitare.
29 **evidence.** Prova.
30 **lest.** Per paura che.
31 **glistened.** Brillava.
32 **sneered.** Sghignazzarono.
33 **half-clad.** Parzialmente vestiti.

After about quarter of an hour, he got the coachman and one of the footmen and crept upstairs. They knocked, but there was no reply. They called out. Everything was still. Finally, after vainly trying to force the door, they got on the roof, and dropped down on to the balcony. The windows yielded easily; their bolts[34] were old.

When they entered they found, hanging upon the wall, a splendid portrait of their master as they had last seen him, in all the wonder of his exquisite youth and beauty. Lying on the floor was a dead man, in evening dress, with a knife in his heart. He was withered, wrinkled, and loathsome of visage. It was not till they had examined the rings that they recognised who it was.

34 **bolts.** Serrature, catenacci.

COMPREHENSION

2 READ the passage and find:

1 what references Dorian Gray makes to his past;
2 how he tries to justify himself;
3 what he thinks about his beauty;
4 what the portrait makes him understand about his recent actions;
5 what he decides to do;
6 why he does this;
7 what happens as a result.

ANALYSIS

3 CONCENTRATE on the character of Dorian Gray.

1 Say what feelings he shows while looking at the picture. How does he judge his own behaviour?
2 What does the portrait mean to Dorian? Does he see it as the reflection of his own soul or as an independent being, extraneous to himself?
3 Read lines 19–118 again. Here Dorian Gray is aware of his sins and crimes, which are reflected on the picture, as well as of the fact that it is impossible to escape old age and death. In the attempt to change his reality, he looks back at his 'unstained' boyhood with a sort of nostalgia and wonders if it is possible to destroy his maturity, which has become hideous to him, and put an end to his life of corruption. Before reaching the final decision to destroy the picture, Dorian's thought follows different steps. Link each of them to the corresponding lines in the passage.

A nostalgia for his pure boyhood — lines ...
B awareness of his corruption — lines ...
C recollection of his pact to keep eternal youth — lines ...
D wish for repentance and purification — lines ...
E awareness that youth and beauty have caused his ruin — lines ...
F wish to free himself from the past — lines ...
G understanding that repentance was pure illusion — lines ...
H decision to destroy the picture — lines ...

4 EXPLAIN. Why does Dorian kill himself in stabbing the portrait? What does the portrait symbolise?

5 EXAMINE the language of the passage.

1 Consider the examples of parallelisms in lines 10–106 and complete the scheme below.
An example has been provided for you:

A wicked people: *always very old and ugly* — line 12
B his beauty: .... — line 43
C his youth: .... — line 43
D his youth: .... — line 44
E the picture: .... — lines 97–98
F the picture: .... — line 106

2 The first parallelism is the creed that has inspired the whole life of Dorian Gray, which seems to be contradicted by the other statements. Why?
3 Which sentences are used to express Dorian's doubts about his salvation? Underline them.
4 Find the references to the mirror. Comment on the meaning of this suggestive detail in the story.
5 Circle the nouns, verbs, adjectives and adverbs which describe the picture in lines 70–82. Which semantic area do they belong to?

YOUR TURN

6 CONSIDER the conclusion of the book. Do you think the Victorian Age, with its taste for purity and respectability, might have influenced Wilde, or do you think that this ending is consistent with Wilde's theories of art and life? Discuss in groups.

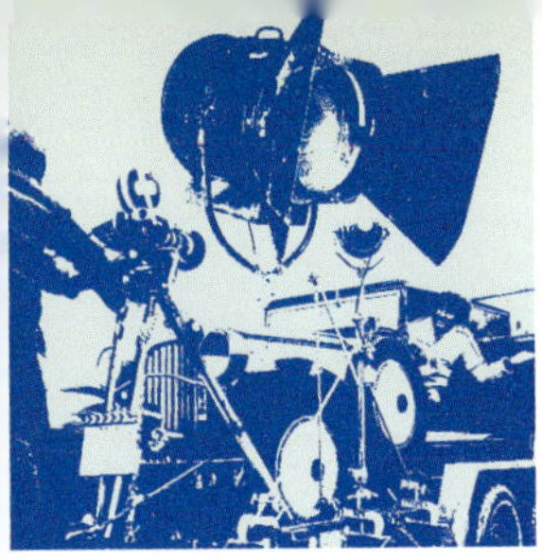

5.15 **Two Films About...**

Oscar Wilde

WARM-UP

1 **DISCUSS.** Wilde was accused of 'committing indecent acts', that is, of homosexuality. Do you think that people who do not accept the more common moral beliefs about sexual behaviour are rejected and punished by society even nowadays?

Wilde

Directed by Brian Gilbert;
USA 1997.
With Stephen Fry (Oscar Wilde);
Jude Law (Bosie).

By 1885, Oscar Wilde's wit and flamboyance are widely renowned. His literary career has earned him fame, and he and his wife Constance have two sons they both love very much. But one evening, Wilde is seduced by the young Robbie Ross, and he is forced to confront his homosexual feelings. In 1892, on the first night of his play *Lady Windermere's Fan*, Oscar is introduced to a handsome young Oxford undergraduate, Lord Alfred Douglas, nicknamed 'Bosie'. Oscar is fascinated by the attractive, intelligent young man, and the risk of a huge scandal becomes greater and greater. Oscar accepts the promiscuous world that excites his lover, neglecting his wife and children. Eventually, Wilde is tried and sentenced to two years of hard labour in Reading Gaol prison. He loses his wife, his children and his reputation, but not Bosie, who waits for him to be released.

What about accuracy?

The film opens with brilliant unexpectedness in the West End, without the rough trade which used to characterise the area in the second half of the 19th century. Fry's Wilde is a credible combination of physical strength and moral weakness, though his hair is wavy and worn insolently longer than even contemporary photographs record. He is a brilliant intellectual, a master of paradox who uses funny and clever remarks every time he opens his mouth. But surely Wilde didn't speak in epigrams all the time.

Dorian Gray

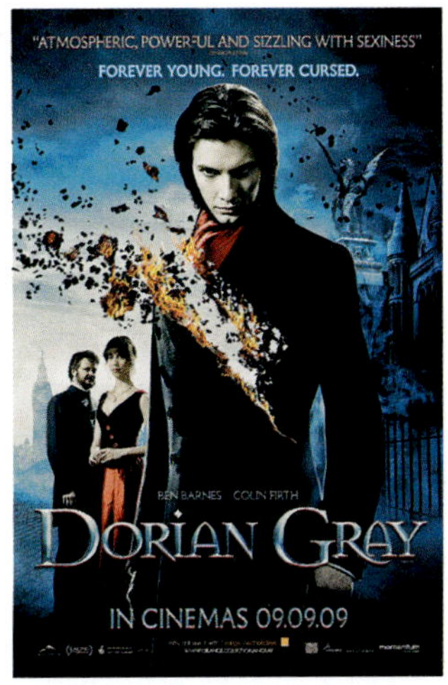

Directed by Oliver Parker;
UK 2009.
With Ben Barnes (Dorian Gray);
Colin Firth (Lord Henry Wotton).

After the death of his grandfather, the vain Dorian Gray returns to Victorian London. He becomes friends with the talented painter Basil Hallward and the corrupt Lord Henry Wotton, who introduces Gray to the hedonistic pleasures of the city. In the meantime, Basil paints Dorian's portrait and gives him the beautiful painting. The young man decides to make a deal with the devil, trading his soul to keep his beauty and youth forever, while his picture ages and shows the effects of his corrupted life. Eventually Dorian's desperate attempts to safeguard his secret turn his once-privileged life into a living hell. Thus, he decides to end it all by stabbing the portrait, but in doing so, his body decays and is consumed in a terrible explosion. A few months later, scarred from the explosion, Lord Henry goes to his attic, where he keeps a now-youthful portrait of Dorian.

What about accuracy?

In the novel, Lord Henry does not have a child. On the contrary, the film reveals one, Emily, who later feels deeply attracted to Dorian, who returns her love.

In the film, instead of using the knife with which he stabbed Hallward, Dorian uses a coal iron to stab the portrait, which materialises and cries out in pain.

Moreover, in the novel, Hallward's character is strongly implied to be sexually interested in Dorian, though this is never explicitly stated; Dorian's feelings are more ambiguous. However, in the film, Dorian initiates a homosexual relationship with the painter at a party and Hallward responds, confused yet willing.

5 Overview

Test what you know

1 COMPLETE the sentences about the Victorian novel:

1 There was a communion of interests between writers and readers because ....
2 Lots of works were published in ....
3 Novelists wanted to reflect ....
4 The narrator was ....
5 The final chapter usually ....
6 The setting was ....
7 The writers were interested in .... of the characters.

2 SAY if the sentences are true or false. Correct the false ones.

1 Britain's imperial activity began in the second half of the 19th century. T F
2 The British occupied only India and parts of China during the Victorian Age. T F
3 Britain took over Egypt to protect its routes to India through the Suez Canal. T F
4 The British were defeated by the Boers in South Africa. T F
5 Victoria was named Empress of India in 1877. T F

Can you do it?

3 SAY why 1851 is considered a milestone in British history.

4 HIGHLIGHT the most important features of Coketown, described by Charles Dickens in his novel *Hard Times*.

5 READ the extract from *Oliver Twist* and answer the questions.

1 Where is Oliver confined to? Who consigned him to that place? What sort of feelings does Oliver express?
2 Pick out the words that belong to the semantic fields of childhood and adulthood. What do they represent?
3 Focus on the setting. What atmosphere does it convey? What sort of feelings does it inspire in Oliver?
4 What do you think the message of the text is?

For a week after the commission of the impious and profane offence of asking for more, Oliver remained a close prisoner in the dark and solitary room to which he had been consigned by the wisdom[1] and mercy of the board[2]. It appears, at first sight, not unreasonable to suppose, that, if he had entertained a becoming[3] feeling of respect for the prediction of the gentleman in the white waistcoat, he would have established that sage individual's prophetic character, once and for ever, by tying one end of his pocket-handkerchief to a hook[4] in the wall, and attaching himself to the other. To the performance of this feat[5], however, there was one obstacle: namely, that pocket-handkerchiefs being decided articles of luxury, had been, for all future times and ages, removed from the noses of paupers by the express order of the board, in council assembled; solemnly given and pronounced under their hands and seals[6]. There was a still greater obstacle in Oliver's youth and childishness. He only cried bitterly all day; and, when the long, dismal[7] night came on, spread his little hands before his eyes to shut out the darkness, and crouching[8] in the corner, tried to sleep: ever and anon[9] waking with a start and tremble, and drawing himself closer and closer[10] to the wall, as if to feel even its cold hard surface were a protection in the gloom[11] and loneliness which surrounded him.

1 **wisdom.** Saggezza.
2 **the board.** Il comitato.
3 **becoming.** Conveniente, appropriato.
4 **hook.** Gancio.
5 **feat.** Impresa.
6 **given ... seals.** Redatto, pronunciato, firmato e sigillato.
7 **dismal.** Terribile.
8 **crouching.** Accovacciandosi per la paura.
9 **ever and anon.** Di tanto in tanto.
10 **drawing himself ... closer.** Avvicinandosi sempre più.
11 **gloom.** Oscurità.

6 EXPLAIN why *Jane Eyre* by Charlotte Brontë can be considered an education novel.

7 EXPLAIN what kind of empire the British created and how they conceived of their role as colonisers.

8 LIST the key ideas of Darwin's theory of evolution and natural selection and explain their implications.

9 DESCRIBE the roots, evolution, philosophy and main theorists of Aestheticism.

Oral test

10 IMAGINE your teacher asks you the following questions in an oral test. For each question, prepare a one-minute turn.

1 What was life in Victorian towns like?
2 What was the Victorian compromise?
3 What was the setting of most of Dickens's novels?
4 What was Dickens's didactic aim?
5 How did Kipling deal with the mission of the coloniser in his poem 'The White Man's Burden'?
6 How did Stevenson use the theme of the double in his novel *Dr Jekyll and Mr Hyde?*
7 What view of beauty did Wilde provide in *The Picture of Dorian Gray?*

The New Frontier

Specification 6 | Homepage

Top News

1855
Walt Whitman publishes the first edition of *Leaves of Grass*

Spotlight

1851 Herman Melville publishes *Moby-Dick*

Top Issue

Being independent

The Arts

American landscape painting: the Hudson River School

Most Popular News

1861 The American Civil War breaks out

1882
Dow, Jones & Company, a financial news service, is established

Cinema

See
the American Civil War on screen

Mapping History

Follow the Trail of Tears

EXPLORE THE CULTURE

Literature | History | Society | The Arts | Two Films About... | Cultural Issues

6.1 **Society**

The beginning of an American identity

ART LAB 11: *AMERICAN HISTORY PAINTING*

WARM-UP

1 **READ the definitions below and discuss what the term 'melting pot' means when applied to a country.**

melting: blending together

pot: container

During the 19th century, America grew as a nation, expanding its territory from the Atlantic to the Pacific Ocean. It developed a true American identity that found its expression also in literature and in the arts. Among the social and cultural factors that helped shape the American mind, Puritanism should be considered. It was the religious faith of the first settlers in the 17th century, the Pilgrim Fathers, who encouraged the spirit of adventure in the name of liberty, and the ethic of hard work to improve each individual's social and financial situation. As the 18th century progressed, more and more immigrants from all over Europe moved to America and settled in the thirteen different colonies along the Atlantic coast. This was fast becoming a 'melting pot', where different races were brought together and were eventually to shape the new 'American'.

The development of the American mind was also influenced by faith in reason and human progress. The belief that man's own efforts can lead him to success was the most important element of the so-called 'American Dream'. The spirit of democracy and the idea of justice and equality were brought about by the War of Independence, where victory saw the birth of a new nation.

Though still influenced by European manners, a new cultural image of America began to take shape. It was dominated by two forces: the East, with Harvard and Yale Universities, the business and cultural centre of New York and its values of wealth and respectability; and the West, characterised by the pioneer spirit, the myth of the frontier and the country's endless possibilities. It was in prose that truly American characteristics emerged. The short story became a distinctive form, mastered by Edgar Allan Poe (1809–49), while James Fenimore Cooper (1789–1851) created the 'epic' of the frontier in his novels.

1 Bird's eye view of New York and Brooklyn, printed by I. Schaerer.

2 English School, *Emigrants leaving old England*, 1869.

3 American School, a picture of Freedom holding the American flag and an eagle, early 19th century. National Gallery of Art, Washington DC, US.

2 **COMPLETE the table below with the correct word.**

Verb	Noun
To expand	
To settle	
To encourage	
To immigrate	
To develop	
To believe	

3 **DECIDE if the following statements are true or false. Correct the false ones.**

1 The work ethic and social make up of the American people prevented the birth of a national identity. T F
2 The Pilgrim Fathers were adventurers who wanted to improve their financial situation. T F
3 The new 'American' was shaped by people with different cultures. T F
4 The development of the American mind was influenced only by religious faith. T F
5 The 'American Dream' only belonged to successful men. T F
6 The independence of the United States was recognised after the war with Britain. T F
7 The pioneer spirit and the myth of the frontier were shared by all American states. T F
8 Both Poe and Cooper wrote short stories. T F

4 **LOOK** at the picture below and point out the main features of the life of the American pioneers when they started to move westwards at the beginning of the 19th century. What frontier landscape is represented in the picture?

FCE Reading and Use of English – Part 6

5 **GAPPED TEXT.** You are going to read a text about the pioneers and the American frontier. SIx sentences have been removed from the text. Choose from the sentences A–G the one which best fits each gap (1–6). There is an extra sentence which you do not need to use.

A This peculiar sense of social place, mission and obligation can be found in Hawkeye, the hero of James Fenimore Cooper's novel *The Last of the Mohicans*.

B Since the expansion to the West and the rapid decimation of Native Americans in the 19th century, an interesting phenomenon has occurred in terms of American society's approach to Native American culture.

C These American colonists were not native to the soil; they desired to prove that they truly belonged to their chosen place, and that bringing Christian civilisation to the wilderness represented the realisation of their own destiny.

D This nature was severe, simple and permanent, used to putting up with difficulties and enduring privations.

E Moving from east to west became faster and easier.

F Although he had a Romantic emotional approach to nature, trust in intuitive wisdom and the ability to feel strong passion, his greatest need was for order.

G He emerged with renewed strength, a superhuman strength from which his land and people would derive sustenance.

The pioneers and the American frontier

One of the most important themes of American culture is that of the pioneers moving westwards and the founding story of the American nation. At the end of the 18th century, the American frontier was facing different problems: the colonial wars involving England, France and Spain; the hostility of the native Indian communities; and the individual spirit of independence of the pioneers who began to explore new lands. **1** ______

The frontier hero was characterised by curiosity and the spirit of adventure, which led him to the Western wilderness. In some cases he was captured by the Indians, initiated and adopted into the tribe, resisted a series of temptations that tested his character, and returned with new wisdom to become the war chief of his people. **2** ______ The frontier hero was sequentially the emigrant, the explorer, the captive, the convert and the hunter. **3** ______ Great passion was necessary for the realisation of his full potential for human feeling, but to attain heroic stature he had to control his emotions, forget private sorrow and dedicate himself to the public good.

The lesson of the frontier experience was that civilisation can only be maintained against the powers of the wilderness through complete knowledge of one's own capacity for good and evil and of the menaces and promises of the environment. **4** ______

The character and habits of the North American Indians were strictly connected with the sublime scenery in which they lived, with its vast lakes, large forests, majestic rivers and trackless plains. **5** ______ In the early periods of colonisation, they were doubly wronged by the white men. They were dispossessed of their hereditary possessions by mercenary and frequent warfare, and their characters were differently described by writers. Not all stereotypes in 19th-century literature depicted American Indians as villains; some portrayed them as naturalistic saints. **6** ______ Some have equated Native Americans with the nature that was threatened by industrialism; they assumed that the Indian did not possess a political and societal structure, and therefore he possessed the 'freedom' that individuals were denied by civilisation. The Indian became a metaphor for the desire for individualism.

4 William Tylee Ranney, *Advice on the Prairie*, 1853. Whitney Gallery of Western Art, Buffalo Bill Historical Center, Cody, Wyoming, US.

6.2 **The Arts**

The Hudson River School

WARM-UP

1 **LOOK** at the title of the text. Which adjectives do you expect to find regarding the American landscape?

majestic • huge • overdeveloped • vast • spoilt • serene • wild • built-up • primitive • dramatic

FCE Reading and Use of English – Part 1

2 **MULTIPLE-CHOICE CLOZE.** For questions 1–8, read the text and decide which answer (A, B, C or D) best fits each gap. There is an example at the beginning (0).

The **(0)** PAINTERS of the Hudson River School constituted the first school of American art **(1)** .... helped to shape the myth of American landscape. The school **(2)** .... with the works of Thomas Cole (1801–48) and Asher B. Durand (1796–1886), and evolved into the Luminist and late Romantic schools. They celebrated their vast nation with a sense of awe for its majestic **(3)** .... resources and a feeling of optimism for the huge potential it held. They **(4)** .... a wilderness in which man was small beside the vastness of creation, but retained that divine quality that completed the circle of harmony. They **(5)** .... the view that painting should become a vehicle through which the universal mind could reach the mind of mankind. For them, art was an agent of moral and spiritual transformation.

Together **(6)** .... Asher B. Durand, Thomas Cole changed not only the styles and themes of American painting, but also the methods. Cole sketched from nature, frequently **(7)** .... vistas in the Catskills or White Mountains, and then returned to his studio to paint his large-scale pictures, alive with tactile brushwork and atmospheric lighting that seemed to breathe. The influence of the Hudson River School continued with artists like John Frederick Kensett and Martin Johnson Heade, who came to be known as 'Luminists' because of their **(8)** .... with the effects of light on water and the sky, and with Frederic Edwin Church. Church, who worked at Olana, his panoramic home in the Catskills, looked for more extensive horizons for his paintings.

0	A writers	B poets	C sculptors	D **painters**
1	A whom	B which	C whose	D how
2	A became	B continued	C began	D born
3	A natural	B raw	C savage	D rich
4	A depicted	B introduced	C coloured	D drew
5	A objected	B thought	C believed	D shared
6	A to	B with	C at	D of
7	A tragic	B strong	C dramatic	D frightened
8	A proofs	B trials	C experiments	D choices

3 **MATCH** the words with their Italian equivalent. Then use them to complete the text below.

1 tiny	A tavolozza
2 framed	B chiavi
3 contemplation	C valle
4 palette	D roccioso
5 keys	E contemplazione
6 reminder	F emblema
7 valley	G ceppo
8 rocky	H promemoria
9 stump	I incorniciato
10 emblem	J piccolissimo

1 Asher B. Durand, *Kindred Spirits*, 1849. Crystal Bridges Museum of American Art, Bentonville, Arkansas, US.

This painting has become a virtual **(1)** .... for the Hudson River School. It shows Durand himself with Cole on a **(2)** .... promontory in serene **(3)** .... of the scene before them: the deep narrow **(4)** .... with its running stream, the Catskill mists shining in a **(5)** .... of subtle colours, **(6)** .... by foliage. In the foreground, stands one of the school's famous symbols – a broken tree **(7)** .... – what Cole called a *memento mori*, or **(8)** .... that life is fragile and impermanent and only nature and the divine within the human soul are eternal. Although human beings are **(9)** ...., they are elevated by the grandeur of the landscape in which they are in harmony. Cole and Durand firmly believed that if the American landscape was a new Garden of Eden, then it was the artists who kept the **(10)** .... of entry.

Manifest Destiny

INTERACTIVE MAP 6: *MANIFEST DESTINY*

WARM-UP

1 LOOK at the painting and in pairs discuss its allegorical meaning.
1 Who do you think the woman is? What is she holding in her hands?
2 Who/what can you see in the foreground and background?

1 John Gast, *American Progress*, ca 1872. Library of Congress, Washington DC, US.

FCE Listening – Part 2

2 5.5 | **SENTENCE COMPLETION. You will hear a talk about the concept of 'Manifest Destiny' in American history. For questions 1–10, complete the sentences.**

The lecturer is talking about 'Manifest Destiny' as a phrase used to justify a sort of **(1)** .... for the expansion of the United States.
The phrase was used for the first time in **(2)** .... in the *United States Magazine and Democratic Review*. The author was **(3)** ....
The article was written for the annexation of **(4)** ....
The notion of Manifest Destiny was then used to justify the annexations of **(5)** .... and of **(6)** ....
The Oregon Trail was established so that more **(7)** .... could settle in Oregon, which officially became a state in 1859.
Around 1846 John C. Freemont and many soldiers invaded California and made it their own **(8)** ....
An effect of Manifest Destiny was that **(9)** .... spread throughout the US, and divided the nation. The philosophy of manifest destiny was adopted by successive **(10)** ....

3 5.5 | **LISTEN again and locate the places mentioned on the map.**

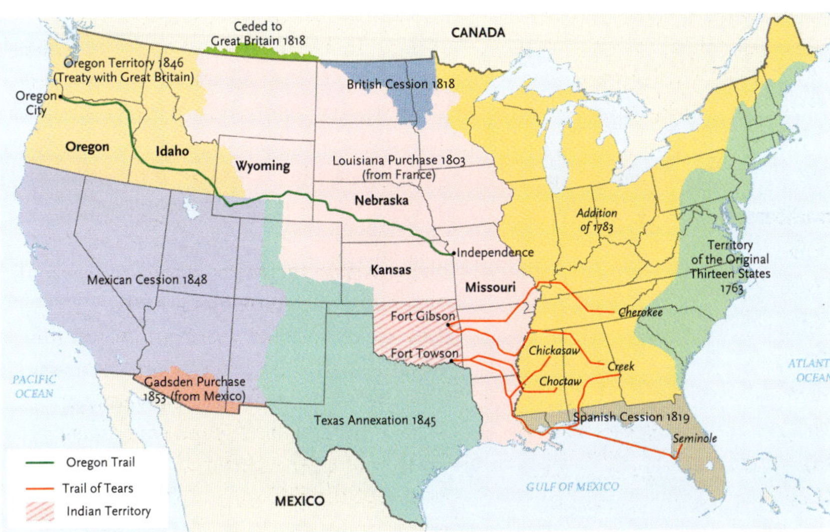

Internet Lab

1 DISCUSS. Manifest Destiny had serious consequences for the American Indians.
1 What do you know about the American Indians?
2 What do you know about their relationship with the US government?

2 BROWSE these websites:
www.indians.org
www.nmai.si.edu
www.history.com/topics/native-american-history/native-american-cultures

3 CARRY OUT a research project about one or more Indian tribe(s) to present to the rest of the class, specifying:
1 where they live today and where they were located in the past;
2 where their name comes from;
3 their chiefs;
4 what men and women were in charge of;
5 their art;
6 other characteristics.

6.4 **History**

The question of slavery

WARM-UP

1 **DISCUSS.** The institution of slavery began before the birth of the United States as a nation. What do you know about its origins?

The political situation in America was tense because of the growing gap between the North and the South. While the North was industrialised, the economy of the South was still based on the vast plantations of tobacco and cotton, and on slavery. The white population constantly increased as immigrants continued to arrive from Europe – though they tended to settle in the North, while in the South there were about 3,500,000 black slaves.

The question of slavery became urgent when several northern states adopted emancipation, while the international demand for cotton meant the economy of the South continued to rely on slave labour. Northern abolitionists, who included writers, intellectuals and religious associations, began to organise themselves into the Republican Party, whose candidate, Abraham Lincoln (1809–65), won the presidential election in 1860.

Lincoln's victory changed the relationship between the American government and the institution of slavery. It led to South Carolina's withdrawal from the Union. Within two months, six other states joined South Carolina in forming an independent 'Confederacy'. War followed because Lincoln, supported by a majority of northerners, refused to concede that any American had the constitutional right to withdraw from the Union, and not certainly in response to a legitimately-won democratic election.

1 A group of captured Africans being taken to become slaves. Print, ca 1860.

2 Slaves on an American cotton plantation, using a cotton gin. Library of Congress, Washington DC, US.

3 William Henry Brown, *Hauling the Whole Week's Picking*, 1842. Collage of a slave harvest crew near Vicksburg, Mississippi, US.

2 **FILL IN** the table to explain the differences between the North and the South in the United States in the 19th century.

North	South

3 **EXPLAIN.** What were the consequences of Lincoln's election?

4 **DISCUSS.** Do you know how the slaves lived on American plantations?

6.5 **History**

Abraham Lincoln

FCE Reading and Use of English – Part 2

1 **OPEN CLOZE.** For questions 1–8, read the text below and think of the word which best fits each gap. Use only one word in each gap. There is an example at the beginning (0).

Abraham Lincoln's life

Born (0) ...ON... 12th February 1809, Lincoln was (1) .... up in rural poverty in Kentucky and Indiana. In 1830 he moved to Illinois, where he practised (2) .... a lawyer in Springfield, served as a Whig in the state legislature and, after a term as a US congressman, largely withdrew from politics.

The threat of the spread west of slavery awoke his interest again. Helping to organise the anti-slavery Republican (3) ...., he won national recognition in his 1858 debates with Senator Stephen Douglas and secured his party's nomination (4) .... the presidency in 1860.

His election victory prompted the secession of the lower South. In the following resort to arms, Lincoln grew into the role of commander-in-chief and skilfully held (5) .... a fragile war coalition. He kept the upper South loyal, prevented the intervention of foreign powers, kept military pressure on the Confederacy across a broad front, and proclaimed the emancipation of the rebels' slaves as a means (6) .... saving the Union. Re-elected to the presidency during the final months of the war, he was shot (7) .... the Confederate sympathiser John Wilkes Booth before he (8) .... develop and implement his policy of national reconstruction.

1 David Gilmour Blythe, *President Lincoln, writing the Proclamation of Freedom*, 1863. Library of Congress, Washington DC, US.

2 The assassination of President Lincoln.

2 **READ** Lincoln's biography again and underline the key phrases. Then compare your work with a classmate.

Insights

The Lincoln Memorial

Located on the National Mall in Washington DC, the Lincoln Memorial is a monument built to honour the 16th president of the United States, Abraham Lincoln. The memorial was the feat of the architect Henry Bacon, and Daniel Chester French made the large seated statue of Abraham Lincoln in 1920. Inside the building, which is in the style of a Greek Doric temple, there are the inscriptions of two famous speeches by Lincoln, 'The Gettysburg Address' and his 'Second Inaugural Address'. The memorial has been the site of seminal historical events, including Martin Luther King's 'I Have a Dream' speech, delivered on 28th August 1963, during the rally at the end of the March on Washington for Jobs and Freedom. The memorial is open to the public twenty-four hours a day.

6.5 Abraham Lincoln

Milestones

1863, the Gettysburg Address
The Gettysburg Address was delivered by Lincoln during the Civil War, in 1863, at the dedication of the Soldiers' National Cemetery in Gettysburg, Pennsylvania. It is one of the most famous speeches in American history, in which Lincoln invoked the principles of human equality contained in the Declaration of Independence and claimed the Civil War was a struggle not merely for the Union, but for 'a new birth of freedom' that would bring true equality to all of its citizens and would also create a unified nation no longer dominated by different states' rights.

The Gettysburg Address

Four score and seven years ago our fathers brought forth, upon this continent, a new nation, conceived in Liberty, and dedicated to the proposition that all men are created equal.

Now we are engaged in a great civil war, testing whether that nation, or any nation so conceived, and so dedicated, can long endure. We are met here on a great battlefield of that war. We have come to dedicate a portion of it as a final resting place for those who here gave their lives that that nation might live. It is altogether fitting and proper that we should do this.

But in a larger sense we can not dedicate – we can not consecrate – we can not hallow this ground. The brave men, living and dead, who struggled, here, have consecrated it far above our poor power to add or detract. The world will little note, nor long remember, what we say here, but can never forget what they did here.

It is for us, the living, rather to be dedicated here to the unfinished work which they have, thus far, so nobly carried on. It is rather for us to be here dedicated to the great task remaining before us – that from these honored dead we take increased devotion to that cause for which they here gave the last full measure of devotion – that we here highly resolve that these dead shall not have died in vain; that this nation shall have a new birth of freedom; and that this government of the people, by the people, for the people, shall not perish from the earth.

1 Statue of Abraham Lincoln reflected in the inscription of the Gettysburg Address at the Lincoln Memorial in Washington DC, US.

2 A portrait of President Abraham Lincoln in 1863 by Alexander Gardner. Library of Congress, Washington DC, US.

3 The Lincoln Memorial and Reflecting Pool, located on the National Mall in Washington DC, US.

O Captain! My Captain!

Walt Whitman

Leaves of Grass (1867)

Sequel to Drum Taps, Parts 1–2

Walt Whitman (1819–92) is one of the most influential poets in American literature. This is one of his most popular poems, reflecting his deep awareness of the significance of the figure of Abraham Lincoln in American history. In 1865 Whitman wrote Drum Taps, *a collection containing lyrics which gave voice to his enthusiasm about the abolition of slavery and the issues of national integrity and democracy promoted by Lincoln. In 1866* Sequel to Drum Taps *followed, to which this poem belongs, and both collections were included in the fourth edition of* Leaves of Grass, *in 1867. The poem was written after Lincoln's assassination. Whitman's lines give Lincoln the stature of a myth, the symbol of American democracy, of that dream which words like those of the Gettysburg Address of 1863 had brought alive.*

5.6

O Captain! my Captain! our fearful trip is done,
The ship has weather'd[1] every rack[2], the prize we sought is won,
The port is near, the bells I hear, the people all exulting,
While follow eyes the steady keel[3], the vessel grim and daring[4];
But O heart! heart! heart!
O the bleeding drops of red,
Where on the deck my Captain lies,
Fallen cold and dead.

O Captain! my Captain! rise up and hear the bells;
Rise up – for you the flag is flung – for you the bugle trills[5],
For you bouquets and ribbon'd wreaths[6] – for you the shores a-crowding;
For you they call, the swaying[7] mass, their eager[8] faces turning;
Here Captain! dear father!
The arm beneath your head!
It is some dream that on the deck,
You've fallen cold and dead.

My Captain does not answer, his lips are pale and still[9],
My father does not feel my arm, he has no pulse nor will,
The ship is anchor'd safe and sound[10], its voyage closed and done,
From fearful trip the victor ship comes in with object won;
Exult O shores, and ring O bells!
But I with mournful tread[11],
Walk the deck my Captain lies,
Fallen cold and dead.

1 **weather'd.** Superato.
2 **rack.** Difficoltà, ostacolo.
3 **steady keel.** Chiglia stabile.
4 **grim and daring.** Risoluto e audace.
5 **the bugle trills.** Squilla la tromba.
6 **ribbon'd wreaths.** Ghirlande con nastri.
7 **swaying.** Ondeggiante.
8 **eager.** Impazienti, desiderose.
9 **still.** Immobili.
10 **safe and sound.** Sana e salva.
11 **with mournful tread.** Con andatura addolorata.

WARM-UP

1 **DISCUSS** in pairs. What are the features of a great political leader?

COMPREHENSION

2 **WRITE** a caption to describe the content of each section of the poem.

Part 1 (lines 1–8) ....

Part 2 (lines 9–16) ....

Part 3 (lines 17–24) ....

ANALYSIS

3 **STATE** whether this poem employs free verse, a device Whitman used in his poems to break down the barriers of form between prose and poetry.

4 **SAY** what tense prevails. What quality does it give to the poem?

5 **IDENTIFY** the main sentence form in the poem.

6 **UNDERLINE** the repetitions.

7 **FIND** the terms referring to President Lincoln. How is he presented? What does the speaker exhort him to do?

8 **EXPLAIN** the following symbols:

trip .... rack ....
prize .... port ....
vessel ....

9 **MARK** the lines describing the people. What are they doing?

YOUR TURN

10 **DISCUSS.** How does the speaker's mood vary throughout the poem? Do you think the poet is simply celebrating a great statesman or is he also speaking in terms of personal loss?

6.6 **History**

The American Civil War

WARM-UP

1 **LOOK** at the pictures (1–3). The American Civil War was the first war to be photographed intensively. Answer the following questions about each picture.

1. What can be seen on the ferry in picture 1?
2. What can be seen in picture 2?
3. Do you think the soldier in picture 3 fought for the North or for the South?

2 **READ** the Q&A text below.

The American Civil War broke out in 1861.

Q How long did the Civil War last?

A It lasted four years, ending in 1865, when the blue Northern troops, commanded by Ulysses Grant (1822–85), defeated the grey Confederates, led by Robert Lee (1807–70). Five days later, President Lincoln was assassinated by a Southern fanatic.

Q What was the most important consequence of the war?

A After the Civil War, the abolition of slavery was sanctioned by the 13th Amendment to the Constitution. However, it did not grant the blacks equality and economic security. They were free but without money and a home. Some migrated to the industrial cities in the North; others remained with their old masters in the South, who, impoverished by the war, could not afford to pay wages but would share the crops with the workers and provide them with tools and a cabin.

Q What frightened the blacks?

A A wave of resentment and violence, embodied by the racist movement the 'Ku Klux Klan', terrorised the blacks and their families. The so-called 'black codes' were created; they segregated the blacks in schools, hospitals and transport.

Q What was the American dream?

A While the economy of the South had collapsed during the war, the Northern states had increased their output to supply military needs. Big fortunes were made, and great financial empires were created by men who rose from nothing, like John Rockefeller, who embodied a new version of the American dream: the myth of the self-made man who went from 'rags to riches'.

Q Who founded the American Federation of Labour?

A The other side of the coin was that the majority of workers were exploited and did not have a share in the wealth and leisure. They soon organised themselves and founded the American Federation of Labor (AFL), which became the strongest group of trade unions.

Q What encouraged the expansion and settlement in the West?

A Expansion and settlement in the West were encouraged above all by the discovery of gold in California in 1848, which resulted in the 'gold rush'. Then the Homestead Act (1862) granted free soil to the first occupants.

Q What did the migration westwards lead to?

A This migration westwards had two main consequences: it led to the disappearance of the frontier, and to the extermination of the buffaloes, with the consequent starvation of the American Indians, who were subjugated, mass-deported or brutally exterminated. Cattlemen became the new Western symbols – the cowboys, so deeply rooted in American tradition.

1 Soldiers and artillery crossing a river on a ferry during the Civil War, photographed by Captain Andrew J. Russell, 1863.

2 The 'Sunken Road' at Antietam, Maryland, showing the aftermath of the bloodiest single-day battle in American history. Photographed by Alexander Gardner in 1862. Library of Congress, Washington DC, US.

3 An African-American soldier in the Union Army.

3 **IN PAIRS** cover the answers (**A**s) in the text. Take turns asking and answering the questions (**Q**s) using the information that you have read.

6.7 Two Films About...

The American Civil War

WARM-UP

1 **DISCUSS.** Do you like historical epic films? Why or why not? Can you give an example of a film belonging to this genre?

Gone with the Wind

Directed by Victor Fleming;
USA 1939.
With Vivien Leigh (Scarlett O'Hara); Clark Gable (Rhett Butler); Leslie Howard (Ashley Wilkes)

'Gone with the Wind' is an historical epic film adapted from Margaret Mitchell's novel of the same title. The film opens on a large cotton plantation, Tara, which fits the audience's expectations of plantation life. So, too, did the sense of propriety that the story portrays as a typical feature of Southern 'civilisation'. Slaves are seen as happy, and some of them are significant characters.

The story focuses on Scarlett O'Hara, a woman of great strength, able to overcome all odds in order to care for her family and herself. The story follows her infatuation with the refined Ashley Wilkes and her marriage to the unscrupulous Rhett Butler. In the midst of this love triangle, there is an account of how the old order was destroyed by the Civil War. The siege and burning of Atlanta are represented vividly.

This is a film about a woman's struggle to survive 'total war', and that was one reason for its great popularity in Britain during World War II.

What about accuracy?

The film portrays the story from a clearly 'Old South' point of view: the South is presented as a great example of civilisation, where the practice of slavery is never questioned. The slaves who escaped or attempted to escape servitude, who deserted their masters' plantations to join Union regiments, have no voice here. Another inaccuracy is linked to the opening scenes, in which blacks pick cotton despite the fact that plantations never harvested cotton in spring.

Cold Mountain

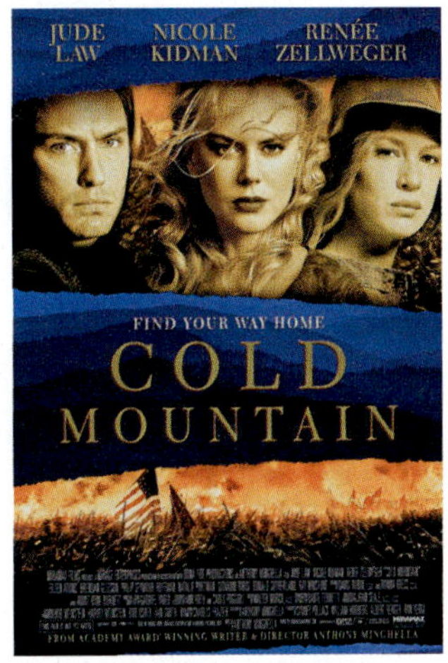

Directed by Anthony Minghella;
UK/USA 2003.
With Nicole Kidman (Ada Monroe); Jude Law (W.P. Inman); Renée Zellweger (Ruby Thewes).

'Cold Mountain' is based on another novel by a Southern author, Charles Frazier, who was interested in the story of his great-great-uncle, a captured Confederate soldier who escaped from a Union prison in Illinois and came back home on foot to North Carolina, only to be shot as a deserter when he was just three miles from home.

The story focuses on a more humble Southern lifestyle and on an unlikely love story between Inman and Ada. The war separates the couple, but the promise of their reunion gives each of them hope and a way of maintaining their humanity amid the brutality of the conflict.

Like 'Gone with the Wind', this is a woman's film and its most interesting characters are a hermit, who nurses Inman, and Ruby, who saves Ada from starving by helping her work the farm.

What about accuracy?

While Inman was based on a real person, the account of his journey is largely imagined and so is the character of Ada. Although one very brief scene shows runaway slaves being shot on the spot, the film seems to omit the slavery issue.
The opening battle sequence realistically portrays Petersburg's 'Battle of the Crater', when Union engineers created a massive crater with explosives in an attempt to penetrate the Confederate lines. Untrained Union soldiers rushed into the crater and got trapped. Confederate soldiers remembered the clash as a 'turkey shoot', with over 5,000 Union soldiers dying. What the film misses are the many black Union soldiers involved in that battle.

TEXT BANK 44: *NATHANIEL HAWTHORNE*

The American Renaissance

1 Thomas Eakins, The Swimming Hole, 1884–85. Amon Carter Museum, US.

The centre of American cultural life in the 19th century remained in New England, where the influence of Puritanism was still very strong. Towards the middle of the century, a group of intellectuals and writers developed the 'New England Renaissance'. 1 The great literary output of the period constituted a sort of reaction against the Puritan doctrine. However, the Puritan heritage can still be traced in the flourishing of symbols and emblems, and in the use of allegory that writers such as Nathaniel Hawthorne and Herman Melville widely employed in their works.

2 The most influential figure in framing the thought of the American Renaissance was Ralph Waldo Emerson (1803–82) who founded the 'Transcendentalist Club', and expressed his philosophy, called Transcendentalism, in the essay *Nature* (1836). 3
The key ideas of Transcendentalism were:

- All reality was seen as a single unity (oneness and multiplicity were the same thing), a concept which well suited the reality of the 'melting pot', of a country where people from all over the world formed a national unity.
- Contact with nature was the best means to reach truth and awareness of the unity of all things. Emerson saw nature according to its 'uses': as a Commodity, as a source of Beauty and symbolic images, as Discipline in educating man to understanding and reason.
- The over-soul was the spiritual principle linking everything together.
- Man was the emanation of the over-soul, and the emphasis lay on his individuality, on his self-education.

4 Transcendentalism praised humankind's ability to transcend the mortal world through reflection and intuition. This belief in the power of human consciousness to discover eternal truths in the natural world became the tenet of Emily Dickinson's poetry.

5 In this work, he described the two years he had lived in a hut in the woods near Walden Pond, Massachusetts, in order to prove that an individual can lead a rich life in solitude or making a living from the land. Thoreau also wrote an essay, *Civil Disobedience* (1849), where he stated his belief in the individual's right to resist the power and the laws of the State when they are in conflict with his honest beliefs. 6

WARM-UP

1 DISCUSS. What does the term 'Renaissance' imply?

FCE Reading and Use of English – Part 6

2 GAPPED TEXT. You are going to read a text about the American Renaissance. Six sentences have been removed from the article. Choose from the sentences A–G the one which fits each gap (1–6). There is one extra sentence which you do not need to use.

- **A** His ideas developed under various influences, including English Romanticism, German Idealism, political liberalism and Eastern mysticism, which Emerson combined in a new, 'American' way.
- **B** This idea of non-violent resistance to authority influenced many thinkers and political activists of the 20th century, from Mahatma Gandhi to Martin Luther King and the demonstrators against the Vietnam War.
- **C** The most faithful follower of Emerson's theories was his friend Henry David Thoreau (1817–62), who published *Walden, or Life in the Woods* (1854).
- **D** Transcendentalism was far broader than a geographical phenomenon or a select club membership.
- **E** The term did not indicate the rebirth of something, but the beginning of a truly American literature, with themes and a style of its own.
- **F** This philosophy encouraged an optimistic and self-reliant point of view, which found expression particularly in the poems of Walt Whitman.
- **G** A great storyteller, Mark Twain is noted for his brilliant depiction of Southern life on the Mississippi river.

3 ANSWER the following questions.

1. What did the term 'American Renaissance' mean?
2. What were the key ideas of Transcendentalism?
3. Who were Emerson's followers?
4. What was the response of Transcendentalism to political preoccupations?

6.9 History

The Gilded Age

WARM-UP

1 **LOOK** up the dictionary definition of 'gilded'. What does this adjective make you think of?

2 **LOOK** at the pictures on pages 205–206 and list the issues they hint at.

3 **READ** the Q&A text.

1 Apache chief Geronimo (right) and his warriors in 1886.

2 Women trimming currency at US Mint, Washington DC, 1907.

The late 19th century witnessed the birth of modern America.

Q Where does the name 'Gilded Age' come from?

A The last three decades of the 19th century were called the 'Gilded Age' from a novel with the same title (1873) by Mark Twain and Charles Dudley Warner (1829–1900). These writers satirised a society whose serious problems had been veiled by a thin layer of gold.

Q What contributed to the growth of American industry?

A From 1870 to 1900, America's industrial economy increased dramatically. Lots of developments contributed to this growth. First of all, the use of machines in manufacturing, which spread throughout American industry after the Civil War, sped up production. Then there was the development of new products, which included the telephone (1876), the electric light (1879) and the petrol-engine car (1885). Advances in communication provided an increase in the economy, too. In fact, in the late 1800s a new nationwide network of railways began distributing goods far and wide. The total distance of railway lines passed from about 14,500 kilometres in 1850 to 320,000 kilometres in 1900. In 1869, the first transcontinental railway line was completed, connecting the east of the country to California. All this was accompanied by a doubling of the population, due both to natural growth and to immigration. More than 25 million immigrants entered the United States from 1870 to 1900.

Q What effects did the industrial boom have on the lives of the American people?

A This industrial boom had important social effects: the new business activity was mainly linked to cities, where people moved in record numbers. New industrial capitalists – like Andrew Carnegie (1835–1919), who built the American steel industry; John D. Rockefeller (1839–1937), an oil magnate; and Cornelius Vanderbilt (1794–1877), a railroad baron – were able to control much of the nation's wealth and power. However, the gap between the rich and the poor became increasingly obvious as only a small percentage of people could live luxuriously while the great mass of city-dwellers lived in poverty.

Q What was the relationship between the government and the people?

A The government of the era had more authority and power but was marked by widespread corruption. Ulysses Grant (1822–85) became the 18th president in 1869 and members of his administration used their political positions for their own financial gain. Corruption also flourished in state and local administrations. As a consequence, these were turbulent years

6.9 The Gilded Age

that saw labour violence, rising racial tension, militancy among workers and farmers and discontent among the unemployed. Burdened by heavy debts and falling prices, many Americans organised themselves in movements like the American Federation of Labor (founded in 1886) and the Farmers' Alliance (from the 1870s to 1880s). They called for changes to reduce poverty, to increase the amount of money in circulation, to get tariff reductions and to implement a graduated income tax.

Q What did the settlement of the West cause?

A The long process of settling the United States from coast to coast brought about the closing of the Western frontier. Between 1865 and the 1890s, Americans settled in the 'Far West', especially after the discovery of gold in the Black Hills of South Dakota. Conflicts with the Plains Indians to push them to restricted reservations began. In 1876, General George Custer and his men found the main encampment of the Sioux and their allies, the Cheyenne, on the Little Bighorn River, but they were completely annihilated by the Indian warriors. Later, in 1881, Sitting Bull surrendered, and Geronimo, the Apache leader, was the last to capitulate to the United States.

Q How did the government try to preserve the wilderness of the West?

A Long before this period, the way of life of the Plains Indians had been destroyed by the massacre of the buffalo, which were almost completely exterminated in the decade after 1870 by indiscriminate hunting. The federal government tried to preserve the disappearing wilderness with the establishment of the first national park at Yellowstone.

Q Did the United States show a great interest in foreign affairs?

A Up until the 1890s, the United States showed little interest in foreign affairs. Its army, with just 28,000 soldiers, was one-twentieth the size of that of France or Germany, and its navy just a sixth the size of Britain's and half the size of Spain's. Towards the end of the 19th century, interest in foreign affairs increased. In 1898, the United States annexed the Hawaiian Islands, and war with Spain led to the acquisition of Puerto Rico and the Philippines. The United States then went on to assist Panama in securing its independence from Colombia in order to build a canal across the Isthmus of Panama. The US also occupied Nicaragua for twenty years, Haiti for nineteen and the Dominican Republic for eight.

4 IN PAIRS cover the answers (A s) in the text above. Take turns asking and answering the questions (Q s) using the information that you have read.

Insights

Yellowstone National Park, Wyoming, Montana and Idaho

In the past, several groups of Native Americans used the park as their home and hunting grounds. These traditional uses of Yellowstone lands continued until the second half of the 19th century, when the first people of European descent found their way into the park. In 1872 Yellowstone became the first national park in the world. A new concept was born and with it a new way for people to preserve and protect the best of what they had for the benefit and enjoyment of future generations. Today the park is home to a large variety of wildlife, including grizzly bears, wolves and bison. Within Yellowstone National Park are: Old Faithful, which is one of the world's most extraordinary geysers; hot springs; and the Grand Canyon of the Yellowstone.

1 Richard Caton Woodville, *War News from Mexico*, 1848.

6.10 **Society**

The new American businesses

WARM-UP

1 **LOOK** at the pictures below and make predictions about the new businesses that changed the American economy in the last part of the 19th century.

1

2

3

GLOSSARY

broker operatore, agente di borsa
bonds obbligazioni, buoni del tesoro
shares azioni
income guadagno
stock market borsa

FCE Reading and Use of English – Part 1

2 **MULTIPLE-CHOICE CLOZE.** For questions 1–8, read the text below and decide which answer (A, B, C or D) best fits each gap. There is an example at the beginning (0).

Dow, Jones & Company, a financial news service, was established in 1882. Neither financier **(0)** ....NOR.... broker, Charles Dow was a journalist. When he came to Wall Street, the investment of choice was bonds. Investors liked shares that were supported by real machineries and factories. They felt reassured by the predictability of income that bonds offered, as **(1)** .... as the specific dates of maturity when their capital **(2)** .... be returned. The stock market, by contrast, dealt in 'shares of ownership' **(3)** .... had no specific claim on anything a company owned. People on Wall Street found it difficult to analyse the daily rising, falling or staying even of stocks. Charles Dow devised his stock average to avoid this confusion. He began in 1884 with eleven stocks, most of them railroads, which were among the biggest companies in America at that time. In May 1896, he introduced the industrial average. Nowadays, there are plenty of indicators to tell investors what the stock market is doing. But most people **(4)** .... on the Dow Jones Industrial Average.

Several **(5)** .... developed in the last three decades of the 19th century, and they really changed the economy of the country. The first real businessman was probably Asa Candler (1851–1929). He had built up one of the largest pharmaceutical businesses in Atlanta and bought the recipe for Coca-Cola for $2,300 in 1887. From that start, he turned Coca-Cola into a nationally recognised brand, marketing his product **(6)** .... no other product had been marketed before. Today, the Coca-Cola brand is known all over the world, and Coke itself has become a US national symbol, just like hot dogs and baseball.

In 1837 William Procter and James Gamble, **(7)** .... immigrants from the United Kingdom, formed Procter & Gamble, a partnership in Cincinnati, Ohio, to manufacture and sell candles and soap. In 1878 Procter & Gamble's White Soap hit the market. The most **(8)** .... characteristic of the product, soon renamed Ivory Soap, was developed by chance. A worker accidentally left a soap mixer on during his lunch break, causing more air than usual to be mixed in. Before long, Procter & Gamble was receiving orders for 'the floating soap'. Soon, P&G's formula for White Soap changed permanently.

In 1891 James C. Fargo (1829–1915), president of the American Express Company, offered the first traveller's cheques to Americans going abroad to help them avoid cash problems.

0	A or	B and	**C nor**	D not
1	A good	B less	C well	D best
2	A will	B had	C used	D would
3	A which	B who	C they	D whom
4	A need	B have faith	C rely	D trust
5	A businesses	B commerce	C business	D trade
6	A which	B like	C what	D that
7	A neither	B and	C either	D both
8	A distincting	B distinguish	C distinctive	D distinction

1 A replica of a share of an oil and mining company belonging to the Rockefeller family.

2 Andy Warhol, *Green Coca-Cola Bottles*, 1962. Whitney Museum, New York, US.

3 This 1898 poster shows a pioneer washing with Ivory soap at his campsite.

6.11 **Literature**

Herman Melville and *Moby-Dick*: an American epic

Herman Melville's life

Herman Melville (1819–91) was born in New York in 1819, into a wealthy merchant family. At the age of twelve, however, he had to leave school because of his father's death and the difficult financial conditions of his family. He took various jobs and in 1839, following his restless nature, he signed on to a merchant ship, and from then on he travelled widely and experienced all kinds of adventures. In 1841, he sailed on his first voyage as a member of the crew of the whaling ship 'Acushnet'. At that time whale-hunting was a flourishing industry in America, but life and discipline on a whaler were hard. So, in 1842, Melville deserted the ship and spent some time in the Marquesas Islands (which now belong to French Polynesia), where he came into contact with the way of life of the Typees, a tribe thought to be cannibals. He then escaped to Tahiti, and later to Hawaii, where he joined a US ship and returned home. His experiences at sea between the age of twenty and twenty-five provided the material for almost all his novels and stories, which made him successful. In 1851 he published *Moby-Dick*, his masterpiece. He died in 1891.

1

2

1 A portrait of Herman Melville in 1885.

2 Gregory Peck as Ahab in the film 'Moby-Dick', directed by John Huston in 1956.

Moby-Dick (1851)

The story
Ahab, the captain of the whaler 'Pequod', has devoted his life to hunting down and killing a white sperm whale, called Moby Dick, which had attacked him and bitten off his leg during a previous whaling expedition.

The crew of the ship consists of a variety of human types of mixed races and religions, like the wise and cautious first mate, Starbuck; the superstitious Queequeg, a Maori whom Ahab has hired because of his skill with the harpoon; and the cabin boy, Pip. Ishmael, the narrator, joins them in Nantucket before the departure of the ship. The story is based on the hunt for the whale, which is eventually seen and then hunted for three days. Finally, Ahab wounds Moby Dick, but in its rage the animal destroys the Pequod and its crew. Only good Ishmael is not caught in the vortex of the sinking ship and manages to float upon a coffin. He survives to tell the story.

Captain Ahab

The character of Ahab has been seen by critics in two different perspectives. One major assumption is that Ahab's quest against the great whale is a blasphemous activity which takes two main forms: the first is the idea that Ahab believes himself to be equal to God; the second type of blasphemy is a rejection of God altogether in favour of an alliance with the devil. In fact, when Ahab receives his harpoon, he asks for it to be baptised in the name of the devil, not in the name of the Father.

According to other critics, like the American contemporary Harold Bloom, Ahab is the voice of the instinctive spirituality of the New World, which rejects the tyranny of nature over man. In this respect Ahab is the American Prometheus: a tragic hero who, in his quest for his enemy, looks for a real apocalypse and takes his crew with him in the final disaster.

The meaning of the white whale

Through Ishmael's description of the sperm whale, Melville approaches the problem of its superiority over all other creatures from a variety of standpoints, both biological and historical. The excellence of the whale serves to place Ahab's quest against Moby Dick as a very hard task in which he is doomed to failure.

An entire chapter is devoted to the whiteness of the whale: Ishmael defines it as absence of colour, and thus finds the whale as having an absence of meaning. This opens up various interpretations for Moby Dick. It is far more than a natural creature; Ahab hates him as the personification of the evil in the world – an active, impersonal force that man has to contend with. It could also represent a sort of mirror in which Ahab and his crew look for their own image, the embodiment of mankind's quest for a reason for existence. But the white whale is also a symbol of the hidden and mysterious forces of nature, a wonderful and powerful nature, capable of sudden and incredible acts of destruction. Therefore the hunt stands for the archetypal conflict between man and nature in an age in which nature was seen as a 'commodity', and whales were considered a source of oil, meat, whalebone and the valuable spermaceti oil.

1 AFTER READING **about Herman Melville and** ***Moby-Dick*****, take turns asking and answering questions about the following:**

1. Ahab's obsession;
2. the reasons for it;
3. Starbuck;
4. Queequeg;
5. Pip;
6. Ishmael;
7. the end of the novel;
8. what Ahab embodies;
9. the different interpretations of the white whale.

3 Gregory Peck, as Captain Ahab, holds a spear to the whale in a scene from the film 'Moby-Dick', directed by John Huston in 1956.

WARM-UP

1 IN PAIRS **discuss what you expect Moby Dick to be like.**

Moby Dick

Herman Melville

Moby-Dick (1851)

Chapter 41

In the following passage, Ishmael reports rumours about Moby Dick, which include half-formed suggestions of supernatural agencies.

5.7

Forced into familiarity, then, with such prodigies as these; and knowing that after repeated, intrepid assaults, the White Whale had escaped alive; it cannot be much matter of surprise that some whalemen should go still further in their superstitions; declaring Moby Dick not only ubiquitous[1], but immortal (for immortality is but ubiquity in time); that though groves of spears[2] should be planted in his flanks, he would still swim away unharmed[3]; or if indeed he should ever be made to spout thick blood, such a sight would be but a ghastly deception[4]; for again in unensanguined billows hundreds of leagues away, his unsullied jet[5] would once more be seen.

But even stripped of these supernatural surmisings[6], there was enough in the earthly make and incontestable character of the monster to strike the imagination with unwonted[7] power. For, it was not so much his uncommon bulk that so much distinguished him from other sperm whales, but, as was elsewhere thrown out – a peculiar snow-white wrinkled[8] forehead, and a high, pyramidical white hump[9]. These were his prominent features; the tokens whereby[10], even in the limitless, uncharted seas, he revealed his identity, at a long distance, to those who knew him.

1 **ubiquitous.** Dotato di ubiquità.
2 **though groves of spears.** Sebbene migliaia di lance.
3 **unharmed.** Illeso.
4 **ghastly deception.** Odioso inganno.
5 **unsullied jet.** Sfiatatoio senza macchia.
6 **surmisings.** Congetture.
7 **unwonted.** Raro.
8 **wrinkled.** Rugosa.
9 **hump.** Gobba.
10 **the tokens whereby.** I segni per mezzo dei quali.

6.11 Herman Melville and *Moby-Dick*: an American epic

The rest of his body was so streaked, and spotted, and marbled with the same shrouded hue[11], that, in the end, he had gained his distinctive appellation of the White Whale; a name, indeed, literally justified by his vivid aspect, when seen gliding at high noon through a dark blue sea, leaving a milky-way wake of creamy foam, all spangled with golden gleamings[12].

Nor was it his unwonted magnitude, nor his remarkable hue, nor yet his deformed lower jaw, that so much invested the whale with natural terror, as that unexampled, intelligent malignity which, according to specific accounts, he had over and over again evinced in his assaults. More than all, his treacherous retreats struck more of dismay[13] than perhaps aught else[14]. For, when swimming before his exulting pursuers, with every apparent symptom of alarm, he had several times been known to turn round suddenly, and, bearing down upon them, either stave their boats to splinters[15], or drive them back in consternation to their ship. [...]

His three boats stove around him, and oars and men both whirling in the eddies[16]; one captain, seizing the line-knife from his broken prow[17], had dashed at the whale, as an Arkansas duellist at his foe, blindly seeking with a six inch blade to reach the fathom-deep[18] life of the whale. That captain was Ahab. And then it was, that suddenly sweeping his sickle-shaped lower jaw[19] beneath him, Moby Dick had reaped away[20] Ahab's leg, as a mower a blade of grass[21] in the field. No turbaned Turk, no hired Venetian or Malay, could have smote[22] him with more seeming malice. Small reason was there to doubt, then, that ever since that almost fatal encounter, Ahab had cherished a wild vindictiveness against the whale, all the more fell for that in his frantic morbidness[23] he at last came to identify with him, not only all his bodily woes, but all his intellectual and spiritual exasperations. The White Whale swam before him as the monomaniac incarnation of all those malicious agencies which some deep men feel eating in them, till they are left living on with half a heart and half a lung.

11 **streaked ... hue.** Striato, e macchiato, e marmoreo dello stesso colore cadaverico.
12 **spangled ... gleamings.** Luccicante di bagliori dorati.
13 **treacherous ... dismay.** Sleali ritirate colpivano più di sorpresa.
14 **aught else.** Qualsiasi altra cosa.
15 **either ... splinters.** Sia sfondare le loro barche riducendole in frantumi.
16 **oars ... eddies.** Remi e uomini entrambi turbinanti nei gorghi.
17 **seizing ... prow.** Afferrando il coltello dalla prua rotta.
18 **fathom-deep.** In profondità.
19 **sickle-shaped lower jaw.** La mascella inferiore a forma di falce.
20 **reaped away.** Tranciato.
21 **as ... grass.** Come una falciatrice un filo d'erba.
22 **smote.** Colpito.
23 **frantic morbidness.** Morbosità frenetica.

COMPREHENSION

2 READ the passage and say whether these statements are true or false. Correct the false ones.

1. The whalemen had never been able to attack the whale. T F
2. The whale spouted thick blood. T F
3. Moby Dick's size was larger than that of other whales. T F
4. He had a protuberance on his back. T F
5. When seen swimming at night, Moby Dick took on the colour of the sea. T F
6. Moby Dick pretended he was swimming away, but suddenly turned back on his pursuers. T F
7. Captain Ahab had tried to kill the whale with his knife. T F
8. The whale had taken away his arm. T F

ANALYSIS

3 POINT OUT the realistic and exaggerated features attributed to Moby Dick. What quality is he given in this way?

4 EXPLAIN what crucial moment in Ahab's life is described. What were its consequences?

5 FIND where the voice of an omniscient narrator can be heard, even though the passage is narrated by Ishmael. Explain the narrator's remarks.

YOUR TURN

6 DISCUSS. What do you think of Ahab's obsession with chasing Moby Dick? Can you justify it? Can you understand his reasons?

7 DISCUSS. Can you think of another symbol as powerful as Moby Dick which could embody evil or the absence of meaning in the contemporary world?

6.12 **Literature**

Walt Whitman: the American bard

Walt Whitman's life

Walt Whitman (1819–92) was born in West Hills on Long Island, New York, in 1819 into a working-class family. He had little formal education, and at the age of eleven, he started to work as an office boy and then became a printer's apprentice for a local newspaper.

Journalism was to become his career as well as a means to support radical democratic causes. When he was about thirty years old, he travelled from New York to New Orleans, returning via Chicago. This journey was a transformative experience since it brought him in touch with the vastness of his country and the variety of its inhabitants. During this period, he read widely, acquiring a self-taught and eccentric education which included the Bible, Homer, Dante, Shakespeare, Carlyle, Goethe, Hegel, Emerson, Eastern religion and philosophy.

In 1855 he published the first edition of *Leaves of Grass*, containing twelve poems about his development as a poet and his experience of the American land. Nine editions followed, each containing new poems. Particularly relevant was the third one, in 1860, which aroused the indignation of puritanical readers and gained Whitman a reputation for obscenity and homosexuality. During the Civil War, he devoted himself to visiting wounded soldiers in army hospitals. He continued to believe in the value of democracy and technological progress. The fourth edition of *Leaves of Grass* (1867) contained poems on the Civil War and on the death of President Lincoln. In 1873 he retired to Camden, New Jersey, where he was visited by admirers and disciples and where he continued to write poetry and some prose essays. He died in 1892.

Whitman's popularity in Europe grew in the 1870s, and he was especially appreciated by the Aesthetic Movement. In America, he had Ralph Waldo Emerson's support during his lifetime and influenced later poets, such as Ezra Pound, Carl Sandburg and, more recently, the Beat Generation. He is generally regarded as the father of American poetry, as the first voice that was distinctly new and 'American'.

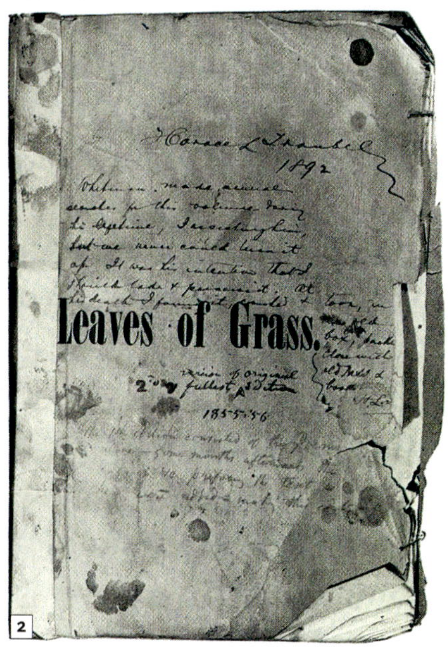

1 An engraving based on the portrait of Walt Whitman by Gabriel Harrison which was published in the first edition of *Leaves of Grass*.

2 Cover of Whitman's personal copy of the first edition of *Leaves of Grass*.

1 READ about Whitman's life and fill in the table below.

Place of birth	
Education	
Readings	
Job experiences	
Beliefs	
Journeys	
Public reaction to his works	
Reputation	

6.12 Walt Whitman: the American bard

The prophet of democracy and individualism

Whitman's poetry is pervaded by optimism and romantic faith in the dynamic future of the American nation. He celebrated America in all its variety – the land itself, its people, its natural life. To him his country represented the expression of the idea of democracy, the incarnation of the 'American dream' which he always believed in.

Another main theme in Whitman's poetry is himself, his task as a poet to respond to the spirit of his country, to give voice to the common man, to reveal the truth like a prophet. In spite of his self-celebration, Whitman sees himself contained in other men and women; he mixes with the crowd, identifies with his neighbour and embraces mankind in brotherly love.

However, he also deals with physical love: Whitman's poetry is a poetry of the body, in which the theme of sex is developed with a directness and frankness that struck puritanical readers as 'immoral'. What Whitman valued most was the dignity of the individual, conceived as the unity of body and soul, with a right to self-expression and personal experience.

I and you, 'whoever you are'

The Transcendentalist philosopher Ralph Waldo Emerson taught self-trust: man should not seek himself outside himself. This religion of self-reliance found its best expression in Whitman's work; however, the shock of overhearing oneself was the realisation of an unexpected otherness. This is the most complex aspect of Whitman's poetry; in *Song of Myself* he divided his being into three: 'my self'; the 'real me' or 'Me self'; and 'my soul'. The 'I' is the 'my self', or Whitman's poetic personality. The 'me self' is his inner personality. Whitman knows these two sides of his map of the mind very well; what seems scarcely known is his soul, which is an enigma, rather like the soul of America.

Song of Myself is the celebration of the meeting between an 'I' whose reality is constantly questioned and a 'you' which is often followed by the phrase 'whoever you are'; it embodies the riddle of the Other. The question is: 'Is there an Other to whom one can speak, a real audience, a real beloved, a real God?' Unless such a 'you' exists, there is no chance of turning private 'vision' into 'public' song. So writing implied, for Whitman, an act of faith that a real 'you' existed somewhere.

New means of expression

The subject matter of Whitman's poetry required new means of expression. *Leaves of Grass* is written in free verse: Whitman rejected rhymes and regular lines with a fixed number of syllables or stresses in favour of long lines where rhythm is naturally determined by the thought or emotion expressed. His poems proceed by accumulation and addition, the participle often replaces the finite verb, and the overall impression is one of fragmentation and lack of unity.

In addition, his language is new: it mixes dialect and common speech with the jargon of science and philosophy. It avoids similes and metaphors because the poet's aim is not to evoke but to assert and celebrate.

2 READ the text about Whitman's work and revise your knowledge using these headings:

1 The uniqueness of *Leaves of Grass*;
2 The reason why Whitman rejected traditional forms;
3 His view of reality;
4 His main themes;
5 His map of the mind;
6 The features of his line.

Milestones

1855, *Leaves of Grass*: a life-long poem

All of Whitman's poetry was incorporated into the various editions of *Leaves of Grass*. The first edition, published on July 4th, American Independence Day, showed a picture of a working man wearing a brown hat, the collar of his shirt open and a long beard. It was a photograph of Whitman himself dressed up as a 'democratic bard'. The work also included a preface where the author introduced the subject matter, the language and the aim of his poetry. *Leaves of Grass* can be regarded not as a collection of poems, but as a life-long poem. Whitman continued to revise and expand it throughout his life, publishing a total of nine different editions of it between 1855 and 1892, the year he died.

This implies a process of development and expansion resulting from the fact that Whitman never lost a Transcendental sense of the unity of all things. All of life and experience – reality itself – were a process, a continuing, all-embracing flow. Whitman, therefore, rejected the traditional forms and structures of 19th-century poetry; such forms and structures were at odds with the notion of poetry as a process, they imposed rigidity and completeness upon reality, which is in fact constantly unfolding.

1 Marilyn Monroe reading *Leaves of Grass*.

I Hear America Singing

Walt Whitman

Leaves of Grass (1855)

The protagonists of this popular poem are all the categories of American workers who are trying to build a better society and to bring the American dream to life.

5.8

I hear America singing, the varied carols[1] I hear,
Those of mechanics, each one singing his as it should be, blithe[2] and strong,
The carpenter singing his as he measures his plank or beam[3],
The mason[4] singing his as he makes ready for work, or leaves off work,
The boatman singing what belongs to him in his boat, the deckhand[5] singing on the steamboat deck.
The shoemaker singing as he sits on his bench, the hatter singing as he stands,
The wood-cutter's song, the ploughboy's on his way in the morning, or at the noon intermission[6] or at sundown;
The delicious singing of the mother, or of the young wife at work, or of the girl sewing or washing.
Each singing what belongs to her, and to none else;
The day what belongs to the day – at night, the party[7] of young fellows, robust, friendly,
Singing with open mouths their strong melodious songs.

1 **carols.** Canzoni tradizionali.
2 **blithe.** Gaia, allegra.
3 **plank or beam.** Tavola di legno o asse.
4 **mason.** Muratore.
5 **deckhand.** Marinaio.
6 **intermission.** Pausa.
7 **party.** Gruppo, comitiva.

2 Charles C. Ebbets, *Lunch atop a Skyscraper (New York Construction Workers Lunching on a Crossbeam)*, 1932.

COMPREHENSION

1 AS YOU READ the poem, note down in the table below the jobs Whitman mentions, together with the actions performed.

Job	Actions

Are women mentioned by the poet? How?

2 UNDERLINE the words referring to time. What image do they convey?

3 DECIDE the subject of the poem. Does it deal with a story or a central idea?

ANALYSIS

4 POINT OUT the layout and the rhyme scheme. Do they respect traditional forms of poetry?

5 THE POET, Whitman, gives unity to his poem through the use of repetition and parallelism, that is, the use of similar syntactic units inside the same line or from line to line. Provide examples from the text.

6 THE VOICES of the people at work are heard both in isolation and fused in a sort of choir. Identify the words conveying the two ideas. How are the individual and the unity of people related?

7 DECIDE. What features of the 'singing America' are stressed in the poem?

8 FOCUS on the 'I' in the poem. Who do you think it stands for?

YOUR TURN

9 DISCUSS the following questions.

1 Do you think Whitman's view of America is exaggeratedly optimistic?
2 Does it correspond to the present reality of American society?

Emily Dickinson: poetry of isolation

Emily Dickinson's life

Emily Dickinson was born into a middle-class Puritan family in Amherst, Massachusetts, in 1830. Her father Edward was a public man, a lawyer and a politician who cast a long shadow on Emily's emotional development and religious beliefs. She received her university education at Mount Holyoke Female Seminary, where she refused to declare her faith in public, as was required by Puritan tradition, and then decided to interrupt her studies and return home. She began a life of seclusion in which she only wore white clothes, as ambiguous emblems of spiritual marriage and singleness, and never left her father's house except for some walks in the garden. She hid her mind as well as her person from everyone but the members of her family, especially her sister Lavinia and a few friends to whom she wrote wonderful letters. Letter-writing became her only form of contact with the world, and her poems also seem to have been written for the purpose of communication rather than for publication.

In fact, during her lifetime she allowed only seven out of more than 2,000 poems to be printed. She died in 1886, and four years later, the literary critic Thomas W. Higginson was asked to make a selection from her work so that a book of her verse might be published. *Poems by Emily Dickinson* appeared in 1890 with some corrections and changes meant to suit the taste of a public accustomed to more traditional rhythms and images. A complete edition of her poems appeared in 1955, edited by Thomas Johnson, who re-established the form in which she wrote them, with the original and eccentric punctuation. A collection of her rich letters was published in 1958.

1

Dickinson's limited vision – 'I see New Englandly,' she wrote – is the poetic antithesis of her contemporary Walt Whitman. If Whitman was the poet of wholeness, she was the poet of what is broken and absent. She knew how the self breaks when it encounters the way things are. However, she possessed the genius to transform a private circumstance into one of general relevance.

Poetry of isolation

Emily Dickinson's poetry was influenced by the reading of the Bible, Shakespeare, Milton, the Metaphysical poets and contemporary writers like Emily Brontë. Along with these, the same forces that had long dominated New England – the Puritan tradition and Emerson's Transcendentalism – contributed to shaping her mind. However, she combined all these influences in a highly original way, detached from contemporary taste and the great events and contrasts of the age, including the campaign for the abolition of slavery, the Civil War and the beginning of the campaign for women's rights.

2

3

The eternal issues of life

Dickinson uses her poetry to challenge received certainties. Her themes are the eternal issues of life: death and loss, love and desire, time, fear, sorrow, despair, God, nature and man's relation to the universe. Though sceptical of established religion, she was deeply interested in spiritual experience and almost obsessed with death. Death elicited her curiosity; she wrote about it from the point of view of the person dying or of a witness. She sometimes felt horror or compassion, and she even wrote about her own death. Yet, death remained the great mystery, connected with the idea of eternity and regarded as a liberation from a state of anxiety. Death is also seen as the place where the human being tends, in order to become one with the universe, to become music, perfume, passion, flight.

1 Emily Dickinson.

2 Emily's father, Edward Dickinson.

3 Emily's sister, Lavinia Dickinson.

4 Michael J. Virzi, *A Poetic Dialogue*, 1995. Amherst, Massachusetts, US. This memorial is a tribute to Emily Dickinson and Robert Frost, who was professor at Amherst College.

5 Emily Dickinson Homestead in Amherst, Massachusetts, US.

The theme of love is explored through a full range of emotions: from ecstatic and sensual celebration to the despair due to separation. In this respect, she deals with the expectation of eternity as the hope of a final spiritual union.

Nature plays an important part in Dickinson's poetry: it is different from man, it is a source of wonder or fear and it can be presented in three ways:

- through an objective description;
- by juxtaposing the thing observed and the soul of the observer, so that the natural object leads to philosophical speculation;
- as a source of imagery to emphasise an abstract concept or theme.

In her poems, the 'I', the speaking voice, becomes a bee (which constantly symbolises the poet), a spider, a bird, a blade of grass or lilacs, in a vision of the world where macrocosm is fitted into microscopic structure.

4

5

Poetry of economy and control

Dickinson's poetry is primarily one of economy and control. Her poems tend to be short and organised in simple quatrains. They are compressed, almost like miniatures, where the faraway and huge are seen in terms of the humble and domestic and vice versa. They do not have a title.

Their language is characterised by monosyllabic words, by terms from various sources – law, geometry, engineering – and by common words that come alive in unusual contexts. Syntax and punctuation are combined in such a way that the meaning of the poems remains ambiguous, highlighting the emotion. Dickinson makes frequent use of rhetorical devices, such as imperfect rhymes, assonance, alliteration, paradox, metaphor, ellipses and capitalisation. The tone can be witty, ironic, cheerful or melancholic.

Dickinson's trademark

She uses the dash, which breaks lines apart, forcing the reader to pause and reconsider and providing a visible, physical space for thought. The dashes often invite the reader to fill in the blanks.

Like Whitman, Dickinson broke away from the stereotypes of poetry, even if, unlike his, her poetry is concerned with questions, intuitions and moods rather than statements and assertions. While her free use of rhyme anticipated modern experimentation, her exploration of universal issues through trivial, everyday imagery makes her the forerunner of the 'minimalist' writers of the 1980s.

1 READ the text about Emily Dickinson's life and work and point out:

1. the influences on her work;
2. how she compares to Whitman;
3. her main themes;
4. the different points of view from which she conveyed death, love and nature;
5. in what sense she broke with the stereotypes of poetry;
6. the function of the dash in her poems.

6.13 Emily Dickinson: poetry of isolation

WARM-UP

1 **DISCUSS in pairs. Emily Dickinson never gave titles to her poems and what is given here as a title is nothing but the first line of the poem itself.**

1 In what way does the presence or absence of a title in a poem affect your expectations about it?

2 What do you think about the 'title' of this poem?

Hope is the thing with feathers[1]

Emily Dickinson

Poem 254

In this poem, Dickinson deals with the fundamental sense of existence and expresses her awareness of the immense importance and dignity of the human soul involved in the adventure of life.

5.9

'Hope' is the thing with feathers –
That perches[2] in the soul –
And sings the tune without the words –
And never stops – at all –

And sweetest – in the Gale[3] – is heard –
And sore[4] must be the storm –
That could abash[5] the little Bird –
That kept so many warm –

I've heard it in the chillest[6] land –
And on the strangest Sea –
Yet, never, in Extremity[7] –
It asked a crumb[8] – of Me.

1 **feathers.** Piume.
2 **perches.** Sta appollaiata.
3 **Gale.** Vento forte.
4 **sore.** Triste, addolorato.
5 **abash.** Sconcertare, confondere.
6 **chillest.** Più fredda.
7 **Extremity.** Grave frangente.
8 **crumb.** Briciola.

COMPREHENSION

2 **READ the poem and write down:**

1 what its subject is;
2 where hope can be found;
3 what qualities it is given by the poet.

ANALYSIS

3 **POINT OUT the distinctive features of Dickinson's poetic form. Consider:**

1 the structure of the poem:
 A number of stanzas;
 B number of lines in each stanza;
 C length of lines;
2 the rhyme scheme;
3 the use of:
 A alliteration;
 B assonance;
 C repetition;
4 other features ....

4 **FOCUS on the vocabulary and syntax of the poem. Choose the correct option to complete the sentences.**

1 The words are *simple* / *complex* and *factual* / *evocative*.
2 There is a prevalence of *nouns* / *adjectives*.
3 The sentences are *simple* / *complex*.

5 **FIND the central metaphor of the poem and analyse its terms.** The vehicle of the metaphor is stated only at the end of the second stanza. What word does the author use at first? Try to explain why, choosing among the following.

- ☐ To create suspense.
- ☐ To make the meaning of the poem unattainable.
- ☐ To leave the image of hope indefinite and therefore more evocative.

6 **FILL IN the table below with the other metaphors contained in the poem and explain what they stand for.**

Metaphor	Stands for

What semantic area does Dickinson draw upon?

YOUR TURN

7 **DISCUSS the similarities and differences between Dickinson's and Whitman's poetry as regards:**

- structure;
- themes;
- language;
- the poet's attitude.

6.14 **Cultural Issues**

The path towards personal independence

WARM-UP

1 **DISCUSS** in pairs what 'being independent' means to you. How do you practise being an independent person concretely in your daily life?

2 **READ** the text about learning how to gain your independence.

3 **IN PAIRS** discuss which of the steps in the text you find most interesting.

Some steps to become independent

Accept yourself.
Accept your body, your personality, your opinions, your choices, your preferences and your life story. Put your mistakes behind you and learn from them. Make an effort to be a better you.

Accept the world.
Independent people are those who see the world, with its good and its bad, and consciously choose to be strong for themselves and others. You are not independent because you do not trust anyone.

Become emotionally independent.
Chances are, you depend on many people for emotional support. It may be your parents, a boyfriend or girlfriend, or good close friends. The only person who will always be with you is you. If you depend on yourself for support, you will never be let down.

Be there.
You don't have to throw away your friends to be independent. In fact, your independence is reinforced with good friends. When your friend needs someone to talk to, be there for them.

Don't settle.
Work hard at everything you do. Defend your opinions.

Leave your friends and family at home.
You must start doing things on your own. Go shopping alone; spend at least one or two evenings a week by yourself. Work on activities that force you to lead, not follow.

Try not to care what others think.
If you depend on others to tell you if your music is cool or if your clothes are trendy, you won't be very happy! As long as you like it, nothing else matters!

Love everyone.
Part of being independent is trying to love people no matter what they think about you.

Have a passion in life.
Choose something you are devoted to, something that you do constantly that takes up some time.

Get rid of the bad influences in your life.
Don't end friendships unless absolutely necessary. Learn to keep a healthy distance.

Take things lightly.
Rome wasn't built in a day, and no one is completely independent.

Good luck on your road to being independent!

Jonathan Livingston Seagull (1970)

The story
Jonathan, the main character of the book, is a seagull who is not happy to live as his peers, who only seem concerned with eating and fighting with one another for food. He dreams of mastering the art of flight and of flying higher and faster than his friends, and, because he tries to reach this goal, he comes to be seen as a nonconformist. He spends all his time practising dives and rolls, so much so that sometimes he even forgets to eat. After the Flock Council witnesses a particularly brave move, Jonathan is sent away. He then spends his days alone but doing what he finds most enjoyable. He keeps his spirit alive and enjoys the freedom from control and restraint. He finds his true freedom living alone and diving for fish below the water's surface and insects on land. One day, Jonathan meets two gulls who claim to be from his former flock. They take Jonathan up into the sky higher than he has ever flown before. Jonathan believes he has entered heaven and his body has transformed into the perfect gull. There are other gulls in this strange new place, and they are all practising flight. One of the gulls, Sullivan, becomes Jonathan's flight instructor and counsellor. When Jonathan asks why so few gulls are in this place, Sullivan answers that it takes most gulls many lifetimes to become ready to seek perfection. After mastering perfect speed, the elder Gull says that one must become ready to fly up to kindness and love. Jonathan decides to go back to his old flock. He supposes there must be other outcasts like himself who are waiting for instruction. Jonathan finds the recently out-cast Fletcher Lynd Seagull and begins to teach him. In a month, Jonathan has seven students. He decides to take them all back to the flock to teach them the limitlessness of flight. They hold flying practice on the beach until all the others join. Once the flock is all practising, Jonathan leaves his flock to teach other flocks. Fletcher is left behind to continue flight instruction.

Richard Bach (1936–)
Richard Bach was born in Oakpark, Illinois, in 1936. He attended college and later became a pilot in the Air Force Reserve. Many of his books contain references to his flying experience. His works include *Stranger to the Ground* (1963), *Biplane* (1966), *Jonathan Livingston Seagull* (1970), *A Gift of Wings* (1974), *Illusions: The Adventures of a Reluctant Messiah* (1977) and *Flying* (2003).

The moral of the story
Jonathan Livingston Seagull is written as a classic children's fable and, as a fable, teaches a lesson. The book has become a bestseller, probably because it opens our eyes to a lot of things in different perspectives. Particularly, Jonathan Livingston Seagull's passion for learning touches the heart of readers, and it inspires them to make changes in their own lives. Jonathan still loves flying even after becoming an outcast. He does not give up, because he has a passion for learning and he is ready to give up everything for his passion. This novel, on a deeper level, explores man's nature to learn and improve and perhaps defy tradition. Deeper still, it is the story of a soul learning to pursue perfection – the ultimate goal.

Bach teaches the reader that through tenacity and perseverance our goals can be achieved and obstacles can be overcome. In addition, the themes of freedom and individuality are explored.

1 Richard Bach in the cockpit of his aeroplane. Photo by John Shearer, 1972.

2 Jonathan, the seagull.

WARM-UP

1 **LOOK** at the epigraph to the book:

To the real Jonathan Seagull, who lives within us all.

Who do you think 'the real Jonathan Seagull' is?

Out by himself

Richard Bach

3 Winslow Homer, *Rocky coast with gulls*, 1869. Museum of Fine Arts, Boston, Massachusetts, US.

Jonathan Livingston Seagull (1970)

Part I

You are going to read the opening pages of the book, where Jonathan Livingstone Seagull is introduced during his first attempt to fly higher.

5.10

It was morning, and the new sun sparkled gold across the ripples[1] of a gentle sea. A mile from shore a fishing boat chummed the water[2] and the word for Breakfast Flock[3] flashed through the air, till a crowd of a thousand seagulls came to dodge[4] and fight for bits of food. It was another busy day beginning.

But way off alone, out by himself beyond boat and shore, Jonathan Livingston Seagull was practicing. A hundred feet in the sky he lowered his webbed feet[5], lifted his beak, and strained to hold a painful hard twisting curve[6] through his wings. The curve meant that he would fly slowly, and now he slowed until the wind was a whisper in his face, until the ocean stood still beneath him. He narrowed his eyes in fierce concentration, held his breath, forced one... single... more... inch... of... curve... Then his featliers ruffled[7], he stalled[8] and fell.

Seagulls, as you know, never falter[9], never stall. To stall in the air is for them disgrace and it is dishonor.

But Jonathan Livingston Seagull, unashamed, stretching his wings again in that trembling hard curve – slowing, slowing, and stalling once more – was no ordinary bird.

Most gulls don't bother[10] to learn more than the simplest facts of flight – how to get from shore to food and back again. For most gulls, it is not flying that matters, but eating. For this gull, though, it was not eating that mattered, but flight. More than anything else, Jonathan Livingston Seagull loved to fly.

This kind of thinking, he found, is not the way to make one's self popular with other birds. Even his parents were dismayed[11] as Jonathan spent whole days alone, making hundreds of low-level glides[12], experimenting.

He didn't know why, for instance, but when he flew at altitudes less than half his wingspan[13] above the water, he could stay in the air longer, with less effort. His glides ended not with the usual feet-down splash into the sea, but with a long flat wake[14] as he touched the surface with his feet tightly streamlined[15] against his body. When he began sliding in to feet-up landings[16] on the beach, then pacing the length of his slide in the sand, his parents were very much dismayed indeed.

'Why, Jon, why?' his mother asked. 'Why is it so hard to be like the rest of the flock, Jon? Why can't you leave low flying to the pelicans, the albatross? Why don't you eat? Son, you're bone and feathers[17]!'

'I don't mind being bone and feathers, mom. I just want to know what I can do in the air and what I can't, that's all. I just want to know.'

'See here, Jonathan,' said his father not unkindly. 'Winter isn't far away. Boats will be few and the surface fish will be swimming deep. If you must study, then study food, and how to get it. This flying business is all very well, but you can't eat a glide, you know. Don't you forget that the reason you fly is to eat.'

Jonathan nodded[18] obediently. For the next few days he tried to behave like the other gulls; he really tried, screeching[19] and fighting with the flock around the piers and fishing boats, diving on scraps[20] of fish and bread. But he couldn't make it work.

1 **sparkled ... ripples.** Luccicava tremolando sulle scaglie.
2 **chummed the water.** Arrancava verso il largo.
3 **Flock.** Stormo.
4 **dodge.** Giostrare.
5 **lowered his webbed feet.** Distese le zampe palmate.
6 **strained ... curve.** Si tese per imprimere una dolorosa torsione.
7 **his featliers ruffled.** Le penne si arruffarono.
8 **he stalled.** Entrò in stallo.
9 **never falter.** Non vacillano mai.
10 **don't bother.** Non si preoccupano.
11 **dismayed.** Afflitti.
12 **low-level glides.** Planate a bassa quota.
13 **wingspan.** Apertura alare.
14 **flat wake.** Scivolata liscia.
15 **tightly streamlined.** Raccolte.
16 **sliding in to feet-up landings.** Ad eseguire planate con atterraggio a zampe retratte.
17 **feathers.** Piume.
18 **nodded.** Annuì.
19 **screeching.** Gettando grida.
20 **scraps.** Avanzi.

6.14 The path towards personal independence

It's all so pointless, he thought, deliberately dropping a hard-won anchovy[21] to a hungry old gull chasing him[22]. I could be spending all this time learning to fly. There's so much to learn!

It wasn't long before Jonathan Gull was off by himself again, far out at sea, hungry, happy, learning.

The subject was speed, and in a week's practice he learned more about speed than the fastest gull alive.

From a thousand feet, flapping his wings as hard as he could, he pushed over into a blazing steep dive[23] toward the waves, and learned why seagulls don't make blazing steep power-dives. In just six seconds he was moving seventy miles per hour, the speed at which one's wing goes unstable on the upstroke[24].

Time after time it happened. Careful as he was, working at the very peak of his ability, he lost control at high speed.

Climb to a thousand feet. Full power straight ahead first, then push over[25], flapping, to a vertical dive. Then, every time, his left wing stalled on an upstroke, he'd roll violently left, stall his right wing recovering, and flick[26] like fire into a wild tumbling spin[27] to the right.

He couldn't be careful enough on that upstroke. Ten times he tried, and all ten times, as he passed through seventy miles per hour, he burst into a churning mass[28] of feathers, out of control, crashing down into the water.

The key, he thought at last, dripping wet, must be to hold the wings still at high speeds – to flap up to fifty and then hold the wings still.

From two thousand feet he tried again, rolling into his dive, beak straight down, wings full out and stable from the moment he passed fifty miles per hour. It took tremendous strength, but it worked. In ten seconds he had blurred through[29] ninety miles per hour. Jonathan had set a world speed record for seagulls!

But victory was short-lived. The instant he began his pullout[30], the instant he changed the angle of his wings, he snapped into[31] that same terrible uncontrolled disaster, and at ninety miles per hour it hit him like dynamite. Jonathan Seagull exploded in midair and smashed down into a brickhard sea.

When he came to[32], it was well after dark, and he floated in moonlight on the surface of the ocean. His wings were ragged bars of lead[33], but the weight of failure was even heavier on his back. He wished, feebly[34], that the weight could be just enough to drag him[35] gently down to the bottom, and end it all.

As he sank low in the water, a strange hollow[36] voice sounded within him. There's no way around it. I am a seagull. I am limited by my nature. If I were meant to learn so much about flying, I'd have charts[37] for brains. If I were meant to fly at speed, I'd have a falcon's short wings, and live on mice instead of fish. My father was right. I must forget this foolishness. I must fly home to the Flock and be content as I am, as a poor limited seagull.

The voice faded, and Jonathan agreed. The place for a seagull at night is on shore, and from this moment forth[38], he vowed[39], he would be a normal gull. It would make everyone happier.

He pushed wearily[40] away from the dark water and flew toward the land, grateful for what he had learned about work-saving low-altitude flying.

But no, he thought. I am done with the way I was[41], I am done with everything I learned. I am a seagull like every other seagull, and I will fly like one. So he climbed painfully to a hundred feet and flapped his wings harder, pressing for shore.

He felt better for his decision to be just another one of the Flock. There would be no ties now to the force that had driven him to learn, there would be no more challenge and no more failure. And it was pretty, just to stop thinking, and fly through the dark, toward the lights above the beach.

Dark! The hollow voice cracked in alarm. Seagulls never fly in the dark!

21 **deliberately ... anchovy.** Lasciando cadere di proposito un'acciuga duramente conquistata.
22 **chasing him.** Che lo inseguiva.
23 **he pushed ... dive.** Si buttò in picchiata.
24 **on the upstroke.** Nella fase ascendente.
25 **push over.** Scivolata d'ala.
26 **flick.** Guizzava.
27 **wild tumbling spin.** Avvitamento selvaggio.
28 **burst into a churning mass.** Si trasformava in una massa arruffata.
29 **he had blurred through.** Era sfrecciato a.
30 **he began his pullout.** Incominciò a risalire.
31 **he snapped into.** Precipitò.
32 **he came to.** Rinvenne.
33 **ragged bars of lead.** Barre sfilacciate di piombo.
34 **feebly.** Debolmente.
35 **to drag him.** A trascinarlo.
36 **hollow.** Cupa.
37 **charts.** Diagrammi.
38 **forth.** In poi.
39 **he vowed.** Giurò.
40 **wearily.** Stancamente.
41 **I am done with the way I was.** Non sono più lo stesso.

Jonathan was not alert to listen. It's pretty, he thought. The moon and the lights twinkling on the water, throwing out little beacon-trails[42] through the night, and all so peaceful and still...

Get down! Seagulls never fly in the dark! If you were meant to fly in the dark, you'd have the eyes of an owl[43]! You'd have charts for brains! You'd have a falcon's short wings!

There in the night, a hundred feet in the air, Jonathan Livingston Seagull – blinked[44]. His pain, his resolutions, vanished.

Short wings. A falcon's short wings!

That's the answer! What a fool I've been! All I need is a tiny little wing, all I need is to fold[45] most of my wings and fly on just the tips[46] alone! Short wings!

42 **beacon-trails.** Scie.
43 **owl.** Civetta.
44 **blinked.** Batté gli occhi.
45 **to fold.** Raccogliere.
46 **tips.** Estremità.

COMPREHENSION

2 AS YOU READ the passage, find details about:
- the setting;
- the characters;
- the main situation.

ANALYSIS

3 SAY what kind of narrator is employed.

4 UNDERLINE the words and phrases connected with the descriptions of Jonathan's flight. The metaphor of flight is powerful in Bach's story.
What idea do these descriptions convey?

5 DISCUSS the difference between the philosophy of the flock and that of Jonathan.

6 DECIDE. Jonathan comments, 'I am a seagull. I am limited by my nature. If I were meant to learn so much about flying, I'd have charts for brains. [...] My father was right. I must forget this foolishness. I must fly home to the Flock and be content as I am, as a poor limited seagull.'
Why has Jonathan given up? What makes him try again?

7 LIST the themes presented in the passage.

FCE Speaking – Part 2

8 INDIVIDUAL LONG TURN. Here are two photographs. They show young people in special moments in their lives. Compare these photos and say how you think these people are feeling.

How do you think these people are feeling?

Process language
Speaking - Part 2

Saying which picture is more effective
- This picture doesn't show / express ... as clearly / effectively as ...
- Picture ... tries to ... but I think picture ... does it more effectively.
- Both photographs are impressive, but ... conveys a stronger idea of ...
- I might be wrong, but I would say that this picture ...

FCE Writing – Part 1

9 AN ESSAY. In class you have been talking about personal independence. Now your teacher has asked you to write an essay. Write your essay using all the notes and giving reasons for your point of view. Read the essay title and write an essay of between 140–190 words.

How can we make ourselves truly free?

Notes:
Write about
- listening to others' advice
- following our dreams
- .... (your ideas)

6 Overview

Test what you know

1 UNDERLINE the correct option in the sentences.

1. The Luminists were called like this because of *the extensive horizons of their paintings / their experiments with the effects of light on water and the sky.*
2. 'Manifest Destiny' was *the Alaska Purchase / a slogan to justify the right to territorial expansion.*
3. The American Civil War lasted from *1860 to 1863 / 1861 to 1865.*
4. The abolition of slavery granted the blacks *freedom without money and a home / equality and economic security.*
5. The American Federation of Labour was founded by *Abraham Lincoln / exploited workers.*

2 DECIDE if the following sentences are true or false. Correct the false ones.

1. The Gilded Age refers to the last three decades of the 19th century. T F
2. New capitalists were able to control the nation's wealth. T F
3. The gap between the rich and the poor disappeared. T F
4. Grant's government was marked by corruption. T F
5. The federal government was not able to preserve the disappearing of the wilderness. T F
6. It was only towards the end of the century that the USA showed interest in foreign affairs. T F
7. In 1898 the USA lost Puerto Rico and the Philippines. T F

Can you do it?

3 DISCUSS the social and cultural factors that helped shape the American mind.

4 TRACE the features of the frontier hero.

5 SUMMARISE the characteristics and aims of the Hudson River School.

6 EXPLAIN the importance of the figure of Abraham Lincoln in the making of the American nation. Describe how Walt Whitman celebrated Lincoln as a leader in his poem 'O Captain! My captain!'.

7 LIST the key ideas of Transcendentalism and say how they affected the American Renaissance.

8 EXPLAIN why Walt Whitman is considered a prophet of democracy and individualism.

9 READ *Poem 77* (ca 1859) by Emily Dickinson and do the following activities.

1. State the subjects of the poem; the reaction produced in the speaker by the word 'escape'; whether the speaker succeeds in breaking free.
2. The poem contains examples of alliteration, assonance and repetition. Point them out. Is the effect of the exclamation mark the same in line 4 as in line 8?
3. Identify contrasting images. What does Dickinson implicitly compare herself to? The poet uses negative structures to state a certain situation. Find the lines where this happens and rephrase them in the form of a positive statement.
4. What insight does the poem provide into the poet's personal experience?

I never hear the word 'escape'
Without a quicker blood[1],
A sudden[2] expectation,
A flying attitude!

I never hear of prisons broad[3]
By soldiers battered down[4],
But I tug childish at my bars[5]
Only to fail again!

1 **Without a quicker blood.** Senza che mi si acceleri il sangue.
2 **sudden.** Improvvisa.
3 **broad.** Ampie.
4 **battered down.** Infrante.
5 **I tug childish at my bars.** Mi aggrappo come un bambino alle mie sbarre.

10 EXPLAIN in what sense the seagull Jonathan Livingston has become a symbol of the struggle towards personal independence.

Oral test

11 IMAGINE your teacher asks you the following questions in an oral test. For each question, prepare a one-minute turn.

1. What two forces dominated the new cultural image of America?
2. What were the consequences of the Civil War?
3. Why is *Moby-Dick* regarded as an American epic?
4. What does Moby Dick's whiteness symbolise?
5. When was the Dow Jones Industrial Average established?
6. What businesses changed the economy of the country in the last three decades of the 19th century?
7. How are Walt Whitman and Emily Dickinson viewed in the context of American literature?

The Great Watershed

Specification 7 | Homepage

Top News

1918 The armistice is signed on 11th November

Top Issue

Moments of being

Most Popular News

1905 Freud publishes *Three Essays on the Theory of Sexuality*

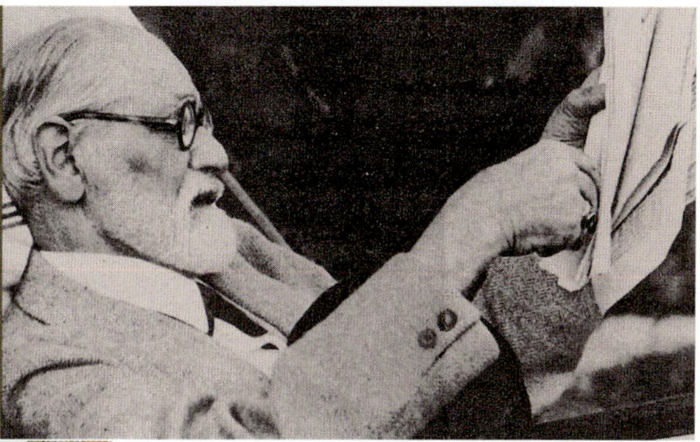

The Arts

World War I in painting

1922
T.S. Eliot publishes *The Waste Land*

Spotlight

Modernist writers give shape to a new consciousness

Cinema

See the Irish Question on screen

Mapping History

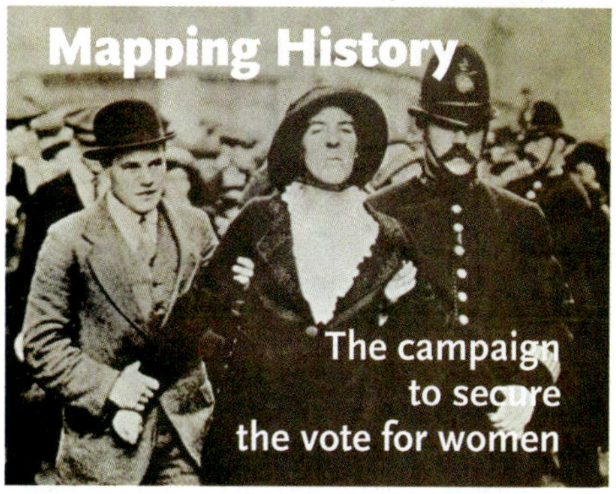

The campaign to secure the vote for women

EXPLORE THE CULTURE

Culture | Literature | History | The Arts | Psychology | Two Films About... | Cultural Issues

INTERACTIVE MAP 7: *SECURING THE VOTE FOR WOMEN*

The Edwardian age

WARM-UP

1 **LOOK** at the pictures (1–6) and match them with the captions (A–E). One caption matches two pictures.

- **A** Women called 'Suffragettes' campaign for the right to vote. ....
- **B** The Liberal government proposes the 'People's Budget', which leads to a constitutional crisis. ....
- **C** The Irish Free State, a new Irish republic, is born. ....
- **D** Edward VII, known as the 'Uncle of Europe', assists in foreign policy. ....
- **E** World War I breaks out in 1914, and Britons of every class and sex are encouraged to support the war. ....

2 **DISCUSS** in pairs. What aspects of Edwardian society are highlighted in the pictures?

3 **READ** the Q&A text.

Q **Who reigned after Queen Victoria's death?**

A On the death of Queen Victoria in 1901, the royal house took the Germanic surname of her consort, Prince Albert of Saxe-Coburg-Gotha. Victoria's son Edward, who reigned until 1910 as Edward VII, was to be the only sovereign of that dynasty in Britain. He was crowned in August 1902.

Q **What were the king's achievements in Europe?**

A He restored energy to a monarchy that had been rather gloomy since his father's death forty years earlier. Related to most European royalty (he was known as the 'Uncle of Europe'), he was able to assist in foreign policy negotiations and his well-received addresses during a state visit to Paris helped pave the way for the Anglo-French *Entente Cordiale*, the agreement reached by France and Britain in April 1904 which settled outstanding colonial disputes. Edward was also the first British monarch to visit Russia. In 1902, he founded the Order of Merit to reward those who distinguished themselves in science, art or literature.

Q **What change was introduced into British politics by the election of 1906?**

A In 1906 the Liberals won the general election and took the first steps towards the creation of a welfare state: national insurance and old-age pensions were introduced.

1 General Kitchener's famous recruiting poster.

2 First World War propaganda poster asking women to support the war effort. Parliamentary Recruiting Committee, London, 1915.

3 Suffragettes protesting for women's right to vote, ca 1914.

4 Edward VII receives maharajahs and other dignitaries from around the Empire before his coronation.

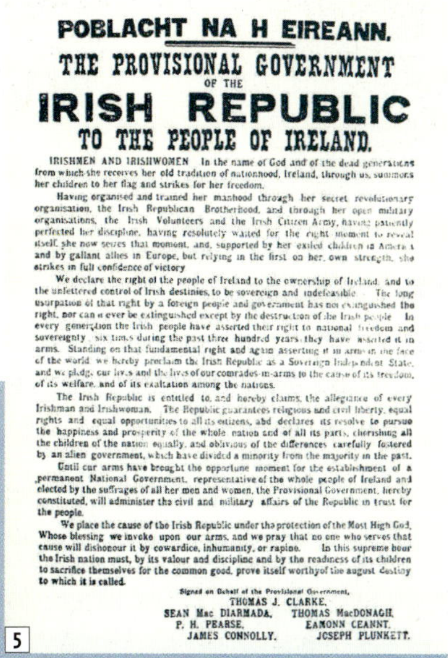

POBLACHT NA H EIREANN.

THE PROVISIONAL GOVERNMENT OF THE IRISH REPUBLIC TO THE PEOPLE OF IRELAND.

IRISHMEN AND IRISHWOMEN: In the name of God and of the dead generations from which she receives her old tradition of nationhood, Ireland, through us, summons her children to her flag and strikes for her freedom.

Having organised and trained her manhood through her secret revolutionary organisation, the Irish Republican Brotherhood, and through her open military organisations, the Irish Volunteers and the Irish Citizen Army, having patiently perfected her discipline, having resolutely waited for the right moment to reveal itself, she now seizes that moment, and, supported by her exiled children in America and by gallant allies in Europe, but relying in the first on her own strength, she strikes in full confidence of victory.

We declare the right of the people of Ireland to the ownership of Ireland, and to the unfettered control of Irish destinies, to be sovereign and indefeasible. The long usurpation of that right by a foreign people and government has not extinguished the right, nor can it ever be extinguished except by the destruction of the Irish people. In every generation the Irish people have asserted their right to national freedom and sovereignty; six times during the past three hundred years they have asserted it in arms. Standing on that fundamental right and again asserting it in arms in the face of the world, we hereby proclaim the Irish Republic as a Sovereign Independent State, and we pledge our lives and the lives of our comrades-in-arms to the cause of its freedom, of its welfare, and of its exaltation among the nations.

The Irish Republic is entitled to, and hereby claims, the allegiance of every Irishman and Irishwoman. The Republic guarantees religious and civil liberty, equal rights and equal opportunities to all its citizens, and declares its resolve to pursue the happiness and prosperity of the whole nation and of all its parts, cherishing all the children of the nation equally, and oblivious of the differences carefully fostered by an alien government, which have divided a minority from the majority in the past.

Until our arms have brought the opportune moment for the establishment of a permanent National Government, representative of the whole people of Ireland and elected by the suffrages of all her men and women, the Provisional Government, hereby constituted, will administer the civil and military affairs of the Republic in trust for the people.

We place the cause of the Irish Republic under the protection of the Most High God, Whose blessing we invoke upon our arms, and we pray that no one who serves that cause will dishonour it by cowardice, inhumanity, or rapine. In this supreme hour the Irish nation must, by its valour and discipline and by the readiness of its children to sacrifice themselves for the common good, prove itself worthy of the august destiny to which it is called.

Signed on Behalf of the Provisional Government,
THOMAS J. CLARKE.
SEAN Mac DIARMADA. THOMAS MacDONAGH.
P. H. PEARSE. EAMONN CEANNT.
JAMES CONNOLLY. JOSEPH PLUNKETT.

5 The Proclamation of the Irish Republic, or 'Easter Proclamation', 1916.

Q Why was Edward's reign characterised by social unrest?

A Although these important measures of social improvement were passed, the Edwardian period was a time of industrial unrest, strikes and violence. The strikes, meant to be weapons against the government, were called because of high prices and low wages. They were remarkable for the number of men involved and for the violence which often accompanied them. Violence came also from women.

Q Who were the Suffragettes?

A They were educated ladies who, together with a very small number of male sympathisers, had been arguing in favour of voting rights for women since the 1860s. However, no one paid much attention to them until 1903, when Mrs Emmeline Pankhurst founded the Women's Social and Political Union. The 'Suffragettes' wanted women to have the vote and soon won massive publicity for their cause.

Q What led to a constitutional crisis?

A The Liberal programme led to a constitutional crisis when the House of Lords refused to pass the Liberal budget of 1909. The budget, called the 'People's Budget', included welfare programmes and unprecedented taxes on the wealthy.

Q Who succeeded Edward VII?

A Edward VII died in 1910 before the situation could be resolved, and was succeeded by his son, who became George V. He maintained a certain informality, which suited his simple, straightforward character and made him popular. On several occasions, he showed that the king's right to advise could be significant. Were he to be judged by posterity, he would prove to be a model monarch by carrying out his royal responsibilities with exemplary dedication while having an irreprehensible family life.

Q How did George V act during World War I?

A In 1914 the First World War broke out. The king made several visits to troops and to hospitals, visiting wounded servicemen; he pressed for proper treatment of German prisoners of war and he also pressed for more humane treatment of conscientious objectors. In 1917, anti-German feeling led him to change the family name to that of Windsor.

Q What did Ireland ask for?

A Support for Home Rule for Ireland, that is, the right of the people to control their own affairs, had grown in the late 19th century. This was opposed by the Unionists in the north and by the Conservative Party.

Q What were the consequences of the Easter Rising in Ireland?

A The 1916 'Easter Rising' in Dublin, and subsequent civil war, resulted in the setting up of the Irish Free State (later to become the Irish Republic) in 1922, while the six northern counties remained part of the United Kingdom. George V played a conciliatory role on this and other occasions, such as the General Strike of 1926.

6 Winston Churchill promotes his Liberal policy from the top of a taxi, Manchester, April 1908.

4 IN PAIRS **cover the answers (A s) in the text. Take turns asking and answering the questions (Q s) using the information that you have read.**

7.2 **History**

World War I

WARM-UP

1 **LOOK** at the pictures (1–3). What issues about World War I do they hint at?

2 **MATCH** the words (1–6) with their meanings (A–F).

1 Allies
2 Warfare
3 Machine gun
4 Tank
5 Shell
6 Treaty

A A formal agreement between two or more states.
B An enclosed combat vehicle that is armed with a cannon and machine guns.
C An artillery projectile containing an explosive charge.
D One in helpful association with another.
E A rapid-firing automatic gun.
F Armed conflict.

3 **READ** the Q&A text.

4 **IN PAIRS** cover the answers (A s) in the text. Take turns asking and answering the questions (Q s) using the information that you have read.

1 Voluntary recruits to the army in Southwark, 1915. At this time, popular enthusiasm for the war was extremely high.

2 British soldiers in a trench near the Somme, 1916.

Q When did the war break out?

A It broke out when the Austrian Archduke Franz Ferdinand was assassinated in Sarajevo in 1914. Germany marched through Belgium, a neutral territory, in order to attack France.

Q What powers were involved in the war?

A The war involved the Central European Powers (Germany and Austria-Hungary) on one side and the Allies, or *Triple Entente*, (Britain and the British Empire, France and Russia and their allies, including later Italy and the United States) on the other.

Q Why did Britain declare war on Germany?

A Britain declared war on Germany in August 1914; Britain justified war on Germany because Britain was a signatory of an agreement to respect Belgium's neutrality. It therefore told the nation that it would defend the weak (Belgium) against the strong (Germany), fighting for democracy and freedom. An increase in patriotism from Ireland as well as from the Dominions enabled Britain to face its ordeal with impressive unity.

Q Why did Germany almost defeat the Allies in the first few weeks of war?

A Germany nearly defeated the Allies in the first few weeks of war in 1914, since it had better equipment, better-trained soldiers and a clear plan of attack. Apart from the Crimean War (➔10.2, 10.14), this was Britain's first European war since the Napoleonic Wars, and the country was unprepared for the terrible, destructive modern artillery, machine guns and tanks, and the use of gas and shells during the attacks.

Q What was 'shell shock'?

A 'Shell shock' was the term used by doctors to allude to the psychological effect of shell explosions, blamed for the frequent cases of psychological disorders among soldiers.

Q When did the United States join the war?

A The United States joined the war on 2nd April 1917, considering it a crusade to make the world 'safe for democracy', a 'war to end all wars'.

Q When did the war end?

A American participation accelerated the German defeat: on 11th November 1918, Allied and German leaders signed an armistice. The peace treaty was signed at Versailles in 1919 by British Prime Minister Lloyd George, Georges Clemenceau of France, American President Woodrow Wilson and Vittorio Emanuele Orlando of Italy.

Q What did President Wilson devise?

A President Wilson proposed 'Fourteen Points' to work out the peace treaty and prevent future occasions of war. He devised a plan to set up the 'League of Nations', an organisation in which the representatives of the world's nations would try to discuss and settle their differences instead of resorting to war. The American Senate, however, voted against permanent involvement in European problems, and the United States never joined the League of Nations.

Q What were the effects of the war?

A The war was a monster which was beyond the control of statesmen or generals, and claimed the lives of about nine million men. It caused the ruin of four great empires, made possible a Communist revolution in Russia, which got rid of the old rule of the tsar, and paved the way for the rise of dictators like Benito Mussolini and Adolf Hitler.

3 Workers, including many women, at the National Shell-fitting Factory in Nottinghamshire, 1917.

Milestones

11th November 1918, the day the guns fell silent

The armistice of 11th November 1918 – 'the eleventh hour of the eleventh day of the eleventh month' – effectively ended the Great War, and many hoped that 'all wars' had ended on that day. However, the conflict was only officially concluded with the signing of the peace treaties in June 1919, and victory parades took place that summer. Although some objected to exultant military parades, and a number of ex-servicemen even refused to participate. As a result, the first Remembrance Day ceremonies were commemorative rather than triumphant; 'Today is Peace Day,' announced the 'Manchester Guardian' on 11th November 1919.

Insights

Remembrance Day

Two features of that first Remembrance Day are central to today's commemorations: the Cenotaph in Whitehall and the two-minutes' silence. The Cenotaph was the place around which people united, and the activity that united them was the silence – the first minute in memory of the nearly twenty million dead, and the second for the living loved ones they left behind. On King George's initiative, people were asked to remain silent and to cease all activity at 11 o'clock. Everything and everyone stopped: buses, trains and factories halted; electricity supplies were cut off to stop the trams; even the ships of the Royal Navy were stopped. Other Remembrance Day traditions developed quickly. In November 1920, the 'Unknown Warrior' was buried in Westminster Abbey. The tomb contained the body of an unknown ordinary serviceman picked at random. It was laid in the abbey in the morning, and tens of thousands of people had walked past the grave by the end of the afternoon. Over a million people visited it in its first week. The poppy campaign was more practical. Starting in 1921, artificial poppies were sold to support the Earl Haig fund for ex-servicemen. Former soldiers made the poppies – and so ensured their own employment – and the profits supported ex-servicemen in need. Still today, the poppy remains a symbol of remembrance.

IELTS Listening – Section 4

5 6.1 **ACADEMIC MONOLOGUE. You are going to hear a lecturer talking about life in the trenches during World War I. Read the questions below carefully. Then listen and answer questions 1–10.**

For questions 1–5, complete the sentences. Write NO MORE THAN THREE WORDS in each space.

The things the soldier remembers most about the trenches are feelings of **(1)** FEAR and DISCONFORT

The trenches themselves were in fact long **(2)** DAG OUT OWLS ...... built to face the enemy lines.

The lines were not necessarily **(3)** STRAIGHT ....

because they followed the lie of the land.

The important thing was that they offered good defence and the possibility to observe **(4)** ENEMY LINE ....

Another important fact is that the trenches were not a continuous line but were **(5)** BUILT in SECTIONS.

For questions 6–8, complete the description of the diagram. Write NO MORE THAN THREE WORDS in each space.

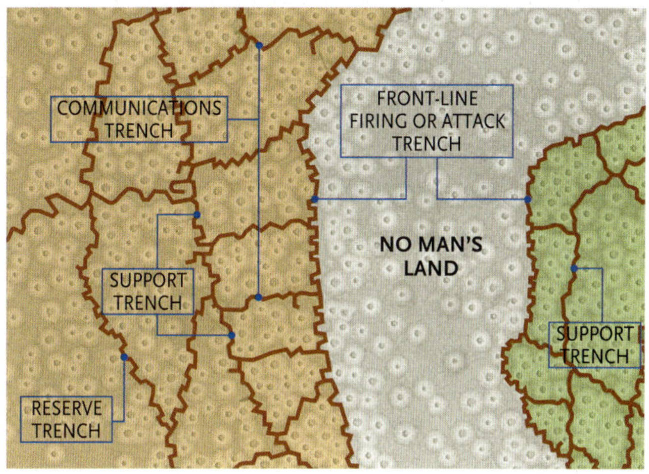

The **(6)** FRONT LINE ...... is the section that faces the enemy line.

The **(7)** SUPPORTED TRENCH is the trench built at some distance behind the main trenches.

The area between the two enemy lines is called **(8)** NO MANS LAND

For questions 9 and 10, complete the notes. Write NO MORE THAN THREE WORDS in each space.

The two main areas of risk in trenches:

(9) DEA ....

The speaker considered the greatest problems in the trenches to come from **(10)** WEATHER ...... PROBLEM

7.2 World War I

WARM-UP

1 **EXPAND** this thinking map with all the words you know relating to war.

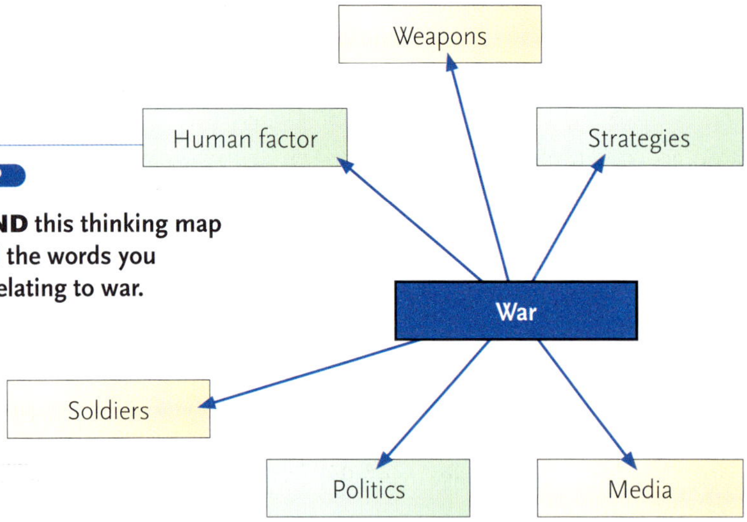

1 German soldiers with machine guns in the trenches, World War I, near Reims, 1914.

There is nothing worse than war

Ernest Hemingway

A Farewell to Arms (1929)

Book I, Chapter 9

In A Farewell to Arms *Ernest Hemingway (1899–1961) tells the story of an American ambulance driver, Lieutenant Henry Frederick, on the Italian front during World War I. In the following passage, Henry and a group of Italian soldiers, Passini, Manera, Gavuzzi and Gordini, are talking about war during a pause before a new attack. The first to speak is Henry. All of a sudden a bomb explodes near them.*

6.3

'I believe we should get the war over[1],' I said. 'It would not finish it if one side[2] stopped fighting. It would only be worse if we stopped fighting.'

'It could not be worse,' Passini said respectfully. 'There is nothing worse than war.'

'Defeat is worse.'

'I do not believe it,' Passini said still respectfully. 'What is defeat? You go home.'

'They come after you[3]. They take your home. They take your sisters.'

'I don't believe it,' Passini said. 'They can't do that to everybody. Let everybody defend his home. Let them keep their sisters in the house.'

'They hang[4] you. They come and make you be a soldier again. Not in the auto-ambulance, in the infantry[5].'

'They can't hang every one.'

'An outside nation[6] can't make you be a soldier,' Manera said. 'At the first battle you all run.'

'Like the Tchecos[7].'

'I think you do not know anything about being conquered and so you think it is not bad.'

'Tenente,' Passini said. 'We understand you let us talk. Listen. There is nothing as bad as war[8]. We in the auto-ambulance cannot even realize at all how bad it is. When people realize how bad it is they cannot do anything to stop it because they go crazy. There are some people who never realize. There are people who are afraid of their officers. It is with them the war is made.'

'I know it is bad but we must finish it.'

'It doesn't finish. There is no finish to a war.'

'Yes there is.'

Passini shook his head.

'War is not won by victory. What if we take San Gabriele[9]? What if we take the Carso and Monfalcone and Trieste? Where are we then? Did you see all the far mountains to-day? Do you think we could take all them too? Only if the Austrians stop fighting. One side must stop

1 **we ... over.** Dovremmo portare a termine la guerra.
2 **one side.** Una delle due forze (belligeranti).
3 **They ... you.** Loro (i nemici) ti inseguono.
4 **They hang.** Impiccano.
5 **infantry.** Fanteria.
6 **An outside nation.** Una nazione straniera.
7 **Tchecos.** Cecoslovacchi (si rifiutarono di appoggiare gli Austriaci che erano stati i loro oppressori).
8 **There is nothing as bad as war.** Non c'è niente di peggio della guerra.
9 **San Gabriele.** La cima di una montagna a Nord-Est d'Italia.
10 **even the peasants ... a war.** Perfino i contadini credono in qualche cosa di meglio della guerra.
11 **We must shut up.** Dobbiamo tacere.

fighting. Why don't we stop fighting? If they come down into Italy they will get tired and go away. They have their own country. But no, instead there is a war.'

'You're an orator.'

'We think. We read. We are not peasants. We are mechanics. But even the peasants know better than to believe in a war[10]. Everybody hates this war.'

'There is a class that controls a country that is stupid and does not realize anything and never can. That is why we have this war.'

'Also they make money out of it.'

'Most of them don't,' said Passini. 'They are too stupid. They do it for nothing. For stupidity.'

'We must shut up[11],' said Manera. 'We talk too much even for the Tenente[12].'

'He likes it,' said Passini. 'We will convert him[13].'

'But now we will shut up,' Manera said.

'Do we eat yet, Tenente?' Gavuzzi asked.

'I will go and see,' I said. Gordini stood up and went ouside with me.

'Is there anything I can do, Tenente? Can I help in any way?' He was the quietest one of the four. 'Come with me if you want,' I said, 'and we'll see.'

It was dark outside and the long light from the search-lights[14] was moving over the mountains. There were big search-lights on that front mounted on camions that you passed sometimes on the road at night, close behind the lines[15], the camion stopped a little off the road[16], an officer directing the light and the crew scared[17]. We crossed the brickyard[18], and stopped at the main dressing station[19]. There was a little shelter of green branches outside over the entrance and in the dark the night wind rustled[20] the leaves dried by the sun. Inside there was a light. The major was at the telephone sitting on a box. One of the medical captains said the attack had been put forward an hour[21]. He offered me a glass of cognac. I looked at the board tables[22], the instruments shining in the light, the basins and the stoppered bottles[23]. Gordini stood behind me. The major got up from the telephone. [...]

I ate the end of my piece of cheese and took a swallow of wine. Through the other noise I heard a cough, then came the chuh-chuh-chuh-chuh – then there was a flash[24], as when a blast-furnace door is swung open[25], and a roar[26] that started white and went red and on and on in a rushing wind. I tried to breathe but my breath would not come and I felt myself rush bodily out of myself[27] and out and out and out and all the time bodily in the wind. I went out swiftly, all of myself, and I knew I was dead and that it had all been a mistake to think you just died. Then I floated[28], and instead of going on I felt myself slide back[29]. I breathed and I was back. The ground was torn up[30] and in front of my head there was a splintered beam of wood[31]. In the jolt of my head[32] I heard somebody crying. I thought somebody was screaming. I tried to move but I could not move. I heard the machine-guns and rifles[33] firing across the river and all along the river. There was a great splashing and I saw the star-shells[34] go up and burst and float whitely[35] and rocks going up and heard the bombs, all this in a moment, and then I heard close to me some one saying 'Mama Mia! Oh, mama Mia!' I pulled and twisted and got my legs loose[36] finally and turned around and touched him. It was Passini and when I touched him he screamed. His legs were toward me and I saw in the dark and the light[37] that they were both smashed above the knee[38]. One leg was gone and the other was held by tendons and part of the trouser and the stump twiched and jerked as though it were not connected[39]. He bit his arm and moaned[40], 'O mama mia, mama Mia,' then, 'Dio te salve, Maria. Dio te salve, Maria. Oh Jesus shoot me Christ shoot me mama mia mama Mia oh purest lovely Mary shoot me. Stop it. Stop it. Oh Jesus lovely Mary stop it. Oh oh oh oh,' then choking[41], 'Mama mama mia.' Then he was quiet, biting his arm, the stump of his leg twitching.

'Porta feriti!' I shouted holding my hands cupped. 'Porta feriti!' I tried to get closer to Passini to try to put a tourniquet[42] on the legs but I could not move. I tried again and my legs moved a

12 **Tenente.** *Henry.*
13 **We will convert him.** Lo convinceremo.
14 **search-lights.** Riflettori.
15 **close behind the lines.** Proprio dietro il fronte.
16 **a little off the road.** Ai margini della strada.
17 **the crew scared.** I soldati si terrorizzarono.
18 **brickyard.** Mattonificio.
19 **main dressing station.** Principale stazione (qui sta per stazione di emergenza, ospedale da campo).
20 **rustled.** Agitava.
21 **the attack ... an hour.** L'attacco era stato anticipato di un'ora.
22 **board tables.** Tavoli di legno (usati come tavoli operatori).
23 **the basins ... stoppered bottles.** Le bacinelle e le bottiglie già pronte.
24 **flash.** Vampata.
25 **When ... swung open.** Quando si spalanca lo sportello di un altoforno.
26 **roar.** Strepito.
27 **I felt ... of myself.** Mi sentii scagliato a tutta forza fuori da me stesso.
28 **I floated.** Tornai a galla.
29 **instead ... slide back.** Invece di risalire mi sentivo scivolare all'indietro.
30 **was torn up.** A pezzi.
31 **a splintered beam of wood.** Una trave schiantata.
32 **In the jolt of my head.** Tra lo stordimento.
33 **machine-guns and rifles.** Mitragliatrici e fucili.
34 **star-shells.** Stelle dei proiettili.
35 **float whitely.** Galleggiavano (in cielo) con una luce bianca.
36 **I pulled ... loose.** Mi stirai, mi contorsi, liberai le gambe.
37 **in the dark and the light.** Negli squarci luminosi.
38 **they ... knee.** Erano sfracellate sopra il ginocchio.
39 **the stump ... connected.** Il moncone strappava e vibrava come se fosse un corpo a sé.
40 **moaned.** Si lamentava.
41 **choking.** Rantolando.
42 **tourniquet.** Laccio emostatico.

little. I could pull backward along with my arms and elbows. Passini was quiet now. I sat beside him, undid my tunic and tried to rip the tail of my shirt[43]. It would not rip and I bit the edge of the cloth to start it. Then I thought of his puttees[44]. I had on wool stockings but Passini wore puttees. All the drivers wore puttees but Passini had only one leg. I unwound the puttee and while I was doing it I saw there was no need to try and make a tourniquet because he was dead already. I made sure he was dead. There were three others to locate. I sat up straight and as I did so something inside my head moved like the weights on a doll's eyes[45] and it hit me inside in the back of my eyeballs. My legs felt warm and wet and my shoes were wet and warm inside. I knew that I was hit and leaned over and put my hand on my knee. My knee wasn't there. My hand went in and my knee was down on my shin[46]. I wiped my hand on my shirt and another floating light came very slowly down and I looked at my leg and was very afraid. Oh, God, I said, get me out of here. I knew, however, that there had been three others. There were four drivers. Passini was dead. That left three. Some one took hold of me under the arms and somebody else lifted my legs.

43 **tried ... my shirt.** Cercai di strappare un pezzo dalla mia camicia.
44 **puttees.** Fasce.
45 **the weights on a doll's eyes.** I meccanismi degli occhi di una bambola.
46 **shin.** Tibia.

COMPREHENSION

2 READ lines 1–41 and complete the following table about the different attitudes to war expressed by the characters.

Characters	Effects of war	Attitude to war
Henry		
Passini		
Manera		
Gavuzzi		
Gordini		

3 NOTE down the setting in time and place, and the place reached by the soldiers in lines 42–51.

4 READ the text to the end and answer the questions.

1 What did Henry see and hear all of a sudden?
2 How did Henry feel?
3 What had happened to the other ambulance driver, Passini?
4 What did the Italian soldier beg Henry to do?
5 Why was there no need to help Passini?
6 Where had Henry been hurt?
7 What happened to Henry at the end?

ANALYSIS

5 DEFINE the role of the narrator. Is he inside or outside the story? Is he the protagonist, a witness or both?

6 FOCUS on the use of 'free direct speech', that is, where dialogue is isolated from the context, in the first section. State how this technique is achieved. What is the effect conveyed by such a technique?

7 CONCENTRATE on the last part, the climax of the extract.

1 Explain how the bombing attack is described.
2 How is the narrator able to increase the tension?

8 BEAR in mind that the whole extract takes place at night, in the dark. Yet, light breaks through the darkness four times in the second and in the third part, revealing something important.

1 Find the words connected to light, the nature of this light and what it reveals.
2 A simile is also used in lines 53–54. Find it and explain what feeling it conveys.

9 UNDERLINE all the words and phrases referring to the five senses employed to describe the explosion, which, at first, is experienced by Henry from the inside.

1 Which sense(s) predominate(s)?
2 Henry then turns his attention to the outside. What causes this shift in his attention? Which sentences uttered by Henry mark his different attitude to the external world?
3 What sort of character does he reveal?

YOUR TURN

10 DISCUSS. *A Farewell to Arms* is one of the most famous war novels ever written. Unlike many war stories, however, the novel does not glorify the experience of combat or offer us portraits of heroes as they are traditionally conceived. What is the novel's attitude towards war?

Ernest Hemingway in a Red Cross Ambulance in Italy, 1918.

7.3 **The Arts**

World War I in English painting

WARM-UP

1 **READ** the quote below, which the British artist Paul Nash wrote to his wife in 1917, and discuss in pairs how war affected his development as an artist.

'I am no longer an artist, interested and curious. I am a messenger who will bring back word from the men who are fighting to those who want the war to go on forever. Feeble, inarticulate, will be my message, but it will have a bitter truth, and may it burn their lousy souls.'

Then read about Paul Nash's life and work.

Paul Nash (1889–1946)

Paul Nash was born in London. In the spring of 1917 he was sent out to the front and, although he hated war and violence, he confessed himself happier in the fighting line than out of it. He did a series of paintings of trench life and no man's land, thus becoming the most individual and expressive of the artists who recorded the battlefields of the First World War. His complete integrity of vision, his individualism and his remarkable ability to evoke the spirit of his subject, set him somewhat apart from his contemporaries. Early in the 1930s, Nash started to paint extraordinary visionary landscapes dealing with the changing of seasons, and a series of equally visionary sunflower paintings on which he was still working at the time of his death.

The Menin Road

The Menin Road was portrayed as an area of devastated chaos by Paul Nash, with no road visible at all. Considered one of the 'hottest' spots of the Western Front in Belgium and France, and certainly in the Ypres Salient in Flanders, the Menin Road was the scene of two battles between the German and British forces.

2 **LOOK** at the painting and complete the following sentences.

1 The line of the road .... the canvas from .... to ....

2 The road surface has been .... and it is .... to distinguish it from the .... ground.

3 Here and there what was once an avenue is pocked with ....

4 It is marked by .... trees.

5 The sky is .... and ....

6 Some .... move towards an .... objective.

7 Stagnant .... lies in .... in the deep ruts of ....

8 Only two .... are alive.

1 Paul Nash, *The Menin Road*, 1919. Imperial War Museum, London.

7.3 World War I in English painting

3 **ANSWER these questions about *The Menin Road*.**

1. What shade of colour prevails in the painting? What mood does it convey?
2. What do the rigid simplification of nature and the deliberate elimination of everything non-essential communicate?
3. Nash wrote in a letter to his wife: *'I have seen the most frightful nightmare of a country more conceived by Dante or Poe than by nature, unspeakable, utterly indescribable.'* How are these words related to the painting? What vision of war emerges?

4 **DISCUSS the way man and the landscape are related in the painting.**

5 **LOOK at this photo of the Menin Road. Which of the two languages, the pictorial or the photographic, do you find more effective?**

1 Frank Hurley, *The Battle of the Menin Road, Chateau Wood, Ypres*, 1917–18. Mitchell Library, State Library of New South Wales.

Internet Lab

1 **SURF these sites to find material about the two paintings below.**
www.iwm.org.uk/collections/item/object/20070
www.tate.org.uk/art/artworks/nash-landscape-from-a-dream-n05667

2 **DESCRIBE them in detail. Do they have anything in common? What is the subject of these paintings? What symbols do they contain?**

2 Paul Nash, *We Are Making a New World*, 1918. Imperial War Museum, London.

3 Paul Nash, *Landscape from a Dream*, 1936–38. Tate Collection, London.

Modern poetry: tradition and experimentation

WARM-UP

1 LOOK at the picture and think about what you have learnt so far in this Specification. What types of changes do you think the war and other social changes might have caused in literature?

1 Percy Wyndham Lewis, *A Battery Shelled*, 1919. Imperial War Museum, London.

The first decades of the 20th century were a period of extraordinary originality and vitality in poetry. A variety of trends and currents gave shape to a changing world and contributed to expressing the nature of the modern experience.

The Georgian poets

The poetry of the years preceding the First World War was characterised by a sharp distinction between the avant-garde groups and those poets that were still influenced by the Victorian Romantic tradition. The latter are usually described as the Georgian poets, owing their name to an anthology, *Georgian Poetry*, published during the reign of George V. Among these were Rupert Brooke and Walter De La Mare (1873–1956), but also Edward Thomas (1878–1917). These poets employed the conventions of diction, looking to the Romantics and the Victorians for guidance. They felt sympathy for specifically English elements, such as the countryside as an idyllic place, and remained indifferent or hostile to the revolution in sensibility and technique started by the Symbolists, including W.B. Yeats, who was a leading figure in the Irish literary revival, and T.S. Eliot.

The War Poets

A whole generation of promising young poets, the so-called 'War Poets', wrote remarkable poetry whose value lies in the unconventional, anti-rhetorical way they dealt with the horrors of modern warfare, and in a certain measure of experimentalism which emerged in the choice of a violent, everyday language.

Imagism and the beginning of modern poetry

Modern poetry officially began with Imagism, a movement which flourished between 1912 and 1917. The name 'Imagiste' was invented by the American poet Ezra Pound (1885–1972). Imagists used hard, clear and precise images, and a rhythm which was freed from metrical regularity. They also felt free in the choice of any subject matter and their poems were usually short and contained no moral comment.

Symbolism and free verse

French Symbolism, a movement which had started in France with Charles Baudelaire's *Les Fleurs du Mal* (1857), also influenced the new poetry. The style of the Symbolist poets was characterised by:

- indirect rather than direct statements;
- the use of allusive language and development of the multiple association of words;
- the importance given to the 'sound' of words as conveying 'the music of ideas';
- the use of quotations from other literatures, revealing cosmopolitan interests;
- the use of free verse;
- the possibility for the reader to bring meaning to the poem.

It was T.S. Eliot who expounded the new poetic theory and practice. In his essay *Tradition and the Individual Talent* (1917), he stated that 'Poetry is not a turning loose of emotion but an escape from emotion; it is not the expression of personality but an escape from personality', thus reversing what had been Wordsworth's definition of poetry as 'emotion recollected in tranquillity'. The poet became the explorer of experience who used language to create rich patterns of meaning that were not made easy for the superficial reader, but required close analysis before they could be understood. T.S. Eliot's poem *The Waste Land* recorded the collapse of Western civilisation and the culture and spiritual waste that characterised the beginning of the century.

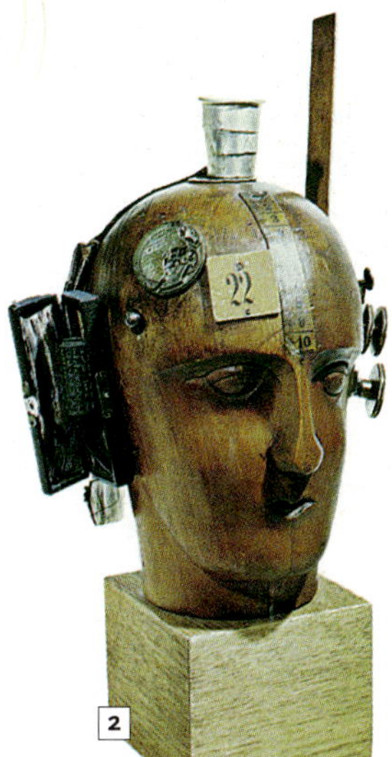

2 Raoul Hausmann, *Mechanical Head (The Spirit of Our Age)*, ca 1920. Musée National d'Art Moderne, Centre Pompidou, Paris.

2 FILL IN the table about modern poetry.

	Georgian poets	War Poets	Imagists	Symbolists
Themes				
Style				
Aim				

7.5 Literature

The War Poets

WARM-UP

1 **LOOK** at the two propaganda posters about World War I and discuss the view of the war they reflect.

1

2

2 **READ** about the War Poets and answer the questions.

1. Why did many young men volunteer for military service when WWI broke out?
2. What did the War Poets manage to do?
3. How can their poetry be considered? Why?

Different attitudes to war

When the First World War broke out, thousands of young men volunteered for military service; most of them regarded the conflict as an adventure undertaken for noble ends. It was not until the slaughter of thousands of British soldiers at the Battle of the Somme in 1916, that this sense of pride and exhilaration was replaced by doubt and disillusionment. The loss of human lives on the so-called 'Western Front', the line of trenches running from northwestern France to Switzerland, was terrible. For the soldiers, life in the trenches was hell because of the rain and mud, the decaying bodies that rats fed on, the repeated bombings and the use of poison gas in warfare. Almost from the beginning, the common soldiers improvised verses which, precisely because they were the rough, genuine, obscene songs of the trenches, did not reach the ears of the literate people living comfortably at home. However, there was a group of poets who actually experienced the fighting, and in most cases lost their lives in the conflict, that managed to represent modern warfare in a realistic and unconventional way, and to awaken the conscience of the readers to the horrors of the war. These poets are known as the War Poets. Theirs can be considered a definite move away from the 19th-century poetic conventions, which could not convey the harsh new reality that faced them and forced them to find another mode of expression.

Rupert Brooke (1887–1915)

Rupert Brooke was born in 1887 into a wealthy family; he was educated at Rugby School and then went to King's College, Cambridge. He was a good student and athlete, and became popular especially for his handsome looks. He was also familiar with literary circles and came to know many important political, literary and social figures before the war. Brooke actually saw little combat during the war since he contracted blood poisoning and died in April 1915, in the Aegean Sea. He was buried on the Greek island of Skyros. Brooke's reputation as a War Poet rests on his five war sonnets of 1914, in which he advanced the idea that war is clean and cleansing. He tried to testify to the safeness of war, in which the only thing that can suffer is the body, and even death is seen as a reward. Traditional not only in form, his poems show a sentimental attitude which was completely lost in the brutal turn that war poetry took in the works of the other War Poets, who lived to witness the horrors of trench warfare. The publication of Brooke's war sonnets coincided with his death and made him immensely popular, turning him into a new symbol of the 'young romantic hero' who inspired patriotism in the early months of the Great War, when England needed a focal point for its sacrifice, ideals and aspirations.

Wilfred Owen (1893–1918)

Born in 1893, Wilfred Owen was working as a teacher of English in France when he visited a hospital for the wounded and decided, in 1915, to return to England and enlist. The year 1917 was an important one: he was sent to France and saw his first action; in March he was injured and sent to Craiglockhart War Hospital in Edinburgh to recover from shell shock. It was there that he met Siegfried Sassoon, who was also a patient and already had a reputation as a poet. He read Owen's poems, encouraged him to continue to write and introduced him to other literary figures. Owen returned to the front in August 1918. On 4th November, just seven days before the Armistice, he was killed in a German machine gun attack.

His poems are painful in their accurate accounts of gas casualties, men who have gone mad and men who are clinically alive although their bodies have been destroyed. He used assonance and alliteration extensively. These devices gave his lines a haunting quality, a gravity and moral force which made them suitable for any situation in which people must suffer and die. In June 1918, Owen was preparing *Disabled and Other Poems* for publication. At that time, he was writing the preface to the book, words which have now become essential in discussing his work and much of the poetry about World War I: 'This book is not about heroes. English poetry is not yet fit to speak of them. Nor is it about deeds, or land, nor anything about glory, honour, might, majesty, dominion, or power, except War. Above all I am not concerned with Poetry. My subject is War, and the pity of War. The Poetry is in the pity. Yet these elegies are to this generation in no sense consolatory. They may be to the next. All a poet can do today is warn. That is why the true Poets must be truthful.'

TEXT BANK 47: *SIEGFRIED SASSOON*
TEXT BANK 48: *ISAAC ROSENBERG*

The Soldier

Rupert Brooke

1914 and Other Poems (1915)

This poem is noted for its lyricism which, together with his handsome appearance and premature death, made Brooke a favourite poet among the young people of his generation.

6.4

If I should die, think only this of me:
That there's some corner of a foreign field
That is for ever England. There shall be
In that rich earth a richer dust[1] concealed[2];
A dust whom England bore[3], shaped, made aware,
Gave, once, her flowers to love, her ways to roam[4],
A body of England's, breathing[5] English air,
Washed by the rivers, blest[6] by suns of home.

And think, this heart, all evil shed away[7],
A pulse[8] in the eternal mind[9], no less
Gives somewhere back the thoughts by England given;
Her sights and sounds; dreams happy as her day;
And laughter, learnt of[10] friends; and gentleness,
In hearts at peace, under an English heaven[11].

1 **dust.** Polvere.
2 **concealed.** Nascosta.
3 **bore.** Generò.
4 **to roam.** Da esplorare, da percorrere.
5 **breathing.** Che respira.
6 **blest.** Benedetto.
7 **shed away.** Liberatosi da.
8 **pulse.** Battito.
9 **mind.** Spirito.
10 **learnt of.** *Learnt from.*
11 **heaven.** Cielo.

WARM-UP

1 **FOCUS** on the title of Rupert Brooke's poem. What traits do you think a good soldier should possess?

COMPREHENSION

2 **READ** the poem and say:
1 who is speaking;
2 if he is afraid of death;
3 where his grave will be;
4 how his dead body will enrich the soil;
5 whether there is any emphasis on war;
6 who you think the poet is speaking to.

ANALYSIS

3 **WORK OUT** the rhyme scheme and say what kind of poem this is.

4 **FIND** the images referring to death. What idea do they suggest?

5 **LIST** the images connected with England under the following headings:
- Landscape
- Inner growth and private feelings

6 **HIGHLIGHT** the view of England conveyed. What traditional qualities does the poet underline?

7 **DEFINE** the tone of the poem and summarise its theme.

3

1 Propaganda poster by Savile Lumley, ca 1915. The Imperial War Museum, London.

2 Propaganda poster, ca 1916.

3 Troops moving up to the Front. Imperial War Museum, London.

Exam Description

What is there in the *Terza Prova* in a foreign language?	The *Terza Prova* is written by the individual commission. The most common types of questions are: • Type A, a short essay of about 200–300 words; • Type B, two or three specific questions to answer in about 10–12 lines each; • Type C, ten multiple-choice questions.
What do I have to focus on?	The emphasis in Types A and B is on producing a concise and coherent written text.
How much time am I allowed?	Three hours for the total test, which includes four to five subjects. The time devoted to the foreign language questions is about forty minutes.

ESAME DI STATO **Terza Prova**

8 **TYPE B.** Read the speech by Winston Churchill that appeared in 'The Times' on 26th April 1915 to commemorate Brooke's death. Write ten to twelve lines explaining whether it is consistent with the poem 'The Soldier' and why.

'The thoughts to which he gave expression in the very few incomparable war sonnets which he has left behind will be shared by many thousands of young men moving resolutely and blithely forward into this, the hardest, cruellest, and the least-rewarded of all the wars that men have fought. They are a whole history and revelation of Rupert Brooke himself. Joyous, fearless, versatile, deeply instructed, with classic symmetry of mind and body, he was all that one would wish England's noblest sons to be in days when no sacrifice but the most precious is acceptable, and the most precious is that which is most freely proffered.'

Dulce et Decorum Est

Wilfred Owen

The Poems of Wilfred Owen (1920)

The following poem is based on the poet's experience of the horrors of war in the trenches, and it is an attempt to communicate the 'pity' of war to future generations. The Latin title means 'it is sweet and honourable'; it is a quotation from the Latin poet Horace (1st century BC), who borrowed the line from the Greek poet Tyrtaeus (7th century BC).

6.5

Bent double, like old beggars[1] under sacks,
Knock-kneed, coughing like hags[2], we cursed through sludge[3],
Till on the haunting flares[4] we turned our backs
And towards our distant rest began to trudge[5].
Men marched asleep. Many had lost their boots
But limped on, blood-shod[6]. All went lame[7]; all blind;
Drunk with fatigue; deaf even to the hoots[8]
Of tired, outstripped Five-Nines[9] that dropped behind.

1 C.R.W. Nevinson, *Returning to the Trenches*, 1914–15. National Gallery of Canada, Ottawa.

WARM-UP

1 **COMPARE** the impact of images of war, which are very frequent on television and in films, with that of words. Which means is most effective, the visual or the verbal? Can you provide an example?

COMPREHENSION

2 **READ** Wilfred Owen's poem and briefly summarise the content of each stanza in your own words.

ANALYSIS

3 **CIRCLE** the personal pronouns in the poem. Then write them down and say to whom they refer. Who do you think the poet is addressing?

4 **FIND** examples of alliteration, repetition of sounds and onomatopoeia.

5 **FOCUS** on the first two stanzas and make a chart with words and phrases referring to physical and psychological suffering.

1 **beggars.** Mendicanti.
2 **Knock-kneed ... hags.** Con le ginocchia che si toccano, tossendo come streghe.
3 **sludge.** Fango.
4 **haunting flares.** Bagliori spaventosi.
5 **trudge.** Trascinarci.
6 **limped on, blood-shod.** Avanzavano zoppicando, calzati di sangue.
7 **lame.** Storpi.
8 **hoots.** Sibili.
9 **outstripped Five-Nines.** Granate (contenenti gas) lasciate indietro.

2 John Singer Sargent, *Gassed*, 1918. Imperial War Museum, London.

Gas! GAS! Quick, boys! – An ecstasy of fumbling[10],
Fitting the clumsy helmets[11] just in time;
But someone still was yelling out and stumbling,
And flound'ring[12] like a man in fire or lime[13]...
Dim, through the misty panes[14] and thick green light,
As under a green sea, I saw him drowning[15].
In all my dreams, before my helpless sight,
He plunges[16] at me, guttering, choking[17], drowning.

If in some smothering[18] dreams you too could pace
Behind the wagon that we flung[19] him in,
And watch the white eyes writhing[20] in his face,
His hanging face, like a devil's sick of sin;
If you could hear, at every jolt[21], the blood
Come gargling from the froth-corrupted lungs[22],
Obscene as cancer, bitter as the cud[23]
Of vile, incurable sores[24] on innocent tongues, –
My friend, you would not tell with such high zest[25]
To children ardent for some desperate glory,
The old Lie: *Dulce et decorum est*
Pro patria mori.

10 **An ecstasy of fumbling.** Un brancolare frenetico.
11 **Fitting the clumsy helmets.** Mettendosi i goffi elmetti.
12 **was yelling out ... flound'ring.** Gridava e inciampava e si dimenava.
13 **lime.** Calce.
14 **misty panes.** Vetri (delle maschere antigas) appannati.
15 **drowning.** Affogare.
16 **plunges.** Si precipita.
17 **guttering, choking.** Barcollando (come la luce di una candela che sta per spegnersi), soffocando.
18 **smothering.** Affannosi.
19 **we flung.** Gettammo.
20 **writhing.** Contorcersi.
21 **jolt.** Sobbalzo.
22 **froth-corrupted lungs.** Polmoni intaccati dal gas.
23 **bitter as the cud.** Amaro come il bolo (di ruminanti).
24 **sores.** Piaghe.
25 **zest.** Entusiasmo.

6 **NOTE DOWN the verbs of movement in the first two stanzas and point out their connotation.**

7 **FIND the similes and metaphors used by the poet at the end of the second stanza to introduce the passage from the real world of the battlefield to an unreal, nightmarish, hallucinatory world. What semantic areas do they belong to?** What is the poet's aim in using them?

8 **EXPLAIN why the final words of the poem are called 'the old Lie' (line 27).** What technique is used by Owen?

9 **SUMMARISE the theme and the message of the poem in your own words.**

10 **COMPARE Owen's poem with Brooke's 'The Soldier'. Analyse the soldier's mood, his attitude to war, the imagery employed and the poet's message.**

ESAME DI STATO Terza Prova

11 **TYPE B. In October 1918 Owen wrote: 'I came out in order to help these boys – directly by leading them as well as an officer can; indirectly, by watching their sufferings that I may speak of them as well as a pleader can. I have done the first.' Write ten to twelve lines explaining whether you find his words relevant to the poem as a whole.**

Exam Reference pag. 355

7.6 **History**

The Easter Rising and the Irish War of Independence

WARM-UP

1 **DISCUSS** what you know about the differences between Northern Ireland and the Republic of Ireland (Eire).

A major issue of British politics in the first two decades of the 20th century was the 'Irish Question'. The term refers to the tragic events regarding the fight for Irish independence. During World War I, the Irish Volunteers (militant Irish nationalists) organised a rebellion on Easter Monday 1916, which inspired Yeats's poem 'Easter 1916', and proclaimed an Irish republic. The uprising was planned to take advantage of Britain's weakness owing to the war, in the expectation that a British defeat in the Great War would bring Irish independence. In this, the Republicans were given military and logistical assistance by the German High Command. About 700 Republicans began the rebellion by seizing strategic points in Dublin, among which foremost was the main Post Office. They held on amidst heavy gunfire for several days, before being defeated. Some died on the spot, others were executed later. They became legendary symbols of Irish heroism in the face of oppression. In the 1918 election, the Sinn Féin party (an Irish name meaning: 'ourselves alone') won nearly all the seats except in the province of Ulster, but instead of going to Westminster, they set up an Irish Parliament in Dublin, the Dáil, and once more proclaimed an Irish Republic. In 1919 the Irish Volunteers became the IRA (Irish Republican Army) and prepared for civil war, which began during Easter, 1920. The war was only ended with the establishment of the Irish Free State (1921), under the leadership of Éamon de Valera (1882–1975) as a dominion of the Empire, while the six predominantly Protestant counties of Ulster remained part of the United Kingdom with their own parliament in Belfast. This partition of the country led to future violence as the tragic events of the 1970s and 1980s, known as 'The Troubles', were to confirm. It was in 1948 that the official Republic of Ireland Act put an end to Commonwealth membership.

2 **READ** about the Irish Question and write notes about:

1 the 1916 rebellion;
2 the developments which took place in Ireland during and after the 1918 election;
3 the settlement of the Irish Question.

1903	King Edward visited Ireland.
1905	Sinn Féin ('Ourselves Alone') was formed by Arthur Griffith. It encouraged the setting up of an Irish parliament.
1908	Patrick Pearse, a poet and teacher, founded St Enda's school to teach the Irish-Ireland spirit. Many of its pupils were to join the Irish Republican Brotherhood.
1912	The third Home Rule Bill passed through the House of Commons.
1913	The Irish Volunteers were founded.
1914	The Home Rule Bill was finally passed by the House of Lords but it was carried out at the end of the war.
1916	The military council planned the Easter Rising. The General Post Office was chosen as the Rising's headquarters and Patrick Pearse proclaimed the Republic. Casualties included 318 civilians, 60 rebels and 130 British troops. The rebellion lasted nearly a week. In May the Rising leaders were executed.
1917	Éamon de Valera became the leader of the new Sinn Féin.
1918	Sinn Féin swept nationalist Ireland in the general election.
1919	An Irish parliament, the Dáil, was established by Sinn Féin. The War of Independence began.
1920	Ireland was partitioned and Northern Ireland was established.
1921	The Anglo-Irish Treaty established the Irish Free State.
1922	The Irish Civil War broke out over the terms of the Anglo-Irish Treaty.
1923	The Free State forces were victorious in the Irish Civil War.
1949	The Free State became the Republic of Ireland.

Postcard with propaganda by Ulster Unionists, ca 1912.

Soldiers in a Dublin street during the Easter Rising, 1916.

Dublin, 1922. IRA members patrolling Grafton Street.

William Butler Yeats and Irish nationalism

W.B. Yeats's life

Born in Dublin in 1865, into a professional middle-class family, William Butler Yeats (1865–1939) inherited the dilemma of the Anglo-Irish Protestant minority to which his parents belonged, feeling as much Irish as British, and remaining largely detached from the Catholic, originally Gaelic-speaking native population. His father, John Butler Yeats, was an artist and a free thinker with an irreligious and at times anti-clerical attitude. He influenced his son in his love for art, particularly painting. When still a student, Yeats was attracted to mystical doctrines and magic, which account for much of his most effective imagery.

A lifelong love and *The Celtic Twilight*

In 1889 Yeats met Maud Gonne, the beautiful actress and fervent patriot with whom he fell in love and who was to dominate his life and poetry for the next half century. She led him deeper into the politics of the Irish Republican Brotherhood, and later disillusioned him by marrying the nationalist John McBride. In the 1890s he met Lady Gregory, an Irish nationalist, dramatist and folklorist, who took him from cottage to cottage to collect Irish folklore and also supported his project regarding the Abbey Theatre: Yeats wanted a literary theatre and fought against the powers of the commercial theatre, the press and the Church to found it. At that time much of native Irish literature was in danger of being lost as the result of England's attempts to anglicise Ireland through a ban on the Gaelic language. So Yeats believed that the role of the artist was to create a new culture, based on Ireland's past, in which all the Irish people alike could share. This hope for an Irish cultural renaissance found expression in a series of essays called *The Celtic Twilight* (1893).

Little by little, his disenchantment with the nationalist movement increased, since he saw it dominated by the values of the Catholic middle classes. However, the cruel treatment by British authorities of the Easter Rising in 1916 brought about a change in his political attitude. He gradually placed his sympathies with the 'moderate' members of the government, and early in 1922 he became a senator in the upper house of the Dáil, something which brought him death threats from the IRA. As a senator, he was concerned with educational policy, in charge of the committee responsible for Ireland's new currency, and spoke out on behalf of the Protestant minority in the divorce debate in the Dáil in 1925.

International recognition

Yeats's greatness as a poet received international recognition with the awarding of the Nobel Prize for Literature in 1923. He died in France in January 1939; he was buried there because of World War II, but in 1948 his body was brought back to Ireland and buried in Drumcliffe Churchyard, County Sligo, exactly in accordance with the instructions in his poem called 'Under Ben Bulben'.

A wide range of themes

Yeats's themes range from his faith in the beauty and eternity of art to the relationship between the poet and the Irish people and tradition. The theme of death is important; unlike the animal, which simply dies, man dies many times before his death. Every defeat, such as an unhappy experience of love, but also every victory, are a series of deaths and rebirths prefiguring the end of life. The idea of the heroic individual also held Yeats's imagination. Loneliness is a feature of his heroes because their superior qualities distinguish them from the common man. Such heroes, by their deeds and deaths, enter a mythical world.

1 A satirical cartoon showing Yeats addressing the audience from the stage of the Abbey Theatre.

Yeats and nationalism

The Yeats' blood had been Anglo-Irish for centuries; the family belonged to that Protestant Irish society owing its position to William of Orange's victory. However, as a poet, Yeats was aware of the ideologies that were troubling Ireland. He experienced 'self-division' because as a Yeats he might have been expected to support the Unionists, but as an Irish poet he aligned himself with the Irish nationalists. He was struggling to create a view of Ireland as 'an independent cultural identity, a state of mind founded on native myths, customs and beliefs that preceded William of Orange and even St Patrick himself'.

As time went by, however, Yeats grew disenchanted with the 'advanced nationalism' that would either resort to armed rebellion or identify Catholic values with the Irish nationality; so he distanced himself from the Celticist atmosphere he had himself tried to create in his younger days.

1 **REVISE your knowledge about the work of W.B. Yeats and explain in your own words:**

1 the link between the poet and Ireland;
2 the variety of his themes;
3 the conflict that Yeats experienced as a poet.

WARM-UP

1 **DISCUSS** whether the people who fight against the oppressor even at the cost of their own life should be regarded as heroes. Would you be ready to do the same for the freedom of your own country?

Easter 1916

William Butler Yeats

Michael Robartes and the Dancer (1921)

The poem was written by Yeats after the Easter Rising in Dublin on 24th April 1916. The Irish leaders celebrated in the poem were: Constance Markievicz, an officer in the Volunteers of the Irish Republican Brotherhood (she was not executed but imprisoned in Holloway Prison in London); Patrick Pearse, a school teacher and poet; Thomas MacDonagh, another intellectual, a dramatist and poet; John MacBride, the husband of Maud Gonne; James Connolly, the leader of the Irish labour movement.

6.6

I have met them at close of day
Coming with vivid faces
From counter[1] or desk among grey
Eighteenth-century houses.
I have passed with a nod[2] of the head
Or polite meaningless words,
Or have lingered awhile[3] and said
Polite meaningless words,
And thought before I had done[4]
Of a mocking tale or a gibe[5]
To please a companion
Around the fire at the club,
Being certain that they and I
But[6] lived where motley is worn[7]:
All changed, changed utterly[8]:
A terrible beauty is born.
That woman's days were spent
In ignorant good-will,
Her nights in argument[9]
Until her voice grew shrill[10].
What voice more sweet than hers
When, young and beautiful,
She rode to harriers[11]?
This man had kept a school
And rode our wingèd[12] horse;
This other his helper and friend
Was coming into his force;
He might have won fame in the end,
So sensitive his nature seemed,
So daring[13] and sweet his thought.
This other man I had dreamed
A drunken, vainglorious lout[14].
He had done most bitter wrong[15]

1 Youth from the Mairead Farrell Sinn Féin Youth Group, with photographs of the signatories of the Irish Proclamation, march during a commemoration of the Easter Rising.

1 **counter.** Bancone.
2 **nod.** Cenno.
3 **have lingered awhile.** Mi sono soffermato per un po'.
4 **before I had done.** *Lett.*: prima di finire; *qui*: prima di andarmene.
5 **a mocking tale or a gibe.** Un racconto beffardo o una battuta di scherno.
6 **But.** Solamente.
7 **motley is worn.** Si indossa la veste dei buffoni.
8 **utterly.** Completamente.
9 **argument.** Discussione.
10 **shrill.** Stridula.
11 **harriers.** Cani per la caccia alla lepre.
12 **wingèd.** Alato (riferimento a Pegaso, il cavallo alato nato dal sangue di Medusa dopo la sua morte).
13 **daring.** Audace.
14 **drunken, vainglorious lout.** Zoticone alcolizzato e vanaglorioso.
15 **most bitter wrong.** Il torto più doloroso.

To some who are near my heart,
Yet I number him in the song;
He, too, has resigned[16] his part
In the casual comedy;
He, too, has been changed in his turn[17],
Transformed utterly:
A terrible beauty is born.

Hearts with one purpose alone
Through summer and winter seem
Enchanted[18] to a stone
To trouble the living stream[19].
The horse that comes from the road,
The rider, the birds that range[20]
From cloud to tumbling[21] cloud,
Minute by minute they change;
A shadow of cloud on the stream
Changes minute by minute;
A horse-hoof slides on the brim[22],
And a horse plashes[23] within it;
The long-legged moor-hens dive[24],
And hens to moor-cocks[25] call;
Minute by minute they live:
The stone's in the midst of all.

Too long a sacrifice
Can make a stone of the heart.
O when may it suffice[26]?
That is Heaven's part, our part
To murmur name upon name,
As a mother names her child
When sleep at last has come
On limbs that had run wild[27].
What is it but nightfall?
No; no, not night but death;
Was it needless[28] death after all?
For England may keep faith[29]
For all that is done and said.
We know their dream; enough
To know they dreamed and are dead;
And what if excess of love
Bewildered them[30] till they died?
I write it out in a verse –
MacDonagh and MacBride
And Connolly and Pearse
Now and in time to be,
Wherever green is worn[31],
Are changed, changed utterly:
A terrible beauty is born.

16 **has resigned.** Ha rinunciato.
17 **in his turn.** A sua volta.
18 **Enchanted.** Incantati, ammaliati.
19 **stream.** Flusso, corrente.
20 **range.** Si muovono liberamente, vagano.
21 **tumbling.** Che si agita.
22 **A horse-hoof ... brim.** Lo zoccolo di un cavallo scivola sulla sponda.
23 **plashes.** Sguazza.
24 **moor-hens dive.** Le gallinelle d'acqua si tuffano.
25 **moor-cocks.** Galli di brughiera.
26 **suffice.** Bastare.
27 **On limbs ... wild.** Su membra che hanno corso all'impazzata.
28 **needless.** Inutile.
29 **faith.** La parola.
30 **Bewildered them.** Li ha disorientati.
31 **Wherever green is worn.** Ovunque il verde sia indossato (il verde è il colore nazionale dell'Irlanda).

COMPREHENSION

2 **READ the first stanza (lines 1–16) and point out:**
1 when the poet used to meet the insurgents;
2 what you are told about their jobs;
3 whether the poet knew them intimately.

3 **READ the second stanza (lines 17–40) and collect information about the insurgents as regards their identity and activities.**

4 **READ the third stanza (lines 41–56) and answer these questions.**
1 What characterises the 'hearts' in line 41?
2 What does 'the living stream' (line 44) stand for? And 'the stone' (lines 43, 56)?

5 **READ the poem to the end.**
1 What does the poet wonder about?
2 Though identifying himself with the nationalist cause, the poet speculates that even now England may grant the Home Rule promised in an act of Parliament in 1914 but deferred by the outbreak of the war. In what lines does this happen? Summarise in your own words the question they point to.

ANALYSIS

6 **LIST the words that characterised the world and life of Dublin before the Rising.** What connotation emerges?

7 **UNDERLINE an example of an oxymoron in the poem.** Explain how the adjective contradicts the noun. What is the function of this line in the text?

8 **STATE the act the poet is performing in line 74. What are the possible effects of such a line?** What is Yeats's attitude towards the idea of revolution?

ESAME DI STATO Terza Prova

9 **TYPE A. Though referring to a specific historical fact, Yeats's poem reflects upon the paradoxes linked to politics, nationalism, fanaticism and heroism. State your opinion on this topic, justifying it with references to recent events you have read about in the newspapers or watched on TV (approximately 200 words).**

Exam Reference pag. 355

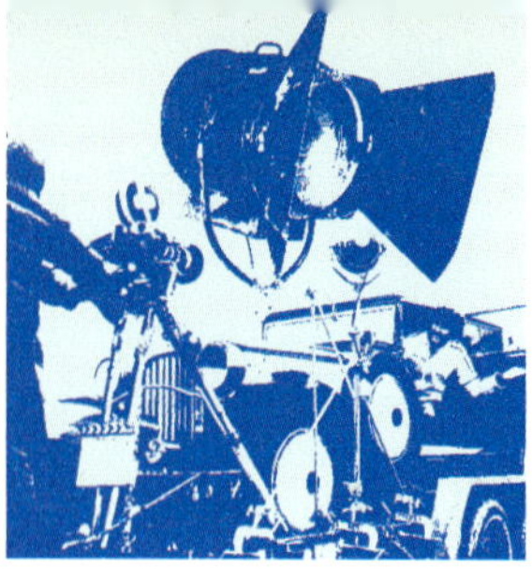

7.8 Two Films About...
The Irish War of Independence

WARM-UP

1 **DISCUSS.** Given what you have studied about the Irish War of Independence, what themes do you think a film about this period might explore?

Michael Collins

Directed by Neil Jordan;
USA 1996.
With Liam Neeson (Michael Collins); Aidan Quinn (Harry Boland); Julia Roberts (Kitty Kiernan).

A powerful film that mixes romance and violence, hope and tragedy and tells the story of the controversial life of Michael Collins, the Irish patriot who inspired a nation to change the course of history. The film takes the audience from the Easter Rising through the terrible years of the Squad, a group of specially trained gunmen, and the elimination of the British intelligence, up to the foundation of the Irish Free State and the conflict with other leaders, such as Éamon de Valera. An important part of the film is dedicated to the relationship between Michael Collins and his best friend, Harry Boland. For four years they are also caught up in a sort of love triangle, as both men love Kitty Kiernan. It takes a while until she confesses that she loves Collins. Her confession is not the only thing that drives the men apart. They are not on the same political page anymore. Best friends become enemies. Michael Collins is shot in 1922 by one of de Valera's men. This is the beginning of the Irish Civil War.

What about accuracy?

The choice to use American actors in Irish roles was considered controversial. The film is shocking in its depiction of the brutality of both the English and the Irish. However, Jordan dissociates his hero from any actual ugliness. He may have been the architect, but Collins is never shown with blood on his hands.

The Wind That Shakes the Barley

Directed by Ken Loach;
UK 2006.
With Cillian Murphy (Damien O'Donovan); Pádraic Delaney (Teddy O'Donovan); Liam Cunningham (Dan).

The film, whose title comes from an old Irish ballad, depicts one stage in the birth of the modern Irish state, including the island's partition by the Anglo-Irish Treaty of 1921, through the lives of two fictional brothers, Damien and Teddy O'Donovan. At the beginning of the war, Damien is about to leave his native Ireland for London, where a position as a doctor at a hospital is waiting for him. Being aware of the brutality and the cruelty his people have to face, and knowing that his brother will be leading a guerrilla group, he decides to stay and join the rebels. At that time the British government has sent the so-called 'Black and Tans' to brutally reinforce their power. The two brothers fight side by side until a truce is reached. But peace doesn't last long, and when one faction of the freedom fighters accepts a treaty with the British that is regarded as unfair by the other faction, a civil war starts, putting Irishmen against Irishmen, brothers against brothers, Teddy against Damien.

What about accuracy?

The director portrays Ireland as a country not only feeling miserable because of military dictatorship, but impoverished by centuries of exploitation. The impression created by this film is that of aversion to the British state, which was not the case; in fact Black and Tan rule was the general state of things in Ireland before independence, fully authorised and sanctioned by the authorities. The film also lacks a detailed analysis of the characters: Damien's companions in the struggle are not distinct; each time one of them is killed, it is difficult for the audience to understand who it was.

TEXT BANK 50: *THE HOLLOW MEN*

Thomas Stearns Eliot and the alienation of modern man

T.S. Eliot's life

Thomas Stearns Eliot (1888–1965) was born in St Louis, Missouri, in 1888. He studied at Harvard, the Sorbonne in Paris, and Oxford, thus giving a cosmopolitan bent to his education. At the outbreak of World War I, he settled in London, where he started to work first as a clerk at Lloyds Bank, then as a director for the publishers Faber & Faber. His first important work was the collection of poems *Prufrock and Other Observations* (1917), which established him as an important avant-garde poet.

Unhappily married, he suffered from a nervous breakdown soon after the war. He wrote most of his masterpiece, *The Waste Land*, while recovering in a sanatorium in Lausanne, Switzerland, at the age of 33. Poetry was, in fact, his only refuge, where he transcended his personal situation in order to represent the general crisis of Western culture. This long poem was published in 1922 after the American poet Ezra Pound had contributed to reduce it to its final form, and Eliot later dedicated it to Pound himself with *'il miglior fabbro – the better craftsman'*, a quotation from Dante's *Purgatory*. In 1925 he published *The Hollow Men*, a poem read as a sequel to *The Waste Land*'s philosophical despair, even if the seeds of his future faith could be found. In 1927 he became a British citizen and in the same year he joined the Church of England, finding the answer to his own uncertainties and to the despair of the modern world's lack of faith and religion.

Eliot was also an influential literary critic: his critical essays on authors, both ancient and modern, as well as on the theory of poetry and on the foundations of literary criticism are both numerous and of primary importance. Most of them are collected in such well-known books as *The Sacred Wood* (1920) and *Selected Essays* (1932). In these essays, he concentrated on specific problems of style and technique; he shared with the modern novelist James Joyce, the view about the importance for the artist to be impersonal and to separate 'the man who suffers' from 'the mind which creates'. In his essay 'Tradition and the Individual Talent' from *The Sacred Wood*, Eliot declared: 'the poet has, not a personality to express, but a particular medium, which is only a medium and not a personality [...] The emotion of art is impersonal.' Thus the characters of his first works are archetypes of 20th-century human beings who turn their own subjective experience into a universal form with which anyone can identify.

In 1948 he was awarded the Nobel Prize for Literature. He died in London in 1965.

1 **WHILE READING T.S. Eliot's biography, fill in the table below. Then use the information you have gathered to organise your knowledge about the author's life.**

His education	
His most important works and what characters he created	
Why he converted to Anglicanism	
How this religious experience is reflected in his works	
What role of the artist he presented in his critical essays	

1 T.S. Eliot in a portrait by Cecil Beaton, 1956. National Portrait Gallery, London.

2 **ANALYSE the picture by the American painter Kitaj. What does it share with the title of T.S. Eliot's poem *The Waste Land*?**

2 R.B. Kitaj, *If Not, Not*, 1975–76. Scottish National Gallery of Modern Art, Edinburgh.

ART LAB 12: *PICASSO AND CUBISM*

The Waste Land (1922)

The structure

The Waste Land consists of 434 lines divided into the following five sections:

I. 'The Burial of the Dead', which centres on the basic opposition between sterility and fertility, life and death.

II. 'A Game of Chess', which juxtaposes the present squalor to a past ambiguous splendour.

III. 'The Fire Sermon', where the theme of present alienation is rendered through the description of a loveless, mechanical, squalid sexual encounter.

IV. 'Death by Water', which reinforces the idea of a spiritual shipwreck.

V. 'What the Thunder Said', which evokes religions from East and West. A possible solution is found in a sort of sympathy with other human beings; however, such a solution does not modify the general atmosphere of utter desolation.

Fragmentation

The poet uses fragmented images of historical narratives such as the quest for the Holy Grail, the Bible, Dante and Shakespeare to mirror his society's reliance on old traditions, customs and aesthetic styles when creating the new Europe. Eliot's fragmentation and reassembly of historical narratives create a poem with new meaning out of something old.

All the fragmentary parts of the poem are connected by one main theme: the contrast between the fertility of a mythical past and the spiritual sterility of the present world, peopled by alienated characters. This poem reflects the breakdown of a historical, social and cultural order, destroyed by the war and by those forces operating under the name of modernity.

Allusion and a new concept of history

The mythical past appears in the allusions to and quotations from many literary works belonging to different traditions and cultures, and religious works, like the Bible and Hindu sacred texts. This use of quotations reflects the concept Eliot had of tradition and history, which he saw as the repetition of the same events, of 'classicism', which he saw as the ability to see the past as a concrete premise for the present, and 'the poetic culture' as a 'living unity' of all the poems written in different periods. Thus the present and past exist simultaneously in *The Waste Land* – just as they do in the mind – and the continuous shifts in time and space are caused by the free associations of ideas and thoughts, as in *Ulysses* by James Joyce.

The mythical method

In his evaluation of Western culture, Eliot went back to its origins, when legends and myths were symptoms of spiritual attitudes which he regarded as extremely important. In modern society, however, old myths are present, but they have lost their deep meaning and it is especially through the mythical allusions that the contrast between the present and past appears. Eliot contrasts the meaninglessness of life with allusions to the Arthurian legend and the quest for the Holy Grail, a metaphor for man's search for spiritual salvation. He makes references to the May festivities celebrating the rebirth of nature, and the Celtic myth, linked to the paradigm of fertility, of the Fisher King, who is awaiting a hero to break the curse of impotence put upon his kingdom.

In the essay 'Ulysses, Order and Myth' (1923) Eliot explained the mythical method which Joyce also employed in *Ulysses*: 'It is simply a way of controlling, of ordering, of giving a shape and a significance to the immense panorama of futility and anarchy which is contemporary history'.

Eliot's innovative style

The style of *The Waste Land* is fragmentary because of the mixture of different poetic styles, such as blank verse, the ode, the quatrain and free verse, thus reproducing the chaos of modern civilisation. The most effective analogies can be found in some Cubist images or in some seemingly unconnected cinematic shots used to express a certain emotional state: the meaning is not in the single fragment but in the whole.

Eliot requires the active participation of the reader/public, who experiences the same world as that of the speaker/poet, by employing the technique of implication. Metaphors and symbols replace direct statements; to this purpose, Eliot adopted the technique of the 'objective correlative', that is, the attempt at communicating philosophical reflections and feelings by means of a simile, a description or a monologue by a character in order to provide a vision of the world or a feeling of the lyrical 'I'. For example, in the text 'The Fire Sermon' the objective correlative of the squalid, passionless present age is the banal and loveless scene of the seduction of a typist by her lover.

From the French Symbolist poet Jules Laforgue (1860–87), Eliot derived the technique of juxtaposition: squalid elements are juxtaposed with poetic ones, trivial elements with sublime ones. Another device widely used by Eliot is the repetition of words, images and phrases from page to page; they all give the impression of the increasing musicality of the poem.

3 **REVISE your knowledge about T.S. Eliot's *The Waste Land* and explain:**

1 how many sections there are in the poem;
2 what the main theme of the whole poem is;
3 what concept of history is developed and how reality is presented;
4 what the mythical method employed by Eliot in this poem is;
5 what innovative techniques characterise the style of this poem.

WARM-UP

1 **READ** these lines. Do you recognise them? Are they consistent with this picture? What do both the picture and these lines celebrate?

When in April the sweet showers fall
And pierce the drought of March to the root, and all
The veins are bathed in liquor of such power
As brings about the engendering of the flower

COMPREHENSION

2 **READ** the first part of 'The Burial of the Dead' and use the lines to write headings for these images.

1 ....

2 ....

3 ....

4 ....

The Burial of the Dead

T.S. Eliot

The Waste Land (1922)
Section I, The Burial of the Dead

A funeral service in the Anglican rite is called 'The Order of the Burial of the Dead'. The title of the first section of The Waste Land *refers to it, since it is a metaphor for the condition of contemporary man, whose life is meaningless, empty, alienating and quite similar to death. The following passage is the opening of the poem; it introduces its most important images and the dominant theme.*

6.7

April is the cruellest month, breeding[1]
Lilacs out of the dead land, mixing
Memory and desire, stirring[2]
Dull roots[3] with spring rain.
Winter kept us warm, covering
Earth in forgetful snow, feeding
A little life with dried tubers. [...]

1 **breeding.** Che genera.
2 **stirring.** Che stimola.
3 **Dull roots.** Sopite radici.

ANALYSIS

3 **ANSWER** these questions.
1 What aspects of spring are singled out as being 'cruel'? What do they evoke?
2 Why is the rebirth of nature 'cruel'?
3 How does the description of winter contradict traditional views?
4 How many speakers can you recognise?

4 **COMPARE** these lines to the opening of Geoffrey Chaucer's ***The Canterbury Tales***, quoted in exercise 1 above, as regards:
1 the speaking voice;
2 the myth of fertility;
3 the general atmosphere.

WARM-UP

1 **DISCUSS** with the rest of the class. Do you think that the actions of men are always governed by an ethical code? What is your ethical code based on?

2 **LOOK** at the painting by Magritte and in pairs discuss what image of love it conveys.

1 René Magritte, *The Lovers*, 1928. Museum of Modern Art, New York.

2 Ernst Ludwig Kirchner, *Women in the Street*, 1914. Von der Heydt-Museum, Wuppertal, Germany.

The Fire Sermon

T.S. Eliot

The Waste Land (1922)
Section III, The Fire Sermon

This passage introduces a key figure of the poem, Tiresias, the Theban prophet who was punished with blindness because he had seen Athena, the goddess of knowledge, bathing naked. In Sophocles's tragedy, Oedipus the King, *Tiresias predicts that Thebes will be destroyed.*

6.8

At the violet hour, when the eyes and back
Turn upward from the desk, when the human engine waits
Like a taxi throbbing[1] waiting,
I Tiresias[2], though blind, throbbing between two lives[3],
Old man with wrinkled female breasts[4], can see
At the violet hour, the evening hour that strives[5]
Homeward, and brings the sailor home from sea,
The typist home at teatime, clears her breakfast, lights
Her stove, and lays out food in tins.
Out of the window perilously spread
Her drying combinations[6] touched by the sun's last rays,
On the divan are piled (at night her bed)
Stockings, slippers, camisoles, and stays[7].
I Tiresias, old man with wrinkled dugs[8]
Perceived the scene, and foretold the rest[9] –
I too awaited the expected guest.
He, the young man carbuncular[10], arrives,
A small house agent's clerk, with one bold stare[11],
One of the low on whom assurance sits
As a silk hat on a Bradford millionaire[12].
The time is now propitious, as he guesses,
The meal is ended, she is bored and tired,
Endeavours[13] to engage her in caresses
Which still are unreproved[14], if undesired.
Flushed[15] and decided, he assaults at once;
Exploring hands encounter no defence;
His vanity requires no response,
And makes a welcome of indifference.

1 **throbbing.** Che pulsa.
2 **Tiresias.** Nelle *Metamorfosi* di Ovidio si racconta come Tiresia fu trasformato in donna da un incantesimo; questa identità fu mantenuta da lui per sette anni, al termine dei quali tornò ad essere un uomo.
3 **between two lives.** Tra due vite, sessi.
4 **wrinkled female breasts.** Vizze mammelle di donna.
5 **strives.** Si strugge.
6 **combinations.** Sottovesti.
7 **Stockings ... stays.** Calze, pantofole, camiciole e fascette.
8 **wrinkled dugs.** Mammelle raggrinzite.
9 **foretold the rest.** Ho predetto il resto.
10 **the young man carbuncular.** Il giovane pieno di foruncoli.
11 **one bold stare.** Un solo sguardo ardito.
12 **As ... millionaire.** Come un cappello di seta su di un milionario di Bradford.
13 **Endeavours.** Tenta.
14 **to engage ... unreproved.** Di coinvolgerla in carezze che non sono ancora respinte.
15 **Flushed.** Eccitato.

(And I Tiresias have foresuffered[16] all
Enacted on this same divan or bed;
I who have sat by Thebes[17] below the wall
And walked among the lowest of the dead[18].)
Bestows[19] one final patronising kiss[20],
And gropes his way, finding the stairs unlit[21]...

She turns and looks a moment in the glass,
Hardly aware of her departed lover;
Her brain allows one half-formed thought to pass:
'Well now that's done: and I'm glad it's over.'
When lovely woman stoops to folly and
Paces about her room again, alone,
She smoothes her hair[22] with automatic hand,
And puts a record on the gramophone.

16 **foresuffered.** Ho presofferto.
17 **Thebes.** Antica città greca che divenne una terra desolata a causa di una maledizione divina.
18 **the lowest of the dead.** Gli infimi tra i morti.
19 **Bestows.** Depone, concede.
20 **patronising kiss.** Bacio condiscendente.
21 **gropes ... unlit.** Si fa strada a tentoni, trovando le scale buie.
22 **smoothes her hair.** Si ravvia i capelli.

3

4

5

COMPREHENSION

3 **WRITE DOWN words and phrases referring to:**

1. Tiresias;
2. the inner setting;
3. the other characters.

4 **ANSWER the questions below.**

1. What are the most significant details of the mythological character?
2. Why do present, past and future coexist in him?
3. What does Tiresias see?
4. What life does the typist lead?
5. How does she feel?
6. What does the estate agent look like? Is he worried about the woman's indifference towards him?
7. What are his feelings when he leaves the typist?
8. Why is Tiresias's role appropriate to the man?
9. How does the typist react to her lover's going away?

ANALYSIS

5 **FOCUS on the typist, an archetype belonging to modern civilisation.** What is she compared to? How does she act? What actions is she associated with?

6 **IDENTIFY the themes developed in these lines.**

7 **DECIDE what language is employed in these lines and provide examples of: symbolism, that is, the use of symbols to represent ideas or qualities; objective correlatives; and juxtaposition, that is, when an author places a person, concept, place, idea or theme parallel to another in order to highlight the contrast between the two and compare them.**

ESAME DI STATO Terza Prova

8 **TYPE A. T.S. Eliot's *The Waste Land* expresses the spiritual sterility of modern life. Develop this statement with reference to the texts by T.S. Eliot you have read and analysed (approximately 200 words).**

Exam Reference pag. 355

3–5 Stills from the film 'Revolutionary Road', directed by Sam Mendes in 2008. The images depict scenes which, like *The Waste Land*, highlight the alienation of modern man.

7.10 Culture

A deep cultural crisis

WARM-UP

1 **DISCUSS** in pairs what issues a 'cultural crisis' may imply.

2 **COMPLETE** the bubbles with the words below.

waste • progress • atrocities • certain • cultural crisis • cynical • hegemony • gap • views • faith • dissolution • concepts • disillusioned • taboo-ridden • frustration

A deep **(1)** .... had been growing since the last two decades of the 19th century and led to the end of the system of Victorian values.

Henri Matisse, *Pink Nude*, 1935. Museum of Art, Baltimore, US.

The private morality of the Victorians had been strict and **(2)** ...., decency had to be maintained, whatever went on under the surface; the positivistic **(3)** .... in **(4)** .... and science had led people to believe that all human misery would be swept away.

The First World War, in which almost a million British soldiers had died, left the country in a **(5)** .... and **(6)** .... mood: stability and prosperity proved to belong only to a privileged class, consciences were haunted by the **(7)** .... of the war.

The **(8)** .... between the generation of the young and the older one, regarded as responsible for the **(9)** .... of lives during the war, grew wider and wider.

English propaganda posters depicting the hardships of veterans after WWI.

An increasing feeling of **(10)** .... led to a remarkable transformation of the notions of Imperial **(11)** .... and white superiority as a result of the slow **(12)** .... of the Empire into a 'Commonwealth of Nations'.

Nothing seemed to be right or **(13)** ....; even science and religion seemed to offer little comfort or security. New **(14)** .... of man and the universe emerged. In 1905 Albert Einstein published his theory of special relativity, which radically changed the **(15)** .... of time and space.

Photo of Albert Einstein working on an equation.

7.11 **Psychology**

Sigmund Freud: a window on the unconscious

WARM-UP

1 **LOOK** at the picture and brainstorm your knowledge about psychoanalysis, with the help of the glossary.

GLOSSARY
complex (*n.*) complesso
psyche psiche
ego io
superego super-io
unconscious inconscio
free association associazione libera

2 **AS YOU READ** the text below, take notes on its main topic and the main points.

Freud and the psyche

The first set of new ideas to have a profound effect on 20th-century thought was introduced by Sigmund Freud (1856–1939). He created a structural model of the psyche where he identified three parts: the id, ego and superego. According to this model, the 'id' is the set of instinctual impulses lacking organisation; the 'ego' is the coordinated, realistic part; and the 'superego' has a critical and moralising role since it includes the constraints imposed on the individual by society, education and moral laws.

Freud explained that the development of the human psyche is deeply affected by the subconscious; the discovery that man's actions could be motivated by irrational forces of which he might know nothing, was very disturbing. Freud's theory also maintained that the superego can profoundly distort man's behaviour. The effects in the sphere of family life were deep: the relationship between parents and children was altered; the conventional models of relationships between the sexes were re-examined. Freud's new method of investigation of the human mind through the analysis of dreams and the concept of 'free association' also influenced the artists and writers of the modern age.

Milestones

1905, Freud publishes *Three Essays on the Theory of Sexuality*

This work contributed to changing the way that people thought, behaved and learnt about sexuality. Its controversial reputation was not due to the first of Freud's three essays, which dealt with perversions. Nor did the last of the *Three Essays*, 'The Transformations of Puberty', seem to be shocking at a time when personal needs, desires and social practices only emphasised the omnipresence of sexuality. Rather, the debate that greeted Freud's work was linked to the second essay, in which he discussed sexuality in infancy and childhood. As a matter of fact, sexuality in infancy and childhood is the central theme of the book. Freud's discussion of adult sexual aberrations links them to unexpected or abnormal events during childhood. He also understood puberty as the sum of changes acting upon infantile sexuality.

3 6.9 | **LISTEN** to the lecture and note down the topic and the main points. How does the information in the lecture add to what was explained in the reading text above?

IELTS **Academic Writing – Task 2**

4 **AN ESSAY.** Write about the following topic:

> As children grow up, their relationship with their parents changes somehow.
> What are the main differences between young children's relationship with their parents and that of young adults?
> Are the changes that take place usually positive?

Give reasons for your answer and include relevant examples from your experience or knowledge. Write at least 250 words.

7.12 Literature

The modern novel

IELTS Academic Reading

1 READ the text and answer questions 1–13.

The passage has SIX paragraphs, A–F. Choose the correct heading for each paragraph from the list of headings below. Write the correct number, i–viii after each question (1–6).

- i Reintroduction of traditional techniques
- ii Experimenting with new narrative techniques
- iii The origins of the English novel
- iv The stream of consciousness
- v Economic forces in the modern novel
- vi Different levels of awareness
- vii A different use of time
- viii The new role of the novelist

1 A ....
2 B ....
3 C ....
4 D ....
5 E ....
6 F ....

For questions 7–9, choose the appropriate letter, A, B, C or D.

7 What was the novelist's new role?
- A To overcome people's boredom with traditional forms of writing.
- B To find new ways to express the uncertainty of the age.
- C To mediate between the different forms of artistic expression.
- D Basically the same as it had always been: to narrate what was happening around them.

8 How was time treated differently by the modern novelists?
- A The passing of time in a chronological sequence was essential.
- B The length of time passing in a novel was a good measure of the characters' maturity.
- C The distinction between past and present was essential.
- D External events in chronological sequence were less important than inner awareness and development.

9 The psychological novelists were mainly concerned with
- A working-class people and the contrast between cultures.
- B the liberating function and mystery of sexuality.
- C the complexity of human relationships and the psychological development of the characters.
- D introducing new narrative techniques and voices from different social classes.

Complete sentences 10–13 with words taken from the reading passage. Use NO MORE THAN THREE WORDS for each answer.

10 .... rejected some of the more traditional narrative techniques like the omniscient narrator.

11 The events of the story might take place just in the course of ...., as in James Joyce's *Ulysses* and in Virginia Woolf's *Mrs Dalloway*.

12 The .... technique was introduced to reproduce the uninterrupted flow of thoughts and sensations of the mind.

13 Some modern novelists were also called .... because they concentrated on the characters' internal development.

Modernist Writers

A. The structure of the English novel remained unaltered till the second decade of the 20th century. Its origins were essentially bourgeois and throughout the 18th and the 19th centuries it was firmly anchored in a social world with the gain or loss of social status as its favourite theme. The novelist was expected to mediate between his characters and the reader, relating in a more or less objective way, significant events and incidents in chronological order. The existence of accepted values and standards of behaviour led to the presentation of a social pattern that was familiar territory to both reader and writer.

B. The shift from the Victorian to the modern novel was caused by a gradual but substantial transformation of British society, which in a few years passed from the comfortable, prosperous world of the Victorians and Edwardians to the inter-war years marked by unrest and ferment. The urgency for social change and, from a literary point of view, the pressing need for different forms of expression forced novelists into a position of moral and psychological uncertainty. The novelists had a new role, which consisted in mediating between the solid and unquestioned values of the past and the confused present.

C. The modern novelist rejected omniscient narration and experimented with new methods to portray the individual consciousness; the viewpoint shifted from the external world to the character's mind. The analysis of a character's consciousness was influenced by the theories about the simultaneous existence of different levels of consciousness and sub-consciousness, where past experience is retained and the existence of the past in the present determines the whole personality of each human being.

D. Their treatment of time was also different. Time was subjective and inner: if the distinction between past and present was meaningless in psychological terms, then there was no use in building a well-structured plot, in leading a character through a chronological sequence of events. It was not necessarily the passing of time that revealed the truth about characters. The story might unfold in the course of a single day, as in James Joyce's *Ulysses* and in Virginia Woolf's *Mrs Dalloway*, by observing the character performing a common action, or by what Joyce called 'epiphany', that is, the sudden revelation of an interior reality caused by the most trivial events of everyday life.

E. The narrative technique that modern novelists mainly employed was the stream-of-consciousness technique or the interior monologue. William James coined the phrase 'stream of consciousness' to define the continuous flow of thoughts and sensations that characterise the human mind.

This definition was applied by literary critics to the kind of 20th-century fiction which focused on this inner process. Interior monologue is the verbal expression of this psychic phenomenon. In his masterpiece *Ulysses*, James Joyce brought to perfection the interior monologue, employing two levels of narration: one external to the character's mind, and the other with the character's thoughts flowing freely.

F. Some novelists were known in particular as psychological novelists because they centred their attention on the development of the character's mind and on human relationships. The most important are: Joseph Conrad, whose novels try to record the mystery of human experience; D.H. Lawrence, who wrote about the inner conflicts of working-class people and the liberating function of sexuality; E.M. Forster, whose recurrent theme is the complexity of human relationships, together with the analysis of the contrast between two different cultures. Other novelists, most notably Joyce and Woolf, experimented with narrative techniques, exploring the mind of one or more characters and giving voice to their thoughts.

Literary language
The interior monologue

The main features of the interior monologue are:
- verbal expression of the stream of consciousness;
- frequent lack of chronological order;
- the narrator may be present;
- formal logical order may be lost or lacking;
- the action takes place within the character's mind;
- speech may be immediate, without introductory expressions.

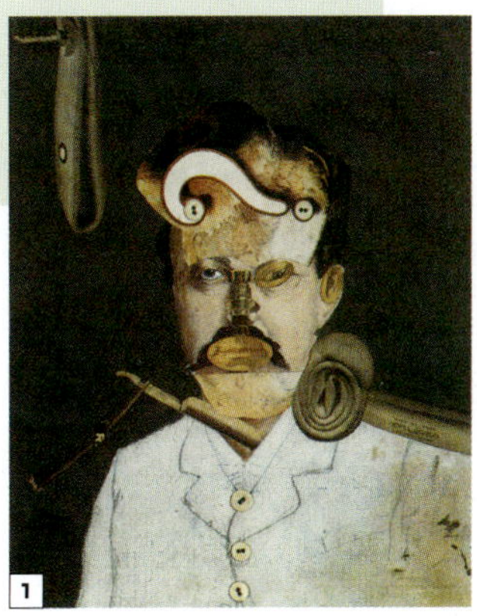

1 George Grosz, *A Victim of Society*, 1919. Courtesy of the Estate of George Grosz.

The funeral

James Joyce

Ulysses (1922)
Part III, Hades: Episode 6

The following extract from James Joyce's Ulysses *(Text Bank 57) is characterised by two levels of narration: one external to the character's mind, the other internal. Here, the protagonist, Leopold Bloom, is on his way to a funeral. The ritual of burial evokes in him a multitude of thoughts on death and human frailty.*

6.10

Mr Bloom stood far back, his hat in his hand, counting the bared heads[1]. Twelve. I'm thirteen. No. The chap in the macintosh[2] is thirteen. Death's number. Where the deuce did he pop out of[3]? He wasn't in the chapel, that I'll swear. Silly superstition that about thirteen.

Nice soft tweed Ned Lambert has in that suit. Tinge of purple[4]. I had one like that when we lived in Lombard street west. Dressy fellow he was once[5]. Used to change three suits in the day. Must get that grey suit of mine turned by Mesias[6]. Hello. It's dyed[7]. His wife I forgot he's not married or his landlady ought to have picked out those threads for him[8].

The coffin dived out of sight[9], eased down by the men straddled on the gravetrestles[10]. They struggled up and out[11]: and all uncovered[12]. Twenty.

Pause.

If we were all suddenly somebody else.

1 CONCENTRATE on the narrative technique of this passage and do the following activities.

1. Has the time of narration got any link with chronological time? Why? Where does the action take place?
2. Some sentences describe the scene from the outside; others reproduce Bloom's thoughts. Underline them with two different colours; then note down the two levels of narration, specifying the points of view adopted.
3. Consider the sentence structure throughout the passage. Some sentences are regular with a conventional use of grammar; others lack subjects, verbs or are made up of only one word. Which level of narration do they belong to?

2 COMPLETE the sequence below in order to get a clearer idea of Mr Bloom's 'flow of thoughts'.
bared heads → thirteen → unlucky number → ...

1 **bared heads.** Teste scoperte.
2 **macintosh.** Tipo di impermeabile.
3 **Where ... out of?** Da dove diavolo è uscito?
4 **Tinge of purple.** Un'ombra di violetto.
5 **Dressy ... once.** Una volta era un elegantone.
6 **Must ... Mesias.** Devo far rivoltare da Mesias quel mio completo grigio.
7 **It's dyed.** E' tinto.
8 **ought to ... for him.** Avrebbero dovuto riprendere quei fili.
9 **The coffin ... sight.** La bara scomparve.
10 **eased down ... gravetrestles.** Fatta scivolare giù dagli uomini a gambe spalancate sopra le assi gettate sulla fossa.
11 **They struggled ... out.** Si rialzarono scostandosi a fatica.
12 **all uncovered.** Tutti si scoprirono.

Joseph Conrad and imperialism

Joseph Conrad's life

Joseph Conrad (1857–1924) was born in 1857, in the territory of Poland, partitioned and occupied since 1795 by Russia, Prussia and Austria. He was brought up within a patriotic and revolutionary household. His father was a national political figure whose activities led him and his family into forced exile in Russia. For Conrad, then, exile and loneliness were almost inborn. After his parents' deaths, he was brought up by an uncle. In 1874 Conrad left for Marseilles, France, to go to sea. In 1878 he joined an English ship sailing to the Far East and Australia. Learning English was required for his Master Mariner qualification, which he achieved in 1886, the same year in which he became a British subject. His career as a seaman put him in contact with men from a different social class and background from his own. From these men, he learnt to appreciate the values of a simple devotion to a demanding, monotonous, dangerous job, and work is a powerful theme in his novels.

In 1890 Conrad received a commission which took him to Africa. A modest inheritance he received from his uncle encouraged him to abandon the sea and devote himself to writing. He contributed some of the major writing of the century. From *The Nigger of the Narcissus* (1897), *Youth* (1898), *Heart of Darkness* (1902) and *Lord Jim* (1900), by way of *Nostromo* (1904), *The Secret Agent* (1907), *The Secret Sharer* (1909) and *Under Western Eyes* (1911), to *Victory* (1915), *The Shadow Line* (1917), *The Rescue* (1920) and *The Rover* (1923), Conrad worked on and out of a society and literary culture which called for a radical reassessment. By the time of his death, which came suddenly from a heart attack in 1924, Conrad had massively answered that demand.

1 Joseph Conrad on board a ship.

The writer's task and experimentation

In the preface to *The Nigger of the Narcissus*, Conrad stated that the writer's task should not be to try to amuse his readers or to teach them a lesson but rather to record the complex pattern of life as he saw it. His aim was to explore the meaning of the human condition. Conrad experimented continually; his main characters are all solitary figures, rooted in no past, committed to an uncertain future. In general they are viewed externally, through the mind of others or through their actions.

Exotic settings

Conrad set his novels and short stories at sea or in exotic latitudes. These were the places he knew well and they enabled him to isolate his characters so that their problems and inner conflicts stood out with particular force. Most extremely, his setting was the ship, which became a sort of microcosm in its isolation, or an African river and the jungle.

Various narrative techniques

Conrad found chronological sequence inadequate, and broke the normal time-sequence and used time shifts to create the illusion of life being lived by a number of very different people at the same time.

He used various narrative techniques: first-person narration, an invisible narrator, journals and letters. Many of his novels and short stories are told by the same narrator, Marlow, or have more than one narrator. The use of several points of view results from Conrad's wish to break free from the constraints of an omniscient narrator so that the reader is left to decide for himself, and it is also to show the relativism of moral values.

The individual consciousness

In almost all his works there is the recurrence of a situation in which a man who relies on the virtues of honesty, courage, pity and fidelity in order to achieve an ideal of conduct is confronted by a sense of evil against which these virtues seem powerless. Conrad is concerned with the conflict between personal feelings and professional duties. It is organised society that gives man confidence, but this confidence fails when man is lonely and surrounded by a wild and hostile background. Thus Conrad points out that reality is indeed the construction of individual consciousness through individual responsibility and self-control.

1 READ about Joseph Conrad's life and works and answer the following questions.

1 How did Conrad's career as a seaman affect him?
2 What features of his works made him different from 19th-century writers?
3 What were the main themes of his works?

2 **FOCUS on the title of Conrad's novel and write down what you associate the phrase 'heart of darkness' with, in the spider chart below.**

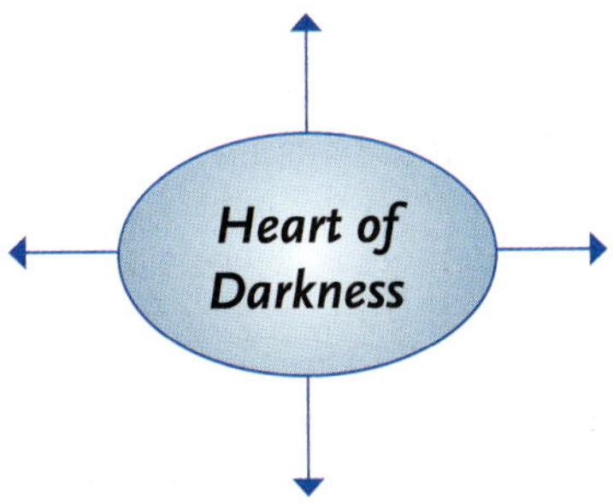

2 Cover of *Heart of Darkness* by Maria Rivans, Penguin Essentials edition.

3 Scene from the film 'Heart of Darkness', directed by Nicolas Roeg, 1993.

Heart of Darkness (1902)

The story

The novel, which consists of three parts, is set at the end of the 19th century, at an unspecified date. The story is told by Marlow, a sailor who, together with the passengers of the 'Nellie', is waiting for the tide which will let the ship sail from London. He talks about his first commission for a Belgian company involved in the ivory trade in the Congo. His task was to carry raw ivory from the heart of the continent to the coast, where it could be loaded on ships bound for Europe. Once in Africa, while he was proceeding down the coast, he encountered a French gun-boat firing into the jungle, though, apparently, there was no enemy and no effect. He then got to the Company Station near the coast, where he was disappointed by the inefficiency and neglect of the organisation and by the cruelty of the colonial exploitation. It was there that he heard Kurtz's name for the first time. Kurtz was a Company agent who managed to supply more ivory than the other agents and had become a sort of idol for the natives. An expedition was arranged to reach Kurtz and bring him back to civilisation, since he was seriously ill. During the voyage, Marlow met several people who referred to Kurtz as 'a very remarkable person' and 'an emissary of pity, and science, and progress'. Marlow found out that Kurtz had even been required by the International Society for the Suppression of Savage Customs to write a report where he put down the noble ideals that had initially brought him to Africa, but which he ended with the postscript: 'Exterminate all the brutes!' Marlow finally met Kurtz and succeeded in taking him on board. However, before he could interrogate him about the 'unspeakable rites' he had taken part in, Kurtz died whispering the ambiguous words 'The horror! The horror!' When Marlow returned to Belgium, he called on Kurtz's fiancée and, instead of telling her the truth about what had happened, he told her that Kurtz had uttered her name while dying.

The historical context of the novel

In 1890 Conrad spent six months in the Congo, employed by the *Société Anonyme Belge pour le Commerce du Haut-Congo*. He therefore witnessed the specific form of colonial imperialism King Leopold II of Belgium practised in his Congo Free State, which he regarded as a personal territorial possession. Moreover, Leopold pursued his interests in the Congo in the name of philanthropy and anti-slavery. He stated that the agents of the State had to accomplish the noble mission of continuing the development of civilisation in Africa, gradually reducing the primitive barbarism and fighting sanguinary customs. They also had to accustom the population to general laws, of which the most needful and salutary was that of work. He set up concession companies controlled by his personal representatives and, to exploit fully the wealth of the Congo State, he instituted a 'labour tax' on natives in the form of forty hours per month of forced labour. In practice this was brutally exacted by the chiefs of the concession companies with the encouragement of Leopold's local army. Increased production of ivory and rubber was their only priority, physical mutilation and abuse their method.

Conrad was writing in a moment of growing doubt about imperialist politics. His indictment of the brutal exercise of law on the natives, of the missionary zeal, the administrative efficiency and search for profit is generalised to all forms of imperialism when he calls the company Marlow works for the 'Continental Trading Company' or when he gives Kurtz a German name, a half-French father and a half-English mother.

A complex structure

The novel presents a series of stories, one embedded within the other. First, there is the frame provided by an anonymous narrator who, on board the 'Nellie' on the Thames, introduces Marlow – an observer-narrator – and formally closes the narrative. Everything else is contained within this frame; minor characters also tell their own stories and state their views of Kurtz. The complex structure of the novel is sustained by the continuous shifts backwards and forwards in Marlow's narrative, by the way he creates suspense and interest by delaying the details of his meeting with Kurtz.

The 'heart of darkness'

During the journey through the forest, most times Marlow is silent, listening, and his worst moments are when he is forced to understand that the great adventure of his life, to which he is devoting much effort, is really a business of death. Throughout the journey, different voices have announced Kurtz as an artist, as an interpreter of life, and Marlow is looking forward to meeting him. Through Conrad's irony, the reader is informed that, at last, Marlow has created an image of Kurtz that may be the prototype of the man he himself would have liked to be. He thinks that Kurtz can tell him things about himself that he does not know. The difference between Marlow and Kurtz is that while Kurtz, through brutal action, has reached new experiences of the self and, against the indifference of the universe, he has felt all the excitement that life can give, Marlow feels he has lived incompletely.

A quest for the self

The 'heart of darkness' evoked by Conrad is hard to understand. The jungle drives white men mad because of its solitude; there is only 'death – the death of many men, the death of ethical behaviour, the death of goodness and civility, the death, crucially, of our authority as selves'. The novel can be read as Marlow's mythical journey in search of the self, in order to bring back a new truth. Kurtz was a progressive and a liberal, a painter, a writer, a musician who was received by the black natives as if he were a god. However, it was perhaps because he went into the jungle without knowing himself, that his inappropriate conduct took him beyond the limits of his heart, paying the price in madness and death. On the contrary, Marlow did not transgress his limits and came back without fully understanding his experience, and although the heart of darkness tried to exercise its influence on him too, he was able to restrain himself – he recognised its fascination and its abomination, but resisted his desire to join in those unspeakable rites. Marlow was saved because his aim was self-knowledge, the mystery of existence, which demands great humility. *Heart of Darkness* ends with the suggestion that it is impossible to penetrate the surface of reality in any meaningful way.

3 ANSWER these questions about *Heart of Darkness*.

1. How did Leopold II justify his kind of colonialism?
2. What is Conrad's attitude towards imperialism?
3. What is the structure of the novel? What sustains it?
4. How can the novel be interpreted?
5. How does Marlow differ from Kurtz?

WARM-UP

1 DESCRIBE the people in this picture.

1

The chain-gang

Joseph Conrad

Heart of Darkness (1902)
Chapter 1

The following passage recounts the moment when Marlow, during his trip up the Congo River in search of Kurtz, reaches the Company Station, where a railroad is being built.

6.11

'A slight clinking[1] behind me made me turn my head. Six black men advanced in a file, toiling up[2] the path. They walked erect and slow, balancing small baskets full of earth on their heads, and the clink kept time with their footsteps. Black rags were wound round their loins[3], and the short ends behind waggled[4] to and fro like tails. I could see every rib, the joints of their limbs[5] were like knots in a rope[6]; each had an iron collar on his neck, and all were connected together with a chain whose bights[7]

1 **A slight clinking.** Un debole tintinnio.
2 **toiling up.** Salendo con fatica.
3 **rags ... loins.** Stracci erano avvolti intorno ai fianchi.
4 **waggled.** Dondolavano.
5 **limbs.** Membra.
6 **knots in a rope.** Nodi su una corda.
7 **bights.** Maglie.

swung between them, rhythmically clinking. Another report[8] from the cliff made me think suddenly of that ship of war[9] I had seen firing into a continent. It was the same kind of ominous[10] voice; but these men could by no stretch of imagination be called enemies. They were called criminals, and the outraged law, like the bursting shells[11], had come to them, an insoluble mystery from the sea. All their meagre breasts panted[12] together, the violently dilated nostrils quivered[13], the eyes stared stonily uphill. They passed me within six inches, without a glance, with that complete, deathlike indifference of unhappy savages. Behind this raw matter[14] one of the reclaimed[15], the product of the new forces at work, strolled despondently[16], carrying a rifle by its middle. He had a uniform jacket with one button off, and seeing a white man on the path, hoisted[17] his weapon to his shoulder with alacrity. This was simple prudence, white men being so much alike at a distance that he could not tell who I might be. He was speedily reassured, and with a large, white, rascally grin[18], and a glance at his charge[19], seemed to take me into partnership in his exalted trust. After all, I also was a part of the great cause of these high and just proceedings.

'Instead of going up, I turned and descended to the left. My idea was to let that chain-gang get out of sight before I climbed the hill. You know I am not particularly tender; I've had to strike and to fend off[20]. I've had to resist and to attack sometimes – that's only one way of resisting – without counting the exact cost, according to the demands of such sort of life as I had blundered into[21]. I've seen the devil of violence, and the devil of greed[22], and the devil of hot desire; but, by all the stars! these were strong, lusty, red-eyed devils, that swayed[23] and drove men – men, I tell you. But as I stood on this hillside, I foresaw[24] that in the blinding sunshine of that land I would become acquainted with a flabby[25], pretending, weak-eyed devil of a rapacious and pitiless folly. How insidious he could be, too, I was only to find out several months later and a thousand miles farther. For a moment I stood appalled[26], as though by a warning. Finally I descended the hill, obliquely, towards the trees I had seen.

'I avoided a vast artificial hole somebody had been digging on the slope[27], the purpose of which I found it impossible to divine. It wasn't a quarry or a sandpit[28], anyhow. It was just a hole. It might have been connected with the philanthropic desire of giving the criminals something to do. I don't know. Then I nearly fell into a very narrow ravine[29], almost no more than a scar[30] in the hillside. I discovered that a lot of imported drainage-pipes[31] for the settlement had been tumbled[32] in there. There wasn't one that was not broken. It was a wanton smash-up[33]. At last I got under the trees. My purpose was to stroll[34] into the shade for a moment; but no sooner within than it seemed to me I had stepped into the gloomy circle of some Inferno. The rapids were near, and an uninterrupted, uniform, headlong, rushing[35] noise filled the mournful stillness of the grove[36], where not a breath stirred, not a leaf moved, with a mysterious sound – as though the tearing pace[37] of the launched earth had suddenly become audible.

'Black shapes crouched[38], lay, sat between the trees, leaning against the trunks, clinging to the earth, half coming out, half effaced[39] within the dim light, in all the attitudes of pain, abandonment, and despair. Another mine on the cliff went off, followed by a slight shudder[40] of the soil under my feet. The work was going on. The work! And this was the place where some of the helpers had withdrawn to die.

'They were dying slowly – it was very clear. They were not enemies, they were not criminals, they were nothing earthly now – nothing but black shadows of disease and starvation, lying confusedly in the greenish gloom. Brought from all the recesses of the coast in all the legality of time contracts, lost in uncongenial surroundings,

8 **report.** Detonazione.
9 **that ship of war.** Marlow si riferisce ad una nave da guerra francese che aveva precedentemente visto sparare verso la giungla, contro un nemico invisibile.
10 **ominous.** Sinistra, inquietante.
11 **bursting shells.** Bombe che esplodevano.
12 **meagre breasts panted.** Toraci scarni ansimavano.
13 **nostrils quivered.** Narici fremevano.
14 **raw matter.** Materia prima.
15 **one of the reclaimed.** Uno dei (nativi) riscattati.
16 **strolled despondently.** Camminava con aria scoraggiata.
17 **hoisted.** Sollevò.
18 **rascally grin.** Largo sorriso da furfante.
19 **at his charge.** Verso i suoi sorvegliati.
20 **to fend off.** Parare i colpi.
21 **I had blundered into.** Mi ero trovato per caso.
22 **greed.** Avidità.
23 **swayed.** Governavano, dominavano.
24 **I foresaw.** Presentii.
25 **flabby.** Flaccido.
26 **appalled.** Sgomento, atterrito.
27 **slope.** Pendio.
28 **a quarry or a sandpit.** Una cava di pietra o di sabbia.
29 **ravine.** Burrone, gola.
30 **scar.** Cicatrice.
31 **drainage-pipes.** Condutture, tubature.
32 **tumbled.** Gettate.
33 **a wanton smash-up.** Uno spreco distruttivo e insensato.
34 **to stroll.** Passeggiare.
35 **headlong, rushing.** Impetuoso, violento.
36 **mournful stillness of the grove.** Lugubre immobilità del boschetto.
37 **tearing pace.** Moto veemente.
38 **crouched.** Accovacciate.
39 **effaced.** Cancellate, confuse.
40 **slight shudder.** Lieve tremolio.

1 Portrait of two manacled men, members of a chain-gang enslaved under King Leopold II's terror regime, ca 1904.

fed on unfamiliar food, they sickened, became inefficient, and were then allowed to crawl away[41] and rest. These moribund shapes were free as air – and nearly as thin. I began to distinguish the gleam[42] of the eyes under the trees. Then, glancing down, I saw a face near my hand. The black bones reclined at full length with one shoulder against the tree, and slowly the eyelids[43] rose and the sunken[44] eyes looked up at me, enormous and vacant, a kind of blind, white flicker[45] in the depths of the orbs, which died out slowly. The man seemed young – almost a boy – but you know with them it's hard to tell. I found nothing else to do but to offer him one of my good Swede's ship's biscuits I had in my pocket. The fingers closed slowly on it and held – there was no other movement and no other glance. He had tied a bit of white worsted[46] round his neck – Why? Where did he get it? Was it a badge – an ornament – a charm[47] – a propitiatory act? Was there any idea at all connected with it? It looked startling round his black neck, this bit of white thread from beyond the seas.

'Near the same tree two more bundles[48] of acute angles sat with their legs drawn up[49]. One, with his chin propped on his knees, stared at nothing, in an intolerable and appalling manner: his brother phantom rested its forehead, as if overcome with a great weariness; and all about others were scattered[50] in every pose of contorted collapse, as in some picture of a massacre or a pestilence. While I stood horrorstruck, one of these creatures rose to his hands and knees, and went off on all-fours[51] towards the river to drink. He lapped[52] out of his hand, then sat up in the sunlight, crossing his shins[53] in front of him, and after a time let his woolly head fall on his breastbone.

'I didn't want any more loitering[54] in the shade, and I made haste[55] towards the station. When near the buildings I met a white man, in such an unexpected elegance of get-up[56] that in the first moment I took him for a sort of vision. I saw a high starched collar, white cuffs[57], a light alpaca jacket, snowy trousers, a clean necktie, and varnished boots. No hat. Hair parted, brushed, oiled, under a green-lined parasol held in a big white hand. He was amazing, and had a pen-holder[58] behind his ear.

'I shook hands with this miracle, and I learned he was the Company's chief accountant, and that all the book-keeping[59] was done at this station. He had come out for a moment, he said, "to get a breath of fresh air". The expression sounded wonderfully odd, with its suggestion of sedentary desk-life. I wouldn't have mentioned the fellow to you at all, only it was from his lips that I first heard the name of the man who is so indissolubly connected with the memories of that time. Moreover, I respected the fellow. Yes; I respected his collars, his vast cuffs, his brushed hair. His appearance was certainly that of a hairdresser's dummy[60], but in the great demoralisation of the land he kept up his appearance. That's backbone[61].

41 **crawl away.** Trascinarsi in disparte.
42 **gleam.** Scintillio, balenio.
43 **eyelids.** Palpebre.
44 **sunken.** Infossati.
45 **flicker.** Barlume.
46 **He had tied ... worsted.** Si era legato del tessuto di lana bianco.
47 **badge ... charm.** Distintivo ... amuleto, portafortuna.
48 **bundles.** Sagome.
49 **drawn up.** Raccolte.
50 **scattered.** Sparsi.
51 **on all-fours.** Carponi.
52 **lapped.** Bevve avidamente.
53 **shins.** Stinchi.
54 **loitering.** Gironzolare, oziare.
55 **I made haste.** Mi affrettai.
56 **get-up.** Abbigliamento.
57 **starched collar, white cuffs.** Colletto inamidato, polsini bianchi.
58 **pen-holder.** Cannuccia per scrivere.
59 **book-keeping.** Contabilità.
60 **a hairdresser's dummy.** Un manichino (nella vetrina) di un parrucchiere.
61 **That's backbone.** Quello è coraggio.

COMPREHENSION

2 READ lines 1–53 and note down:

1 what the narrator saw when he turned his head;
2 what caused the clinking;
3 how the narrator defined himself and why;
4 what kind of landscape was described;
5 what the narrator saw between the trees;
6 what was going on at the station.

3 READ the second section (lines 54–93) and answer the following questions.

1 What does the narrator gradually make out 'in the greenish gloom'?
2 Is the narrator passive in front of the scene?
3 What strikes him about the boy? What does he wonder about?
4 Can you find out the identity of the man the narrator meets near the buildings?
5 Why is he mentioned?

ANALYSIS

4 FOCUS on the shocking description of the natives: the six black men and the shapes in the grove of death.

1 What details does Conrad concentrate upon?
2 Circle the verbs conveying their actions. What is their main connotation?
3 Are these people given proper names? Write down the expressions Marlow, the narrator, uses to mention them.
4 Note down the words referring to the mood of the natives. Then summarise it in your own words.

5 FIND the similes in the extract and explain what they mean.

6 LOOK at the description of the chain-gang overseer. What insight does this 'product of the new forces at work' give into the relationship between the natives and the white colonisers?

7 CHOOSE the ways in which the chief accountant is characterised from the list and provide the relevant details from the passage. Then answer the questions below.

- □ Name ....
- □ Nationality ....
- □ Age ....
- □ Sex ....
- □ Physical appearance ....
- □ Clothes ....
- □ Job ....
- □ Thoughts ....
- □ Words ....
- □ Actions ....

1 What kind of images does Conrad use to connote him? Discuss their possible symbolic implications.
2 This character embodies one of the striking paradoxes Marlow faces on his journey. Can you explain why?
3 However, Marlow says: 'I respected the fellow.' What justifies this attitude?

8 FOCUS on Marlow's method of narration and tick the correct statements.

- □ He says what he sees directly.
- □ He withholds information.
- □ He delays the recognition of objects.
- □ He makes ironic remarks.
- □ He keeps a self-distancing position of marginality.
- □ He vehemently expresses his indignation towards what he witnesses.
- □ He asks questions.

Can you think of the advantages and disadvantages of this narrative method?

9 EXPLAIN what evidence of the devastating effects of colonial exploitation you can find in the text. Provide examples of the following:

1 military and administrative control;
2 exploitation of the native labour force to obtain the country's natural resources;
3 physical violence;
4 devastation of the natural environment;
5 inefficiency and waste.

10 THE NARRATOR, Marlow, makes sarcastic comments that imply a severe judgement of European colonisation. Underline these remarks and identify the metaphor used by the narrator to convey his opinion.

11 SAY what the opposition between 'black' and 'white' symbolises in the passage.

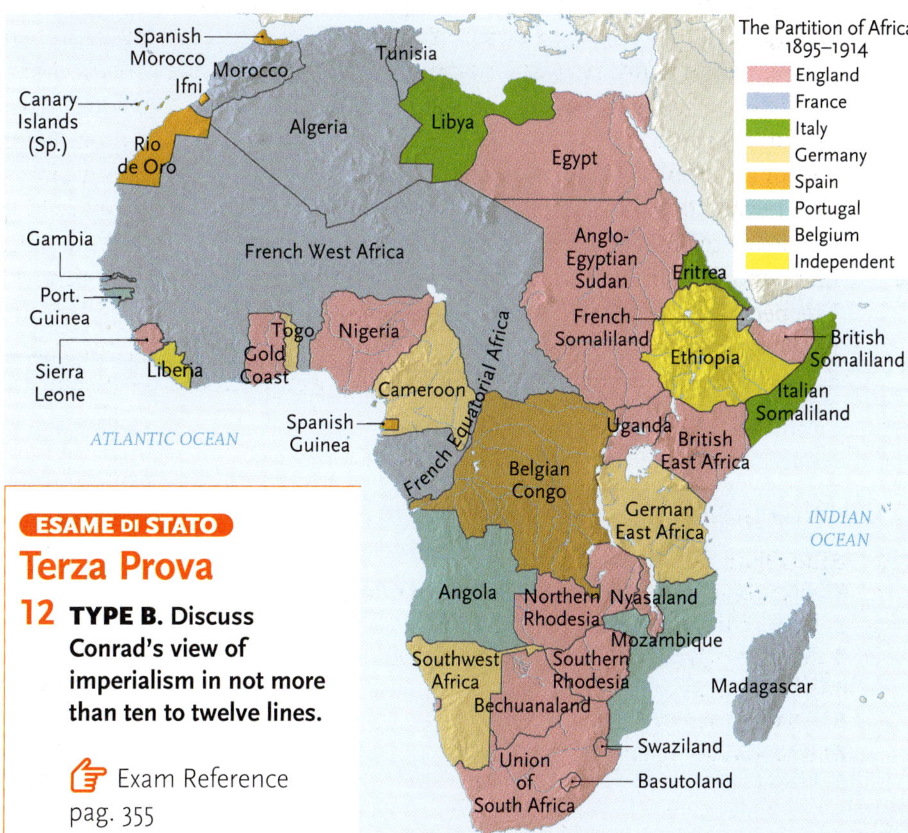

ESAME DI STATO

Terza Prova

12 TYPE B. Discuss Conrad's view of imperialism in not more than ten to twelve lines.

Exam Reference pag. 355

TEXT BANK 54: *A PASSAGE TO INDIA*

Edward Morgan Forster and the contact between different cultures

E.M. Forster's life

Edward Morgan Forster (1879–1970) was born in London in 1879. His father died soon after, and he was brought up by his mother and his great-aunt, whose financial help enabled him to live comfortably all his life. He was educated by his mother until the age of eleven, after which he was sent to Eastbourne, a strict preparatory school, and then to Tonbridge School. He experienced both periods as a sort of spiritual imprisonment until, in 1897, he entered King's College, Cambridge. After leaving Cambridge – which he returned to in 1946 as an Honorary Fellow of King's College, and where he was to spend the rest of his life – he lived for a time in Italy, the background of his first and third novels: *Where Angels Fear to Tread* (1905) and *A Room with a View* (1908). In both works he explored the differences between the strictness of English conventions and upper-middle-class codes of social behaviour and the more spontaneous and relaxed way of life of the Italians. Between these two books, he published *The Longest Journey* (1907), a novel about English life, perhaps the most autobiographical of the three. Then followed the first of his two masterpieces, *Howards End* (1910).

In 1912 Forster went to India for the first time, and in 1914 he began to work on the novel *A Passage to India*, which was finally published in 1924. He also published: two volumes of short stories; *Aspects of the Novel* (1927), a series of lectures on modern aesthetics; and two books of collected essays.

He died in 1970, and the following year *Maurice* was published. He had written the novel as early as 1914 to release and overcome his sense of guilt about his homosexuality, which at that time was still regarded as a criminal offence.

1 Portrait of E.M. Forster in Indian clothing, 1921.

A balance of traditional and modern elements

Forster's work presents an interesting balance of traditional and modern elements, especially in his last two novels, *Howards End* and *A Passage to India*. He was, first of all, a writer of comedies of manners who was interested in the society of his time. He derived much from the Victorian tradition – the plot arrangement and the presence of an omniscient narrator that occasionally becomes obtrusive – but the optimism about the future that one finds in most 19th-century fiction was already being questioned in his work before World War I, through the technique of irony, reminiscent of Jane Austen's. Forster laid emphasis on personal relationships, on personal vision as the only way to 'connect', to find harmony in the face of the increasing disintegration of the world. His complexity derived from his talent for self-scrutiny, from his power to question the culture to which he remained, however, attached. His early books were more humorous; in the last two novels there was an attempt to approach through sensation and experience what gives meaning to life and affords a visionary understanding of it.

1 READ **E.M. Forster's biography and find evidence that:**
- He was influenced by female figures.
- He was annoyed by restrictions.
- He was attracted to dualities.
- He was a prolific writer.
- He was a critic and an essayist.
- He was indebted to the 19th-century novel.
- His works showed a modern complexity.

A Passage to India (1924)

The story

The novel is set in the fictional Indian town of Chandrapore, which is divided into the old Indian quarter and a British Civil Station. The City Magistrate, Ronny Heaslop, is engaged to Miss Adela Quested, who decides to visit India accompanied by Ronny's mother, Mrs Moore. One night Mrs Moore meets a Muslim doctor, Aziz, at the mosque. They soon become friends and he invites Mrs Moore and Adela to visit the Marabar Caves, which are about twenty miles away from the town. The visit to the caves proves to be a disrupting incident. Mrs Moore suffers a nervous breakdown and loses the will to go on living. A moment before she experiences this terrifying sense of emptiness, she suggests that Aziz and Adela should continue the exploration of the caves without her. Forster does not explicitly say what happens in the cave, but when Adela emerges in the sunlight again, she is in a state of confusion and accuses Aziz of physical assault. Aziz is arrested and a trial ensues. Cyril Fielding, the headmaster of the local college, sides with the Indians because he believes Aziz is innocent; Mrs Moore shows none of her former understanding but is hard, irritable and takes no interest in the victim (later she leaves for England and dies during her voyage); and Adela is surrounded by the formal concern of the British community. At the trial she is in a state of nervous collapse; finally she declares that she has made a mistake. Aziz is released; Adela is disowned by her own people, except Fielding, and the man's kindness makes Aziz and his compatriots suspicious towards him. The rest of the plot deals with the aftermath of the broken friendship between Aziz and Fielding.

2 Scene of the tour at the 'Marabar Caves' in the film 'A Passage to India', filmed on location at the Barabar Caves.

Insights

The Barabar Caves

The Barabar Caves are some 35 km north of Gaya in northeastern India. They were visited by Forster on one of his two visits to India. Struck by their curious echo, he used them as a central location in his book *A Passage To India*, renaming them the 'Marabar Caves' for the story. The Barabar Caves were carved during the first phase of development of Buddhism in the 2nd century BC. These caves were meant for ascetic spiritual Buddhist monks who were truth seekers and wanted isolation and seclusion. The Barabar Caves have been cut so sharply that they give the illusion of modern-day laser cutting. The beauty of the decorations is so effective that from inside the caves they give the semblance of wooden crafting. The caves are important from the point of view of historical writings of Buddhism. Many Buddhist tales have been portrayed on the walls of the caves which are relevant to understanding the development of Buddhism in different phases.

The belief in goodwill

Forster began to develop the novel in 1913, after visiting India. He was concerned with the issue of 'connection', as well as with the desire to overcome social and racial differences. This is why he named the novel after Walt Whitman's poem 'Passage to India' (1871), which celebrated the opening of the Suez Canal as a bridge between Europe and India. Personal relationships were, for Forster, a fundamental value which led him to believe in a general need for tolerance, good temper and sympathy. What remains strong in the novel is the belief in 'goodwill', be it a religious belief as for Mrs Moore, or a secular, personal one as for Fielding.

India as a physical and mental landscape

A Passage to India is told by an omniscient narrator, whose voice intrudes from time to time to comment on the situation, while the point of view shifts from character to character. The novel deals with the clash between Western and Eastern cultures, and at the end it declares the impossibility of establishing an understanding relationship on an equal basis. On a more general level, it also explores the difficulties man faces in trying to come to terms with himself and the universe. The Indian landscape dominates the novel from the beginning to the end, challenging the established values of Western civilisation. The reader is constantly reminded of the many inhabitants of India: the crowds of people, the animals, the plants, the birds, the stones. One of the basic qualities of Forster's India is that it has no interiors or exteriors, nothing is private there, everyone can see you and know even your secrets, weaknesses and failures. As a matter of fact, it is Ronny's job to make sure there is no privacy – at least amongst the Indians in his jurisdiction. The mission of the Anglo-Indian establishment is to create a relationship of power where the Indians are the looked at, while the English are the spectators or the inspectors. Another aspect of India is that it awakens desire. Adela's experience of certain events in the Indian landscape is linked to her realisation that she does not love Ronny.

The Marabar Caves

The Marabar Caves, which Forster based on the real-life Barabar Caves, have a central role in the development of the novel. First of all, they are enclosed spaces that are, however, public spaces. There are no paintings, decorations or other signs of human presence, and Mrs Moore and Adela both have traumatic experiences inside them. For both, the transformative experience comes in the form of an 'echo'. In Hindu mythology the caves represent the 'womb of the universe', from which all forms of created life emanated. A psychological explanation would identify this idea with the notion of the subconscious. According to literary tradition, the echo is the symbol of nature's benevolence which often acts as a reminder of the harmonies in creation, but Forster gives the echo in the cave a dehumanising quality.

Forster's view of imperialism

The novel deals with the dissolution of British dominion over India. The typical attitude of the British in India was that they were undertaking the 'white man's burden'. This was a system of distant, condescending sovereignty in which the English bureaucracy did not associate with the people they ruled, and it finds its expression in the character of Ronny Heaslop. The non-cooperation movement and Mohandas Gandhi wanted complete social equality between the British and the Indians. Forster shared this view and criticised imperialistic policies of discrimination under which personal relations were spoilt. The isolation of the British community in Chandrapore, the atrocities suffered by the Indians, the agitation of the natives, all these issues are present in the novel. The development of an Indian national consciousness is described by Forster in the character of Aziz.

2 **ANSWER the following questions about the novel *A Passage to India*.**

1. Who are the most important characters within the English and the Indian communities?
2. What is Forster's main concern in the novel?
3. Why did Forster set the novel in India? What are the features of his India?
4. Why is the visit to the Marabar Caves a turning point?
5. How did Forster portray the colonial experience?

7.14 Edward Morgan Forster and the contact between different cultures

Aziz and Mrs Moore

E.M. Forster

A Passage to India (1924)
Chapter 2

This passage deals with the meeting between Aziz and Mrs Moore, who are both trying to escape from an alien environment. Aziz, who has been treated rudely by Major Callendar and his wife, comforts himself with the thought of 'shaking the dust of Anglo-India off his feet'. Mrs Moore seeks relief from the heat and from having to sit through a stage comedy she has already seen in London.

WARM-UP

1 **DISCUSS.** Do sincere personal relationships overcome the obstacles between different peoples and civilisations?

1 Peggy Ashcroft as Mrs Moore in the film 'A Passage to India', directed by David Lean, 1984.

6.12

He was an athletic little man, daintily[1] put together, but really very strong. Nevertheless walking fatigued him, as it fatigues everyone in India except the newcomer. There is something hostile in that soil. It either yields[2], and the foot sinks into a depression, or else it is unexpectedly rigid and sharp, pressing stones or crystals against the tread[3]. A series of these little surprises exhausts; and he was wearing pumps[4], a poor preparation for any country. At the edge of the Civil Station he turned into a mosque to rest.

He had always liked this mosque. It was gracious, and the arrangement pleased him. The courtyard – entered through a ruined gate – contained an ablution-tank of fresh clear water, which was always in motion, being indeed part of a conduit that supplied the city. The courtyard was paved with broken slabs[5]. The covered part of the mosque was deeper than is usual; its effect was that of an English parish church whose side has been taken out. Where he sat, he looked into three arcades whose darkness was illuminated by a small hanging lamp and by the moon. The front – in full moonlight – had the appearance of marble, and the ninety-nine names of God on the frieze[6] stood out black, as the frieze stood out white against the sky. The contrast between this dualism and the contention[7] of shadows within pleased Aziz, and he tried to symbolize the whole into some truth of religion or love. A mosque by winning his approval let loose his imagination. The temple of another creed, Hindu, Christian or Greek, would have bored him and failed to awaken his sense of beauty. Here was Islam, his own country, more than a Faith, more than a battle-cry, more, much more... Islam, an attitude towards life both exquisite and durable, where his body and his thoughts found their home.

His seat was the low wall that bounded[8] the courtyard on the left. The ground fell away beneath him towards the city, visible as a blur[9] of trees, and in the stillness he heard many small sounds. On the right, over in the Club, the English community contributed an amateur orchestra. Elsewhere some Hindus were drumming – he knew they were Hindus, because the rhythm was uncongenial to him – and others were bewailing a corpse[10] – he knew whose, having certified it in the afternoon. There were owls[11], the Punjab[12] mail... and flowers smelt deliciously in the station-master's garden. But the mosque – that alone signified, and he returned to it from the complex appeal of the night, and decked it[13] with meanings the builder had never intended. Some day he too would build a mosque, smaller than this but in perfect taste, so that all who passed by should experience the happiness he felt now. And near it, under a low dome[14], should be his tomb, with a Persian inscription:

Alas, without me for thousands of years
The Rose will blossom and the Spring will bloom,
But those who have secretly understood my heart –
They will approach and visit the grave where I lie.

1 **daintily.** Con grazia, delicatamente.
2 **yields.** Cede.
3 **tread.** Passo.
4 **pumps.** Scarpe scollate, leggere.
5 **slabs.** Lastre.
6 **frieze.** Fregio.
7 **contention.** Contesa, contrasto.
8 **bounded.** Delimitava.
9 **blur.** Macchia, visione indistinta.
10 **were bewailing a corpse.** Stavano facendo un lamento funebre.
11 **owls.** Gufi.
12 **Punjab.** Regione dell'India nord-occidentale.
13 **decked it.** La rivestì.
14 **dome.** Cupola.

He had seen the quatrain on the tomb of a Deccan[15] king and regarded it as profound philosophy – he always held pathos to be profound. The secret understanding of the heart! He repeated the phrase with tears in his eyes, and as he did so one of the pillars[16] of the mosque seemed to quiver. It swayed[17] in the gloom and detached itself. Belief in ghosts ran in his blood, but he sat firm. Another pillar moved, a third, and then an Englishwoman stepped out into the moonlight. Suddenly he was furiously angry and shouted: 'Madam! Madam! Madam!'

'Oh! Oh!' the woman gasped[18].

'Madam, this is a mosque, you have no right here at all; you should have taken off your shoes; this is a holy place for Moslems.'

'I have taken them off.'

'You have?'

'I left them at the entrance.'

'Then I ask your pardon.'

Still startled[19], the woman moved out, keeping the ablution-tank between them. He called after her, 'I am truly sorry for speaking.'

'Yes, I was right, was I not? If I remove my shoes, I am allowed?'

'Of course, but so few ladies take the trouble, especially if thinking no one is there to see.'

'That makes no difference. God is here.'

'Madam!'

'Please let me go.'

'Oh, can I do you some service now or at any time?'

'No, thank you, really none – good night.'

'May I know your name?'

She was now in the shadow of the gateway, so that he could not see her face, but she saw his, and she said with a change of voice, 'Mrs Moore.'

'Mrs–' Advancing, he found that she was old. A fabric[20] bigger than the mosque fell to pieces, and he did not know whether he was glad or sorry. She was older than Hamidullah Begum, with a red face and white hair. Her voice had deceived him.

'Mrs Moore, I am afraid I startled you. I shall tell our community – my friends – about you. That God is here – very good, very fine indeed. I think you are newly arrived in India.'

'Yes – how did you know?'

'By the way you address me. No, but can I call you a carriage?'

'I have only come from the Club. They are doing a play that I have seen in London, and it was so hot.'

'What was the name of the play?'

'*Cousin Kate*.'

'I think you ought not to walk at night alone, Mrs Moore. There are bad characters about and leopards may come across from the Marabar Hills. Snakes also.'

She exclaimed; she had forgotten the snakes.

'For example, a six-spot beetle[21],' he continued. 'You pick it up, it bites, you die.'

'But you walk alone yourself.'

'Oh, I am used to it.'

'Used to snakes?'

They both laughed. 'I'm a doctor,' he said. 'Snakes don't dare bite me.' They sat down side by side in the entrance, and slipped on their evening shoes. 'Please may I ask you a

15 **Deccan.** La penisola indiana a sud del fiume Narbada.
16 **pillars.** Colonne.
17 **swayed.** Oscillò.
18 **gasped.** Disse ansando.
19 **startled.** Spaventata.
20 **fabric.** Edificio.
21 **six-spot beetle.** Scarabeo a sei macchie.

2 Judy Davis, Alec Guinness and Victor Banerjee in a scene from the film 'A Passage to India', directed by David Lean, 1984.

question now? Why do you come to India at this time of year, just as the cold weather is ending?'

'I intended to start earlier, but there was an unavoidable delay.'

'It will soon be so unhealthy for you! And why ever do you come to Chandrapore?'

'To visit my son. He is the City Magistrate here.'

'Oh no, excuse me, that is quite impossible. Our City Magistrate's name is Mr Heaslop. I know him intimately.'

'He's my son all the same,' she said, smiling.

'But, Mrs Moore, how can he be?'

'I was married twice.'

'Yes, now I see, and your first husband died.'

'He did, and so did my second husband.'

'Then we are in the same box[22],' he said cryptically[23]. 'Then is the City Magistrate the entire of your family now?'

'No, there are the younger ones – Ralph and Stella in England.'

'And the gentleman here, is he Ralph and Stella's half-brother?'

'Quite right.'

'Mrs Moore, this is all extremely strange, because like yourself I have also two sons and a daughter. Is not this the same box with a vengeance[24]?'

'What are their names? Not also Ronny, Ralph and Stella, surely?'

The suggestion delighted him. 'No, indeed. How funny it sounds! Their names are quite different and will surprise you. Listen, please. I am about to tell you my children's names. The first is called Ahmed, the second is called Karim, the third – she is the eldest – Jamila. Three children are enough. Do not you agree with me?'

'I do.'

They were both silent for a little, thinking of their respective families. She sighed and rose to go.

'Would you care to see over the Minto Hospital one morning?' he inquired. 'I have nothing else to offer at Chandrapore.'

'Thank you, I have seen it already, or I should have liked to come with you very much.'

'I suppose the Civil Surgeon took you.'

'Yes, and Mrs Callendar.'

His voice altered. 'Ah! A very charming lady.'

'Possibly, when one knows her better.'

'What? What? You didn't like her?'

'She was certainly intending to be kind, but I did not find her exactly charming.'

He burst out with: 'She has just taken my tonga[25] without my permission – do you call that being charming? – and Major Callendar interrupts me night after night from where I am dining with my friends and I go at once, breaking up a most pleasant entertainment, and he is not there and not even a message. Is this charming, pray[26]? But what does it matter? I can do nothing and he knows it. I am just a subordinate, my time is of no value, the veranda is good enough for an Indian, yes, yes, let him stand, and Mrs Callendar takes my carriage and cuts me dead[27]...'

She listened.

He was excited partly by his wrongs, but much more by the knowledge that someone sympathized with them. It was this that led him to repeat, exaggerate, contradict. She had proved her sympathy by criticizing her fellow country-woman to him, but even earlier he

22 **we are in the same box.** Sta per *"we are in the same boat"* (Abbiamo tante cose in comune).
23 **cryptically.** Enigmaticamente.
24 **with a vengeance.** Abbondantemente.
25 **tonga.** Veicolo leggero a due ruote trainato da cavalli.
26 **pray.** Di grazia.
27 **cuts me dead.** Fa come se io non esistessi.

1 Another scene from the film.

had known. The flame that not even beauty can nourish was springing up[28], and though his words were querulous[29] his heart began to glow secretly. Presently it burst into speech.

'You understand me, you know what I feel. Oh, if others resembled you!'

Rather surprised, she replied: 'I don't think I understand people very well. I only know whether I like or dislike them.'

'Then you are an Oriental.'

She accepted his escort back to the Club, and said at the gate that she wished she was a member, so that she could have asked him in.

'Indians are not allowed into the Chandrapore Club even as guests,' he said simply. He did not expatiate[30] on his wrongs now, being happy. As he strolled[31] downhill beneath the lovely moon, and again saw the lovely mosque, he seemed to own the land as much as anyone owned it. What did it matter if a few flabby[32] Hindus had preceded him there, and a few chilly[33] English succeeded?

28 **was springing up.** Stava crescendo.
29 **querulous.** Lamentose.
30 **expatiate.** Dilungarsi.
31 **strolled.** Passeggiava.
32 **flabby.** Fiacchi, deboli.
33 **chilly.** Freddi.

COMPREHENSION

2 READ the extract up to line 37 and focus on the elements that make up the setting. Write down the details concerning:

1 the time;
2 the place;
3 the architecture;
4 the elements belonging to the natural landscape;
5 the feelings the place arouses in Aziz.

3 READ the passage to the end and answer the following questions.

1 How does Aziz react when Mrs Moore suddenly appears?
2 What makes him change his attitude?
3 What is the subject of the conversation?
4 Do the two characters have anything in common? Collect information about:
- their age;
- nationality;
- family;
- religion;
- relationship with the community they belong to.

ANALYSIS

4 IDENTIFY the kind of narrator used. From whose point of view is the scene described?

5 GO THROUGH the dialogue again and focus on the way Forster portrays the two characters showing them both as individuals and as members of a group and therefore conditioned by their own culture.

1 Trace the emotional changes Aziz and Mrs Moore undergo during their conversation.
2 Find the references to the two characters' cultural background and say if they appear to be conditioned by it in their behaviour or not.
3 Underline in the text the sentences expressing the understanding reached by these two dissimilar people.
4 Which aspects of their personality bring them close to each other?

6 READ the Persian inscription Aziz would like on his own tomb carefully. It introduces a theme Forster will develop in the novel. Identify it.

7 THE UNDERSTANDING between Aziz and Mrs Moore does not exclude all those elements that will threaten personal relations later in the novel. Find the details connected with the ideas of:

1 the hostility of nature;
2 the conflict between cultures;
3 difficulty of communication.

8 DISCUSS the insight the passage gives into the relationship between the British and the Indians. Does the narrator seem to suggest that there are many more divisions in India than the Empire can be held responsible for?

ESAME DI STATO Terza Prova

9 TYPE B. Explain how Forster deals with the theme of 'Only connect...' (the words chosen for the epigraph of *Howards End*) in *A Passage to India*. What kind of connections does he present and what characters try or manage to connect? Write ten to twelve lines.

☞ Exam Reference pag. 355

TEXT BANK 55: *A PORTRAIT OF THE ARTIST AS A YOUNG MAN*
TEXT BANK 56: *DUBLINERS*
TEXT BANK 57: *ULYSSES*

James Joyce and Dublin

He uses Dubliners because is the city were he was born.

James Joyce's life

James Joyce (1882–1941) was born in Dublin in 1882, one of a large family. He was educated at Jesuit schools, including University College, Dublin. Here he studied the French, Italian and German languages and literatures and English literature, and graduated in modern languages in 1902. Those movements, whether political or literary, which had as their objective the freeing of Ireland from English dominance, held very little attraction for him. His interest was for a broader European culture, and this led him to begin to think of himself as a European rather than an Irishman. His attitude contrasted greatly with that of his literary contemporaries, like W.B. Yeats, who were leading the Irish Literary Revival and were trying to rediscover the Irish Celtic identity by referring back to the past in order to create a national conscience. Joyce, on the contrary, believed that the only way to increase Ireland's awareness was by offering a realistic portrait of its life from a European, cosmopolitan viewpoint.

He established himself on the Continent and spent some time in Paris, but his mother's fatal illness in 1903 brought him back to Dublin. In June 1904 he met and fell in love with Nora Barnacle, a twenty-year-old girl who was working as a chambermaid in a hotel. They had their first date on 16th June, which was to become the 'Bloomsday' of *Ulysses*. In October they moved to Italy, settling in Trieste where Joyce began teaching English and became friends with Italo Svevo. Joyce and Nora had two children, Giorgio and Lucia, and eventually married in 1931. The years in Trieste were difficult, filled with disappointment and financial problems; in fact, Joyce was in trouble with publishers and printers from early on due to supposedly obscene elements in his prose, and as a consequence of this the first of his works to appear in book form was thirty-six short poems, *Chamber Music* (1907). *Dubliners* (1914), a collection of short stories all about Dublin and Dublin life, was completed in 1905 but only published on the eve of the First World War. In 1916 Joyce published *A Portrait of the Artist as a Young Man*, his semi-autobiographical novel. In 1914 Joyce wrote most of his naturalistic drama *Exiles*, and in the following year he moved to Zurich together with his family, since his position as a British national in Austrian-occupied Trieste left him no alternative.

Although *Dubliners* and *A Portrait* had established him as a writer, they had done little to alleviate his financial difficulties. In 1917 he received the first of several anonymous donations which enabled him to continue writing *Ulysses*, which was published in Paris in 1922. In March 1923 he began to work on what was eventually to be published as *Finnegans Wake* in 1939. Hitler's advances in Europe forced the Joyces to flee from France to neutral Switzerland, where the writer died in January 1941.

1 Jacques-Emile Blanche, *Portrait of James Joyce*, 1935. National Portrait Gallery, London.

Ordinary Dublin

Though Joyce went into voluntary exile at the age of twenty-two, he set all his works in Ireland and mostly in the city of Dublin. His effort was to give a realistic portrait of the life of ordinary people doing ordinary things and living ordinary lives. By portraying these ordinary Dubliners, he succeeded in representing the whole of man's mental, emotional and biological reality, fusing it with the cultural heritage of modern civilisation and with the reality of the natural world around him.

Style and technique

He uses different point of view x every character.

For Joyce, the artist's task was to render life objectively in order to give back to the readers a true image of it. As his works did not have to express the author's point of view, Joyce used different points of view and narrative techniques appropriate to the several characters portrayed.

His style, technique and language developed from the realism and the disciplined prose of *Dubliners*, through an exploration of the characters' impressions and points of view, through the use of free direct speech and the epiphany, to the interior monologue with two levels of narration – a device used to give a realistic framework to each character's formless thoughts – up to the extreme interior monologue. So language broke down into a succession of words without punctuation or grammatical connections, into infinite puns, and reality became the place of psychological projections, of symbolic archetypes and cultural knowledge.

1 **REVISE your knowledge about James Joyce's life and works by using these hints:**

1. the education he received;
2. his interests;
3. what became the 'Bloomsday' in his novel *Ulysses*;
4. where he settled;
5. his most important works;
6. why he chose Dublin as the setting of all his works;
7. the main features of his style.

Dubliners (1914)

The origin of the collection

It was the oppressive effects of religious, political, cultural and economic forces on the lives of lower-middle-class Dubliners that provided Joyce with the raw material for a psychologically realistic picture of Dubliners as afflicted people.

Dubliners consists of fifteen short stories; they all lack obvious action, but they disclose human situations and moments of intensity and lead to a moral, social or spiritual revelation. The opening stories deal with childhood and youth in Dublin; the others, advancing in time and expanding in scope, concern the middle years of characters and their social, political or religious affairs. The stories are arranged into four groups, as Joyce explained: 'My intention was to write a chapter of the moral history of my country and I chose Dublin for the scene because that city seemed to me the centre of paralysis. I have tried to present it to the indifferent public under four of its aspects: childhood, adolescence, maturity and public life. The stories are arranged in this order.'

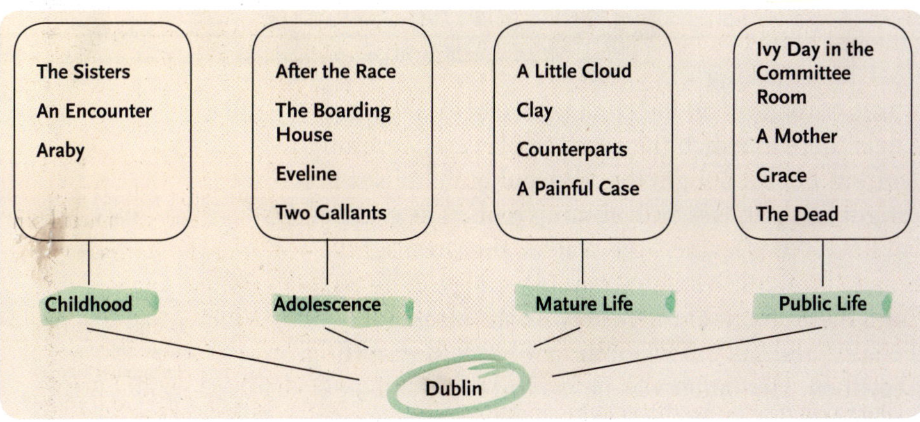

The last story, 'The Dead', can be considered Joyce's first masterpiece. It stands out from the other fourteen stories of the collection because, however similar in theme, it is denser, more elaborate and more remarkable; it is at once the summary and climax of *Dubliners*. What holds all these stories together is a particular structure and the presence of the same themes, symbols and narrative techniques.

The use of epiphany

The description in each story is realistic and extremely concise, with an abundance of external details, even the most unpleasant and depressing ones. The use of realism is mixed with symbolism, since external details generally have a deeper meaning. In fact, Joyce thought his function was to take the reader beyond the usual aspects of life and he employed a peculiar technique to reach his purpose, the 'epiphany', that is, 'the sudden spiritual manifestation' caused by a trivial gesture, an external object or a banal situation, which is used to lead the character to a sudden self-realisation about himself/herself or about the reality surrounding him/her. Indeed, this motif is central to the collection, since it is revelation, not the plot, that drives the stories. Since these epiphanic moments are unveiled by both the character who experiences them and by the reader who perceives them, the whole process, in turn, becomes an epiphany for him. *Dubliners* can therefore be seen as a sequence of multiple epiphanies that offer a revelation of the city in its intellectual, moral and spiritual paralysis.

A pervasive theme: paralysis

The paralysis of Dublin which Joyce wanted to portray is both physical, resulting from external forces, and moral, linked to religion, politics and culture. Joyce's Dubliners either accept their condition because they are not aware of it or because they lack the courage to break the chains that bind them. All the Dubliners are spiritually weak and scared people, they are to some extent slaves of their familiar, moral, cultural, religious and political lives. However, the moral centre of *Dubliners* is not paralysis alone but its revelation to its victims. Coming to awareness or self-realisation marks the climax of these stories, since knowing oneself is a basis of morality if not morality itself. However, Joyce is far from being didactic and appears to be detached. The main theme is the failure to find a way out of 'paralysis'. The opposite of paralysis is 'escape' and its consequent failure. It originates from an impulse caused by a sense of enclosure that many characters experience, but none of them succeeds in overcoming; they live as exiles at home, unable to cut the bonds that tie them to their own world.

Narrative techniques

The omniscient narrator and the single point of view are rejected: each story is told from the perspective of a character. Narrated monologue in the form of free direct speech, and often of free direct thought, is widely used; it consists of the direct presentation of the protagonist's thoughts, through limited mediation on the part of the narrator, and allows the reader to acquire direct knowledge of the character. The linguistic register is varied, since the language used in all the stories suits the age, the social class and the role of the characters.

2 **ANSWER the following questions to organise your knowledge about *Dubliners*.**

1 How are the stories arranged?
2 What sort of description is employed in each story?
3 What is meant by the term 'epiphany'?
4 What are the main themes of the stories?
5 Which techniques are employed by Joyce to tell his stories?

7.15 James Joyce and Dublin

WARM-UP

1 **DISCUSS** in pairs. Do you remember the first time you fell in love? How did your parents react to it? Recollect your experience focusing on your feelings, fears and desires and how they alternated inside you.

Eveline

James Joyce

Dubliners (1914)
'Eveline'

This short story describes the life of a nineteen-year-old girl who has the opportunity to change her routine life but she is unable to leave her familiar community in Dublin.

1 Sackville Street and O'Connell Bridge, Dublin, ca 1899.

7.1

She sat at the window watching the evening invade the avenue. Her head was leaned[1] against the window curtains, and in her nostrils[2] was the odour of dusty cretonne[3]. She was tired.

Few people passed. The man out of the last house passed on his way home; she heard his footsteps clacking along the concrete pavement[4] and afterwards crunching on the cinder path[5] before the new red houses. One time there used to be a field there in which they used to play every evening with other people's children. Then a man from Belfast bought the field and built houses in it – not like their little brown houses, but bright brick houses with shining roofs. The children of the avenue used to play together in that field – the Devines, the Waters, the Dunns, little Keogh the cripple[6], she and her brothers and sisters. Ernest, however, never played: he was too grown up. Her father used often to hunt them in out of the field[7] with his blackthorn stick[8]; but usually little Keogh used to keep nix[9] and call out when he saw her father coming. Still they seemed to have been rather happy then. Her father was not so bad then; and besides, her mother was alive. That was a long time ago; she and her brothers and sisters were all grown up; her mother was dead. Tizzie Dunn was dead, too, and the Waters had gone back to England. Everything changes. Now she was going to go away like the others, to leave her home.

Home! She looked round the room, reviewing all its familiar objects which she had dusted once a week for so many years, wondering where on earth all the dust came from. Perhaps she would never see again those familiar objects from which she had never dreamed of being divided. And yet during all those years she had never found out the name of the priest whose yellowing photograph hung on the wall above the broken harmonium[10] beside the coloured print of the promises made to Blessed Margaret Mary Alacoque[11]. He had been a school friend of her father. Whenever he showed the photograph to a visitor her father used to pass it with a casual word:

'He is in Melbourne now.'

She had consented to go away, to leave her home. Was that wise? She tried to weigh[12] each side of the question. In her home anyway she had shelter[13] and food; she had those whom she had known all her life about her. Of course she had to work hard, both in the house and at business. What would they say of her in the Stores[14] when they found out that she had run away with a fellow? Say[15] she was a fool, perhaps; and her place would be filled

1 **leaned.** Appoggiata.
2 **nostrils.** Narici.
3 **dusty cretonne.** Cretonne polveroso.
4 **clacking ... pavement.** Risuonare sul marciapiede di cemento.
5 **crunching ... path.** Cigolare sul sentiero di detriti.
6 **the cripple.** Lo storpio.
7 **hunt ... field.** Cacciarli fuori dal campo.
8 **blackthorn stick.** Bastone di pruno.
9 **used ... nix.** Faceva da palo.
10 **broken harmonium.** Armonium rotto.
11 **Blessed ... Alacoque.** Beata Margherita Maria Alacoque (monaca francese, 1647–90, che aveva avuto visioni del Sacro Cuore di Gesù).
12 **tried to weigh.** Cercava di valutare.
13 **shelter.** Protezione.
14 **the Stores.** Il negozio in cui Eveline lavorava.
15 **Say.** Avrebbero detto.

up[16] by advertisement. Miss Gavan would be glad. She had always had an edge on her[17], especially whenever there were people listening.

'Miss Hill, don't you see these ladies are waiting?'

'Look lively[18], Miss Hill, please.'

She would not cry many tears at leaving the Stores.

But in her new home, in a distant unknown country, it would not be like that. Then she would be married – she, Eveline. People would treat her with respect then. She would not be treated as her mother had been. Even now, though she was over nineteen, she sometimes felt herself in danger of her father's violence. She knew it was that that had given her the palpitations. When they were growing up he had never gone for her[19], like he used to go for Harry and Ernest, because she was a girl; but latterly[20] he had begun to threaten her and say what he would do to her only for her dead mother's sake[21]. And now she had nobody to protect her, Ernest was dead and Harry, who was in the church decorating business[22], was nearly always down somewhere in the country[23]. Besides, the invariable squabble[24] for money on Saturday nights had begun to weary her unspeakably. She always gave her entire wages – seven shillings – and Harry always sent up what he could, but the trouble was to get any money from her father. He said she used to squander[25] the money, that she had no head, that he wasn't going to give her his hard-earned money to throw about the streets, and much more, for he was usually fairly bad[26] on Saturday night. In the end he would give her the money and ask her had she any intention of buying Sunday's dinner. Then she had to rush out[27] as quickly as she could and do her marketing[28], holding her black leather purse tightly in her hand as she elbowed her way[29] through the crowds and returning home late under her load of provisions[30]. She had hard work to keep the house together and to see that the two young children who had been left to her charge went to school regularly and got their meals regularly. It was hard work – a hard life – but now that she was about to leave it she did not find it a wholly undesirable life.

She was about to explore another life with Frank. Frank was very kind, manly, open-hearted. She was to go away with him by the night-boat to be his wife and to live with him in Buenos Aires, where he had a home waiting for her. How well she remembered the first time she had seen him; he was lodging[31] in a house on the main road where she used to visit. It seemed a few weeks ago. He was standing at the gate, his peaked cap pushed back[32] on his head and his hair tumbled forward over a face of bronze[33]. Then they had come to know each other. He used to meet her outside the Stores every evening and see her home. He took her to see *The Bohemian Girl*[34] and she felt elated[35] as she sat in an unaccustomed[36] part of the theatre with him. He was awfully fond of music and sang a little. People knew that they were courting[37], and, when he sang about the lass[38] that loves a sailor, she always felt pleasantly confused. He used to call her Poppens out of fun[39]. First of all it had been an excitement for her to have a fellow and then she had begun to like him. He had tales of distant countries. He had started as a deck boy at a pound a month on a ship of the Allan Line[40] going out to Canada. He told her the names of the ships he had been on and the names of the different services. He had sailed through the Straits of Magellan and he told her stories of the terrible Patagonians. He had fallen on his feet[41] in Buenos Aires, he said, and had come over to the old country just for a holiday. Of course, her father had found out the affair and had forbidden her to have anything to say to him.

'I know these sailor chaps,' he said.

One day he had quarrelled with Frank, and after that she had to meet her lover secretly.

The evening deepened[42] in the avenue. The white of two letters in her lap[43] grew indistinct. One was to Harry; the other was to her father. Ernest had been her favourite, but she liked Harry too. Her father was becoming old lately, she noticed; he would miss her.

16 **would ... up.** Sarebbe stato rimpiazzato.
17 **She ... her.** L'aveva sempre presa di punta.
18 **Look lively.** Si muova.
19 **When ... her.** Quando erano piccoli, non se l'era mai presa con lei.
20 **latterly.** Poi.
21 **her ... sake.** La memoria di sua madre morta.
22 **was in the church ... business.** Lavorava come decoratore di chiese.
23 **down ... country.** Da qualche parte del paese (fuori da Dublino).
24 **invariable squabble.** Eterne discussioni.
25 **to squander.** Dilapidare.
26 **fairly bad.** Ubriaco.
27 **to rush out.** Precipitarsi fuori.
28 **and do her marketing.** A fare la spesa.
29 **elbowed her way.** Si apriva un varco.
30 **load of provisions.** Carico di provviste.
31 **lodging.** Alloggiando.
32 **his ... pushed back.** Il suo cappello a visiera gettato all'indietro.
33 **his hair ... bronze.** I capelli che ricadevano sul volto abbronzato.
34 ***The Bohemien Girl.*** *La ragazza di Boemia* o *La Zingara*, opera in tre atti del compositore irlandese Michael W. Balfe (1808–70).
35 **she felt elated.** Si sentì felice.
36 **unaccustomed.** Non abituale.
37 **they were courting.** Uscivano insieme.
38 **the lass.** La ragazza.
39 **Poppens out of fun.** Bambolina tanto per ridere.
40 **Allan Line.** Compagnia Allan (con sede a Liverpool).
41 **had ... feet.** Gli era andata bene.
42 **deepened.** Si incupiva.
43 **lap.** Grembo.

7.15 James Joyce and Dublin

Sometimes he could be very nice. Not long before, when she had been laid up[44] for a day, he had read her out a ghost story and made toast[45] for her at the fire. Another day, when their mother was alive, they had all gone for a picnic to the Hill of Howth. She remembered her father putting on her mother's bonnet[46] to make the children laugh.

Her time was running out, but she continued to sit by the window, leaning her head against the window curtain, inhaling the odour of dusty cretonne. Down far in the avenue she could hear a street organ playing. She knew the air. Strange that it should come that very night to remind her of the promise to her mother, her promise to keep the home together as long as she could. She remembered the last night of her mother's illness; she was again in the close, dark room at the other side of the hall and outside she heard a melancholy air of Italy. The organ-player had been ordered to go away and given sixpence. She remembered her father strutting back[47] into the sick-room saying:

'Damned Italians[48]! coming over here!'

As she mused[49] the pitiful vision of her mother's life laid its spell on the very quick of her being[50] – that life of commonplace[51] sacrifices closing in final craziness. She trembled as she heard again her mother's voice saying constantly with foolish insistence:

'Derevaun Seraun[52]! Derevaun Seraun!'

She stood up in a sudden impulse of terror. Escape! She must escape! Frank would save her. He would give her life, perhaps love, too. But she wanted to live. Why should she be unhappy? She had a right to happiness. Frank would take her in his arms, fold her in his arms. He would save her.

1 Amedeo Modigliani, *Portrait of Thora Klinckowstrom*, 1919. Private Collection.

44 **she had ... up.** Era rimasta a letto ammalata.
45 **made toast.** Abbrustolito il pane.
46 **bonnet.** Cappellino.
47 **strutting back.** Rientrare impettito.
48 **Damned Italians.** Dannati italiani (l'imprecazione del padre risuona come una presa in giro poiché l'immigrazione italiana in Irlanda era modesta).
49 **she mused.** Meditava.
50 **laid ... being.** Tesseva un incantesimo nel suo intimo.
51 **commonplace.** Banali.
52 **Derevaun Seraun.** La fine del piacere è il dolore (frase in Gaelico).

COMPREHENSION (I)

2 READ lines 1–111 and do the following activities.

1. Write a heading for this section.
2. Find out: the setting in time and place; how the interior of the room is described; how Eveline feels.
3. Say:
   - **A** what the world outside her window makes her think about;
   - **B** what role Eveline's father played in the past;
   - **C** what objects the girl notices in her room and what feature these things share;
   - **D** how Eveline considers her job and what she thinks about her superior;
   - **E** what she has agreed to become and why;
   - **F** who Frank is and what his job is;
   - **G** what the girl remembers about him;
   - **H** whether Eveline's father accepted the young man;
   - **I** what the sound of the organ reminds her of;
   - **J** how she sees her mother's life and what her last words really meant for Eveline;
   - **K** what Eveline is caught between throughout this part;
   - **L** what the girl experiences and what she perceives as her fate if she remains in Ireland;
   - **M** what Frank represents to her.

ANALYSIS (I)

3 FOCUS on lines 93–111.
The access to the character's consciousness is provided by Joyce through the technique of 'epiphany', that is, 'the sudden revelation of a hidden reality' through 'casual words or events'.

1. Explain what revelation the girl has.
2. The miserable life of Eveline's mother has influenced her decisions. Sum up the different phases of the girl's decisions up to the final failure.

7.2

She stood among the swaying[53] crowd in the station at the North Wall[54]. He held her hand and she knew that he was speaking to her, saying something about the passage over and over again. The station was full of soldiers with brown baggages. Through the wide doors of the sheds[55] she caught a glimpse[56] of the black mass of the boat, lying in beside the quay wall[57], with illumined portholes[58]. She answered nothing. She felt her cheek pale and cold and, out of a maze of distress[59], she prayed to God to direct her, to show her what was her duty. The boat blew a long mournful whistle[60] into the mist. If she went, tomorrow she would be on the sea with Frank, steaming[61] towards Buenos Aires. Their passage had been booked. Could she still draw back after all he had done for her? Her distress awoke a nausea in her body and she kept moving her lips in silent fervent prayer.

A bell clanged[62] upon her heart. She felt him seize her hand: 'Come!'

All the seas of the world tumbled about[63] her heart. He was drawing her into them: he would drown her. She gripped with both hands at the iron railing.

'Come!'

No! No! No! It was impossible. Her hands clutched the iron in frenzy[64]. Amid the seas she sent a cry of anguish.

'Eveline! Evvy!'

He rushed beyond the barrier and called to her to follow. He was shouted at to go on, but he still called to her. She set her white face to him, passive, like a helpless animal. Her eyes gave him no sign of love or farewell or recognition.

53 **swaying.** Ondeggiante.
54 **North Wall.** La stazione di North Wall (sul fiume Liffey).
55 **sheds.** Capannoni.
56 **caught a glimpse of.** Intravide.
57 **quay wall.** Murata della banchina.
58 **portholes.** Oblò.
59 **out of a maze of distress.** In un groviglio di angoscia.
60 **mournful whistle.** Sibilo lamentoso.
61 **steaming.** Diretta.
62 **clanged.** Risuonò.
63 **tumbled about.** Si abbatterono su.
64 **clutched ... frenzy.** Afferrarono con violenza la ringhiera.

COMPREHENSION (II)

4 READ up to the end of the story and do the following activities.

1 Write a heading for this section.
2 Now answer the questions.
  A Where is Eveline?
  B Who surrounds her?
  C What happens when she is on the quayside?
  D How does her relationship with Frank turn out to be?
  E What does she understand about her affections for her family and surroundings?
  F What is the effect produced by the last words of the story?

6 FOCUS on the character of Eveline.

1 Does Joyce introduce her in a traditional way? What is the reader obliged to do?
2 How does she appear? Why?
3 Most of the story takes place in Eveline's mind; however, her thoughts are not arranged in chronological order and they wander from past to present and future. Fill in the table below with her most important thoughts.

Past	Present	Future

4 Point out the most important images connected with these time references.
5 A simile is used in line 130 to describe Eveline. Identify it. What does it add to the description of her character?

7 DISCUSS. 'Eveline' is a story of paralysis. Has this state of mind been determined by her conflict between love and duty or familiar boredom and a courageous break?

ANALYSIS (II)

5 CONCENTRATE on the narrator. Note down:

1 what kind of narrator it is;
2 whose point of view is adopted;
3 what technique is employed to give voice to Eveline's thoughts.

ESAME DI STATO Terza Prova

8 TYPE B. In not more than ten to twelve lines, clarify the most important stylistic devices and the themes of *Dubliners* present in 'Eveline'.

Exam Reference pag. 355

YOUR TURN

9 DISCUSS with the rest of the class. Does 'Eveline' still exist in our contemporary society?

ART LAB 13: *BLOOMSBURY ARTISTS*

Virginia Woolf and 'moments of being'

Virginia Woolf's life

1 Portrait of Virginia Woolf by George Charles Beresford, 1902.

Virginia Woolf (1882–1941) was born in 1882. Her father, Leslie Stephen, was an eminent Victorian man of letters. Thus, she grew up in a literary and intellectual atmosphere and, apart from a few courses at King's College, London, her education consisted of private Greek lessons and, above all, access to her father's library, where she read whatever she liked. She spent her summers at St Ives, Cornwall, and the sea remained central to her art as a symbol. For Virginia, water represented two things: on the one hand, it represented what is harmonious and feminine; on the other hand, it stood for the possibility of the resolution of intolerable conflicts in death. The death of her mother in 1895, when Virginia was only thirteen, affected her deeply and brought about her first nervous breakdown. She began to revolt against her father's tyrannical character and his idealisation of the domesticated woman.

It was only with her father's death in 1904 that Virginia began her own literary life and career. She decided to move to Bloomsbury and, together with her sister, the artist Vanessa Bell, she became a member of the Bloomsbury Group, which included the avant-garde of early 20th-century London. In 1912 Virginia married Leonard Woolf, and in 1915 she published *The Voyage Out*, her first novel, which still followed a traditional pattern. At this time, she entered a nursing home and attempted suicide by taking drugs. In 1925 the novel *Mrs Dalloway* appeared, in which Virginia successfully experimented with new narrative techniques, followed by *To the Lighthouse* (1927) and *Orlando* (1928), which was devoted to Vita Sackville-West, a novelist and biographer with whom she had an intense relationship. She was also a very talented literary critic and a brilliant essayist, as her volume of literary essays, *The Common Reader* (1925), shows.

In October 1929 she delivered two lectures at Cambridge which later became *A Room of One's Own* (1929), a work of great impact on the feminist movement of the 1960s and 1970s, in which she explored many issues connected with women and writing but above all insisted on the inseparable link between economic independence and artistic independence. In 1929 she began to work on her novel *The Waves* (1931), in which she seemed to recognise that there was a link between her creative process and her illness. The Second World War increased her anxiety and fears. She became haunted by the terror of losing her mind. Finally she could stand it no longer and drowned herself in the River Ouse. She was fifty-nine.

A modernist novelist

Woolf was interested in giving voice to the complex inner world of feeling and memory and conceived the human personality as a continuous shift of impressions and emotions. So the events that traditionally made up a story were no longer important for her; what mattered was the impression they made on the characters who experienced them. In her novels the omniscient narrator disappeared and the point of view shifted inside the characters' minds through flashbacks, associations of ideas and momentary impressions presented as a continuous flux. Her contribution to modernism is made clear by a statement contained in her essay *Modern Fiction* (1919): '*Examine for a moment an ordinary mind on an ordinary day. The mind receives a myriad impressions – trivial, fantastic, evanescent, or engraved with the sharpness of steel. From all sides they come, an incessant shower of innumerable atoms; and as they fall, as they shape themselves into the life of Monday or Tuesday, the accent falls differently from of old; the moment of importance came not here but there; so that, if a writer were a free man and not a slave, if he could write what he chose, not what he must, if he could base his work upon his own feeling and not upon convention, there would be no plot, no comedy, no tragedy, no love interest or catastrophe in the accepted style, and perhaps not a single button sewn on as the Bond Street tailors would have it. Life is not a series of gig-lamps symmetrically arranged; life is a luminous halo, a semi-transparent envelope surrounding us from the beginning to the end.*'

Woolf vs Joyce

As for James Joyce, also for Virginia Woolf, subjective reality came to be identified with the technique called 'stream of consciousness'. However, differently from Joyce's characters, who show their thoughts directly through interior monologue and sometimes in an incoherent and syntactically unorthodox way, Woolf never lets her characters' thoughts flow without control, and she maintains logical and grammatical organisation. Her technique is based on the fusion of streams of thought into a third-person, past tense narrative. Thus she gives the impression of simultaneous connections between the inner and the outer world, the past and the present, speech and silence.

Similar to Joyce's 'epiphanies' are Woolf's 'moments of being', rare moments of insight during the characters' daily life when they can see reality behind appearances. While Joyce was more interested in language experimentation and worked through the accumulation of details, Woolf's use of words was almost poetic, allusive and emotional. Fluidity is the quality of the language which flows following the most intricate thoughts and stretches to express the most intimate feelings.

1 ANSWER the following questions about Virginia Woolf.

1. What kind of education did Woolf receive?
2. How did her life change after her father's death?
3. How did she contribute to the modernist novel?
4. What aspects of tradition did she reject?
5. How did her narrative technique differ from Joyce's?

Mrs Dalloway (1925)

2 A scene from the film 'Mrs Dalloway', directed by Marleen Gorris, 1997.

The story

At 10 a.m. on a Wednesday early in June of 1923, Clarissa Dalloway, the protagonist of the novel, goes to Bond Street to buy some flowers for a party she is giving that evening at her house. While she is in the flower shop, a car drives noisily past and shifts the attention to the street, where Septimus and Lucrezia Warren Smith are walking; he is an estate agent's clerk and shell-shocked veteran of the First World War, she is an Italian girl. Septimus's mental disorder has necessitated the calling in of doctors, first Dr Holmes, and now Sir William Bradshaw, a famous nerve specialist. Clarissa walks back home and there she receives an unexpected visit from Peter Walsh, the man she used to love in her youth. He then leaves Clarissa's house and goes to Regent's Park, where he catches a glimpse of the Warren Smiths, who are going to Sir William Bradshaw's for an interview. The interview lasts three-quarters of an hour and results in Sir William's arranging for Septimus to go into one of his clinics. At 6 p.m. Septimus jumps out of the window of his room, and the ambulance carrying his body passes by Peter Walsh, who is going back to his hotel. All the characters who have been in some way important during the day are present at Clarissa's party. The Bradshaws arrive and Clarissa hears from them of Septimus's death, with which she feels a strong connection.

The setting

Mrs Dalloway takes place on a single ordinary day in June of 1923, and it follows the protagonist through a very small area of London, from the morning to the evening of the day on which she gives a large formal party. Unlike Joyce, Woolf does not elevate her characters to the level of myth, but shows their deep humanity behind their social mask. They all enjoy the sights and sounds in London, its parks, its changing life, its flavour. Moreover, through what she defined as the 'tunnelling technique', she allows the reader to experience the characters' recollection of their past, thus providing a sense of their background and personal history. Clarissa Dalloway's party is the climax of the novel and unifies the narrative by gathering all the people Clarissa thinks about during the day.

A changing society

The novel also deals with the way people react to new situations, and provides insight into some of the most significant changes in the social life of the time, for instance the spread of newspapers, the increasing use of cars and planes, new standards in marital relationships. Woolf also adopts a motif, the striking of Big Ben and of clocks in general, which acts at the same time as a structural connection and symbol. The insistent chiming of clocks reminds the reader of the temporal grid which organises the narrative, of the passing of the time of life and of its flowing into death. So life expresses itself in moments of vision which are at the same time objective (the clocks, the streets, the cars, the flowers) and yet subjectively creative, since they are recreated every moment by active consciousness.

The connection between Clarissa and Septimus

Clarissa is a London society lady of fifty-one, the wife of a Conservative MP who has extremely conventional views on politics and women's rights. The influence of a possessive father, the frustration of a genuine love, the need to refuse Peter Walsh, a man who would force her to share everything – all this has weakened her emotional self and split her in two. She is characterised by opposing feelings: her need for freedom and independence and her class consciousness. Her life appears to be an effort towards order and peace, an attempt to overcome her weakness and sense of failure. She needs to make her home perfect to become an ideal human being, but she imposes severe restrictions on her spontaneous feelings.

Septimus Warren Smith is an extremely sensitive man who can suddenly fall prey to panic and fear or feelings of guilt. The cause of these feelings lies in the death of his best friend, Evans, during the war. He is a 'shell-shock' case, one of the victims of industrialised warfare. After the war, Septimus is haunted by the spectre of Evans; he suffers from headaches and insomnia. He cannot stand the idea of having a child; he is sexually impotent.

The plot does not connect Clarissa and Septimus, apart from the news of his death at her party. However, they are similar in many respects: their response to experience is always given in physical terms, and they depend upon their partners for stability and protection. There is a fundamental difference, however, which has given rise to the theory that Septimus is Clarissa's double. He is not always able to distinguish between his personal response and external reality. His psychic paralysis leads him to suicide, whereas Clarissa never loses her awareness of the outside world as something external to herself. In the end, she recognises her deceptions, accepts the idea of death, and is prepared to go on.

2 ANSWER the following questions about *Mrs Dalloway*.

1. What is the setting in time and place?
2. What is the role of clocks in the novel?
3. What kind of woman is Clarissa Dalloway?
4. What is the function of the character of Septimus?
5. How are the two protagonists of the novel connected?

7.16 Virginia Woolf and 'moments of being'

WARM-UP

1 **DISCUSS** in pairs the difference between the external and the internal portions of the self. What do they consist of? Complete the spider charts.

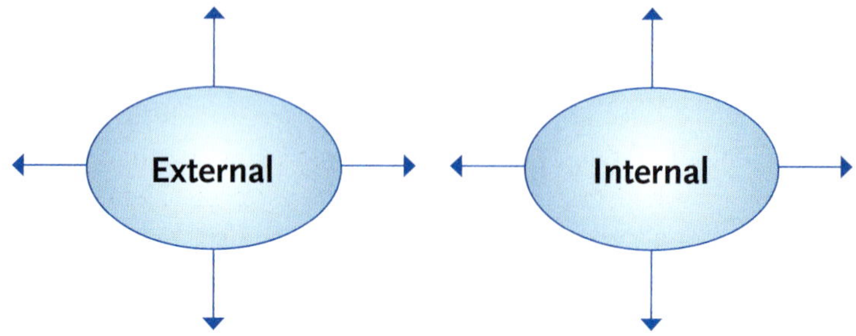

Clarissa and Septimus

Virginia Woolf

Mrs Dalloway (1925)
Part I

'Mrs Dalloway said she would buy the flowers herself'; this is how the novel opens, and in the following thirty pages Clarissa Dalloway is seen walking through Green Park, then up Bond Street to the flower shop. She perceives sights and sounds, thinking and remembering. Just before reaching the shop, Clarissa is thinking about the relationship between her seventeen-year-old daughter, Elizabeth, and her disagreeable history teacher – whom Mrs Dalloway feels to be her enemy. This thought arouses a feeling of hatred in her, which she calls 'this brutal monster'.

1 Vanessa Bell, *Still Life on the Corner of a Mantelpiece*, 1914. Tate Gallery, London.

7.3

Nonsense, nonsense! she cried to herself, pushing through the swing doors of Mulberry's the florists.

She advanced, light, tall, very upright, to be greeted at once by button-faced[1] Miss Pym, whose hands were always bright red, as if they had been stood in cold water with the flowers.

There were flowers: delphiniums, sweet peas, bunches of lilac; and carnations[2], masses of carnations. There were roses; there were irises. Ah yes – so she breathed in the earthy garden sweet smell as she stood talking to Miss Pym who owed her help, and thought her kind, for kind she had been years ago; very kind, but she looked older, this year, turning her head from side to side among the irises and roses and nodding tufts[3] of lilac with her eyes half closed, snuffing in[4], after the street uproar[5], the delicious scent[6], the exquisite coolness. And then, opening her eyes, how fresh, like frilled linen clean from a laundry laid in wicker trays[7], the roses looked; and dark and prim[8] the red carnations, holding their heads up; and all the sweet peas spreading in their bowls, tinged violet, snow white, pale – as if it were the evening and girls in muslin frocks[9] came out to pick sweet peas and roses after the superb summer's day, with its almost blue-black sky, its delphiniums, its carnations, its arum lilies was over; and it was the moment between six and seven when every flower – roses, carnations, irises, lilac – glows; white, violet, red, deep orange; every flower seems to burn by itself, softly, purely in the misty beds; and how she loved the grey white moths spinning[10] in and out, over the cherry pie, over the evening primroses[11]!

And as she began to go with Miss Pym from jar[12] to jar, choosing, nonsense, nonsense, she said to herself, more and more gently, as if this beauty, this scent, this colour, and Miss Pym liking her, trusting her, were a wave which she let flow over her and surmount that hatred, that monster, surmount it all; and it lifted her up and up when – oh! a pistol shot in the street outside!

'Dear, those motor cars,' said Miss Pym, going to the window to look, and coming back and smiling apologetically[13] with her hands full of sweet peas, as if those motor cars, those tyres[14] of motor cars, were all *her* fault.

The violent explosion which made Mrs Dalloway jump and Miss Pym go to the window

1 **button-faced.** Dalla faccia inespressiva.
2 **delphiniums ... and carnations.** Delfini, piselli odorosi, mazzi di lillà e garofani.
3 **nodding tufts.** Ciuffi svolazzanti, ondeggianti.
4 **snuffing in.** Inalando.
5 **uproar.** Frastuono.
6 **scent.** Profumo.
7 **frilled ... wicker trays.** Biancheria increspata, lavata di fresco e riposta in ceste di vimini.
8 **prim.** Cerimoniosi.
9 **muslin frocks.** Abiti di mussola.
10 **moths spinning.** Falene che giravano in tondo.
11 **primroses.** Primule.
12 **jar.** Vaso.
13 **apologetically.** A mo' di scusa.
14 **tyres.** Pneumatici.

and apologise came from a motor car which had drawn to the side of the pavement[15] precisely opposite Mulberry's shop window. Passers-by who, of course, stopped and stared, had just time to see a face of the very greatest importance against the dove-grey upholstery[16], before a male hand drew the blind[17] and there was nothing to be seen except a square of dove grey.

Yet rumours[18] were at once in circulation from the middle of Bond Street to Oxford Street on one side, to Atkinson's scent shop on the other, passing invisibly, inaudibly, like a cloud, swift[19], veil-like upon hills, falling indeed with something of a cloud's sudden sobriety and stillness upon faces which a second before had been utterly disorderly[20]. But now mystery had brushed them with her wing[21]; they had heard the voice of authority; the spirit of religion was abroad[22] with her eyes bandaged tight and her lips gaping wide[23]. But nobody knew whose face had been seen. Was it the Prince of Wales's, the Queen's, the Prime Minister's? Whose face was it? Nobody knew.

Edgar J. Watkiss, with his roll of lead piping[24] round his arm, said audibly, humorously of course: 'The Proime Minister's kyar[25].'

Septimus Warren Smith, who found himself unable to pass, heard him.

Septimus Warren Smith, aged about thirty, pale-faced, beak-nosed[26], wearing brown shoes and a shabby[27] overcoat, with hazel eyes[28] which had that look of apprehension in them which makes complete strangers apprehensive too. The world has raised its whip[29], where will it descend?

Everything had come to a standstill[30]. The throb[31] of the motor engines sounded like a pulse irregularly drumming through an entire body. The sun became extraordinarily hot because the motor car had stopped outside Mulberry's shop window; old ladies on the tops of omnibuses spread their black parasols; here a green, here a red parasol opened with a little pop. Mrs Dalloway, coming to the window with her arms full of sweet peas, looked out with her little pink face pursed in enquiry[32]. Every one looked at the motor car. Septimus looked. Boys on bicycles sprang off[33]. Traffic accumulated. And there the motor car stood, with drawn blinds, and upon them a curious pattern like a tree, Septimus thought, and this gradual drawing together of everything to one centre before his eyes, as if some horror had come almost to the surface and was about to burst into flames, terrified him. The world wavered and quivered[34] and threatened to burst into flames. It is I who am blocking the way, he thought. Was he not being looked at and pointed at; was he not weighted there, rooted to the pavement, for a purpose? But for what purpose?

'Let us go on, Septimus.' said his wife, a little woman, with large eyes in a sallow[35] pointed face; an Italian girl.

But Lucrezia herself could not help looking at the motor car and the tree pattern on the blinds. Was it the Queen in there – the Queen going shopping?

The chauffeur, who had been opening something, turning something, shutting something, got on to the box[36].

'Come on,' said Lucrezia.

But her husband, for they had been married four, five years now, jumped, started, and said, 'All right!' angrily, as if she had interrupted him.

People must notice; people must see. People, she thought, looking at the crowd staring at the motor car; the English people, with their children and their horses and their clothes, which she admired in a way; but they were 'people' now, because Septimus had said, 'I will kill myself'; an awful thing to say. Suppose they had heard him? She looked at the crowd. Help, help! she wanted to cry out to butchers' boys and women. Help! Only last autumn she and Septimus had stood on the Embankment wrapped in the same cloak[37] and, Septimus reading a paper instead of talking, she had snatched it from him[38] and laughed in the old

15 **had drawn ... the pavement.** S'era accostata al marciapiede.
16 **the dove-grey upholstery.** Imbottitura grigio tortora.
17 **the blind.** La tendina.
18 **rumours.** Dicerie.
19 **swift.** Veloce.
20 **disorderly.** Turbolente.
21 **brushed ... wing.** Li aveva sfiorati con la sua ala.
22 **was abroad.** Era in giro, aleggiava.
23 **with her eyes ... gaping wide.** Con gli occhi bendati stretti e la bocca spalancata.
24 **roll of lead piping.** Rotolo di tubatura di piombo.
25 **The Proime Minister's kyar.** La macchina del Primo Ministro (la pronuncia viene storpiata).
26 **beak-nosed.** Con il naso aquilino.
27 **shabby.** Trasandato.
28 **hazel eyes.** Occhi color nocciola.
29 **whip.** Frusta.
30 **had come to a standstill.** Si era fermata.
31 **throb.** Battito.
32 **pursed in enquiry.** Corrugato per la curiosità (cioè nello sforzo per vedere).
33 **sprang off.** Sfrecciavano.
34 **wavered and quivered.** Ondeggiava e tremava.
35 **sallow.** Terreo.
36 **box.** Volante.
37 **on the Embankment ... in the same cloak.** Sulla riva del Tamigi avvolti nello stesso mantello.
38 **she had snatched it from him.** Glielo aveva strappato di mano.

7.16 Virginia Woolf and 'moments of being'

man's face who saw them! But failure one conceals[39]. She must take him away into some park.

'Now we will cross,' she said.

She had a right to his arm, though it was without feeling. He would give her, who was so simple, so impulsive, only twenty-four, without friends in England, who had left Italy for his sake, a piece of bone.

39 **conceals.** Cela, nasconde.

1 Meryl Streep as Clarissa Vaughan, a modern-day version of Clarissa Dalloway, in the film 'The Hours', directed by Stephen Daldry, 2002.

COMPREHENSION

2 **READ the passage. It can be divided into five sections. Write a caption to describe the content of each section.**

3 **AS YOU READ, make notes about the setting in time and place.**

4 **FOCUS on the flower shop in lines 1–20. Underline the phrases referring to the florist and then fill in the table below about the flowers.**

Flowers	Their colours

5 **WRITE DOWN the main event in the passage. Then, in your own words, summarise the various people's reactions to it.**

6 **CONSIDER how the car is described and list the inferences people make about who may be in the car.**

7 **COLLECT the details concerning the description of Septimus Warren Smith and his wife in lines 45–86. Fill in the table below.**

	Septimus Warren Smith	His wife
Age		
Nationality		
Appearance		
Attitude		

8 **UNDERLINE the words and phrases which give insight into a changing society.**

ANALYSIS

9 **TICK as appropriate to say how the narrative is organised.**
- ☐ Following chronological order.
- ☐ Respecting a logical pattern.
- ☐ Piece by piece, through association.

10 **SAY what kind of narrator and point of view Woolf uses. What is the author's aim in using this method?**

11 **LOOK at the diagram below.** How much action can you find in the passage? What does the extract mostly consist of?

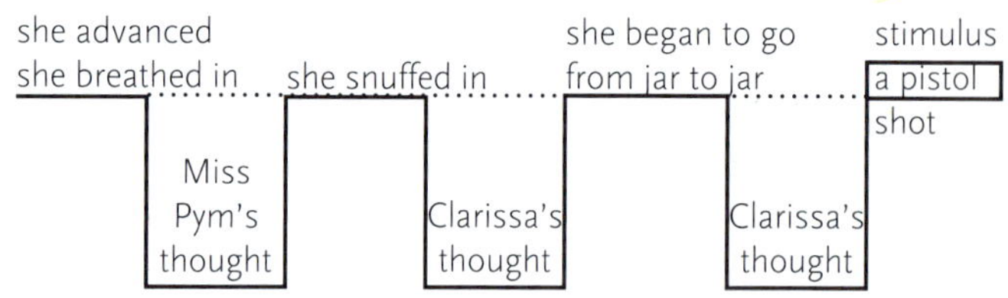

12 **POINT OUT the main aspects of Clarissa's personality.**

13 **FOCUS on lines 45–75 and list the sentences that convey the idea that Septimus is in the grip of a very serious mental illness. Match them with the corresponding states of mind:**
- Alienation
- Panic
- Feelings of guilt
- Terror and anger
- Madness

14 **THE CHARACTERS' RESPONSE to the world around them is both emotional and physical. Go through lines 1–68 and find words and phrases referring to sensory experience.** Which sense is predominant?

ESAME DI STATO **Terza Prova**

15 **TYPE B. Compare Woolf's way of writing with that of James Joyce as regards analogies and differences (10–12 lines).**

Exam Reference pag. 355

7.17 Cultural Issues

Moments of being: one moment in time

Virginia Woolf first mentioned moments of being in her essay 'A Sketch of the Past', where she wondered why some moments are so powerful and memorable – even if the events themselves are unimportant – that they can be vividly recalled, while other events are easily forgotten. She concluded that there are two kinds of experiences: moments of being and moments of non-being.

Moments of being are acts experienced intensely and with awareness; instead, moments of non-being appear to be moments that the individual is not consciously aware of even as he or she experiences them. It is not the nature of the actions that separates moments of being from moments of non-being. One activity is not more extraordinary than the other. Instead, it is the intensity of feeling, one's consciousness of the experience, that separates the two moments. Woolf asserted that a moment of being is a moment when an individual is fully conscious of his experience, a moment when he is not only aware of himself but catches a glimpse of his connection to a larger pattern hidden behind the opaque surface of daily life.

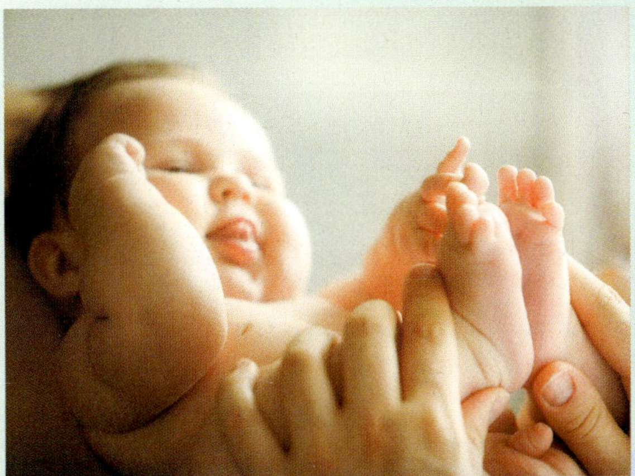

1 **ANSWER** the following questions.

1. Do you ever try to find a moment in your day when you can do what you want, think or simply do nothing?
2. How do you identify 'your' moment and make it count?
3. Can you take an ordinary event and turn it into something extraordinary or more meaningful?
4. Have you ever experienced a 'moment of being', that is, one of those rare moments in which you suddenly seem to understand reality beyond its surface?

7.17 Moments of being: one moment in time

The Hours (1998)

The Hours was written by Michael Cunningham (1952–), an American author who was brought up in Los Angeles and lives in New York. He has published the following novels: *Golden States* (1984), *A Home at the End of the World* (1990), *Flesh and Blood* (1995), *The Hours* (1998), *Specimen Days* (2005) and *By Nightfall* (2010).

In *The Hours*, his Pulitzer Prize-winning novel, Michael Cunningham revisits Virginia Woolf's *Mrs Dalloway*, bringing the past into the present for contemporary readers. The book presents three generations of women affected by Virginia Woolf's novel. The first is Woolf herself in 1923, writing and coping with her own mental illness. The second is Mrs Brown, the wife of a World War II veteran, who is reading *Mrs Dalloway* in 1949 in Los Angeles as she makes plans for her husband's birthday party. The third is Clarissa Vaughan, who, in 2001, is arranging a party to celebrate her good friend and former lover Richard. He is a poet who has just received an important literary award and who is dying of AIDS. All three characters live the situations experienced by Woolf's character Clarissa Dalloway in *Mrs Dalloway*.

Mrs Brown

Michael Cunningham

The Hours (1998)

Chapter 1

These lines deal with one of the characters, Mrs Laura Brown, caught in the act of reading the opening page of Virginia Woolf's novel Mrs Dalloway.

1 Nicole Kidman as Virginia Woolf in the film 'The Hours', directed by Stephen Daldry, 2002.

7.4

Mrs Dalloway said she would buy the flowers herself.

For Lucy had her work cut out for her[1]. The doors would have to be taken off their hinges[2]; Rumpelmayer's men were coming. And then, thought Clarissa Dalloway, what a morning – fresh as if issued[3] to children on a beach.

It is Los Angeles. It is 1949.

Laura Brown is trying to lose herself[4]. No, that's not it exactly – she is trying to keep herself[5] by gaining entry[6] into a parallel world. She lays the book face down on her chest[7]. Already her bedroom (no, *their* bedroom) feels more densely inhabited, more actual, because a character named Mrs Dalloway is on her way to buy flowers. Laura glances at the clock on the nightstand[8]. It's well past seven. Why did she buy this clock, this hideous thing, with its square green face in a rectangular black Bakelite sarcophagus – how could she ever have thought it was smart? She should not be permitting herself to read, not this morning of all mornings; not on Dan's birthday. She should be out of bed, showered and dressed, fixing[9] breakfast for Dan and Richie. She can hear them downstairs, her husband making his own breakfast, ministering[10] to Richie. She should be there, shouldn't she? She should be standing before the stove in her new robe[11], full of simple, encouraging talk. Still, when she opened her eyes a few minutes ago (after seven already!) – when she still half inhabited her dream, some sort of pulsating machinery in the remote distance, a steady pounding[12] like a gigantic mechanical heart, which seemed to be drawing nearer[13] – she felt the dank[14] sensation around her, the nowhere feeling, and knew it was going to be a difficult day. She knew she was going to have trouble believing in herself, in the rooms of her house, and when she glanced over at this new book on her nightstand, stacked atop the one[15] she finished last night, she reached for it automatically, as if reading were the singular and obvious first task of the day, the only viable[16] way to negotiate the transit from sleep to obligation. Because she is pregnant, she is allowed these lapses[17]. She is allowed, for now, to read unreasonably, to linger[18] in bed, to cry or grow furious over nothing.

1. **had ... for her.** Aveva troppo lavoro.
2. **to be ... hinges.** Essere tolte dai cardini.
3. **issued.** Donata.
4. **to lose herself.** Perdersi.
5. **to keep herself.** Rimanere in sé.
6. **gaining entry.** Entrando.
7. **chest.** Petto.
8. **nightstand.** Comodino.
9. **fixing.** A preparare.
10. **ministering.** Dà da mangiare.
11. **robe.** Vestaglia.
12. **a steady pounding.** Un battito costante.
13. **be drawing nearer.** Avvicinarsi.
14. **dank.** Umida.
15. **stacked atop the one.** Impilato sull'altro.
16. **viable.** Praticabile.
17. **lapses.** Errori.
18. **linger.** Oziare.

She will make up for breakfast by baking Dan a perfect birthday cake; by ironing the good cloth; by setting a big bouquet of flowers (roses?) in the middle of the table, and surrounding it with gifts. That should compensate, shouldn't it?

She will read one more page. One more page, to calm and locate herself, then she'll get out of bed.

What a lark[19]*! What a plunge*[20]*! For so it had always seemed to her, when, with a little squeak*[21] *of the hinges, which she could hear now, she had burst open the French windows and plunged at Bourton into the open air. How fresh, how calm, stiller than this of course, the air was in the early morning; like the flap*[22] *of a wave; the kiss of a wave; chill and sharp and yet (for a girl of eighteen as she then was) solemn, feeling as she did, standing there at the open window, that something awful was about to happen;* [...]

She inhales[23] deeply. It is so beautiful; it is so much more than... well, than almost anything, really. In another world, she might have spent her whole life reading. But this is the new world, the rescued world – there's not much room for idleness[24].

19 **lark.** Spasso.
20 **plunge.** Salto.
21 **squeak.** Cigolio.
22 **flap.** Flusso.
23 **inhales.** Inspira.
24 **idleness.** Inattività.

COMPREHENSION

1 READ the extract and make notes about:

1 where Laura is;
2 what time it is exactly;
3 how she feels and why;
4 what she should be doing;
5 what she had realised after waking up;
6 what Laura's present condition is;
7 what she is going to do to make up for her delay in getting up;
8 what the new world is like.

ANALYSIS

2 EXPLAIN in what sense Laura Brown fights the pressures of society's expectations.

3 POINT OUT the features of Cunningham's style.

IELTS Speaking – Part 1

4 INTERVIEW. Answer these questions.

1 Do you like reading? Do you sometimes read in English? Do you find it easy?
2 Do you read for pleasure or for study/work? Why/Why not?
3 Did your parents/grandparents read to you when you were a child?
4 Do you consider the act of listening to stories important for children?

2 Poster for 'The Hours', directed by Stephen Daldry, 2002.

Exam Description

What is there in the *Prova Orale*?	The *Prova Orale* consists of three parts: 1. the presentation of a cross-curricular project by the candidate using visual aids and/or PowerPoint; 2. an oral interview on all the subjects studied during the student's last school year; 3. a brief discussion of the candidate's written papers.
What do I have to focus on?	The emphasis is on content, communication and presentation skills, as well as fluency.
How much time am I allowed?	About an hour.

Process language
Prova Orale – Part 1

Starting your talk
- The topic of my talk is ...
- I would like to talk about ...
- What I'm going to talk about is ...
- My choice of topic is ...

Stating intentions
- My purpose/aim is to show ...
- My main objective/goal is ...
- I've chosen this topic because ...

ESAME DI STATO Prova Orale – Part 1

5 SURF the net to find information about the novel *The Hours* and the film version directed by Stephen Daldry in 2002. Create your own PowerPoint presentation using the material from the Internet.

6 SHOW your presentation to the class.

Exam Reference pag. 355

ESAME DI STATO

7 Prova Orale – Part 2

Test yourself

Tip

The second part of the oral test at the *Esame di Stato* revolves around set questions. When you prepare for the *colloquio*, remember that each question asks you to carry out specific tasks. The question might:

- contain words which require a definition;
- raise established views on a specific issue;
- require examples to illustrate specific points;
- imply the knowledge of crucial technical terms;
- be linked to a specific historical context which needs to be introduced in order to develop the topic.

1 **HIGHLIGHT the main features of the Edwardian Age.**

2 **EXPLAIN the causes and effects of World War I.**

3 **EXPLAIN what traditional features were subverted by modern poets.**

4 **USE the quotations to discuss different attitudes to war. Identify their authors.**

If I should die, think only this of me:
That there's some corner of a foreign field
That is for ever England.

My friend, you would not tell with such high zest
To children ardent for some desperate glory,
The old Lie:

Too long a sacrifice
Can make a stone of the heart.
O when may it suffice?

5 **IDENTIFY the literary device used by T.S. Eliot in these lines. Provide a definition and explain its meaning in the context of the lines.**

A crowd flowed over London Bridge, so many,
I had not thought death had undone so many.
Sighs, short and infrequent, were exhaled,
And each man fixed his eyes before his feet.

6 **EXPLAIN the new concept of history expressed in the following lines.**

There I saw one I knew, and stopped him, crying: 'Stetson!
'You who were with me in the ships at Mylae!

7 **DISCUSS how the Irish Question has been presented in poetry and film.**

8 **EXPLAIN Sigmund Freud's theory of the human psyche. Use this image for help.**

9 **HIGHLIGHT the differences between the traditional and the modern novel. Organise your knowledge in a table like the one below.**

	Traditional novel	Modern novel
Main theme		
Novelist's task		
Treatment of time		
Narrative technique		

10 **POINT OUT the modern elements in Joseph Conrad's novel *Heart of Darkness*.**

11 **READ this short extract from E.M. Forster's novel *A Passage to India* and answer the following questions.**

1 What attributes does Forster assign to India?
2 What themes did he develop in this vast physical and mental landscape?

How can the mind take hold of such a country? Generations of invaders have tried, but they remain in exile. The important towns they build are only retreats, their quarrels the malaise of men who cannot find their way home. India knows of their trouble. She knows of the whole world's trouble, to its uttermost depth. She calls 'Come' through her hundred mouths, through objects ridiculous and august. But come to what? She has never defined. She is not a promise, only an appeal.

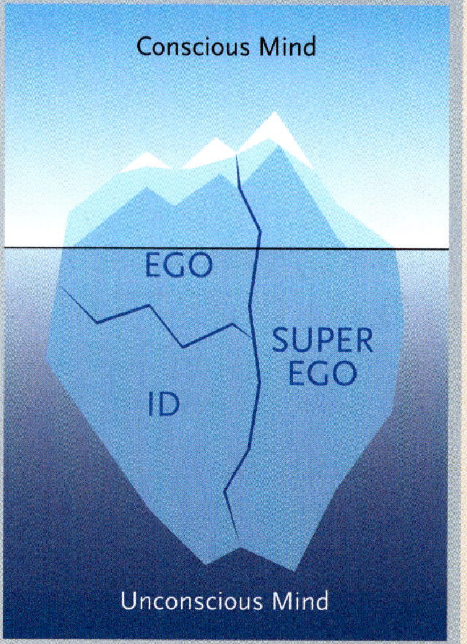

12 **DESCRIBE James Joyce's use of the 'epiphany' and the interior monologue.**

13 **EXPLAIN how Virginia Woolf's technique differs from Joyce's.**

A New World Order

Specification 8 | Homepage

Top News

1929
The Wall Street Crash

1945
The end of World War II

Top Issue

Imagining the future

Most Popular News

1925
The Great Gatsby is published

Spotlight

The United Nations Organisation is founded

The Arts

Edward Hopper: the poetry of silence

Cinema

See World War II on screen

Mapping History

The Blitz

EXPLORE THE CULTURE

Literature | History | Society | The Arts | Two Films About... | Cultural Issues

8.1 **History**

The USA in the first decades of the 20th century

WARM-UP

1 **MATCH** these key terms about this historical period to the correct definition. Then link each term to a picture (1–7).

1 Prohibition
2 Muckraking
3 The Red Scare
4 The Jazz Age
5 The Dust Bowl
6 Black Thursday
7 The New Deal

A President Roosevelt's economic programme.
B The stock market crash.
C A ban on alcohol.
D A period when jazz music and dance became popular also called the 'Roaring Twenties'.
E Investigative journalism.
F A period of severe dust storms, causing major ecological and agricultural damage.
G Fear of communism.

2

2 Walter Thornton tries to sell a luxury roadster after the 1929 stock market crash, in New York City.

2 **READ** the Q&A text.

1

1 Dust storm approaching Stratford, Texas, 1935. Photo courtesy of NOAA George E. Marsh Album.

Q What were the contradictions within American society at the end of the 19th century and in the early 20th century?

A By the end of the 19th century, the United States had become the richest country in the world, with its economic power based on agricultural prosperity, massive industrial output, the rich mineral resources available and the rise of 'trusts', the huge corporations of firms in the same trade, which gradually came to dominate the market. The economic boom, however, had not prevented the spread of poverty. In the industrial areas of the North – like the metropolises of Chicago, Pittsburgh, New York and Boston – workers lived in dirty, overcrowded slums and toiled long hours for low wages.

Q How were these contradictions brought to light?

A In the early years of the 20th century, a large number of national problems, like the conditions of life in the city slums or corruption in the government, were brought to light by books and articles written by investigative journalists called 'muckrakers'. Their reports shocked most of the American people, who started to think that the government should take action to eliminate the problems of society through reform.

Q Who became president at the beginning of the century?

A The 19th-century belief in *laissez-faire* was supplanted by 'progressivism', which found a leader in the Republican Theodore Roosevelt (1858–1919), who became the 26th president of the United States, from 1901–09. An 'expansionist', he made the navy stronger, insisted on the regulation of trusts and carried out a moderate programme of social legislation.

3

Q What was the US foreign policy?

A The United States had pursued a policy of imperial expansion. In 1867 America had bought Alaska from Russia, and from 1895 attention was focused on the Spanish colony of Cuba, where the United States supported the Cuban rebellion against Spain. The Spanish-American War (1898) ended with the defeat of Spain, and the United States acquired most of its overseas empire, including Cuba, Puerto Rico and the Philippines.

Q Why did the US grant independence to all dominions except for Cuba?

A Imperialism, however, was regarded as contrary to the democratic values of the American constitution. This is why the United States gradually began to grant independence to their dominions except for Cuba, where they maintained the control of Guantanamo Bay to build a large naval base.

3 *Freedom from Want*, one of four paintings by Norman Rockwell inspired by Franklin Roosevelt's 'Four Freedoms' speech. Norman Rockwell Museum, Stockbridge, Massachusetts, US.

4 A protest against Prohibition, 1931.

5 Poster in favour of the freeing of Sacco and Vanzetti, anarchists who were sentenced to death for homicide in the 1920s.

6 Cover of 'Life' magazine from the 1920s. Library of Congress, Washington DC, US.

7 A photo by Lewis Hine, famed 'muckraking' photojournalist, for the National Child Labor Committee. 'A little spinner in the Mollohan Mills, Newberry, South Carolina, 1908.'

Q How did America get involved in World War I?

A When the First World War broke out, America initially held to its policy of isolationism. However, after the British liner the 'Lusitania' was sunk, the United States joined the war (1917), considering it a 'war to end all wars'. When the armistice was signed in 1918, American President Woodrow Wilson (1856–1924) proposed 'Fourteen Points' to work out the peace treaty and devised a plan to set up the 'League of Nations'.

Q Why were the 1920s a good time for many Americans?

A During the 1920s, confidence in the US was high and the economy grew quickly. This was due to many reasons: vast resources were invested to create new industries; there was little competition from Europe; the population was increasing; and taxes on profits and industries were cut by the Republican government. However, large groups, like miners, farmers and urban industrial workers, remained untouched by wealth.

Q Why were the 1920s known as the 'Jazz Age' or the 'Roaring Twenties'?

A Because the economic prosperity in large parts of the US gave rise to a feeling of euphoria and experimentation in music, with new styles like jazz, as well as dance and fashion.

Q What was the so-called 'Red Scare'?

A The Twenties were also characterised by reactionary attitudes such as the fear of socialism, or the so-called 'Red Scare', which led to the imprisonment and persecution of political activists with radical or labour backgrounds. The most famous case, on a charge of murder, was that of the Italian anarchists Sacco and Vanzetti, whose execution in 1927 divided American public opinion.

Q Why was the manufacture of alcohol prohibited?

A A revival of puritanical attitudes brought about the Eighteenth Amendment to the Constitution, which prohibited the manufacture, consumption and import of alcohol. This drastic step, which was taken to fight the problem of alcohol addiction among the poor, encouraged the illegal traffic of 'bootleggers', who imported or produced liquor illegally, and increased the phenomenon of gangsterism.

Q What happened in 1929?

A In 1929 the American stock market collapsed. It was known as the 'Great Wall Street Crash', since Wall Street was (and is) the home of the New York Stock Exchange. It marked the end of the prosperous Twenties and the beginning of the Great Depression.

Q What were the consequences of the Wall Street Crash?

A Thousands of businessmen were ruined, and millions of common people who had invested their savings in shares found themselves facing debt and ruin. Factories shut down, banks crashed, goods were produced but no longer sold.

(Continued on page 282)

8.1 The USA in the first decades of the 20th century

Nearly 8 million Americans were unemployed in the 1930s and spent hours queuing in 'breadlines', where they received free rations of food.

Q What about the situation in agriculture?

A The 'Dust Bowl' was the name given to an ecological disaster: the frenzied wheat boom of the 'Great Plow-Up' was followed by a decade-long drought in the 1930s, during which winds nearly swept away the breadbasket of the nation. The agricultural devastation helped to lengthen the Depression, the effects of which were felt worldwide.

Q How did Roosevelt's 'New Deal' try to solve the problem of unemployment?

A In 1932 Franklin D. Roosevelt (1882–1945) became president and promised the Americans a 'New Deal' of reforms. The three aims of the New Deal were 'relief, recovery, reform'. The federal government spent billions of dollars on relief for the unemployed, on public works and on the conservation of natural resources.

3 **IN PAIRS** cover the answers (As) in the text. Take turns asking and answering the questions (Qs) using the information that you have read.

1 Crowd gathering in Wall Street after the stock market crash of October 1929.

2 Wall Street today.

Milestones

1929, the Wall Street Crash

The American economy had been enjoying a boom throughout the Roaring Twenties. The introduction of consumer goods not only created more jobs but also helped the American economy rise. However, the benefits of economic growth were not equally distributed. There was a widening gap between the rich and the poor: 42% of all Americans were living below the poverty line, and new immigrants and farmers never enjoyed the boom.

A 1919 act had placed a high tariff on foreign imports into America, and European nations had responded with their own high tariffs on American exports. The demand for goods decreased both because of a reduction in the volume of international trade and in consumerism. All this caused a fall in prices and industrial instability.

However, these were not the whole of America's problems. Better technology was increasing supply, but the demand for food was not increasing at the same rate. Therefore, prices fell and farmers' incomes dropped. The Dust Bowl had also hit the farming industry hard. Poor farming methods and bad soil erosion had left the ground infertile. Winds swept the dust all over, especially around Oklahoma, where farmers were struggling to survive.

The inflated economy of the 1920s had also led to inflated share prices. In the autumn of 1929 some businessmen decided that the market could not remain so artificially high and decided to sell their shares. This led to a massive panic and the selling of shares. On Thursday, 24th October 1929, Wall Street crashed. This day became known as 'Black Thursday' as it sealed America's fall into depression.

Insights

The history of Wall Street

Wall Street can trace its name back to 1644, when a wall was built on the lower end of Manhattan Island by the Dutch to protect it against British attacks. This wall lasted a good while, until 1685, when a new street was built. The British called it Wall Street.

In 1792 New York City's population was about 34,000. Much of Manhattan had just been rebuilt with brick buildings after the devastating Great Fire of 1776, and Wall Street was New York's centre of commerce. There were warehouses for furs, coffee and tea, and other goods from all over the world. Wealthy businessmen, along with their ordinary trade, would sell lottery tickets, bonds and shares of stocks in the new banks that were forming. The most popular trading and speculating was in treasury bonds issued by the new Bank of the United States. The first organised stock exchange was created in 1792 when, under a tree in Castle Garden (now called Battery Park), some financial leaders signed an agreement of rules, regulations and fees. Then, in a building at 22 Wall Street, securities were sold every day beginning at noon, to whoever offered the most. The seller paid the Exchange a commission on each stock or bond sold.

They originally called this group the 'Stock Exchange Office'. This was a very exclusive organisation, allowing only the elite of New York's financial community to join. In 1863, the Board changed its name to the New York Stock Exchange and moved into the majestic building at the corner of Wall Street and Broad Street, where the exchange still does business today.

TEXT BANK 59: *LANGSTON HUGHES*

A new generation of American writers

1 Jasper Johns, *Three Flags*, 1958. Whitney Museum, New York.

WARM-UP

1 DISCUSS. What does the phrase 'Lost Generation' make you think of? What do you think was 'lost'?

2 READ the text and write a heading to each paragraph in the spaces provided.

1 ....

The First World War swept away the influences of Europe and New England that had dominated American letters since colonial times and created a new generation of intellectuals.

2 ....

The so-called 'Jazz Age' of the 1920s was full of excitement and contradictions due to the radical changes in the way people behaved and thought. The new manners were a reaction against the strict Puritan morality of the previous century. They were especially evident among young people, with their roaring cars and new daring dances like the Charleston. In spite of Prohibition, parties and cocktails became smart and women began to wear their hair and dresses short. The new novelists dealt with the Jazz Age, sometimes, as in the case of F. Scott Fitzgerald, describing its glamour with the awareness of the moral desert it was hiding. More often, however, they openly attacked the rich businessmen and the superficial hedonism of the period, as in the case of the naturalistic novels of Sherwood Anderson (1876–1941) and Sinclair Lewis (1885–1951).

3 ....

Many disillusioned writers and intellectuals emigrated to Europe, chiefly to Paris because of its stimulating atmosphere for the arts. These writers and artists were usually referred to as the 'Lost Generation', after a term coined by the American experimental writer Gertrude Stein (1874–1946), whose salon in Paris was an important meeting point for young talent. World War I seemed to have destroyed the idea that if you acted virtuously, good things would happen. Many good, young men went to war and died, or returned home physically or mentally wounded, and their faith in the moral ideals that had earlier given them hope, was 'lost'. Among the writers of the Lost Generation were F. Scott Fitzgerald, Ernest Hemingway and the poet and novelist E.E. Cummings (1894–1962).

4 ....

In poetry, the 1920s were an age of experimentation. Apart from a few traditionalists like Robert Frost (1874–1963), American poets wrote in free verse, abandoning conventional verse forms, experimenting with syntax, punctuation and typography. Some of them, like Carl Sandburg (1878–1967), used the rhythms of everyday speech.

5 ....

A remarkable contribution to the writing of the age was given by the sudden awakening and flourishing of Afro-American literature, which found its fullest expression in the Harlem Renaissance. In the Twenties, Harlem became the 'Black Paris', where every sort of amusement could be found. Afro-American artists, like Langston Hughes (1902–67) and Zora Neale Hurston (1901–60), had to face the problem of self-definition through a new evaluation of their past. The moment was favourable since the Western world was discovering black art in all its forms. Jazz, in particular, helped to make black music famous all over the world; it represented a revolution in the aesthetics of musical rhythm and a rebellion against the conventions of the past in favour of a new scale of values.

6 ....

As a consequence of the Great Depression, much of the literature of the Thirties and Forties was characterised by a resentful and bitter pessimism. A new social consciousness, a feeling of political responsibility and a deeper interest in psychology, pervaded the works of the period. Having discovered their true national idiom during the Twenties, American writers of the 1940s focused on refining their literary techniques. Among the greatest writers of this decade were John Steinbeck (1902–68) and the regionalist William Faulkner (1897–1962), who depicted the violent reality of the American South. Experimentation characterised the work of John Dos Passos (1896–1970), who drew inspiration from the cinema, advertising, newspapers and songs to recreate the atmosphere of the nation during the period between the wars.

3 COMPLETE the following activities about this period in American literature.

1. Describe the mood of the Jazz Age.
2. Explain why the writers who emigrated to Europe were called the 'Lost Generation'.
3. Point out the contributions to the modernisation of American literature as regards style.
4. Explain how black artists contributed to the development of an American literary identity.
5. Say what mood characterised the literature of the 1930s and 1940s.

8.3 **Literature**

Francis Scott Fitzgerald: the writer of the Jazz Age

F. Scott Fitzgerald's life

Francis Scott Fitzgerald (1896–1940) was born in 1896 in Minnesota. He studied in a Catholic boarding school in New Jersey, and, in 1913, he went to Princeton University to complete his education. There he began to write and had the opportunity to associate with rich young men. When the United States entered the First World War, he joined the army and began to work on his first novel, which he published in 1920 with the title *This Side of Paradise*. The book gave a forceful picture of the lifestyle of young people in the Roaring Twenties, and also captured the sense of loss and emptiness hiding behind the cult of wealth and materialism. The novel was an extraordinary success; it gave him fame and money. In 1921 he married Zelda Sayre. They settled in New York, where they led a glamorous life spending a lot of money on amusements, parties, alcohol and drugs. Fitzgerald worked hard to keep up with their expensive lifestyle. In 1922 he published *Tales of the Jazz Age* and the novel *The Beautiful and Damned*, where he portrayed the hedonism, corruption and loss of ideals of the Lost Generation. In the same year, the Fitzgeralds went to Europe and spent some time in Paris and on the French Riviera, where Scott finished writing *The Great Gatsby*, published in 1925. Though regarded as his finest work, the novel was not a commercial success and marked the beginning of the decline of the author's popularity. Back in the United States, Fitzgerald started to write film scripts to pay his debts. He was by now an alcoholic, and his wife suffered from mental instability. In 1934 Fitzgerald published *Tender is the Night*, where he dealt with the failure of the dreams and ideals of the Twenties. The book was coolly received, perhaps because the tastes of the public had changed owing to the Great Depression. In 1939 Fitzgerald began his last novel, *The Last Tycoon*, but he died of a heart attack in 1940 before completing it.

1 A portrait of Zelda and F. Scott Fitzgerald, ca 1920.

1 FILL IN the table with details about F. Scott Fitzgerald's life.

Education	
Married life	
Themes of his works	
Reputation	
Death	

The Great Gatsby (1925)

The story

Nick Carraway, a young stockbroker from the Midwest, moves to New York in the summer of 1922. He rents a house in the wealthy West Egg district of Long Island. His next-door neighbour is Jay Gatsby, a mysterious man who gives extravagant parties every Saturday night. Nick's cousin, Daisy Buchanan, and her husband, Tom, a former classmate of Nick's at Yale, introduce Nick to Jordan Baker, a beautiful, cynical young woman with whom Nick begins a romantic relationship. Jordan tells Nick that Tom has a lover, Myrtle Wilson, who lives in the valley of ashes, an industrial area between West Egg and New York City. Nick receives an invitation to one of Gatsby's parties. There he sees Jordan Baker and they meet Gatsby himself. Gatsby speaks to Jordan alone and tells her that he is still in love with Daisy, whom he met in 1917. Every night he stares at the green light at the end of her dock, across the bay from his house. Gatsby's extravagant lifestyle is an attempt to impress Daisy and his parties are simply a means to meet her. Gatsby asks Nick to help him get back together with Daisy. Nick invites both of them to have tea at his house and they begin an affair. Tom grows suspicious of the relationship between Gatsby and his wife and finally confronts them in a suite at the Plaza Hotel in New York; he reveals that Gatsby is a criminal, that his fortune comes from bootlegging alcohol and other illegal activities. While driving back to Gatsby's house, Daisy runs over Tom's mistress, Myrtle. She does not stop, and Gatsby hides the car. Myrtle's husband finds out that the car which killed his wife is Gatsby's. Gatsby does not protest his innocence because he wants to defend Daisy, but she deserts him and reconciles with her husband. Gatsby is finally shot in his garden by Myrtle's husband. Only Nick tries to defend Gatsby's name and arranges his funeral but, in stark contrast to the parties, nobody comes. Nick ends his relationship with Jordan and moves back to the Midwest. He reflects that just as Gatsby's dream of Daisy was corrupted by money and dishonesty, the American dream of happiness and individualism is over.

2–3 Scenes from the 2013 film adaption of *The Great Gatsby*, directed by Baz Luhrmann, starring Leonardo DiCaprio as Gatsby, Tobey Maguire as Nick and Carey Mulligan as Daisy.

2

The decay of the American Dream

The Great Gatsby contains many enlightening descriptions and criticisms of American life in the Jazz Age. The 'American-ness' of the novel is emphasised by such themes as the move from West to East; the confrontation between the romantic ideals of courage, honour and beauty, and the corrupted world of greed and money; the relationship of Gatsby's material achievements to the myth of going from 'rags to riches'; the tremendous growth of the car industry; the corrupting effects of Prohibition; the poverty of spiritual life in America during its most hedonistic decade.

Blindness is another central theme: the characters in the novel do not wish to see. They seek out blindness: they use drunkenness, like Daisy and the guests at Gatsby's parties; Jordan, Daisy, Tom and many others drive carelessly; they remain blind to danger, so caught up are they with the selfish pursuit of pleasure. Only Nick truly *sees*. He is Fitzgerald's spokesman in his representation of the decay of his generation.

Jay Gatsby and Nick Carraway

Jay Gatsby is presented as a mysterious character, since he seldom takes part in the lavish parties he organises. Rich and attractive, with some secret hidden in his past, he has the stature of a romantic hero who dies for his dream; yet he also embodies the 'self-made man' who tries to recreate the past through the power of money, and is destroyed in the end. Fitzgerald puts forth the idea that the American dream has been corrupted by the desire for materialism. We see that Gatsby had a pure dream, but became corrupt in his quest towards that dream.

Nick Carraway is both observer and participant in the novel. He is the only character in the novel to show and hold on to a sense of morals and decency. Nick can be seen as representing the outsider that Fitzgerald felt himself to be. Both Fitzgerald and Carraway found themselves surrounded by high society and dishonest people, and neither fit in with that kind of lifestyle. Nick is also linked to one of the major themes in the novel: the opposition between East and West. He comes from the West, and returns to it at the novel's end. Through Carraway, Fitzgerald shows his fondness for the West, which he idealised as being more moral than the East.

3

Retrospective narration

Nick Carraway is the narrator from whose point of view all the events and characters of the story are presented. Nick is a retrospective narrator who, after going through an experience, looks back on it with a better understanding. Fitzgerald rejects chronological order and uses the fragmentation of time and frequent flashbacks to represent the inner world of his characters and the way knowledge is normally acquired in real life. Gatsby's personality, therefore, is not developed through explicit statements but rather through implication, in the footsteps of Nick's own experience.

Symbolic images

Fitzgerald's style is characterised by frequent appeals to the senses, by the suggestive use of colours, and poetic devices such as repetition, simile and metaphor. The language blends realism and symbolism. The description of the society of the Jazz Age is extremely detailed and it is scattered with symbolic images, like the car, which stands for the destructive power of modern society and money. The most impressive description is perhaps that of the 'valley of ashes', a stretch of land full of rubbish, waste and ashes, lying between the city and the suburb where Gatsby lives. It stands for the emotional and spiritual sterility which is a counterpart to the bright lights of the modern metropolis. Gatsby's house too is at the same time real and symbolic: carefully described in its various rooms and acres of garden, it celebrates Gatsby's luck and success during the parties, but embodies his melancholy and loneliness when it is empty.

2 REVISE your knowledge about *The Great Gatsby* by answering the following questions.

1 How does the character of Gatsby develop throughout the story?
2 What is his relationship with Daisy?
3 How is American life described in the novel?
4 What is the role of Nick Carraway?
5 What is Fitzgerald's narrative technique?
6 What are the most important symbols in the novel?

1 Two competitors in a Charleston dance contest, Los Angeles, 1926.

WARM-UP

1 **DISCUSS** in pairs. How do you feel/act at a party if you don't know most of the people there? What do you do if you've never met the host?

Nick meets Gatsby

F. Scott Fitzgerald

The Great Gatsby (1925)
Chapter III

Gatsby, Nick's neighbour, gives very big parties every weekend in his large house. Most of the people who attend them have not been invited. There is always plenty of good food to eat, alcohol to drink and an orchestra playing jazz. Nick actually receives an invitation to one weekend party, so he decides to go.

7.5

Dressed up in white flannels[1] I went over to his lawn[2] a little after seven, and wandered around rather ill at ease[3] among swirls and eddies[4] of people I didn't know – though here and there was a face I had noticed on the commuting train[5]. I was immediately struck by the number of young Englishmen dotted about[6]; all well dressed, all looking a little hungry, and all talking in low, earnest voices to solid and prosperous Americans. I was sure that they were selling something: bonds or insurance or automobiles. They were at least agonizingly aware of the easy money in the vicinity and convinced that it was theirs for a few words in the right key[7].

As soon as I arrived I made an attempt to find my host, but the two or three people of whom I asked his whereabouts[8] stared at me in such an amazed way, and denied so vehemently any knowledge of his movements, that I slunk off[9] in the direction of the cocktail table – the only place in the garden where a single man could linger without looking purposeless[10] and alone.

I was on my way to get roaring drunk from sheer embarrassment[11] when Jordan Baker came out of the house and stood at the head of the marble steps, leaning a little backward[12] and looking with contemptuous[13] interest down into the garden.

Welcome or not, I found it necessary to attach myself to someone before I should begin to address cordial remarks to the passers-by.

'Hello!' I roared[14], advancing toward her. My voice seemed unnaturally loud across the garden.

'I thought you might be here,' she responded absently as I came up. 'I remembered you lived next door to –'

She held my hand impersonally, as a promise that she'd take care of me in a minute, and gave ear to two girls in twin yellow dresses, who stopped at the foot of the steps.

'Hello!' they cried together. 'Sorry you didn't win.'

That was for the golf tournament[15]. She had lost in the finals the week before.

'You don't know who we are,' said one of the girls in yellow, 'but we met you here about a month ago.'

'You've dyed[16] your hair since then,' remarked Jordan, and I started[17], but the girls had moved casually on and her remark was addressed to the premature moon, produced like the supper, no doubt, out of a caterer's[18] basket. With Jordan's slender golden arm resting in mine, we descended the steps and sauntered about[19] the garden. A tray of cocktails floated at us through the twilight[20], and we sat down at a table with the two girls in yellow and three men, each one introduced to us as Mr Mumble.

'Do you come to these parties often?' inquired Jordan of the girl beside her.

1 **flannels.** Flanella.
2 **lawn.** Prato.
3 **rather ill at ease.** Piuttosto a disagio.
4 **among ... eddies.** Tra turbini.
5 **commuting train.** Treno dei pendolari.
6 **dotted about.** Sparsi in giro.
7 **in the right key.** Dette nel modo giusto.
8 **his whereabouts.** Dove fosse.
9 **I slunk off.** Sgattaiolai.
10 **could ... purposeless.** Potesse indugiare senza sembrare spaesato.
11 **to get ... from sheer embarrassment.** Di ubriacarmi a morte per sfuggire all'imbarazzo.
12 **leaning a little backward.** Pendendo un po' all'indietro.
13 **contemptuous.** Sprezzante.
14 **roared.** Gridai.
15 **tournament.** Torneo.
16 **dyed.** Tinto.
17 **I started.** Sussultai.
18 **a caterer's.** Di un fornitore.
19 **sauntered about.** Gironzolammo per.
20 **A tray ... twilight.** Un vassoio di cocktails fluttuò verso di noi nel crepuscolo.

'The last one was the one I met you at,' answered the girl, in an alert confident voice. She turned to her companion: 'Wasn't it for you, Lucille?'

It was for Lucille, too.

'I like to come,' Lucille said. 'I never care what I do, so I always have a good time. When I was here last I tore my gown[21] on a chair, and he asked me my name and address – inside of a week I got a package from Croirier's with a new evening gown in it.'

'Did you keep it?' asked Jordan.

'Sure I did. I was going to wear it to-night, but it was too big in the bust[22] and had to be altered. It was gas blue with lavender beads[23]. Two hundred and sixty-five dollars.'

'There's something funny about a fellow that'll do a thing like that,' said the other girl eagerly[24]. 'He doesn't want any trouble with *any*body.'

'Who doesn't?' I inquired.

'Gatsby. Somebody told me –'

The two girls and Jordan leaned together confidentially.

'Somebody told me they thought he killed a man once.'

A thrill passed over all of us. The three Mr Mumbles bent forward[25] and listened eagerly.

'I don't think it's so much *that*,' argued Lucille sceptically; 'it's more that he was a German spy during the war.'

One of the men nodded in confirmation.

'I heard that from a man who knew all about him, grew up with him in Germany,' he assured us positively.

'Oh, no,' said the first girl, 'it couldn't be that, because he was in the American army during the war.' As our credulity switched back[26] to her she leaned forward with enthusiasm. 'You look at him sometimes when he thinks nobody's looking at him. I'll bet[27] he killed a man.'

She narrowed her eyes and shivered[28]. Lucille shivered. We all turned and looked around for Gatsby. It was testimony to the romantic speculation he inspired that there were whispers[29] about him from those who found little that it was necessary to whisper about in this world. [...]

There was dancing now on the canvas[30] in the garden; old men pushing young girls backward in eternal graceless circles, superior[31] couples holding each other tortuously, fashionably, and keeping in the corners – and a great number of single girls dancing individualistically or relieving[32] the orchestra for a moment of the burden[33] of the banjo or the traps[34]. By midnight the hilarity had increased. A celebrated tenor had sung in Italian, and a notorious contralto had sung in jazz, and between the numbers people were doing 'stunts[35]' all over the garden, while happy, vacuous bursts of laughter[36] rose toward the summer sky. A pair of stage twins, who turned out to be the girls in yellow, did a baby act in costume, and champagne was served in glasses bigger than finger-bowls[37]. The moon had risen higher, and floating in the Sound[38] was a triangle of silver scales[39], trembling a little to the stiff, tinny drip[40] of the banjoes on the lawn.

I was still with Jordan Baker. We were sitting at a table with a man of about my age and a rowdy[41] little girl, who gave way upon the slightest provocation to uncontrollable laughter. I was enjoying myself now. I had taken two finger-bowls of champagne, and the scene had changed before my eyes into something significant, elemental, and profound.

At a lull in the entertainment[42] the man looked at me and smiled.

'Your face is familiar,' he said, politely. 'Weren't you in the First Division during the war?'

'Why, yes. I was in the Twenty-eighth Infantry[43].'

'I was in the Sixteenth until June nineteen-eighteen. I knew I'd seen you somewhere before.'

We talked for a moment about some wet, gray little villages in France. Evidently he lived in this vicinity, for he told me that he had just bought a hydroplane[44], and was going to try it out in the morning.

21 **I tore my gown.** Mi strappai il vestito.
22 **bust.** Busto, corpetto.
23 **lavender beads.** Perline di colore lavanda.
24 **eagerly.** Con entusiasmo.
25 **bent forward.** Si curvarono in avanti.
26 **switched back.** Si spostava di nuovo.
27 **I'll bet.** Scommetto che.
28 **shivered.** Rabbrividì.
29 **there were whispers.** Si bisbigliava.
30 **canvas.** Tela.
31 **superior.** Di classe.
32 **relieving.** Sollevando.
33 **burden.** Onere, preoccupazione.
34 **the traps.** La batteria.
35 **stunts.** Numeri, esibizioni.
36 **vacuous burst of laughter.** Superficiali scoppi di risa.
37 **finger-bowls.** Lavadito di vetro usate come coppe da champagne.
38 **the Sound.** Lo stretto.
39 **scales.** Scaglie.
40 **stiff, tinny drip.** Sgocciolio rigido e metallico.
41 **rowdy.** Scalmanata.
42 **At a lull in the entertainment.** In una pausa dell'intrattenimento.
43 **Infantry.** Fanteria.
44 **hydroplane.** Idrovolante.

'Want to go with me, old sport[45]? Just near the shore along the Sound.'

'What time?'

'Any time that suits you best[46].'

It was on the tip of my tongue[47] to ask his name when Jordan looked around and smiled.

'Having a gay time now?' she inquired.

'Much better.' I turned again to my new acquaintance. 'This is an unusual party for me. I haven't even seen the host. I live over there –' I waved my hand at the invisible hedge in the distance, 'and this man Gatsby sent over his chauffeur[48] with an invitation.' For a moment he looked at me as if he failed to understand.

'I'm Gatsby,' he said suddenly.

'What!' I exclaimed. 'Oh, I beg your pardon.'

'I thought you knew, old sport. I'm afraid I'm not a very good host.'

He smiled understandingly – much more than understandingly. It was one of those rare smiles with a quality of eternal reassurance in it, that you may come across[49] four or five times in life. It faced – or seemed to face – the whole external world for an instant, and then concentrated on you with an irresistible prejudice in your favor. It understood you just so far as you wanted to be understood, believed in you as you would like to believe in yourself, and assured you that it had precisely the impression of you that, at your best, you hoped to convey[50]. Precisely at that point it vanished – and I was looking at an elegant young rough-neck[51], a year or two over thirty, whose elaborate formality of speech just missed being absurd[52]. Some time before he introduced himself I'd got a strong impression that he was picking[53] his words with care.

Almost at the moment when Mr Gatsby identified himself, a butler[54] hurried toward him with the information that Chicago was calling him on the wire[55]. He excused himself with a small bow[56] that included each of us in turn.

'If you want anything just ask for it, old sport,' he urged me. 'Excuse me. I will rejoin you later.'

45 **old sport.** Vecchio mio.
46 **that suits you best.** Che preferisci.
47 **tip of my tongue.** Punta della lingua.
48 **chauffeur.** Autista.
49 **come across.** Incontrare.
50 **to convey.** Di trasmettere.
51 **rough-neck.** *Lett.:* teppista; *qui:* tipo manierato.
52 **formality ... absurd.** Ricercatezza nel parlare rasentava l'assurdo.
53 **he was picking.** Scegliesse.
54 **butler.** Maggiordomo.
55 **wire.** Telefono.
56 **bow.** Inchino.

COMPREHENSION

2 READ the text and point out: the setting in time and place, the people involved, the main situation.

ANALYSIS

3 ANALYSE the extract by doing the following activities.

1 Make notes about Nick's character, his appearance and his feelings. How does he compare to the other people at the party?
2 Gather information about Jordan Baker. What impression do you get of her character?
3 How is Gatsby introduced throughout the text? What sort of man is he? What does Nick think of him?
4 Find references to the moon and say what it symbolises.
5 Describe the topics of conversation and the type of behaviour at Gatsby's party that convey the mood of the society of the 1920s in America.

ESAME DI STATO

Prova Orale – Part 1

4 RESEARCH information about:

- the biography of F. Scott Fitzgerald;
- *The Great Gatsby* (the plot, the characters, the themes);
- American writers from the beginning of the 20th century and the Lost Generation;
- the music, dances, clothing, prohibition and/or other cultural elements of the Jazz Age;
- film adaptations of the novel.

Then create your own PowerPoint presentation using the material you have gathered from the Internet.

Tip

Motivate the choice of your topic.
Your motivations may be:

- readings, poems, films or songs that are not included in the syllabus but connected to it;
- the fact that the topic has real connections with other subjects studied during the current school year;
- different points of view on a specific topic in different school subjects;
- the fact that your topic anticipates your future university choice.

5 SHOW your presentation to the class.

Exam Reference pag. 355

8.4 **The Arts**

Edward Hopper and the poetry of silence

Edward Hopper (1882–1967) was born in the small Hudson River town of Nyack, New York State, in 1882. By 1899 he had already decided to become an artist. He first attended the New York School of Illustrating; then, in 1900, he transferred to the New York School of Art. Here he worked under Robert Henri (1869–1929), one of the fathers of American Realism, who preached the importance of everyday life and the avoidance of historical, mythological subjects. Like the majority of young American artists of the time, he went to study in Paris in 1906.

His paintings combine seemingly contrasting qualities. Modern in their bleakness and simplicity, they are also full of nostalgia for the Puritan virtues of the American past – the kind of 19th-century architecture Hopper liked to paint, for instance, could not have been more out of fashion than it was in the 1920s. Even if his compositions are supposed to be realist, they also make frequent use of symbolism. Hopper became a pictorial poet who recorded the bareness and vastness of America. Sometimes he painted traditional aspects, such as lighthouses and landscapes, sometimes the city – New York, in particular, was his context – showing deserted streets at night and stressing the theme of monotony and loneliness.

1 **READ about Edward Hopper above and fill in the table.**

Education	
Themes of his paintings	

2 **LOOK at the paintings and do the activities.**

1 Edward Hopper, *Gas*, 1940. Museum of Modern Art, New York City, New York, US.

2 Edward Hopper, *Nighthawks*, 1942. The Art Institute of Chicago, Chicago, Illinois, US.

1 In *Gas*, Hopper represented one of the many gas stations he had studied during his trips around the United States, but he gave it a light which is only apparently realistic.

A Focus on the man in the picture. Is he consistent with the place? What is strange about him?

B Where does the light come from in the picture? How does it affect the representation?

C What is the role of the road? What contrast does it define?

2 One of the best-known images of 20th-century art, *Nighthawks* was inspired by a restaurant on New York's Greenwich Avenue where two streets meet, but it has a timeless quality that transcends its particular locale.

A How many people are represented? Describe their pose. On which figure does the picture pivot?

B What encloses the snackbar?

C Light plays an essential role in Hopper's paintings. Define its exact nature, source, direction and colour in *Nighthawks*. What function does the light fulfil?

D *Nighthawks* is the clearest example of a more complex kind of design employed by Hopper, the 'wedge design'. A wedge is a piece of wood, plastic or metal which has one pointed edge and one thick edge. Identify it in the picture. Then say where it thrusts from and what meets it.

E Do the individuals appear just as parts of the whole scene or in leading roles? What condition do they symbolise?

ESAME DI STATO **Terza Prova**

3 **TYPE B. Write a paragraph about Hopper's paintings of modern America and its inhabitants and the moods he wanted to convey. Write ten to twelve lines.**

Exam Reference pag. 355

8.5 **History**

The Great Depression of the 1930s in the USA

IELTS Academic Reading

1 **READ the passage about the Great Depression and answer questions 1–13.**

The passage has SIX paragraphs, A–F. Choose the correct heading (i–viii) for each paragraph from the list of headings below. Write the correct number, i-viii, in the spaces below.

List of Headings
- **i** An oversupply of goods and credit sales
- **ii** The effect on production
- **iii** The worst crisis in American history
- **iv** An extended period of poor performance
- **v** The gap between social classes grows wider and wider
- **vi** A policy for maintaining economic growth
- **vii** The fall of production and rise of unemployment
- **viii** The release of foreign exchange rates

1 Paragraph **A** ....
2 Paragraph **B** ....
3 Paragraph **C** ....
4 Paragraph **D** ....
5 Paragraph **E** ....
6 Paragraph **F** ....

Choose the correct letter, A, B, C or D, to complete the sentences (7–9).

7 The Great Depression was
- A the worst economic crisis in world history.
- B followed by inflation.
- C also the cause of economic problems in Europe.
- D caused by the war.

8 The Great Depression was caused by
- A a balance of wealth.
- B economic instability.
- C decreased industrial production.
- D the fast rate of increase of wages.

9 In the 1920s
- A there was an excessive production of goods.
- B people bought and paid straightaway.
- C the economy did not depend on luxury goods.
- D people could afford to buy anything.

Complete sentences 10–13 with words taken from the reading passage. Use NO MORE THAN THREE WORDS for each answer.

10 .... concerning technological industries was that they were limited in their expansion by the fact that people could not buy too many luxury goods.

11 Industrial production fell because people stopped buying things ....

12 Foreign countries gave up importing American products because the US imposed higher .... to protect the national economy.

13 The Fed was devised .... sudden widespread alarm concerning finance and decreased business activity.

GLOSSARY
- **slump** caduta dei prezzi
- **loans** prestiti
- **aftermath** conseguenza
- **imbalance** sbilancio
- **output** produzione
- **oversupply** quantità eccessiva
- **credit sales** vendita a credito
- **inflate** inflazionare

AN ECONOMIC CATASTROPHE

A. The Wall Street Crash of 1929 started an economic crisis known as the Great Depression. It was the worst economic slump in American history. It was not a novelty, because previous economic declines had afflicted the world. They were usually preceded by speculation and inflation. Between 1924 and 1930 both the US and most parts of Europe enjoyed favourable economic conditions, but it soon became clear that this prosperity depended on American loans and American markets, which almost vanished in late 1929. The European economy, still recovering from the trauma of the World War I and its aftermath, was too weak to face this crisis.

1 New Yorkers queuing at an unemployment agency, 1932.

B. Many factors brought about the Great Depression; however, the main cause was the combination of the unequal distribution of wealth throughout the 1920s and the extensive stock market speculation that took place during the latter part of that same decade. Money was distributed unequally between the rich and the working classes, between industry and agriculture within the United States, and between the US and Europe. This imbalance of wealth created an unstable economy. The excessive speculation in the late 1920s kept the stock

2 Ben Shahn, *Unemployment*, ca 1940 (detail).

3 Front page of a newspaper from 28th October 1929.

The FIRST with the LATEST
Full United Press leased wire

Santa Ana Register

People's Paper — Orange County — Daily Evening

FINAL EDITION

VOL. XXIV. NO. 285. SANTA ANA, CALIFORNIA, MONDAY, OCTOBER 28, 1929 — 20 PAGES — 3c Per Copy. 65c Per Month

BILLIONS LOST AS STOCKS CRASH

Pantages In Jail Awaits Sentence To State Prison

GUILTY SAYS JURY AFTER MANY HOURS

SENATE "FARM BLOC" STARTS BATTLE FOR HIGHER TARIFFS

JURY BELIEVES HER STORY

MAINSTAYS OF MARKET IN PLUNGE

STATE PLANS TO ROUND UP

Friend Brings Man To Jail

BINGHAM TAKES EXCEPTION TO Alliance Of Two Factions

market artificially high, and it eventually led to large market crashes. A major reason for this large and growing gap between the rich and the working class was the increased manufacturing output throughout this period. Therefore wages increased at a lower rate than productivity.

C. Total demand must equal total supply for an economy to function properly. In the 1920s there was an oversupply of goods. There was too much bread, wheat, corn, meat and oil and almost every other commodity required by man for his subsistence and material happiness. One obvious solution to the problem of the vast majority of the population not having enough money to satisfy all their needs was to allow credit sales. The concept of buying now and paying later became popular. This strategy created artificial demand for products which people could not ordinarily afford. The US economy also relied upon luxury spending and investments from the rich during the 1920s.

D. While the automobile and radio industries were booming in the 1920s, some economic areas, like agriculture in particular, were declining steadily. Several factors had caused prosperity in these two industries: first, during World War I both the automobile and the radio had been significantly improved. If those two industries were to slow down or stop, so would the entire economy. The fundamental problem with the automobile and radio industries was that they could not expand *ad infinitum* for the simple reason that people could not buy too many cars and radios. When the automotive and radio industries went down, all their employees suffered. Because it had been ignored, agriculture, which was still a fairly large segment of the economy, was already in ruins when American industry declined.

E. At the end of the decade, the rich stopped spending on luxury items, and slowed investments; the working class and poor stopped buying things on credit for fear of losing their jobs and not being able to pay the interest. As a result, industrial production fell by more than 9% between the market crashes in October and December of 1929. To protect the nation's businesses the US imposed higher trade taxes, and foreigners stopped buying American products. Jobs were lost, stores were closed, banks crashed and factories shut down. Unemployment grew to 5 million in 1930, and up to 13 million in 1932. The country moved into a catastrophe. The Great Depression had begun.

F. The Federal Reserve Board had been created to prevent bank panics and depressions. The first thing it did was inflate the money supply by about 60% during the 1920s. In early 1931 the Fed raised interest rates, exactly the wrong thing to do during an economic contraction. When Franklin Delano Roosevelt became President in 1933, he embarked on a programme of active state economic involvement known as the 'New Deal'. The most important initiatives included the National Industrial Recovery Act (1933), the Agricultural Adjustment Act (1933), the National Youth Administration (1935), the National Labor Relations Act (1935) and the Social Security Act (1935).

IELTS Academic Writing – Task 1

2 **A SUMMARY. The graph to the right shows the percentage of the rate of unemployment in the US between 1929 and 1939. Summarise the information by selecting and reporting the main features, and make comparisons where necessary. Write at least 150 words.**

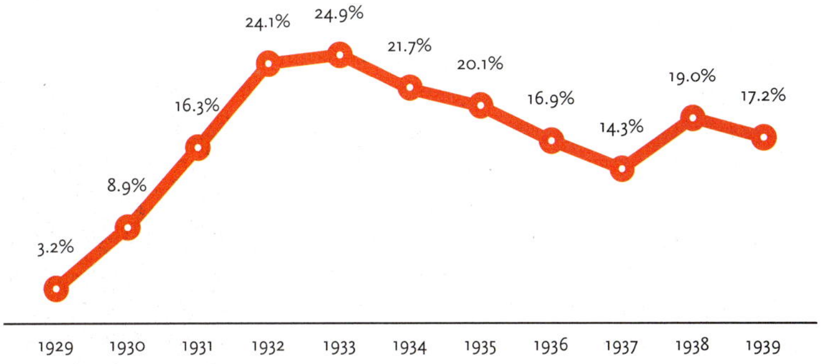

Average rate of unemployment in the US

7.6 DICTATION: *THE HEIGHT OF FASHION – THE CHRYSLER BUILDING*

TEXT BANK 61: *JOHN STEINBECK*

Internet Lab

1 Walker Evans, *Floyd Burroughs and his children – Tengle, Alabama*, 1936. Library of Congress, Washington, DC, US.

WARM-UP

1 **LOOK** at the photographs and describe the people's faces. Think about the emotions they express. What do you think the artists wanted to convey?

2 Dorothea Lange, *Migrant Mother*, 1936, Nipomo, California. Library of Congress, Washington DC, US.

3 Margaret Bourke-White, *Bread line during the Louisville flood*, Kentucky, 1937. Whitney Museum of American Art, New York, US.

2 **BROWSE** these websites and carry out a research project on the American Social Realist photographers whose pictures are shown above. Then present your findings to the rest of the class.

www.metmuseum.org/toah/hd/evan/hd_evan.htm

www.moma.org/collection/artist.php?artist_id=3373

www.loc.gov/rr/print/list/128_migm.html

myhero.com/go/hero.asp?hero=d_lange

www.smartwomeninvest.com/peoplepics.htm

American Social Realism in photography

During America's Great Depression of the 1930s and 1940s, the Farm Security Administration (FSA) employed photographers to document the rural poverty and exploitation of small farmers and migrant labourers, in an attempt to gain support for President Roosevelt's New Deal. The photographs were distributed free of charge to newspapers across the country and brought the life of displaced farming communities to the public's attention. The most famous images were made by Dorothea Lange (1895–1965), Walker Evans (1903–1975) and Margaret Bourke-White (1904–1971), whose black-and-white photos of starving fruit-pickers, farmers and impoverished workers became iconic symbols of the Great Depression.

8.6 **Society**

Britain between the wars

WARM-UP

1 **LOOK at pictures 1–5 on pages 293–294 and match them with the captions (A–E). Then discuss how you think Britain was changing between the two wars.**

A Experience and education were no protection against unemployement during the depression. ....

B The 'modern' suburban lifestyle: a man and a woman polish a car in front of a semi-detached house. ....

C Between 1941 and 1943, George Orwell worked on propaganda for the BBC. ....

D Wallis Simpson and the Duke of Windsor (formerly King Edward VIII) on their wedding day, 1937. ....

E Joan Miró, *Help Spain (Aidez L'Espagne)*, 1937. The artist designed this one franc stamp to be sold for the benefit of the Republican Government during the Spanish Civil War. ....

2 **READ the text on pages 293–294 and check your answers to exercise 1.**

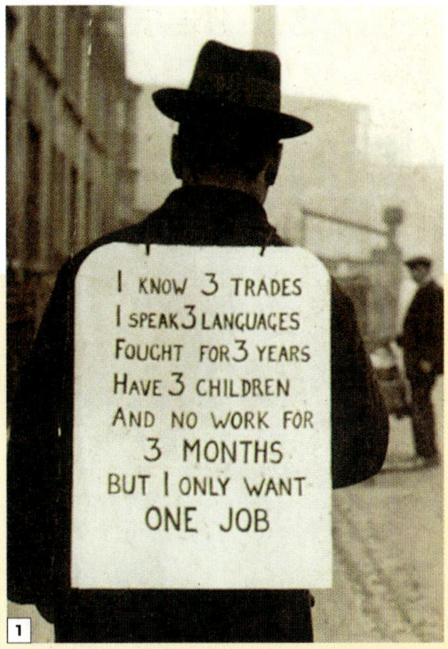

1

A. After World War I the Labour Party rose rapidly and the trade unions became more active in trying to get better pay and conditions by holding strikes. During the 1920s, the constant disputes between the coal miners and the mine owners eventually led to the General Strike of 1926. The families of coal miners, shipbuilders and cotton operatives experienced prolonged periods of hardship, and the areas in the North of England, South Wales and central Scotland became depressed. For the unemployed, there was misery and often abject poverty. They spent their time hanging around at street corners, waiting in queues for food and sheltering for warmth in the reading room of the public library. The unemployment of the 1920s and 1930s was certainly one of the most shocking phenomena of the first half of the 20th century.

2

B. All over Europe and America a serious crisis, known as the Great Depression, was taking place. During the second half of the decade the economy recovered somewhat, mostly because of the boom owing to rearmament for the impending war against Germany. In the South East of England, for example, new light industries such as chemicals, electrical goods and automobiles developed and families became affluent.

C. The creation of the British Commonwealth of Nations was formalised by the Statute of Westminster in 1931. This marked the end of the British Empire and the recognition of equal status for all member states of the new organisation. The year 1936, when Neville Chamberlain (1869–1940), leader of the Conservative Party, became prime minister, was one of crisis – with the abdication of King Edward VIII (1894–1972), who had succeeded his father George V (1865–1936), and the outbreak of the Spanish Civil War (1936–39). When King Edward VIII announced his intention to marry Wallis Simpson, a divorced American woman, he met opposition from all parties. Rather than renounce his intentions, he abdicated and was succeeded by his brother George VI (1894–1952).

D. The Spanish Civil War went on until April 1939, and was won by the fascist rebel General Francisco Franco (1892–1975) with the assistance of Benito Mussolini (1883–1945) and Adolf Hitler (1889–1945). The left-wing movements in Britain supported the Spanish republican government and many committed intellectuals like the poet W.H. Auden and the novelists George Orwell and Ernest Hemingway, joined the anti-fascist International Brigades. Inspired by contemporary politics, the themes of nation-building and dictatorship would heavily influence the writing of the period, especially in the form of so-called dystopian literature.

E. The 1930s brought about important social transformations. The growth of the population slowed down, mainly thanks to birth-control practices, families became smaller and women were more and more independent. The drift

3

4

of the population from the South to the North, which had been a characteristic of the Industrial Revolution, was reversed as heavy industry in the North declined and light industry in the South and the Midlands expanded. The other significant development was that fewer people lived in the centres of towns. Managers and professionals moved out to the suburbs and dormitory towns, and many working-class families went to live in new subsidised housing estates on the edges of towns.

F. One of the most striking social changes was the boom in the sales of the daily press. The serious 'quality' newspapers, like 'The Times' and 'The Daily Telegraph', retained their traditional character, while new 'popular' newspapers appeared, such as the 'Daily News', the 'Daily Chronicle', the 'Daily Express' and the 'Daily Herald'. Newspapers, which had been almost the only means of mass communication before the First World War, were supplemented in the 1920s by the development of radio broadcasting. In 1926 the British Broadcasting Corporation (BBC) was created.

5

IELTS Academic Reading

3 **READ** the text on pages 293–294 again and answer questions 1–14.

The passage has SIX paragraphs, A–F. Which paragraph contains the following information?

1 support of left-wing politics by British and American intellectuals
2 the drift to the suburbs
3 the spread of mass communication
4 reference to the effects of unemployment
5 reference to the way industry was evolving

Do the statements 6–11 agree with the information given in the passage? Write: *TRUE* if the statement agrees with the information; *FALSE* if the statement contradicts the information; *NOT GIVEN* if there is no information on this.

6 The northern areas of the country were more depressed than the southern ones.
7 The oncoming war with Germany affected industry negatively.
8 Edward VIII and Wallis Simpson moved to France.
9 The size of families doubled.
10 People began to move out of town centres.
11 All the newspapers had the same format.

For questions 12–14, complete the summary below. Choose ONE WORD ONLY from the passage to write in each gap.

British society in the 1930s

It is generally agreed that important social changes took place in the 1930s and that British society was transformed. After the **(12)** .... of 1926, many families lived long periods of terrible **(13)** .... During the second half of the decade, the economy started to recover as a result of **(14)** .... in the expectation of a new war.

ESAME DI STATO Terza Prova

4 **TYPE B.** Write ten to twelve lines explaining the changes that took place in British society in the 1920s and 1930s.

Exam Reference pag. 355

Insights

The British Commonwealth of Nations

6

The British Commonwealth of Nations, normally referred to today as 'The Commonwealth', is an intergovernmental organisation including fifty-four countries led by the United Kingdom. All members except Mozambique and Rwanda were part of the British Empire, out of which the Commonwealth developed. Recognition of the changed status of the British Empire came in the Balfour Declaration at the 1926 Imperial Conference, where Britain and its dominions agreed they were 'equal in status, in no way subordinate one to another in any aspect of their domestic or external affairs, though united by common allegiance to the Crown'. The Commonwealth countries recognise the queen as their head of state and are bound to Britain by trading agreements. The member states cooperate within a framework of common values and goals, which include the promotion of democracy, human rights, good governance, the rule of law, individual liberty, egalitarianism, free trade, multilateralism and world peace.

6 The flag of the British Commonwealth of Nations.

TEXT BANK 62–63: *W.H. AUDEN*

Wystan Hugh Auden and the committed writers

IELTS Listening – Section 4

1 7.7 | **ACADEMIC MONOLOGUE. Listen to the lecture and complete the notes below. Write NO MORE THAN TWO WORDS for each answer.**

The literature of commitment

Historical context
The deep sense of crisis created by World War I became more intense with the worldwide **(1)** .... of the late 1920s and 1930s and the Spanish Civil War (1936–39).
Prospect of another **(2)** .... in Europe.
Unemployment, Nazism and Fascism, were inescapable.

Inter-war literature
A **(3)** .... characterised much of the writing of the 1930s.
Themes in the fiction of the 1930s: divisions **(4)** .... and the burden of sexual repression.
In poetry: great variety, from modernist **(5)** .... to a new **(6)** .... realism.

Committed poetry
A group of poets joined together as undergraduates at **(7)** .... to write left-wing propaganda.
The four most famous poets: W.H. Auden, Stephen Spender (1909–95), Louis MacNeice (1907–63) and Cecil Day-Lewis (1904–72).
Concerned themselves with the social and **(8)** .... of human life.
Belonged to a generation which had been encouraged by its teachers to develop a **(9)** ....
Avoided **(10)** .... and allusiveness to communicate with their readers and encourage them to follow certain morally right courses of action.

Literary language
Committed poetry

The main features of committed poetry are:
- the poet seldom intrudes as a speaker using the pronoun 'I';
- scepticism about contemporary society;
- openness to new ideas and a broad range of life experiences;
- a social commentary which is not limited to politics – for example, it explores Freudianism, the inadequacies of the British government, war;
- a variety of forms and techniques;
- a very colloquial tone, which complements the satirical subject matter;
- powerful imagery, the use of juxtaposition and contrast;
- a unique and inspiring perspective on the human condition.

W.H. Auden's life

Wystan Hugh Auden was born in York in 1907, to middle-class High Church Anglican parents. While studying at Oxford, Auden became familiar with modernist poetry and he was the leader of the so-called 'Oxford poets', a group of young intellectuals who expressed a left-winged viewpoint, while continuing the artistic revolution started by T.S. Eliot, James Joyce and Ezra Pound. As a young man, he was deeply committed to social and political issues. During the General Strike of 1926 he worked for the strikers. In 1928 he went to Berlin, where he witnessed the rise of Nazism. During the Spanish Civil War he served as an ambulance driver. He showed his solidarity with the Jews persecuted by Hitler after 1933: in 1935 he married the German writer Thomas Mann's daughter, Erika, only to provide her with a British passport to enable her to escape from Nazi Germany.

Auden was also becoming increasingly concerned about his homosexuality. Homosexuality was condemned by the standards of his religious upbringing and was regarded as a criminal offence in England. In 1939 he moved to New York and settled in a house in Brooklyn which he ran as a sort of intellectual commune. In 1940 he began teaching in New York and published what is probably his best volume of the decade, *Another Time*. He was still to write much social poetry but his 'political' period was over; from then on his social poetry was to be anti-ideological, anti-political. It was at about this same time that he returned to the religion of his youth, Anglicanism.

He developed a growing concern with poetics. *New Year Letter* (1941), *For the Time Being: a Christian Oratorio* (1944), and the 1948 Pulitzer Prize-winning *The Age of Anxiety* (1948) are all characterised by extremely difficult verse forms. These works are also marked by his religious reaffirmation, even if this is expressed through questions concerning existence rather than by discussing his own spiritual struggles and achievements. In 1946 Auden became a citizen of the US, and in 1956 he was elected Professor of Poetry at Oxford. He died of a heart attack after giving a poetry reading in Vienna in 1973.

2 **READ W.H. Auden's biography and justify these statements.**
1 He was one of the Oxford poets.
2 He was deeply committed to social and political issues.
3 He was a homosexual.
4 He started a new life in New York.
5 He changed his poetic attitude.
6 He returned to Anglicanism.

1 W.H. Auden during a stateside CBS radio interview, 1940.

Another Time (1940)

This collection of poems deserves a special place in Auden's production – first of all, because of the period of its composition and publication, which covered the eve and the beginning of World War II, and also because it was the moment when the poet decided to leave England and emigrate to the United States. The title of the collection is symbolic: the poet entered 'another time' through the exile which he shared with many other refugees and that would eventually lead to his becoming an American citizen. The collection is viewed by critics as a pivotal one that marks Auden's turn from secular political interests towards ethical concerns, often addressed by Christianity. The work contains some of Auden's most famous poems and shows the main features of his poetry: it combines intellectual rigour and social conscience with a mixture of styles. The form may be that of free verse, metre, rhyme; Auden also uses simple popular forms such as ballads and songs. The poems are less radically political and are organised into three sections. The first, 'People and Places', is the most complex and meditative, where the poet deals with the theme of sorrow and the relationship between man and nature. The second section is called 'Lighter Poems' and includes some poems that may surprise readers with their light comic tone and domesticity. Finally, the third section, 'Occasional Poems', both celebrates the death of great figures like Freud and Yeats – in whom Auden recognises examples of transgression, of moral and artistic renewal – and tries to interpret great historical events such as the German invasion of Poland.

The English period

At the beginning of his career, the English period, Auden was deeply influenced by Freud and psychoanalysis but thought about psychological models in relation to the customs and rituals of an entire society, rather than exclusively with reference to the personal history of the individual. He believed that the role of poetry was 'to tell stories of particular people and experiences, from which each according to his own immediate and peculiar needs may draw his own conclusions'. Another influence that meant much to Auden in this period was that of Karl Marx. His way of arguing took for granted the engagement of the individual with history, to continually question the social and political climate in which one lived. So the poet's task was to act as a public voice, to support the causes for freedom against tyranny, to express the anxieties of the contemporary left-wing intellectuals.

Auden in America

The second period of Auden's poetry started with his move to America in 1939 and his withdrawal from political commitment. Auden's description of the Thirties as 'a low dishonest decade' reveals his disillusionment with political events such as the Republican defeat in Spain, the Moscow Trials ordered by Stalin from 1936 to 1938 and the Soviet-German Non-Aggression Pact of 1939, which was concluded just a few days before the beginning of World War II and which divided Eastern Europe into German and Soviet spheres of influence. The move to America freed him from the burden of social responsibility, of being the leader of the intellectual left rather than simply a verbal artist. He developed a style that refused identification with a single poetic culture or nation. He came to believe that improvement must begin within the self, not within society. The theme of the quest recurs in both the earlier and later periods, but the message differs. In the English period, the quest is for a new society and a new self. Later on, it becomes a quest for a new life.

3 **ANSWER the following questions about the work of W.H. Auden.**

1 What characterised the works of the English period?
2 What was the poet's task?
3 What did his move to America coincide with?
4 How did this change affect him?
5 What is the symbolic meaning of the title *Another Time*?
6 What is the style of this collection like?
7 How is it organised?

WARM-UP

1 **IN PAIRS** provide a definition of a 'refugee'. Then discuss the problems refugees encounter while living in different places throughout the world. How can state bureaucracies help refugees?

Refugee Blues

W.H. Auden

Another Time (1940)

Written in 1939, this poem employs a modified blues form to deal with the escape of Jewish refugees from Nazi Germany.

7.8

Say this city has ten million souls.
Some are living in mansions, some are living in holes[1]:
Yet there's no place for us, my dear, yet there's no place for us.

Once we had a country and we thought it fair.
Look in the atlas[2] and you'll find it there:
We cannot go there now, my dear, we cannot go there now.

In the village churchyard there grows an old yew[3].
Every spring it blossoms[4] anew:
Old passports can't do that, my dear, old passports can't do that.

The consul banged the table[5] and said.
'If you've got no passport you're officially dead':
But we are still alive, my dear, but we are still alive.

Went to a committee: they offered me a chair:
Asked me politely to return next year:
But where shall we go to-day, my dear, but where shall we go to-day?

Came to a public meeting: the speaker got up and said:
'If we let them in, they will steal our daily bread':
He was talking of you and me, my dear, he was talking of you and me.

Thought I heard the thunder rumbling[6] in the sky:
It was Hitler over Europe, saying. 'They must die':
O we were in his mind, my dear. O we were in his mind.

Saw a poodle[7] in a jacket fastened with a pin[8].
Saw a door opened and a cat let in:
But they weren't German Jews, my dear, but they weren't German Jews.

Went down the harbour[9] and stood upon the quay[10].
Saw the fish swimming as if they were free:
Only ten feet away, my dear, only ten feet away.

Walked through a wood, saw the birds in the trees:
They had no politicians and sang at their ease[11]:
They weren't the human race, my dear, they weren't the human race.

1 **mansions ... holes.** Ville ... buchi.
2 **atlas.** Atlante.
3 **yew.** Albero di tasso.
4 **blossoms.** Fiorisce.
5 **banged the table.** Batté il pugno sul tavolo.
6 **the thunder rumbling.** Il tuono rombare.
7 **poodle.** Cane barboncino.
8 **fastened with a pin.** Chiusa con uno spillo.
9 **harbour.** Porto.
10 **quay.** Banchina, molo.
11 **at their ease.** A loro agio.
12 **plain.** Pianura.
13 **to and fro.** Avanti e indietro.

Dreamed I saw a building with a thousand floors.
A thousand windows and a thousand doors:
Not one of them was ours, my dear, not one of them was ours.

Stood on a great plain[12] in the falling snow:
Ten thousand soldiers marched to and fro[13]:
Looking for you and me, my dear, looking for you and me.

COMPREHENSION

2 READ the poem and identify the three protagonists whose destinies will sadly cross.
- The victims ....
- The perpetrators ....
- The spectators ....

3 MATCH these various aspects of the refugees' situation with the corresponding stanzas:
A They are homeless.
B They have no passport.
C They are seen as intruders in the country they flee to.
D Pets are treated better than they are and enjoy greater freedom.
E They are persecuted.

4 IDENTIFY the different functionaries or objects that represent bureaucracy in the poem.

ANALYSIS

5 POINT OUT: 1) the stanza form; 2) the rhyme scheme; 3) the use of repetition; 4) the presence of a refrain.

6 FOCUS ON the first line of each stanza. Do you notice a device which is common to almost all of them? What effect does the poem achieve? Tick as appropriate.
□ It conveys the idea of improvisation and common speech.
□ It gives a glimpse into the social status of the speaker.
□ It suggests that the speaker may not be a well-educated person.

7 UNDERLINE images that can be defined as 'poetic' and images belonging to everyday life. Which prevail?

8 WRITE DOWN the contrasting images the poem is built upon and explain their meaning. An example has been provided:
(line 2) mansion / holes = It refers to the gap between the rich and the poor.

9 SUM UP the issues having a more general relevance that are hinted at in the poem.

YOUR TURN

10 DISCUSS. Who are 'the refugees' nowadays? Does your country experience this situation directly? What should the role of society be in absorbing refugees? Do you agree with the statement in line 17?

11 LOOK at the paintings *The Refugees* (1941) by the realist painter Lucian Freud and *The Refugee* (1939) by Felix Nussbaum. How did the painters portray their subjects? Do you think the pictures can be related to the poem you have just read? If so, how? Do the paintings affect you in a different way than the poem?

1

2

1 Lucian Freud, *The Refugees*, 1941. Private Collection.

2 Felix Nussbaum, *The Refugee*, 1939. Courtesy of the Felix Nussbaum Foundation.

8.8 History

INTERACTIVE MAP 8: *THE BLITZ*

World War II and after

WARM-UP

1 **DISCUSS** what you know about WWII, the term 'Welfare State' and Queen Elizabeth II. Use the pictures on pages 299–301 for help.

2 **READ** the Q&A text.

1 The Japanese attack the US naval base at Pearl Harbor, Hawaii, 7th December 1941.

2 The mushroom cloud created by the atomic bomb dropped on Hiroshima, Japan, 6th August 1945.

3 Stalin, Roosevelt and Churchill at the Yalta Conference, February 1945.

Q When did World War II start?

A In September 1939 Germany invaded Poland and the Second World War started.

Q Did it gain more popular support than in 1914?

A Yes, a vast majority thought that it was a necessary war and, even in the darkest days, very few thought of giving in. Government controls, conscription, rationing and air raids also brought everyone into the firing-line.

Q What successes did Germany have from 1939 to 1940?

A From September 1939 to June 1940 Germany had many successes: Poland fell in September 1939; Belgium, Holland and Norway fell in 1940; France surrendered in June 1940 after British and French soldiers retreated from Dunkirk.

Q Who became prime minister in 1940?

A The Conservative Winston Churchill (1874–1965) became prime minister in 1940; he appointed ministers from all the political parties and established a 'War Cabinet' of five to take important decisions.

Q What were the key points leading to the German defeat?

A The German defeat was due to several reasons. One important factor was that Germany did not manage to get control of the air over the English Channel. Hitler's greatest misstep, however, was his decision to invade the USSR in June 1941. The German army was destroyed by the long Russian winter and by resistance in the sieges of Leningrad, Moscow and Stalingrad, where it was forced to surrender in January 1943. The Russians then marched through Eastern Europe to liberate the countries invaded by the Germans.

Q What events paved the way to the final victory?

A American intervention in 1941, which followed a Japanese attack on Pearl Harbor in Hawaii, and the advance of Montgomery's army in North Africa (1942), which proved disastrous for the German and Italian troops, marked a turning point which paved the way to the final victory, which was inaugurated by D-Day (D for Deliverance). On 6th June 1944, the Allies touched down on the coasts of Normandy and managed to liberate France.

Q When did Germany and Japan surrender?

A In 1945 Germany finally surrendered, after Hitler's suicide. Japan remained at war, but in August 1945 US President Harry Truman (1884–1972) ordered the dropping of the atomic bomb on the Japanese cities of Hiroshima and Nagasaki.

Q What were the main consequences of the war?

A The power of the European empires was weakened by the war. The French, the Dutch and the British had to abandon some of their colonies. Britain withdrew from India, Burma, Ceylon, Malaya and Singapore, since all the people from the colonies who had fought for Britain against Germany wanted independence as a reward. Britain's foreign trading position was also weakened by the huge debts to pay for the war and extensive bomb damage which made it very difficult for many industries to readjust to peacetime conditions.

Q Who won the general election in July 1945?

A The general election in July 1945 was won by the Labour Party under the leadership of Clement Attlee (1945–1961).

Q What was the US Marshall Plan and what were its aims?

A The US Marshall Aid Plan (1947) was the American programme to help European countries recover economically and prevent the weaker ones from falling under Russian influence. Thanks to this plan, which was in operation for four years, Britain received large US loans, but recovery was slow.

8.8 World War II and after

1 A Labour Party poster for the General Election of 1945.

2 A poster promoting the US Marshall Aid Plan for European economic recovery.

3 The coronation of Queen Elizabeth II, 2nd June 1953.

1

2

Q In which other ways did US foreign policy demonstrate a new opening towards Europe?

A The US signed an agreement of mutual defense with Western Europe, the North Atlantic Treaty Organisation, known as NATO. This was in addition to the United Nations Organisation (1945), which replaced the League of Nations created after the First World War.

Q What new policies did the new government offer to overcome these problems?

A The Labour Party offered new policies which focused on the new role of the government in looking after the interests and welfare of its citizens in such areas as health, unemployment and pensions. This new kind of state intervention became known as the 'Welfare State'.

Q What other important step was taken by the Labour government?

A The next important step of the Labour government was to take over the control of power and natural resources, transport (airlines and railways) and credit (the Bank of England). This process of nationalisation meant that the government bought all the shares of the companies in these fields in exchange for government bonds.

Q What was the 'Cold War'?

A The only country which could counterbalance America's powerful position was the Soviet Union. Competition and fear between these two powerful nations was known as the 'Cold War', which was to dominate international affairs for decades when many major crises occurred, like the wars in Korea (1949–53) and the Vietnam War (1957–75).

Q What was central to the Cold War?

A The nuclear arms race was central to the Cold War. Both the US and the Soviet Union massively built up nuclear weapons. The world greatly changed when the US exploded the H-bomb in 1952. This bomb was smaller in size than the Hiroshima atomic bomb but 2,500 times more powerful. The Russians produced an H-bomb in 1953 and the world became a much more dangerous place.

Q How did the conflict between the US and the Soviet Union lead to McCarthyism?

A Fear of Communism, seen as a threat both to the freedom of the individual and the capitalist system, swept across the US and led to 'McCarthyism', where the politician Joseph McCarthy (1909–57) started a public 'witch hunt' investigating intellectuals, scientists, public officers and others, though he was eventually discredited and censured by the Senate.

Q What events led to the Suez Crisis of 1956?

A After World War II, Egypt, which had been an important British colony, gained independence and a British-friendly government was set up. In 1952 there was a revolution and Britain agreed to withdraw from the Canal Zone but kept its shares in the Canal. In July 1956 President Nasser of Egypt nationalised the company that owned the Suez Canal, which was jointly owned by the British and French governments.

Q What was the impact of the Suez Crisis on Britain?

A British and French forces bombed and invaded Egypt in October 1956. There was an international outcry, strong opposition from all the political parties in Britain and France, condemnation from the United Nations and from the US. The value of sterling collapsed and the invaders were obliged to withdraw their troops by the United Nations. This showed that Britain was no longer a world power and was unable to manage international relations without US support.

Q When did Elizabeth II ascend the throne and who did she succeed?

3

A When George VI died in February 1952, there was a widespread sense of loss and shock. His support and loyalty to his people during the war had made him a respected and popular figure.
He was succeeded by his daughter Elizabeth II (1926–), who was crowned in 1953.

Q What were the most important features of the New Elizabethan Age?

A Despite the heralding of a 'New Elizabethan Age', the general euphoria was mingled with a sense of anguish and rootlessness, especially among the young, caused by the aftermath of the Second World War and increased by the Cold War. Disillusionment came also at the realisation that Britain was gradually being reduced to a second-class power dependent on the United States. Moreover, Britain no longer had an empire, accelerating the plan to hand over the government of the various colonies to local rulers.

3 **FIND** the words in the text on pages 299–300 which mean the following:

1 the practice of ordering people by law to serve in the armed forces;
2 the policy of limiting the amount of food, fuel;
3 attacks by a number of aircraft dropping many bombs on a place;
4 to be in a position where you can be shot at;
5 military operations in which enemy forces surround towns or buildings;
6 created a situation in which something can happen.

4 **IN PAIRS** cover the answers (As) in the text on pages 299–300. Take turns asking and answering the questions (Qs) using the information that you have read.

ESAME DI STATO **Terza Prova**

5 **TYPE A.** Write a 200-word essay about the key events of World War II and the main consequences of the conflict.

Exam Reference pag. 355

Internet Lab

1 **BROWSE** the website www.un.org/en and carry out a research project on the following:

1 the UN structure and organisation;
2 the present Secretary-General;
3 the UN process of renewal;
4 the thematic issues linked to peace and security;
5 the thematic issues linked to humanitarian affairs.

2 **PRESENT** your findings to the rest of the class.

Milestones

1946, the National Health Service Act

Britain's health care system before 1948 had been inefficient. The main weaknesses were the lack of access to hospital care and health care for the families of working men. The National Health Service Act was passed in 1946, although the service began in 1948. It gave free medical, dental, optical and hospital care to everyone. Almost all hospitals were nationalised and run by fourteen regional hospital boards. Maternity care, health visitors and child welfare clinics were set up, too, and run by local authorities. The man in charge of these reforms was the minister of Health, Aneurin Bevan.

Previously, doctors, dentists and opticians had charged their patients; and Bevan had first thought of paying them salaries, making them employees of the state, but later got them to support the National Health Service (NHS) by paying them a fee based on the number of patients they had. Totally free treatment in the NHS did not last long, as charges for glasses and prescriptions were introduced as early as 1952, but overall the NHS massively improved the health of the British people and provided a model for similar schemes in other countries.

4

4 Minister of Health Aneurin Bevan opens Park Hospital in Manchester, 1948.

5 The office of the United Nations in New York City.

Insights

The United Nations Organisation

5

The United Nations (UN) is an international organisation designed to facilitate cooperation in international law, security, economic development, social progress and human rights, as well as keep peace throughout the world. The name 'United Nations' was first used by Winston Churchill and Franklin D. Roosevelt in the 'Declaration by United Nations' in 1942. This declaration was made to officially state the cooperation of the Allies (Great Britain, the United States and the Union of Soviet Socialist Republics) during World War II. The UN was founded in 1945, when the representatives of fifty countries met in San Francisco at the UN Conference on International Organisation to draw up the UN Charter. Its forerunner was the League of Nations, an organisation conceived in similar circumstances at the end of World War I and established in 1919 under the Treaty of Versailles. The present UN includes 193 member states and its main headquarters are in New York City. UN Day is celebrated on 24th October each year.

8.9 Two Films About... World War II

WARM-UP

1 **DISCUSS** in pairs. Think about films based on true stories you have already seen. Should filmmakers deliberately avoid historical accuracy in favour of an entertaining film?

Pearl Harbor

Directed by Michael Bay;
USA 2001.
With Ben Affleck (Rafe McCawley);
Josh Hartnett (Danny Walker);
Kate Beckinsale (Evelyn Johnson).

The film is a tribute to the men and women who served their country during wartime. The battle scenes and the reenactment of Japan's attack on Pearl Harbor are really impressive but act as background for the main story, which is a love story. The protagonists, Rafe and his best friend Danny, grow up together on a farm, both live to fly and become fighter pilots, and both fall in love with Evelyn, who is the nurse at their medical pilot's examination. However, it is Rafe who soon begins dating Evelyn. Rafe volunteers to go to fight in Europe with the British Royal Air Force, while Evelyn and Danny are assigned to Pearl Harbor.

Believing that Rafe has died in action, Danny and Evelyn begin a love affair and she is pregnant when Rafe returns home, miraculously saved by a fisherman after crashing into the Atlantic. Danny and Rafe fight and get drunk and are sleeping it off when the attack on Pearl Harbor begins. They participate in the battle, and because of their heroism they are both sent on a secret mission to Japan. They are captured and about to be shot, but Danny protects his friend and ends up dying in his arms. The final scene of the film shows Rafe with Evelyn and their little son Danny, standing by Danny's grave.

What about accuracy?

The history lesson included in the film is oversimplified even though it is based on the actual events of the 7th December 1941 bombing of Hawaii's Pearl Harbor, where, during World War II, the American Armed Forces had a lot of their troops and ships stationed. The Japanese bombed the harbour, killing over 3,000 officers and civilians. The film stirs emotions with massive war scenes and the romantic love story. As regards historical accuracy, the dates and the order of events are right, but the film is very pro-American. Pearl Harbor was a tragedy, but the film does not mention the dropping of nuclear bombs on Japan which followed.

The King's Speech

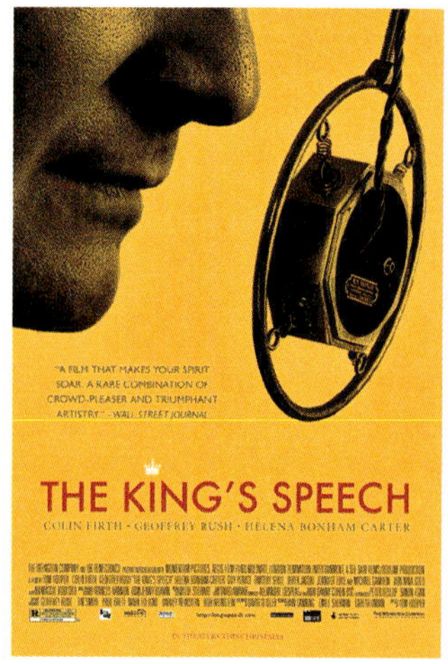

Directed by Tom Hopper;
UK 2010.
With Colin Firth (King George VI);
Geoffrey Rush (Lionel Logue);
Helena Bonham Carter
(Queen Elizabeth).

This historical drama film tells the story of the man who became King George VI, the father of Queen Elizabeth II. After the death of his father, King George V, and the scandalous abdication of his brother, King Edward VIII, Albert, or 'Bertie', reluctantly assumes the throne as King George VI. Plagued by a terrible stammer and considered unfit to be king, Bertie engages the help of an unorthodox Australian speech therapist, Lionel Logue. Through a set of unexpected techniques, and as a result of an unlikely friendship, Bertie is able to find his voice. With the support of Logue, his family, his government and Winston Churchill, the king is able to overcome his stammer and deliver a radio address that inspires his people and unites them to face the battle ahead.

What about accuracy?

The most widely criticised inaccuracy in the film is Bertie's political affiliation. While the film portrays the king as having a close relationship with Winston Churchill, in reality Bertie and his wife were supporters of the previous prime minister, Neville Chamberlain, and advocated his policy of negotiating with a political adversary in order to avoid war. Moreover, some critics criticise the film for inaccurately portraying the severity of the king's stammer. In fact, it was not severe, and when he was concentrating hard on what he was saying it disappeared altogether. However, Bertie's 1925 speech at the British Empire Exhibition at Wembley, which opens the film, has been described in various publications as 'humiliating', 'disastrous' and 'painful', which is certainly how it is depicted in the film. Another inaccuracy of the film regards exactly when Logue and the king met, which was in 1926, after Bertie's disastrous speech at Wembley. In the film their meeting is postponed until the late 1930s.

8.10 **Literature**

The dystopian novel

TEXT BANK 64: *ALDOUS HUXLEY*

WARM-UP

1 **LOOK UP the word 'utopia' in the dictionary and write down its definition. Then provide your own definition of 'dystopia'.**

For most of the 19th-century writers and thinkers, utopia was a thing of the future, the culmination of the forces of historical evolution, prepared by the most powerful and progressive tendencies of modem times: democracy, science and socialism. The renewal of utopia also stimulated its counter-force: anti-utopia, or dystopia. As utopia concentrated on the positive, so dystopia painted the most negative, the blackest picture possible of the present and the future to come. Just as utopia lent the persuasive techniques of the literary imagination to the cause of modern ideas of science and socialism, so dystopia lent the same techniques to the revolt against modernity. Like utopia, dystopia invented whole social orders, in all their particularity. But while the utopian order was perfect in the moral sense, the dystopian order was merely perfected in the social sense. It was the dreadful perfection of some modern system or idea. And while utopian societies were ideal, in the sense of 'the best possible', dystopian society represented the victory or tyranny of the idea. In both cases, the reader was invited to live the life of a society based on some principles, but in the one case the expected response to the experience was delight, in the other, horror.

In the eyes of 20th-century intellectuals, the industrial society seemed to have overreached itself and was preparing its own destruction, as it is reflected in Yeats's poems. America and the Soviet Union inspired the hopes and designs of utopian experiments, but they could inspire dystopia as well. Aldous Huxley's (1894–1963) novel *Brave New World* (1932) drew largely upon American practices for its picture of a benighted future world, sunk in consumerism. George Orwell's *Animal Farm* (1945) and *Nineteen Eighty-Four* (1949) were the precise and passionate expression of the writer's bitter feelings about the failure of a socialist utopia in the Soviet Union. However, in these novels utopia and dystopia flow into and out of each other in intricate patterns of affirmation mixed with bleak pessimism.

The 1950s proclaimed 'the end of ideology'; in the new utopian conception, science and technology played a major role to which fears about nuclear war were the persistent dystopian undercurrent. Horror of the present and fear of the future concerned writers such as William Golding (1911–93) who, in his novel *Lord of the Flies* (1954), expressed his view of the thinness of the protective civilised layer keeping man from barbarism and the brutal annihilation of his own kind.

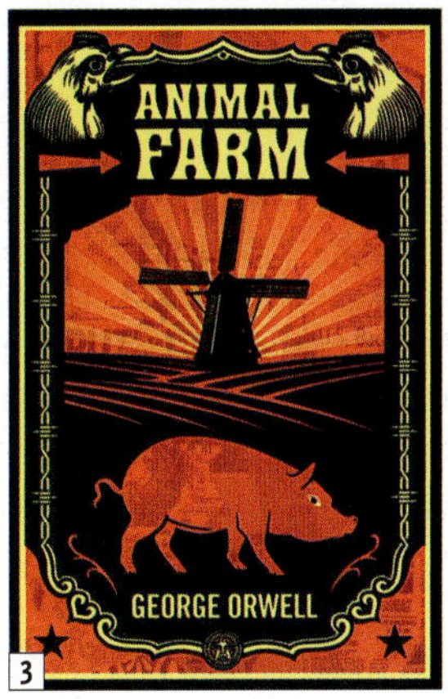

1 Animated sequence by Gerald Scarfe from the film 'Pink Floyd – The Wall', directed by Alan Parker, 1982.

2 The cover of Aldous Huxley's *Brave New World*, 1932.

3 Cover for the new Penguin edition of George Orwell's *Animal Farm* designed by the street artist Shepard Fairey, 2010.

2 **READ the text and answer the following questions.**

1. What did 'utopia' mean to 19th-century writers?
2. How did utopia and dystopia differ? Fill in the table below.

Utopia	Dystopia

3. How did America and the Soviet Union inspire the dystopian novelists of the 1930s and 1940s?
4. How did the concept of utopia change in the novels of the 1950s?

YOUR TURN

3 **DISCUSS. Can you think of other examples of dystopian books, films and TV programmes? Why do you think this genre has been so popular in the 20th and 21st centuries?**

TEXT BANK 65: *ANIMAL FARM*

George Orwell and political dystopia

George Orwell's life

Born Eric Blair in India in 1903, George Orwell (1903–50) was the son of a minor colonial official. As a small child, he was taken to England by his mother, and was educated first at a preparatory school, St Cyprian's, in Eastbourne, then at Eton College. He could not stand the lack of privacy, the humiliating punishments, the pressure to conform to the values of the English public school tradition – such as the development of 'character', a spirit of competition and a rigid adherence to discipline – and to the prevailing moral code. At Eton he began to develop an independent-minded personality, indifference to accepted values, and professed atheism and socialism.

On leaving school, he passed the India Office examinations for the Indian Imperial Police, opting to serve in Burma (also called Myanmar), where he remained from 1922 to 1927. In 1927 he went on leave and decided not to return; it was not simply that he wished to break away from British Imperialism in India, he wished to 'escape from ... every form of man's dominion over man', as he said in the *Road to Wigan Pier* (1937), and the social structure from which he came.

Back in London, he started a social experiment: wearing second-hand clothes, he spent short periods living in common lodging-houses in the East End, seeking the company of 'down-and-outs'. In this way, he directly experienced poverty and learnt how institutions for the poor, such as hostels, prisons, lodging-houses and hospitals, worked. After a period in Paris where he worked as a dishwasher in a hotel, he decided to begin publishing his works with the pseudonym of George Orwell. He chose 'George' because it had an Englishness about it, suggesting plain speaking and common sense, and 'Orwell' because it was the name of a river he was fond of. *Down and Out in Paris and London* (1933) was his first non-fiction narrative, in which he described his experiences among the poor; it was followed by *Burmese Days* (1934), a book based on his time in the colonial service. In 1936 he married Eileen O'Shaughnessy, an Oxford graduate who shared his interests in literature and socialism. In the same year, Orwell was commissioned by a left-wing publisher to investigate conditions among the miners, factory workers and unemployed in the industrial North, where he stayed for two months. His report, *The Road to Wigan Pier*, was published in 1937.

In December 1936 Orwell went to Catalonia with his wife to report on the Spanish Civil War. In Barcelona he joined the militia of the POUM (Workers' Party of Marxist Unification) and fought in the trenches of the Aragon front. In *Homage to Catalonia* (1938) he recalled this experience as the time of his true conversion to socialism and the ideals of brotherhood and equality. Back in England, the Orwells adopted an infant child and called him Richard. They both had poor health: George suffered from bronchitis and pneumonia, and Eileen was to die during an operation in 1945.

1 A passport photo showing George Orwell during his time in Burma.

When the Second World War broke out, Orwell moved to London and, in 1941, he joined the BBC, broadcasting cultural and political programmes to India. In 1943 he resigned and became the literary editor of the 'Tribune', an influential socialist weekly. He also began writing *Animal Farm,* which was published in 1945, just when the Iron Curtain was beginning to fall on Eastern Europe, and it made Orwell internationally known and financially secure. Orwell's last book, *Nineteen Eighty-Four*, was his most original novel; it was published in 1949 and soon became a bestseller. Orwell died of tuberculosis the following year.

The artist's development

Orwell had a deep understanding of the English character, of its tolerance, its dislike of abstract theories and insistence on common sense and fair play. On the other hand, his various experiences abroad contributed to his unusual ability to see his country from the outside and to judge its strengths and weaknesses. He chose to reject his background and to establish a separate identity of his own. As a consequence, he was receptive to new ideas and impressions. Orwell's life and work were marked by the unresolved conflict between his middle-class upbringing and education and his emotional identification with the working class. He believed that writing interpreted reality and therefore served a useful social function. This explains why his most successful novels express political themes. However, Orwell believed that the writer should be independent, and that no good writing could come from following a party line.

Social themes

Orwell was a prolific book-reviewer, critic, political journalist and pamphleteer in the tradition of Swift and Defoe. Indebted to Dickens in his choice of social themes and the use of realistic and factual language, he conveyed a vision of human fraternity and of the misery caused by poverty and deprivation. He insisted on tolerance, justice and decency in human relationships, and warned against the increasing artificiality of urban civilisation. Above all, he presented a devastating critique of totalitarianism, warning against the violation of liberty and helping his readers to recognise tyranny in all its forms.

1 ANSWER the following questions about the life and work of George Orwell.

1 How did Orwell view his country?
2 What conflict did he experience?
3 What social experiments did he make?
4 What did he believe about writing?
5 What themes did he deal with?

2–3 Scenes from the film adaptation of *Nineteen Eighty-Four* directed by Michael Radford, 1984.

Nineteen Eighty-Four (1949)

The story

The novel describes a future world divided into three blocks: Oceania, an Empire of which England, 'Airstrip One', is no longer the head but just an outpost; Eurasia, including Russia and Europe; and Eastasia, that is, Asia and the Far East. The regimented, oppressive world of Oceania is ruled by 'the Party', which is led by a figure called 'Big Brother', and is continuously at war with the other two states. In order to control people's lives, the Party is implementing 'Newspeak', an invented language with a limited number of words, and threatening them through the 'Thought Police'. Free thought, sex and any expression of individuality are forbidden, but the protagonist, Winston Smith, illegally buys a diary in which he begins to write his thoughts and memories, addressing them to the future generations.

At the 'Ministry of Truth', where he rewrites historical records to suit the needs of the Party, Winston notices an attractive dark-haired girl staring at him, and is afraid she might be an informant who will prove him guilty of 'thoughtcrime'. The girl's name is Julia; she proves to also have a rebellious attitude, and they begin a secret affair. One day O'Brien, a member of the powerful 'Inner Party', summons them to his luxury flat and tells them that he too hates the Party and works against it as a member of the 'Brotherhood', led by Emmanuel Goldstein. This mysterious group is trying to overthrow the Party. O'Brien gives Winston a copy of Goldstein's book, the manifesto of the Brotherhood. Winston is reading it to Julia in their room when some soldiers suddenly break in and arrest them. He is taken to the 'Ministry of Love', where he finds out that O'Brien is a Party spy. O'Brien tortures and brainwashes Winston for months, but he struggles to resist. At last, O'Brien sends him to 'Room 101', the final destination for those who oppose the Party. Here, Winston is forced to confront his worst fear: rats on his head, ready to eat his face. Winston's will is broken and he is released to the outside world. He meets Julia, but no longer loves her. He has completely given up his identity and has learnt to love Big Brother.

A dystopian novel

Set in a grotesque, squalid and menacing London, *Nineteen Eighty-Four* is a dystopian novel. Orwell presents a frightening picture of the future as being under the constant control of Big Brother. There is no privacy because there are monitors called 'telescreens' watching every step people take; love is forbidden but there is the 'Two Minutes Hate' and the country is in a perpetual state of war. The Party has absolute control of the press, communication and propaganda; language, history and thought are controlled in the interests of the state through the gradual introduction of Newspeak, whose lexis is so limited that people find it impossible to express their own ideas. Any form of rebellion against the rules is punished with prison, torture and liquidation. The novel does not offer consolation but reveals the author's acute sense of history and his sympathy with the millions of people persecuted and murdered in the name of the totalitarian ideologies of the 20th century.

Winston Smith

The overwhelming impression made by *Nineteen Eighty-Four* is one of a sense of loss, a feeling that beauty and truth, and all finer emotions and values, belong to the past. This is symbolised by the protagonist, Winston Smith, the last man to believe in humane values in a totalitarian age. 'Smith', the commonest English surname, suggests his symbolic value; 'Winston' evokes Churchill's patriotic appeals for 'blood, toil, tears and sweat' during the Second World War. Winston is middle-aged and physically weak; he experiences alienation from society and feels a desire for spiritual and moral integrity. In the first two parts of the novel, it is likely that Winston and the narrator are one, and that he expresses Orwell's views.

Themes

Nineteen Eighty-Four is a satire on hierarchical societies which destroy fraternity. The dictator is called 'Big Brother', but he actually does not watch over his people as a brother should. 'Watching' here does not mean 'taking care of' but 'controlling'. Memory and mutual trust become positive themes in the struggle where Winston attempts to maintain his individuality. Orwell believed that if man has someone to trust, his individuality cannot be destroyed because his identity arises from interaction, not autonomy or isolation. Decency is mutual trust, tolerance, behaving responsibly towards other people and acting with empathy; it is extremely important for political action and any civic culture. The major theme of memory is linked to a view of morality. An egalitarian post-revolutionary society would not change values or expect them to be different but would put an end to exploitation and draw on the best of the past. Thus Winston attempts to write a diary in which his private memory is defended against the official attempts to rewrite history.

2 **ANSWER the following questions about *Nineteen Eighty-Four*.**

1. In what sense is *Nineteen Eighty-Four* a dystopian novel?
2. What sort of society does it describe?
3. What is the protagonist like and what does he symbolise?
4. What are its main themes?

WARM-UP

1 **DISCUSS.** Do you think the question of privacy is a pressing one in contemporary society? Can you provide examples of ways in which technology has changed access to our private lives and information?

Big Brother is watching you

George Orwell

Nineteen Eighty-Four (1949)
Part I, Chapter I

This extract gives an insight into the life in London, the capital of Airstrip One in Oceania, a totalitarian state where men have lost control of their inner being. The only person who tries to resist indoctrination is the protagonist of the book, Winston Smith.

7.9

Inside the flat a fruity[1] voice was reading out a list of figures which had something to do with the production of pig-iron[2]. The voice came from an oblong metal plaque like a dulled[3] mirror which formed part of the surface of the right-hand wall. Winston turned a switch and the voice sank somewhat, though the words were still distinguishable. The instrument (the telescreen, it was called) could be dimmed[4], but there was no way of shutting it off completely. He moved over to the window: a smallish, frail figure, the meagreness[5] of his body merely emphasized by the blue overalls[6] which were the uniform of the Party. His hair was very fair, his face naturally sanguine, his skin roughened by coarse[7] soap and blunt razor blades[8] and the cold of the winter that had just ended.

Outside, even through the shut window-pane, the world looked cold. Down in the street little eddies[9] of wind were whirling dust and torn paper into spirals, and though the sun was shining and the sky a harsh blue, there seemed to be no colour in anything, except the posters that were plastered everywhere. The blackmoustachio'd[10] face gazed down from every commanding corner. There was one on the house-front immediately opposite. BIG BROTHER IS WATCHING YOU, the caption said, while the dark eyes looked deep into Winston's own. Down at street level another poster, torn at one corner, flapped fitfully[11] in the wind, alternately covering and uncovering the single word INGSOC. In the far distance a helicopter skimmed down[12] between the roofs, hovered[13] for an instant like a bluebottle[14], and darted[15] away again with a curving flight. It was the police patrol[16], snooping[17] into people's windows. The patrols did not matter, however. Only the Thought Police mattered.

Behind Winston's back the voice from the telescreen was still babbling away about pig-iron and the overfulfilment of the Ninth Three-Year Plan. The telescreen received and transmitted simultaneously. Any sound that Winston made, above the level of a very low whisper, would be picked up by it; moreover, so long as he remained within the field of vision which the metal plaque commanded, he could be seen as well as heard. There was of course no way of knowing whether you were being watched at any given moment. How often, or on what system, the Thought Police plugged in[18] on any individual wire was guesswork[19]. It was even conceivable that they watched everybody all the time. But at any rate they could plug in your wire whenever they wanted to. You had to live – did live, from habit that became instinct – in the assumption that every sound you made was overheard, and, except in darkness, every movement scrutinized.

Winston kept his back turned to the telescreen. It was safer; though, as he well knew, even a back can be revealing. A kilometre away the Ministry of Truth, his place of work, towered vast

1 Poster of Big Brother as it appears in the film adaptation of *Nineteen Eighty-Four* directed by Michael Anderson, 1956.

1 **fruity.** Melliflua.
2 **pig-iron.** Ghisa.
3 **dulled.** Offuscato.
4 **dimmed.** Oscurato.
5 **meagreness.** Magrezza.
6 **overalls.** Tuta da lavoro.
7 **coarse.** Scadente.
8 **blunt razor blades.** Lamette non affilate.
9 **eddies.** Turbini.
10 **blackmoustachio'd.** Con i baffi neri.
11 **flapped fitfully.** Sbatteva in modo intermittente.
12 **skimmed down.** Volava basso.
13 **hovered.** Volteggiò.
14 **bluebottle.** Tafano, moscone.
15 **darted.** Sfrecciò.
16 **patrol.** Pattuglia.
17 **snooping.** Che ficcava il naso.
18 **plugged in.** Si sintonizzava.
19 **was guesswork.** Era un mistero.

and white above the grimy[20] landscape. This, he thought with a sort of vague distaste – this was London, chief city of Airstrip One, itself the third most populous of the provinces of Oceania. He tried to squeeze out some childhood memory that should tell him whether London had always been quite like this. Were there always these vistas of rotting[21] nineteenth-century houses, their sides shored up with baulks of timber[22], their windows patched[23] with cardboard and their roofs with corrugated iron, their crazy garden walls sagging[24] in all directions? And the bombed sites where the plaster dust swirled in the air and the willow-herb straggled over the heaps of rubble[25]; and the places where the bombs had cleared a larger patch and there had sprung up sordid colonies of wooden dwellings[26] like chicken-houses? But it was no use, he could not remember: nothing remained of his childhood except a series of bright-lit tableaux[27], occurring against no background and mostly unintelligible.

The Ministry of Truth – Minitrue, in Newspeak[28] – was startlingly different from any other object in sight. It was an enormous pyramidal structure of glittering white concrete[29], soaring up[30], terrace after terrace, 300 metres into the air. From where Winston stood it was just possible to read, picked out on its white face in elegant lettering, the three slogans of the Party:

WAR IS PEACE
FREEDOM IS SLAVERY
IGNORANCE IS STRENGTH

20 **grimy.** Sudicio.
21 **rotting.** Imputridite, cadenti.
22 **shored up ... timber.** Puntellati con travi di legno.
23 **patched.** Rappezzate.
24 **sagging.** Inclinate.
25 **the willow-herb ... rubble.** La salcerella (un'erba selvatica) cresceva disordinatamente sui mucchi di macerie.
26 **dwellings.** Abitazioni, dimore.
27 **tableaux.** Quadri plastici.
28 **Newspeak.** Si tratta della lingua ufficiale di Oceania.
29 **glittering ... concrete.** Scintillante ... cemento.
30 **soaring up.** Che si innalzava.

COMPREHENSION

2 READ and gather information about the social and political organisation of Oceania as regards: security and control; people's private lives; language; politics.

3 NOTE DOWN the details the passage gives you about the protagonist. Consider: his name; physical appearance; clothes; mood; job.

2 Komar & Melamid, *Stalin in Front of Mirror*, 1983. Private Collection.

ANALYSIS

4 DISCUSS the symbolic meaning of the elements concerning Winston Smith's description.

1. His name 'Winston': who may have inspired Orwell in the choice of such a name?
2. His surname 'Smith': how would you explain the choice of such a common British surname?
3. His age and appearance: do they correspond to the traditional features of the 'hero'?
4. His memories: can he remember anything about his past?

5 ANALYSE the presence of Big Brother in the extract.

1. Through what device is Big Brother conveyed? What does this method remind you of?
2. Big Brother is also the parody of a historical figure. Single out the details of his description and try to guess who he is.

6 POINT OUT what features of the life in the city of the future created by Orwell particularly strike you.

7 ANALYSE the three slogans of the Party.

1. What kind of words does Orwell employ?
2. How does this affect the meaning of each slogan?

8 DISCUSS. What does Orwell attack in the passage? What danger does he warn the reader against?

YOUR TURN

9 DISCUSS in pairs. What does 'having an identity' mean to you? Do you think it is important to preserve the memory of the past? If so, why and how?

ESAME DI STATO **Terza Prova**

10 TYPE B. Write ten to twelve lines presenting the totalitarian society described by George Orwell in *Nineteen Eighty-Four*.

Exam Reference pag. 355

8.12 **Cultural Issues**

Imagining the future

WARM-UP

1 **IN PAIRS** make a list of what you think the most important issues concerning the future are.

IELTS
Speaking – Part 2

2 **INDIVIDUAL LONG TURN.** Draw a spider chart to present your dreams and your fears about a possible future society. You have one minute to prepare; then you have two minutes to talk.

My ideal future society

My future dystopia

Cormac McCarthy and *The Road* (2006)

The Road, by the American novelist and playwright Cormac McCarthy (1933–), is a novel that describes a terrifyingly devastated world but ends with an optimistic belief in humanity that allows us some hope for the future. The protagonists are a father and his son who live in a post-apocalyptic America. The father and son set off towards the south to find some warmth. They walk along the road, avoiding jackals, thieves and worse, with nothing but a shopping trolley containing their last meagre possessions and the love that keeps them together and gives them the strength to go on. In the desolate world that the two main characters are crossing, the hardest commitment of all is sticking to one's humanity, renouncing violence, but also holding on to the affectionate everyday life that binds the man and the child.

You have to carry the fire

Cormac McCarthy

The Road (2006)

In this excerpt the father knows he is dying and has little time left. He wants to give his son the only gift he has left to give – some hope for the future, some hope that he will survive.

8.1

The boy thought he smelled wet ash[1] on the wind. He went up the road and come dragging back a piece of plywood[2] from the roadside trash[3] and he drove sticks into the ground with a rock and made of the plywood a rickety leanto[4] but in the end it didnt rain. He left the flarepistol[5] and took the revolver with him and he scoured[6] the countryside for anything to eat but he came back emptyhanded. The man took his hand, wheezing[7]. You need to go on, he said. I cant go with you. You need to keep going. You dont know what might be down the road. We were always lucky. You'll be lucky again. You'll see. Just go. It's all right.

I cant.

It's all right. This has been a long time coming. Now it's here. Keep going south. Do everything the way we did it.

You're going to be okay, Papa. You have to.

No, I'm not. Keep the gun with you at all times. You need to find the good guys but you cant take any chances. No chances. Do you hear?

I want to be with you.

You cant.

Please.

You cant. You have to carry the fire.

I don't know how to.

Yes you do.

Is it real? The fire?

Yes it is.

1 Cover of Cormac McCarthy's *The Road*.

2 Scene from the film adaptation of *The Road* directed by John Hillcoat, 2009.

1 **ash.** Ceneri.
2 **plywood.** Legno compensato.
3 **trash.** Spazzatura.
4 **rickety leanto.** Riparo traballante.
5 **flarepistol.** Razzo.
6 **scoured.** Perlustrò.
7 **wheezing.** Ansimando.

Where is it? I dont know where it is.

Yes you do. It's inside you. It was always there. I can see it.

Just take me with you. Please.

I cant.

Please. Papa.

I cant. I cant hold my son dead in my arms. I thought I could but I cant.

You said you wouldnt ever leave me.

I know. I'm sorry. You have my whole heart. You always did. You're the best guy. You always were. If I'm not here you can still talk to me. You can talk to me and I'll talk to you. You'll see.

Will I hear you?

Yes. You will. You have to make it like talk that you imagine. And you'll hear me. You have to practice. Just dont give up. Okay?

Okay.

Okay.

I'm really scared Papa.

I know. But you'll be okay. You're going to be lucky. I know you are. I've got to stop talking. I'm going to start coughing again.

It's okay Papa. You don't have to talk. It's okay. [...]

He went down the road as far as he dared and then he came back. His father was asleep. He sat with him under the plywood and watched him. He closed his eyes and talked to him and he kept his eyes closed and listened. Then he tried again. [...]

Do you remember that little boy, Papa?

Yes. I remember him.

Do you think that he's all right that little boy?

Oh yes. I think he's all right.

Do you think he was lost?

No. I dont think he was lost.

I'm scared that he was lost.

I think he's all right.

But who will find him if he's lost? Who will find the little boy?

Goodness will find the little boy. It always has. It will again.

3 The boy and his father as represented in the film adaptation of *The Road* directed by John Hillcoat, 2009.

COMPREHENSION

1 READ the passage and answer the questions.

1. Who is active at the beginning of the passage and what is he doing?
2. What is the fire the father refers to and where is it?
3. What promise did the father make to his son?
4. Why won't he keep this promise?
5. How will the father and son continue to talk to each other?
6. Why does the father have to stop talking?
7. What does the boy do when he returns and finds his father asleep?
8. Who is the boy thinking of when he asks about the 'little boy'?

ANALYSIS

2 COMMENT on: the language and style; the atmosphere created at the end of the passage.

YOUR TURN

3 DISCUSS. How important is having hope for the future? Do you think it is necessary for mankind to think things can get better? What might happen if all hope were lost?

8.13 **Literature**

The Theatre of the Absurd and Samuel Beckett

The Theatre of the Absurd

Samuel Beckett's *Waiting for Godot*, which was first performed in Paris in 1953 and in London in 1955, is generally considered the starting point of Absurdist drama. The literary critic Martin Esslin applied the term 'absurd' to the works of a group of dramatists who emerged in the 1950s: the Irish writer Samuel Beckett, the Russian-born Arthur Adamov (1908–70) and the French and Romanian Eugène Ionesco (1912–94). They did not form a school, since each playwright regarded himself as an outsider, with his own roots and background and a personal approach to form and subject matter. Ionesco defined 'absurd' as 'that which is devoid of purpose [...] Cut off from religious, metaphysical and transcendental roots, man is lost; all his actions become senseless, absurd, useless'. This sense of metaphysical anguish, rootlessness, lack of purpose and inaction, is the theme of the plays of Beckett, Harold Pinter (1930–2008) and Tom Stoppard (1937–). These dramatists do not argue about the absurdity of the human condition, they simply present it in concrete situations on the stage.

Literary language
The Theatre of the Absurd

The main features of the Theatre of the Absurd are:
- absence of a real story or plot;
- vagueness about time, place and the characters;
- the value of language is reduced – in fact, what happens on the stage transcends, and often contradicts, the words spoken by the characters;
- extensive use of pauses, silences, miming and farcical situations which reflect a sense of anguish;
- incoherent babbling makes up the dialogue.

Samuel Beckett's life

Samuel Beckett (1906–89) was born in 1906 in a Dublin suburb, into a Protestant middle-class family. He was educated at a boarding school, where he was a brilliant student, and then at Trinity College, Dublin. After taking his B.A. degree in French and Italian, he moved to Paris, where he had been appointed as a lecturer in English and became closely associated with the Irish novelist James Joyce and his circle. He settled permanently in Paris in 1937, and wrote most of his works first in French, then translated them into English.

He began his literary career as a short-story writer and a novelist, however his international reputation was established by his plays. He was one of a group of dramatists who developed the so-called 'Theatre of the Absurd', with the common basic belief that man's life appears to be meaningless and purposeless and that human beings cannot communicate and understand each other. Beckett's play *Waiting for Godot* (1952) was the first play in this style. Though it puzzled some critics and shocked the public, it achieved immense success; it was regarded as the most original, influential play of the time and its protagonists, the tramps Vladimir and Estragon, became the emblems of the Absurd.

Beckett's further plays develop the character of the naked, helpless, static being: *Endgame* (1958) deals with the dissolution of the relationship between the physical and the intellectual sides man experiences at the very moment of his death; *Krapp's Last Tape* (1959) is a monologue which stresses the impossibility for a man to find an identity; *Happy Days* (1961) reveals the playwright's tendency to reduce characters to motionless individuals. One of his last plays, *Breath* (1970), shows how human life has become mere sounds, if not silence.

In 1969 he was awarded the Nobel Prize for Literature. He died in December 1989.

1

1 Caricature of Samuel Beckett by Edmund Valtman, 1969. Library of Congress, Washington DC, US.

2

2 Photo of Samuel Beckett by Jerry Bauer.

1 READ the text about the Theatre of the Absurd and make notes under the following headings:
- Main representatives
- Subject matter
- Style
- Aim

2 READ the biography of Samuel Beckett and point out:
1. the education he received;
2. how he started his literary career;
3. the features of his masterpiece, *Waiting for Godot*;
4. whether he was successful in his lifetime.

3 Scene from Samuel Beckett's *Waiting for Godot*. Théâtre de Gennevilliers, 2002.

3 **LOOK at the photograph from a production of *Waiting for Godot*. Describe the scenery in detail. What kind of characters are there on the stage?**

Waiting for Godot (1952)

The story

The play is divided into two acts. In Act I, two tramps, Vladimir and Estragon, or 'Didi' and 'Gogo', are waiting on a country road for a mysterious Godot, who eventually sends a boy to inform them he is not coming but will surely come the following day. The tramps are continually aware of cold, hunger and pain; they quarrel and think about separation and even suicide in each act, yet remain dependent on each other and never do anything. As opposed to the two protagonists, the other characters in the play, Pozzo and Lucky, who are physically linked to each other by a rope as well as by a tyrannical relationship of master and servant, make continuous purposeless journeys to fill their existence. Act II differs only apparently from the first, and the play ends with the two tramps still waiting for Godot, who never comes.

Absence of a traditional structure

The play has no development in time, since there seems to be no past or future, just a repetitive present, and a dreary stability characterises the world portrayed. It has no setting but a country road and a bare tree; it has no plot, because events do not mean anything in the course of time. It has no characters in the traditional sense, as a character presupposes some personality. It has no action, since the static situation of waiting is described; it has no dialogue in the conventional sense, because the characters are unable to provide each other with information either about their present situation, or about their recent experiences and current events in the world outside.

The symmetrical structure

The two acts are symmetrically built. The play unit effect is, in fact, its symmetry: the stage is divided into two halves by the tree; the human race is divided into two, Didi and Gogo, then into four, Didi-Gogo and Pozzo-Lucky; then, with the boy's arrival, into two again, mankind and Godot. The characters' actions are also symmetrical: throughout the play Estragon tries to take off one of his boots, while Vladimir takes off his hat and peers into it. Both tramps need to take off their hat to think, whereas Lucky and Pozzo need to do the opposite.

Vladimir and Estragon

Vladimir and Estragon are never described as tramps; they are two human beings perpetually concerned with questions about the nature of the self, the world and God. They are complementary, since they are different aspects of a single whole. Vladimir is more practical, he never dreams and he keeps waiting; Estragon is a dreamer, sceptical about Godot and always complaining about mysterious people who beat him during the night. As the passing of time is their mutual occupation, Estragon struggles to find games to help them reach their goal. Thus they engage in insulting one another, in asking each other questions, creating a grotesque, humorous atmosphere. The difficulty for Beckett of keeping a dialogue running for so long is overcome by making his characters forget everything. Estragon cannot remember anything about his past; Vladimir, although possessing a better memory, distrusts what he remembers. Estragon needs his friend to tell him his history; it is as if Vladimir establishes Estragon's identity by remembering for him. Estragon also serves as a reminder for Vladimir of all the things they have done together. Thus both men serve to remind the other man of his very existence.

The meaninglessness of time

Time is meaningless as a direct result of chance, which is at the basis of human existence. This is why there is a cyclic pattern to events in *Waiting for Godot*. Vladimir and Estragon return to the same place each day to wait for Godot and experience the same general events with variations each time. It is not known for how long they have been doing this, or for how long they will continue to do so: time essentially is chaos. Human life is treated arbitrarily and is characterised by suffering, but Beckett does not want to offer any solution because when you try to systemise, you simplify and stop understanding the truth. The fundamental question is: *Is there a God?* The evidence seems to be that there is no God, but Beckett leaves the question open because it is impossible to know.

The language

The language of the play is informal, but it does not serve the purpose of communication: dialogue is only sketched and each character, who usually follows his own thoughts, appears to be perfectly aware that the words he produces are just a way to fill his endless waiting. Another device used to show the lack of communication between characters is the use of para-verbal language, such as pauses, silences and gaps.

4 **ANSWER the following questions about the play *Waiting for Godot*.**

1. What is the setting of the play?
2. Who are the protagonists?
3. Why are the main characters complementary?
4. What are the most important themes?
5. What is the main feature of Beckett's language?

1 Roger Rees as Vladimir and Ian McKellen as Estragon in Sean Mathias's production of *Waiting for Godot* at the Sydney Opera House, 2010.

WARM-UP

1 **REFER** to the introduction to ***Waiting for Godot*** **on the previous page and discuss the following questions.**

1. What do you think the function of the audience is in this play?
2. Do you think we can be caught up in Vladimir's and Estragon's dilemmas?
3. Are we supposed to be as confused as these two characters are?

Nothing to be done

Samuel Beckett

Waiting for Godot (1952)

Act I

The following extract is the beginning of the play; the two tramps are alone. The stage directions read: 'A country road. A tree. Evening. Estragon, sitting on a low mound[1]*, is trying to take off his boot. He pulls at it with both hands, panting*[2]*. He gives up, exhausted, rests, tries again. As before. Enter Vladimir.'*

8.2

ESTRAGON [*giving up again*] Nothing to be done.

VLADIMIR [*advancing with short, stiff strides*[3]*, legs wide apart*] I'm beginning to come round to that opinion. All my life I've tried to put it from me[4], saying Vladimir, be reasonable, you haven't yet tried everything. And I resumed[5] the struggle. [*He broods, musing on*[6] *the struggle. Turning to Estragon.*] So there you are again.

ESTRAGON Am I?

VLADIMIR I'm glad to see you back. I thought you were gone forever.

ESTRAGON Me too.

VLADIMIR Together again at last! We'll have to celebrate this. But how? [*He reflects.*] Get up till I embrace you.

ESTRAGON [*irritably*] Not now, not now.

VLADIMIR [*hurt, coldly*] May one inquire where His Highness spent the night?

ESTRAGON In a ditch[7].

VLADIMIR [*admiringly*] A ditch! Where?

ESTRAGON [*without gesture*] Over there.

VLADIMIR And they didn't beat you?

ESTRAGON Beat me? Certainly they beat me.

VLADIMIR The same lot as usual?

ESTRAGON The same? I don't know.

VLADIMIR When I think of it ... all these years ... but for me ... where would you be ... [*Decisively.*] You'd be nothing more than a little heap of bones[8] at the present minute, no doubt about it.

ESTRAGON And what of it?

VLADIMIR [*gloomily*[9]] It's too much for one man. [*Pause. Cheerfully.*] On the other hand what's the good of losing heart now, that's what I say. We should have thought of it a million years ago, in the nineties.

ESTRAGON Ah stop blathering[10] and help me off with this bloody thing.

VLADIMIR Hand in hand from the top of the Eiffel Tower, among the first. We were respectable in those days. Now it's too late. They wouldn't even let us up. [*Estragon tears at his boot.*] What are you doing?

ESTRAGON Taking off my boot. Did that never happen to you?

VLADIMIR Boots must be taken off every day, I'm tired telling you that. Why don't you listen to me?

ESTRAGON [*feebly*] Help me!

VLADIMIR It hurts?

1 *low mound.* Monticello di terra.
2 *panting.* Ansimando.
3 *advancing ... strides.* Avanzando a piccoli passi rigidi.
4 **put it from me.** Allontanarlo (il pensiero) da me.
5 **resumed.** Riprendevo.
6 **broods ... on.** Prende un'aria assorta, pensando a.
7 **ditch.** Fossato.
8 **a little heap of bones.** Un mucchietto di ossa.
9 *gloomily.* Malinconicamente.
10 **blathering.** Parlare a vanvera.

ESTRAGON [*angrily*] Hurts! He wants to know if it hurts!

VLADIMIR [*angrily*] No one ever suffers but you. I don't count. I'd like to hear what you'd say if you had what I have.

ESTRAGON It hurts?

VLADIMIR [*angrily*] Hurts! He wants to know if it hurts!

ESTRAGON [*pointing*] You might button it all the same.

VLADIMIR [*stooping*[11]] True. [*He buttons his fly*[12].] Never neglect the little things of life.

ESTRAGON What do you expect, you always wait till the last moment.

VLADIMIR [*musingly*] The last moment ... [*He meditates.*] Hope deferred maketh the something sick[13], who said that?

ESTRAGON Why don't you help me?

VLADIMIR Sometimes I feel it coming all the same. Then I go all queer[14]. [*He takes off his hat, peers inside it*[15]*, feels about inside it, shakes it, puts it on again.*] How shall I say? Relieved[16] and at the same time ... [*he searches for the word*] ... appalled[17]. [*With emphasis.*] AP-PALLED. [*He takes off his hat again, peers inside it.*] Funny. [*He knocks on the crown as though to dislodge a foreign body*[18]*, peers into it again, puts it on again.*] Nothing to be done. [*Estragon with a supreme effort succeeds in pulling off his boot. He peers inside it, feels about inside it, turns it upside down, shakes it, looks on the ground to see if anything has fallen out, finds nothing, feels inside it again, staring sightlessly*[19] *before him.*] Well?

ESTRAGON Nothing.

VLADIMIR Show me.

ESTRAGON There's nothing to show.

11 ***stooping.*** Chinandosi.
12 ***buttons his fly.*** Si abbottona la patta (dei pantaloni).
13 **Hope ... sick.** La speranza rinviata rende le cose negative.
14 **queer.** Strano.
15 ***peers inside it.*** Guarda all'interno di esso (del cappello).
16 **Relieved.** Sollevato.
17 **appalled.** Spaventato, scioccato.
18 ***on the crown ... body.*** Sul cocuzzolo come per sloggiare un corpo estraneo.
19 ***staring sightlessly.*** Guardando da non vedente.

COMPREHENSION

2 **READ the text and find out:**

1 where the two characters are;
2 what Estragon is trying to do;
3 what they have to celebrate;
4 where Estragon spent the night;
5 what / who beat him during the night;
6 whether they have a clear memory of their past;
7 what their main occupation is;
8 what Estragon and Valdimir do at the end;
9 whether their actions are meaningful.

ANALYSIS

3 **FOCUS on the dialogue between the two characters.**

1 State the most important features of the language employed.
2 Clues like the phrases 'The same' and 'Nothing to be done' are repeated several times in this extract. What effect is achieved? What do these sentences stand for?

4 **CONCENTRATE on the stage directions. What do they mostly refer to?**

5 **DESCRIBE Vladimir and Estragon in a few sentences.**

6 **POINT OUT the devising games which will help the two characters pass the time. What are they the result of?**

7 **IDENTIFY the theme developed in this extract.**

8 **CONSIDER the language used in this scene. How would you define it?**

ESAME DI STATO Terza Prova

9 **TYPE B. Explain in not more than ten to twelve lines how Beckett moved away from the traditional features of drama as regards: plot, characters, message, setting, dialogue and stage directions.**

Exam Reference pag. 355

Process language
Terza Prova

Introducing and supporting the topic

- First of all ...
- It is important ...
- I think/believe that
- For example/instance ...
- On the other hand ...
- What's more ...

8 Prova Orale – Part 2

ESAME DI STATO

Test yourself

Tip

Among the set questions you may be asked to analyse and comment on a few lines from a particular passage. When you prepare to answer such questions:

- provide information about the main situation, the context and the characters involved;
- link the passage to the work it belongs to;
- highlight the key words and concepts through an analysis of the language;
- comment on the issue(s) developed and the technique employed.

1 EXPLAIN why the first decades of the 20th century in America were a good period but were also full of contradictions.

2 READ the short extract from Chapter III of ***The Great Gatsby*** by F. Scott Fitzgerald and explain what aspects of the Jazz Age are described in the novel.

There was music from my neighbor's house through the summer nights. In his blue gardens men and girls came and went like moths among the whisperings and the champagne and the stars. At high tide in the afternoon I watched his guests diving from the tower of his raft, or taking the sun on the hot sand of his beach while his two motor-boats slit the waters of the Sound, drawing aquaplanes over cataracts of foam. On week-ends his Rolls-Royce became an omnibus, bearing parties to and from the city between nine in the morning and long past midnight, while his station wagon scampered like a brisk yellow bug to meet all trains. And on Mondays eight servants, including an extra gardener, toiled all day with mops and scrubbing-brushes and hammers and garden-shears, repairing the ravages of the night before.

3 LOOK AT this painting and point out Edward Hopper's use of symbolism.

1 Edward Hopper, *Nighthawks*, 1942.
The Art Institute of Chicago, Chicago, Illinois, US.

4 DISCUSS the causes and consequences of the Great Depression.

5 EXPLAIN how the Great Depression was reflected in the different arts.

6 PROVIDE a general view of the 1930s in England.

7 READ the poem 'Epitaph on a Tyrant' below, which appeared in the section 'Lighter Poems' of Auden's collection ***Another Time***, and do the following activities.

1 Describe the layout of the poem as regards: number and length of lines, rhyme scheme, punctuation.
2 Say what portrait of the tyrant Auden provides.
3 Explain how you would link this poem to the historical context.

Perfection, of a kind, was what he was after[1]
And the poetry he invented was easy to understand;
He knew human folly like the back of his hand,
And was greatly interested in armies and fleets;
When he laughed, respectable senators burst with
 laughter[2],
And when he cried the little children died in the
 streets.

1 **what he was after.** Ciò che gli stava a cuore.
2 **burst with laughter.** Scoppiavano a ridere.

2 'The Führer', Adolf Hitler, climbing the steps at the Nazi Party's Harvest Festival celebration in Bückeberg, Germany, 1934.

8 TRACE the most important events of World War II.

9 DISCUSS the consequences of the victory of the Labour Party in the 1945 general election in Britain.

10 EXPLAIN the difference between utopia and dystopia. What is meant by a 'dystopian novel'?

11 DEFINE the role of the artist according to George Orwell.

12 DISCUSS. Is Winston Smith in ***Nineteen Eighty-Four*** a hero or an anti-hero?

13 TRACE the features of Absurdist drama in Samuel Beckett's ***Waiting for Godot***.

Moving Forward

Specification 9 | Homepage

Top News

1967
The *annus mirabilis* of social legislation in Britain

9/11/2001

Top Issue

Visions of Peace

Most Popular News

1963
Martin Luther King, Jr., delivers his famous 'I Have a Dream' speech

1979 Margaret Thatcher becomes prime minister

Spotlight

1957
Jack Kerouac publishes *On the Road*

1989 The fall of the Berlin Wall

Cinema

See the Sixties on screen

The Arts

Pop Art

Mapping Music

The Beatles' Liverpool

EXPLORE THE CULTURE

Culture | Literature | History | Society | The Arts | Two Films About... | Cultural Issues

9.1 History

Turbulent times in Britain

WARM-UP

1 **LOOK** at pictures 1–5. Discuss what they tell you about the 1960s and 1970s in Britain.

1 The front pages of the major British newspapers on the 1st of January 1973.

2 A box of Tide laundry detergent, 1958. Procter & Gamble Archives, Cincinnati, US.

3 Women queuing at a clinic to receive the birth control pill. Photo by Jim Mahan.

4 A protest in Trafalgar Square, London, against the use of the atomic bomb, during the Cuban Missile Crisis, October 1962.

5 Black and Asian Britons on a protest march from Hyde Park to Downing Street, London, March 1971.

2 **MATCH** the words (1–4) to their definitions (A–D).

1 Convenience foods
2 Permissiveness
3 Mores
4 Sit-in

A Characterised by freedom of behaviour.
B Form of protest in which demonstrators occupy a place until their demands are met.
C Items that are pre-prepared or pre-cooked commercially.
D Customs and conventions of a community.

3 **READ** the Q&A text.

2

The middle of the 20th century was a time of profound changes in Britain: on a national level, due to the destabilising effects of World War II and the process of decolonisation, as well as in the private sphere.

1

Q What technological changes characterised Britain in the 1960s?

A Technological changes influenced social organisation in Britain in the 1960s and could be seen in many areas, from detergents to freezing and drying methods of producing convenience foods. These developments ran parallel to a social reality where a greater proportion of women were going out to work.

Q What did the social reforms passed in the 1960s mark?

A The rapid changes and multiplicity of new inputs created an ever increasing gap between those who proposed the new culture and the older generation. Pressure from the young and from social movements influenced politicians already campaigning for a more civilised and tolerant society. The reforms passed in the 1960s marked a retreat from the social controls imposed in the Victorian age in favour of what came to be termed 'permissiveness'. The abolition of capital punishment in 1969 was the most significant of all the pieces of civil legislation.

Q Why was 1967 an *annus mirabilis* for social legislation?

A The year 1967 was an *annus mirabilis* as regards sexual mores. First, the Abortion Act made it possible to get an abortion on the National Health Service; then the National Health Service (Family Planning) Act allowed local authorities to provide contraceptives. The Sexual Offences Act stated that a homosexual act between two consenting adults in private was no longer a criminal offence.
The Divorce Reform Act of 1969 made divorce possible after the couple had lived apart for two years, while the Matrimonial Property Act of 1970 established that a wife's work should be regarded as an equal contribution towards creating the family home.

Q What did the Campaign for Nuclear Disarmament anticipate?

A This new social awareness was mirrored in the Campaign for Nuclear Disarmament (CND), which anticipated a decade of popular participation and public involvement in social causes. In 1958 the young supporters of the CND marched from the nuclear research establishment at Aldermaston in southeast England, while the pacifists, led by the elderly philosopher Bertrand Russell (1872–1970), organised a 'sit-in' in Trafalgar Square. These actions provided the model for the marches, demonstrations and occupations of the universities by the students in the 1960s.

Q What was a new source of open social conflict?

A Race was also a new source of open social conflict in Britain. Immigrants were making a valuable contribution to the British economy, but usually in the lowest-paid jobs. They also had deeply felt cultural and religious traditions. The final goal would be integration, meaning equal opportunity, accompanied by cultural diversity in an atmosphere of mutual tolerance. In 1968 a bill against discrimination was

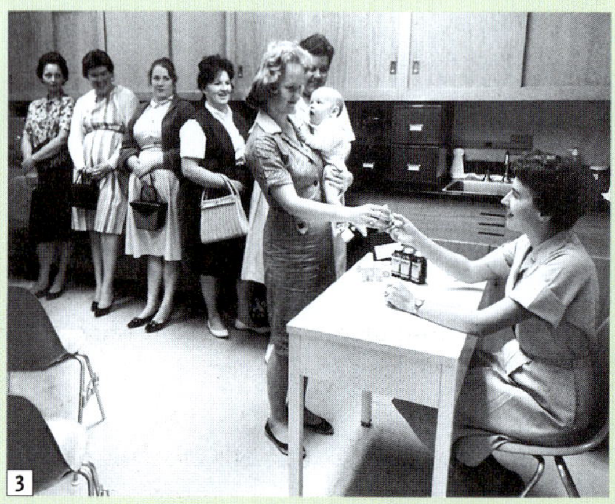
3

TEXT BANK 67: *JOHN OSBORNE*

4

coupled with new legislation to control entry. The new Act aimed at fighting discrimination in employment and housing.

Q What marked the Seventies?

A A worsening economy and declining living standards marked the middle and late 1970s in Britain. There were increasing episodes of violence, racial tension and terrorism, as well as revelations of corruption in local and national government, which all contributed to a lessening of the optimistic consensus that had carried England through the difficult post-war years.

Q Why was 1974 a critical year?

A In 1974 the Irish Republican Army's campaign of violence in Britain materialised. The Conservative government of Edward Heath (1970–74) found itself in confrontation with the miners and involved in an international energy crisis where the main industries were reduced to a three-day week. Unemployment rose steadily. The winter of discontent had begun, with new social problems like: the first urban race riots; a new generation strongly influenced by drugs; juvenile violence; and the new dangers of pollution created by widespread consumerism.

5

Q Why did Britain join the European Community in 1973?

A Britain was doing less well economically than its European neighbours and, partly to share the new European wealth, the country joined the European Community in 1973. The crisis was to last for some time, although Margaret Thatcher's call on individual enterprise and responsibility gave English society the illusion of a new start in the 1980s.

4 IN PAIRS cover the answers (As) in the text. Take turns asking and answering the questions (Qs) using the information that you have read.

ESAME DI STATO Terza Prova

5 TYPE A. Write a 200-word essay about the key concepts regarding British society in the 1960s and 1970s.

Exam Reference pag. 355

ESAME DI STATO Prova Orale – Part 1

6 SURF the Internet to find information about Bertrand Russell regarding:
- his biography;
- his works on logic;
- his works on pacifism;
- his lecture when he was awarded the Nobel Prize for Literature.

7 CREATE your own PowerPoint presentation using the material from the Internet.

8 SHOW your presentation to the class.

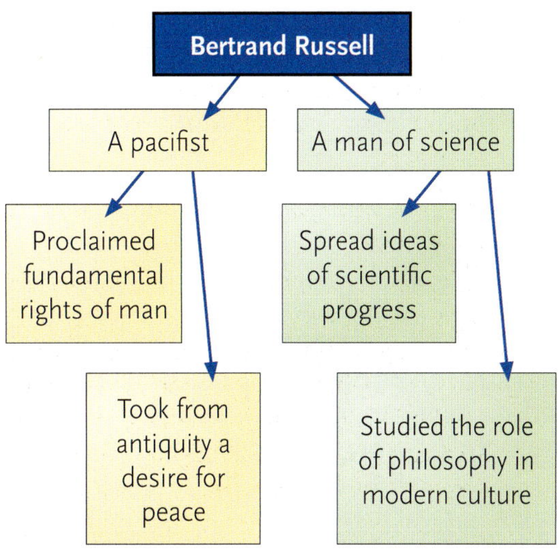

Tip
Create a mind map of your chosen topic:
- Choose a title for your map and write it in the middle of the page as in the example here.
- Write down the headings/main ideas below the title and use lines to link them to the central title bubble.
- Add information for each heading or idea in the bubbles.
- Leave space for adding more ideas and more information in the headings you have already found.

9.2 History
Mid-century America

WARM-UP

1 **LOOK** at pictures 1–5. Discuss what they tell you about the 1960s and 1970s in the US.

2 **READ** the Q&A text.

1 The funeral of President John F. Kennedy, 1963.

2 Claes Oldenburg, *French Fries and Ketchup*, 1963. The Whitney Museum of American Art, New York.

3 An American soldier in the Vietnam War, late 1960s.

4 American athletes Tommie Smith and John Carlos giving the 'Black Power salute' at the 1968 Olympic Games.

Q How did World War II make the US a prosperous country?

A World War II made the Americans the most prosperous people in the world. Apart from Pearl Harbor, they did not suffer bombings or invasions, and the war brought economic advantages, such as increased production and higher wages. Between 1947 and 1971, Americans bought more and more consumer goods like cars, television sets, refrigerators and washing machines.

Q Who won the US elections in 1961?

A In 1961 John Fitzgerald Kennedy (1961–63), the Democratic candidate, won the elections with 50% of the votes. He was the first Catholic and the youngest president ever elected. He saw that the nation, though economically prosperous, was facing social problems such as poverty in the crowded city slums and racial discrimination.

Q What were the key issues in US foreign policy in the early Sixties?

A American foreign policy was defined by the Cold War and the United States' perceived antagonism towards communist nations and leaders. There were moments of tension with the building of the Berlin Wall (1961) and the Cuban Missile Crisis (1962), which ended with the withdrawal of Russian missiles from the island. Moreover, America's advisory role in the war between South Vietnam and communist North Vietnam became militarised.

Q What happened in Dallas on 22nd November 1963?

A Kennedy was assassinated in Dallas on 22nd November 1963; his death put an end to the social hopes his election had awakened.

Q What did Kennedy's successor manage to carry forward?

A His vice president, Lyndon Johnson (1963–69), took over the presidency and managed to carry forward some reforms. He persuaded Congress to pass the Civil Rights Act of 1964, which prohibited discrimination of all kinds based on race, colour, religion or national origin. The law also provided the federal government with the powers to impose desegregation. He also started a programme of health care for the elderly and the poor.

Q What was the social climate in the 1960s?

A The United States of the 1960s was also a troubled society and saw parallel protests in university campuses and among minorities. American Indians reaffirmed the separateness and superiority of traditional Indian culture. Leaders like Martin Luther King, Jr., (1929–68) fronted the African-American Civil Rights Movement, adopting Gandhi's philosophy of non-violent resistance. Other groups adopted more radical ideologies: the revolutionary movement of the 'Black Panthers' was against integration and resorted to violence in the struggle for freedom; the 'Black Muslims', led by Malcolm X (1926–65), advocated

TEXT BANK 68: *J.D. SALINGER*

separateness from the whites and the assertion of racial identity through a return to African roots. Both Malcolm X and Martin Luther King were assassinated.

Q What did Richard Nixon have to face during his presidency?

A America's involvement in the Vietnam War caused many to question American participation in foreign conflicts and gave rise to the greatest anti-war movement the nation had ever experienced. Richard Nixon (1969–74), who replaced Johnson as President in 1969, worked to put an end to the conflict and finally, in 1973, the last American soldiers left Vietnam. Though marked by the success in the 'space race' with the USSR and the first landing on the moon in 1969, Nixon's presidency saw severe economic recession, with inflation and growing unemployment. In 1973 the US even suffered a fuel shortage and began to import large quantities of oil.

Q Why was Richard Nixon impeached?

A The Watergate scandal had occurred at the Democratic National Committee headquarters at the Watergate office complex in Washington DC. It had brought to light political espionage and illegal contributions by the Republican administration to win the election and obliged Nixon to resign in 1974 rather than face impeachment. Nixon's place was taken by Vice President Gerald Ford (1974–77), who aimed at reasserting the qualities of honesty and reliability in high office.

Q What was Jimmy Carter's main achievement?

A In 1976 the Democratic candidate, Jimmy Carter (1977–81), won the elections. His greatest achievement was certainly the Camp David Agreements between Egypt and Israel, preparing the ground for a possible settlement of the Middle East question. But Carter did not succeed in obtaining the release of a group of American citizens held hostage by Iranian leader Ayatollah Khomeini (1900–89). This contributed to his defeat in the elections in 1980 by the Republican Ronald Reagan (1981–89).

5 President Lyndon Johnson giving a televised address to the nation, 1968.

3 IN PAIRS cover the answers (As) in the text. Take turns asking and answering the questions (Qs) using the information that you have read.

Internet Lab

WARM-UP

1 LOOK at the picture and say what it shows.

6 The Apollo 11 moon landing, July 1969.

2 SURF the Internet to find information about: NASA; the 'space race' between the US and the USSR; and the Apollo 11 moon landing, including the astronauts, the purpose of the mission, the famous quotes from the event, and the conspiracy theories which question the truthfulness of the event.
Two examples have been provided:
www.history.com/topics/space-race
www.nasa.gov/home/index.html

3 PRESENT your findings to the rest of the class.

9.3 **Culture**

The cultural revolution

1 **IN PAIRS** discuss what a 'cultural revolution' usually implies.

IELTS Academic Reading

2 **READ** the article and then answer questions 1–13.

Questions 1–4

Do the following statements agree with the information given in the reading passage? Write *TRUE* if the statement agrees with the information; *FALSE* if the statement contradicts the information; *NOT GIVEN* if there is no information about this.

1 After the two world wars people returned to the secure traditions of Victorian values.

2 The middle classes felt the greatest need to modify their way of life.

3 The working-class young became an economically important section of society.

4 The 'Swinging Sixties' were characterised by greater sexual and individual freedom.

Questions 5–9

Choose the correct letter A, B, C or D.

5 The word 'rootlessness' in paragraph 1 is closest in meaning to
- A the decline of agriculture after the war.
- B a feeling of restlessness and the desire to emigrate.
- C more people wanting to move to the country.
- D a feeling of having lost your native culture or country.

6 Which ONE of the following statements is NOT true of the post-war period?
- A The pre-war class structure disappeared completely.
- B The accession of a young female monarch initially gave rise to optimism.
- C The implementation of the Welfare State encouraged expectations.
- D The working-class young became an economically important section of society.

7 According to the passage, what prompted the rise of a service market specialised in music, fashion, cosmetics, drinks, cars and the motorcycle trade?
- A The end of the war made people more willing to spend money on pleasure.
- B Production in industry needed new markets.
- C Young people had money to spend on themselves for the first time.
- D World markets were in the process of expansion.

8 In the author's view, the successful social revolution of the Sixties brought the greatest changes in which area of society?
- A The introduction of a new political freedom.
- B Social attitudes and behaviour changed dramatically and permanently.
- C The total acceptance and integration of the racial minorities.
- D The medical field introduced reforms and new laws.

9 According to the text, pacifism was gradually replaced by
- A American rock-and-roll music.
- B feminism and the Women's Liberation Movement.
- C politically motivated demonstrations and university occupations.
- D over-permissiveness in films, plays and magazines.

Questions 10–13

Complete the summary below. Choose NO MORE THAN TWO WORDS from the passage for each answer.

The Sixties in Britain saw important social changes due to a tangible desire for change in the aftermath of the two **(10)** .... and a rise in the spending possibilities of the young. London became the new fashion capital of the world with its rejection of **(11)** .... and the introduction of the miniskirt. Young people also found a form of protest in their choice of music, and popular bands from this period became famous nationally and internationally. Drugs and sexual permissiveness were the predominant elements of the **(12)** .... revolution of this period. The Sixties were years of lasting gains in sexual and **(13)** .... , but they were followed by a period of disillusion and increasing egoism.

The two traumatic world wars that began the twentieth century changed the social landscape in Britain forever. The rigid values of Victorian morality gave way to a widespread feeling that a rapidly changing civilisation called for more fluid values. The aftermath of the Second World War brought a sense of anguish, and a feeling of rootlessness and frustration as a consequence of the loss of the Empire and the numerous displaced persons for whom life would never be the same again. The accession of a new, young queen, Elizabeth II, and the numerous conquests of the Welfare State, created an atmosphere of expectation of social justice, but this led to disillusionment and apathy when people realised that the old class system still survived. Much of the social frustration became increasingly evident in the young. For the first time in British history, there were working-class adolescents who could spend considerable sums of money on their own pleasure. The result was a distinctive culture and the rise of a service market specialised in music, fashion, cosmetics,

drinks, the car and motorcycle trade. In the 1960s, London replaced Paris as the leader of fashion and boutiques came to symbolise a reaction against the mass presentation of department stores. Mary Quant had opened her first Bazaar shop in King's Road in 1955 and began to popularise the 'miniskirt'. Just a year later, John Stephen came from Glasgow and opened the first shop in Carnaby Street, soon to become a symbol of 'Swinging London'.

Another clear example of the cultural revolution was the transformation of the popular music scene. Pop music was genuinely innovative and protested against established society although it quickly became a massive commercial enterprise. In the mid-Fifties American rock-and-roll music had hit Britain with Bill Haley's 'Rock Around the Clock' and Elvis Presley's songs. This music had a distinctive influence on a little-known group playing in Liverpool clubs called the Quarrymen. The group changed its name to the Silver Beatles and then 'The Beatles' before releasing their first record, *Love Me Do*, in 1962. Fame and fortune followed with the spread of 'Beatlemania' in the UK and also the US. Their only rivals were the London-based rhythm-and-blues group the Rolling Stones, who had a stronger anti-establishment and wilder image than the 'Fab Four'.

Marked by a mood of irreverence, rebellion, and of the general effort to move away from all artificial constraints and to 'do your own thing', the 'Swinging Sixties' in Britain were characterised by an increase in drug consumption, permissiveness in films, plays and magazines, and in sexual attitudes and behaviour, as well as progressiveness in educational practice and theory. It is because of the successful social revolution of the Sixties that social mores changed so dramatically and to such a lasting effect. Living together outside marriage, children born out of marriage, one-parent families supported by public services and the official acceptance of same-sex partnerships have all come down to us from this time. The introduction and spread of the contraceptive pill and family planning clinics revolutionised the sexual climate, especially for women. In 1968 the Women's Liberation Movement was formed to fight for equal rights with men in the home and the workplace.

The quest for self-expression and liberation in the 1960s was replaced in the 1970s by an increasing loss of trust in the values of collectivism and corporatism. The beginning of the 1970s announced the so-called 'me-decade', marked by individualism, egoism or, as in the emergence of punk culture in the late 1970s, by nihilism. Pacifism was replaced by radical demonstrations and occupations on the university campuses, and by political struggle. It also became increasingly evident that racial minorities would no longer tolerate the second-class status assigned to them. Both in the UK and the US, second and third generation immigrants began fighting for their rightful position in the new society.

(From top to bottom)
Marlon Brando in the film 'The Wild One', 1953.
Two hippies during the 'Summer of Love' of 1967.
Jim Dine, *Double Isometric Self Portrait*, 1964.
Andy Warhol, *Big Campbell's Soup Can, 19¢*, 1962.
Roy Lichtenstein, *World's Fair Girl*, 1963.
Poster and album cover for the Woodstock festival, 1969.

8.4 DICTATION: *THE WOODSTOCK FESTIVAL*

Youth culture and street style in Britain

The post-war period saw the emergence in Britain of a youth culture which distinguished itself by its behaviour, musical tastes and body symbolism, all of which took on the tribal significance of belonging to a group. The street became the focus of life, a metaphor for all that was presumed to be real and happening in the world.

1 A Teddy boy and his future wife, in a London street. Photo by Roger Mayne.

Insights

Carnaby Street

Carnaby Street, parallel to Regent Street and near Oxford Circus, is one of the most famous shopping streets for fashion in London. In the 1960s several important independent fashion boutiques and designers, such as Mary Quant, Marion Foale and Sally Tuffin, Lord John, Merc, Take Six and Irvine Sellars, opened shops there. It became a popular shopping area for followers of both the 'mod' and 'hippie' styles. There were also underground music bars in the surrounding streets, and the legendary Marquee Club was just around the corner. With bands such as the Rolling Stones appearing in the area to work, shop and socialise, it became one of the 'coolest' destinations associated with the Swinging London of the 1960s. *Time* magazine helped make the street internationally famous in 1966 with a picture of Carnaby Street on the cover and an enthusiastic article describing its attractions: 'Perhaps nothing illustrates the new Swinging London better than narrow, three-block-long Carnaby Street, which is crammed with a cluster of the "gear" boutiques where the girls and boys buy each other clothing.'

2 *Time* magazine cover of an issue about Swinging London, from 1966.

IELTS Listening – Section 4

3 8.3 | **ACADEMIC MONOLOGUE. You are going to hear a lecturer talking about youth culture and street style in Britain. Read the questions below carefully. Then listen and answer questions 1–10.**

Questions 1–6

Complete the sentences. Write NO MORE THAN THREE WORDS in each space.

The ideological differences in the youth movements of the Sixties and Seventies were evident from their **(1)** ....

Teddy boys, or Teds, liked to dress in a fancy way, cut **(2)** .... in a particular style and had a reputation for violence.

Bikers or rockers rode motorcycles and wore rough working-class clothes, but both **(3)** .... they were considered outsiders.

Bikers participated in many **(4)** .... activities, which included racing along major streets, getting into fights and stealing from bars. They held sexist views about women and racist views about **(5)** ....

A less violent youth movement and rivals of the bikers, were **(6)** .... who dressed smartly, rode scooters and enjoyed many types of typical Sixties music.

For questions 7–10, choose the correct letter, A, B or C.

7 Which is the best definition of a hippy?
- **A** Hippies believed in tolerance, peace and freedom from consumerism.
- **B** Hippies strove to achieve social harmony even at the cost of violence.
- **C** Hippies had a clear idea of the time needed to bring peace.

8 According to the speaker, skinheads became associated with racism because
- **A** they became increasingly political and anti-social.
- **B** they were known for their hooliganism at football matches.
- **C** they had been known to attack coloured immigrants.

9 What does the speaker mean when he calls the punks 'nihilistic'?
- **A** Their political creed was to do nothing.
- **B** They believed in nothing and were against everything.
- **C** They wanted the total destruction of society as it was.

10 What happened to the punk movement in the Seventies?
- **A** They transformed their violent rebellion into popular music genres.
- **B** They became known as Sex Pistols.
- **C** Their extravagant style attracted visitors to a particular part of London.

ART LAB 15: *MID-CENTURY AMERICAN ART*
INTERACTIVE MAP 9: *THE BEATLES' LIVERPOOL*

Annus Mirabilis

Philip Larkin

High Windows (1974)

Philip Larkin (1922–85) was a member of the 'Movement' poets, who refused the committed poetry of the 1930s and the Neo-Romanticism of the 1940s; his casual style and melancholic themes mirrored the period in which he wrote. The poem you are going to read belongs to the collection High Windows *(1974), where 1963, the year of sexual liberation, is described as 'Annus Mirabilis'.*

8.5

Sexual intercourse began
In nineteen sixty-three
(Which was rather late for me) –
Between the end of the *Chatterley* ban[1]
And The Beatles' first LP.

Up till then there'd only been
A sort of bargaining[2],
A wrangle[3] for a ring,
A shame that started at sixteen
And spread to everything.

Then all at once the quarrel sank:
Everyone felt the same,
And every life became
A brilliant breaking of the bank[4],
A quite unlosable[5] game.

So life was never better than
In nineteen sixty-three
(Though just too late for me) –
Between the end of the *Chatterley* ban
And The Beatles' first LP.

1 ***Chatterley* ban.** La censura de *L'amante di Lady Chatterley*, romanzo di D.H. Lawrence, a causa dei riferimenti espliciti di carattere sessuale.
2 **bargaining.** Contrattazione.
3 **wrangle.** Azzuffarsi.
4 **breaking of the bank.** Far saltare il banco, sbancare (nel gioco d'azzardo).
5 **unlosable.** Che non si può perdere.

WARM-UP

1 DISCUSS. What was blocking sexual liberation before the Sixties? What happened to change the situation?

COMPREHENSION

2 READ the poem and do the following activities.

1 What have you learnt about 1963? Underline specific details of this year in the poem.
2 Make notes under these two headings: past and present (=1963).
3 Complete the following sentences.
   A In 1963 there was an important change in .... because the contraception pill was made freely available.
   B A different attitude towards sex in literature was shown by ....
   C It was also the beginning of a new young scene in music as the ....
   D Before that time sex had been ....
   E The new atmosphere of sexual freedom ....
   F The poem ends by saying that life was so much better for everyone except for ....

ANALYSIS

3 SAY what you notice in:

1 the structure of the poem;
2 the length of the lines;
3 the use of rhyme scheme;
4 other sound devices.

4 CONCENTRATE on the opening and closing stanzas. What is their function?

5 FOCUS on the language of this poem.

1 Do you find this language ordinary or 'poetic'? Would you describe the general tone as conversational or formal?
2 What are the most important stylistic features of the poem?
3 Lines 3 and 18 contain the poet's comments. What do they suggest about his personality and attitude to life?

ESAME DI STATO Terza Prova

6 TYPE B. On the basis of the elements you have gathered so far, write ten to twelve lines about the changed ethics of the 1960s and the new sexual freedom celebrated by Larkin in this poem.

Exam Reference pag. 355

Process language
Terza Prova

Referring to texts and using quotes

- According to ... the Sixties was a time when ...
- In the opinion of many ...
- Most people at the time believed ...
- It is clear from events like ... and ... that ...
- As Philip Larkin so rightly says: '...'
- I think everyone would agree with the idea that '...'
- In the words of *Time Magazine* in 1966, Carnaby Street was: '...'

9.4 Literature

Jack Kerouac and the Beat Generation

WARM-UP

1 LOOK up the definition of the word 'beat' in the dictionary and discuss how it could be connected to the cultural context of the Sixties.

The Beat Generation

Jack Kerouac (1922–69) was born in Massachusetts in 1922, the son of French-Canadian immigrants. After the war, he began travelling back and forth across the States, starting lasting friendships with the poet Allen Ginsberg (1926–97), the experimental novelist William S. Burroughs (1914–97) and the writer Neal Cassady (1926–68). This circle, along with other friends, became known as the centre of the Beat movement. In their writings, they chronicled their own wild and rebellious lifestyles in the late 1950s and early 1960s, paving the way for the cultural revolution.

The word 'beat' was a slang term used by post-war jazz musicians to mean 'down and out', or poor and exhausted. Jack Kerouac claimed that the word meant both exhausted, at the bottom of the world, rejected by society, and also beatitude or beatific. The key ideas of the Beat Generation were:

- rebellion and bohemian living;
- refusal to conform to traditional middle-class puritanical values;
- rejection of materialism and organised religion;
- the search for alternative ways to find spiritual understanding, like Eastern religion, with its emphasis on meditation and communion with nature, and mind-altering drugs.

The beatniks

With the popularity of Beat literature, a new countercultural 'type' arose: the beatnik. It was a journalist of the *San Francisco Chronicle* who created the term 'Beatnik' in 1958. The '-nik' suffix was borrowed from 'Sputnik', a satellite that had just been launched by the Soviet Union, striking fear into the hearts of many Communist-fearing Americans.

The beatniks:

- lived in dirty apartments, selling drugs or committing crimes for money, hitchhiking across the country along Route 66;
- acted on impulse, did whatever they felt like doing, explored nudity, sexuality;
- pushed their senses to the limits of understanding;
- used hallucinogenic drugs and alcohol to expand their world;
- attracted attention because of their being different, disregarding the conventions of dress and personal cleanliness;
- wore their hair long, grew beards and considered worn-out jeans, old T-shirts and sandals their standard uniform;
- advocated escapism and created a so-called 'underground culture', which included jazz (highly appreciated because of its spontaneous flow and its freedom of expression), poetry and the Eastern philosophy of Zen Buddhism;
- had their reference place in the City Lights bookstore in San Francisco, founded by the poet Lawrence Ferlinghetti (1919–) in 1953, where the Beat poets and novelists used to read their works in public;
- transitioned and transformed into the hippie movement of the Sixties.

2 ANSWER the following questions about the Beat Generation and the beatniks.

1 What are the different connotations of the word 'beat'?
2 What were the key ideas of the Beat Generation?
3 Where did the term 'beatnik' come from?
4 What were the beatniks' typical actions and clothing?
5 What did they advocate?

Insights

City Lights Booksellers & Publishers, San Francisco

City Lights is more than a bookshop and publishing house: it is a literary landmark and an iconic reminder of the Beat Generation. The store was founded by Lawrence Ferlinghetti and Peter D. Martin in 1953, and was followed by the opening of City Lights Publishers in 1955 with the publication of the soon-to-be-famous 'Pocket Poets Series'. The series included Allen Ginsberg's masterpiece 'Howl' (1956) and introduced the public to many avant-garde writers. The bookstore became a meeting place and stage for the Beat writers, and many like-minded booklovers have enjoyed its unique atmosphere ever since. The ideals of anti-authoritarian politics and revolutionary thinking continue to play an important role in the selection of titles that City Lights publishes and sells. The store now covers three floors, offering an impressive range of both national and international authors and a wide variety of titles in literature, politics and history. It remains a truly independent bookstore which has never lost its commitment to opposing censorship and encouraging progressive ideals and literary innovation.

1 A Beat poetry reading in New York, 1959.

2 City Lights bookstore.

3 **DISCUSS in pairs. The myth of the journey has been dealt with in many different ways: from epic to autobiographical report, with introspective or exotic tones. In what literary works and films that you know does a journey play an important role?**

On the Road (1957)

The story

The novel is the story of a friendship and a diary-like account of Kerouac's wanderings across North America with his friend, Neal Cassady. It lacks a central plot, since its structure is episodic. However, some structural elements give it cohesion:

- the theme of the journey, a symbol of the escape from the city and from one's own past;
- the narrator Sal Paradise, who stands for Kerouac himself;
- the character of Dean Moriarty, a fictionalised Cassady – Sal idolises him for his cowboy style, his ease with women and his exuberant joy in living;
- the same group of friends who reveal a chronic restlessness, an uneasiness that manifests itself in a desire to get going and keep moving – they do not always have a destination in mind and find nothing at the end of their journey.

The characters

The hero of the book is Dean Moriarty, who lives for 'kicks', as he describes those moments of intense experience and pleasure, free from all social and economic restraints. He symbolises the desperate attempt of the post-war generation to live every moment with extreme intensity so as to overcome the sense of void and fear. It is only 'on the road' that Dean and Sal live wild and free. The music the two friends listen to and the people they meet during their journeys are described in a detailed and fascinating way.

Style

Kerouac's style is 'spontaneous' and episodic. He thought writing meant expressing whatever came into one's mind: a thought, an idea, a scene or an episode, ordered as the mind recalls it. The writer saw this exposure of feeling as a significant break with the escape from emotion. The unsophisticated language used in this novel has been defined as 'hip talk' (meaning 'street' language) and identified with the language of jazz musicians in so far as it is based on spontaneity and on mostly monosyllabic words.

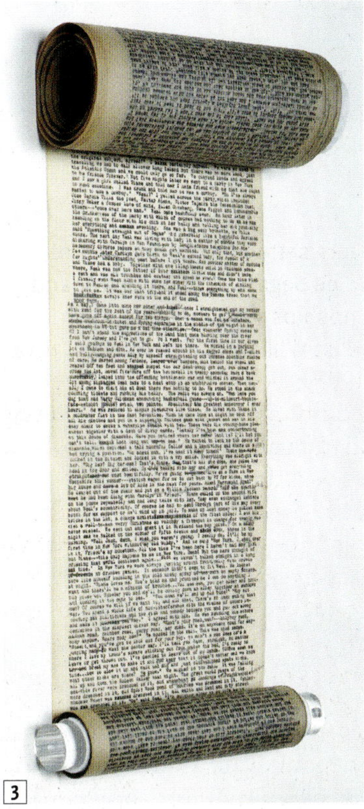

3

4

3 The original manuscript of *On the Road* (1957) as exhibited at the Boott Cotton Mills Museum, Lowell (USA).

4 Photo of Jack Kerouac, right, and Neal Cassady in 1952.

4 **ANSWER these questions about *On the Road*.**

1. Who is the narrator of the novel?
2. What is the most important theme?
3. Who is the hero?
4. What language is employed?

Insights

Route 66

Route 66 is a famous American highway that once stretched from Chicago to Los Angeles. It was opened in 1926 and covered almost 4,000 kilometres, passing through the centre of many cities and towns, and crossing deserts, mountains, valleys and rivers. During the Great Depression many poor families lost their farms in Oklahoma because of dust storms, so they travelled west to California on Route 66 in search of a better life. In the 1950s and 1960s holiday travel brought more and more families to the West to explore the area, and Route 66 represented the spirit of movement and excitement. Over the years it underwent many improvements and realignments, changing its overall length and moving its endpoint farther west to Santa Monica. Finally, in 1985, it was officially removed from the national highway system. However, people have formed groups to save parts of the old Sixty-Six and many of the interesting places to eat and stay can still be seen along the way.

5

5 Route 66, the famous highway linking Chicago to Los Angeles.

1

Into the West

Jack Kerouac

On the Road (1957)
Part One, Chapter 3

In the following passage the protagonist reports his travel Westwards by hitchhiking along Route 66.

8.6

2

It was an ordinary bus trip with crying babies and hot sun, and countryfolk[1] getting on at one Penn[2] town after another, till we got on the plain of Ohio and really rolled[3], up by Ashtabula[4] and straight across Indiana in the night. I arrived in Chi[5] quite early in the morning, got a room in the Y[6], and went to bed with a very few dollars in my pocket. I dug[7] Chicago after a good day's sleep.

The wind from Lake Michigan, bop[8] at the Loop[9], long walks around South Halsted and North Clark[10], and one long walk after midnight into the jungles[11], where a cruising car[12] followed me as a suspicious character. At this time, 1947, bop was going like mad all over America. The fellows at the Loop blew[13], but with a tired air, because bop was somewhere between its Charlie Parker *Ornithology*[14] period and another period that began with Miles Davis[15]. And as I sat there listening to that sound of the light which bop has come to represent for all of us, I thought of all my friends from one end of the country to the other and how they were really all in the same vast backyard[16] doing something so frantic[17] and rushing-about. And for the first time in my life, the following afternoon, I went into the West. It was a warm and beautiful day for hitchhiking[18]. To get out of the impossible complexities of Chicago traffic I took a bus to Joliet, Illinois, went by the Joliet pen[19], stationed myself[20] just outside town after a walk through its leafy rickety[21] streets behind, and pointed my way. All the way from New York to Joliet by bus, and I had spent more than half my money.

My first ride was a dynamite truck[22] with a red flag, about thirty miles into great green Illinois, the truckdriver pointing out the place where Route 6[23], which we were on, intersects Route 66 before they both shoot west for incredible distances. Along about three in the afternoon, after an apple pie and ice cream in a roadside stand[24], a woman stopped for me in a little coupe[25]. I had a twinge[26] of hard joy as I ran after the car. But she was a middle-aged woman, actually the mother of sons my age, and wanted somebody to help her drive to Iowa[27]. I was all for it[28]. Iowa! Not so far from Denver, and once I got to Denver I could relax. She drove the first few hours, at one point insisted on visiting an old church somewhere, as if we were tourists, and then I took over the wheel[29] and, though I'm not much of a driver, drove clear through the rest of Illinois to Davenport, Iowa, via[30] Rock Island. And here for the first time in my life I saw my beloved Mississippi River, dry in the summer haze[31], low water, with its big rank smell[32] that smells like the raw body of America itself because it washes it up. Rock Island – railroad tracks, shacks, small downtown section; and over the bridge to Davenport, same kind of town, all smelling of sawdust[33] in the warm Midwest sun. Here the lady had to go on to her Iowa hometown by another route, and I got out.

The sun was going down. I walked, after a few cold beers, to the edge of town, and it was a

1 **countryfolk.** Gente di paese.
2 **Penn.** Pennsylvania.
3 **rolled.** Viaggiavamo molto velocemente.
4 **Ashtabula.** Città Americana.
5 **Chi.** Chicago.
6 **Y.** Forma abbreviata di YMCA (Young Men's Christian Association) che offre ai giovani alloggio a buon prezzo.
7 **dug.** Apprezzai.
8 **bop.** Stile di musica jazz.
9 **Loop.** Il centro di Chicago, così chiamato perché circondato da un anello di ferrovia.
10 **South ... Clark.** Due strade centrali di Chicago.
11 **jungles.** Quartieri poveri.
12 **cruising car.** Macchina della polizia.
13 **blew.** Suonavano strumenti a fiato.
14 **Charlie ... *Ornithology*.** Il titolo di un pezzo jazz di Charlie Parker.
15 **Miles Davis.** Famoso trombettista.
16 **backyard.** Giardino sul retro di una casa; qui usato con senso metaforico di un posto comune.
17 **frantic.** Pazzo.
18 **hitchhiking.** Fare l'autostop.
19 **Joliet pen.** Il penitenziario di Joliet.
20 **stationed myself.** Mi piantai.
21 **leafy rickety.** Ombrose sconnesse.
22 **truck.** Autocarro.
23 **Route 6.** Statale 6.
24 **roadside stand.** Chiosco sulla strada.
25 **coupe.** Vettura piccola chiusa.
26 **twinge.** Fitta.
27 **to help ... Iowa.** Aiutarla a guidare fino allo Iowa.

long walk. All the men were driving home from work, wearing railroad hats, baseball hats, all kinds of hats, just like after work in any town anywhere. One of them gave me a ride up the hill and left me at a lonely crossroads on the edge of the prairie. It was beautiful there. The only cars that came by were farmer-cars; they gave me suspicious looks, they clanked along[34], the cows were coming home. Not a truck. A few cars zipped by[35]. A hotrod kid[36] came by with his scarf flying. The sun went all the way down and I was standing in the purple darkness. Now I was scared. There weren't even any lights in the Iowa countryside; in a minute nobody would be able to see me. Luckily a man going back to Davenport gave me a lift downtown. But I was right where I started from.

1–2 Scenes from the film 'On the Road' directed by Walter Salles, 2012.

3 Jasper Johns, *Map*, 1962. The Museum of Contemporary Art, Los Angeles, US.

28 **I ... for it.** Mi ci buttai a pesce.
29 **took ... wheel.** Presi io il volante.
30 **via.** Passando per.
31 **haze.** Caligine, foschia.
32 **rank smell.** Forte odore.
33 **smelling of sawdust.** Odorosa di segatura.
34 **clanked along.** Passavano sferragliando.
35 **zipped by.** Sfrecciarono via.
36 **hotrod kid.** Un ragazzo su una macchina dal motore truccato.

3

COMPREHENSION

1 WRITE a heading for each of the three sections into which the text can be divided.

1 Part 1: lines 1–24 ....
2 Part 2: lines 25–39 ....
3 Part 3: lines 40–49 ....

2 READ the first section and answer the following questions.

1 Who was travelling on an ordinary bus?
2 Which city did the protagonist reach?
3 Where did he stay for the night?
4 How did he spend the following day?
5 What did he do while listening to 'bop' sounds?
6 What was he going to do the following afternoon?

3 NOTE DOWN in lines 25–39:

1 the protagonist's first ride;
2 who gave him a lift afterwards;
3 whether he 'took over the wheel';
4 what he saw for the first time in his life;
5 which place he reached.

4 READ the text from line 40 to the end and say if the following statements are true or false. Correct the false ones.

1 He walked to the edge of the town. T F
2 Lots of men driving home from work passed him by without stopping. T F
3 The narrator was afraid of not being seen, since there were no lights in the countryside. T F
4 He decided to walk downtown. T F

ANALYSIS

5 FOCUS on the narrative method.

1 Who narrates the events?
2 How does the narrative technique affect the way the reader perceives the whole scene?
3 The narrator is presented through his actions. List them and say who/what they are related to.
4 From what he does, what kind of man do you think he is?
5 What does travelling mean for him?

6 DEFINE the language used by Kerouac in this extract.

7 CIRCLE all the descriptions of nature. How is nature perceived by the narrator?

ESAME DI STATO Terza Prova

8 TYPE B. Write a ten- to twelve-line paragraph explaining the reasons why *On the Road* became a 'cult' book of the Sixties.

Exam Reference pag. 355

9.5 **History**

The Civil Rights Movement in the USA

WARM-UP

1 **GIVE** your own definition of racism and expand the following vocabulary network; then share your answers with your classmates.

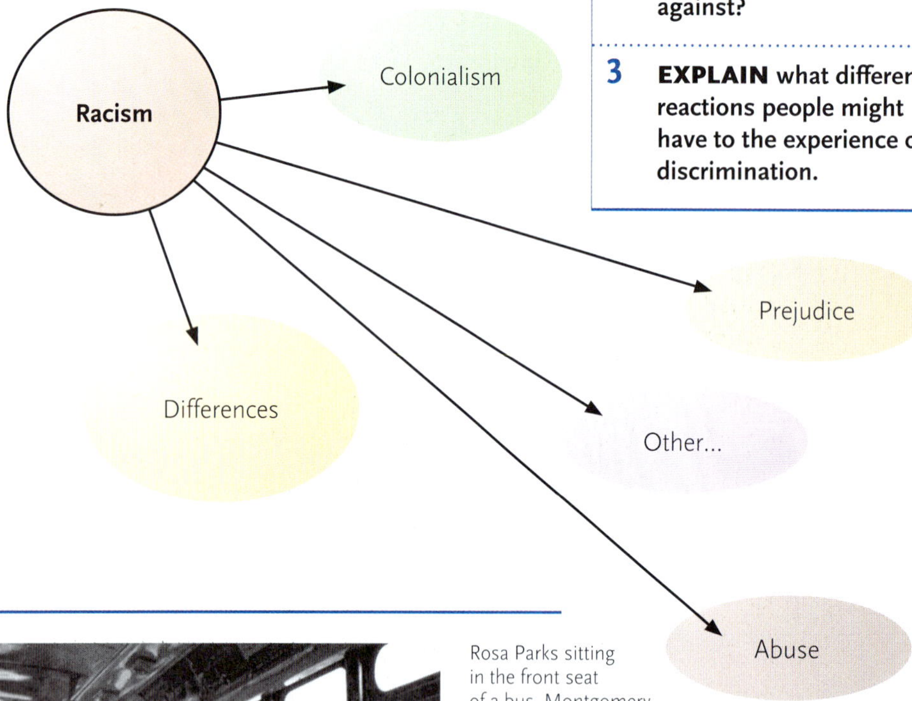

2 **DISCUSS.** What is the difference between discrimination and prejudice? What groups do people discriminate against?

3 **EXPLAIN** what different reactions people might have to the experience of discrimination.

1

One hundred years had passed since the Emancipation Proclamation, but African Americans living in Southern states still suffered from segregation and various forms of oppression, including race-inspired violence. 'Jim Crow' laws, enacted between 1876 and 1965, barred them from classrooms and bathrooms, from theatres and train cars, from juries and legislatures. Starting from the 1950s, Civil Rights activists used non-violent protest and civil disobedience to bring about change, and the federal government passed the

Rosa Parks sitting in the front seat of a bus, Montgomery, Alabama, 1956.

1955

In Montgomery, Alabama, Rosa Parks refused to give up her seat at the front of the 'coloured section' of a bus to a white passenger. In response to her arrest the black community began a bus boycott, led by the Reverend Martin Luther King, Jr., which lasted for more than a year. The buses were desegregated in 1956.

1957

Martin Luther King, Charles K. Steele and Fred L. Shuttlesworth established the Southern Christian Leadership Conference. The SCLC became a major force in organising the Civil Rights Movement and founded its principles on non-violent and civil disobedience.

1962

James Meredith was the first black student to enroll at the University of Mississippi. President Kennedy had to send 5,000 federal troops to deal with the violence and riots that surrounded the event.

Martin Luther King, Jr., during the 1963 March on Washington.

1963

About 200,000 people joined the March on Washington. The participants assembled at the Lincoln Memorial to listen to Martin Luther King deliver his famous 'I Have a Dream' speech.

1964

President Lyndon Johnson signed the Civil Rights Act, which outlawed major forms of discrimination and ended many areas of segregation.

2

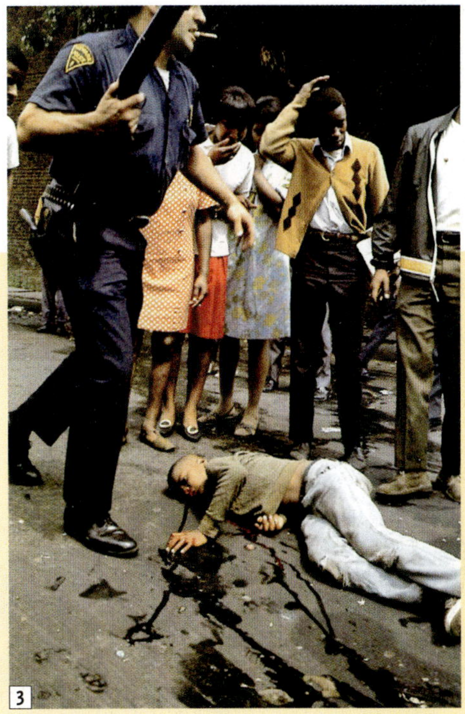

3

1 The Ku Klux Klan in the 1920s.

2 Harassment of Elizabeth Eckford, age 15, one of the first black students to attend Central High School in Little Rock, Arkansas, 1957.

3 A wounded bystander during a riot in Newark, New Jersey, 1967, which broke out after the police beat a black motorist.

Voting Rights Act of 1965, which outlawed discriminatory practices in voting and voter registration, and the Civil Rights Act of 1968. Many leaders within the African-American community and beyond rose, risked and sometimes lost their lives in the name of freedom and equality during the Civil Rights era, including Martin Luther King, Jr., Rosa Parks (1913–2005), Malcolm X and Andrew Goodman (1943–64).

After the 1960s there was a decline in protest activity but the Afro-American freedom struggle left a permanent mark on American society. Overt forms of racial discrimination and government-supported segregation of public facilities came to an end, although segregation persisted in northern as well as southern public school systems and in other areas of American society. Anti-black violence declined in the South, while black candidates were elected to political offices in communities where blacks had once been barred from voting. Southern colleges and universities that once excluded blacks began to recruit them.

Malcolm X with his wife, Betty Shabazz, and their daughters, 1965.

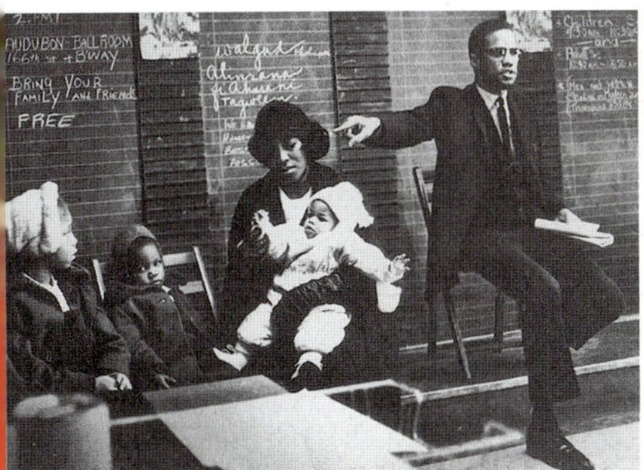

1965

Black nationalist and founder of the Organization of Afro-American Unity, Malcolm X was shot dead in Harlem, New York. It was believed that the aggressors were members of the Black Muslim faith, which Malcolm had recently abandoned in favour of orthodox Islam.

Button protesting the trial of radical black activist Angela Davis, ca 1970.

1966

The militant Black Panthers were founded by Huey Newton and Bobby Seale in Oakland, California. The Panthers' strategy of 'picking up the gun' reflected the feelings of many inner-city blacks.

1967

Stokely Carmichael, a leader of the Student Nonviolent Coordinating Committee (SNCC), used the phrase 'black power' for the first time. He meant it as an assertion of black pride and 'the coming together of black people to fight for their liberation by any means necessary'. The term alarmed many who believed the Civil Rights Movement's effectiveness and moral authority crucially depended on non-violent civil disobedience.

Moments after the shooting of Martin Luther King, Jr., 1968.

1968

Martin Luther King was shot as he stood on the balcony outside his hotel room in Memphis,Tennessee. President Johnson signed the Civil Rights Act of 1968, which prohibited discrimination in the sale, rental and financing of housing.

1

4 **DISCUSS. You are now going to read Martin Luther King's famous 'I Have a Dream' speech, which he delivered on the steps of the Lincoln Memorial in Washington DC on 28th August 1963.** What is the American dream? Where did it come from? Is it a realistic dream to hold on to? Why or why not? How do you think young people define the American dream today?

I HAVE A DREAM

So we have come here today to dramatize an appalling[1] condition. In a sense we have come to our nation's capital to cash a check[2]. When the architects of our republic wrote the magnificent words of the Constitution and the Declaration of Independence, they were signing a promissory note[3] to which every American was to fall heir[4].

This note was a promise that all men would be guaranteed the inalienable rights of life, liberty, and the pursuit of happiness. It is obvious today that America has defaulted on[5] this promissory note insofar as her citizens of color are concerned[6]. Instead of honoring this sacred obligation, America has given the Negro people a bad check which has come back marked 'insufficient funds'. But we refuse to believe that the bank of justice is bankrupt. We refuse to believe that there are insufficient funds in the great vaults[7] of opportunity of this nation.

So we have come to cash this check – a check that will give us upon demand the riches of freedom and the security of justice. We have also come to this hallowed spot[8] to remind America of the fierce urgency of now. This is no time to engage in the luxury of cooling off[9] or to take the tranquilizing drug of gradualism. Now is the time to rise from the dark and desolate valley of segregation to the sunlit path of racial justice. Now is the time to open the doors of opportunity to all of God's children. Now is the time to lift our nation from the quicksands[10] of racial injustice to the solid rock of brotherhood.

It would be fatal for the nation to overlook[11] the urgency of the moment and to underestimate the determination of the Negro. This sweltering[12] summer of the Negro's legitimate discontent will not pass until there is an invigorating autumn of freedom and equality. Nineteen sixty-three is not an end, but a beginning. Those who hope that the Negro needed to blow off steam[13] and will now be content will have a rude awakening[14] if the nation returns to business as usual. There will be neither rest nor tranquility in America until the Negro is granted his citizenship rights.

The whirlwinds[15] of revolt will continue to shake the foundations of our nation until the bright day of justice emerges. But there is something that I must say to my people who stand on the warm threshold[16] which leads into the palace of justice. In the process of gaining our rightful place[17] we must not be guilty of wrongful deeds[18]. Let us not seek[19] to satisfy our thirst for freedom by drinking from the cup of bitterness and hatred[20]. We must forever conduct our struggle on the high plane of dignity and discipline. We must not allow our

1 **appalling.** Terribile.
2 **check.** Assegno.
3 **promissory note.** Vaglia cambiario.
4 **to which ... heir.** Che ogni Americano ha ereditato.
5 **has defaulted on.** Non ha pagato.
6 **insofar ... concerned.** Per quanto riguarda.
7 **vaults.** Camere blindate, caveau.
8 **hallowed spot.** Luogo consacrato.
9 **cooling off.** Sbollire, calmarsi.
10 **quicksands.** Sabbie mobili.
11 **overlook.** Sottovalutare.
12 **sweltering.** Soffocante.
13 **to blow off steam.** Scaricarsi, sbollire.
14 **rude awakening.** Brusco risveglio.
15 **whirlwinds.** Venti forti.
16 **threshold.** Soglia.
17 **our rightful place.** Il posto che ci spetta.
18 **wrongful deeds.** Azioni illegali.
19 **Let us not seek.** Non cerchiamo.
20 **bitterness and hatred.** Amarezza e odio.

creative protest to degenerate into physical violence. Again and again we must rise to the majestic heights of meeting physical force with soul force.

The marvelous new militancy which has engulfed the Negro community must not lead us to distrust of all white people, for many of our white brothers, as evidenced[21] by their presence here today, have come to realize that their destiny is tied up[22] with our destiny and their freedom is inextricably bound to[23] our freedom. We cannot walk alone. And as we walk, we must make the pledge[24] that we shall march ahead. We cannot turn back. There are those who are asking the devotees of civil rights, 'When will you be satisfied?' we can never be satisfied as long as our bodies, heavy with the fatigue of travel, cannot gain lodging in the motels of the highways and the hotels of the cities. We cannot be satisfied as long as the Negro's basic mobility is from a smaller ghetto to a larger one. We can never be satisfied as long as a Negro in Mississippi cannot vote and a Negro in New York believes he has nothing for which to vote. No, no, we are not satisfied, and we will not be satisfied until justice rolls down like waters and righteousness[25] like a mighty stream[26]. [...] I still have a dream. It is a dream deeply rooted in the American dream.

I have a dream that one day this nation will rise up and live out the true meaning of its creed: 'We hold these truths to be self-evident: that all men are created equal.' I have a dream that one day on the red hills of Georgia the sons of former slaves and the sons of former slaveowners will be able to sit down together at a table of brotherhood. I have a dream that one day even the state of Mississippi, a desert state, sweltering with the heat[27] of injustice and oppression, will be transformed into an oasis of freedom and justice. I have a dream that my four children will one day live in a nation where they will not be judged by the color of their skin but by the content of their character. I have a dream today.

21 **evidenced.** Provato.
22 **tied up.** Legato.
23 **bound to.** Legata a.
24 **make the pledge.** Prendere l'impegno.
25 **righteousness.** Onestà, rettitudine.
26 **mighty stream.** Fiume potente.
27 **sweltering with the heat.** Che é oppresso dal caldo.

1 Martin Luther King, Jr., at the March on Washington, 1963.

2 Norman Rockwell, *The Problem We All Live With*, 1964. Norman Rockwell Museum, Stockbridge, Massachusetts, US (on loan to the White House).

5 **READ the text up to line 37 and answer the following questions.**

1 What semantic area does the speaker employ in lines 1–17 to point out the reason why the blacks have gathered?
2 What appeal does King make in lines 16–29? Why?
3 What kind of struggle does he call for in lines 34–37?

6 **READ the rest of the text and say:**

1 what he thinks of the white brothers;
2 when civil rights will be granted;
3 what his dream is and where it is rooted.

IELTS Academic Writing – Task 2

7 **AN ESSAY.** Write about the following topic.

What is the best way to protest for one's rights?

Give reasons for your answer and include relevant examples from your experience or knowledge to support your response. Write at least 250 words.

9.6 **The Arts**

Pop Art and Andy Warhol

ART LAB 16: *POP ART*

WARM-UP

1 **DISCUSS in pairs what you know about Marilyn Monroe.**

2 **LOOK at the painting below and do the activities.** Marilyn Monroe died in August 1962. In the following four months, Warhol made more than twenty silkscreen paintings of her, all based on the same publicity photograph from the 1953 film 'Niagara'.

1 Describe Marilyn Monroe's physical features in detail.
2 Say whether all the images are identical. What modifies the outline of Marilyn Monroe's oval face?
3 Tick the suitable alternative(s) to define the kind of images produced by Warhol's method of work.

□ lively	□ realistic
□ impersonal	□ mechanical
□ unreal	□ visual jokes
□ illusionistic	□ flat

Which techniques and styles does this painting recall?
4 State the colours used and their connotation.

YOUR TURN

3 **EXPLAIN what you think Marilyn Monroe's myth meant for Andy Warhol.**

ESAME DI STATO **Terza Prova**

4 **TYPE A. Write a twenty-line essay commenting on this quote by Warhol from his book *Exposures* (1979): 'In the future everyone will be famous for fifteen minutes.' What is the real meaning of these words? Why did they undermine assumptions about art practice and the role of the artist in society?**

Exam Reference pag. 355

In the late 1950s, at first in Britain but soon in the US too, a new surprising development took place in the field of art. It was named 'Pop Art' because it adopted as its subject matter the imagery of popular culture as defined by the powerful advertising industry. The public adopted it with enthusiasm because it was lively, colourful and decorative; it could be easily collected and fitted into modern interiors. Pop artists employed various techniques from collage to assemblage, silkscreen and encaustic.

Andy Warhol (1928–87), whose real name was Andrew Warhola, was born in Pittsburgh, Pennsylvania, where he studied art. He practiced commercial art in New York City and he started to attract attention in the early 1960s with exhibitions of Pop Art objects from daily life. He chose to present his obsessions, real or induced; among the first of these were *Green Coca-Cola Bottles* (1962), *Campbell's Soup Cans* (1962) and film stars, which he treated in single or multiple images. His art, and from 1965 his experimental underground films, such as 'The Chelsea Girls' (1966), 'Lonesome Cowboys' (1968) and 'Trash' (1970), his personal lifestyle and his determination to remain an inarticulate enigma made him fascinating to a wide public. In 1994 the Andy Warhol Museum, the largest single-artist museum in the United States, opened in Pittsburgh.

1 A photograph of Andy Warhol in New York City in the 1960s.

2 Andy Warhol, *Marilyn Diptych*, 1962. Tate Gallery, London.

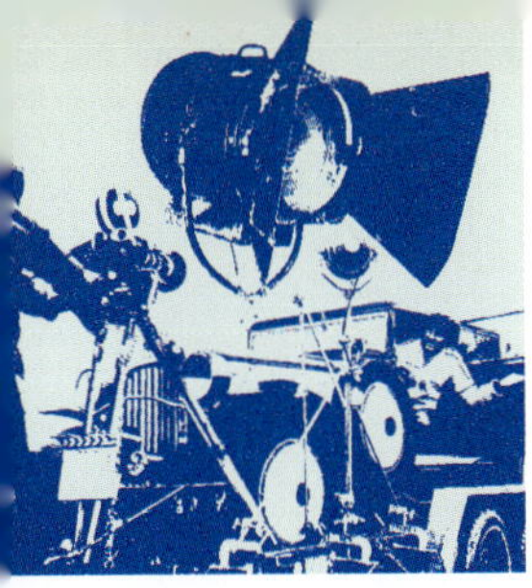

9.7 Two Films About...

The Sixties

WARM-UP

1 **DISCUSS** in pairs.

1 What kind of music do you associate with the Sixties? Why do you think so many of the songs and musical artists from this period are still popular today?

2 By the 1960s, film had become an important artistic medium, and much of what we think about the decade comes from images in films. What images do you associate with the Sixties?

Dirty Dancing

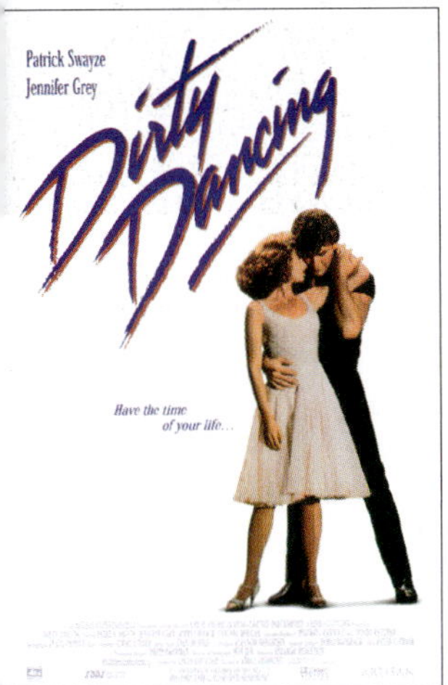

Directed by Emile Ardolino; USA 1987.
With Patrick Swayze (Johnny Castle); Jennifer Grey (Frances 'Baby' Houseman); Jerry Orbach (Dr Jake Houseman); Cynthia Rhodes (Penny Johnson).

The film takes place in the summer of 1963 and tells the story of seventeen-year-old New Yorker Frances 'Baby' Houseman, who is on holiday with her affluent family at a resort in the Catskill Mountains where her father, Dr Jake Houseman, is the personal physician of the resort's owner. Baby, who is about to go to a prestigious college to study economics, develops a crush on the resort's dance instructor, Johnny Castle, a leader of the working-class entertainment staff. At a secret staff party she observes 'dirty dancing' (the mambo) for the first time. She is intrigued by the sexy dancing, and receives a brief lesson from Johnny. Johnny's dance partner, Penny Johnson, discovers she is pregnant by Robbie, a womanising waiter who dates (and cheats on) Baby's sister, Lisa. When Baby learns that Robbie plans to do nothing about the pregnancy, she secures the money from her father to pay for Penny's illegal abortion. Baby also takes over as Johnny's dance partner and, while he trains her for an exhibition performance, their romance blossoms. The situation becomes complicated when Baby's father has to step in to save Penny after a misguided backstreet abortion. Believing Johnny is responsible for the pregnancy, he forbids Baby to see him. The truth eventually emerges but Johnny has lost his job, returning only for the finale: a magnificent dance performance to the song 'The Time of My Life'.

What about accuracy?

'Dirty Dancing' is in large part based on screenwriter Eleanor Bergstein's own childhood: she is the younger daughter of a Jewish doctor from New York who spent summers with her family in the Catskills, participated in 'dirty dancing' competitions, and was herself called 'Baby' as a girl. The film is set in 1963 and it mirrors the new sexual freedom and social mobility that characterised the time. The character of Johnny was based on the stories of Michael Terrace, a dance instructor whom Bergstein met in the Catskills in 1985 while she was researching the story.

Across the Universe

Directed by Julie Taymor; USA 2007.
With Jim Sturgess (Jude); Evan Rachel Wood (Lucy); Joe Anderson (Max); Dana Fuchs (Sadie).

'Across the Universe' is a 2007 musical romantic drama where the plot is built around Beatles songs. The story is loosely about a young Liverpool shipyard worker called Jude who jumps ship in New Jersey from the Merchant Navy in search of a father he has never met. He finds his father working as a janitor at Princeton University and meets a series of young Americans including Lucy, whose boyfriend, Daniel, is about to leave for Vietnam. Jude joins the anti-war protest marches and goes to live in Greenwich Village with Lucy's brother, Max, and an aspiring singer, Sadie. Max drops out of school and becomes a taxi driver, while Jude finds work as a freelance artist. Daniel is killed in Vietnam, and Lucy and Jude fall in love. At a New York book function they all take punch laced with LSD and have psychedelic experiences. Jude is deported back to Liverpool, but returns to win Lucy back in a touching rooftop scene.

What about accuracy?

The film received mixed reviews from critics but needs to be seen not as a story but as a tribute to the 1960s and 1970s and The Beatles' songbook. It presents a broad picture of many aspects of the time, including the Vietnam War and the violent anti-war protests, as well as the hippie lifestyle in Greenwich Village, the drug scene and the sexual permissiveness. Characters in the film die and are wounded in Vietnam, drop out of school, take drugs, are beaten up by the police and are blown up by a homemade bomb. Negative reviews criticised a lack of coherence in the plot and an overly literal interpretation of The Beatles' songs, but for many it is a historical document and a genuine tribute to the Fab Four.

9.8 **History**

The Irish Troubles

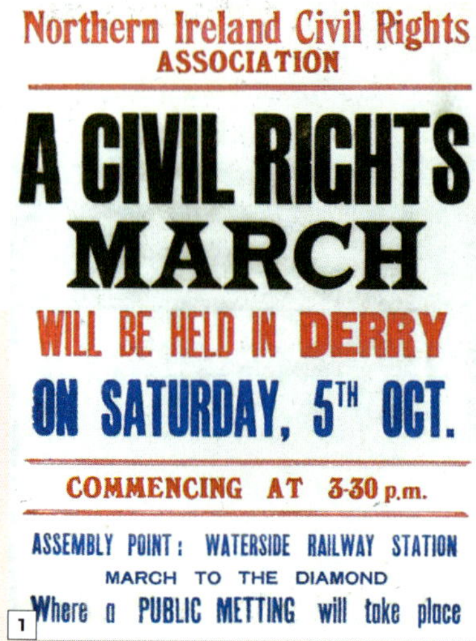

WARM-UP

1 **LOOK** at pictures 1–2. Discuss what they tell you about this period in Ireland.

1 A poster which was hung in Derry to organise a civil rights march in 1968. The march ended with an outburst of violence.

2 Fighting between the British Army and the IRA in a street in Belfast during what came to be known as 'The Troubles'.

The history of Ireland in the early 20th century saw the country split into two parts with separate Parliaments in Dublin and Belfast. The Irish were themselves divided: many wanted Ireland to be a united country under one government, but the Protestant majority in Northern Ireland wished to keep the 'Union' with Britain. The conflict between the Unionists and the Republicans, or Nationalists, was bitter.

After the Second World War, new factors strengthened the power of Protestants and made a united Ireland less possible. The introduction of the Welfare State made a powerful argument for keeping the Union with Britain, since Northern Ireland was guaranteed higher living standards than the Republic of Ireland, and Catholics, considered potential enemies of the state, were kept out of responsible positions. When the British economy weakened, as in the late Sixties and Seventies, Northern Ireland suffered most, and the Catholics of Northern Ireland most of all. Catholics also protested that Unionist authorities did not give Catholic families their fair share of council houses. Finally, not only were most members of the armed police force, the 'Royal Ulster Constabulary', Protestants, but the part-time policemen, the 'B-Specials', were exclusively Protestants and against Catholics.

In 1968 the Catholics organised a civil rights movement, taking inspiration from the black Civil Rights Movement in the United States. The events that would become known as 'The Troubles' began. A 'People's Democracy' march from Belfast to Londonderry in January 1969 was attacked and broken up by Protestants. In the summer of the same year, tension led to rioting between the communities in Londonderry and Belfast. In two nights of rioting in Belfast in August 1969, whole streets of houses were burnt and dozens of Catholic and Protestant families moved to the comparative safety of their own communities. The British sent troops to ensure peace between the Catholics and the Protestants. After being welcomed by the Catholics, these soldiers came to be seen as representatives of the British control of Northern Ireland. The B-Specials were disbanded in 1970 and the 'Ulster Defence Regiment' was formed, dominated by the Protestants.

To counter the threat of terrorism, internment without trial was introduced in Northern Ireland in August 1971 and lasted until December 1975. There was also a deterioration in the relations between the army and the Catholic population, and in January 1972, thirteen people were shot dead by British troops during a civil rights march in Londonderry. This event is known as 'Bloody Sunday'. In 1976, a group of IRA prisoners in Maze Prison in Belfast claimed special status because they said they had committed their crimes for political reasons. They took to wearing only their blankets, then soiling their cells with excrement, and finally in 1981 they went on hunger strike. Ten of the prisoners died before the hunger strike was called off. The first to die was Bobby Sands (1954–81), who became a symbol and martyr of the IRA.

In 1985, Britain and Ireland made a formal agreement to involve the Dublin government in the affairs of Northern Ireland. But violence continued and was experienced both in Britain and in Ireland. IRA targets included Lord Mountbatten, the uncle of Prince Philip, who was murdered in 1979. Finally, in December 1993, British Prime Minister John Major and his Irish counterpart, Albert Reynolds, signed a historic declaration affirming the right of self-determination for the people of Northern Ireland. It was only on 31st August 1994 that Sinn Féin, the IRA's political wing, announced a cease-fire.

2 **MAKE** a table comparing the different positions of Unionists, or 'Protestants', and Republicans, or 'Catholics', specifying the different causes leading to the conflict.

3 **WRITE** a summary of the main events of 'The Troubles' and their consequences.

Seamus Heaney and Irish politics

1 Seamus Heaney relaxes in a London park, 1995. Photo by Johnny Eggitt.

1 READ the text about Seamus Heaney and answer the following questions.

1 What was the poet's relationship to the Irish Troubles?
2 What did the bog victims represent for him?

The poet Seamus Heaney (1939–2013) was born in the county of Derry, Northern Ireland. Always present in his poetry is the shadow of the violent conflict between Protestant Unionists and Catholic Nationalists in Northern Ireland. Being born into a society deeply divided along religious and political lines had the effect not only of darkening the mood of Heaney's work in the 1970s, but also of giving him concerns about the question of poetry's responsibilities in the world, since poetry is split between a need for creative freedom and pressure to express the sense of social obligation felt by the poet as a citizen. Heaney was attacked by both sides: Unionists accused him of being a Catholic poet; Republican sympathisers emphasised his political ambivalence, blaming him for not taking a clear stance supporting the movement for independence from Britain.

People have also criticised his comparison of the conflict in Northern Ireland to prehistoric religious struggles and blood sacrifices, as in his poem about the 'Tollund Man', the corpse of a sacrificial victim found buried in a peat bog. 'When I saw photos of Tollund Man for the first time, I had the same impression as if I had opened a chestnut and found a truth and palpable beauty hidden inside,' the poet said in an interview. 'The man had been killed as a fertility sacrifice. He could have been one of my ancestors. In a flash, I realised the connection between the mutilations of that long-ago epoch with the martyrs of the Easter 1916 uprising in Ireland and all the reprisals and repercussions visited on both communities.' Heaney was deeply impressed by *The Bog People*, a book by the Danish archaeologist P.V. Glob dealing with the discovery, in peat bogs, of the preserved bodies of people sacrificed over 2,000 years ago during tribal rituals. To the poet, the bog victims became archetypal symbols for the enduring need of communities to exact blood sacrifice. Repulsive as these impulses may be, the poet's task is not to condemn, but to draw back and examine the historical reasons and psychological consequences behind them. This gives his work universal meaning and almost mythic resonance.

His apparent detachment is also functional to his poetic vision: in his Nobel Prize speech (1995), Heaney evoked the image of a bombed bus with a dying Protestant man reaching out to shake the hand of a Catholic. He pointed out that this fragile gesture symbolised the power of art, because the mission of poetry is not to make peace – poetry is peace in itself.

WARM-UP

1 LOOK at the picture and describe it in detail. What does it represent?

2 A picture of the Tollund Man: a mummified 'bog body' from 220–40 BC, which was discovered in Jutland, Denmark.

The Tollund Man

Seamus Heaney

Wintering Out (1972)

This poem is from the collection Wintering Out. *In Ulster, the verb 'to winter out' means to see through and survive a crisis. This poem is a seminal one in Heaney's work, since it explores the connection between the aesthetic and the political.*

8.7

I

Some day I will go to Aarhus[1]
To see his peat-brown[2] head,
The mild pods of his eye-lids[3],
His pointed skin cap[4].
In the flat country nearby
Where they dug him out,
His last gruel of winter seeds
Caked[5] in his stomach,
Naked except for
The cap, noose and girdle[6],
I will stand a long time.
Bridegroom to the goddess[7],

1 **Aarhus.** Località dello Jutland dove sono conservati i reperti.
2 **peat-brown.** Marrone come la torba.
3 **The mild ... eye-lids.** I gusci delicati delle sue palpebre.
4 **pointed skin cap.** Cappuccio di pelle appuntito.
5 **gruel ... Caked.** Farinata di semi invernali incrostata.
6 **noose and girdle.** Cappio e cordiglio.
7 **Bridegroom to the goddess.** Si riferisce al rito in cui la dea Terra richiedeva ogni inverno nuovi sposi nel suo letto sacro, la torbiera, per rinnovare la fertilità della terra.

TEXT BANK 69: *SEAMUS HEANEY*

She tightened her torc[8] on him
And opened her fen[9],
Those dark juices working
Him to a saint's kept body,
Trove of the turfcutters'
Honeycombed workings[10].
Now his stained[11] face
Reposes at Aarhus.

II

I could risk blasphemy,
Consecrate the cauldron bog[12]
Our holy ground and pray
Him to make germinate
The scattered, ambushed
Flesh of labourers[13],
Stockinged corpses[14]
Laid out in the farmyards,

Tell-tale[15] skin and teeth
Flecking[16] the sleepers
Of four young brothers, trailed[17]
For miles along the lines.

III

Something of his sad freedom
As he rode the tumbril[18]
Should come to me, driving,
Saying the names
Tollund, Grauballe, Nebelgard[19],
Watching the pointing hands
Of country people,
Not knowing their tongue.
Out here in Jutland[20]
In the old man-killing parishes[21]
I will feel lost,
Unhappy and at home.

8 **tightened her torc.** Strinse la sua collana metallica.
9 **fen.** Palude.
10 **Trove ... workings.** Tesoro rinvenuto nelle aree di lavoro crivellate dai tagliatori di torba.
11 **stained.** Macchiata.
12 **Consacrate the cauldron bog.** A consacrare il calderone della palude.
13 **The scattered ... labourers.** Si riferisce alle esecuzioni faziose degli anni Venti in Irlanda; *lett.*: carne di lavoratori sbaragliata in un agguato.
14 **Stockinged corpses.** Cadaveri con le calze.
15 **Tell-tale.** Spia, rivelatori.
16 **Flecking.** Che macchiano.
17 **trailed.** Trascinati.
18 **tumbril.** Carretta per il trasporto dei condannati.
19 **Tollund, Grauballe, Nebelgard.** Paesi della Danimarca dove sono state trovate le mummie di palude.
20 **Jutland.** Penisola del Nord Europa comprendente la parte continentale della Danimarca e la parte più settentrionale della Germania.
21 **parishes.** Distretti.

COMPREHENSION

2 READ the poem and explain:
1 how it opens;
2 what exactly had happened to the Tollund Man;
3 what the poet suggests in the second stanza;
4 why the poet invokes him as if in prayer;
5 what he imagines in the third stanza;
6 how the poet thinks he will feel.

ANALYSIS

3 ANALYSE the poem's layout. Consider:
1 the division into stanzas;
2 the length of the lines and of the words;
3 the rhyme scheme;
4 the use of punctuation.

4 FOCUS on the use of tenses in the poem. Which tenses are employed? What do they tell you about the speaking 'I' and the Tollund Man?

5 FIND words and phrases referring to the Tollund Man and explain their connotation.

6 POINT OUT the lines where the poet draws an analogy between the bog man and the victims of sectarian atrocities in Northern Ireland. Can you see any difference in the way the poet speaks about prehistoric and contemporary violence?

7 DISCUSS. Why do you think the poet appeals to the Tollund Man to 'make germinate' the contemporary victims?

8 CONSIDER the poet's identification with the Tollund Man in the last part of the poem.
1 Why do you think he chose to speak about him?
2 In what sense are the last four lines ambiguous?

YOUR TURN

9 DISCUSS. How much should an artist respond to the social and political context in which he lives? Is it the artist's responsibility to question it, to make moral comments, or more?

ESAME DI STATO

Terza Prova

10 TYPE B. Write ten to twelve lines comparing Heaney's 'Irishness' with Yeats's. Consider the two poets' upbringing, interests, imagery and aims.

Exam Reference pag. 355

9.10 **History**

Britain: the Thatcher years and beyond

WARM-UP

1 **LOOK** at pictures 1–6 on pages 337–338. Discuss what they tell you about the last few decades in Britain.

2 **MATCH** the years (A–F) to the events shown in the pictures 1–6 on pages 337–338. Then read the Q&A text and check your answers.

A 1982 ....
B 1997 ....
C 1979 ....
D 1989 ....
E 2010 ....
F 1990 ....

1 Margaret Thatcher waiting for election results. Photo by Herbie Knott.

2 The 'Canberra' returns from the Falklands. Photo by Lionel Cherrault.

3 London's Poll Tax riot. Photo by Nick Hider.

Q Who won the 1979 general election?

A The 1979 general election was won by the Conservative Party led by Margaret Thatcher (1979–90), making her the country's first woman prime minister. She can be defined as a 19th-century liberal rather than a conservative because she advocated free trade, that is, low protective tariffs, and as little government interference as possible in business and domestic matters. Her strong will and determination earned her the nickname 'the Iron Lady'.

Q What were the most important features of her home policy?

A To lower government spending, industries were denationalised; the Conservatives believed that industry would be more efficient and competitive in private hands. Margaret Thatcher made a series of reforms to develop private enterprise and to reduce the power of the trade unions.

Q What were the Eighties characterised by?

A The Eighties brought with them an increase in material wealth as well as the emergence of an underclass of poor people with low-paid jobs or no job, a poor home or no home. Thatcher encouraged the young in particular to take up their own responsibilities, to try to make a good career and to value the freedom of self-employment. In this climate, professional choices changed: law, finance, accounting, medicine and advertising were regarded as steady jobs with the prospect of high salaries.

Q Who were the 'yuppies'?

A The ambitious urban professionals, whose main interests were high-earning professions and the acquisition of impressive status symbols such as expensive clothes and sports cars, became a social phenomenon known as 'yuppies' (young urban professionals).

Q Why did the Falklands War break out?

A The Falkland Islands (or Malvinas) in the South Atlantic were one of the last British dominions. In 1982 they were claimed by Argentina as part of its national territory and were invaded by the Argentine army. The British response was immediate: a task force was sent to reclaim the islands, and after a two-month campaign, Argentina surrendered.

Q Which tax required sacrifices mainly from the poor?

A In 1987 Thatcher introduced the unpopular 'poll tax', a local tax on individuals and no longer on properties, which was to be paid by all citizens enrolled to vote. Poorer people considered this tax extremely unfair, but Thatcher refused to back down. In April 1990 her reputation for invincibility was shaken by a London poll tax demonstration that degenerated into a riot.

Q What marked the changes taking place from the 1980s to the 1990s?

A Two of the biggest changes were the fall of

the Berlin Wall in 1989, marking the end of the Cold War, and Margaret Thatcher's resignation in November 1990. She was succeeded as party leader and prime minister by John Major (1990–97). His programme was to follow Margaret Thatcher's ideas, but not to attack certain social policies quite so strongly.

Q Which party did Tony Blair belong to? What were his political views?

A Tony Blair (1997–2007), leader of the Labour Party, won the elections in May 1997. He held liberal views on matters of education, welfare and technological change, but conservative views on law and order issues and family values. His government produced constitutional reforms that partially decentralised the UK, leading to the formation of separate parliaments in Wales and Scotland by 1999. Blair won two further electoral victories with the Labour Party in June 2001 and May 2005.

Q Who replaced Tony Blair in 2007?

A Gordon Brown became the leader of the Labour Party and prime minister in 2007, when Tony Blair resigned.

4

Q Who won the 2010 general election?

A In the 2010 general election no party won an overall majority and the Conservatives, under their leader David Cameron, formed a coalition government together with the Liberals.

5

4 Tony Blair. Photo by Toby Melville.

5 David Cameron makes his first speech as prime minister, outside 10 Downing Street. Photo by Tristan Fewings.

6 East German guards knock down a part of the Berlin Wall near Potsdamer Platz. Photo by Gérard Malié.

3 **MATCH the words (1–4) from the text to their definition (A–D).**

1 Nickname
2 Accounting
3 Steady
4 Back down

A Reliable and not likely to change.
B Change or withdraw from a chosen direction.
C An informal name that takes the place of the proper name.
D The action of keeping financial accounts.

4 **IN PAIRS cover the answers (As) in the text. Take turns asking and answering the questions (Qs) using the information that you have read.**

ESAME DI STATO **Terza Prova**

5 **TYPE A. Write a 20-line essay in which you discuss the key ideas of the Thatcher years.**

Exam Reference pag. 355

Milestones

6

1989, the fall of the Berlin Wall

Berlin had been politically divided since the end of World War II, with the eastern part of the city serving as the capital of the German Democratic Republic. The two parts of the city were physically divided in 1961 with the building of the Berlin Wall, made up of large concrete walls, barbed wire and guard towers. This wall became part of the 'Iron Curtain' which separated the communist eastern bloc of Europe from the West during the Cold War. The East German authorities claimed that the wall defended communist East Berlin from the capitalist western section of the city. However, it was really built to stop thousands of East Berliners from emigrating to the free western part of the city in search of a better life. In 1989 rebellions against communism spread all over Eastern Europe, and all the gates in the Wall were opened for free access on 9th November of that year. This event became the symbol of the end of the Cold War, and East and West Berlin became one undivided city.

TEXT BANK 70: *BLACK DOGS*

Ian McEwan and Thatcher's England

an McEwan's life

an McEwan (1948–) started writing in 1970, after studying at he University of Sussex and at the University of East Anglia. In 975 he published his first collection of short stories, *First Love, .ast Rites*, which are concerned with degenerate or dislocated ›ehaviour. A second collection, *In Between the Sheets*, appeared in 978, and was followed in the same year by *The Cement Garden*, menacing novel of psychological penetration. His second iovel, *The Comfort of Strangers* (1981), was followed by *The Child n Time* (1987), which was characterised by a humanity and a :apacity to feel and to arouse feelings and emotions that had been ·ather absent from his earlier works. In *The Innocent* (1990) and *3lack Dogs* (1992), McEwan showed greater social and political awareness, though he tried to preserve that ·ather mysterious element he regards as so important in fiction. In *The Daydreamer* (1994) he returned to the form of the short story and took up one of his dearest themes: that of childhood. McEwan's latest works include the novels: *Enduring Love* (1997), a thriller where he explores contemporary neurosis and 'new age' spirituality; *Amsterdam* (1998), an allegory of the moral desert in which modern man lives; *Atonement* (2001), regarded as his masterpiece by many critics; *Saturday* (2005), a day-in-the-life novel that follows one character from the early hours of Saturday morning to the dawn of Sunday; *Chesil Beach* (2007), dealing with a couple's worries about the wedding night to come; *Solar* (2010), a satirical novel which focuses on climate change; and *Sweet Tooth* (2012), a spy story.

1

1 Ian McEwan. Photo by Robert Judges.

2 Cover of *The Child in Time*.

The Child in Time (1987)

The story

Stephen Lewis writes books for children. He is married to Julie, a musician, and they have a three-year-old daughter, Kate. One Saturday morning, Stephen takes Kate with him to a local supermarket. He lifts Kate from the shopping cart and begins unloading the groceries at the checkout. When he turns to check on Kate, she has disappeared. No trace of Kate is found and no ransom note is ever received. After Kate's loss, Stephen and Julie split up. Stephen starts drinking and gets involved in a British government committee which is preparing a report on childcare. The right-wing government has decided to make disciplined childcare part of its policy. Stephen's best friend, Charles, is a politician, and despite being the prime minister's favourite, he is heading towards a nervous breakdown. He eventually retires from political life because of his fragile mental condition; he rejects his own adult state, moving to the countryside and regressing back to a fantasy childhood. As the novel moves to its end, Charles commits suicide, and Stephen and Julie are reunited. Julie gets pregnant, and Stephen helps at the delivery of their child.

2

1 **ANSWER the questions about *The Child in Time*.**

1 What traumatic experience do Stephen Lewis and his wife go through?
2 Why does Stephen get involved in a British government committee?
3 What is the setting of the novel?
4 What is history associated with in the book?
5 How does the narrative technique affect the reader?

Themes

Set in England in a near dystopian future, the novel offers McEwan's view of Thatcher's England – a country where poverty and squalor are to be found everywhere amidst affluence, and where control is exercised in the name of freedom. Stephen acts as an observer stuck in a state of unreality who feels perpetually 'outside' of time, as if it had stopped at the moment of Kate's disappearance. Childhood and its idealisation is a major theme. Kate is frozen in time: she is always the perfect three-year-old in Stephen's mind.

History seems to be connected with loss, with the radical change which has transformed the face of Britain, filling the cities with beggars, causing the collapse of public transport and running down educational provision. The past has been destroyed in the name of efficiency and individual freedom. The figure of the child of the title, however, suggests that the world can be redeemed, that loss is real but not necessarily permanent. Julie and Stephen's child at the end of the book represents this hope.

The style

The story is narrated by an anonymous third-person narrator from the point of view of Stephen Lewis. This perspective means that the reader is very limited in the understanding of anything that does not occur in the direct sight of Stephen. There are, however, occasions where the narrator speaks directly to the reader.

1 Jenny Holzer, *Truisms*, 1982. Spectacolor signboard, Time Square, New York.

WARM-UP

1 DISCUSS. What is a writer likely to want to achieve with the opening of a novel?

A sense of loss

Ian McEwan

The Child in Time (1987)
Chapter One

You are going to read the opening pages of the novel. The protagonist, Stephen, is walking down a street through central London. McEwan uses the scene to present the character and his sense of loss for the abduction of his daughter.

8.8

Subsiding[1] public transport had long been associated in the minds of both Government and the majority of its public with the denial[2] of individual liberty. The various services collapsed twice a day at rush hour and it was quicker, Stephen found, to walk from his flat to Whitehall than to take a taxi. It was late May, barely[3] nine-thirty, and already the temperature was nudging the eighties[4]. He strode[5] towards Vauxhall Bridge past double and treble files of trapped, throbbing[6] cars, each with its solitary driver. In tone the pursuit[7] of liberty was more resigned[8] than passionate. Ringed fingers drummed[9] patiently on the sill of a hot tin roof[10], white-shirted elbows poked[11] through rolled-down windows. There were newspapers spread over steering wheels[12]. Stephen stepped quickly through the crowds, through layers of in-car radio blather – jingles[13], high-energy breakfast DJs, news-flashes, traffic 'alerts'[14]. Those drivers not reading listened stolidly[15]. The steady forward press[16] of the pavement crowds must have conveyed to them a sense of relative motion, of drifting slowly backwards[17].

Jigging and weaving to overtake[18], Stephen remained as always, though barely consciously, on the watch for children, for a five-year-old girl. It was more than a habit, for a habit could be broken. This was a deep disposition, the outline experience had stenciled[19] on character. It was not principally a search, though it had once been an obsessive hunt, and for a long time too. Two years on, only vestiges of that remained; now it was a longing[20], a dry hunger. There was a biological clock, dispassionate in its unstoppability, which let his daughter go on growing, extended and complicated her simple vocabulary, made her stronger, her movements surer. The clock, sinewy[21] like a heart, kept faith with an unceasing[22] conditional; she would be drawing, she would be starting to read; she would be losing a milktooth[23]. She would be familiar, taken for granted. It seemed as though the proliferating instances might wear down[24] this conditional, the frail[25], semi-opaque screen, whose fine tissues[26] of time and chance separated her from him; she is home from school and tired, her tooth is under the pillow, she is looking for her daddy.

Any five-year-old girl – though boys would do[27] – gave substance to her continued existence. In shops, past playgrounds, at the houses of friends, he could not fail to watch out for Kate in other children, or ignore in them the slow changes, the accruing[28] competences, or fail to feel the untapped potency[29] of weeks and months, the time that should have been hers. Kate's growing up had become the essence of time itself. Her phantom growth, the product of an obsessive sorrow, was not only inevitable – nothing could stop the sinewy clock – but necessary. Without the fantasy of her continued existence he was lost, time would stop. He was the father of an invisible child.

But here on Millbank there were only ex-children shuffling[30] to work. Further up, just before Parliament Square, was a group of licensed beggars. They were not permitted anywhere near Parliament or Whitehall or within sight of the square. But a few were taking advantage of the confluence of commuter routes[31]. He saw their bright badges from a couple of hundred yards away. This was their weather and they looked cocky[32] with their freedom. The wage earners had to give way[33]. A dozen beggars were working both sides of the street, moving towards him steadily against the surge[34]. It was a child Stephen was watching now,

1 **Subsiding.** Sovvenzionare.
2 **denial.** Negazione.
3 **barely.** Da poco passate.
4 **nudging the eighties.** Sfiorava i 25°.
5 **He strode.** Si diresse a grandi passi.
6 **trapped, throbbing.** Intrappolate, vibranti.
7 **pursuit.** Perseguimento.
8 **resigned.** Rassegnato.
9 **Ringed ... drummed.** Dita inanellate tamburellavano.
10 **sill ... roof.** Bordo del tettuccio metallico rovente.
11 **poked.** Spuntavano.
12 **steering wheels.** Volanti.
13 **layers ... blather – jingles.** Blaterare da autoradio – motivi pubblicitari.
14 **alerts.** Bollettini.
15 **stolidly.** Con indifferenza.
16 **The steady forward press.** L'avanzare regolare e compatto.
17 **drifting slowly backwards.** Lenta deriva all'indietro.
18 **Jigging ... overtake.** Avanzando a saltelli e zig-zag per superare.
19 **had stenciled.** Aveva lasciato un'impronta indelebile.
20 **longing.** Desiderio intenso.
21 **sinewy.** Elastico e forte.
22 **kept faith ... unceasing.** Si manteneva fedele a un continuo.
23 **milktooth.** Dente da latte.
24 **It seemed ... down.** Era come se le molte ipotesi potessero logorare.
25 **frail.** Fragile.
26 **tissues.** Membrane.
27 **would do.** Andassero bene.
28 **accruing.** Che maturavano.
29 **untapped potency.** Potenziale inutilizzato.
30 **shuffling.** Che si trascinavano.
31 **commuter routes.** Percorsi dei pendolari.
32 **cocky.** Impertinenti.
33 **to give way.** Cedere il passo.
34 **steadily ... surge.** Fermamente contro le ondate di folla.

not a five-year-old but a skinny prepubescent. She had registered him at some distance. She walked slowly, somnambulantly, the regulation black bowl[35] extended. The office workers parted and converged about her. Her eyes were fixed on Stephen as she came. He felt the usual ambivalence. To give money ensured the success of the Government programme. Not to give involved some determined facing away from private distress[36]. There was no way out. The art of bad government was to sever[37] the line between public policy and intimate feeling, the instinct for what was right. These days he left the matter to chance. If he had small change[38] in his pocket he gave it. If not, he gave nothing. He never handed out banknotes.

The girl was brown-skinned from sunny days on the street. She wore a grubby yellow cotton frock[39] and her hair severely cropped[40]. Perhaps she had been deloused[41]. As the distance closed he saw she was pretty, impish and freckled[42], with a pointed chin. She was no more than twenty feet away when she ran forward and took from the pavement a lump of still glistening chewing gum[43]. She popped it in her mouth and began to chew. The little head tilted defiantly[44] as she looked again in his direction.

Then she was before him, the standard-issue bowl[45] held before her. She had chosen him minutes ago, it was a trick they had. Appalled, he had reached into his back pocket for a five pound note. She looked on with neutral expression as he set it down on top of the coins.

As soon as his hand was clear, the girl picked the note rolled it tight into her fist[46] and said, 'Fuck you, mister.' She was edging round him[47].

Stephen put his hand on the hard, narrow shoulder and gripped[48]. 'What was that you said?'

The girl turned and pulled away. The eyes had shrunk, the voice was reedy[49]. 'I said fank you mister.' She was out of reach when she added, 'Rich creep![50]'

Stephen showed empty palms in mild rebuke[51]. He smiled without parting his lips to convey his immunity to the insult. But the kid had resumed her steady, sleep-walker's step along the street. He watched her for a full minute before he lost her in the crowd. She did not glance back.

35 **the regulation black bowl.** La ciotola nera regolamentare.
36 **facing ... distress.** Ignorare l'indigenza dell'individuo.
37 **to sever.** Rendere netta.
38 **small change.** Spiccioli.
39 **grubby ... frock.** Abito sudicio di cotone giallo.
40 **severely cropped.** Tagliati cortissimi.
41 **deloused.** Rasata per i pidocchi.
42 **impish and freckled.** Con il viso malizioso coperto di lentiggini.
43 **a lump ... gum.** Una gomma da masticare ancora luccicante.
44 **tilted defiantly.** Si piegò indietro con aria di sfida.
45 **the standard-issue bowl.** La ciotola regolamentare.
46 **rolled it tight into her fist.** La accartocciò stretta in un pugno.
47 **She ... him.** Lo stava lentamente oltrepassando.
48 **gripped.** Strinse.
49 **had shrunk ... reedy.** Si erano assottigliati ... flebile.
50 **Rich creep!** Sporco capitalista!
51 **mild rebuke.** Mite rimprovero.

COMPREHENSION

2 READ up to line 33 and note down:

1. the setting in time and place;
2. the situation of public transport;
3. the people's attitude;
4. what Stephen was watching out for;
5. how he had come to regard time;
6. what the essence of time had become for him;
7. how he would have felt without that fantasy.

3 READ the rest of the passage and answer the questions.

1. Who did Stephen meet on his way to Whitehall?
2. What did they look like?
3. Whom did Stephen spot among them?
4. How did he usually behave with beggars?
5. What did the girl suddenly pick up from the pavement?
6. What did Stephen give her? How did she react?
7. What did he do then?

ANALYSIS

4 ANALYSE the passage by doing the following activities.

1. Underline the words which describe Stephen looking for his daughter. How long has it been since his daughter disappeared? How is his search connoted?
2. Make notes about the beggar girl's age, physical appearance, clothes, personal belongings, attitude.
3. Read lines 43–48. What is the narrator's opinion of the government?
4. Describe the view of London in the 1980s presented by McEwan. What strikes you most?

ESAME DI STATO **Terza Prova**

5 TYPE B. In ten to twelve lines, explain what McEwan achieves in the opening pages of the novel in terms of setting the tone, point of view, presentation of character and themes.

Exam Reference pag. 355

2 Barbara Kruger, *Untitled (We are not what we seem)*, 1988.

9.12 **History**

The USA: from Reagan to Obama

1

WARM-UP

1 DISCUSS what you know about the American presidency.

1 How long are American presidents elected for?
2 How many times can they be re-elected?
3 What time of year is the American presidential election?
4 Are they elected directly by the American people?
5 Can you name any recent presidents?

1 Margaret Thatcher and Ronald Reagan at a meeting in Tokyo, 1986.

2 Yitzhak Rabin, Bill Clinton and Yasser Arafat in 1993.

3 Barack Obama and George W. Bush at the White House in 2008.

A former film actor and a brilliant talker, Ronald Reagan (1981–89) won the consent of many Americans through his policy of 'stand on your own feet and act tough', which had much in common with Thatcherism in England. His economic policy encouraged free enterprise and the rise of young, very competitive professionals, or 'yuppies', and brought about cuts in government spending. Millions of dollars were spent on developing powerful missiles and on space research. This created employment and businessmen made big profits, and probably contributed to Reagan's re-election in 1984 with the biggest majority in American history.

2

He was followed in the presidency by the Republican George H.W. Bush (1989–93), who led the United States in its involvement in the Persian Gulf crisis in 1990, after Iraq's President Saddam Hussein invaded and annexed Kuwait. The Gulf War began on 16th January 1991, when Hussein refused to comply with the United Nations' demand to withdraw from Kuwait. US General Norman Schwarzkopf led the military operation 'Desert Storm', and on 3rd March 1991 he dictated the cease-fire terms that put an end to the war.

The Democrat Bill Clinton (1993–2001) won the presidential elections in 1992. Political commentators compared him to John F. Kennedy because of his youth, charisma, his liberal policies and reform programme. An achievement in foreign affairs was marked by the peace agreement signed between Yasser Arafat's PLO (Palestine Liberation Organisation) and Yitzhak Rabin of Israel at the White House in 1993. Clinton was re-elected on 7th November 1996.

In 2001 Clinton was succeeded by the Republican George W. Bush (2001–09). During the first year of Bush's presidency the country was stunned by the September 11th attacks on the Twin Towers of the World Trade Center, in New York, and on the Pentagon, the headquarters of the US Department of Defense, in Virginia. All the buildings were hit by American passenger planes which had been hijacked by Al-Qaeda terrorists. The collapse of the two towers caused the deaths of thousands of civilians. President Bush ordered a retaliatory attack in Afghanistan, which was thought to contain Al-Qaeda bases, and in 2003 he declared war against Iraq, accusing Saddam Hussein of having large quantities of weapons of mass destruction. The American invasion had limited international support and proved very costly in terms of military expense and lives lost, as well as undermining American prestige abroad.

Bush's presidency ended in November 2008, which marked a unique moment in American history: on a popular wave of renewed enthusiasm, the Democratic nominee Barack Hussein Obama, a young African American, became the 44th US president and the first ever black American to hold the office. He was re-elected for a second term in 2012.

3

2 ANSWER the questions about the text.

1 In which way was Ronald Reagan already well known before he became president?
2 Why was his political stance seen as similar to Thatcherism in the UK?
3 In which areas was government money invested during Reagan's presidency?
4 Why did George H.W. Bush take America into war with Iraq?
5 Why was Bill Clinton compared to John F. Kennedy?
6 What was Clinton's greatest achievement in foreign policy?
7 What dramatic event happened at the beginning of George W. Bush's presidency?
8 Why did Bush attack Afghanistan and Iraq?
9 In which ways has the war in Iraq proved costly?
10 What happened in November 2008 to improve American morale?

IELTS Listening – Section 3

3 8.9 | **ACADEMIC DISCUSSION. You are going to hear two students, Geraldine and Toby, in a tutorial about an American president. Before you listen, read the questions (1–10) below, and then complete them while you listen.**

Answer questions 1–3.

1 What happened in November 2008?
2 What was significant about the election?
3 Which political party does Barack Obama belong to?

4 Choose which THREE of the following are true of Barack Obama's background.

A His father was Malaysian.
B He grew up in Texas.
C He was brought up by his grandparents.
D His first degree was from Harvard Law School.
E He hardly knew his African father.
F He spent time in both Hawaii and Jakarta as a child.

For questions 5–9, complete the following sentences using a maximum of THREE words for each gap.

In his first term as president, Barack Obama introduced social legislation including the **(5)** .... Reform Act and the American **(6)** .... Act in 2009. In response to the continued recession, he also signed a **(7)** .... in 2010. His foreign policy included the **(8)** .... troops from Iraq, but he **(9)** .... in Afghanistan.

10 Complete the labels (A–B) on the pie chart.

The US presidential election, November 2012
Electoral College result
Add the correct label:
Democrat or Republican.

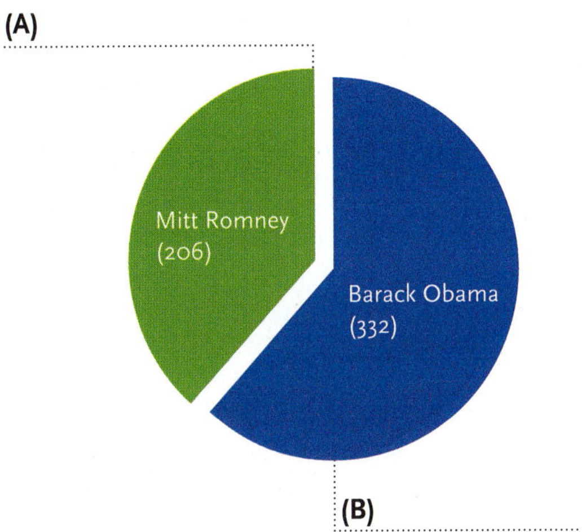

Milestones

11th September 2001

On 11th September 2001, terrorists attacked the Unites States. They hijacked four airplanes in mid-flight and flew two of the planes into two skyscrapers, the World Trade Center, in New York City. The impact caused the buildings to catch fire and collapse. Another plane crashed into the western wall of the Pentagon in Arlington, Virginia. The fourth plane crashed in Shanksville, Pennsylvania. Officials believe that the terrorists on that plane intended to destroy either the White House or the US Capitol. Passengers on the plane fought the terrorists and prevented them from reaching their goal. In all, nearly 3,000 people were killed in the 9/11 attacks. Following 9/11, the US government took many steps to try to make the country safer. It tightened security at airports and in public buildings, and a new cabinet-level ministry, the Department of Homeland Security, was created to protect the United States from terrorism.

4 Smoke coming out from the Southwest E-ring of the Pentagon, after a plane crashed into the building and set off a huge explosion. Photo by Alex Wong.

5 The North Tower of the World Trade Center on fire, while the South Tower is about to be hit by the second plane. Photo by Sean Adain.

9.13 **Literature**

Don DeLillo and 9/11 America

1 Don DeLillo in 2009. Photo by Giovanni Giovannetti.

2 Cover of *Falling Man*. Design by Noma Bar for Picador.

Don DeLillo's life

Don DeLillo was born in 1936, in the New York City borough of the Bronx, to Italian immigrants. He attended Fordham University in New York, and soon got interested in experimental art, jazz and the cinema. He worked in the advertising world for a while, and his obsession with the media and American culture may find its roots there, as well as in his immigrant background. DeLillo's first novel, *Americana* (1971), explores issues of the media and culture through the experiences of a television executive who travels to rediscover America through a film project. *End Zone* (1972) and *Great Jones Street* (1973) are about celebrities – a football player and a rock star – and deal with questions of death, celebrity, cults and consumerism.

In the 1980s, DeLillo moved to Greece for several years; then he returned to the US and wrote *White Noise* (1985). He later published *Libra* (1988) and *Mao II* (1991). His greatest achievement, *Underworld* (1998), spans the latter half of the 20th century and explores celebrity, consumerism and waste. His novel *Falling Man* (2007) takes its title from the image of an unidentified man who fell from the Twin Towers on September 11th after the planes struck. DeLillo has also written two plays, *The Day Room* (1986) and *Valparaiso* (1999).

Falling Man (2007)

The story

It is the morning of September 11th, 2001, and the World Trade Center is collapsing. Keith Neudecker, a lawyer in his late thirties who worked in the North Tower, walks towards the flat of his estranged wife, Lianne, and their son, Justin. Keith feels terribly disoriented; he is covered in blood, and moving with him are all the rest of the characters, including a performance artist – the 'falling man' of the title – who will appear around the city in the weeks after 9/11, dressed like a businessman, leaping from high places only to be caught by a safety harness and suspended, mid-air, in the posture of someone falling from the World Trade Center. Lianne takes Keith to the hospital to be treated, then waits and watches as their separation turns into a new type of relationship. They look like a family again, but there are many psychological scars, as well as new wounds that are slowly opening. Keith disappears at times. Lianne almost cracks under the pressure of their new relationship and the fear that her whole world, like the towers, may someday come crashing down.

At the end of each of the three parts of the book, the narrator abandons Keith and his family to take us inside the mind of one of the 9/11 hijackers, Hammad, a member of the Hamburg cell – a terrorist group – who struggles with his doubts. DeLillo does not present the terrorists as villains; instead, he gives us a taste of the power of 9/11 from the other side.

Themes

DeLillo focuses on the psychological damage that his characters have suffered beyond the mourning. He shows how they try to deal with it or how they change their lives in order to avoid it. In the course of the novel, the subjects of religion, terrorism, death and the meaning of life are dealt with but never resolved. Even the hijackers appear momentarily, as DeLillo attempts to give them faces and a reason for doing what they felt was right. Everyone in this story tries to move forward, tries to extract him or herself from the past. In *Falling Man*, the real effect of 9/11 is not political but existential. The planes cut everyone loose from whatever anchors of normality allowed them to relate to each other and the world.

The structure

Falling Man does not have a linear plot. The form is circular, moving the reader around and around a central point and then ending up where he started: at the falling Twin Towers after jet airliners have been hijacked and crashed into them. In the ruins of 9/11, relationships are interrupted. Disconnectedness is the new currency. Language is fragmented. Vision is distorted. Even when the characters look at the bottles and jars in the composition of a Giorgio Morandi still life, they still cannot help seeing the towers. The whole city, not just its centre, is in the physical and emotional limbo of a frozen zone.

1 ANSWER the questions about *Falling Man.*

1 What does Keith do after the collapse of the tower?
2 How does DeLillo present the terrorists?
3 What is the subject of the novel?
4 What is the real effect of 9/11?
5 What characterises the structure of the novel?

WARM-UP

1 **DISCUSS.** Do you think that art should deal with such events as 9/11? Could it be too painful or rather exploitative, healing or wounding? And what can art possibly add to the event itself?

3 *The Falling Man*, photographed by Richard Drew for the Associated Press.

Down the Tower

Don DeLillo

Falling Man (2007)
Chapter 14

You are going to read the last pages of the novel: the tower, where Keith Neudecker works, has just been struck by one of the planes.

8.10

Paper was flying down the hallway, rattling in[1] a wind that seemed to wash down[2] from above.

There were dead, faintly seen[3], in offices to either side.

He climbed out over a fallen wall and made his way slowly toward the voices.

In the stairwell[4], in near dark, a woman carried a small tricycle tight to her chest, a thing for a three-year-old, handlebars framing her ribs[5].

They walked down, thousands, and he was in there with them. He walked in a long sleep, one step and then the next.

There was water running somewhere and voices in an odd[6] distance, coming from another stairwell or an elevator bank, out in the dark somewhere.

It was hot and crowded and the pain in his face seemed to shrink[7] his head. He thought his eyes and mouth were sinking into his skin.

Things came back to him in hazy[8] visions, like half an eye staring. These were moments he'd lost as they were happening and he had to stop walking in order to stop seeing them. He stood looking into nothing. The woman with the tricycle, alongside, spoke to him, going past.

He smelled something dismal[9] and understood it was him, things sticking to his skin, dust particles, smoke, some kind of oily grit[10] on his face and hands mixing with the body slop[11], paste-like, with the blood and saliva and cold sweat, and it was himself he smelled, and Rumsey[12].

The size of it, the sheer[13] physical dimensions, and he saw himself in it, the mass and scale, and the way the thing swayed[14], the slow and ghostly lean[15].

Someone took his arm and led him forward for a few steps and then he walked on his own, in his sleep, and for an instant he saw it again, going past the window, and this time he thought it was Rumsey. He confused it with Rumsey, the man falling sideways, arm out and up, like pointed up, like why am I here instead of there.

They had to wait at times, long stalled[16] moments, and he looked straight ahead. When the line moved again he took a step down and then another. They talked to him several times, different people, and when this happened he closed his eyes, maybe because it meant he didn't have to reply.

There was a man on the landing ahead, old man, smallish, sitting in shadow, knees up, resting. Some people spoke and he nodded his head okay, he waved them on nodding[17].

There was a woman's shoe nearby, upside down. There was a briefcase[18] on its side and the man had to lean to reach it. He extended a hand and pushed it with some effort toward the advancing line.

He said, 'I don't know what I'm supposed to do with this. She fell and left it.'

People didn't hear this or retain it[19] or want to and they moved past, Keith moved past, the line beginning to wind down toward an area of some light.

It did not seem forever to him, the passage down. He had no sense of pace or rate. There was a glow stripe[20] on the stairs that he hadn't seen before and someone praying back in the

1 **rattling in.** Scossa rumorosamente da.
2 **to wash down.** Riversarsi.
3 **faintly seen.** Appena visibili.
4 **In the stairwell.** Nella tromba delle scale.
5 **handlebars ... ribs.** Con il manubrio che le incorniciava il torace.
6 **odd.** Strana.
7 **seemed to shrink.** Sembrava che gli contraesse.
8 **hazy.** Sfocate.
9 **dismal.** Lugubre.
10 **oily grit.** Ghiaia oleosa.
11 **body slop.** Poltiglia del corpo.
12 **Rumsey.** Il più caro amico di Keith e suo compagno nelle partite a poker.
13 **sheer.** Pure e semplici.
14 **swayed.** Oscillava.
15 **ghostly lean.** Sinistro piegarsi.
16 **stalled.** Di stallo.
17 **he waved ... nodding.** Annuendo fece segno di proseguire.
18 **briefcase.** Valigetta.
19 **retain it.** Non ne colsero il senso.
20 **glow stripe.** Striscia fluorescente.

line somewhere, in Spanish.

A man came up, moving quickly, in a hard hat[21], and they cleared a space[22], and then there were firemen, in full bulk[23], and they cleared a space.

Rumsey was the one in the chair. He understood that now. He had set him back down in the chair and they would find him and bring him down, and others.

There were voices up behind him, back on the stairs, one and then another in near echo, fugue voices[24], song voices in the rhythms of natural speech.

This goes down.

This goes down.

Pass it down.

He stopped again, second time or third, and people pushed around him and looked at him and told him to move. A woman took his arm to help and he didn't move and she went on.

Pass it down.

This goes down.

This goes down.

The briefcase came down and around the stairwell, hand to hand, somebody left this, somebody lost this, this goes down, and he stood looking straight ahead and when the briefcase came to him, he reached his right hand across his body to take it, blankly[25], and then started down the stairs again.

There were long waits and others not so long and in time they were led down to the concourse level[26], beneath the plaza, and they moved past empty shops, locked shops, and they were running now, some of them, with water pouring in from somewhere. They came out onto the street, looking back, both towers burning, and soon they heard a high drumming rumble[27] and saw smoke rolling down from the top of one tower, billowing[28] out and down, methodically, floor to floor, and the tower falling, the south tower diving into the smoke, and they were running again.

The windblast[29] sent people to the ground. A thunderhead[30] of smoke and ash came moving toward them. The light drained dead away[31], bright day gone. They ran and fell and tried to get up, men with toweled[32] heads, a woman blinded by debris[33], a woman calling someone's name. The only light was vestigial[34] now, the light of what comes after, carried in the residue of smashed matter, in the ash ruins of what was various and human, hovering[35] in the air above.

He took one step and then the next, smoke blowing over him. He felt rubble[36] underfoot and there was motion everywhere, people running, things flying past. He walked by the Easy Park sign, the Breakfast Special and Three Suits Cheap, and they went running past, losing shoes and money. He saw a woman with her hand in the air, like running to catch a bus.

He went past a line of fire trucks and they stood empty now, headlights flashing. He could not find himself in the things he saw and heard. Two men ran by with a stretcher[37], someone facedown, smoke seeping[38] out of his hair and clothes. He watched them move into the stunned[39] distance. That's where everything was, all around him, falling away, street signs, people, things he could not name.

Then he saw a shirt come down out of the sky. He walked and saw it fall, arms waving like nothing in this life.

21 **in a hard hat.** Con un elmetto protettivo.
22 **they ... space.** Aprirono un varco.
23 **in full bulk.** In massa.
24 **fugue voices.** Una fuga di voci.
25 **blankly.** Senza espressione.
26 **concourse level.** Atrio.
27 **drumming rumble.** Rombo percussivo.
28 **billowing.** Gonfiandosi.
29 **windblast.** Massa d'aria.
30 **thunderhead.** Nube gigantesca.
31 **drained dead away.** Si prosciugò del tutto.
32 **toweled.** Avvolte in asciugamani.
33 **debris.** Detriti.
34 **vestigial.** Residua.
35 **hovering.** Sospeso.
36 **rubble.** Pietrisco, macerie.
37 **stretcher.** Barella.
38 **seeping.** Che filtrava.
39 **stunned.** Sbiadita.

COMPREHENSION

2 **READ** the passage and say what situation is described.

3 **IDENTIFY** the people that are involved in the scene.

ANALYSIS

4 **ANALYSE** the passage by doing the following activities.

1. Say from whose point of view the story is told.
2. Underline the words and phrases referring to the setting in place.
3. Focus on Keith's perceptions and actions. How would you define his mood?
4. Pick out the objects or people that acquire a symbolic meaning in the scene.
5. Define the tone of the narration. What strikes you the most in DeLillo's descriptive technique?

YOUR TURN

5 **DISCUSS** the impact that September 11th has had on our daily lives.

9.14 **Literature**

TEXT BANK 71: *J.M. COETZEE*
TEXT BANK 72: *DORIS LESSING*

Voices from English-speaking countries

WARM-UP

1 DISCUSS. **What is a *lingua franca*? What are its advantages?**

1 Neels Britz's illustration from *Madiba Magic: Nelson Mandela's Favourite Stories for Children*, 2002.

2 READ the text and answer the following questions.

1 What factors led to the use of English as a sort of *lingua franca*?
2 What new contributions have enriched English-language literature since World War II?
3 What are the reasons why non-English writers write in English?
4 What do African-English literatures have in common?

During the past five hundred years, English has developed into a language used all over the world. This was made possible, first of all, by historical events: the settlement of English-speaking people in newly discovered lands; the massive emigration of people from England, Ireland and Scotland to North America, Canada, Australia, New Zealand and Africa during the 18th and 19th centuries; the increase of the world power of the United States since World War II. In the 20th century, English became the language of political and financial transactions, of study and research; it is now a sort of *lingua franca* which people of different nations use to communicate. This is certainly due to the adaptability and flexibility of the language itself, and increasingly to the domination of English on the Internet.

Recently the scope, audience and significance of English-language literature have been enlarged by the contributions of countries such as South Africa and Nigeria, the West Indies, Australia and Canada, which used to be part of the British Empire; nowadays they belong to the Commonwealth of Nations. A lot of authors writing outside of Britain and the United States use the resources of English to embody their experience and view of life. Other new voices, like Salman Rushdie (1947–), are part of the waves of immigration into England – often from ex-colonies and Commonwealth countries – which have added new perspectives to British literature. At times they find themselves torn between their two cultures; they judge their countries of origin both as insiders and as Westerners.

On the other hand, writers who come from countries where indigenous languages are still mainly oral and not mutually comprehensible have quickly realised that if they wish to communicate not only with the English-speaking world at large, but also with considerable numbers of their fellow countrymen, they have to use English. For many of them, the popular tradition of their country, with its folk songs, dialects and regional customs, is in contrast to the great tradition of English literature, with its conventions and its European influences. Therefore each writer tries to make a specific adjustment to this conflict, shaping it by personal and national circumstances, and by his or her creativity.

Since World War II there has been a considerable output of high literary quality from such writers, and some of them have been awarded the Nobel Prize for Literature, including: the Australian Patrick White (1912–90) in 1973, the Nigerian Wole Soyinka (1934–) in 1986, the South African Nadine Gordimer (1923–2014) in 1991, the West Indian Derek Walcott (1930–) in 1992, the Trinidadian V.S. Naipaul (1932–) in 2001 and the South African J.M. Coetzee (1940–) in 2003.

The emergence of a strong and independent English literature from black African writers has been one of the most exciting postwar cultural developments. All the new African-English literatures have shared similar styles and approaches, dealt with many of the same basic themes and gone through the same phases of development – from initial revulsion against colonialism and passionate reassertion of indigenous cultural values, through disillusionment with the fruits of independence, and thereafter either to a growing sense of alienation, to silence or to further explosions of anger and radicalism. Another general point is that the rapid political and social changes in Africa are likely to exert considerable pressure on African writers, so that they are less interested in introspection and psychological analysis or in elaborate experiments in language and structure. The Nigerian writer Chinua Achebe (1930–2013) deals with a central problem facing African writers: one of his greatest achievements is the creation of a prose style which, while incorporating African customs and thought patterns, is in fluent and impeccably good English.

White is instead the colour of three other major writers: 2007 Nobel-Prize winner Doris Lessing (1919–2013) who, after being brought up in Southern Rhodesia (now Zimbabwe), decided to live and work in Great Britain, and the South Africans Nadine Gordimer and J.M. Coetzee. The special historical and racial features of South Africa differentiate their work from that of other African writers. Moreover, their European heritage and the fact that they were brought up in an environment where English was often the first language, has meant that their work is closer in form and narrative modes to that of Europe than is the case with many black African writers.

9.15 **Literature**

Nadine Gordimer and post-apartheid South Africa

1 A portrait of Nadine Gordimer, 1993. Photo by Ulf Andersen.

Nadine Gordimer's life

South African writer Nadine Gordimer (1923–2014) was a long-time active campaigner against policies of racial segregation in South Africa and fought for tolerance, free speech and understanding. She always refused to become an exile, despite the banning of three of her works by the South African regime. After the fall of apartheid, she became active in HIV/AIDS causes. In 1991 Gordimer received the Nobel Prize for Literature.

A Soldier's Embrace (1980)

Gordimer wrote this short story before the lifting of the racist apartheid laws in South Africa. The main characters, who are never given a name, are a woman and her lawyer husband. Although they are liberals who have sympathised with the local freedom fighters, their lives change when native Africans take over the unnamed African country. This story is about the removal of the white colonials from their positions and homes in an era of black power. It begins with the experience of an embrace: the lawyer's wife, meeting two celebrants of the cease-fire – one white, one black – kisses them both on the cheek. She kisses one on the left cheek and one on the right cheek, as if they were two sides of the same face. However, the couple gradually begin to experience a growing sense of fear and alienation. Three black Africans who were once the couple's friends change their attitudes with the revolution. First, there is Father Mulumbua, a priest from the slums who had been sent to prison in the past for shouting freedom slogans. Then there is Chipande, who has come in out of the bush after being forced to leave by the old white regime. Now he has a job in the new government, but feels uncomfortable when he comes to visit them. Finally, there is Muchanga, an old servant, who makes them feel guilty.

The lawyer loses clients as more and more white colonials move across the border. In the end he realises that there is no longer a place for him in the country and decides to accept a position in a neighbouring country, but Chipande begs the couple to stay. The wife sets up a hawker's license for Muchanga and, as she waves goodbye to him, she does not know what to say. It looks as if the right words are left behind forever. From a symbol of unity in the beginning of the story, the embrace turns into an ironic and complex marker for what separates whites and blacks in the emerging country.

Insights

The system of apartheid

Racial segregation was a social and political reality in South Africa from the earliest colonial times under Dutch and British rule, but it became institutionalised after the Second World War in a system called 'apartheid'. The name came from a word in the South African Dutch settlers' language, Afrikaans; it means 'aparthood', or separateness. The system of apartheid was government enforced racial discrimination laid down by the National Party, which ruled the country from 1948 until 1994. Through a series of laws, the period of apartheid maintained white supremacy and Afrikaner minority rule by suppressing the rights of the black majority. The discrimination imposed covered all areas of public and private life. It affected housing, schooling, medical care and the use of public transport, as well as creating white only areas on beaches and other public areas.

The system of apartheid gave rise to significant internal resistance and violence among the black population, as well as a long international arms and trade embargo against South Africa. There were numerous uprisings and protests that were put down with force. Any opposition was forbidden, and anti-apartheid leaders were banned, arrested and sent to jail. The best-known example was the militant activist Nelson Mandela (1918–2013), who spent twenty-seven years in prison. In 1994, the year apartheid ended, he became the first black president of South Africa.

2 An armoured vehicle greets a mother and her children out for a stroll in Soweto, Johannesburg, South Africa.

3 Nelson Mandela, the first democratically elected president of South Africa, 1996. Courtesy of Adrian de Kock.

4 Leon Golub, *Mercenaries V*, 1984. Formerly Saatchi Collection, London.

WARM-UP

1 **DISCUSS.** What happens when the white minority finds itself out of power? What do they do?

A change of life

Nadine Gordimer

A Soldier's Embrace (1980)

After the day of the cease-fire, a white woman and her husband, a lawyer, have to face a severe change in their lives.

8.11

The lawyer had more free time than he'd ever remembered. So many of his clients had left; he was deputed[1] to collect their rents and pay their taxes for them, in the hope that their property wasn't going to be confiscated – there had been alarmist rumours among such people since the day of the cease-fire. But without the rich whites there was little litigation over possessions, whether in the form of the children of dissolved marriages or the houses and cars claimed by divorced wives. The Africans had their own ways of resolving such redistribution of goods. And a gathering of elders[2] under a tree was sufficient to settle[3] a dispute over boundaries[4] or argue for and against the guilt of a woman accused of adultery. He had had a message, in a round-about way[5], that he might be asked to be consultant on constitutional law to the Party, but nothing seemed to come of it. He took home with him the proposals for the draft constitution[6] he had managed to get hold of. He spent whole afternoons in his study making notes for counter or improved proposals he thought he would send to Chipande or one of the other people he knew in high positions: every time he glanced up[7], there through his open windows was Muchanga's little company at the bottom of the garden. Once, when he saw they had straggled off[8], he wandered down himself[9] to clear his head (he got drowsy[10], as he never did when he used to work twelve hours a day at the office). They ate dried shrimps[11], from the market: that's what they were doing! The ground was full of bitten-off[12] heads and black eyes on stalks[13]. His wife smiled. 'They bring them. Muchanga won't go near the market since the riot[14].' 'It's ridiculous. Who's going to harm him[15]?'

There was even a suggestion that the lawyer might apply for a professorship at the university. The chair of the Faculty of Law was vacant, since the students had demanded the expulsion of certain professors engaged during the colonial regime – in particular of the fuddy-duddy[16] (good riddance[17]) who had gathered dust[18] in the Law chair, and the quite decent young man (pity[19] about him) who had had Political Science. But what professor of Political Science could expect to survive both a colonial regime and the revolutionary regime that defeated it? The lawyer and his wife decided that since he might still be appointed in some consultative capacity to the new government it would be better to keep out of the university context, where the students were shouting for Africanization, and even an appointee[20] with his credentials as a fighter of legal battles for blacks against the colonial regime in the past might not escape their ire[21].

Newspapers sent by friends from over the border gave statistics for the number of what they termed 'refugees' who were entering the neighbouring country. The papers from outside also featured sensationally the inevitable mistakes and misunderstandings, in a new administration, that led to several foreign businessmen being held for investigation by the new regime. For the last fifteen years of colonial rule, Gulf had been drilling for oil[22] in the territory, and just as inevitably it was certain that all sorts of questionable people, from the point of view of the regime's determination not to be exploited preferentially, below the open market for the highest bidder[23] in ideological as well as economic terms, would try to gain[24] concessions.

His wife said, 'The butcher's gone.'

1 **deputed.** Addetto a.
2 **a gathering of elders.** Una riunione dei più anziani.
3 **to settle.** Per risolvere.
4 **boundaries.** Confini.
5 **in a round-about way.** Per via traversa.
6 **draft constitution.** Bozza della costituzione.
7 **he glanced up.** Alzava lo sguardo.
8 **had straggled off.** Si erano dispersi.
9 **he wandered down himself.** Si diresse lì lui stesso.
10 **drowsy.** Assonnato.
11 **shrimps.** Gamberi.
12 **bitten-off.** Morsicate.
13 **stalks.** Steli.
14 **riot.** Rivolta.
15 **Who ... harm him.** Chi gli farà del male.
16 **fuddy-duddy.** Matusa.
17 **riddance.** Liberazione, espulsione.
18 **gathered dust.** *Lett:* raccolto polvere; *qui:* rimasto troppo tempo.
19 **pity.** Peccato.
20 **appointee.** Candidato.
21 **ire.** Collera.
22 **drilling for oil.** Trivellato per trovare il petrolio.
23 **bidder.** Offerente.
24 **to gain.** Ottenere.

9.15 Nadine Gordimer and post-apartheid South Africa

He was home, reading at his desk; he could spend the day more usefully there than at the office, most of the time. She had left after breakfast with her fisherman's basket that she liked to use for shopping, she wasn't away twenty minutes. 'You mean the shop's closed?' There was nothing in the basket. She must have turned and come straight home.

'Gone. It's empty. He's cleared out[25] over the weekend.' She sat down suddenly on the edge of the desk; and after a moment of silence, both laughed shortly, a strange, secret, complicit[26] laugh. 'Why, do you think?' 'Can't say. He certainly charged[27], if you wanted a decent cut[28]. But meat's so hard to get, now; I thought it was worth it[29] – justified.'

The lawyer raised his eyebrows and pulled down his mouth: 'Exactly.' They understood; the man probably knew he was marked to run into trouble for profiteering[30] – he must have been paying through the nose[31] for his supplies on the black market, anyway, didn't have much choice.

Shops were being looted[32] by the unemployed and loafers[33] (there had always been a lot of unemployed hanging around for the pickings[34] of the town) who felt the new regime should entitle[35] them to take what they dared not[36] before. Radio and television shops were the most favoured objective for gangs who adopted the freedom fighters' slogans. Transistor radios were the portable luxuries of street life; the new regime issued solemn warnings[37], over those same radios, that looting and violence would be firmly dealt with but it was difficult for the police to be everywhere at once. Sometimes their actions became street battles, since the struggle with the looters changed character as supporters of the Party's rival political factions joined in with the thieves against the police. It was necessary to be ready to reverse direction, quickly turning down a side street in detour[38] if one encountered such disturbances while driving around town. There were bodies sometimes; both husband and wife had been fortunate enough not to see any close up, so far. A company of the freedom fighters' army was brought down from the north and installed in the barracks[39] to supplement the police force; they patrolled[40] the Quarter, mainly.

25. **He's cleared out.** Ha sbaraccato.
26. **complicit.** Complice.
27. **charged.** Faceva pagare caro.
28. **cut.** Taglio di carne.
29. **it was worth it.** Ne valesse la pena.
30. **profiteering.** Aver lucrato.
31. **must ... nose.** Deve aver pagato un occhio della testa.
32. **looted.** Saccheggiati.
33. **loafers.** Fannulloni.
34. **pickings.** Avanzi.
35. **entitle.** Autorizzare.
36. **dared not.** Non osavano.
37. **issued solemn warnings.** Emanava avvertimenti solenni.
38. **in detour.** Come deviazione.
39. **barracks.** Caserme.
40. **they patrolled.** Pattugliavano.

1 Jean-Michel Basquiat, *Self Portrait*, 1986. MACBA Collection, Government of Catalonia Art.

COMPREHENSION

2 **READ the extract and answer the following questions.**

1. What happened to the white lawyer after the revolution?
2. How did the white law and the black way differ?
3. What did the lawyer expect or hope for?
4. What other suggestion came to him?
5. What news did the wife have when she came back home?
6. What was happening in the streets?

ANALYSIS

3 **SAY why the wife and husband do not have a name.**

4 **EXPLAIN why the position of the progressive white couple is ambivalent.**

5 **TAKE NOTE of the manner in which the newspapers deal with the events.**

6 **SAY whether the story communicates by implication or by direct statement.** From whose point of view is it narrated?

7 **DISCUSS the theme of the extract.**

9.16 Cultural Issues

Building peace

WARM-UP

1 **DISCUSS** in pairs the difference between 'peacebuilding' and 'peacemaking'.

2 **READ** the following quotation by Martin Luther King, Jr., and then make a list of possible peacemaking activities.
'Peace is not merely a distant goal that we seek, but a means by which we arrive at that goal.'

Insights

The International Day of Peace

The International Day of Peace, or 'Peace Day', was established by a United Nations resolution in 1981 to coincide with the opening of the General Assembly. The first Peace Day was celebrated in September 1982.

In 2002 the General Assembly officially declared 21st September as the permanent date for the International Day of Peace.

3 **READ** the following list of ways to be a peacebuilder and identify the one which you think is most suitable for you. Then explain why to the rest of the class.

1 BECOME AN INFORMED CITIZEN:
Keep up to date on global news and events related to the management of international conflicts. Try to find out the role your government plays as a peacebuilder in conflict situations around the world. Share that knowledge with others to get them involved.

2 GET INSPIRED BY FAMOUS PEACEBUILDERS:
Interview your relatives or teachers and ask them who the famous peacebuilders of their generation were when they were growing up. Then do some research about these people to learn about the role they played in building peace.

3 RAISE PEACEBUILDING ISSUES AT YOUR SCHOOL:
Organise discussions in your classes about issues of international peacebuilding and conflicts happening in the world.

4 FOLLOW PEACEBUILDING ORGANISATIONS AND PEOPLE ON SOCIAL MEDIA:
Do some research into organisations or individuals that build peace and follow them on networks like Twitter or Facebook. Share relevant updates with your social contacts.

5 FOUND A FILM OR BOOK CLUB:
Create a group to read and discuss peacebuilding books or watch and discuss peacebuilding films from around the world.

6 STUDY ABROAD:
Explore options for studying abroad as an opportunity to learn firsthand about other cultures and to gain or improve important cross-cultural communication skills.

(Adapted from www.buildingpeace.org)

IELTS Speaking – Part 3

4 **TWO-WAY DISCUSSION.** Consider these questions and then answer them.

1. How can charities and international organisations help people? Do you think they have an important role in contemporary society?
2. Can they be more effective than government organisations?
3. Have you ever supported any charities? How important is it for people to support them?

5 **READ** the extract from the speech (2009) below, and note down its main ideas. Then discuss your notes with the class.

1 Barack Obama at the Nobel Peace Prize ceremony, 2009. Photo by Pete Souza, Official White House Photostream.

Barack Obama's Nobel speech

[This award] speaks to our highest aspirations – that for all the cruelty and hardship[1] of our world, we are not mere prisoners of fate. Our actions matter[2], and can bend history in the direction of justice. [...]

I do not bring with me today a definitive solution to the problems of war. What I do know is that meeting these challenges will require the same vision, hard work, and persistence of those men and women who acted so boldly decades ago. And it will require us to think in new ways about the notions of just war and the imperatives of a just peace.

We must begin by acknowledging[3] the hard truth that we will not eradicate violent conflict in our lifetimes. There will be times when nations – acting individually or in concert – will find the use of force not only necessary but morally justified.

I make this statement mindful[4] of what Martin Luther King said in this same ceremony years ago – 'Violence never brings permanent peace. It solves no social problem: it merely creates new and more complicated ones.' As someone who stands here as a direct consequence of Dr King's life's work, I am living testimony to the moral force of non-violence. [...]

[But] yes, the instruments of war do have a role to play in preserving the peace. And yet this truth must coexist with another – that no matter how justified, war promises human tragedy. [...]

But let me turn now to our effort to avoid such tragic choices, and speak of three ways that we can build a just and lasting[5] peace.

First, in dealing with those nations that break rules and laws, I believe that we must develop alternatives to violence that are tough[6] enough to change behavior – for if we want a lasting peace, then the words of the international community must mean something. Those regimes that break the rules must be held accountable[7]. Sanctions must exact a real price. Intransigence must be met with increased pressure – and such pressure exists only when the world stands together as one. [...]

This brings me to a second point – the nature of the peace that we seek[8]. For peace is not merely the absence of visible conflict. Only a just peace based upon the inherent rights and dignity of every individual can truly be lasting.

It was this insight[9] that drove drafters[10] of the Universal Declaration of Human Rights after the Second World War. In the wake of devastation, they recognized that if human rights are not protected, peace is a hollow[11] promise. [...]

Third, a just peace includes not only civil and political rights – it must encompass[12] economic security and opportunity. For true peace is not just freedom from fear, but freedom from want[13].

It is undoubtedly true that development rarely takes root without security; it is also true that security does not exist where human beings do not have access to enough food, or clean water, or the medicine they need to survive. It does not exist where children cannot aspire to a decent education or a job that supports a family. The absence of hope can rot[14] a society from within. [...]

We can acknowledge that oppression will always be with us, and still strive[15] for justice. We can admit the intractability of depravation, and still strive for dignity. We can understand that there will be war, and still strive for peace. We can do that – for that is the story of human progress; that is the hope of all the world; and at this moment of challenge, that must be our work here on Earth.

1 **hardship.** Sofferenza.
2 **Our actions matter.** Le nostre azioni sono importanti.
3 **by acknowledging.** Ammettendo, riconoscendo.
4 **mindful.** Consapevole.
5 **lasting.** Duratura.
6 **tough.** Dure, severe.
7 **held accountable.** Ritenuti responsabili.
8 **we seek.** Cerchiamo.
9 **insight.** Intuizione.
10 **drafters.** Autori.
11 **hollow.** Vuota.
12 **encompass.** Includere.
13 **want.** Miseria.
14 **rot.** Far marcire.
15 **strive.** Lottare.

The Season of Phantasmal Peace

Derek Walcott

The Fortunate Traveller (1981)

The poem conveys Walcott's belief in love. Love is made seasonless, an elevation of the tropical climate to a metaphysical symbol.

8.12

Then all the nations of birds lifted together
the huge net of the shadows of this earth
in multitudinous dialects, twittering[1] tongues,
stitching and crossing it[2]. They lifted up
the shadows of long pines down trackless slopes[3],
the shadows of glass-faced towers down evening streets,
the shadow of a frail plant on a city sill[4] –
the net rising soundless as night, the birds' cries soundless, until
there was no longer dusk, or season, decline, or weather,
only this passage of phantasmal light
that not the narrowest shadow dared to sever[5].
And men could not see, looking up, what the wild geese drew[6],
what the ospreys trailed behind[7] them in silvery ropes
that flashed in the icy sunlight; they could not hear
battalions of starlings waging peaceful cries[8],
bearing the net higher, covering this world
like the vines of an orchard, or a mother drawing
the trembling gauze[9] over the trembling eyes
of a child fluttering to sleep[10];
it was the light
that you will see at evening on the side of a hill
in yellow October, and no one hearing knew
what change had brought into the raven's cawing[11],
the killdeer's screech, the ember-circling chough[12]
such an immense, soundless, and high concern
for the fields and cities where the birds belong,
except it was their seasonal passing, Love,
made seasonless, or, from the high privilege of their birth,
something brighter than pity for the wingless ones
below them who shared dark holes in windows and in houses,
and higher they lifted the net with soundless voices
above all change, betrayals of falling suns,
and this season lasted one moment, like the pause
between dusk and darkness, between fury and peace,
but, for such as our earth is now, it lasted long.

1 **twittering.** Cinguettanti.
2 **stitching ... it.** Cucendola e intrecciandola.
3 **trackless slopes.** Pendii impraticabili.
4 **frail ... sill.** Fragile ... davanzale.
5 **dared to sever.** Osava spezzare.
6 **the wild geese drew.** Le oche selvatiche tiravano.
7 **ospreys trailed behind.** Falchi pescatori tiravano dietro.
8 **starlings ... cries.** Storni che lanciavano grida di pace.
9 **gauze.** Velo, mussolina.
10 **fluttering to sleep.** Che si agita prima di addormentarsi.
11 **the raven's cawing.** Il gracchiare del corvo.
12 **the killdeer's ... chough.** Lo strillo acuto del piviere, il gracchio che vola in tondo sulle braci.

WARM-UP

1 **IMAGINE** you have to create your own symbol for peace. What image would you choose?

COMPREHENSION

2 **ANSWER** the questions.
1. What did the birds do together?
2. How did this affect the landscape?
3. Did humans take part?
4. Where were the birds flying?
5. Did the event last long?

3 **CIRCLE** the words and phrases connected with 'light'. What kind of landscape do they evoke?

ANALYSIS

4 **FOCUS** on the layout of the poem. What do you notice about it? How does it contribute to its development?

5 **UNDERLINE** examples of repetition and say what their function is.

6 **WRITE DOWN** what is described as 'soundless'. Then note down the different 'shadows' mentioned in the poem. What connotation does the emphasis on these two qualities give the scenery?

7 **POINT OUT** the verbs connected with the human presence in the poem. What pattern do they share? What impression of mankind does the poet create?

ESAME DI STATO **Terza Prova**

8 **TYPE B.** In ten to twelve lines, discuss the poet's remark in the last line of the poem as regards the historical context of the contemporary age.

Exam Reference pag. 355

ESAME DI STATO

9 Prova Orale – Part 2

Test yourself

Tip

- After answering the set question, think about possible links within the culture curriculum that you have studied.
- Consider whether the moment in time (History), the place (Geography), the text/author (Literature) are relevant to a possible link.
- Remember that a mind map is a good way of organising your ideas when you study in order to think about what to say in more detail.

1 **DISCUSS the social developments in England in the 1960s and the sources of social conflict in the 1970s.**

2 **TRACE the main events which marked American history in the 1960s and 1970s.**

3 **EXPLAIN how the face of British society changed in the 1960s regarding:**
- moral values;
- family and sex;
- entertainment and fashion.

4 **READ this quote below from *On the Road* by Jack Kerouac and do the following activities.**
1. Identify the key words of these sentences. What do they reveal about the speaker's character?
2. What does *On the Road* deal with?
3. What is the main theme developed in this novel?
4. Who is the protagonist? What generation does he represent?
5. What is the style employed in this novel?

I like too many things and get all confused and hung up running from one falling star to another till I drop. This is the night, what it does to you. I had nothing to offer anybody except my own confusion.

5 **TRACE the development of the Civil Rights Movement in the US in the 1950s and 1960s.**

6 **HIGHLIGHT the key ideas in Martin Luther King's 'I Have a Dream' speech.**

1 Andy Warhol, *Nine Jackies*, 1964. Private Collection.

2 An expression of anger from a protester towards a policeman during a march for peace in England in 1967.

7 **LOOK AT Andy Warhol's painting *Nine Jackies* (1964) and trace the features of his art.**

1

8 **POINT OUT the events that marked the so-called 'Troubles' in Northern Ireland. Say how Britain tried to solve the problem.**

2

9 **DISCUSS how the Irish poet Seamus Heaney responded to the political context of his country.**

10 **DISCUSS the features of Margaret Thatcher's policies in Britain in the 1980s.**

11 **EXPLAIN how McEwan's *The Child in Time* reflects Thatcher's England.**

12 **TRACE the main events in US history from Ronald Reagan's presidency to Barack Obama's.**

13 **JUSTIFY why many writers from around the world use English to write their works.**

14 **HIGHLIGHT the key ideas in the passage 'A change of life' from Nadine Gordimer's *A Soldier's Embrace*.**

15 **DISCUSS the reflections on peace expressed by Barack Obama in his Nobel Prize acceptance speech and by Derek Walcott in his poem 'The Season of Phantasmal Peace'.**

Process language
Prova Orale – Part 2

Asking for repetition or clarification
- Could you repeat the question?
- I'm sorry, I didn't catch that.

Buying time to organise your answer
- Well, let me think ...

Circumscribing the topic
- Are you referring to ... ?
- Shall I speak about...?

Creating a link
- This is also related to ...

Quoting from a passage to support your statement
- Do you mind if I get a text?
- Evidence of this can be found in ...

Exam Reference

English in the Esame di Stato

The Terza Prova

The third part of the final school exam is based on four/five different subjects and is not written by the Education Ministry but by the exam commission in each school or institute. Questions regarding the study of a foreign language in this part of the exam are of one of three possible ways of testing:

- **Type A:** a short essay for each subject where students are asked to give a complete answer in a set number of words or lines (approximately 20 lines, or 200–300 words). There can be no more than four to five questions.
- **Type B:** single-answer questions where students are asked to answer in a set number of words or lines (approximately 10–12 lines). There are usually two to three questions for each subject. There are between ten to fifteen questions.
- **Type C:** multiple-choice questions on four to five subjects. There are between thirty and forty questions.

Duration of exam: a maximum of three hours.

Monolingual and bilingual dictionaries can be used.

The Prova Orale

There are three parts in the oral test, or *colloquio*. These are:

1. **A presentation:** an individual cross-curricular research project by the candidate. This is a project chosen by the candidate who can decide to present it with visual aids and/or using multimedia like PowerPoint. The topic chosen should be one that the student is genuinely interested in and one that can be extended to include other subjects. The connections made with other subjects must be genuine and not forced or too many. The choice of the topic must be motivated and must be given an appealing title. Students can choose to present their project in the foreign language of their choice.
2. **An oral interview:** a discussion initiated by the examiners on any of the subjects presented by the candidate. The subjects can be introduced through texts or other documents. Some of the examiners' questions can be in the foreign language studied.
3. **A brief discussion:** a conversation in Italian initiated by the examiners concerning the written papers presented by the candidate. If the written papers have been presented in a foreign language, this language will also be used in this part of the oral test.

Example question and answer

Step 1
Although this is a short essay, the preparation and planning are similar to a longer one.

Write a short essay in which you discuss the key ideas of the Thatcher years.

Step 2
You should start by reading the task carefully and underline or highlight key words.

Write a short essay in which you discuss the key ideas of the Thatcher years.

key ideas = main policies →

- de-nationalisation of industry and public services
- self-sufficiency (especially for young people)
- less power to the trade unions
- less government
- poll tax (local tax on individuals rather than property)
- aggressive foreign policy (towards Europe and the Falkland Islands)

Thatcher years

- became Prime Minister in 1979 (until 1990)
- eighties years of economic boom (but widening gap between rich and poor)
- 'yuppies' emerged

Step 3
Organise your plan or brainstorm into the order you wish to follow.

Step 4
Even a short essay must have an introduction (even if it is just one sentence), a development and a conclusion.

Step 5
Write a rough version and then check on the accuracy of your grammar, spelling and vocabulary before writing a final version.

Margaret Thatcher was an influential and at times polarizing politician whose policies earned her the nickname the 'Iron Lady'.

Thatcher became prime minister, the first woman to do so in Britain, in 1979. The Eighties brought with them an increase in material wealth, as well as the emergence of an underclass of poor people with low-paid jobs or no job, a poor home or no home.

Thatcher believed in minimum government involvement and encouraged the young in particular to take up their own responsibilities, to try to make a good career and to value the freedom of self-employment. In this climate, professional choices changed: law, finance, accounting, medicine and advertising were regarded as steady jobs with the prospect of high salaries. Her main aim was to reduce government spending, so she set out on a programme of de-nationalising public services and industry. The Conservatives believed that industry would be more efficient and competitive in private hands. Margaret Thatcher made a series of reforms to develop private enterprise and to reduce the power of the trade unions.

She also introduced the much-criticised poll tax in 1987. This was a local tax on individuals which had previously been on property and had to be paid by all citizens enrolled to vote. Poorer people considered this tax extremely unfair, but Thatcher refused to back down. In April 1990 her reputation for invincibility was shaken by a London poll tax demonstration that degenerated into a riot.

Her aggressive attitude was also seen in her foreign policy – in her rigid stance in Europe and her sending a task force to reclaim the Falkland Islands.

The ambitious urban professionals known as yuppies did well under Thatcher, but many sections of the population suffered and became bitter.

Terza Prova
Type B

Example question and answer

Step 1
Ten to twelve lines means you will write about eight sentences.

Write ten to twelve lines to present the totalitarian society described by George Orwell in *Nineteen Eighty-Four.*

Step 2
The question here will always be quite specific and require a precise answer relating to a text.

Step 3
Your starting point, once again, is the question. Read the question carefully and underline or highlight key words. Make sure you understand what is required of you.

Write ten to twelve lines to present the totalitarian society described by George Orwell in *Nineteen Eighty-Four*.

Step 4
Use the key words to help you make a short plan or brainstorm.

totalitarian society → dictatorship

- authoritarian regime
- no democracy
- no civil rights/freedom
- based on fear or military

Orwell in ***Nineteen Eighty-Four*** = Big Brother

- use of technology to watch and control
- thought police / no freedom
- based on fear and propaganda
- no room for individual thoughts or emotions

Step 5
Write out your ideas clearly in the brief paragraph.

Step 6
Write a rough version and then check on the accuracy of your grammar, spelling and vocabulary before writing a final version.

The society Orwell describes in *Nineteen Eighty-Four* is one of fear and monotony. There is no room for any individuality of any kind, whether it be in thought or in action. It is a society that is completely controlled through fear and punishment. There is the constant awareness of being watched and controlled all the time through the 'telescreens' that also serve to pump out endless propaganda, by helicopters and the 'thought police'. It is a society where everyone is expected to conform and thoughts and expressive language are contrary to what is accepted by the omnipresent 'Big Brother'. Personal memories and individual emotional attraction are banned and punished. It is a cold, impersonal, heartless and inhuman vision of society.

Prova Orale

Part 1

How to do it

In the oral exam you will be assessed on content, communication and presentation skills as well as fluency. The best way to prepare for this part of the exam is through your presentation. First of all, make sure:

- the topic you have chosen is one that you are genuinely interested in and one that can be extended to include other subjects as the presentation should be interdisciplinary;
- any connections that you make with other subjects are genuine and not forced or too many;
- you motivate your choice of topic and grab viewers' attention with an interesting title and pictures;
- you have done your research thoroughly, have panned your presentation and feel confident about what you say;
- you communicate your information clearly using bullet points, numbered lists and putting key ideas in bold or coloured text and use appropriate visual aids like pictures or charts to add interest and variety;
- talk with enthusiasm;
- avoid digressions;
- practise your presentation on a willing friend or parent.

You will normally be given about 10 minutes to present your topic.

Remember that non-verbal communication is important too, so you must be relaxed but formal. Stand straight and remember to look at your listeners and to smile. Be enthusiastic about your topic, after all you chose it!

Language tips

In Part 1 of the oral test, you will be presenting and explaining your topic. Here are some useful phrases:

Introduction

I would like to begin by (+ gerund) ...

I'm going to talk about ...

The idea of this presentation came from ...

There are many reasons why I choose this particular topic, perhaps the most important is/are ...

My presentation will cover ...

Sequencing

To begin with, I'd like to ...

Then ...

In addition ...

I will now explain/discuss ...

Using visual aids

This picture/slide shows ...

Here you can see ...

As you can see from ...

This is ...

Here is what I mean by ...

This is an example of ...

Adding emphasis

Obviously ...

Naturally ...

In fact ...

Actually ...

It is important to bear in mind that ...

I would like to emphasise/highlight/underline that ...

Concluding

I would like to finish/conclude by ...

To summarise ...

So ...

Finally ...

Therefore ...

In conclusion ...

Prova Orale

Part 2

How to do it

In the second part of the oral test you will be answering questions asked directly by the examiners. It is very important here to listen carefully and make sure you understand the question. If you have any doubts, ask the examiner to repeat the question rather than risk answering incorrectly.

Language tips

Answering questions

I think/believe that ...

This is an interesting question because ...

The answer is quite complex. First of all ...

If I understand you correctly, the question is about ...

This is an area I feel very confident in because ...

This particular question refers to ...

On this particular point I would like to say ...

There are several different ways of approaching this argument. Firstly ... Then ... And finally ...

It is clear that ...

Asking for the question to be repeated

I'm not sure I have completely understood the question. Would you mind repeating it, please?

Could you please repeat the question?

Did you mean the ... ?

I'm afraid I didn't hear the question properly. Can you please repeat it?

Quoting authors or texts

According to ... in the novel/poem/essay ...

As ... says in the novel/poem/essay ...

The novelist/playwright/poet ... sums up this point when he/she says '...'

The novelist/playwright/poet ... made this point very clearly when he/she said '...'

The main character in the novel/poem/play ... often says '...'

Literary Genre Reference

HOW TO READ A POETIC TEXT

Step 1

When reading a poem, first try to answer questions about its content:

- Who is the speaking voice in the poem?
- What is the setting in time and place?
- What is the poem about?
- How is the reader supposed to react?
- Does the poem seem to have a moral message?

Step 2

Next analyse the sound features and consider their effect.

- How is the poem organised?
- Does it have a fixed poetic form?
- Do its stanzas contrast with each other?
- Does the poem have a regular rhythm or metre?
- Is there any sound device such as alliteration, assonance or onomatopoeia?

A Slumber Did My Spirit Seal

William Wordsworth

Lucy Poems (1799)

What follows is one of a group of five poems dedicated to a girl, Lucy, who was never identified. A Slumber *was written in 1799 and it appeared in the collection* Lyrical Ballads.

a line: the basic unit of poetry

alliteration of /s/

rhyme scheme

A slumber did my spirit seal; A
I had no human fears: B
She seemed a thing that could not feel A
The touch of earthly years. B

No motion has she now, no force;
She neither hears nor sees;
Rolled round[1] in earth's diurnal course[2],
With rocks, and stones, and trees.

assonance of 'ee' /iː/

a four-line **stanza**

enjambement or **run-on line**

repetition of 'no'

sound devices increase the musicality of the poem and highlight particular feelings

1 **Rolled round.** Avvolta.
2 **earth's diurnal course.** Corso diurno della terra.

Dreams

Langston Hughes

Selected Poems (1959)

In this poem, the Afro-American poet Langston Hughes (1902–67) speaks of the importance of having a dream.

Hold fast to[1] **dreams**
For[2] if dreams die
Life is a broken-winged bird
That cannot fly.

Hold fast to dreams
For when dreams go
Life is a barren[3] field
Frozen with snow.

1 **Hold fast to.** Tienti stretti.
2 **For.** Poiché.
3 **barren.** Desolato, spoglio.

theme of the poem

metaphor of life compared to a bird that cannot fly and be free

metaphor of life compared to a barren field lacking meaning, warmth and happiness

January

R.S. Thomas

New Poetry (1962)

This poem was published in the anthology New Poetry *by the British critic A. Alvarez in 1962. It is one of the best examples of Thomas's nature poetry.*

The fox[1] drags[2] its wounded belly[3]
Over the snow, the **crimson** seeds[4],
Of blood burst with a mild explosion[5],
Soft as excrement, bold[6] as roses.

Over the snow that feels no pity,
Whose **white** hands can give no healing[7],
The fox drags its wounded belly.

1 **fox.** Volpe.
2 **drags.** Trascina.
3 **wounded belly.** Ventre ferito.
4 **crimson seeds.** Semi rosso vivo.
5 **mild explosion.** Blanda esplosione.
6 **bold.** Audace.
7 **healing.** Guarigione.

two opposing **colours**: white symbolises the purity of the snow but also coldness and the lack of life; red stands for suffering and death

two **similes**

personification of the snow

repetition of the first line → inevitability of death in the monotonous winter landscape

Step 3

Then analyse the most important linguistic features and imagery, and consider their effect on the general meaning of the poem.

- Is the language formal or informal, simple or complex?
- Are there any groups of words with the same connotation?
- Are there any single words or phrases that particularly stand out?
- Are there any contrasting images?

Imagery

- Does the poem contain any linguistic devices, such as similes, metaphors, personification or symbols?
- What is/are its/their effect/s?

Theme and message

- What is the theme of the poem?
- Does it have a message to convey? If so, what is it?

Step 4

Finally, your personal response is also important.

- Do you like the poem?
- Do you find it effective?
- Can you link it to your own personal experience or with contemporary reality?

Murderous Plans

William Shakespeare

Macbeth (1606)
Act I, Scene VII

stage directions provide information about the setting and the characters on the stage

The scene opens with the arrangement of a banquet in Duncan's honour. In one of the rooms of Macbeth's castle, he is already considering the killing of Duncan, in a monologue that is regarded by many critics as the birth of evil ambition in Macbeth.

HOW TO RECOGNISE A TRAGEDY

The typical elements of a tragedy include:

- a solemn style and elevated language;
- the struggle between good and evil;
- the characters are never common people but kings, princes and warriors;
- there is a villain who is generally guilty of some action which he must expiate.

[A room in the castle.]

Hautboys[1] and torches. Enter, and pass over the stage, a sewer[2], and divers servants[3] with dishes and service. Then enter Macbeth.

MACBETH If it were done, when 'tis done then 'twere well
It were done quickly[4]: if th'assassination
Could trammel up[5] the consequence, and catch
With his surcease[6] success; that but this blow[7]
Might be the be-all and the end-all[8] here,
But here, upon this bank and shoal of time[9],
We'd jump the life to come[10]. But in these cases,
We still have judgement here; that we but teach
Bloody instructions, which, being taught, return
To plague[11] th'inventor: this even-handed[12] justice
Commends th'ingredience of our poison'd chalice
To our own lips. He[13]'s here in double trust:
First, as I am his kinsman and his subject,
Strong both against the deed[14]; then, as his host,
Who should against his murtherer[15] shut the door,
Not bear the knife myself. Besides, this Duncan
Hath borne his faculties so meek[16], hath been
So clear in his great office, that his virtues
Will plead like angels, trumpet-tongu'd[17], against
The deep damnation of his taking off[18];
And pity, like a naked new-born babe,
Striding the blast[19], or heaven's cherubins, hors'd
Upon the sightless couriers of the air[20],
Shall blow the horrid, deed in every eye,
That tears shall drown[21] the wind. I have no spur[22]
To prick the sides of my intent[23], but only
Vaulting ambition, which o'erleaps itself
And falls on th'other[24].

Macbeth's **monologue** reveals his thoughts about a problem and his plans

the **main topic** of the monologue: the murder of the king

conscience and sense of guilt

virtues of the king

solemn style and **elevated language**

tragedy

main theme: ambition

1 **Hautboys.** Suoni di oboe.
2 **sewer.** Cerimoniere, colui che assaggiava il cibo del re.
3 **divers servants.** Parecchi Servitori.
4 **If it ... quickly.** Se tutto fosse finito, quando è fatto, allora sarebbe bene che fosse fatto velocemente.
5 **trammel up.** Accalappiare.
6 **surcease.** Estinzione.
7 **blow.** Colpo; *qui*: assassinio.
8 **the be-all and the end-all.** L'inizio e il compimento.
9 **shoal of time.** La secca del tempo; *qui*: gli ostacoli del tempo.
10 **We'd ... to come.** Noi correremmo il rischio di gettarci nella vita futura.
11 **return To plague.** Si ritorcono.
12 **even-handed.** Imparziale.
13 **He.** Il re Duncan.
14 **the deed.** Azione; *qui*: omicidio.
15 **murtherer.** Assassino.
16 **meek.** Mite.
17 **his virtues ... trumpet-tongu'd.** Le sue virtù simili ad angeli dalla voce di tromba invocheranno.
18 **taking-off.** Soppressione.
19 **Striding the blast.** Scavalcando la tempesta.
20 **hors'd ... the air.** A cavallo sugli invisibili corrieri dell'aria.
21 **shall drown.** Affogheranno.
22 **spur.** Sprone.
23 **To prick ... my intent.** Da cacciare nei fianchi del mio progetto.
24 **o'erleaps itself ... th'other.** Salta oltre se stessa e cade dall'altra parte.

The buttonhole

Oscar Wilde

An Ideal Husband (1895)
Act 3, Scene I

stage directions provide information about the setting and the characters on the stage

The characters of the play, set in London in the last decade of the 19th century, are presented according to their fortune, their marital status, their virtues and their vices. Lady Chiltern is a righteous woman whose handsome, loving husband, Sir Robert Chiltern, has secured a perfectly dignified living as a dedicated politician. His best friend is the elegant Arthur Goring who resists the mere thought of losing his bachelorhood.

HOW TO RECOGNISE A COMEDY

The typical elements of a comedy include:

- ordinary characters set in everyday situations in an amusing way;
- the playwright generally mocks the vices and follies of the society he belongs to;
- specific sets of comic characters are developed – they do not evolve in the course of the play and their names sometimes reveal their nature;
- the plots rely on witty dialogue.

The Library in Lord Goring's house. An Adam room. On the right is the door leading into the hall. On the left, the door of the smoking-room. A pair of folding doors[1] at the back open into the drawing-room. The fire is lit. Phipps, the butler[2], is arranging some newspapers on the writing-table. The distinction of Phipps is his impassivity. He has been termed[3] by enthusiasts the Ideal Butler. The Sphinx is not so incommunicable. He is a mask with a manner. Of his intellectual or emotional life, history knows nothing. He represents the dominance of form.
Enter Lord Goring *in evening dress with a buttonhole[4]. He is wearing a silk hat and Inverness cape[5]. White-gloved, he carries a Louis Seize cane[6]. His are all the delicate fopperies[7] of Fashion. One sees that he stands in immediate relation to modern life, makes it indeed, and so masters it[8]. He is the first well-dressed philosopher in the history of thought.*

the **topic of the dialogue** between Lord Goring and his butler

Lord Goring — Got my second buttonhole for me, Phipps?
Phipps — Yes, my lord. [*Takes his hat, cane, and cape, and presents new buttonhole on salver[9].*]
Lord Goring — Rather distinguished thing, Phipps. I am the only person of the smallest importance in London at present who wears a buttonhole.
Phipps — Yes, my lord. I have observed that.
Lord Goring — [*Taking out old buttonhole.*] You see, Phipps, Fashion is what one wears oneself. What is unfashionable is what other people wear.
Phipps — Yes, my lord.
Lord Goring — Just as vulgarity is simply the conduct of other people.
Phipps — Yes, my lord.
Lord Goring — [*Putting in a new buttonhole.*] And falsehoods[10] the truths of other people.
Phipps — Yes, my lord.
Lord Goring — Other people are quite dreadful[11]. The only possible society is oneself.
Phipps — Yes, my lord.
Lord Goring — To love oneself is the beginning of a lifelong romance, Phipps.
Phipps — Yes, my lord.
Lord Goring — [*Looking at himself in the glass.*] Don't think I quite like this buttonhole, Phipps. Makes me look a little too old. Makes me almost in the prime of life[12], eh, Phipps?
Phipps — I don't observe any alteration in your lordship's appearance.
Lord Goring — You don't, Phipps?
Phipps — No, my lord.
Lord Goring — I am not quite sure. For the future a more trivial[13] buttonhole, Phipps, on Thursday evenings.

Lord Goring uses **aphorisms**

He is interested in changing his buttonhole according to the day of the week and the people he is going to see.

1 **folding doors.** Porte a libro.
2 **butler.** Maggiordomo.
3 **has been termed.** È stato definito.
4 **buttonhole.** Fiore portato all'occhiello.
5 **Inverness cape.** Soprabito da uomo con mantellina staccabile.
6 **Louis Seize cane.** Tipo di bastone da passeggio.
7 **fopperies.** Frivolezze.
8 **masters it.** La padroneggia.
9 **salver.** Vassoio.
10 **falsehoods.** Falsità.
11 **dreadful.** Terribili.
12 **in the prime of life.** Nel fiore degli anni.
13 **trivial.** Frivolo.

PHIPPS	I will speak to the florist, my lord. She has had a loss in her family lately, which perhaps accounts for the lack of triviality your lordship complains of in the buttonhole.
LORD GORING	Extraordinary thing about the lower classes in England – they are always losing their relations.
PHIPPS	Yes, my lord! They are extremely fortunate in that respect.
LORD GORING	[*Turns round and looks at him. PHIPPS remains impassive.*] Hum! Any letters, Phipps?
PHIPPS	Three, my lord. [*Hands letters on a salver.*]
LORD GORING	[*Takes letters.*] Want my cab round in twenty minutes.
PHIPPS	Yes, my lord. [*Goes towards door*]
LORD GORING	[*Holds up letter in pink envelope.*] Ahem! Phipps, when did this letter arrive?
PHIPPS	It was brought by hand just after your lordship went to the club.

The **situation** is everyday and amusing.

The **language** employed is witty.

comedy

HOW TO READ A NARRATIVE TEXT

Step 1

Start with questions about its content:

- What is the setting in time and place?
- Who are the characters?
- What is the text about?

Step 2

Then analyse:

- the narrative mode (dialogue, narration or description);
- the narrator and the point of view;
- the characters.

Step 3

Next analyse:

- the features of the language;
- the theme and the message that are conveyed by the author.

Step 4

The last step should be the contextualization of the text:

- first with reference to the work it belongs to and to the author's background;
- and then, when possible, by reference to the personal experience of the reader.

The wind-swept ash-tree

David Herbert Lawrence

Sons and Lovers (1913)

Chapter 4

The extract belongs to D.H. Lawrence's novel Sons and Lovers *(1913). The novel deals with the writer's personal experiences in the working-class environment in Nottinghamshire and its protagonists are the members of the Morel family. Mr and Mrs Morel do not get on well with each other, and quarrels are the order of the day. In this text, Paul Morel, his brothers, William and Arthur, and his sister, Annie, are upstairs in their bedroom and overhear a quarrel between their drunk father and their mother.*

third-person narrator

characters involved

setting: the place where the story takes place

When William was growing up, the family moved from the Bottoms to a house on the brow[1] of the hill, commanding a view of the valley, which spread out like a convex cockle-shell[2], or a clamp-shell[3], before it. In front of the house was a huge old ash-tree[4]. The west wind, sweeping from Derbyshire, caught the houses with full force, and the tree shrieked[5] again. Morel liked it.

personification of nature

1. **brow.** Ciglio.
2. **convex cockle-shell.** Conchiglia convessa.
3. **clamp-shell.** Guscio della vongola.
4. **ash-tree.** Frassino.
5. **shrieked.** Scricchiolava.

characters involved

Paul's **point of view**

It is night, the children have gone to bed to sleep. They are woken by their drunk father and the sharp voice of their mother. There are a lot of words linked to the darkness and silence of the night.

The children lay still and listened to what was happening downstairs.

'It' s music,' he said. 'It sends me to **sleep**.'

But Paul and Arthur and Annie hated it. To Paul it became almost a **demoniacal noise**. The winter of their first year in the new house their father was very bad. The children played in the street, on the brim[6] of the wide, **dark valley**, until eight o'clock. Then they **went to bed**. Their mother sat sewing[7] below. Having such a great space in front of the house gave the children a **feeling** of **night**, of vastness[8], and **of terror**. **This terror came in from the shrieking of the tree and the anguish of the home discord**[9]. Often Paul would wake up[10], after he had been **asleep** a long time, aware of thuds[11] downstairs. Instantly he was wide awake. Then he heard the booming[12] shouts of his father, come home nearly drunk, then the sharp replies of his mother, then the bang[13], bang of his father's fist[14] on the table, and the nasty snarling shout[15] as the man's voice got higher. And then the whole **was drowned**[16] **in a piercing medley**[17] **of shrieks and cries from the great**, **wind-swept ash-tree.** The children lay **silent in suspense**, waiting for a lull[18] in the wind to hear what their father was doing. He might hit their mother again. **There was a feeling of horror**, a kind of bristling[19] in the **darkness**, and **a sense of blood**. They lay with their hearts in the grip of an **intense anguish**. The wind came through **the tree fiercer and fiercer**. All the cords of the great harp hummed[20], whistled[21], and shrieked. And then **came the horror** of the sudden **silence, silence everywhere**, outside and downstairs. What was it? Was it a **silence of blood**? What had he done?

The children lay and breathed the **darkness**. And then, at last, they heard their father throw down[22] his boots and tramp upstairs in his stockinged feet[23]. Still they listened. Then at last, if the wind allowed, they heard the water of the tap drumming[24] into the kettle[25], which their mother was filling for morning, and they could go **to sleep in peace**.

So they were happy in the morning – happy, very happy playing, dancing at night round the lonely lamp-post[26] in the midst of the **darkness**. But they had one tight place[27] of anxiety in their hearts, one darkness in their eyes, which showed all their lives. Paul hated his father.

feelings of fear and anguish

words linked to the **sense of hearing**: they refer to the noises downstairs

Paul's **feelings** towards his father

6 **brim.** Orlo.
7 **sewing.** Cucendo.
8 **vastness.** Immensità.
9 **discord.** Disaccordo.
10 **would wake up.** Soleva svegliarsi.
11 **thuds.** Rumori sordi.
12 **booming.** Che rimbombavano.
13 **bang.** Battere.
14 **fist.** Pugno.
15 **nasty snarling shout.** Lo stridulo parlare rabbiosamente.
16 **was drowned.** Veniva annegato.
17 **piercing medley.** Penetrante mescolanza.
18 **lull.** Momento di calma.
19 **bristling.** Ira.
20 **hummed.** Emettevano un rumore sordo.
21 **whistled.** Fischiavano.
22 **throw down.** Che si toglieva.
23 **tramp ... feet.** Che saliva di sopra con passo pesante scalzo.
24 **drumming.** Scorrere.
25 **kettle.** Bollitore.
26 **lamp-post.** Lampione.
27 **tight place.** Nodo.

Literary Language Reference

Aestheticism: a literary and artistic style linked to the Aesthetic Movement, which flourished in England in the 1880s. The Movement's motto was 'art for art's sake'. It rejected the traditional notion that art should have a social or moral purpose. Its main representatives included Oscar Wilde in literature and Aubrey Beardsley in the visual arts.

A number of features can be distinguished in the works of Aesthetic artists:
- evocative use of the language of the senses;
- excessive attention to the self;
- a hedonistic attitude;
- perversity in subject matter;
- disenchantment with contemporary society;
- absence of any didactic aim.

Allegory: a combination of a number of different symbols into a totality, often a story. For example, in *The Canterbury Tales*: the pilgrimage to Canterbury = allegory of the journey towards the celestial city.

Alliteration: a poetic sound device; the repetition of the same initial consonant sound in consecutive words or words which are close together.

Grendel they called this cruel spirit,
the fell and fen his fastness was,
the march his haunt.
(Anonymous, *Beowulf*)

Sometimes the alliteration can come in the middle or at the end of words too. It can help create the tone of the poem or affect the regularity of rhythm.

Allusive language: when an author uses suggestion rather than explicit mention.

Anonymous narrator: when the person telling the story is not identified or known to the reader.

Anti-hero: a protagonist of a story who lacks traditional heroic characteristics.

Archaism: very old words which are often out of use; conscious imitation of old styles and forms.

Archetype: a very typical (or the original) example of a recurrent symbol, motif or character.

Aside: a dramatic technique; a short comment made by a character in a play that is intended to be heard by the audience but unheard by the other characters on the stage. It usually occurs in or between speeches. Its purpose can be:
- to reveal the nature of the speaker;
- to draw the attention of the audience to the importance of what has been said or to explain developments;
- to create humour by introducing the unexpected.

Assonance: a poetic sound device; the repetition of the same vowel sound which 'colours' part of a poem with that vowel quality. The repetition of the sound is in non-rhyming stressed syllables which are near to each other.

He was sad at heart,
Unsettled yet ready, sensing his death.
(Anonymous, *Beowulf*)

Ballad: a form of poetry generally meant to be sung and used to express basic human emotions, such as love and hate or fear and wonder at physical and supernatural worlds.

Its features include:
- short narrative song, usually comes from a 'folk' or 'popular' tradition, preserved and transmitted orally, traditionally of unknown authorship;
- composed of short stanzas of two or four lines;
- impersonal – narrator or singer rarely interferes with the story;
- the 'I' is one that represents a party or a community;
- repetition of words or lines;
- dialogue is often used;
- the story focuses on a single crucial episode or situation;
- little description of the setting;
- the characters can be both fantastical creatures and human beings;
- the language is generally plain and formulaic;
- the themes deal with the supernatural, love, war and dramatic events;

Beat Generation: a circle of writers and friends which included Jack Kerouac, Allen Ginsberg and William S. Burroughs. In their writings, they chronicled their own wild and rebellious lifestyles in the late 1950s and early 1960s, paving the way for the cultural revolution. The word 'beat' was a slang term used by post-war jazz musicians to mean 'down and out', or poor and exhausted. Jack Kerouac claimed that the word meant both exhausted, at the bottom of the world, rejected by society, and also beatitude or beatific. The key ideas of the Beat Generation were:
- rebellion and bohemian living;
- refusal to conform to traditional middle-class puritanical values;
- rejection of materialism and organised religion;
- the search for alternative ways to find spiritual understanding, like Eastern religion, with its emphasis on meditation and communion with nature, and mind-altering drugs.

Blank verse: verse without rhyme. It is a common poetic form based on iambic pentameter, usually in lines of five iambic feet. The use of blank verse achieves extreme flexibility, almost giving poetry the quality of everyday speech. This is why it is often found in Elizabethan drama, for example in *Macbeth* by William Shakespeare.

Characters: in drama, they are the people in the play. The number of characters, which in the past were called *Drámatis Personae*, may vary but always include:
- a hero;
- a heroine;
- in the tragedies, a villain who does all sorts of evil actions.

Characters can be divided into main or minor according to how important they are for the story.

In fiction, they are the people who appear in a novel. They represent the most important ingredient in the world of fiction. The presentation of a character can be 'direct' (through what the writer tells the reader of his/her personality and appearance) or 'indirect' (when the reader has to infer the features of the character from his/her interaction with other characters, feelings and thoughts). The two methods of presentation are often mixed by authors in order to create portraits that are realistic but also provide psychological insight into the inner life of the characters.

Depending on their role in the story there can be 'major' and 'minor' characters. A further distinction can be made between 'round' and 'flat' characters.

Cinematic technique: a narrative technique in which an author describes a scene using a 'camera-eye' and 'camera movement'. For example, the writer may move into their subjects from the city into the street, from the street into the house, taking the reader from room to room.

Specific techniques include:
- The camera eye: its perspective mimics ordinary human vision, offering an image that seems like reality rather than an artificial system of signs.
- Wide, panoramic, aerial views: ways of introducing an action, which give a broad vision of the setting or scene. There may also be a 'bird's-eye' view, that is, a view on a scene from a position that is not too high, simply from elevated ground.
- Zooming in: the narrator focuses on some detail.
- Low-angle shot: the narrator looks at its subject from below.
- Close-up: the narrator identifies the characters and highlights their faces.
- Zooming-in: the eyes of the characters zoom in on something.

Climax: the most intense, exciting or important point in the story.

Colloquialism: informal or non-literary term which comes from everyday speech.

Comedy: a story which is generally intended to make the reader or audience laugh. The word 'comedy' comes from the Greek word *comodìa*, probably meaning 'Dionysiac feast song'. It was generally linked to village feasts celebrating the rite of fecundity.

The comedy has maintained some fixed features through the centuries:
- It generally deals with ordinary characters set in everyday situations in an amusing way.
- It begins with misfortunes but does not end with the death of the main character.
- The playwright generally mocks the vices and follies of the society he belongs to.
- Specific sets of comic characters are developed. They do not evolve in the course of the play and their names sometimes reveal their nature.
- The plots are mainly based on love and rely on witty dialogue.

Committed poetry: poets devoted to left-wing propaganda after World War I. The most famous was W.H. Auden. They concerned themselves with the social and political aspects of human life. This was partly because the brutal facts of the day, such as unemployment, Nazism and Fascism, were inescapable, and partly because they belonged to a generation which had been encouraged by its teachers to develop a social conscience. They turned away from complexity and allusiveness in order that they might communicate with their fellow men and encourage them to follow certain morally right courses of action. They also used slang and jazz rhythms and drew their images from the world of technology. The main features of committed poetry are:
- the poet seldom intrudes as a speaker using the pronoun 'I';
- scepticism about contemporary society;
- openness to new ideas and a broad range of life experiences;
- a social commentary which is not limited to politics – for example, it explores Freudianism, the inadequacies of the British government, war;
- a variety of forms and techniques;
- a very colloquial tone, which complements the satirical subject matter;
- powerful imagery, the use of juxtaposition and contrast;
- a unique and inspiring perspective on the human condition.

Contrast: when an author describes or calls attention to the differences between two things. It is the opposite of simile.

Couplet: a two-line stanza in a poem. They are usually in the same meter and joined by rhyme.

Dialect: language that is specific to a certain geographical area, culture or ethnic group.

Dialogue: coversation between two or more people in a book or play. The dialogue is the main support of drama since:
- it creates the action;
- it provides details about the characters and their relationships;
- it shows what a character thinks about another;
- it gives information about the past and can foreshadow subsequent events.

Dialogue can have a similar function in novels.

Drama: a play or story, an exciting, emotional or unexpected series of events or set of circumstances. The Greeks were the first in Europe to stage theatrical performances. In ancient Greece, drama was a collective and ritual phenomenon. The word 'theatre' comes from the Greek verb *theàomai*, 'to watch', and it referred to the group of spectators gathered for the religious ceremonies and the rites to honour Dionysus in the belief of the continuity between life and death. The origins of drama lie in the solemn chorus which accompanied sacrifices and in the procession organised by the citizens to propitiate fecundity in nature.

The most unique feature of drama is its non-repetitiveness: this is a consequence of the fact that any dramatic work is a collective event which involves various elements:
- a playwright – the addresser;
- a written text (the play) – the message;
- actors, director, designers, musicians – the performance;
- audience – the addressee.

Drama implies a real moment of communication from author to audience through the actors, and it depends on the immediate response of the public. In addition, the same work can be performed in a different way according to the period and the sensibility of the director, the actors and the audience.

A dramatic work consists of a number of acts divided into scenes. All Shakespearean plays, for example, are made up of five acts:
- Act 1: introduction;
- Act 2: development;
- Act 3: crisis or turning point;
- Act 4: complications;
- Act 5: *denouement*, that is, the resolving of all difficulties.

A dramatic text contains a variety of points of view, giving drama a special vitality:
- the character's, depending on his/her knowledge of facts and his/her opinions;
- the playwright's, who does not interfere either directly or indirectly but determines the development of the story;
- the audience's, influenced by what they watch and know.

Dramatic language: the language of drama; it is particularly intense and variegated because it can share the features of everyday speech, of poetry or prose.

Dystopian novel: a story which painted the most negative, the blackest picture possible of the present and the future to come. Just as utopia lent the persuasive techniques of the literary imagination to the cause of modern ideas of science and socialism, so dystopia lent the same techniques to the revolt against modernity. Like utopia, dystopia invented whole social orders, in all their particularity. But while the utopian order was perfect in the moral sense, the dystopian order was merely perfected in the social sense. It was the dreadful perfection of some modern system or idea. And while utopian societies were ideal, in the sense of 'the best possible', dystopian society represented the victory or tyranny of the idea. In both cases, the reader was invited to live the life of a society based on some principles, but in the one case the expected response to the experience was delight, in the other, horror. One example is George Orwell's *Nineteen Eighty-Four.*

Eighteenth-century novel: the novel came to prominence in the 18th century. Novels of the period, though different, shared the following features:
- Events were usually narrated in chronological sequence.
- Narration was in the 1st person or the 3rd person.
- The setting was given great attention, with specific references to names of countries, streets and towns.
- References were made to particular times of the year or of the day.
- All the characters were given contemporary names and surnames to reinforce the impression of realism, and they struggled either for survival or for social success.
- The hero of the novel was always the 'bourgeois man', with his problems. He was generally the mouthpiece of his author and the reader was expected to sympathise with him.
- The language was simple and factual.

Elegy: a poem of serious reflection; it often combines natural settings with poetic lamentation or speculation on death.

End-rhyme: a poetic device; when the last word of two or more lines has the same ending sound.

> *When in April the sweet showers fall*
> *And pierce the drought of March to the root, and all*
> (Geoffrey Chaucer, *The Canterbury Tales*)

End-stopped lines: a poetic sound device; this is when the end of a line coincides with a grammatical pause, usually marked by a punctuation mark. In poetry, lines are usually end-stopped.

English sonnet: see Shakespearean sonnet.

Enjambement: a French word meaning 'run-on line' (a poetic sound device); when a line ends in the middle of a phrase and the meaning break comes in the next line.

> *So the company of men led a careless life,*
> *All was well with them: until One began*
> *To encompass evil, an enemy from hell.*
> (Anonymous, *Beowulf*)

Epic poem: a long narrative poem, typically derived from ancient oral tradition. The word 'epic' comes from the Greek noun *épos*, which means 'the poet's oral exposition'. The two major epic poems in the Western tradition are the *Iliad* and the *Odyssey* by the Greek poet Homer.

The epic poem is a long narrative poetical composition dealing with the recollection of a glorious past in the national history of a country, the praise of the brave deeds of heroes, and the lament at the death of a hero. The main features of an epic poem include:

- History is the frame and the background of an epic poem, since the 'canvas' is occupied by supernatural folk-tales and mythological events.
- The society described is aristocratic and military. There is no attempt to deal with the story of a single human being; common people exist because they are related to heroes.
- The narrative is made up of a series of vivid, pictorial flashes against an unstable moving background. These 'type-scenes' include the banquet, the battle, the voyage and the funeral, and they are a meditation upon an event rather than its 'visual' description.
- The epic poem is an objective narration, since the poet's point of view coincides with the ones of the literary characters described; neither the poet nor his characters criticise the ideals and the customs of the country they belong to.
- The main theme is the nature of heroic life, more specifically, the function and character of leadership in heroic society.
- The didactic aim is linked to the celebration of the heroic ethic: all men should direct themselves to actions which lead to glory and praise.
- The style is elevated, the vocabulary is extremely rich and various.
- Each line of a poem is divided into two halves by a break and has four stresses; alliteration links the two halves of the line.

Epiphany: a technique used by James Joyce which implied 'the sudden revelation of a hidden reality' through 'casual words or events'. He described it as a 'sudden spiritual manifestation' in a character, caused by a trivial gesture, an external object or a banal situation, and used it to lead the character to a sudden self-realisation about himself/herself or about the reality surrounding him/her.

External narrator: a narrator that is a voice outside of the story who tells of events he has not taken part in.

First-person narrator: when a story is recounted in the 'I' mode. In fiction, it can coincide with a character in the story or the protagonist who tells about his life. The choice of this narrator can have the following functions:

- to bring the reader close to the mind and feelings of the narrator;
- to convey an impression of reality;
- to restrict the reader's perspective.

Flashback: a scene in a play or novel which is set in an earlier time than that of the main story.

Flat characters: also called 'types' or 'caricatures', are built around a single psychological trait or quality. They are easy to recognise and do not develop throughout the story, even if they experience different relationships and situations. This does not mean they are always artistically inferior to 'round characters'. As a matter of fact, the author can use them to create a particular atmosphere inside a complex narrative frame. They can be easily presented in a few sentences.

> *She was a woman of mean understanding, little information, and uncertain temper. When she was discontented she fancied herself nervous. The business of her life was to get her daughters married; its solace was visiting and news.*
> (Jane Austen, *Pride and Prejudice*)

Foot: group of two syllables in a line, one of which is stressed. The pattern may be either:

1. unstress-stress;
2. stress-unstress.

The unstress-stress pattern (˘/¯) is called an iamb, and it is the commonest foot in English poetry. The stress-unstress pattern (¯/˘) is called a trochee.

Lines of poetry in Latin were divided into feet, with different names according to the arrangement of syllables. Adapted into English, the long syllables became the stressed syllables, marked with a ¯, and the short syllables became unstressed syllables, marked with a ˘.

> *A˘nd m¯akes/ ˘us r¯a/th˘er b¯ear/ th˘ose ¯ılls/ w˘e h¯ave*
> *th˘an fl¯y/ t˘o ¯o/th˘ers th¯at/ w˘e kn¯ow/ n˘ot ¯of.*
> (William Shakespeare, *Hamlet*, Act 3)

'And makes' is a segment, or foot, which contains an unstressed syllable (˘), and a stressed syllable (¯).

Foreshadowing: hints in the early parts of a novel or play about an important thing or event that is going to happen later on in the story.

Free direct speech: where dialogue is isolated from the context, often used by modern novelists like Ernest Hemingway and James Joyce.

Free verse: a poem without a metre. Free verse rejects the conventional patterns of regular verse. The only unifying element in free verse is the use of the poetic line. The free verse line might consist of a complete sentence or of a single word. The traditional metre and rhyme scheme are absent; alliteration and assonance compensate for the absence of the other traditional musical devices.

Georgian poets: poetry of the years preceding the First World War influenced by the Victorian Romantic tradition. The name comes from an anthology, *Georgian Poetry*, published during the reign of George V. Among these poets was Rupert Brooke. They employed the conventions of diction, looking to the Romantics and the Victorians for guidance. They felt sympathy for specifically English elements, such as the countryside as an idyllic place, and remained indifferent or hostile to the revolution in sensibility and technique started by avant-garde movements of the period.

Gothic novel: an English genre of fiction which came to popularity at the end of the 18th century. It reflected a specific historical moment characterised by an increasing disillusionment with the Enlightenment and rationality, and was a reaction against industrialisation. The first novel of this kind was *The Castle of Otranto* (1764) by Horace Walpole. *Frankenstein* (1818) by Mary Shelley is the most notable.

The main features of the Gothic novel include:

- A setting which evokes an atmosphere of horror and fear, like isolated castles, mysterious abbeys and convents with hidden passages, dungeons and secret rooms. Darkness is a key element for creating a mysterious, gloomy atmosphere. Catholic countries are often the setting of the most terrible crimes, due to Protestant prejudices against Catholicism.
- The story is marked by obscurity, uncertainty and horror, often caused by evil and atrocity.
- The characters are dominated by exaggerated reactions in front of mysterious situations or events.

- There are often supernatural beings: vampires, monsters and ghosts.
- The hero is a sensitive man who saves a heroine.
- The heroine is both stricken with unreal terrors and persecuted by a villain.
- The villain is the embodiment of evil, either by his own fall from grace, or by some implicit malevolence. He is usually a satanic, terrifying male character who is a victim of his negative impulses.
- The wanderer or outcast of many Gothic tales, is the symbol of isolation as he wanders the earth in perpetual exile, usually as a form of divine punishment.
- The language often refers to emotions and feelings, and is capable of evoking anxiety, fear or horror.
- The plot itself mirrors the ruined world since it deals with the protagonist's fall from grace after his succumbing to temptation from a villain.

Harlem Renaissance: also known as the 'New Negro Movement', was a literary, artistic, cultural and intellectual movement that began in Harlem, New York City, after World War I and ended around 1935 during the Great Depression. The movement raised important issues affecting the lives of African Americans through various forms of literature, art, music, drama, painting, sculpture, films and protests. Its writers exalted the heritage of African Americans and tried to use their unique culture as a means to re-define African-American literary expression. The literature of this period helped to shape the psychology of the 'New Negro', characterised as self-assertive, racially conscious and articulate. With greater possibilities for artistic self-determination, the writers of the Harlem Renaissance produced works which explored such themes as alienation and marginalisation. Several writers, including Langston Hughes, relied particularly on the rich folk tradition – oral culture, folktales, black dialect, jazz and blues composition – to create unique literary forms.

Humour: the quality of being amusing or comic. Humour differs from both satire and irony because it does not deride or hint at anything – it simply evokes laughter as an end in itself. The humorist sees the faults of his subject but accepts them and laughs at them.

Hyperbole: the exaggeration of a quantity, a quality or a concept. The statement is usually not meant to be taken literally. It is often used in everyday language.

I've told you a thousand times

Iamb: a poetic foot which has an unstressed-stressed pattern (◡˘/¯). It is the commonest foot in English poetry.

Imagism: a poetic movement which flourished between 1912 and 1917. The name 'Imagiste' was invented by the American poet Ezra Pound. Imagists used hard, clear and precise images, and a rhythm which was freed from metrical regularity. They also felt free in the choice of any subject matter and their poems were usually short and contained no moral comment.

Incremental repetition: when a phrase recurs with minor differences as the story progresses.

Interior monologue: often confused with the stream of consciousness, although they are not in fact the same thing: the former is the verbal expression of a psychic phenomenon, while the latter is the psychic phenomenon itself. The main features of the interior monologue are:
- verbal expression of the stream of consciousness;
- frequent lack of chronological order;
- the narrator may be present;
- formal logical order may be lost or lacking;
- the action takes place within the character's mind;
- speech may be immediate, without introductory expressions.

Internal narrator: a narrator whose point of view is internal to the story, that is, a character in the story, either the protagonist or a witness.

Internal rhyme: a poetic sound device; when rhyme is used within a line.

Her breath was strang, her hair was lang
(Anonymous, *Kemp Owyne*)

Irony: a manner typically used to add humour or emphasis. When irony is used as a literary tool, what is said is not a direct, open attack on the subject. The ironist wishes to surprise the reader; he/she does not want to change or reform, but simply to create awareness in the reader.

There are three kinds of irony.

1. Verbal irony, in which the writer says one thing and means something completely different. An example of verbal irony can be found in 'The Wife of Bath' from *The Canterbury Tales* by Chaucer.

In all the parish not a dame dared stir
Towards the altar steps in front of her,
And if indeed they did, so wrath was she
As to be quite put out of charity.

2. Dramatic irony, in which the reader or the audience perceives something which a character does not know. An example of dramatic irony can be found in *Macbeth*, Act 1, Scene 6, in which Duncan visits Macbeth's castle where later he will be murdered.

Duncan: *This castle hath a pleasant seat; the air*
Nimbly and sweetly recommends itself

3. Situational irony, in which a discrepancy between the expected results of a situation and its actual results is shown. An example of situational irony can be found in *Gulliver's Travels*, where there is a discrepancy between the Lilliputians' description of the objects they find on Gulliver's body and what they actually find.

Italian sonnet: see Petrarchan sonnet.

Juxtaposition: when an author places a person, concept, place, idea or theme parallel to another in order to highlight the contrast between the two and compare them.

Language of sense impressions: words and expressions which generate visual, auditory, olfactory or tactile images, used by a poet to convey his perception of reality. The poet uses nouns, adjectives and verbs which refer to the five senses (sight, hearing, smell, taste, touch) in order to recreate his/her own physical experience. Verbs such as 'to see', 'to look', 'to stare' may introduce the sense of sight together with adjectives referring to colours. Temperature, texture and materials convey touch, while verbs of sound are linked to hearing.

Layout: the way the parts of something are arranged; in reference to poetry, it implies the organisation of the words, lines and stanzas on the page.

Line: the basic unit of poetry. In English poetry a line is usually from eight to twelve syllables in length.

Litotes: the opposite of hyperbole; a rhetorical understatement in which the negative of the opposite of what is meant to be said is used to express that idea.

You will find him not ill-disposed. (= *He will be favourably disposed.*)

Lost Generation: disillusioned American writers and intellectuals who emigrated to Europe after World War I, chiefly to Paris because of its stimulating atmosphere for the arts. Among the writers of the Lost Generation were F. Scott Fitzgerald and Ernest Hemingway.

Metaphor: while a simile establishes a comparison between two separate things, a metaphor describes something as if it were something else. It is a means of comparison between two things that are basically dissimilar without connective words such as 'like' or 'as'.

Life's but a walking shadow, a poor player
(William Shakespeare, *Macbeth*, Act 5)

The elements of a metaphor are:
- the tenor: the subject of the metaphor;
- the vehicle: what the subject is compared to;
- the common ground: the analogy between them, the ideas they share.

This scheme can also be applied to the simile. Simile and metaphor have more or less the same functions but the latter has a stronger emotional impact.

Metonymy: a subtype of metaphor in which a word, name or expression is used as a substitute for something else. The substitute is often an attribute or something closely associated with what is substituted (a 'suit' = a business executive). An example in literature is the following metonymies for doom and gloom which suggest elements of mystery, danger or the supernatural and are common in Gothic novels.

> Doom and gloom = *doors grating on rusty hinges, clanking chains, lights in abandoned rooms, doors suddenly slamming shut, ruins of buildings, barking of distant dogs*

Metre: a regular arrangement of stressed and unstressed syllables. It is an important part of rhythm; it is the 'beat' of a poem, that is, the distribution within the line of stressed and unstressed syllables. Metre is measured in feet (groups of two syllables in a line, one of which is stressed).

For many centuries the use of the iambic foot, particularly iambic pentameter (generally corresponding to ten syllables), has been the commonest metre in English poetry.

> *Will I / with wine / and was / sails so / convince*
> (William Shakespeare, *Macbeth*, Act 1)

Modern novel: brought about by a transformation of British society, from the comfortable world of the Victorians to the inter-war years, marked by unrest and ferment, and Freud's new theory of the psyche and a new concept of time introduced by the philosophers William James and Henri Bergson. The new role of the novelist consisted in mediating between the solid and unquestioned values of the past and the confused present. The novelist rejected omniscient narration and experimented with new methods to portray individual consciousness; the viewpoint shifted from the external world to the character's mind. Time was subjective and internal: if the distinction between past and present was meaningless in psychological terms, then there was no use in building a well-structured plot, with a chronological sequence of events. The stream of consciousness technique, or the interior monologue, was introduced to reproduce the flow of thoughts quite similar to the mind's activity. The most important modern novelists include: Joseph Conrad, Edward Morgan Forster, James Joyce and Virginia Woolf.

Monologue: a dramatic technique; a long speech by a character in a play which is ignored by the other characters on the stage. This device enables the playwright to let the audience know the character's:
- thoughts about a specific problem;
- plans for the future;
- feelings and reactions;
- explanation of what happens between scenes.

Motif: a recurring element or image which often has symbolic meaning within a work.

Narrative poem: a spoken or written account of events told in verse, in other words, poetry that has a plot. The poems may be short or long and simple or complex. They usually have a regular rhyme scheme and metre. Narrative poetry includes such forms as epics and ballads. Some narrative poems are like novels in verse. Shorter narrative poems are often similar in style to the short story. Short narrative poems may be collected into interrelated groups, like Geoffrey Chaucer's *The Canterbury Tales*, which is considered the greatest example of a narrative poem in English literature.

Here are the features of the narrative poem:
- variety of narrative elements (such as: the setting in time and place; the description of characters; the use of a narrator, often in the first person);
- links with the moral views of the time;
- insight into individual characters as regards their lifestyles, their psychology and their experiences;
- usually recounts a story using a poetic theme;
- the focus is often the pros and cons of life.

Narrator: an essential element of a narrative text; the speaking voice. The narrator is not the author of a book (the author is a real person, with his own experiences, personality and ideas). The narrator is the voice who tells the story and gives the point of view from which the story is told. The narrator can be 'internal' or 'external', 'first-person' or 'third-person'.

Novel: a long fictitious prose narrative which usually maintains a certain level of realism. It is the commonest form of fiction as a genre. It emerged in its modern form in 18th-century Europe.

The main features of the novel include:
- It is fictitious (fiction comes from the Latin word *fingere*) – it tells about imaginary events and characters.
- It is in some sense 'representative of real life', since it can bear an important resemblance to reality.
- It is written in prose, rather than verse, even if it can include very poetic elements as far as its language is concerned.
- It has a narrative: in other words it is a 'telling'.
- It has characters, actions and a plot.
- It involves people who act in a context ruled by some sort of connective logic (chronology, cause-and-effect).
- It involves the investigation of an issue of human importance whose complexity requires a certain length.

Objective correlative: a sequence of events, a cluster of images, a setting, used to express a certain emotion and evoke it in the reader.

Obtrusive narrator: the omniscient third-person narrator when he addresses the reader directly by making personal remarks and digressions or by providing a comment on the society of the time or on some of the characters. The obtrusive narrator takes away the realistic illusion and reduces the emotional intensity of what is being told by focusing on the act of narrating.

Octave: an eight-line stanza in a poem.

Ode: a classical form of poetry which is quite long and complex. Its form is determined by the theme (usually the celebration of an abstract concept) and situation.

Omniscient narrator: a third-person narrator who knows everything about the events and the characters' thoughts and intentions. Can be 'obtrusive' or 'unobtrusive'.

Onomatopoeia: a word whose sound illustrates its meaning.

> *crack, screech, bang, snuffle*

Oxymoron: a rhetorical device in which two incongruous or contradictory terms are combined. This combination of two usually contradictory things is sometimes used to express extreme feelings.

> *dear enemy, sweet sorrow*

Paradox: a statement or proposition that may at first seem contradictory, unbelievable, absurd or that leads to illogical or self-contradictory conclusions, but, when investigated or explained, it may prove to be true and often reveals a deeper truth.

Parallelism: a poetic device; a similarity of structure in a pair or series of related words, phrases or clauses. It is the use of similar syntactic units inside the same line or from line to line.

Parody: an imitation which deliberately exagerates certain characteristics in order to achieve a comic effect.

Personification: a form of imagery which attributes the characteristics of a living being to abstract things or inanimate objects. In these lines Chaucer speaks about the spring wind:

When also Zephyrus with his sweet breath
Exhales an air in every grove and heath
(Geoffrey Chaucer, *The Canterbury Tales*)

Personification can often be recognised by the use of capital letters, possessive adjectives and verbs referring to human actions.

Petrarchan sonnet: a form of sonnet, also called the Italian sonnet. Its main features include:

- fourteen lines of iambic pentameter;
- division into two sections;
- an octave which presents a problem or situation;
- a sestet which solves or clarifies the situation;
- rhyme scheme:
  - ABBAABBA for the octave;
  - CDECDE or CDCDCD for the sestet;
- a turning point at the end of the eighth line and the ninth (sometimes introduced by words like: *and, if, so, but, then, when*);
- language full of oxymora;
- themes of love and faith, beauty.

The octave has the purpose of: introducing a problem; expressing a desire; reflecting on reality; presenting a situation that causes doubt or conflict in the poet.

The first quatrain introduces the problem. The second quatrain develops the problem.

The beginning of the sestet is known as the *volta*, and it introduces a pronounced change in tone in the sonnet. The sestet's purpose is to make a comment on the problem or to apply a solution to it.

Plot: the story; the main events of a play or novel. The sequence of events does not always have to be presented in chronological order. The author can combine these events in different ways using flashbacks, anticipation of events or by omitting details of the story.

Poetry: a literary genre in which special emphasis is given to the expression of feelings and ideas through the use of different styles and rhythms. It derives its name from the Greek verb *poiêin*, which means 'to create'. It was born as an oral art, generally accompanied by dancing and music, and is the oldest form of literature. People use poetry as a means to express the most remarkable events in their lives and to convey the feelings associated with them.

The three most important elements of poetry are:

- its sound;
- its visual layout;
- the special way it uses language.

Poetry is characterised by musical patterns of sounds which are based on the natural qualities of spoken language. Its language is far more condensed and intensified than in other genres. The poet combines words to make his reader feel what he has felt and experience what he has experienced.

The structural units of poetry are:

- the line;
- the stanza;
- the canto or book.

All these can vary almost infinitely.

A poem conveys its meaning through words chosen and arranged in images. Three elements characterise each word in a poem:

- the denotation: dictionary definition;
- the connotation: the associations and feelings evoked in the reader's mind;
- the sound.

Point of view: the angle(s) from which the scene in a narrative text is described and the story is told. It is influenced by the kind of narrator. The point of view does not simply refer to the description or perception of facts and events, but also to their interpretation. Narrative voice and point of view do not always coincide. The narrative voice belongs to the person who is speaking, be it an internal or an external narrator. The point of view regards the person who, inside the story, sees the facts, thinks and judges. It may vary more often than the narrative voice.

The point of view can be:

1. fixed and therefore restricted;
2. shifting from the narrator's to the character's, or from one character's to another's.

Pun: word play which exploits the multiple meanings of a word or words with different meanings that sound alike.

Quatrain: a four-line stanza in a poem.

Realism: a movement or style which aims to represent things as they truly are.

Refrain: a poetic sound device; when phrases or lines are repeated in the course of a poem to create a musical effect. Refrain is similar to repetition, but is often called refrain when it comes in ballads, as in the question repeated at the beginning of every stanza.

O where ha' you been, Lord Randal my son?
And where ha' you been, my handsome young man?
(Anonymous, *Lord Randal*)

Register: the variety or level of language, which can be determined by the degree of formality or other social or artistic markers.

Repetition: a poetic sound device; when phrases or lines are repeated in the course of a poem to create a musical effect. This device is sometimes called refrain.

Rhyme: a poetic sound device; when the last word of two or more lines has the same ending sound (end-rhyme).

When in April the sweet showers fall
And pierce the drought of March to the root, and all
(Geoffrey Chaucer, *The Canterbury Tales*)

Conventionally, rhyme has often been used to mark the end of the line of verse (which also makes the poem easier to memorise). When rhyme is used within the line, it is called internal rhyme.

Her breath was strang, her hair was lang
(Anonymous, *Kemp Owyne*)

Rhymes are identified by the letters of the alphabet. The pattern they create is called rhyme scheme.

Rhyme scheme: the pattern created by the rhyme in a poem. Rhymes are identified by the letters of the alphabet (i.e. AABB).

Rhyming couplet: a unit of verse consisting of two lines, usually in the same metre, which are joined by rhyme.

Rhythm: a regular repeated pattern of sound. It is a natural feature of language. It is most apparent in poetry, although it is part of all good writing, and gives it a distinct musical quality. Rhythm also refers to the pace or speed.

Unlike the Italian language, which is syllable-timed, English is stress-timed; therefore stress is always much more important to rhythm than syllables.

Like other aspects of a poem, rhythm helps give form to its meaning. The quality of rhythm – regular and irregular, slow and fast, flowing and quick, smooth and hammering – is usually linked to the subject matter and emotional content of a poem.

Round characters: characters which pass through the crucial events of the story, and are remembered by the reader in connection with those scenes. Their personality is modified by experience, and they are likely to influence the development of the story. They are fit to surprise the reader in a convincing way. They bring the variety of real life into the novel. They are more complex than flat characters and have more than one facet, like human beings. An example of a round character is Elizabeth Bennet, in Jane Austen's *Pride and Prejudice*, when she realises she has been prejudiced towards Mr Darcy:

> *I have courted prepossession and ignorance, and driven reason away, where either were concerned. Till this moment, I never knew myself.*

Run-on line: a poetic sound device; when a line ends in the middle of a phrase and the meaning break comes in the next line, also called *enjambement*.

> *So the company of men led a careless life,*
> *All was well with them: until One began*
> *To encompass evil, an enemy from hell.*
> (Anonymous, *Beowulf*)

Satire: the use of humour, irony or exaggeration to expose or criticise certain qualities or behaviour. Two ideas of satire come from Roman culture: one expresses a basic instinct for comedy through the mockery of human beings; the other implies the desire of the satirist to instruct his readers by setting moral standards to reform social conduct or by denouncing everything in human nature that he finds distasteful. No sharp distinction can be made between these two kinds of satire since the tone of the satirist's attack can range from light humour to biting sarcasm according to the degree of indignation. Satire has been used since the beginnings of English literature. For example, Chaucer satirised the corruption of the Church in *The Canterbury Tales*. The 18th century is considered the golden age of satire, with artists like William Hogarth and authors like Jonathan Swift.

Sestet: a six-line stanza in a poem.

Setting: the place and time of the story. In drama, the setting can be inferred both from the dialogue and the stage directions.

> *(A Heath)*
> *A storm, with thunder and lightning. Enter Kent and a Gentleman, meeting*
> (William Shakespeare, *King Lear*, Act 3, Scene I)

Time setting usually refers to the time of the day, the season or the year. It is important to be aware of the context within which the action of a novel or play takes place, thus social and historical factors are also important.

In fiction, place setting can be interior or exterior and it deals with the description of the landscape, interiors and objects. A novel may begin with the description of a town or a landscape, which is the 'primary setting' of the story and also provides important information about the characters who live in it. When the description is very detailed, depending on the language of the senses or metaphorical expressions, the setting may acquire the status of a character, it may become almost like a protagonist of the story.

Shakespearean sonnet: is a type of sonnet, also called the English sonnet; its main features include:

- fourteen lines of iambic pentameter;
- division into four sections: three quatrains that present a problem or situation and a couplet that solves or summarises the problem;
- rhyme scheme:
  - Quatrain I: ABAB
  - Quatrain II: CDCD
  - Quatrain II: EFEF
  - Couplet: GG
- a turning point at the end of the eighth line and the ninth (sometimes introduced by words like: *and, if, so, but, then, when, yet, nor*);
- language full of oxymora;
- themes of love and faith, beauty and art.

The first quatrain introduces an idea. The second quatrain complicates it. The third complicates it still further. The final epigrammatic couplet resolves the whole thing.

Simile: a comparison of two things which is made explicit through the use of 'like', 'as', 'than' or 'resembles'. A simile is usually more striking if it compares two essentially unlike things.

> *And though so much distinguished, he was wise*
> *And in his bearing modest as a maid*
> (Geoffrey Chaucer, *The Canterbury Tales*)

The functions of a simile are:

- to convey a more vivid idea of the scene or object;
- to make the meaning easier to understand;
- to introduce an element of surprise;
- to create an emotional response in the reader.

Solecism: a mistake in grammar.

Soliloquy: a dramatic technique; when a character speaks his or her thoughts aloud. It is a special convention of drama: the character speaks even though he is alone on stage, thus his words are truly meant for the audience. It enables the playwright to let the audience know the character's:

- thoughts about a specific problem;
- plans for the future;
- feelings and reactions;
- explanation of what happens between scenes.

Sonnet: a fouteen-line poem, usually in iambic pentameter, which may follow a number of formal rhyme schemes, such as the Petrarchan or Shakespearean. It is the most formal among the lyric poems, but it is capable of great variety and intensity. The sonnet was invented by the Italian Iacopo da Lentini in the first half of the 13th century. It was introduced into England by Sir Thomas Wyatt.

Stage directions: instructions in the text of a play. They are open interventions of the playwright to provide information that cannot be conveyed through the dialogue. They allow the playwright to tell the director and the actors about how a play should be staged. They provide information about: the setting; the characters' actions and movements; and the style of acting.

> *Exeunt all but TITANIA [and the sentinel]. Enter Oberon.*
> *He drops the juice on TITANIA's eyelids.*
> (William Shakespeare, *A Midsummer Night's Dream*, Act 2, Sc II)

Stanza: a section of a poem which consists of several lines. In English poetry stanzas are normally from two to twelve lines long.

The types of stanzas are:

- the couplet (two lines);
- the tercet (three lines);
- the quatrain (four lines);
- the sestet (six lines);
- the octave (eight lines).

Stream of consciousness: phrase coined by William James to define the continuous flow of thoughts and sensations that characterise the human mind. This definition was applied by literary critics to a kind of 20th-century fiction which focused on this inner process. Interior monologue is often confused with the stream of consciousness, although they are not in fact the same thing: the former is the verbal expression of a psychic phenomenon, while the latter is the psychic phenomenon itself.

Subject matter: the topic(s) dealt with or presented in a work.

Sub-plot: a secondary plot. It usually mirrors the themes of the main plot but presents them from a different perspective.

Symbol: any thing, person, place or action that has a literal meaning and also stands for something else, such as a quality, an attitude, a belief or a value. Most symbols are shared by the members of the same cultural community and are therefore easy to understand. For example:

a rose = love and beauty;
a skull = death;
spring and winter = youth and old age.

There are symbols, however, which are the individual creation of a writer.

Symbolism: an artistic movement which started in France with Charles Baudelaire's *Les Fleurs du Mal*. The style of the Symbolist poets was characterised by:
- indirect rather than direct statements;
- the use of allusive language and development of the multiple association of words;
- the importance given to the 'sound' of words as conveying 'the music of ideas';
- the use of quotations from other literatures, revealing cosmopolitan interests;
- the use of free verse;
- the possibility for the reader to bring meaning to the poem.

Symbolism: a literary device, the use of symbols to represent ideas or qualities.

Tercet: a three-line stanza in a poem.

Theatre of the Absurd: a movement which had it's starting point in Samuel Beckett's *Waiting for Godot*. It denotes a group of dramatists who emerged in the 1950s. They did not form a school, since each playwright regarded himself as an outsider, with his own roots and background and a personal approach to form and subject matter, but they shared the common basic belief that man's life appears to be meaningless and purposeless and that human beings cannot communicate and understand each other.

Theme: a subject or topic on which one writes or speaks. However, the term can be intended in a wider perspective as:
- a proposition for discussion or argument;
- a key idea which acquires moral, philosophical or psychological value and offers hints for personal reflection;
- a subject of fictional or artistic representation, a visual motif or figure that forms a component of design in plastic arts, a melodic subject of a musical composition.

Themes can be presented by following different approaches:
- visual – with the aid of photos, images, paintings;
- auditory – through songs or pieces of music;
- verbal – by means of written documents (newspaper articles, literary texts, essays).

Third-person narrator: a person who tells the story and knows everything about the events and the characters' thoughts and intentions. Such a narrator is also called 'omniscient'.

Tragedy: a work, typically dramatic, involving suffering, destruction, death or distress. The word 'tragedy' comes from the Greek word *tràgos*, meaning 'goat', and *odé*, meaning 'song'. The goat was, in fact, considered a lascivious animal, sacrificed by the ancients who intended in this way to obtain purification from all their sins. This rite of sacrifice was generally accompanied by singing.

Some of the main features of the classical tragedies are:
- a prologue, which sets the scene of the story, introduces the characters and the main themes;
- a chorus which, in classical Greek drama is a group of actors who comment on the main action or advise the main characters;
- Aristotelian unities: one time, one action, and one place;
- the concept of catharsis (a Greek word which means 'purification'), a process in which strong emotions are experienced by the audience through the identification with the characters so that, in the end, they lose their power;
- a solemn style and elevated language;
- a representation of the struggle between good and evil;
- heroes and heroines who are never common people, but kings, princes and warriors, and they are not free but dominated by fate;
- the hero sometimes presents a flaw (ambition, weakness, jealousy) which leads him to suffering, madness or suicide (in this case the character is called a tragic hero because, after coming close to success and showing courage, he experiences destruction);
- generally also a villain who is guilty of some action which he must expiate through death.

Trochee: a poetic foot which has a stressed-unstressed pattern (¯/˘∪).

Unobtrusive narrator: an omniscient third-person narrator who shows what happens but does not interfere with the story – he acts like a camera.

Victorian novel: a novel produced during the reign of Queen Victoria which relates to the attitudes and values of this period.

The main features of the Victorian novel include:
- The voice of an omniscient narrator provides a comment on the plot and erects a rigid barrier between 'right' and 'wrong', light and darkness.
- The setting chosen by most Victorian novelists is the city, which was the main symbol of industrial civilisation as well as the expression of anonymous lives and lost identities.
- The plot is long and often complicated by subplots.
- Victorian writers concentrated on the creation of characters and thus achieved deeper analysis of the characters' inner life.
- Retribution and punishment are usually to be found in the final chapter, where the whole texture of events, adventures and incidents is explained and justified.

War Poets: a whole generation of promising young poets, who wrote remarkable poetry whose value lies in the unconventional, anti-rhetorical way they dealt with the horrors of modern warfare, and in a certain measure of experimentalism which emerged in the choice of a violent, everyday language.

Index

Acknowledgements

Texts

pp. 12–13: 'Lord Randal' in *The Oxford Book of Ballads*, edited by J. Kinsley, Oxford University Press, London, 1989. pp. 18–20: 'When in April' and 'The Wife of Bath', in G. Chaucer, *The Canterbury Tales*, General Prologue, translated into modern English by N. Coghill, Penguin Books, Harmondsworth, Middlesex, England, 1977. pp. 21–22: 'The Wife of Bafa' in P. Agbabi, *Transformatrix*, Canongate, Edinburgh, 2010. p. 34: 'My Mistress' Eyes' by W. Shakespeare, Sonnet CXXX in *The Arden Edition of Works of William Shakespeare*, Routledge, London and New York, 1988. p. 35: 'Anne Hathaway' in C.A. Duffy, *The World's Wife*, Picador, London, 1999. p. 43: 'What shall I swear by?' from W. Shakespeare, *Romeo and Juliet*, Act II, Scene I in *The Arden Edition of Works of William Shakespeare*, Routledge, London and New York, 1988. p. 44: 'To be or not to be' from W. Shakespeare, *Hamlet*, Act III, Scene I in *The Arden Edition of Works of William Shakespeare*, Routledge, London and New York, 1988. p. 45: 'The bond' from W. Shakespeare, *The Merchant of Venice*, Act I, Scene III in *The Arden Edition of Works of William Shakespeare*, Routledge, London and New York, 1988. p. 45: 'My hands are of your colour' from W. Shakespeare, *Macbeth*, Act II, Scene II, in *The Arden Edition of Works of William Shakespeare*, Routledge, London and New York, 1988. pp. 48–51: 'Two households', 'The ball' and 'The balcony scene' from W. Shakespeare, *Romeo and Juliet*, Prologue in *The Arden Edition of Works of William Shakespeare*, Routledge, London and New York, 1988. pp. 54–57: 'The three witches', 'Duncan's murder' and 'Macbeth's last monologue' from W. Shakespeare, *Macbeth*, Act I, Scene I in *The Arden Edition of Works of William Shakespeare*, Routledge, London and New York, 1988. pp. 59–64: 'The tempest', 'Prospero and Caliban' and 'Prospero renounces his magic powers' from W. Shakespeare, *The Tempest*, Act I, Scene I in *The Arden Edition of Works of William Shakespeare*, Routledge, London and New York, 1988 p. 111: p. 72 'Satan's speech' in J. Milton, *Paradise Lost and Regained*, Book I, Signet Classic, New York, 1968. pp. 83–86: 'The journal', 'Man Friday' in D. Defoe, *Robinson Crusoe*, Chapter V, Penguin Books, London, 1981. pp. 89–90: 'Gulliver and the Lilliputians' in J. Swift, *Gulliver's Travels*, Book 1, Penguin Books, London, 1981. p. 92: 'About movers' in S. Rushdie, *Shame*, Jonathan Cape, London, 1983. p. 101: 'London' in W. Blake, *The Complete Poems*, Penguin, London, 1968. pp. 109–110: 'The creation of the monster' in M. Shelley, *Frankenstein*, Chapter 5, The New American Inc., New York, 1965. p. 117: 'Daffodils' from W. Wordsworth, *Poems in Two Volumes* in Bloom, Trilling, *The Oxford Anthology of English Literature*, Oxford University Press, New York, 1974. pp. 120–123: 'The killing of the Albatross' in S.T. Coleridge, *The Rime of the Ancient Mariner*, Part I, Einaudi, Torino, 1964. pp. 127–128: 'Apostrophe to the ocean' from G.G. Byron, *Childe Harold's Pilgrimage*, Canto IV in G.G. Byron, *The Complete Poetical Works*, edited by J.J. McGann, Volume II, Oxford at the Clarendon Press, Oxford, England, 1980. p. 130: 'Bright Star' by J. Keats in *The Norton Anthology of English Literature*, Volume II, W.W. Norton & Company, New York, 1993. pp. 132–134: 'Ode to the West Wind' by P.B. Shelley in *The Penguin Book of English Romantic Verse*, Penguin Books, London, 1972. pp. 137–141: 'Mr and Mrs Bennet' and 'Darcy proposes to Elizabeth' in J. Austen, *Pride and Prejudice*, Chapter XXXIV, Penguin Classics, London, 2003. pp. 144–145: 'Any wife is better than no wife' in M. Ali, *Brick Lane*, Doubleday, New York, 2003. pp. 151–153: 'Coketown' in C. Dickens, *Hard Times*, Book I, Chapter 5, Penguin Books, London, 1976. pp. 158–159: 'Oliver wants some more' in C. Dickens, *Oliver Twist*, Chapter 2, Oxford University Press, Oxford, England, 1987. pp. 161–163: 'The definition of a horse' in C. Dickens, *Hard Times*, Chapter 2, Penguin Books, London, 2000. pp. 164–166: 'Punishment' in C. Brontë, *Jane Eyre*, Chapter 7, Everyman's Library, London, 1991. pp. 170–172: 'Becoming a nurse' in I. McEwan, *Atonement*, Jonathan Cape, Random House, London, 2001. p. 175: 'The White Man's Burden' in R. Kipling, *The White Man's Burden* (abridged), 1899. pp. 179–181: 'The story of the door' in R.L. Stevenson, *Dr Jekyll and Mr Hyde and Other Stories*, Chapter I, Penguin Books, London, 1967. pp. 187–190: 'Dorian's death' in O. Wilde, *Complete Works*, Chapter 1, Chapter 2, Collins, New York, 1977. p. 201: 'O Captain! My Captain!' in W. Whitman, *American Verse*, edited by O. Williams, Simon and Schuster, New York, 1978. pp. 209–210: 'Moby Dick' in H. Melville, *Moby-Dick*, Chapter 41, Bantman Books, New York, 1971. p. 213 : 'I Hear America Singing' in W. Whitman, *American Verse*, edited by O. Williams, Simon and Schuster, New York, 1978. p. 216: 'Hope is the thing with feathers' in E. Dickinson, *Poesie*, Poem 254, Poem 258, Rizzoli, Milano, 1979. pp. 219–221: 'Out by himself' in R. Bach, *Jonathan Livingston Seagull*, Macmillan Publishers, New York, 1970. pp. 228–230: 'There is nothing worse than war' in E. Hemingway, *A Farewell to Arms*, Charles Scribner's Sons, New York, NY, 2012. p. 235: 'The Soldier' by R. Brooke from *The New Oxford Book of English Verse*, edited by H. Gardner, Oxford University Press, London, 1990. pp. 236–237: 'Dulce et Decorum Est' by W. Owen, from *The Poems of Wilfred Owen*, Chatto & Windus, London, 1992. pp. 240–241: 'Easter 1916' by W.B. Yeats, from *The New Oxford Book of English Verse*, edited by H. Gardner, Oxford University Press, London, 1990. pp. 245–247: 'The Burial of the Dead' and 'The Fire Sermon' in T.S. Eliot, *The Waste Land and Other Poems*, Faber and Faber, London, 1940. p. 251: 'The funeral' in J. Joyce, *Ulysses*, Seeker and Wauburg, London, 1992. pp. 254–257: 'The chain-gang' in J. Conrad, *Heart of Darkness*, Milan, Mursia, 1985. pp. 260–263: 'Aziz and Mrs Moore' in E.M. Forster, *A Passage to India*, London, Penguin Books Ltd., pp. 266–268: 'Eveline' in J. Joyce, *Dubliners*, Panther Books; Frogmore, St Albans, 1977. pp. 272–274: 'Clarissa and Septimus' in V. Woolf, *Mrs Dalloway*, London, Penguin Books Ltd., 1992. pp. 276–277: 'Mrs Brown' in M. Cunningham, *The Hours*, Fourth Estate Limited, London, 1999. pp. 286–287: 'Nick meets Gatsby' in F. S. Fitzgerald, *The Great Gatsby*, Penguin Books, London, 1980. pp. 297–298: 'Refugee Blues' by W. H. Auden from *The New Oxford Book of Light Verse*, edited by K. Amis, Oxford University Press, London, 1979. pp. 306–307: 'Big Brother is watching you' in G. Orwell, *Nineteen Eighty-Four*, Penguin Books, London, 1980. pp. 308–309: 'You have to carry the fire' in C. McCarthy, *The Road*, Alfred A. Knopf, USA, 2006. pp. 312–313: 'Nothing to be done' in S. Beckett, *Waiting for Godot*, Faber and Faber, London, 1965. p. 323: 'Annus Mirabilis' by P. Larkin, from *The Less Deceived*, The Marvell Press, Hessle, 1966. pp. 326–327: 'Into the West' in J. Kerouac, *On the Road*, Penguin Books, London, 1973. pp. 330–331: 'I Have a Dream' from M.L. King, Jr, *The Peaceful Warrior*, Pocket Books, New York, 1968. pp. 335–336: 'The Tollund Man' by S. Heaney, from *Wintering Out*, Faber and Faber, London, 2002. pp. 340–341: 'A sense of loss' in I. McEwan, *The Child in Time*, Vintage, London, 1992. pp. 345–346: 'Down the Towere' in D. DeLillo, *Falling Man*, Picador, New York, 2011. pp. 349–350: 'A change of life' in N. Gordimer, *A Soldier's Embrace*, The Viking Press, New York, 1980. p. 352: 'Barack Obama's Nobel speech' downloaded from www.huffingtonpost.com/2009/12/10/obama-nobel-peace-prize-a_n_386837.html"http://www.huffingtonpost.com/2009/12/10/obama-nobel-peace-prize-a_n_386837.html. p. 353: 'The Season of Phantasmal Peace' by D. Walcott, from *Collected Poems 1948-1984*, Faber and Faber, London, 1992.

Illustrations

1 Suzanne Plunkett/Bloomberg Via Getty Images; The British Museum, London; Telepress, Rome; Gail Johnson/Shutterstock. **2** Skyscan Photolibrary/Alamy; The Trustees Of The British Museum. **3** Maria Gioberti/Shutterstock; Hemis/Alamy; Subbotina Anna/Shutterstock. **4** Holmes Garden Photos/Alamy; Ian Mcdonald/Shutterstock. **5** Brian Maudsley/Shutterstock; Roy Strong, *The Story Of Britain*, Pimlico, London, 1998. **6** Michael Holdford. **7** The British Library Board; Ann Ronan/Heritage Images/Scala, Firenze. **8** Angelo Hornak/Corbis; The Thirdman/Shutterstock. **9** Alinari Archives. **10** INTERFOTO/Alamy; Telepress, Rome. **11** 'Robin Hood: Prince Of Thieves', Warner Bros. Pictures 1991; 'Robin Hood', Universal Pictures 2010. **12** Dagli Orti/The Art Archive. **14** Vinicius Tupinamba/Shutterstock. **15** Moviestore Collection Ltd/Alamy; AF Archive/Alamy. **16** Artistes Associes/PEA/The Kobal Collection. **19** PEA Produzioni Europee Associate. **20** PEA Produzioni Europee Associate. **21** Ragne Kabanova/Shutterstock; Mshep2/Istockphoto; L'Express 2010, Paris; Yevgen Kotyuk/Shutterstock; Suzanne Plunkett/Bloomberg Via Getty Images. **22** Karen Kasmauski/Getty Images. **25** The Guildhall Library, London; Classical Comics; 'Romeo e Giulietta', BHE Films, Dino De Laurentiis Cinematografica, Paramount Pictures, Verona Produzione, 1968; 'Romeo + Juliet', Bazmark Films, Twentieth Century Fox Film Corporation, 1996; Chris Green/Shutterstock.Com. Rob Kints/Shutterstock. **26** The Bridgeman Art Library; The National Portrait Gallery, London. **27** The National Portrait Gallery, London. **28** The National Portrait Gallery, London. **29** Jeff Banke/Shutterstock; Twin Design/Shutterstock. **31** Bridgeman Art Library/Alinari; Darren Pierce Kelly/Shutterstock. **33** The Bridgeman Art Library, London. **34** Succession Picasso, by SIAE 2015. **35** AF Archive/Alamy. **36** Fiat Group Automobiles S.P.A.; Classical Comics; 'Hamlet', Canal+; Carolco Pictures, Icon Entertainment International, Marquis, Nelson Entertainment, Sovereign Pictures, Warner Bros. Pictures, 1990. **37** Henrietta Butler/Redferns/Getty. **39** Jorisvo/Shutterstock. **41** United Archives Gmbh/Alamy; AF Archive/Alamy. **42** AF Archive/Alamy. **43** Moviestore Collection Ltd/Alamy. **44** SIAE 2015. **46** 'Maqbool', Kaleidoscope Entertainment Pvt. Ltd., Vishal Bhardwaj Pictures, 2004. **49** 'Romeo + Juliet', Bazmark Films, Twentieth Century Fox Film Corporation, 1996. **51** Houston Rogers, 1960. **52** 'Romeo e Giulietta', BHE Films, Dino De Laurentiis Cinematografica, Paramount Pictures, Verona Produzione, 1968; 'Romeo + Juliet', Bazmark Films, Twentieth Century Fox Film Corporation, 1996. **53** AF Archive/Alamy. **54** Encyclopaedia Britannica/The Kobal Collection. **56** Henry Fuseli/Tate Gallery. **57** AF Archive/Alamy. **58** 'The Tempest', Miramax Films, Talkstory Productions, Artemis Films, Mumbai Mantra Media, Prologue Films, Chartoff Hendee Productions, Touchstone Pictures, 2010. **62** The Kobal Collection/Touchstone Pictures. **67** Painted Hall by John Thornhill, Greenwich, Royal Naval College, London; National Portrait Gallery, London; 'Cromwell', Irving Allen Productions, 1970; Reuters 2009; Daniel Defoe, *Robinson Crusoe*, Silva, Zurich, 1951; Illustration by Hugo Laubi; Ihilliard/Bigstockphoto. **68** Buckingham Palace, Royal Collection. **69** Cromwell, Irving Allen Productions, 1970; To Kill A King, Filmfour, Iac Film, Natural Nylon Entertainment, Rockwood Edge, Scion Films, Screenland Movieworld Gmbh, 2003. **70** Museums Sheffield/The Bridgeman Art Library. **73** Bridgeman Art Library/Alinari. **74** British Museum, London. **75** The Bridgeman Art Library; The British Museum, London. **76** National Portrait Gallery, London; Scottish National Portrait Gallery, Edinburgh. **77** 'Tom Jones', Woodfall Film Productions, 1963. **80** The Mansell Collection, London; Imperial Brewing & Leisure Ltd, Photo F.T. Archive. Roy Strong, *The Story Of Britain*, Pimlico, London, 1998. **81** The British Library, London; PhotoSky 4t com/Shutterstock. **83** 'Cast Away', Twentieth Century Fox Film Corporation, Dreamworks SKG, Imagemovers, Playtone, 2000. **84** Daniel Defoe, *Robinson Crusoe*, Silva, Zurich, 1951. Illustration by Hugo Laubi. **86** Daniel Defoe, *Robinson Crusoe*, Silva, Zurich, 1951. Illustration by Hugo Laubi. **87** National Portrait Gallery, London. **88** *Gulliver Nei Paesi Dei Nani*, Genio, Milano, 1934; Classic Comics, 1943. **89** AF Archive/Alamy. **90** Royal Collection/Her Majesty Queen Elizabeth II. **91** Oleg_Mit/Shutterstock; Zejko Radojko/Shutterstock; Maridav/Shutterstock; Pixinity/Shutterstock; Fotohunter/Shutterstock. **92** Nancy Kaszerman/ZUMA Press/Corbis. **95** Bridgeman Art Library/Alinari; The Bridgeman Art Library/Alinari Getty Images; R. Hamlyn and M. Phillips, *William Blake*, Harry N. Abrams Inc., New York; Penguin Books Ltd., 1981; Look and Learn/The Bridgeman Art Library/Alinari, Cassandra Austen, 1810; Shestakoff/Shutterstock; 'Pride and Prejudice', BBC, Chestermead, 1995. **96** M&N/Alamy; Gillian Darley/Corbis. **97** M& Bridgeman/Alinari. **98** Mary Evans Picture Library. **99** National Portrait Gallery, London; R. Hamlyn and M. Phillips, *William Blake*, Harry N. Abrams Inc., New York. **102** The Bridgeman Art Library/Alinari Getty Images. **103** Henrik Lehnerer/Shutterstock. **106** Philip de Bay/©Historical Picture Archives/Corbis; Bridgeman Art Library/Alinari. **107** Universal Picture; Telepresse, Rome. **108** Telepresse, Rome. **109** Il Cinema, Vol. 1, n. 6, Istituto Geografico De Agostini, Novara. **110** Moviestore Collection Ltd/Alamy. **111** 'Casablanca', Warner Bros. Pictures, 1942. **114** The Bridgeman Art Library. **116** Creativeoneuk/Shutterstock. **117** The Bridgeman Art Library. **118** The Bridgeman Art Library. **119** S.T. Coleridge, *La Ballata del Vecchio Marinaio*, Rizzoli, Milan, 1973. **121** Look and Learn/The Bridgeman Art Library. **122** Look and Learn/The Bridgeman Art Library. **123** David Hughes/Shutterstock. **127** The Bridgeman Art Library. **130** 01 Distribution. **131** Bridgeman/Alinari. **136** 'Pride & Prejudice', Focus Features, Universal Pictures, Studio Canal, Working Title Films, Scion Films, 2005. **139** 'Pride & Prejudice', Focus Features, Universal Pictures, Studio Canal, Working Title Films, Scion Films, 2005. **140** Look and Learn/The Bridgeman Art Library. **141** AF Archive/Alamy. **142** 'Pride and Prejudice', BBC, Chestermead, 1995; 'Pride & Prejudice', Focus Features, Universal Pictures, Studio Canal, Working Title Films, Scion Films, 2005. **143** Stephane Lehr/Corbis; Robert Wallis/Corbis; Athar Hussain/Reuters/Contrasto; Karen Kasmauski/Corbis; Eurekaimages.com/Alamy; Darron R. Silva/Aurora/Olycom. **144** 'Brick Lane', Film4, Ingenious Film Partners, Ruby Films, Seven Seas Productions, UK Film Council, 2007. **147** Photo Prof. Peter W.E. Smith; Dickens House, London; 'Oliver Twist', R.P. Productions, Runteam II Ltd., ETIC Films, Medusa Produzione, Runteam, 2005; The National Portrait Gallery, London, Photo to Evelyn George Carey; 'Wilde', BBC, Capitol Films, Dove International, NDF International, Pandora Filmproduktion, Pony Canyon, Samuelson Entertainment, The Greenlight Fund, Wall to Wall Television, 1997. **148** Bridgeman Art Library/Alinari; Getty Images; Felice Beato/Getty Images; Albert Fenn/Time-Life Picture Agency. National Geographic Photographer. **149** Hulton Getty Picture Library; Getty Images. **150** The Bridgeman Art Library. **154** Bridgeman/Alinari. **156** Getty Images. **157** Medusa Web Photo; 'Oliver Twist', R.P. Productions, Runteam II Ltd., ETIC Films, Medusa Produzione, Runteam, 2005. **158** Time&Life Picture/Getty Images. **160** T.E. Duverger, *The Naughty Schoolchildren*. **161** Look and Learn/Bridgeman Art Library/Alinari. **162** Look and Learn/Bridgeman Art Library/Alinari. **166** 'Jane Eyre', Cineritino S.R.L. Flach Film, Mediaset, Miramax Films, RCS Editori S.P.A., Rochester, 1996. **167** Bridgeman Art Library/Alinari; Marka, Milan. **168** Beryl Peters Collection/Alamy 4. Archive Images/Alamy. **169** Bridgeman Art Library/Alinari, The Art Gallery Collection/Alamy. **170** 'Atonement', Universal Pictures, Studio Canal, Relativity Media, Working Title Films, 2007. **171** 'Atonement', Universal Pictures, Studio Canal, Relativity Media, Working Title Films, 2007. **173** Bodleian Library, Oxford. **174** Albert Fenn/Time-Life Picture Agency; E. Duyckinick, *Portrait Gallery of Eminent Men and Women in Europe and America*, Johnson, Wilson & Company, New York, 1873; Magnum Photos/Contrasto. **175** Photo E. Tweedy, Courtesy of the Kipling Society and the Royal Commonwealth Society. **176** *Atlante della Storia d'Europa*, Zanichelli, Bologna, 1997; The National Portrait Gallery, London. **179** Bodley Head, London. **180** Telepresse, Rome. **186** AF Archive/Alamy, Bridgeman Art Library/Alinari. **189** AF Archive/Alamy. **191** Andresr/Shutterstock; Telepresse, Rome; 'Gone with the Wind', Selznick International Pictures, Metro-Goldwyn-Mayer, 1939. **194** The Bridgeman Art Library/Alinari. **197** Indians.Org © 2011. **198** Mary Evans Picture Library; National Geographic Photographer; The Historic New Orleans Collection, New Orleans. **199** Hulton Archives/Getty Images; Bridgeman Art Library/Alinari. **200** Washington D.C., Digital Stock; Solana Beach, CA, 1996. **202** Library of Congress. **203** 'Gone with the Wind', Selznick International Pictures, Metro-Goldwyn-Mayer, 1939; 'Cold Mountain', Miramax Films, Mirage Enterprises, Bona Fide, Castel Film Romania, Cattleya, 2003. **205** Eastvillage Images/Shutterstock. **207** Photri Images/Alamy. **209** Archive Photos/stringer/Photo by Warner Brothers/Getty Images. **213** Bettman Archive. **215** James Marshall/Corbis. **218** John Shearer/Time Life Pictures/Getty Images. **221** Runzelkorn/Shutterstock; Andresr/Shutterstock. **223** Percy Wyndham Lewis, *T.S. Eliot*, 1938; Paul Nash, The Menin Road, 1919. Imperial War Museum, London; 'Michael Collins' Warner Bros. Pictures, Geffen Pictures, 1996; Salvador Dalì, Gala-Salvador Dalì Foundation, by SIAE 2015; René Magritte by SIAE 2015. **224** The Imperial War Museum; Parliamentary Recruiting Committee,London; Hulton Deutsch Collection. **225** Edward VII receiving Maharajahs and Dignitaries Prior to his Coronation, Harris, Albert E. (fl.1917) / Roy Miles Fine Paintings. **226** Imperial War Museum. **227** Shutterstock / Chris Howey. **231** Bridgeman / Alinari. **232** Frank Hurley, *The Battle of the Menin Road*, Chateau Wood, Ypres, 1917–18. Mitchell Library, State Library of New South Wales; Paul Nash, *We Are Making a New World*, 1918. Imperial War Museum, London; Paul Nash, *Landscape from a Dream*, 1936–38. Tate Collection, London. **233** Musée National d'Art Moderne, Centre Pompidou, Paris. **236** National Gallery of Canada, Ottawa. **240** Stephen Barnes/NI Politics / Alamy. **242** 'Michael Collins' Warner Bros. Pictures, Geffen Pictures, 1996; 'The Wind That Shakes the Barley' Sixteen Films, Matador Pictures, Regent Capital, 2006. **245** Shutterstock / Songchai W; The Industrial Environment, Brand X, Culver City, CA, 2001; Shutterstock / Mazzzur; Shutterstock / Sebastian Knight; Brand X, Four Seasons, Culver City, CA, 2001. **246** René Magritte by SIAE 2015. **247** 'Revolutionary Road', DreamWorks SKG, BBC Films, Evamere Entertainment, 2008. **248** Succession H. Matisse, by SIAE 2015. **251** George Grosz by SIAE 2015. **252** Lebrecht Music and Arts Photo Library / Alamy. **253** AF archive / Alamy.259 'A Passage to India' EMI Films, Home Box Office (HBO), Thorn EMI Screen Entertainment, 1984. **260** 'A Passage to India' EMI Films, Home Box Office (HBO), Thorn EMI Screen Entertainment, 1984. **261** 'A Passage to India' EMI Films, Home Box Office (HBO), Thorn EMI Screen Entertainment, 1984. **262** 'A Passage to India' EMI Films, Home Box Office (HBO), Thorn EMI Screen Entertainment, 1984. **271** AF Archive / Alamy. **274** 'The Hours' Paramount Pictures, Miramax Films, Scott Rudin Productions, 2002. **275** Shutterstock; PT Images / Shutterstock; Oskin Pavel / Shutterstock; oliveromg / Shutterstock. **276** 'The Hours', Paramount Pictures, Miramax Films, Scott Rudin Productions, 2002. **277** 'The Hours', Paramount Pictures, Miramax Films, Scott Rudin Productions, 2002. **279** Museum of Modern Art, New York; Alfred Eisenstaedt—Time & Life Pictures / Getty Images; Cristapper / Shutterstock; **282** Songquan Deng / Shutterstock. **285** 'The Great Gatsby', Bazmark Films, Red Wagon Productions, Village Roadshow Pictures, 2013. **290** Corbis / Bettman-Upi. **298** The Refugees, 1941 (panel), Freud, Lucian (1922-2011) / Private Collection / The Bridgeman Art Library / Archivi Alinari; Felix Nussbaum / VG Bild-Kunst/akg-images. **301** SVLUMA / Shutterstock. **302** 'Pearl Harbor' Touchstone Pictures, Jerry Bruckheimer Films, 2001; 'The King's Speech' Weinstein Company, The, UK Film Council, Momentum Pictures, 2010. **303** 'Pink Floyd The Wall' Goldcrest Films International, Metro-Goldwyn-Mayer (MGM), Tin Blue, 1982. **305** 'Nineteen Eighty-Four' Umbrella-Rosenblum Films Production, Virgin Benelux, Virgin Schallplatten, 1984. **307** Komar & Melamid / Collezione Privata. **308** 'The Road' Dimension Films, 2929 Productions, Nick Wechsler Productions, 2009. **309** 'The Road' Dimension Films, 2929 Productions, Nick Wechsler Productions, 2009. **315** Sean Pavone / Shutterstock; Kienzle, T. / Associated Press; Andy Warhol Foundation for the Visual Arts, by SIAE 2015. **319** Corbis / Encinitas, CA, 1999. **321** Andy Warhol Foundation for the Visual Arts, by SIAE 2015; Estate of Roy Lichtenstein, by SIAE 2015. **326** 'On the Road' MK2 Productions, American Zoetrope, Jerry Leider Company, 2012. **332** Andy Warhol Foundation for the Visual Arts, by SIAE 2015. **333** 'Dirty Dancing' Great American Films Limited Partnership, Vestron Pictures, 1987; 'Across the Universe' Revolution Studios, Gross Entertainment, Team Todd, 2007. **339** Robert Judges / Rex Features. **342** Bettmann / Corbis; Getty Images. **348** Durand / Sipa Press. **349** Leon Golub by SIAE 2015. **350** Jean-Michel Basquiat / Scala Archives The Estate of Jean-Michel Basquiat, by SIAE 2015. **354** Andy Warhol Foundation for the Visual Arts, by SIAE 2015.